Materials for
Sustainable Sites

*A Complete Guide to the Evaluation, Selection, and Use
of Sustainable Construction Materials*

by Meg Calkins

WILEY

John Wiley & Sons, Inc.

Published by John Wiley & Sons, Inc., Hoboken, New Jersey

Published simultaneously in Canada.

For general information about our other products and services, please contact our Customer Care Department within the United States at (800) 762-2974, outside the United States at (317) 572-3993 or fax (317) 572-4002.

Wiley also publishes its books in a variety of electronic formats. Some content that appears in print may not be available in electronic books. For more information about Wiley products, visit our web site at www.wiley.com.

Library of Congress Cataloging-in-Publication Data:

Calkins, Meg, 1965–
    Materials for sustainable sites: a complete guide to the evaluation, selection, and use of sustainable construction materials / by Meg Calkins.
        p. cm.
    Includes bibliographical references and index.
    ISBN 978-0-470-13455-9 (cloth)
1. Sustainable buildings—Materials.   2. Building materials.   I. Title.
    TH880.C35 2009
    691—dc22
                                                            2008002722

Printed in the United States of America

10 9 8 7 6 5 4 3 2 1

Contents

Preface

Environmental and human health impacts of materials are a hidden cost of our built environment. Impacts during manufacture, transport, installation, use, and disposal of construction materials can be significant, yet often invisible. A broad and complex web of environmental and human health impacts occurs for each of the materials and products used in any built landscape, a web that extends far beyond any project site. Construction materials and products can be manufactured hundreds, even thousands, of miles from a project site, affecting ecosystems at the extraction and manufacturing locations, but unseen from the project location. Likewise, extraction of raw materials for these products can occur far from the point of manufacture, affecting that local environment. Transportation throughout all phases consumes fuel and contributes pollutants to the atmosphere. Disposal of manufacturing waste and used construction materials will affect still another environment. These impacts are "invisible" because they are likely remote from the site under construction and the designer's locale. For example, the impact of destroying a wetland on the site can be clearly demonstrated and understood, but it is difficult to see the effects of global warming resulting from the release of CO_2 during concrete manufacture, or the destruction of a rainforest halfway around the world from bauxite mining for aluminum.

Despite the fact that we can't see their impacts, materials used in construction of the built environment are damaging the world's ecosystems at an alarming rate. Most materials are made from nonrenewable resources, and their extraction disrupts habitats; impacts soil, air, and water; and affects human health either directly or indirectly through environmental damage.

These high costs have contributed to an increased interest in green design, and the rapid adoption of the U.S. Green Building Council's LEED™ system; however, material selection and specification remains a challenging, sometimes even contentious issue. Many designers experience difficulty understanding the full extent of environmental and human health impacts of building materials as they are not easily quantified. Complete and accurate information is elusive. Life-cycle assessment (LCA), a thorough accounting of environmental and human health impacts of a material, is the best tool for truly evaluating materials. Yet LCAs for materials and products used in site construction are limited, and wide variations between proprietary products, manufacturing methods and study boundaries can make comparisons difficult.

And the right answer may not always lie in a new, green material, but instead in a conventional, tried-and-true material used in green ways. This book is written with the assumption that conventional materials may eventually be replaced by greener alternatives, but for the time being, designers must take steps to specify conventional materials in such a way as to minimize their environmental and human health impacts. For example, in the future there may be a material that performs better than asphalt, costs less, is widely accepted by the road building industry, *and* is better for the environment and human health, but in the meantime designers can take steps to specify asphalt in such a way that the impacts are minimized by incorporating recycled aggregates such as tires, glass, and reclaimed asphalt; cooling the mix; and making it porous.

This book provides detailed and current information on construction materials for sustainable sites. The first four chapters of the book discuss general environmental and human health impacts of the materials and products industry; provide tools, techniques, ideologies, and resources for evaluating, sourcing, and specifying sustainable site materials. The second part of the book devotes a chapter each to nine basic types of site construction materials—both conventional and emerging green materials. These are concrete, earthen materials, brick masonry, asphalt, aggregates and stone, wood, metals, plastics, and nonliving biobased materials. Each chapter discusses environmental and human health impacts of the material at all phases of its life cycle, and presents detailed strategies to minimize these impacts.

It is important to note that this book does not provide definitive answers for "right" and "wrong" materials and products. It is an impossible task to determine what is right or wrong for every situation—climate, application, site conditions, aesthetic, and performance requirements—across the board. Requirements vary. No one aesthetic will work everywhere so nor should one for "green" materials. Nor should this ever be the goal. The FSC-certified wood harvested from local forests may be the right material for a camp on Bainbridge Island, Washington, but it is not right for an intensively used public plaza 3,000 miles away in New York City.

This book will equip the reader with knowledge and skills for "life-cycle thinking"—techniques to evaluate and minimize the environmental and human health impacts of materials and products for a particular climate, application, and location. This book is not a substitute for true LCA techniques, and where they are available they should be the primary method of evaluation.

This book emphasizes the following four major principles:

- *Choose materials and products that use resources efficiently.* Reduce, reuse, and recycle materials in order to reduce resource consumption and habitat destruction and ecosystem disruption that result from extracting and harvesting the resources. Use of durable, reusable, recyclable, and renewable materials can support this principle as can reducing the amount of material used

- *Choose materials and products that minimize embodied energy and embodied carbon.* Use of local, low embodied energy materials can support this principle. Materials that are manufactured with nonfossil fuel–based renewable energy sources can also contribute.

- *Avoid materials and products that can harm human or environmental health at any phase of their life cycle.* Materials or by-products from materials that hold potential to emit toxins, pollutants, and heavy metals to air, water, or soil where they can impact ecological and human health should be avoided.

- *Choose materials that assist with sustainable site design strategies.* Some materials may not be "green" themselves, but if they are used to construct a sustainable site design feature, they may be.

Acknowledgments

The seeds of inspiration for this book were planted by many mentors, colleagues, and friends. Several years ago, Linda Jewell inspired my interest in construction materials—both their aesthetic possibilities and their environmental impacts. This led to one of the book's major undercurrents—that "green" materials can and should be aesthetically pleasing; this will hasten their adoption. Linda, a very supportive mentor over the years, introduced me to Bill Thompson, editor of *Landscape Architecture* magazine—a major forum for the preliminary material of this book. Bill allowed me wide rein to explore many topics related to materials and sustainability while asking valuable questions about some of my conclusions.

With training in both architecture and landscape architecture, one of my main career goals has been to strengthen connections between the two professions in areas of green building. This book is an attempt to create common ground between site and building in the area of green building materials. As such, the book is inspired by others exploring these issues in both professions: Alex Wilson and all the writers of *Environmental Building News*, Tom Lent, Bill Walsh, Charles Kibert, Kim Sorvig, Bruce Ferguson, Daniel Winterbottom, and my knowledgeable inspiring colleagues on the Sustainable Sites Initiative (SSI) Materials Technical Subcommittee.

The broad reach of this book has been made possible by the following chapter and manuscript reviewers who gave freely and generously of their great expertise: Alex Wilson, Bob Falk, Tom Lent, Bruce Ferguson, Kim Sorvig, Daniel Winterbottom, Scott Shell, Jean Schwab, Kimberly Cochran, John Motloch, Howard Marks, Margaret Cervarich, Nathan Imm, and Charles Kibert.

Professional colleagues and students at Ball State University, The University of Illinois at Urbana-Champaign, and The University of California at Berkeley helped to foster many concepts and ideas in this book through both formal and informal interchanges. I am indebted to the unflagging enthusiasm and dedication of graduate assistants Ruth Stafford, Dena Shelley, Scott Minor, Jessica Clement, Brent Krieg, and Kyle Barrett.

Editor Margaret Cummins at Wiley has shown unflagging enthusiasm and support for this book project from the first pitch. Her straightforward and always friendly approach, as well as that of her Wiley colleagues Lauren Poplawski and Alda Trabucchi, is much appreciated.

This book is dedicated to my children, Annie and Jack. My concern for the future of their earth is the impetus for this book. I am particularly grateful for the support of my family during the germination and growth of this book. My parents, lifelong learners themselves, fostered in me a love of inquiry that sustained the creation of this book. More practically, my parents lent endless moral support and childcare and my children provided much needed comic relief and great artwork at the end of a long day. I thank George Elvin for his calm encouragement, steady belief in my abilities, good humor, and his willingness to go beyond his share of the parenting during the many deadlines.

chapter 1

Materials for Sustainable Sites Defined

Since the mid-nineteenth century when Olmsted excavated stone from the meadows of Central Park to build the park's bridges, walls, and stairs, the construction materials industry has undergone major changes. There has been a shift away from localized use of materials to centralized large-scale production and global distribution; from minimally processed materials to highly processed ones; and from simple materials to engineered composites, mixed materials assemblies, and liberal use of chemical additives to impart a wide array of properties.

Materials of site construction have evolved in response to many twentieth-century trends: the shift from skilled craftsmen to cheap labor in construction, increasingly nationalized standards that do not specifically address regional materials or conditions, centralized production of building materials and products, cheap and abundant resources where "real" costs of ecosystem destruction and pollution are not factored in, increasing use of composite materials, and huge growth in the global materials industry.

The result has been a consumptive and sometimes wasteful materials industry with use of a limited palette of nationally standardized site construction materials (e.g., concrete, asphalt, pressure-treated lumber, powder-coated steel). Local, low embodied energy structures, such as earthen construction in the Southwest or dry stone construction in New England, have decreased in use as labor costs are high, workers skilled in these techniques are increasingly scarce, and national building codes hamper their use.

Abundant resources, inexpensive labor, and minimal environmental regulations in developing countries have shifted production of many building materials overseas. This has further reduced designers' capacity to understand the impacts of construction material production, or even to know where they come from. Aggregate may come by train from a quarry 200 miles from the site, while the aluminum for the handrails may have visited three continents before it arrived at the site. This means that today, a far greater portion of the impacts of building materials are those related to energy consumption incurred in trucking, shipping, and train transport. These are not insignificant, given the weight of many site construction materials.

Site construction materials of the twenty-first century must respond to an entirely different set of forces—global climate change, air pollution, rising fuel costs, ecological destruction, and loss of biodiversity. These forces are shaping the site and building construction industry through the rapidly growing sustainable development movement.

And they will necessitate significant changes in the materials industry. These changes may involve closed-loop material manufacturing systems that eliminate waste; use of renewable energy sources for manufacturing, processing, finishing, and transport activities; "mining" of construction demolition sites for "raw materials"; substantial reductions of pollution from material manufacture, use, and disposal; an emphasis on minimally processed local or regional materials; and greater reuse of site structures in place or on-site.

To address the goal of sustainable development, the construction material production and construction industries must shift their use of resources and fuels from nonrenewables to renewables, from waste production to reuse and recycling, from an emphasis on first costs to life-cycle costs and full-cost accounting, where all costs such as waste, emissions, and pollution are factored into the price of materials (Kibert et al. 2002).

And this shift has already begun. The first decade of the twenty-first century has seen the start of what will be significant changes to the construction materials industry:

- Global warming is well acknowledged by global decision makers and treaties such as the Kyoto Protocol for greenhouse gas reduction.
- Policies for waste reduction and reuse in the European Union and to a lesser degree in the United States are fostering growth in salvage, recycling, and industrial materials exchange industries.
- In the EU, policies are increasing the responsibility of producers to reduce and recycle packaging, increase the recycled content of their products, recycle more of their waste, and even take back and recycle components of their own products.
- Industrial designers and product manufacturers are looking to natural systems for closed-loop design, new material compositions, and green chemistry to reduce waste and pollution of their product production.
- Standards and criteria for reducing the environmental and human health impacts of materials and products are being developed and increasingly used by product specifiers to make decisions. The LEED system, Cradle to Cradle Certification, Greenguard, EPA Comprehensive Procurement Guidelines, Green Globes, and others offer criteria and standards for material or product selection.

- Life-cycle assessment (LCA) studies are increasingly available, yet still limited, for construction materials and products. In the United States, BEES and the Athena Environmental Impact Estimator interpret and weigh LCA results for building assemblies and some site construction materials.

Yet while progress is being made, selection of materials and products with the least environmental and human health impacts remains a challenging, confusing, and sometimes even contentious issue. The appropriate materials for sustainable sites will vary by impact priorities, regional issues, project budgets, and performance requirements. Some will emphasize materials that conserve resources by being reused without remanufacturing, by being extremely durable, or by closing material loops with high recycled content and manufacturer take-back programs. Others place great emphasis on low toxicity of products and emissions throughout their life cycle, while others may regard low ecological impacts or conservation of water as the highest priority. With this wide variety of priorities comes an even wider variety of "right answers." Portland cement concrete may appear to be a "green" material for those with durability or regionally produced materials as a priority, whereas it might be rejected by those who are concerned about the global warming impacts of material manufacture or high embodied energy materials. Composite lumber (a mix of recycled plastic and wood fibers) seems like a good alternative to wood lumber for those concerned with the ecological impacts of clear-cutting forestry practices, but it may be rejected for its mixed material composition by those concerned with the closed-loop recyclability of materials.

In addition to varying priorities and goals in green material selection, there are shades of green. For instance, the ideal green material might be a natural, renewable, local and indigenous, nontoxic, low embodied energy material such as willow cuttings for slope stabilization or rammed earth for a retaining wall; however, these materials may not be feasible in all situations. They may not be able to perform to current construction standards, construction workers may not be skilled in techniques to build structures with these materials, or they may not be appropriate for the scale of construction or performance requirements.

Claims of green abound as product manufacturers capitalize on the rapidly growing "green" segment of the construction materials industry. Yet it can be difficult for designers to cut through the hype and determine just how green the product is, let alone compare it with six or seven alternatives. Evaluating multiple products for a given use can be like comparing apples and oranges. One product may pose global warming impacts while another may involve a known human carcinogen; a third product may require large amounts of fossil fuel–powered energy to produce, but it may be more durable with the potential to last twice as long as the first two alternatives.

True life-cycle assessment (LCA), an accounting of all inputs and outputs through a product's life cycle, can potentially offer some answers for sustainable site material selection. But it is outside the time and skill constraints of most designers. And while LCA information is becoming available for a wide variety of products through Athena or BEES in the United States, to date these tools have focused on evaluating building assemblies and materials with only minimal analysis of site construction materials.

Materials for Sustainable Sites Defined

This section defines characteristics of materials for sustainable sites. It is important to note that all of the strategies summarized below and addressed in this book are not equal. Just diverting a waste material from the landfill is not always enough. While it is a step in the right direction, what is actually done with the diverted material will determine whether it is a large or small step. In resource conservation, as in other aspects of designing for sustainable sites, there are shades of green from light to dark. For example, chipping a reclaimed old-growth oak beam into mulch is not the highest and best use of the material. Instead, reusing it in whole form is the best use. Better yet, if the beam came from an old barn that is no longer needed, keeping the beam in place and adapting the barn structure to another use will maintain the resource in place, incurring no transportation costs and maintaining the integrity of the beam—and the old structure.

So the definition of materials for sustainable sites can vary widely, and some materials or products will be slightly green while others may be dark green. It can all be a step in the right direction, and taking the largest step possible in a given situation will help push the site construction industry incrementally toward substantial changes.

Materials and products for sustainable sites are those that minimize resource use, have low ecological impacts, pose no or low human and environmental health risks, and assist with sustainable site strategies. Within this definition, specific characteristics of materials for sustainable sites are summarized below. These attributes are also woven throughout the chapters on individual materials in this book, and are discussed there in greater detail.

Characteristics of "green materials" listed below are not in a ranked order as priorities will vary among projects. Environmental priorities as ranked by the EPA Science Advisory Board are discussed in Chapter 3 and a hierarchy of waste reduction strategies is discussed in Chapter 4.

MATERIALS OR PRODUCTS THAT REDUCE RESOURCE USE

Reducing use of virgin natural resources in the production and use of construction materials can substantially reduce their environmental impacts. Using fewer materials in construction by reducing the size of a structure or by retrofitting an existing one will not only save virgin resource use for the new product or material, but it will also reduce the "ecological rucksack" of waste, often many more times than the actual product entails, that is created through the raw material acquisition and manufacturing processes. Reusing materials or using waste as feedstock for new products will reduce virgin resource impacts as well.

Impacts associated with virgin resource use will also be reduced with reuse or recycling of resources. Habitat destruction, waste generation, energy, and air and water pollution are minimized with reduced use of virgin resources. Energy is saved in the processing and manufacture of new materials as primary processing steps are often eliminated with use of recycled materials. And, if materials are reused on-site or even in place, transportation impacts can be eliminated. Use of reclaimed, refurbished, and recycled content materials is discussed in greater detail in Chapter 4.

Use No New Materials, Don't Rebuild

While not always feasible or appropriate, this is the best way to minimize use of resources. This might mean a choice is made not to build or rebuild a structure, and a site can be used as is. Designing sites for adaptability with open plans and multiuse spaces, so the site and its structures do not require adaptation in a short period of time, can help minimize future use of resources.

Reuse Existing Structures in Place

Adapting or retrofitting existing structures without deconstruction and rebuilding can give them new life with minimal use of new materials. For example, the cracked concrete deck of an old loading dock might be stained with a natural iron oxide pigment (which is a by-product of iron ore production) to become a terrace for a new condo in the adjacent warehouse. Reuse of existing structures on-site can enhance the design of the site by referencing the identity of the previous intervention. At the start of the project, evaluate project sites and old buildings for materials to reuse. Include known subgrade structures in the evaluation as well.

Reduce Material Use

Designing smaller structures (e.g., smaller decks, thinner slabs and walls, flexible footings, cable balustrades rather than hollow steel tube rails, smaller parking lots and spaces, narrower roads) with fewer elements (e.g., excessive finishes or ornaments) and smaller members (e.g., 4 × 4 posts, not 6 × 6 unless structurally necessary) can substantially reduce use of materials. Designing structures to modular material sizes can minimize construction waste (e.g., cutoffs). For instance, wood decks should be sized based on available board lengths.

Use Durable Materials

Designing and detailing site structures with durable materials that will last the life of the site and beyond to other structures will reduce virgin resource use. Ease of repair of the structure will also extend the life. Brick or concrete bricks are durable materials and when sand-set can be easily repaired, replaced, or re-leveled without removal of the entire installation. After the useful life of the paving they can be removed and reused in another installation.

Reclaim and Reuse Materials or Products in Whole Form

Deconstructing previously developed sites rather than demolishing them can allow for reclamation of materials and products that can be reused in new site structures or applications. In addition to reducing use of virgin resources and saving manufacturing energy and pollution, reuse of materials on-site can save energy and costs of transporting new materials to the site. Reduced demolition waste can save on landfill fees, which may offset the increased cost of deconstruction over demolition. A major consideration is storage of reclaimed materials during the construction process. It is important that storage facilities on or near the site maintain the integrity of the material (e.g., recovered wood should be protected from excess moisture) without negatively impacting the site itself (e.g., avoid stockpiles on tree roots). Where deconstructed materials can't be reused on-site, they can be taken to local salvage or reprocessing facilities.

Use Reclaimed Materials from Other Sources

The only major impacts of reused materials are energy consumption in transport, reworking and refinishing, and installation. Reclaimed materials can be obtained from numerous sources beyond the project site. Materials exchanges are increasing in areas of the country with higher landfill fees, and many municipalities will list recycling and salvage facilities in the region. There are many Internet materials exchange websites as well. Materials should be obtained from local sources as fuel use for transport can be considerable with heavy landscape materials.

Reprocess Existing Structures and Materials for Use On-site

Reprocessed materials are those that are broken down or size reduced from their unit or standard size. Although downcycled, reprocessing materials uses less energy and produces fewer emissions than remanufacturing for recycling. Bringing crushing or other processing equipment to the site rather than hauling the materials to a reprocessing facility can save transport fuel use and costs. Plan for processed material stockpiles during construction.

Use Reprocessed Materials from Other Sites

Material reprocessing facilities are growing in number as landfill costs increase. Crushed concrete, tires, asphalt, glass, and other materials can be obtained from reprocessing facilities for use as aggregates or concrete or asphalt ingredients. Care should be taken to minimize haul distances.

Specify Materials and Products with Reuse Potential and Design for Disassembly (DfD)

Materials that are installed in such a way that they can be easily removed at the end of the life of the landscape and reused elsewhere may not be green themselves, but the way that they are assembled is. For example, masonry installations where no mortar is used, such as interlocking retaining wall units, allow for easy disassembly and reuse of the materials. Also, use of metal fasteners rather than welding, where applicable, facilitates removal of reusable parts.

Specify Recycled-content Materials and Products

Recycled-content materials or products are manufactured using reclaimed materials, scrap, or waste as the feedstock. Some energy is used and emissions and waste result from manufacturing of the new product; however, it is often less than with use of virgin feedstocks. Use of recycled materials will also divert waste from landfills or incinerators. Post-consumer recycled content is preferable to pre-consumer as it is more likely to have been diverted from landfills. Pre-consumer recycled content often can be reused in other industrial processes. With the exception of metals and some plastics, most recycled-content products are downcycled from their original use (e.g., wood joists chipped for mulch). An overemphasis on recycled-content materials can result in greater environmental impacts for a given structure. For example, use of steel with a relatively high recycled content may be chosen over wood that has no recycled content, yet even the recycled steel can result in greater energy use, emissions, and waste than a comparable wood member.

Use Materials and Products with Recycling Potential

In an effort to close materials loops, thinking ahead to the end of a structure's useful life and the recyclability of materials used to build it is an important step in resource minimization. Simple materials such as concrete, asphalt, wood, and polyethylene plastics (e.g., HDPE, PE, LDPE) are easily reprocessed and recycled. Composite materials such as mixed plastic and wood fiber composite lumber or coated metals have no or limited recycling potential. PVC, a common site construction material for pipes, fences, and decking, is technically recyclable, but many plastics recycling facilities consider it a contaminant to other plastics recycling and will not take it.

Specify Materials and Products Made from Renewable Resources

Materials and products made from renewable resources offer the opportunity for closed-loop material systems. A number of site construction products are made from renewable, biobased resources; however, some will decompose and biodegrade if not preserved in some way. Wood is the most common site construction material that is renewable. It is considered to be a "long-cycle" renewable material as the average regrowth time from trees used for lumber is 25 years for softwoods. Rapidly renewable materials are primarily plants that are harvested in cycles shorter than ten years. Coir and jute are used for geotextiles; succulents are used as stabilizers for loose aggregate paving; and plant oils are used in form-release agents. Bamboo and willow can be used in landscape structures, and fiber from processed crops is used in engineered wood products. Living materials (e.g., slope stabilization with plants, willow wattles, willow fences and domes) are renewable in place. Recycling of renewable materials can often be accomplished by composting or aerobic/anaerobic digestion, using minimal energy and chemicals.

Specify Materials or Products from Manufacturers with Product Take-back Programs

Product or packaging take-back programs are a new trend in manufacturing, particularly in EU legislation and incentive programs. In many EU countries, some manufacturers are required to take back and reuse or recycle the packing for their products. This has resulted in more efficient packaging methods and greater use of recyclable packaging materials. Some manufacturers offer take-back programs for their product as well. Construction material take-back programs are starting to be seen among carpeting and flooring manufacturers.

MATERIALS OR PRODUCTS THAT MINIMIZE ENVIRONMENTAL IMPACTS

Materials and products can cause negative impacts to ecosystems and the environment during all phases of their life cycle. In the materials acquisition phase, mining and harvesting practices can impact habitats and removal of vegetation increases runoff, loss of topsoil, and sedimentation of waterways. Waste piles from mining can leach heavy metals into the soil and ground and surface waters. Emissions and waste from manufacturing can impact air, water, and soil both near and far from the facility. Transport of materials and products between all life-cycle phases uses nonrenewable fuel and releases emissions. Construction and maintenance of materials and products can involve solvents, adhesives, sealers, and finishes that off-gas VOCs or release toxic chemicals to the environment. Dust from unstabilized roads can impact air quality and adjacent vegetation and crops. And disposal of materials and products after their use can fill landfills, impact soil and water around poorly managed landfills, and impact air quality if incinerated.

Use Sustainably Harvested or Mined Materials

Some manufacturers take steps to eliminate or mitigate air, water, and soil pollution from their raw material acquisition processes. While mining operations are largely unregulated, some companies make efforts to protect or remediate negative effects from their mining activities. Growth and harvesting of renewable materials can have environmental impacts from fertilizer and pesticide use, impacting soil health and resulting in eutrophication of nearby water bodies. Attention should be paid to farming and harvesting practices of renewable materials.

Use Certified Wood

As it is renewable and has relatively low embodied energy, wood can be considered a green material if it comes from well-managed forests and is harvested sustainably. Environmentally responsible forest management includes practices that protect the functional integrity and diversity of tree stands, minimize clearcutting, protect old-growth forests, and minimize wasteful harvesting and milling techniques (Forest Stewardship Council [FSC]). The Forest Stewardship Council (FSC) has developed standards for third-party certification of sustainably harvested wood. Certification of lumber should be made by an FSC-certified independent party. Chapter 10 discusses other forest certification organizations.

Use Minimally Processed Materials

Materials and products that are minimally processed (e.g., uncut stone, earth materials, wood, bamboo) often pose fewer ecological impacts. Reduced manufacturing and processing can conserve energy use and potentially harmful emissions and wastes. Minimally processed materials are usually associated with fewer hidden wastes.

Specify Low Embodied Energy Materials

Products that are minimally processed, such as stone and wood, usually have lower embodied energy than highly processed materials such as plastics and metals. Embodied energy is the total energy required to produce and install a material or product during all stages of the life cycle. Evaluating the embodied energy of materials can be a useful baseline for comparing two different materials; however, this type of analysis does not take into account other factors of production such as pollutants and toxins released, resources used, or habitats disturbed. If a product is complex (made from more than one material, such as a steel and wood bench), the embodied energy of the bench would include the energy inputs from both the wood and steel components plus the energy inputs to assemble and finish them.

Specify Materials Produced with Energy from Renewable Sources

Materials and products produced using renewable energy sources (e.g., solar, wind, hydroelectric, biofuels, geothermal) can have reduced environmental impacts. Combustion of fossil fuels, the primary energy source in a high percentage of manufacturing activities, releases greenhouse gases and air pollutants contributing to global climate change, acid rain, and human respiratory health problems. Any comparison of embodied energy of materials should include an examination of energy sources as a product with relatively high embodied energy may be considered lower impact if it is produced with energy from renewable sources. Aluminum requires around eight times as much energy to produce as a comparable amount of steel, yet its primary energy source is renewable hydroelectric power, whereas the primary fuel energy source of steel is coal.

Use Local Materials

Transport of building materials, especially heavy or bulky ones, not only requires a tremendous amount of fuel energy, but also contributes to air and water pollution. Using regionally extracted and manufactured materials can help lessen the environmental impact of a material, by reducing environmental impacts of transport. Transportation costs may also be reduced; at the same time the local economy is supported. Availability of regionally manufactured materials depends on the project location. Ideally, heavy materials such as aggregate, concrete, and brick should be procured within 100 miles, medium-weight materials within 500 miles and lightweight materials within 1000 miles of the project site (Living Building Challenge). Distances between raw material extraction locations and manufacturing/processing facilities should be included in these calculations. Researching regionally available materials and products during the schematic design phase can facilitate use of local materials. Creating databases of regional materials and products can save time on future projects within the same region.

Specify Low-polluting Materials

Some raw material extraction, manufacturing, or disposal processes for construction materials produce waste, by-products, and emissions that can contribute harmful pollutants and particulates to air, water, and soil. Some manufacturers minimize pollution from their processes through equipment or process improvement or state-of-the-art pollution controls. Materials with relatively high-polluting processes are metals mining, primary metal production, metal finishing, cement production, and PVC production and disposal.

Specify Low-water Use and Low–water-polluting Materials

Some materials and products require large amounts of water during processing, manufacturing, or construction. The used water is often contaminated with heavy metals, hazardous chemicals, or particulates and sediments, and is a disposal risk if not treated and remediated. Material manufacturing processes that use large amounts of water or can result in water pollution are metal mining and primary processing, PVC production, stone working, brick making, and lumber processing. Disposal of some materials, such as PVC pipes, can affect groundwater quality. Some manufacturers recycle wastewater back into manufacturing processes. Some employ chemical and heavy metal removal techniques to safely dispose of potential pollutants.

MATERIALS OR PRODUCTS THAT POSE NO OR LOW HUMAN HEALTH RISKS

Low-emitting Materials and Products

Many adhesives, sealers, finishes, and coatings contain volatile organic compounds (VOCs) and other harmful chemical ingredients that can off-gas in use, leading to air pollution, or leach into soil and groundwater in disposal. Construction workers and end users exposed to these chemicals can be adversely affected in many ways. Products containing synthetic chemicals should be carefully examined for harmful effects. Many synthetic chemicals are not biodegradable or easily broken down. The National Research Council estimated that over 65,000 synthetic chemical compounds introduced and in use since 1950 have not been tested on humans (INFORM 1995). Nontoxic, organic, or natural alternative products are increasingly available.

Specify Materials or Products That Avoid Toxic Chemicals or By-products

Materials can contain or emit known toxins during life-cycle phases of manufacture, use, or disposal. Persistent bioaccumulative toxins (PBTs), known and suspected carcinogens, teratogens, and products with hazardous chemicals should be avoided. For example, dioxin, a known carcinogen, is released during the manufacture and incineration of polyvinylchloride (PVC) products such as rigid pipe, plastic fencing and railings, drip irrigation tubing, garden hoses, and lawn edging. The EPA's Toxic Release Inventory (TRI) maintains manufacturer's self-reported data on their toxic releases by compound.

MATERIALS OR PRODUCTS THAT ASSIST WITH SUSTAINABLE SITE DESIGN STRATEGIES

Some site structures may be constructed from materials that are not in and of themselves green, but the way in which they are used contributes to the sustainable function of the site. For instance, use of highly reflective white portland cement concrete, not considered a "green" material because of its relatively high embodied energy, will aid in reducing the urban heat island effect over the life of a pavement, potentially saving energy to cool adjacent buildings. Over the long life of a site, the impacts from manufacture of the material may be minimized with the benefits it can provide for the site's environment.

Products That Promote a Site's Hydrologic Health

Design of sites to respect natural drainage patterns, minimize impermeable surfaces, maximize storm water infiltration, and improve storm water quality can protect the hydrologic health of a site and a region. While polyethylene filter fabric would not be considered a green material, it can go a long way toward ensuring the appropriate function of storm water structures such as bioswales or rain gardens. Green roof products can also promote hydrologic health.

Materials and Products That Sequester Carbon

Lumber, engineered wood products, and many bio-based products sequester carbon until they decay; then it is released. New technologies are in development that capture carbon, reducing CO_2 from other sources such as carbon-sequestering concrete.

Products That Reduce the Urban Heat Island Effect

Heat island effects result from solar energy retention on constructed surfaces in urban areas, elevating the temperature differential between urban and rural environments. Streets, sidewalks, parking lots, and roofs are the primary contributors to the heat island effect. Use of highly reflective paving materials or open grid pavement structures with vegetation in the cells can reduce the heat island effect. Pervious pavements will cool pavement by allowing air and water to circulate through them.

Products That Reduce Energy Consumption of Site Operation

Products such as solar lights, high-efficiency lights, Energy Star pumps, and irrigation controllers will reduce a site's energy consumption over the life of the site.

Products That Reduce Water Consumption of Site Operation

Products that use water efficiently, such as drip irrigation, irrigation sensors and timers, and rainwater collection barrels, will reduce the site's water consumption.

MATERIALS OR PRODUCTS FROM COMPANIES WITH SUSTAINABLE SOCIAL, ENVIRONMENTAL, AND CORPORATE PRACTICES

Social, environmental, and corporate practices of a product manufacturer or distributor can impact the sustainability of a product. Products should be sourced from companies that take responsibility for the environmental and human health impacts of their operations; protect the health, safety, and well-being of their employees; provide fair compensation and equal opportunity for all workers; protect consumer health and safety; and contribute positively to community health and well-being (Pharos Project). Ask manufacturers for corporate ethics statements, fair labor statements, and the location (if applicable, country) of raw material acquisition and production.

The Contents and Structure of This Book

Materials for Sustainable Sites is intended to fill a critically important gap in the literature on sustainable site design. This book aims to be a comprehensive resource that clarifies the environmental and human health impacts of site construction materials and products and, maybe more importantly, provides designers, specifiers, and educators specific and detailed strategies to reduce these impacts. This book does not contain definitive answers for the "best" and "worst" site construction materials to use. This is an impossible goal given the wide range of performance expectations, site conditions, project constraints, and client priorities within which construction materials must be evaluated.

Table 1–1 Materials for Sustainable Sites Defined

Materials or products that minimize resource use:

Products that use less material
Reused material and products
Reprocessed materials
Post-consumer recycled-content materials
Pre-consumer recycled-content materials
Products made from agricultural waste
Materials or products with reuse potential
Materials or products with recycling potential
Renewable materials
Rapidly renewable materials
Durable materials
Materials or products from manufacturers with product take-back programs

Materials or products with low environmental impacts:

Sustainably harvested or mined materials
Minimally processed materials
Low-polluting materials in extraction, manufacture, use, or disposal
Low water use materials in extraction, manufacture, use, or disposal
Low energy use materials in extraction, manufacture, use, or disposal
Materials made with energy from renewable sources (e.g., wind, solar)
Local materials

Materials or products posing no or low human and environmental health risks:

Low-emitting materials and products
Materials or products that avoid toxic chemicals or by-products in their entire life cycle

Materials or products that assist with sustainable site design strategies:

Products that promote a site's hydrological health by reducing storm water runoff quantities and improving hydrologic qualities
Products that reduce the urban heat island effect
Products that reduce energy consumption of site operation
Products that reduce water consumption of site operation

Materials or products from companies with sustainable social, environmental, and corporate practices

This book takes the approach that no effort to reduce environmental and human health impacts is too small, even though larger steps may be preferable. There are many shades of green in construction materials, from use of a small amount of recycled content in a standard material such as concrete to use of on-site earth materials to construct site pavements and walls.

Changes can occur incrementally through small steps or may be achieved more drastically through larger steps. Therefore, this book presents a range of options for "greening" the standard materials of site construction in addition to offering information on alternative "dark green" materials such as earthen materials, bamboo, or high-volume fly ash concrete. The aim is to encourage both small and large efforts to minimize the environmental and human health impacts of construction materials. Nearly any material can be "greened" and a small step in the right direction is better than no step if the big step is not acceptable. Many small steps can add up to big impacts, and small steps over and over can result in a changed material industry—an industry that closes material loops; eliminates toxins and toxic wastes; and uses durable, local materials.

For example, if at first concrete is specified with 30% fly ash substituted for portland cement, and it performs well, then for the next project it is 40% fly ash with 10% recycled concrete for aggregate, progress has been made. Then as the clients, contractors, and structural engineers grow more familiar with these alternatives and 60% Class C fly ash, 40% recycled concrete for coarse aggregate, or 40% spent foundry sand for fine aggregate are specified to achieve a more durable concrete wall, substantial changes with far-reaching positive impacts will have been accomplished.

This incremental approach to change is the basic premise of this book. Radical change, if it can be accomplished, can be a good thing, but the reality is that the small steps of incremental change may be a much more realistic approach within the mainstream construction industry.

This book devotes one chapter each to the basic materials of site construction: concrete, asphalt, aggregates and stone, brick masonry, earthen materials, lumber and wood products, metals, plastics, and biobased materials. Each chapter discusses basic attributes of the material, and environmental and human health impacts during all phases of its life cycle. Then it provides detailed discussion of strategies and technologies to reduce these impacts, and current standards, resources, and items for consideration during specification of these materials and products.

This book is intended for all professionals who design, specify, educate, or regulate sustainable sites. Professionals and educators in landscape architecture, architecture, civil engineering, urban design, and construction management will find valuable information to assist them in material and product selection and evaluation.

And, while this book addresses site construction materials, there is a substantial overlap with many architectural building materials such as concrete, brick, lumber and wood products, metals, plastics, aggregates and stone, earthen materials, and biobased materials. They are used differently in buildings than in site applications, but their life-cycle impacts and some strategies for reducing the impacts are similar. Therefore, this book can be of value to architects as they make decisions about building construction materials as well.

This chapter, Chapter 1, "Materials for Sustainable Sites Defined," has identified the basic tenets of materials for sustainable sites. These have been carried into each individual material chapter and have shaped the content and issues discussed. There has been no attempt to rank the attributes here because their relative importance will vary by material and site conditions. Discussions of ranking priorities follow in subsequent chapters.

Chapter 2, "Background: Inputs, Outputs, and Impacts of Construction Materials," begins with a summary of environmental and human health impacts resulting from the production, use, and disposal of construction materials. Relationships between the impacts and materials are illustrated and the life-cycle phases of materials and products are defined. Chapter 2 reveals the sheer magnitude of resources and waste that result from material production and begins to pinpoint the major problem areas to address with material and product selection. The chapter concludes with a hopeful discussion of recent trends in industrial ecology and material manufacture, and ideologies, principles, and policies relating to the sustainable use of construction materials.

Chapter 3, "Evaluating the Environmental and Human Health Impacts of Materials," takes the position that with careful attention to environmental and human health costs throughout their life cycle, one can minimize their impacts. Therefore chapter 3 discusses the practice of life-cycle assessment (LCA) and offers techniques for sustainability assessment (SA) and embodied energy and carbon analysis of building materials. Acknowledging that an LCA is outside the skills and scope of most designers, the chapter provides explanations of current LCA tools and other information sources to assist designers with material and product evaluation. Establishment of environmental and human health priorities and weightings is also discussed.

Chapter 4, "Resource Reuse: Designing with and Specifying Reclaimed, Reprocessed, and Recycled-content Materials," addresses one of the most critical and far-reaching principles of materials for sustainable sites—the reuse and recycling of materials and products. The importance of this activity is manifest not only in the conservation of natural resource use, but also in the related reductions of habitat destruction of energy use for primary processing of raw materials, waste, and pollution. The chapter discusses priorities and a hierarchy for reduction of resource use from reusing existing structures in place to recycling down to energy recovery. The chapter provides techniques of design for disassembly and deconstruction so that our existing built environment can be "mined" for resources after its useful life.

Chapter 5 leads the individual materials chapters with the most commonly used construction material in the world: concrete. The many advantages of concrete are weighed against the severe energy consumption and pollution resulting from cement manufacture. The main focus of the chapter is on use of pozzolanic and cementitious substitutes for portland cement, followed by a discussion of recycled materials that can be substituted for natural aggregates in a concrete mix. Considerations for the specification of porous concrete are provided.

Chapter 6 reintroduces earthen building materials for consideration in the modern site construction material palette. The chapter defines and discusses specification considerations for rammed earth, compressed earth blocks, adobe, sprayed earth, cob, rammed earth tires, earthbag, and soil cement construction methods.

It discusses soils, soil testing and amendments, and stabilizing additives and finishes to allow use of relatively low-impact earthen structures in any climate.

Chapter 7 discusses methods to balance the environmental impacts of brick production by maximizing longevity of the brick product. Clay bricks are known for their durability and when used appropriately can be used over and over again in many different structures, often outlasting the life of a landscape and giving new life to another. Strategies to minimize quantities of bricks used through perforated walls and single-wythe serpentine walls or pier and panel walls are discussed, along with techniques for reducing a wall's structural materials and footings.

Chapter 8 addresses the most ubiquitous paving material, asphalt concrete pavement, and provides many techniques to minimize its environmental impacts, from cooling the mix to recycling asphalt in place to making asphalt porous, supporting sustainable storm water strategies and reducing the pavement's contribution to the urban heat island effect. The chapter concludes that there is much that can be done to reduce the environmental and human health impacts of asphalt pavements.

Chapter 9 provides strategies for efficient use of stone and aggregates with both natural and recycled materials. While aggregate and stone are relatively low-impact materials to produce compared with cement or metals, the sheer volume of aggregate used in construction poses resource consumption and habitat destruction impacts. Use of a wide variety of recycled materials for aggregates in base materials and as block materials in surface pavement and walls is discussed along with techniques to reduce material use with gravel pavements, dry stack walls, gabions, and gravel-based wall foundations. Sustainable site strategies are supported with discussions of porous gravel pavements and structural soils.

Chapter 10 explores the often controversial topic of wood use for sustainable sites and concludes that wood offers the potential to be an extremely sustainable and renewable construction material if it is grown and harvested sustainably or reclaimed from other structures, naturally decay resistant, or treated with one of the newer low-toxicity treatments, finished with a renewable low-VOC finish, and detailed to conserve wood resources. The value of efficient wood use and potential impacts of engineered wood products are discussed along with the role that forests and even harvested wood play in carbon sequestration. Emphasis throughout the chapter is on detailing wood structures to last long enough to ensure that the equivalent tree can be grown to replace the lumber used, making wood a truly renewable material.

Chapter 11 addresses metals, the group of materials with the largest environmental and human health impacts of any site construction material. The chapter begins with an extensive explanation of the impacts that metals pose, primarily in the mining and primary processing phases, and to a lesser degree in the finishing phase. Strategies for metal product specification focus on ensuring a long use life for metal products by inhibiting corrosion in an attempt to offset the huge environmental impacts of their manufacture. Benefits and drawbacks of metal recycling are discussed along with the wide variety of available metal finishes.

The wide range of plastics used in site construction materials is the topic of chapter 12. While all are petroleum-based products, impacts from plastics manufacture, use, and disposal vary widely. HDPE plastic is a relatively benign plastic with the ability to be easily recycled into new plastic products—many of which are used in site construction. At the other end of the impact spectrum is polyvinyl chloride (PVC), the most commonly used plastic in construction, which poses severe impacts in manufacture and disposal and is virtually unrecyclable. The chapter discusses the often-contested impacts of PVC and provides alternative materials to consider.

Chapter 13 discusses the expanding range of non-living, biobased materials for site construction. Short-cycle materials grown on a ten-year or shorter rotation—such as fiber crops, bamboo, agricultural residues, and plant seed oils—are discussed along with impacts of their growth and processing. Some biobased site construction materials discussed are coir and jute erosion control products; straw mulch and straw bale; cellulose fiber mulch; compost; bamboo products; and plant-based soil stabilizers, form-release agents, finishes, and sealants.

REFERENCES

Cascadia Chapter, U.S. Green Building Council. Living Building Challenge (LBC). http://www.cascadiagbc.org/lbc (accessed April 6, 2008).

Forest Stewardship Council (FSC). http://www.fsc.org.

Healthy Building Network. Pharos Project. Institute for Local Self-Reliance. www.pharosproject.net (accessed April 6, 2008).

INFORM, Inc. 1995. *Toxics Watch 1995*. New York: INFORM, Inc.

Kibert, C. J., J. Sendzimir, and B. Guy, eds. 2002. *Construction Ecology: Nature as the Basis for Green Building*. London: Routledge.

2

Background: Inputs, Outputs, and Impacts of Construction Materials

The typical site construction product is composed of a variety of constituents, each with its own complex web of inputs, outputs, and impacts that led to their existence. This broad web can extend hundreds of miles, across the country, or even around the world—and is largely invisible to those who specify the product. Impacts—both to the environment and to human health—begin during the raw material extraction phase with destruction of ecosystems and habitats to extract mostly nonrenewable materials from the earth. They continue in processing, manufacturing, and fabricating phases, using energy and producing emissions, effluents, and waste. Transport impacts of materials between phases are often significant because many site construction materials are bulky and heavy. Compared with the average consumer product, the use phase of site materials is relatively long, yet maintenance activities can pose risks to the environment and to human health. After the useful life of the material, disposal will pose another set of impacts, yet a recent increase in recycling and reuse of materials such as asphalt and concrete has substantially reduced disposal to landfills.

The inputs (resources, energy, and water) and outputs (emissions, effluents, and solid waste) that occur during the phases of a product's life cycle result in a variety of impacts that affect the health of our ecosystems, our planet, and ourselves. The burning of fossil fuels and even some material processing activities contribute greenhouse gases to the atmosphere and acid deposition on water and land. Extensive quantities of water are consumed to produce some products and wastewater effluents from their processing can carry pollutants, acids, and heavy metals into the environment. Some air and water emissions contain biological toxins, carcinogens, or mutagens that find their way into the human body, potentially producing a range of negative health effects. And the amount of waste that results from each phase places a burden on the adjacent ecosystem, sometimes through pollution, other times just through sheer volume.

But changes in the ways that products are made and specified are starting to occur—changes that pay more attention to these impacts and attempt to reduce them. Growing recognition of the immensity of the above impacts, coupled with rising fuel costs, is leading to practices, sometimes policies, of pollution prevention, waste reduction, and energy conservation in the manufacturing industry. Some new ideologies of product manufacture draw inspiration from nature's closed-loop processes, in which waste from one process is "food" for another. Others acknowledge the health risks of hazardous chemical use and are attempting to reduce their use.

This chapter begins by summarizing environmental and human health issues related to construction materials and their production. Typical phases of the life cycle of a material or product are discussed along with general impacts of inputs and outputs of construction materials and products. Trends in industrial ecology and material manufacture conclude the chapter along with ideologies, principles, and policies relating to the sustainable use of construction materials.

Major Environmental and Human Health Concerns Resulting from Construction Materials and Products

In material and product production, interaction with the environment occurs in two distinct ways. The earth is the *source* of all material resources and a *sink* for emissions, effluents, and solid wastes. It is in both of these ways that the use of materials impacts the environment. Overuse at sources depletes both the quantity and quality of available resources. And extraction of resources degrades ecosystems at the source location. Overuse of sinks from overgeneration, and careless disposal of emissions and waste, impact the balance of natural processes and ecosystems.

Construction materials are a major market segment, with 24% of Total Domestic Output (by weight) of all materials manufactured for construction-related activities (World Resources Institute [WRI] 2000). The environmental and human health concerns discussed in this section have been identified as partially resulting from overuse of sources and sinks. Table 2–1 lists these concerns and their linkages to manufacturing processes. The table and information presented in this chapter demonstrate that many environmental problems are partially related to material manufacture, use, and disposal. It is important to note that the severity of impacts among materials and products varies widely. Discussion of severity of risks and priorities for reducing the impacts summarized below is included in chapter 3, "Evaluating the Environmental and Human Health Impacts of Materials."

GLOBAL CLIMATE CHANGE

Global climate change is defined as long-term fluctuations in temperature, precipitation, wind, and all other aspects of the earth's climate. Climate change holds potential to impact many aspects of life on the planet with rising sea levels, melting glaciers, more violent storms, loss of biodiversity, reduced food supplies, and displaced populations. Global warming, one type of global climate change, is the increase in average temperature of the earth's near-surface air and oceans. Global warming occurs when energy from the earth is reradiated as heat and is absorbed and trapped by greenhouse gases in the atmosphere. This greenhouse effect reduces heat loss to space, resulting in warmer temperatures on Earth.

The Intergovernmental Panel on Climate Change (IPCC) concludes, "Most of the observed increase in globally averaged temperatures since the mid-20th century is very likely due to the observed increase in anthropogenic greenhouse gas concentrations," which leads to warming of the surface and lower atmosphere by increasing the greenhouse effect (IPCC 2007b). Greenhouse gases (GHG) include carbon dioxide (CO_2), methane, nitrous oxide, ozone, sulfur hexafluoride, hydrofluorocarbons, perfluorocarbons, and chlorofluorocarbons. In addition, there are several gases that do not have a direct global warming effect but indirectly impact solar radiation absorption by influencing the formation of greenhouse gases, including ground-level and stratospheric ozone. They are carbon monoxide (CO), oxides of nitrogen (NO_x), and non-CH_4 volatile organic compounds (NMVOCs). The IPCC predicts that a rise in mean global temperatures of between 2 and 11 degrees Celsius could be expected by the end of the twenty-first century (IPCC 2007b).

The global carbon cycle, made up of large carbon flows and reservoirs, involves billions of tons of carbon in the form of CO_2. CO_2 is absorbed by sinks (e.g.,

Table 2–1 Environmental Concerns and Connections to Construction Materials

Environmental Concerns	Connections to Construction Materials
Global climate change	Greenhouse gas (GHG) emissions from energy use, non-fossil fuel emissions from material manufacture (eg. cement production, iron and steel processing), transportation of materials, landfill gases
Fossil fuel depletion	Electricity and direct fossil fuel usage (e.g., power and heating requirements), feedstock for plastics, asphalt cement, and sealants, solvents, adhesives
Stratospheric ozone depletion	Emissions of CFCs, HCFCs, halons, nitrous oxides (e.g., cooling requirements, cleaning methods, use of fluorine compounds, aluminum production, steel production)
Air pollution	Fossil fuel combustion, mining, material processing, manufacturing processes, transport, construction and demolition
Smog	Fossil fuel combustion, mining, material processing, manufacturing processes, transport, construction and demolition
Acidification	Sulfur and NO_x emissions from fossil fuel combustion, smelting, acid leaching, acid mine drainage and cleaning
Eutrophication	Manufacturing effluents, nutrients from nonpoint source runoff, fertilizers, waste disposal
Deforestation, desertification, and soil erosion	Commercial forestry and agriculture, resource extraction, mining, dredging
Habitat alteration	Land appropriated for mining, excavating, and harvesting materials. Growing of biomaterials, manufacturing, waste disposal
Loss of biodiversity	Resource extraction, water usage, acid deposition, thermal pollution
Water resource depletion	Water usage and effluent discharges of processing and manufacturing
Ecological toxicity	Solid waste and emissions from mining and manufacturing, use, maintenance and disposal of construction materials

Sources: Ayers 2002; Azapagic et al. 2004; Graedel and Allenby 1996; Gutowski 2004; UNEP 1999

oceans and living biomass) and emitted to the atmosphere by sources in natural processes such as decomposition of plant or animal matter. In equilibrium, carbon fluxes are somewhat balanced; however, since the Industrial Revolution, global atmospheric concentrations of CO_2 have risen around 35% (IPCC 2001). This rise is due largely to the combustion of fossil fuels.

In the United States in 2005, fossil fuel combustion accounted for 94% of CO_2 emissions, with the remainder from sources such as chemical conversions (e.g., cement, iron, and steel production), forestry, and land clearing for development. Globally, the United States contributed 22% of CO_2 emissions in 2004 (IPCC 2007b) while the U.S. population is just 4.5% of the worldwide population.

Three-quarters of anthropogenic greenhouse gas emissions are generated from fossil fuel combustion to power vehicles and power generation plants, and as raw material for production of synthetic polymers (IPCC 2007a). Other major greenhouse gas releases result from the conversion of limestone into lime for cement manufacture, from animal agriculture, and from deforestation. Table 2–3 contains greenhouse gas contributions of major industrial sectors involved in material production related to construction materials.

Greenhouse gas emissions are often directly related to the embodied energy of a construction material, as for most materials the emissions stem from the fossil fuel combustion required in their production. For instance, steel requires a relatively high amount of energy to produce—energy derived primarily from coal combustion processes, so the greenhouse gas emissions are directly related. Aluminum and concrete are the two main construction material exceptions to this, for

Table 2–2 Global Warming Potentials (GWPs) and Atmospheric Lifetimes (Years) of GHG[a]

Gas	Atmospheric Lifetime In Years	GWP[b]
CO_2	50–200	1
CH_4	12 ± 3	21
N_2O	120	310
HFC-23	264	11,700
CF_4	50,000	6,500
C_2F_6	10,000	9,200
C_2F_{10}	2,600	7,000
C_6F_{14}	3,200	7,400
SF_6	3,200	23,900

[a]100-year time horizon

[b]The GWP of CH_4 includes the direct effects and those indirect effects due to the production of tropospheric ozone and stratospheric water vapor. The indirect effect due to the production of CO_2 is not included.

Source: U.S. EPA 2007c

different reasons. Because the energy requirements to produce aluminum are so great, hydroelectric power is the primary power source (55%). While hydroelectric power poses other environmental concerns, CO_2 release

is relatively low compared to coal combustion or even natural gas; therefore, pound for pound steel has a lower embodied energy than aluminum, but higher GHG emissions. Greenhouse gas emissions for concrete are about twice the embodied energy, as almost equal amounts of CO_2 are released in the conversion of limestone to lime as in the fossil fuel combustion to heat the limestone.

FOSSIL FUEL DEPLETION

Fossil fuels, the primary source of energy for the industrialized world, are being extracted at a rate thousands of times faster than the time taken for them to renew. They are considered to be nonrenewable resources because they take millions of years to renew. As fuel reserves decrease, it is expected that extraction and refinement costs will increase. Fossil fuels are used throughout a product's life cycle to power vehicles (used in extraction, transportation, construction, and maintenance); to produce steam or heat for industrial processes; for electricity; to power machinery; and as raw material for production of plastics, other synthetic polymers (e.g., fibers), and solvents. Besides the impacts associated with extraction and combustion of fossil

Table 2–3 Greenhouse Gas Emissions by Industrial Sector in the United States

Industry	1990 Tg CO_2 Eq	2005 Tg CO_2 Eq	Percent Change
Fuel-related GHG emissions from industrial processes	1,539.8	1,575.2	2.3
Nonfuel GHG from industrial processes:			
Iron and steel production	86.2	46.2	−46.4
Cement manufacture	33.3	45.9	37.8
Lime manufacture	11.3	13.7	21.2
Aluminum production	25.3	8.7	−65.6
Limestone and dolomite use	5.5	7.4	34.5
Titanium dioxide production	1.3	1.9	46.2
Ferroalloy production	2.2	1.4	−36.4
Zinc production	0.9	0.5	−44.4
Petrochemical production	2.3	4.0	74.0
Total GHG emissions from all sources	4,724.1	5,751.2	21.7

Source: U.S. EPA 2007c.

fuels, there are no direct environmental impacts of depletion per se.

There is widespread disagreement about the finite nature of fossil fuels, and if and when they will be depleted. Some scientists warn that the effects of current levels of fossil fuel combustion will wreak havoc on climate and the environment before fossil fuel supplies are depleted.

Political concerns over ownership of fossil fuel reserves and concerns about the environmental and human health impacts of combustion have led to increased policy interest in renewable energy sources such as biofuels, geothermal, wind, and solar power in some countries. In the industrial sector, as costs of fossil fuels and purchased electricity increase, some manufacturers are looking to alternative energy sources such as wind power, hydroelectric power, landfill methane capture, or energy recovery from incineration of waste.

STRATOSPHERIC OZONE DEPLETION

The naturally occurring ozone layer of the stratosphere is a critical barrier that prevents harmful shortwave ultraviolet radiation from reaching the earth. Human-caused emissions of ozone-depleting substances, such as chlorofluorocarbons (CFCs; used as a propellant in manufacturing and a refrigerant) and halons (used in fire suppression systems), can cause a thinning of the ozone layer, resulting in more shortwave radiation on Earth. This has a number of potentially negative consequences, such as impacts on plants and agriculture, and increases in cancer and cataracts in people. Additional effects on climate and the functioning of different ecosystems may exist, although the nature of these effects is less clear.

In 1987, over 190 countries, including the United States, signed the Montreal Protocol calling for elimination of CFCs and other stratospheric ozone-depleting substances (ODSs). Since that time, the production of ODSs has been in the process of being phased out. Use of substitutes for CFCs and HCFCs such as hydrofluorocarbons (HFCs) and perfluorocarbons (PFCs) has grown; while they do not contribute to ozone depletion, they are powerful greenhouse gases with high global warming potential (GWP) and long atmospheric lifetimes.

AIR POLLUTION

Air pollutants are airborne solid and liquid particles and gases that can pose risks to the environment and human health. Fugitive emissions result from many activities, including production of electricity; operation of equipment used in manufacture, transport, construction, and maintenance; manufacturing processes; and mining and crushing of materials. Air pollution from manufacturing processes related to site construction materials is discussed in greater detail later in this chapter under outputs from manufacturing.

Amendments to the Clean Air Act were passed in 1990, giving the U.S. EPA rights to restrict levels of criteria air pollutants and emissions of hazardous air pollutants from sources such as power plants and manufacturing facilities. *Criteria air pollutants (CAPs)* are particulate matter (both PM_{10} and $PM_{2.5}$), ground-level ozone, carbon monoxide (CO), sulfur dioxides (SO_2), nitrogen oxides (NO_x), and lead. VOCs and ammonia are also monitored along with CAPs, as they contribute to human and environmental health risks. CAPs, particularly particulate matter and ground-level ozone, are considered by the EPA to be widespread human and environmental health threats (U.S. EPA Air and Radiation). Release of CAPs such as particulate matter, CO, lead, and ozone can contribute to asthma, or more serious respiratory illnesses such as permanent lung damage, and heart disease. SO_2, NO_x, and ozone can contribute to acid rain and ground-level ozone, damaging trees, crops, wildlife, water bodies, and aquatic species. The EPA regulates release of CAPs by setting permissible levels for geographic areas.

Hazardous air pollutants (HAPs), also called toxic air pollutants or air toxics, are pollutants that can cause negative human or environmental health effects. They may cause cancer or other serious health effects such as reproductive effects or birth defects; damage to the immune system; or developmental, respiratory, or neurological problems in humans and other species (U.S. EPA Air and Radiation). Airborne HAPs can deposit onto soils or surface waters, where they are taken up by plants and ingested by animals, and are magnified as they move up the food chain.

Human exposure to toxic air pollutants can occur by breathing contaminated air; eating contaminated food products such as fish from polluted waters or vegetables grown in contaminated soil; drinking water contaminated by toxic air pollutants; or touching contaminated soil, dust, or water. HAPs released into the air such as vinyl chloride (the precursor to PVC) are toxic and can cause cancer, birth defects, long-term injury to the lungs or brain, and nerve damage (U.S. EPA Air and Radiation).

SMOG

Smog is a type of air pollution, resulting when industrial and fuel emissions become trapped at ground level and are transformed after reacting with sunlight. For example, ozone is one component of smog and occurs when volatile organic compounds (VOCs) react with oxides of nitrogen (NO_x). Transport of materials and equipment used in landscape construction and maintenance contributes to smog-producing emissions. Like air pollutants and acidification compounds, smog can have negative effects on the health of people and other biotic communities.

ACIDIFICATION

Acidification occurs in surface waters and soils as acidifying gases, primarily sulfur and nitrogen compounds, either dissolve in water or adhere to solid particles. These compounds reach ecosystems primarily in the form of acid rain, through either a dry or wet deposition process. The primary sources of acid rain are emissions of sulfur dioxide and nitrogen oxide from fossil fuel combustion, although they can also result from natural processes of decaying vegetation and volcanoes. In the United States, roughly two-thirds of all SO_2 and one quarter of all NO_x emissions result from electric power generation, primarily from coal-fired power plants, while another primary source is motor vehicle fuel combustion. In material manufacture, fossil fuels are burned to produce electricity and to power equipment used in raw material extraction, manufacture, transportation, construction, and maintenance. Winds can blow these emissions from power and manufacturing plants over hundreds of miles before they are deposited (U.S. EPA Air and Radiation).

Acid rain causes acidification of rivers, streams, and oceans, lowering the pH and causing damage to fish and other aquatic animals. This can lower the biodiversity of the water body. Soil biology is also negatively affected by acid rain with the consumption of acids by microbes killing some. Some acids in soil can mobilize toxins and leach essential nutrients and minerals.

Sulfur dioxide can interfere with photosynthesis of vegetation, slowing the growth of forests. Trees, particularly those at higher altitudes surrounded by clouds and fog that are more acidic, may be weakened and made more susceptible to other threats. Impacted soils can also contribute to vegetation impacts. Nitrogen oxides affect animals (and humans) through respiratory irritation. In addition, interaction of these compounds with other atmospheric pollutants can have toxic effects on animals and plants through formation of photochemical smog.

Acid rain also accelerates weathering of building materials such as granite, limestone, concrete, and metals. It may even cause some stainless steels to stain. This can cause premature removal and replacement of some building materials.

EUTROPHICATION

Eutrophication is the addition of nutrients, such as nitrogen and phosphorus, to soil or water resulting in overstimulation of plant growth. Eutrophication is a natural process; however, it is accelerated by human activities, causing species composition alterations and reducing ecological diversity. In water, it promotes algal blooms that can cloud the water, blocking sunlight and causing underwater grasses to die. Loss of the grasses reduces habitat and food for aquatic species, sometimes causing their death. As algae die, oxygen in water is depleted, also affecting the health of fish and aquatic species. Eutrophication impacts affect humans by affecting the taste of water (even after treatment) and by negative impacts on swimming, boating, and fishing.

Eutrophication results from the release of pollutants, such as nitrogen and phosphorus, to surface waters from fertilizers, sewage effluent, and manufacturing wastewater. Nitrogen and phosphorus are major components of synthetic fertilizers used in landscape maintenance and agriculture. Unchecked nutrients from nonpoint source pollution in stormwater runoff are also a cause of eutrophication. A 1993 survey of lakes worldwide showed that 54% of lakes in Asia are eu- trophic; in Europe, 53%; in North America, 48%; in South America, 41%; and in Africa, 28% (ILEC 1993).

DEFORESTATION, DESERTIFICATION, AND SOIL EROSION

Only 36% of the world's primary forests remain as of 2005, yet forests play a key role in the health of the planet by containing half of the world's biodiversity and sequestering large quantities of carbon dioxide. Defor- estation, the large-scale removal of forests, contributes to negative environmental impacts such as loss of bio- diversity, global warming, soil erosion, and desertifica- tion. Deforestation is driven by factors such as poverty, economic growth, government policies, technological change, and cultural factors (Food and Agriculture Or- ganization of the United Nations [FAO] 2005). Defor- estation occurs when forested land is cleared for agriculture, mining, new construction of buildings, or roads, or when trees are harvested for fuel or lumber. For site construction materials, forest harvesting for lumber and land clearing for mining of metal ore, min- erals, stone, and gravel are the primary activities that contribute to deforestation. Lumber from some forests, particularly in developing countries, holds substantial economic value and is sometimes harvested illegally. Agricultural expansion was involved in 96% of defor- estation cases in a 2001 study, but it was not the sole

cause, as timber harvesting and road building were often the reason for the cutting. Expansion of cattle op- erations in Brazil is a significant cause of deforestation in the Amazon, with a 3.2% total loss of forests be- tween 2000 and 2005 (FAO 2005).

Nearly 37 million hectares, or just under 1% of the global forested area, was lost between 2000 and 2005. While this is about 19% less than the shrinkage rate of the 1990s, it is still substantial, with largest losses in African, South American, and Southeast Asian coun- tries that contain valuable rain forests. Europe and China both had a net gain of forest land, with a 10% gain in China due to an aggressive reforestation pro- gram (FAO 2005).

When forests are eliminated, they no longer provide ecological services such as carbon sequestration, habitat, erosion control, and regulation of the hydrological cycle. Forests play a vital role in stabilizing the climate by sequestering atmospheric carbon. The FAO estimates that between 1990 and 2005, the carbon storage capac- ity of forests declined by more than 5%. When forests are cut, they can be a significant source of carbon emis- sions from rotting branches and debris that gives off car- bon dioxide. Lumber and other wood products continue to sequester carbon until they decay. Estimates attribute 25% of human-caused carbon emissions to deforesta- tion (FAO 2005). On a global scale, deforestation can affect the albedo, or reflectivity, of the earth, altering

Table 2–4 Change in Extent of Forest, 1990–2005

Region	1990 Area (1,000 ha)	2005 Area (1,000 ha)	Change in Area (1,000 ha)	Change in Area (%)
South America	890,818	831,540	−59,278	−6.65
Africa	699,361	635,412	−63,949	−9.14
Oceania	212,514	206,254	−6,260	−2.95
Central America and Caribbean	32,989	28,385	−4,604	−13.96
North America	677,801	677,464	−337	−0.05
Europe	989,320	1,001,394	+12,073	+1.22
Asia	574,487	571,577	−2,910	−0.51
World	4,077,291	3,952,025	−125,265	−3.07

Source: Adapted from FAO 2005, Annex 3, Table 4

surface temperatures, water evaporation, and rainfall patterns.

Deforestation causes soil erosion, resulting in topsoil loss and sedimentation of water bodies. Increased runoff volume from deforested land can carry topsoil and pollutants into surface waters, causing reduced light penetration, increased turbidity, increased biochemical oxygen demand (BOD), and deoxygenation. These stressors can result in a loss of faunal diversity and possible fish kill. The EPA has estimated that erosion from clear-cut forests can be as much as 12,000 tons per square mile per year. This is 500 times the erosion rate of undisturbed forests.

In arid and semiarid regions, removal of natural forest cover can lead to desertification by exposing soil to wind, erosion, salinization, and rapid evaporation of soil moisture—all of which alter biodiversity and habitats. Desertification is estimated to have affected over 250 million people with potential to affect over a billion, as 40% of the earth's surface is drylands susceptible to desertification (United Nations Convention to Combat Desertification [UNCCD] 2007).

HABITAT ALTERATION

Habitats are altered or destroyed when human activity results in a change in the species composition of plant and animal communities. This can occur through practices that change environmental conditions and reduce habitat, as well as through differential removal or introduction of species. Habitat alteration is a primary impact resulting from mining and harvesting of materials for the manufacture of construction materials. Habitat alteration also can occur as a result of air, water, and land releases from industrial processes that change environmental conditions, such as water quality and quantity, in naturally occurring communities. Effects of habitat alteration include changes in ecosystem function and possible reduced biodiversity.

LOSS OF BIODIVERSITY

Global climate change, the destruction of forests and habitats, and air, water, and soil pollution have all contributed to a loss of biodiversity over the past few centuries. The Millennium Ecosystem Assessment estimates that "extinction rates are [currently] around 100 times greater that rates characteristic of species in the fossil record" (World Resource Assessment 2005). Biodiversity was defined at the UN Earth Summit in 1992 as "the variability among living organisms from all sources including, inter alia, terrestrial, marine, and other aquatic organisms, and the ecological complexes of which they are part: this includes diversity within species, between species and of ecosystems" (United Nations Environment Programme [UNEP] 1999). The stability of an ecosystem is compromised as its species are made extinct and it decreases in complexity. An example of this is monoculture plantings following deforestation for lumber.

Biodiversity is critical to the health of the ecosystems that provide many services keeping humans and the environment in relative balance. The biodiversity of ecosystems plays a role in regulating the chemistry of the atmosphere and water supply, recycling nutrients, and providing fertile soils. Biodiversity controls the spread of diseases, provides food and drugs for humans, and provides resources for industrial materials such as fibers, dyes, resins, gums, adhesives, rubber, and oils.

WATER RESOURCE DEPLETION

Human activities and land uses can deplete water resources, through use rates that exceed groundwater reserves and through practices that prevent aquifer recharge. Product manufacturing activities use water, and effluent wastes that are released to water bodies reduce water resources through pollution. In addition, the use of impervious surfaces (such as concrete and asphalt) seriously reduces groundwater recharge, as do storm water management strategies that convey runoff away from the site. Water resource depletion has serious consequences, by disrupting hydrological cycles, reducing the water available to dilute pollutants, and decreasing water for human consumption and for plant and animal communities that require more abundant and constant water supplies.

ECOLOGICAL TOXICITY

Toxic materials can be released into ecosystems as by-products of manufacturing processes and fossil fuel combustion, and from direct environmental application of toxic pesticides. Like substances that have negative effects on human health, these can also harm animals and plants, with potential impacts on ecosystem function and loss of biodiversity.

HUMAN HEALTH DAMAGE

Negative human health effects can result from exposure to toxic materials, either human-made or naturally occurring. Toxic chemicals and substances can be encountered in all phases of the life cycle of construction materials. Many of these substances result from manufacturing, using, or disposing of plastics (e.g., PVC, polystyrene, ABS), metals, metal finishes, solvents, and adhesives. The effects of these substances vary from momentary irritation (acute) to prolonged illness and disease (chronic) to death. Some compounds are carcinogens, persistent bioaccumulative toxins (PBTs), mutagens, endocrine disruptors, reproductive toxicants, teratogens, or acute or chronic toxicants.

Humans are exposed through numerous pathways to toxic substances, and because the effects are not always noticeable, they are often overlooked. Some mine tailings left from extraction of raw materials can pollute habitats and watersheds, concentrating in fish and working their way up the food chain. Harmful chemicals can be released into water from processing and manufacture and find their way into the drinking water supply. Some manufacturing processes can pose a risk to worker health through exposure. And during use, materials such as asphalt sealants and CCA-treated lumber pose toxic risks to people in contact with the materials. Commonly used adhesives, finishes, sealants, and maintenance products can contain hazardous chemicals and VOCs. During landfill disposal, some materials can threaten drinking water supplies, while incineration of some materials such as PVC can release hazardous chemicals and PBTs into the air and eventually the food supply. Material safety data sheets are mandated by the Occupational Safety and Health Administration's (OSHA) hazard communication standard and are available for all materials/products that may pose risks to human health. Table 2–5 defines classifications of toxins and provides sources of information on each.

Table 2–5 Classifications and Listings of Toxic Substances

PERSISTENT BIOACCUMULATIVE TOXINS (PBTs)

PBTs such as mercury and DDT last for a long time in the environment with little change in their structure or toxic effects. This means that a persistent toxic chemical transported in the wind can be just as toxic 10,000 miles away as it was at the smokestack from which it was released. Some PBTs, such as polychlorinated biphenyls (PCBs), have been found in remote parts of the Arctic, far away from the industrial sources that produce them.

Some of the PBTs that move through the air are deposited into water bodies and concentrate up through the food chain, harming fish-eating animals and people. Small fish may consume plants that live in water contaminated by PBTs, which are absorbed into plant tissues. Larger fish eat smaller fish and as the PBTs pass up the food chain, their levels go up. So a large fish consumed by people may have PBT levels thousands of times in its tissues than those found in the contaminated water. Over 2,000 U.S. water bodies are covered by fish consumption advisories, warning people not to eat the fish because of contamination with chemicals, often PBTs. These compounds have been linked to illnesses such as cancer, birth defects, and nervous system disorders (U.S. EPA Air and Radiation).

PBTs of concern for site construction materials include dioxin emissions from PVC and cement manufacture and PVC disposal, and heavy metals such as lead, mercury, chromium, and cadmium from metal production and finishing.

U.S. EPA Priority PBTs. http://www.epa.gov/pbt/pubs/cheminfo.htm

U.S. EPA Great Lakes Pollution Prevention and Toxics Reduction, The Great Lakes Binational Toxics Strategy http://www.epa.gov/grtlakes/p2/bns.html

Washington State PBT list. http://www.ecy.wa.gov/programs/eap/pbt/pbtfaq.html

Continued

Table 2–5 Classifications and Listings of Toxic Substances *(Continued)*

Stockholm Convention on Persistent Organic Pollutants http://www.pops.int/ and http://www.pops.int/documents/convtext/convtext_en.pdf

European Chemicals Bureau, European Union Status report on PBTs and vPvBs for new and existing substances. http://www.defra.gov.uk/environment/chemicals/achs/060606/achs0614d.pdf

CARCINOGENS

Carcinogens are defined as substances that cause or increase the risk of cancer. The International Agency for Research on Cancer (IARC) classifies substances as to carcinogenic risk in the following categories:

Group 1: The agent is *carcinogenic to humans.*

Group 2A: The agent is *probably carcinogenic to humans.*

Group 2B: The agent is *possibly carcinogenic to humans.*

Group 3: The agent is *not classifiable as to its carcinogenicity to humans.*

Group 4: The agent is *probably not carcinogenic to humans.*

Some chemicals in construction materials, or released during their processing, manufacture, or disposal, are known or suspected carcinogens. Vinyl chloride (used to produce PVC) can cause liver cancer, formaldehyde is linked to cancers of the sinuses and brain, and heavy metal fumes such as chromium, nickel, and cadmium can cause lung cancer (Healthy Building Network 2007).

International Agency for Research on Cancer (IARC), World Health Organization

http://monographs.iarc.fr/ENG/Classification/index.php. Provides monographs on substances that are or may be carcinogens.

National Toxicology Program (NTP), Department of Health and Human Services

Report on Carcinogens, 11th edition; U.S. Department of Health and Human Services, Public Health Service, National Toxicology Program. Lists both known and suspected carcinogens. http://ntp.niehs.nih.gov/

National Institute for Occupational Safety and Health, Centers for Disease Control

List of suspected carcinogens found in the workplace. http://www.cdc.gov/niosh/npotocca.html

State of California, EPA, Office of Environmental Health Hazard Assessment, Safe Drinking Water and Toxic Enforcement Act of 1986. Proposition 65, Chemicals Known to the State to Cause Cancer or Reproductive Toxicity. http://www.oehha.ca.gov/prop65/prop65_list/Newlist.html

Brookhaven National Labs, Department of Energy

Standard carcinogen list that is a compilation of listings by Occupational Safety and Health Administration (OSHA), International Agency for Research on Cancer (IARC), National Toxicology Program (NTP), and American Conference of Industrial Hygienists (ACGIH).

http://www.bnl.gov/esh/shsd/Programs/Program_Area_Chemicals_LabStd_Carcinogens.asp

REPRODUCTIVE TOXIN LISTINGS

Reproductive toxins disrupt both male and female reproductive systems. A teratogen is a substance that causes defects in development between conception and birth or a substance that causes a structural or functional birth defect (Agency for Toxic Substances and Disease Registry [ATSDR]). Lead and mercury, released from fossil fuel combustion and the processing of metals and metal finishes, are examples of reproductive toxins.

Table 2–5 Classifications and Listings of Toxic Substances *(Continued)*

Brookhaven National Labs, Department of Energy

Reproductive toxins table that is a compilation of toxin ratings by Occupational Safety and Health Administration (OSHA), National Toxicology Program (NTP), and American Conference of Industrial Hygienists (ACGIH).

http://www.bnl.gov/esh/shsd/Programs/Program_Area_Chemicals_ReproToxins.asp

State of California, EPA, Office of Environmental Health Hazard Assessment, Safe Drinking Water and Toxic Enforcement Act of 1986. Proposition 65, Chemicals Known to the State to Cause Cancer or Reproductive Toxicity.

http://www.oehha.ca.gov/prop65.html

HIGHLY ACUTE LISTINGS

OSHA defines substances that are considered to have a high degree of acute toxicity as those substances which are highly toxic or toxic and may be fatal or cause damage to target organs as a result of a single exposure or exposures of short duration. OSHA has set thresholds by dose and weight of receiving body (http://www.osha.gov/SLTC/hazardoustoxicsubstances/index.html). Some listings, such as the Comprehensive Environmental Response, Compensation, and Liability Act (CERCLA) Priority List of Hazardous Substances, rank substances based on a combination of their threat to public health and their presence in the environment and potential for human exposure (CERCLA 2005).

Brookhaven National Labs, Department of Energy, Highly Acute Toxins Table

http://www.bnl.gov/esh/shsd/Programs/Program_Area_Chemicals_Highly_Acute_Toxins.asp

CERCLA Priority List of Hazardous Substances, Agency for Toxic Substances and Disease Registry, Department of Health and Human Services. http://www.atsdr.cdc.gov/cercla/

Databases of Chemical Toxicity Profiles

Toxicological Profile Information Sheets, Agency for Toxic Substances and Disease Registry, Department of Health and Human Services. http://www.atsdr.cdc.gov/toxpro2.html

Intergovernmental Programme on Chemical Safety, Database of Chemical Safety Information from Governmental Organizations. Canadian Centre for Occupational Health and Safety (CCOHS); World Health Organization; International Labour Organization; United Nations Environment Programme. http://www.inchem.org/

National Library of Medicine Toxicology Network (TOXNET) Hazardous Substances Data Bank (HSDB) is an online database of peer-reviewed toxicology data for about 5,000 chemicals. http://toxnet.nlm.nih.gov/.

REACH European Commission on the Environment, EUROPA. REACH is a new European Community Regulation on chemicals and their safe use (EC 1907/2006). It deals with the Registration, Evaluation, Authorisation and Restriction of Chemical substances. http://ec.europa.eu/environment/chemicals/reach.htm

IRIS (Integrated Risk Information System), National Center for Environmental Assessment, U.S. EPA. IRIS is a compilation of electronic reports on specific substances found in the environment and their potential to cause human health effects. IRIS was initially developed for EPA staff in response to a growing demand for consistent information on substances for use in risk assessments, decisionmaking, and regulatory activities. The information in IRIS is intended for those without extensive training in toxicology, but with some knowledge of health sciences. http://cfpub.epa.gov/ncea/iris/index.cfm

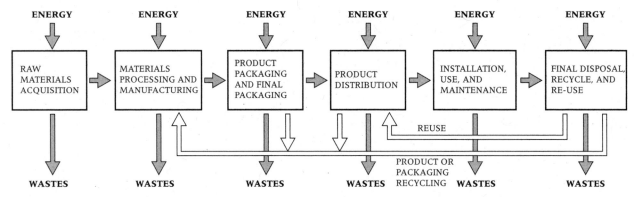

Figure 2–1.

Typical phases of a material or product's life cycle are illustrated, along with energy inputs and waste outputs at each phase. The disposal phase can involve reuse or recycling. (George C. Ramsey. Copyright © 2005, John Wiley & Sons, Inc. Reprinted with the permission of John Wiley & Sons, Inc.)

Life-cycle Phases of a Construction Material or Product

The typical life cycle of materials and products begins with the extraction of raw materials from the earth and ends with the disposal of waste products back to the earth or recycled into other materials. Most material life-cycle flows are relatively linear, where materials move through the cycle once and are then disposed of; however, some are circular with product reuse, component remanufacturing, and material recycling. The ideal material life cycle would be a closed-loop circular flow where waste from one process or product is "food" or feedstock for another, and waste released to the environment does not exist (see Table 2–6).

Inputs and Waste Outputs Associated with Building Materials/Products

A construction material or product is produced through multiple unit processes with inputs from both nature and industry. These processes result in outputs back to nature and the technosphere. Inputs include raw materials, either from virgin or recycled resources; energy; and water. Waste outputs include air emissions, water effluents, releases to land, or otherwise managed

wastes. The intermediate material or the final product is also an output (National Renewable Energy Laboratory [NREL] 2007).

Material flows for a product or process are divided into direct and indirect flows. Direct flows, normally accounted for in material analyses, are fuels, minerals, biological materials, metals, and water. Indirect flows, also called hidden flows, are materials such as mining overburden, soil erosion, ore waste, vegetation waste, and emissions and effluents that are released to air, land, or water. Hidden flows never enter the economy as traded commodities, yet they are substantially greater than direct flows for most products (Azapagic et al 2004). Most hidden flows remain on land, although some enter water bodies as sediments or particulates. Figure 2–2 illustrates the annual proportion of hidden to direct flows in metric tons per capita in the United States, Germany, Japan, and the Netherlands.

INPUT: RESOURCES

The United States uses far more materials than other industrialized nations, with 10.3 metric tons per person in 1995 and a world average of 1.7 metric tons per capita. Between 1992 and 2001 U.S. raw material use increased by 10% and this trend is expected to continue (WRI 2000).

Most resources used today are nonrenewable, with only 5% of our material flow from renewable resources.

Table 2–6 Life-cycle Phases of Construction Materials and Products

Raw Materials Acquisition The acquisition phase includes drilling, mining, dredging, and harvesting.	Many environmental impacts associated with materials occur very early in their life cycle as large amounts of material are harvested or mined to obtain the actual material. Habitats are often destroyed at the point of extraction, and surrounding ecosystems are impacted through dispersion of emissions and wastes released to air, land, and water. This can be particularly serious if the wastes are toxic, such as the mineral ore waste extracted along with metals that can oxidize upon exposure to air, resulting in acid mine drainage. Soil erosion from forest clear-cutting or mining can result in sedimentation of waterways and loss of topsoil. Gravel mining and stone quarrying can destroy habitats directly and indirectly through dust settling on vegetation and blocking photosynthesis processes. Increasingly, raw materials are "mined" from both industrial (also called pre-consumer) and post-consumer wastes. Reclaimed and recycled materials are discussed in greater detail in Chapter 4.
Primary Processing and Refining of Materials	This phase can be very waste intensive, as large amounts of material are handled and a good portion of it discarded prior to reaching the manufacturing stage. For example, metal mining produces ore waste to metals ratios of 3:1 for iron and aluminum and far greater for copper. Emissions, effluents, and solid wastes, some of which are toxic, are generated. Fugitive emissions, those not contained, are released to air, water, and soil. Emissions and waste that are contained are disposed of in controlled releases or recycled. Toxic waste types and quantities vary widely by industry, with the metals sector producing relatively large amounts. The stone industry produces large amounts of waste in the form of overburden, but with minimal toxicity. Primary materials processing and refining can be very energy intensive, resulting in additional energy-related emissions. For example, the production of 1kg of aluminum uses 12 kg of input materials and 290 MJ of energy. This leads to the release of about 15 kg of CO_2 equivalents per kilogram of aluminum produced (Gutowski 2004). The substitution of recycled materials for primary materials can greatly reduce virgin material and energy requirements. Substitution of recycled aluminum for virgin uses only about 5% of the energy and resources and produces less than 5% of greenhouse gas emissions (Aluminum Association 2003).
Manufacturing The manufacturing phase includes secondary processing, fabrication, assembly, and finishing.	Compared with primary processing, manufacturing processes pose fewer impacts, partially because the volume of materials processed is smaller; however, it is the design of manufacturing processes that sets many of the requirements for primary process outputs. Manufacturing processes that can use large amounts of recycled materials will have greatly reduced energy and resource impacts in primary processing. A large environmental and human health concern in the manufacturing phase is the use of cleaning fluids and coatings. Solvents are used for cleaning and preparation of surfaces and as carriers for coatings. Many oil-based solvents contain toxic constituents and release volatile organic compounds (VOCs), impacting human health and air quality. Some manufacturers take steps toward minimizing the environmental and human health impacts of their materials/products by incorporating recycled materials and by-products into their products; minimizing energy and water use in manufacturing processes; using organic and water-based solvents; using mechanical cleaning methods; burning waste as fuel; using alternative energy sources; and capturing, recycling, or safely disposing of toxic emissions and wastes.

Continued

Table 2–6 Life-cycle Phases of Construction Materials and Products *(Continued)*

Product Delivery The product delivery phase involves packaging and transportation. Materials and products are transported from the extraction point to the manufacturer, then to the distributor and site, and after use, to the disposal point.	Transport fuel uses nonrenewable resources and releases by-products (VOCs, CO_2, carbon monoxide, particulates, and sulfur and nitrogen compounds) from internal combustion engines, substantially contributing to air pollution, human respiratory problems, and global climate change. All transportation activities accounted for 28% of all greenhouse gas emissions in 2005, having risen 32% since 1990 (U.S. EPA 2007c). Transport emissions of trucks, ships and boats, and trains accounted for 53% of the total. Most fuels used in transport were petroleum-based products such as gasoline for cars and light trucks, diesel fuel for heavy trucks, or jet fuel for airplanes. Our materials economy is increasingly global, where natural resources are extracted in one country, processed in another, and consumed in a third. Materials production often takes place near where the resources exist. For example, lumber is processed in the regions where it is harvested. Transport distances may be among the most important considerations for site designers because materials/products used in site construction are often heavy and bulky. Energy used in transport, especially by less efficient trucks and airplanes, can be greater than energy used in production if the manufacturer is located too far from the site. For example, energy used to transport a truckload of bricks 350 miles is equal to the energy used to produce and fire them (Thompson and Sorvig 2000). Use of local materials can significantly reduce nonrenewable fossil fuel use and related air pollution and greenhouse gases. Whenever possible, materials and products should be mined, processed, and manufactured within the following distances: heavy materials such as aggregate, concrete, and brick within 100 miles, medium weight materials within 500 miles and lightweight materials within 1000 miles of the project site (Living Building Challenge). Packaging of products can use a large amount of materials with only a short use life. Packaging is manufactured, used, and discarded in a very short time period and the majority of packaging is disposed of rather than reused or recycled. Some site construction materials such as aggregates are not packaged; instead they are transported directly to the site in trucks.
Construction, Use, and Maintenance	The use and maintenance phase can be important when considering the environmental and human health impacts of building materials and products, as they tend to be in use for very long periods of time. Durability of the product is therefore one of the most important concerns because the longer the installation lasts, the less need for replacements that use more resources and produce more waste. It is important to match the expected life of the product with the expected life of the site or structure, and to ensure that the product is recyclable. Adhesives, finishes, sealants, and cleaners used in construction and maintenance can contain hazardous chemicals, including VOCs. Steps should be taken to specify materials and products that require few chemicals to maintain, or low-VOC and nontoxic cleaners and sealers should be used. Products including lights, pumps, and controllers that use electricity can pose large environmental impacts in the use phase as they are generally in use for a long time. Therefore, energy efficiency may be the most important concern in their selection.
Final Disposition	The final disposition phase may include "backflows" such as reuse, reprocessing, or material recycling, but it more often includes disposal directly to landfills or incinerators, then landfills.

Table 2–6 Life-cycle Phases of Construction Materials and Products *(Continued)*

Landfill access in the United States is diminishing in some regions, particularly in the well-populated Northeast. Some states have moratoriums on new landfill development or waste reduction mandates that make recycling efforts more economical than landfill disposal. Lined landfills for the disposition of hazardous waste are limited, resulting in increased costs of disposal and transport of hazardous waste long distances.

Waste incineration is not a popular option in the United States due to pollution concerns. Incineration can be combined with an electrical generation facility or even a material-processing facility to produce power. This is called energy recovery. Emissions can be captured or "scrubbed," but pollution control equipment is an expensive capital investment and it is difficult to control the incoming waste stream, so a variety of unanticipated emissions can occur. In the United States, municipal incinerators are one of the largest sources of dioxin—a hazardous chemical and carcinogen that is expensive to scrub (U.S. EPA 2003).

Some construction materials can outlast the life of a site or structure, so planning for their reuse is an important consideration. "Deconstruction" is the term used to refer to the disassembly and salvage of materials from a building or site, as opposed to "demolition," where materials and products are destroyed and hauled to a landfill. While deconstruction takes more time and incurs higher labor costs than demolition, it may ultimately be less expensive than paying landfill costs. Resale of the materials, either whole or ground, can generate additional income.

The life-cycle impact of materials depends strongly on how they are handled after the use phase. Extending the life of materials through reuse or recycling can go a long way toward offsetting the environmental and human health impacts of their initial extraction, processing, and manufacture.

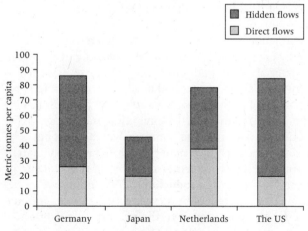

Figure 2–2.

Hidden and direct flows in the United States and other countries are shown in metric tons per capita. Note the very high ratio of hidden to direct flows in the United States. (Azapagic, A., Perdan, S. & Clift, R., eds. Copyright © 2004. John Wiley & Sons, Inc. Reprinted with the permission of John Wiley & Sons, Inc.)

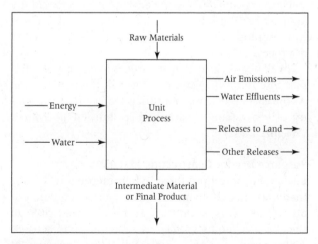

Figure 2–3.

The BEES inventory data categories diagram illustrates the flow items of a given unit process within the life cycle of a material or product. There will likely be several unit processes for a given material or product. (Lippiatt 2007)

Over the twentieth century as the U.S. economy shifted from an agricultural to an industrial one, use of nonrenewable resources increased from 59% to 95% (Wagner 2002). With the exception of timber, plant, and fiber products, most materials in construction are nonrenewable. While some materials such as iron ore are considered unlimited, others such as chromium are being depleted.

An environmental footprint of worldwide resource consumption conducted in 1996 concluded that humans now consume more resources than the earth can replace. The study, published by the National Academy of Sciences, found that we are currently exceeding the earth's carrying capacity by 20%. Americans use four times as many resources as the global average—the most of any country in the world. If every country used as many resources as Western countries do, three Earths would be required to sustain our survival (Wackernagel and Rees 1996).

The focus on consumption of resources has shifted from scarcity concerns to include the environmental degradation that occurs with raw material extraction, processing, use, and disposal. As the flow of materials increases to meet our consumption, impacts on the environment are also increasing. The mining of geologic materials alters habitats, causes increased runoff and soil erosion, and disrupts the ecological processes of the land where the mining occurs. Reduced forest cover from mining may negatively affect the planet's ability to process CO_2.

In all phases, growth in quantities of waste and residuals intensifies burdens from their disposal or release. As the earth is essentially a closed-loop system, the ability of ecosystems to absorb these burdens is limited (Wagner 2002).

Resource Use for Construction Materials

Each year more than three billion metric tons of raw materials are used to manufacture construction materials and products worldwide. This is about 40–50% of the global economy's total flow (Roodman and Lenssen 1995; Anink, Boonstra, and Mak 1996). Inclusion of hidden flows is estimated to more than double the consumption of resources for construction materials. Total quantities of materials used for construction in the U.S. economy has increased from about 35% in 1900 to 60% of nonfood, nonfuel raw materials in 1995 (U.S. Geological Survey 1998).

Crushed stone, sand, and gravel account for as much as three-fourths by weight of new resources used each year in the United States. Consumption reached the highest level ever in 2006, totaling 2.9 billion metric tons (USGS 2007). Cement is another major industrial commodity produced, with 103.8 million metric tons produced in 2002 in the United States (Portland Cement Association). Metals involve substantial material flows, both direct and indirect. Use of metals has declined slightly due to increased use of lighter weight metals such as aluminum and the availability of substitute materials such as plastics and composites (Wagner 2002).

Relative to other consumer products, most site construction materials are heavy; however, the trend toward lighter weight materials can still be seen with increased use of plastics in infrastructure (e.g., drain grates, tree grates, piping), and increased use of corrosion-resistant aluminum in traditionally iron-based applications such as site furnishings, overhead structures, and railings. In 2002, over 10.5 billion pounds of PVC were produced in the United States for construction materials such as pipe, siding, flooring, windows, fencing, and decking. And an estimated seven billion pounds are discarded each year with less than 1% recycled (Healthy Building Network 2007).

Reusing, reprocessing, or recycling materials reduces extraction of resources and associated resources for energy generation—sometimes substantially. It also keeps materials and pollutants out of waste streams. A Swedish study of two buildings, one with a large proportion of recycled materials and the other with all new materials, found that the environmental impacts of the building with recycled materials were only about 55% of the one with new materials. Use of recycled materials could save between 12 and 40% of the total energy used for material production. This number varies because of differences in recycling rates, forms, and material composition; nevertheless, this is a substantial potential energy savings (Thomark 2000).

INPUT: ENERGY

The industrial sector is the largest end user of energy, greater even than the transportation sector or building operations. Nonrenewable fossil fuels are the primary fuel source for industrial processes in the United States, including manufacture of construction materials (U.S. EPA 2007b). U.S. industry produces much of its power through direct fuel inputs and cogeneration as opposed to purchasing electricity. While use of direct fuel inputs can mean greater energy efficiency as there is less energy loss from power plant to industrial facility, it can result in greater air pollution as some industrial facilities are not equipped with the state-of-the-art pollution control equipment that some power plants are.

Cogeneration involves generation of both heat (usually steam) and power (electricity) that produces both thermal and electric energy through a single fuel source. The most common form of cogeneration, called combined heat and power (CHP), is a relatively energy-efficient opportunity for industrial processes with high thermal and electricity loads such as iron and steel making, chemical manufacturing, and petroleum refining

(U.S. EPA 2007b). Another form of cogeneration is capture of process heat and reuse in other processes. For instance, heat loss from cooling bricks post-firing is captured and fed back into brick kilns that are heated to temperatures in excess of 2,500°F.

The recent rise in fuel prices may make the business case for more fuel-efficient practices or use of alternative fuel sources within industry. This is particularly important for the energy-intensive cement and metal processing sectors. Table 2–7 illustrates the energy consumption and intensity per dollar value of some manufacturing sectors involved with the production of construction materials. Energy intensity is defined as the ratio of fuel-related energy consumption to economic production in terms of dollar value of shipments.

Generally materials and products with high energy intensity will have greater environmental impacts from fuel consumption and related air emissions. There are some exceptions to this. For example, production of

Table 2–7 Energy Consumption and Intensity of Select Manufacturing Sectors in 2002

NAICS	Sector[a]	Total Energy Consumption (Trillion Btu)[b]	Energy Consumption per Dollar Value of Shipments (Thousand Btu)[c]
325	Chemical manufacturing—includes solvents, cleaners, adhesives, paints, stains, dyes, and many other compounds used in site construction products	3,769	8.5
324110	Petroleum refining—includes transportation fuel and polymer production	3,086	16.1
331111	Iron and steel	1,455	27.8
327310	Cement—includes portland, natural, masonry, pozzolanic, and other hydraulic cements	409	56.0
332	Fabricated metal products—includes industries that transform metals into intermediate or end products	387	1.7
321	Wood products—includes lumber processing and engineered wood products	375	4.2
3313	Alumina and aluminum	351	12.2
3315	Metal casting	157	5.6

[a]Definitions from NAICS 2002

[b]TBtu is equal to Trillion British Thermal Units.

[c]Energy intensity is the ratio of fuel-related energy consumption to economic production in terms of dollar value of shipments.

Source: Adapted from U.S. EPA 2007b

wood products is somewhat energy intensive, yet the primary fuel source is renewable biomass fuels that are by-products from wood processing; therefore environmental impacts and economic costs may be less. Aluminum production also requires a high amount of energy, yet many aluminum producers are colocated with hydroelectric plants and utilize their relatively clean energy.

The U.S. EPA's *Energy Trends in Selected Manufacturing Sectors: Opportunities and Challenges for Environmentally Preferable Energy Outcomes,* published in 2007, discusses opportunities for increased energy efficiency and cleaner energy for manufacturing sectors that are major energy users. Opportunities include use of cleaner fuels that produce lower GHG and criteria air pollutant (CAP) emissions such as natural gas, biomass, wind, solar, or geothermal power; increased use of cogeneration such as combined heat and power (CHP) systems and captured process heat; upgrades to equipment and improvements or changes to processes for energy efficiency; and increased research and development of higher-efficiency technologies and processes (U.S. EPA 2007b).

Fuel Type
Fuel type is a major factor in the equation of environmental impacts from energy use. For example, manufacturing sectors that rely on coal for energy, such as the cement manufacturing sector, will have greater impacts than those that rely more on natural gas. Coal is still an important fuel source in some industries; however, its use as a direct fuel input has declined from its peak in 1950 to a relatively small fraction of industrial inputs today. At the same time, coal use in electrical power generation has increased rapidly to more than 50% of inputs for electrical power generation, so it is still a major source of energy for industrial sectors (U.S. EPA 2007b). And with rising natural gas prices, many manufacturing facilities that can switch to coal energy sources are doing so.

The industrial sector is the largest user of renewable energy sources. This is due in part to the extensive use of biomass fuels (e.g., sawdust, wood waste) in the forest products industry. Renewable energy is also represented in the purchased electricity figure primarily

through hydropower. Table 2–8 illustrates the percentage of fuel types used by industry as a whole and discusses the major environmental and human health impacts of the fuel use. Impacts from renewable energy sources such as biofuels and solar, wind, and geothermal power can be considerably less than nonrenewable fossil fuels both from a resource use and emissions standpoint. Renewable energy sources are discussed along with fossil fuel sources in Table 2–8. Table 2–9 illustrates percentages of fuel use by select manufacturing sectors related to construction material manufacture and production.

Embodied Energy of Materials and Products
The total energy used during all stages of a material's life is known as *embodied energy.* If the product is complex—made from more than one material, such as a steel and wood bench—then the embodied energy of the bench includes all of the energy inputs from both the wood and steel components and the energy inputs to assemble them. It is virtually impossible to quantify all the embodied energy of a product, and embodied energy estimates for materials can vary widely, sometimes by 100%. Variables include regional and national conditions, manufacturing processes, recycled content, energy sources, and study parameters (e.g., cradle to gate, cradle to cradle). Therefore embodied energy figures should be used with caution. In addition, energy use is only one measure by which to evaluate materials and products. Pollution, environmental impacts, resource use, waste produced, and human health impacts are other important measures.

Embodied energy figures in Appendix A are from a variety of sources and measured in a variety of units—either by weight or by volume. Some are from Athena Environmental Impact Estimator, reports by the Athena Sustainable Materials Institute and the National Institute of Standards and Technology's BEES (Building for Economic and Environmental Sustainability). As the product types in these sources are limited to architectural applications, embodied energy and embodied carbon figures were also drawn from a study at the University of Bath of multiple EU and worldwide figures for embodied energy and carbon loads of construction materials. The Bath study developed figures based on the number of records, the date of the records, sources, and averages.

Table 2–8 Percentage of Total Energy Demand of Industrial End Uses in 2004 and Impacts of Fuel Use by Type

Fuel Type and Percentage of Use by U.S. Industry[a]	Environmental and Human Health Impacts from Fuel Use
Purchased electricity 33.5%	Most purchased electricity is produced in fossil fuel–burning power plants. These plants burn coal (49.7% of all electricity produced in 2005), fuel oil (3%), or natural gas (18.7%). In the United States, average efficiency of power plants is 35%. Combustion of fossil fuels contributes to acid rain, global warming, and air pollution.
	Emissions vary by fuel type and power plant. Coal combustion releases on average almost twice as much CO_2 as natural gas per Btu generated and nearly 400 times as many particulates.
	Some electricity is generated at power plants with non-fossil fuel–burning sources such as hydroelectric (6.5% of all electricity generated at power plants in 2005) and nuclear (19.3%) power. Other sources of electricity (totaling 2.9%) are waste to energy, solar, wind, and geothermal power. Impacts of specific fuels and sources of power will be discussed individually below (U.S. DOE 2007b).
	A primary issue with purchased electricity use is the low efficiency levels and power loss from power plant to the end user.
Coal 6.1%	Combustion of coal produces carbon dioxide (CO_2), particulate matter containing heavy metals, nitrogen oxides (NO_x), and varying amounts of sulfur dioxide (SO_2) depending on the composition of the coal. Emissions from coal-fired power plants are one of the two largest sources of carbon dioxide emissions, the primary cause of global warming.
	Coal and coal waste products such as fly ash, bottom ash, boiler slag, and flue gas desulfurization contain heavy metals including arsenic, lead, mercury, nickel, vanadium, beryllium, cadmium, barium, chromium, copper, molybdenum, zinc, selenium, and radium. Some of these are persistent and accumulate in fatty tissues of humans and organisms, producing a wide variety of negative health effects. Coal-fired power plants are one of the largest emitters of mercury in the United States, releasing forty-eight tons annually. Coal contains low levels of uranium, thorium, and other naturally occurring radioactive isotopes (USGS 1997).
	Clean coal, a process in development, is chemically washed of minerals and impurities, sometimes gasified, burned, and treated with steam to remove sulfur dioxide and make CO_2 in the flue gas recoverable. Some scientists warn that it still produces emissions and wastes, yet transfers them to another waste stream.
Coal coke 0.4%	Coal coke is used as a fuel and as a reducing agent in smelting iron ore in blast furnaces. Hydrocarbons are major byproducts of coke-making facilities. Many are captured and beneficially used in other processes.
Natural gas 25.6%	Natural gas is the cleanest burning of all fossil fuels as it is composed primarily of methane. Combustion products are carbon dioxide, produced at a much lower level per unit of energy produced than coal or oil, and water vapor. Fuel cell technology, currently not price-competitive, is a potentially cleaner and more efficient option for use of natural gas for electricity.
	The rising cost of natural gas and somewhat limited supply means that it is not as broadly used as it might be. It is projected that the world's supply of natural gas could be exhausted by the year 2085. Landfills are a potential source of methane for energy. A brick manufacturer, a relatively energy-intensive industry, colocated a manufacturing plant in 2007 in Florida adjacent to a landfill to use the methane generated there for kiln fuel in the brick-firing process.
Petroleum[b] 29.3%	Burning oil for power releases CO_2 into the atmosphere, contributing to global warming. Per unit of energy it releases less CO_2 than coal, but more than natural gas. It releases far fewer particulates than coal and about half the sulfur dioxide. Petroleum is characterized as a limited resource.

Continued

Table 2–8 Percentage of Total Energy Demand of Industrial End Uses in 2004 and Impacts of Fuel Use by Type *(Continued)*

Renewable 5.0%	Renewable energy technologies include solar power, wind power, hydroelectric power, geothermal heat, biomass, and biofuels. While in 2004 only 5% of energy for industrial processes was produced from renewables (in addition to some from purchased electricity sources), the potential for their use is great. And with limited fossil fuel supplies and rising costs, some renewable energy technologies may soon gain wider use.
	Solar power, also called solar energy, uses radiation emitted by the sun. Costs of solar energy–produced electricity are currently higher than for fossil fuels; however, as technology improves, use is increasing and costs are decreasing. Solar power does not produce pollution in use, but materials and manufacture of the equipment can result in pollution.
	There is some criticism that solar power facilities are land consumptive; however, solar power plants use less land than a comparable coal or hydroelectric power plant. And prime land for solar power is the sparsely populated desert. One study estimated that just over 4,000 square miles, 3.4% of land in New Mexico, would be required to supply 30% of U.S. electricity through solar power.
	Wind energy is potentially plentiful, widely distributed, clean, and nonpolluting. Some pollution can result from fossil fuel–based backup energy systems for wind power. Wind turbines do not require water to generate electricity.
	There are some concerns that turbines might kill bird or bat species; however, one study found that on average one bird was killed per thirty turbines each year (Marris and Fairless 2007). This is far less than the number of birds and other species killed by habitat loss from acid rain and coal mining for fossil fuel energy.
	Wind farms occupy less land area per kilowatt-hour (kWh) of electricity than any other energy conversion system aside from rooftop solar energy. Wind farms are compatible with grazing and crops.
	Aesthetic issues are a drawback with wind energy, as many farms are best located in open, often scenic, areas.
	Hydroelectric power offers advantages of a renewable source of power, low costs, longer life than fuel-fired generation, and recreational opportunities. Environmental impacts from hydroelectric energy production are far less than those of coal, yet it is not without risks. Hydroelectric power plants don't release the high sulfur, nitrogen, and carbon gas emissions of fossil fuel–burning plants. However, a few recent studies of large reservoirs behind hydroelectric dams have suggested that the submerged decaying vegetation may give off quantities of greenhouse gases similar to other sources of electricity. Other major impacts of hydroelectric power are flooding of vast areas of land for reservoirs, watershed impacts from amount and quality of downstream waters and soil, and fish migration barriers.
	Geothermal energy is obtained by capturing heat from the earth's crust. Large amounts of water are piped kilometers deep into the earth and then warmed by the earth's heat to produce energy. Estimates of geothermal energy potential worldwide are the highest of any renewable fuel technology as there are many potentially appropriate sites. Capital costs of geothermal plants are high, but operating costs are minimal.
	Geothermal sites are not completely renewable energy sources. They can be depleted after decades as the ground cools. Some additional environmental concerns with geothermal power plants are adverse effects of plant construction on land stability in the region, as seismic activity can increase and land can subside as older wells cool down; and emissions of low levels of CO_2, nitric oxide, and sulfur. However, these emissions occur at levels of 5% of fossil fuel plants.
	Biofuels are liquid fuels derived from crops and agricultural wastes. They are a means of converting the sun's energy into fuel through plant photosynthesis. They can be produced in many locations. Ethanol, a form of alcohol derived from corn in the United States and sugar cane in Brazil, is the predominant biofuel in use today. Biodiesel is made from bioesters derived from vegetable oils.

Table 2–8 Percentage of Total Energy Demand of Industrial End Uses in 2004 and Impacts of Fuel Use by Type *(Continued)*

Biofuels burn more cleanly and produce less CO_2 than fossil fuels, yet are not without environmental impacts. One concern about biofuels is their net energy balance as their production requires a certain amount of fossil fuel energy inputs (e.g., fertilizers, herbicides, fuel for machines). Bioenergy is increasingly used for feedstock processing and refining. Another concern is the effect of land- and fossil fuel–consumptive agriculture practices on soil and water quality, local ecosystems, and even global climate.

[a]U.S. EPA 2007b

[b]This figure does not include petroleum use in transportation of materials and industrial products.

OUTPUTS: WASTE

Along with excessive consumption of resources comes generation of wastes. In the United States, the amount of waste generated by industrial processes, including construction, far outweighs the amount of municipal solid waste (MSW) generated by consumers each year, with thirty tons of industrial waste for every ton of MSW in U.S. landfills (U.S. EPA 2006b). While not as well documented as MSW statistics, estimates of total waste generated and disposed of by industry each year is 7.6 billion tons (U.S. EPA Industrial Waste Management). In 2005, MSW generated was 245 million tons (U.S. EPA 2006a).

Waste is an output generated at all phases of a material's life cycle, resulting in both human and environmental health impacts. Waste can be in gaseous, liquid, or solid form. It is released to air, water, or land, through fugitive releases or controlled disposal, or is contained and recycled into other processes. The World Resources Institute (WRI) estimates that one-half to three-quarters of annual resource inputs to industrial economies are returned to the environment within a year. In the United States this is about twenty-five metric tons of waste per person per year (WRI 2000). This figure does not include waste that is recycled back into other processes or hidden flows such as mine tailings or excavated soil.

Table 2–9 Fuel Type Use by Manufacturing Sector (2005)

NAICS	Sector	Net Electricity	Natural Gas	Petroleum	Coal	Coke & Breeze	Other
325	Chemical manufacturing	13.8%	44.5%	2.5%	8.3%	0.0%	30.7%[a]
324110	Petroleum refining	3.9%	26.6%	1.5%	0.0%	0.0%	68.0%[b]
331111	Iron and steel	12.6%	26.7%	0.8%	2.5%	36.2%	21.4%[c]
327310	Cement	10.5%	5.1%	1.7%	57.7%	2.0%	23.2%[d]
332	Fabricated metal products	41.6%	54.0%	2.4%	0.3%	—	0.5%
321	Wood products	19.2%	15.2%	4.3%	0.3%	0.0%	61.1%[e]
3313	Alumina and aluminum	55%[f]	37.0%	0.6%	0.0%	—	7.4%
3315	Metal casting	34.4%	49.0%	1.2%	0.6%	14.6%	—

[a]Other fuels include petroleum-derived by-product gases and solids, woody materials, hydrogen, and waste materials.

[b]Primarily fuel gas generated in the refining process.

[c]By-product fuels such as coke oven gas and blast furnace gas (coal based in origin).

[d]Includes petroleum coke and waste materials that are incinerated for fuel such as old tires and municipal solid waste.

[e]Primarily biomass fuels such as black liquor, pulping liquor, wood residues, and by-products of wood processing.

[f]Primarily source is hydroelectric power.

Source: U.S. EPA 2007b

The atmosphere is the largest dumping ground for industrial wastes. Sixty-eight percent of waste is in the form of emissions released to air, 22% is released to land, less than 1% is released to water, and 10% is unaccounted for due to incomplete data. When oxygen is included, 87% of waste is released to air and 9% is released to land (WRI 2000). Waste types, sources, and potential human and environmental health impacts are discussed in Appendix B.

The often substantial "hidden flows" of waste generated during raw material acquisition, manufacturing, or processing of materials is known as the "ecological rucksack" of a material. Ecological rucksack is defined by the Wuppertal Institute as the primary resource extractions required to produce a product minus the weight of the product (Moll, Bringezu, and Schutz 2005).

The ecological rucksack of minimally processed materials such as gravel and stone is not large; however, more processed materials such as metals, concrete, and plastics have larger associated hidden flows. For instance, the production of one ton of cement requires 5.5 tons of fuel and 1.8 tons of raw materials and releases about .5 ton of CO_2. A ton of steel requires removal of 1.1 tons of overburden, and results in 1.5 tons of ore concentration waste and 1 ton of CO_2 released (Ayers 2002). Aluminum requires the excavation and use of 80 tons of material to produce one ton (Kibert 2005).

The ecological rucksack of a product can be substantially reduced with substitution of recycled content for virgin materials in a product. For instance, each ton of iron that is recycled saves 12.5 tons of overburden, 2.8 tons of iron ore, 0.8 tons of coal, and many other inputs. It also avoids release of a ton of carbon dioxide and additional pollution from coking, pickling, and other processing activities (Ayers 2002).

It is important to note that all releases are not the same and small releases of a particular chemical can be more hazardous than large amounts of another type of waste. For instance, fugitive (uncaptured) air releases of mercury, a persistent bioaccumulative toxin, from iron and steel smelting holds potential for more damage to human health than overburden and waste rock from limestone mining.

In addition, while outputs of some hazardous materials from manufacturing processes have been reduced or stabilized through regulation, other hazardous material flows are poorly controlled because they occur outside the traditional area of regulatory scrutiny in extraction, use, or disposal phases (WRI 2000).

The U.S. Pollution Prevention Act of 1990 requires manufacturing facilities to report information about certain hazardous waste they release, recycle, or dispose of. Facilities self-report information on over 650 chemicals. The annually updated data is available through the Toxics Release Inventory (TRI) database and is searchable by industrial sector, individual facility, state, chemical, or group of chemicals (e.g., HAPs, heavy metals, PBTs).

In 2005, disposal or other releases of TRI chemicals and wastes to the environment totaled almost 4.34 billion pounds from almost 23,500 U.S. facilities. This total had increased by 79% since 1996. Of the 2005 total, 88% was disposed of or released on-site, while 12% was sent off-site for disposal. TRI data have shown that in many cases pollutant releases have been reduced quite a bit from historic levels. For example, VOC re-

Figure 2–4.

Information collected under the Toxics Release Inventory (TRI) under requirements by the Pollution Prevention Act of 1990 (PPA) is self-reported in quantities of TRI chemicals managed in waste, both on- and off-site, including amounts reported as recycled, burned for energy recovery, and treated or disposed of or otherwise released. The total of these amounts is called total production-related waste.

leases from paints and coatings have been substantially reduced as regulations in California have spurred manufacturers to develop new low-VOC products. Lead releases from gasoline combustion are down with conversion to unleaded; however, lead releases are still an issue from the primary metal sector in air emissions and from electrical utilities in surface water discharges (Kapur and Keoelian 2005). In addition, new chemicals have been introduced, some of which persist in the environment and bioaccumulate. Others have not been tested for their impact on the environment or on human health, yet they are in use.

OUTPUTS TO AIR

Wastes released to air include greenhouse gases, particulates, criteria air pollutants (CAPs), and hazardous air pollutants (HAPs). Many fugitive emissions released to air can travel, sometimes substantial distances, then settle on land or in water, affecting ecosystems distant from the source. Some waste is inert with little effect on the environment and human health, but much waste either by its chemical makeup or just sheer volume will pose risks—some of which are substantial.

While air emissions can occur during the construction, use, and disposal phases of a product's life cycle, emissions from manufacturing are the best documented and regulated. Air emissions from industrial processes result from fossil fuel combustion for energy, nonenergy uses of fossil fuels, chemical conversion of materials, dust in processing operations, fumes, and many other sources.

Table 2–10 Fossil Fuel Emission Levels in Pounds per Billion Btu of Energy Output

Emission type	Natural Gas	Oil (Petroleum)	Coal
Carbon dioxide (CO_2)	117,000	164,000	208,000
Carbon monoxide (CO)	40	33	208
Nitrogen oxides (NO_x)	92	448	457
Sulfur dioxide (SO_2)	1	1,122	2,591
Particulates (NMVOCs)	7	84	2,744
Mercury (Hg)	0.000	0.007	0.016

Source: U.S. DOE 1998

Greenhouse Gas (GHG) Emissions from Industrial Processes

The extraction and use of fossil fuel resources dominate materials output flows with release of carbon dioxide (CO_2) accounting for 80% by weight of all industrial waste. This makes the atmosphere the largest dumping ground for industrial wastes (WRI 2000).

GHG emissions from fossil fuel combustion In the industrial sector, greenhouse gas emissions result directly from the combustion of fossil fuels and indirectly from the generation of electricity that is consumed by industry. Combined, these accounted for 27% of all CO_2 emissions in 2005. Emissions vary widely by industry due to the volume of material produced, the energy requirements to produce the material, and the type of fuel used (see Table 2–10).

GHG emissions from nonenergy-related industrial processes Greenhouse gases and precursors are also released as by-products of nonenergy-related industrial processes. These accounted for 5% of all U.S. GHG emissions in 2005 (U.S. EPA 2007c). Some industrial processes chemically transform materials, releasing waste gases such as CO_2, CH_4 and N_2O. Manufacturing processes related to construction material production that release significant amounts of nonenergy-related GHGs are iron and steel production, cement manufacture, lime manufacture, limestone and dolomite use (in flux stone and glass), titanium dioxide production (for paint and plastic pigments), ferroalloy production (for stainless steels and other steel alloys), aluminum production, and zinc production (for galvanizing coatings and alloys). Table 2–12 details the nonenergy-related GHG emissions and sinks by industrial sectors related to construction material manufacture. Nonenergy use of fossil fuels in industry can result in both GWP emissions and in carbon sinks.

Fossil fuels, primarily petroleum, are used as raw materials in the manufacture of asphalt, plastics, synthetic rubber, adhesives, joint compounds, and solvents. GWP emissions can occur during the manufacture of a product, such as occurs in plastics, or emissions can occur during the product's lifetime, as in the off-gassing during solvent use. In 2005, nonenergy use of fossil fuels resulted in emissions of 142.4Tg CO_2 equivalents,

Table 2–11 Sources and Impacts of Greenhouse Gases and Precursors

Greenhouse Gas or Precursor[a]	Major Sources (Related to Power Generation and Construction Material Production)	Health Impacts	Environmental Impacts
Carbon dioxide (CO_2) GHG	Sources include combustion of fossil fuels (oil, natural gas, coal), solid waste, and wood products, and chemical reactions such as conversion of lime. Carbon dioxide is also removed from the atmosphere (or "sequestered") when it is absorbed by plants as part of the biological carbon cycle.[b]	None, except impacts from global climate change	Greenhouse gas that contributes to global warming
Nitrous oxide (N_2O) GHG	Emitted from fossil fuel combustion of both mobile and stationary sources	Causes poor air quality leading to possible respiratory illness or lung damage[c]	Contributes to global warming. Contributes to acid rain that degrades soil and water quality; forms acid aerosols that reduce visibility; contributes to fine particulates and ozone[c]
Fluorinated gases— hydrofluorocarbons, perfluorocarbons, and sulfur hexafluoride (SF_6) High GWP	Electric power transmission; magnesium production; aluminum smelting emissions; replacements for ozone-depleting substances such as CFCs, HCFCs, halons; HFC-23 production as feedstock for some synthetic polymers	Perfluorocarbons are persistent and accumulative. They have been found in increasing concentrations in human blood, and have been linked to bladder cancer and reproductive toxicity.	High global warming potential gases. Perfluorocarbons are persistent in environment. Not easily broken down. SF_6 is the most potent greenhouse gas evaluated by the IPCC.
Methane (CH_4) GHG	Emitted during the production and transport of coal, natural gas, and oil; iron and steel production; decay of organic waste in municipal solid waste landfills. Natural sources are wetlands, termites, and oceans.	Methane is nontoxic, but an asphyxiant so it is a concern for indoor air quality or enclosed spaces. It is highly flammable.	Contributes to global warming
Sulfur dioxide (SO_2) CAP I-GHG	Mostly results from combustion of sulfur-containing fuels, primarily coal	Major component of smog, which causes respiratory illness and may lead to lung damage[c]	Contributes to acid rain that degrades soil and water quality, leading to acidification; forms acid aerosols that reduce visibility; contributes to fine particulates[c]
Volatile organic compounds (VOCs) I-GHG CAP	Largest energy-related sources are fugitive emissions from fuel storage tanks and pipelines; also from solvent use; incomplete combustion	Cause respiratory illness including asthma; irritate eyes and respiratory system; some VOCs are known or suspected carcinogens[c]	React with nitrogen oxides to form ground-level ozone; some VOCs damage vegetation[c]

Table 2–11 Sources and Impacts of Greenhouse Gases and Precursors *(Continued)*

Greenhouse Gas or Precursor[a]	Major Sources (Related to Power Generation and Construction Material Production)	Health Impacts	Environmental Impacts
Carbon monoxide (CO) I-GHG CAP	Product of incomplete combustion. The largest source is vehicles. Some is from stationary sources.	Reduces blood's capacity for carrying oxygen to body cells and tissues, and is particularly damaging for people with impaired cardiovascular and lung function.[c]	A greenhouse gas precursor that contributes to the formation of methane[c]

[a]U.S. EPA classifications:
   GHG = Principal greenhouse gases
   High GWP = High global warming potential gases
   I-GHG = Indirect greenhouse gases
   CAP = Criteria air pollutant
[b]U.S. EPA Climate Change—Greenhouse Gas Emissions
[c]Adapted from U.S. EPA 2007b

Table 2–12 Nonenergy-related U.S. Greenhouse Gas Emissions and Sinks from Industrial Processes in Select Manufacturing Sectors (Tg CO_2 Equivalents)[a,b]

Sector	1990	2005	Percent Change	Processes
CO_2				
Nonenergy use of fuels	117.3	142.4	+21	Fossil fuels are used in solvents, adhesives, and coatings and as feedstocks in plastics, synthetic rubber, and asphalt, releasing CO_2 and other GHG and emissions.
Cement manufacture	33.3	45.9	+38	Heating calcium carbonate to produce lime, then clinker production releases about one ton of CO_2 for every ton of cement produced.
Iron and steel production	84.9	45.2	−47	Pig iron production and thermal processes used to create sinter and metallurgical coke release CO_2 and CH_4.
Lime manufacture	11.3	13.7	+21	Chemical conversion of lime releases CO_2.
Limestone and dolomite use	5.5	7.4	+34	Heated limestone reacts with metal impurities to form and release CO_2.
Aluminum production	6.8	4.2	−38	CO_2 is emitted when alumina is reduced to aluminum.
Titanium dioxide production (used as a pigment in white paint and plastics)	1.3	1.9	+47	CO_2 is emitted from the chloride process that uses petroleum coke and chlorine as raw materials.

Continued

Table 2–12 Nonenergy-related U.S. Greenhouse Gas Emissions and Sinks from Industrial Processes in Select Manufacturing Sectors (Tg CO_2 Equivalents)[a,b] *(Continued)*

Sector	1990	2005	Percent Change	Processes
Ferroalloy production (e.g., steel and iron alloys)	2.2	1.4	−35	CO_2 is emitted from the production of several ferroalloys including stainless steel.
Zinc production	0.9	0.5	−51	CO_2 emissions occur in the primary and secondary production of zinc through the electrothermal production process.
Petrochemical production	2.2	2.9	+31.8%	CO_2 results from polymer production.
CH_4				
Iron and steel production	1.3	1.0	−28	Pig iron production and thermal processes used to create sinter and metallurgical coke release CO_2 and CH_4.
HFCs, PFCs, SF_6				
Aluminum production	18.5	3.0	−84	Tetrafluoromethane (CF_4), hexafluoroethane (C_2F_6), and PFCs are emitted as intermittent by-products of the smelting process.
Sinks				
Forests	(598.5)[c]	(698.7)	±16.7	Forests (including vegetation, soils, and harvested wood) accounted for 85% of total CO_2 sequestration in 2005. Harvested wood still sequesters carbon until it decomposes or is burned.
Urban trees	(57.5)	(88.5)	+53.9	Accounted for 11% of total CO_2 sequestration in 2005.
Asphalt and road oil[d]	(85)[e]	(100.0)[e]	+17.6%	Major source of sequestration.
Petrochemical feed (includes plastic feedstocks)	(46.0)[e]	(64.2)[e]	+39.5%	CO_2 is sequestered until plastics are burned; then it is released.

[a]Units are teragrams of CO_2 equivalents.

[b]Figures for industrial sectors are for nonfuel combustion emissions from industrial processes.

[c]Parentheses indicate negative values or sequestration.

[d]U.S. DOE 2006

[e]Figures are in million metric tons of CO_2 equivalents.

Source: Adapted from U.S. EPA 2007c

about 2% of total CO_2 emissions, a 21% increase from 1990 (U.S. EPA 2007c).

Nonfuel use of fossil fuels can also sequester carbon. In 2005, nonfuel use of fossil fuels resulted in sequestration equal to 300.9 MMT CO_2 equivalents (U.S. EPA 2007c). Asphalt and road oils are a major source of carbon sequestration in the use phase. *The Inventory of U.S. Greenhouse Gas Emissions and Sinks: 1990–2005* estimates that asphalt sequestered 100 million metric tons (MMT) of

CO_2 in 2005 (U.S. EPA 2007c). It is not certain whether the carbon continues to be stored as the asphalt pavement deteriorates over time or if it is released to the air or soil.

Criteria and Hazardous Air Pollutant Releases from Industrial Processes

Criteria air pollutants (CAPs) are considered by the EPA to be widespread human and environmental health threats (U.S. EPA Air and Radiation).

Criteria air pollutants (CAPs) are particulate matter (both PM10 and PM2.5), ground-level ozone, carbon monoxide (CO), sulfur oxides (S_2O), nitrogen oxides (NO_x) and lead. VOCs and ammonia are also monitored along with CAPs, as they contribute to human and environmental health risks. CAP emissions from energy-related and nonenergy-related sectors involved in construction material manufacture are summarized in Table 2–13.

Releases of hazardous air pollutants (HAPs) and other air emissions accounted for 35% of Toxics Release Inventory (TRI)–reported chemical releases in 2005 (U.S. EPA 2007a). While these air releases are of great concern, improvements in pollution control equipment, fuels, equipment, and manufacturing processes have reduced them by 8.6%, or 106 million pounds, beyond 2001 levels.

The 1990 Clean Air Act Amendment directs the EPA to set standards for all major sources of HAPs and some area sources that are of particular concern. The EPA has tar-geted 188 HAPs for reduction by setting thresholds for some of the "major" sources of HAPs by industrial sector. "Major" sources of HAPs emissions are those facilities that emit ten tons per year of any of the listed toxic air pollutants, or twenty-five tons per year of a mixture of air toxics. "Area" sources are facilities that emit less than the major source thresholds (U.S. EPA Air and Radiation).

Table 2–15 summarizes total HAPS released from industrial sectors involved in construction material manufacture. The figures are based on manufacturers' self-reported data. Appendix B lists select HAPs and their potential environmental and human health impacts. Many are from the subset of HAPs that the EPA selected for the National Scale Air Toxics Study for their possible effect on human health, and frequency and persistence in the environment (U.S. EPA Air and Radiation).

Outputs and Releases to Water

Water is impacted by all phases of a material's life cycle. Emissions to water are primarily through wastewater release and while the contaminant loading is minor in quantity as compared with air emissions, it may have some important large-scale environmental impacts given the critical role that water plays in the health of living things (WRI 2000). While releases to water are less than 1% of all toxic releases, toxic releases to air can drift, sometimes for substantial distances, to settle on water bodies. And releases to land can find their way into ground- and surface waters.

While quantities are still small, the resulting impacts to water quality and aquatic health can be large. Raw material extraction can affect water quality through habitat alteration, which increases runoff, contributing sediment and pollutants to streams, rivers, lakes, and wetlands. Processing and manufacturing of materials/products use water and create wastewater, which can pollute water bodies. Installation of materials and products can affect water quality around the site (e.g., on-site cleanup from concrete or mortar), and disposal of materials/products can affect groundwater and surface water quality.

Outputs and Releases to Land

Industrial waste releases to land, totaling about 15% of total TRI releases, amounted to 643 million pounds in

Table 2–13 Energy-Related and Total CAP Emissions by Sector in 2002

NAICS	Sector	All Energy-related CAPs (TPY)	All CAP Emissions (TPY)
3313	Alumina and aluminum	72,736	538,841
327310	Cement	41,477	544,501
325	Chemical manufacturing	739,123	1,536,183
331111	Iron and steel	227,808	850,644
332813	Metal finishing	111	374
3315	Metal casting	5,225	72,645
324110	Petroleum refining	298,838	788,985
321	Wood products (within-forest products)	183,285	289,727
Total	**All manufacturing sectors including some not listed above**	**2,549,362**	**6,252,816**

Source: U.S. EPA 2007b, Table 13

Table 2–14 Criteria Air Pollutants (CAPs)—Environmental and Human Health Impacts

Pollutant and EPA or Other Classification[a]	Major Sources (Related to Power Generation and Construction Materials)	Health Impacts	Environmental Impacts
Carbon monoxide (CO) I-GHG CAP	Product of incomplete combustion. The largest source is vehicles. Some is from stationary sources.	Reduces blood's capacity for carrying oxygen to body cells and tissues. Can adversely affect nervous, pulmonary, or cardiovascular systems.[b]	A greenhouse gas precursor that contributes to the formation of methane[b]
Nitrogen oxides (NO$_x$) CAP	Result from fossil fuel combustion of both mobile and stationary sources	Causes poor air quality, leading to possible respiratory illness or lung damage[b]	Contributes to acid rain that degrades soil and water quality; forms acid aerosols that reduce visibility; contributes to fine particulates and ozone[b]
Particulate matter (PM)— PM10, PM2.5 CAP	Ash and dust from the combustion of coal or heavy oil. Very fine particulates (PM2.5) are largely composed of aerosols formed by nitrogen oxide and sulfur dioxide emissions.	Can cause respiratory system irritation and illness and/or lung damage.[b] Some are heavy metals or toxins considered to be hazardous air pollutants (HAPs) by the EPA.	Forms haze that reduces visibility[b]
Sulfur dioxide (SO$_2$) CAP I-GHG	Primarily results from combustion of sulfur-containing fuels, primarily coal	Major component of smog, which causes respiratory illness and may lead to lung damage[b]	Contributes to acid rain that degrades soil and water quality; forms acid aerosols that reduce visibility; contributes to fine particulates[b]
Ozone (ground level) CAP	Created by a chemical reaction between oxides of nitrogen (NO$_x$) and volatile organic compounds (VOC) in the presence of sunlight	Can cause respiratory illnesses including asthma; irritates eyes and respiratory system[b]	Forms smog that reduces visibility; damages vegetation[b]; in urban areas traps radiated heat from dark and impervious surfaces, causing the urban heat island effect
Lead CAP P-PBT W-PBT HAP	Lead is also used in the production of metal products, such as sheet lead, solder (but no longer in food cans), and pipes, and in ceramic glazes, paint, ammunition, cable covering, and other products (http://www.epa.gov/ttn/atw/hlthef/lead.html). Emissions from iron and steel production and lead smelters[c]	Exposure to lead can occur from lead particulates in air, water, food, and soil. Lead is a very toxic element, causing a variety of effects at low dose levels. Brain damage, kidney damage, and gastrointestinal distress are seen from acute (short-term) exposure to high levels of lead in humans. Chronic (long-term) exposure to lead in humans results in effects on the blood, central nervous system (CNS), blood pressure, kidneys, and Vitamin D metabolism. Children are	

Table 2–14 Criteria Air Pollutants (CAPs)—Environmental and Human Health Impacts *(Continued)*

Pollutant and EPA or Other Classification[a]	Major Sources (Related to Power Generation and Construction Materials)	Health Impacts	Environmental Impacts
		particularly sensitive to the chronic effects of lead, with slowed cognitive development, reduced growth, and other effects reported.[c]	

[a]U.S. EPA classifications:

   GHG = Principal greenhouse gases

   High GWP = High global warming potential gases

   I-GHG = Indirect greenhouse gases

   CAP = Criteria air pollutant

   HAP = Hazardous air pollutant

   PBT = Persistent bioaccumulative toxin

   P-PBT = Priority persistent bioaccumulative toxin by EPA

   W-PBT = Washington State PBT list

[b]Adapted from U.S. EPA 2007b

[c]ATSDR

Table 2–15 Total Hazardous Air Pollutant Emissions from Sectors Involved in Construction Material Manufacture from TRI Inventory (2005)

Sector	Total Releases (lb./year)			
	PBTs	Carcinogens	HAPs	Metal/Metal Cmpds.
Metal mining (SIC Code 10)	398,211,474	578,351,390	616,455,614	1,157,980,596
Lumber (SIC Code 24)	74,594 (Dioxin-like cmpds.: 600.7629700 grams)	5,925,583 (Dioxin-like cmpds.: 594.0384500 grams)	19,936,261	980,166
Plastics (SIC Code 30)	223,839 (Dioxin-like cmpds.: 598.01677 grams)	20,101,387	35,340,970	5,581,859
Stone, glass, clay (SIC Code 32)	4,588,815 (Dioxin-like cmpds.: 45.0407133 grams)	25,065,414 (Dioxin-like cmpds.: 5.6137 grams)	47,084,439	14,090,345
Primary metals (SIC Code 33)	36,132,900 (Dioxin-like cmpds.: 323.0093 grams)	70,236,802 (Dioxin-like cmpds.: 315.7128 grams)	151,206,333	438,851,373
Fabricated metals (SIC Code 34)	36,731,349 (Dioxin-like cmpds.: 323.0093 grams)	70,573,173 (Dioxin-like cmpds.: 315.7128 grams)	151,287,177	441,402,331

* Figures based on "Total On- and Off-site Disposal or Other Releases"

Source: U.S. EPA TRI Explorer 2005

2005. These releases were disposed of in waste piles, spills, or leaks, some of which worked their way into ground- or surface waters, or into the soil. Another 18%, 787 million pounds, were disposed of in surface impoundments or landfills, and 972 million pounds were disposed of in Class I underground injection wells or hazardous waste landfills either on- or off-site. Seventy-three million pounds of TRI-reported chemicals were metals sent for solidification or stabilization. Surface water releases increased by 24% from 1990 to 2005 and land releases other than to landfills or underground injection increased 350% (U.S. EPA 2007a).

Construction and demolition (C&D) waste resulting from both construction and demolition phases of the built environment is primarily released to land either directly to landfills or to incineration, then landfill. An estimated 136 million tons of construction and demolition waste is disposed of each year in the United States alone. This is about 26% of the total municipal waste stream. Only 20–30% of C&D waste is reused or recycled. Demolition waste from buildings and sites accounts for 92% of all C&D waste (U.S. EPA 1998). Chapter 4 addresses waste reduction hierarchies and techniques for recovering, reusing, and recycling construction and demolition wastes.

Creating Change: Ideologies, Trends, and Policies to Improve the Environmental and Human Health Performance of Materials and Products

Along with recognition of excessive resource use are the immediate concerns of poor air quality and global climate change, all of which are combining to initiate changes in industrial design and manufacturing industries. Trends and policies in industrial manufacturing and product design, including construction products, are discussed in this section. Many have originated in European countries and are being implemented there through policy measures to varying degrees.

Natural ecosystems with their mass conservation properties are a model used to explore ideas of dematerializa-

tion, closed-loop manufacturing systems, energy conservation, and waste reduction (Allen 2004). In their book *Construction Ecology,* Kibert et al. suggest natural processes, from which industry and sustainable development can draw lessons. They are predominantly cyclic rather than linear; operate off solar energy flux and organic storages; promote resilience within each range of scales by diversifying the execution of functions into arrays of narrow niches; maintain resilience across all scales by operating functions redundantly over different ranges of scale; promote efficient use of materials by developing cooperative webs of interactions between members of complex communities; and sustain diversity of information and function to adapt and evolve in response to changes in their external environment (Kibert, Sendzimir, and Guy 2002). The emerging field of industrial ecology in addition to several ideologies such as cradle-to-cradle design, biomimicry, the Natural Step, and eco-efficiency look to ecosystem processes as a model for industrial material systems. These are discussed below followed by a discussion of the green chemistry movement and trends in extended producer responsibilities.

INDUSTRIAL ECOLOGY

Industrial ecology views industrial systems as being part of and intertwined with the biosphere, and it draws biological analogies to help industry become more efficient and sustainable. The most common definition of industrial ecology is "the idea that nature (specifically nature at its higher levels of organization such as communities and ecosystems) can serve as a useful metaphor for industrial systems" (Allen 2004). It also refers to the study of physical, chemical, and biological interactions and interrelationships both within and among industrial and ecological systems.

Most specifically it involves the shifting of industrial processes from linear, open-loop systems where resources move through the system to become waste, to a closed-loop system where wastes are used as inputs for new processes.

Industrial Symbiosis

A major aim of industrial ecology is waste reduction, a response to the massive quantities of waste generated in product manufacture. Like natural ecosystems where

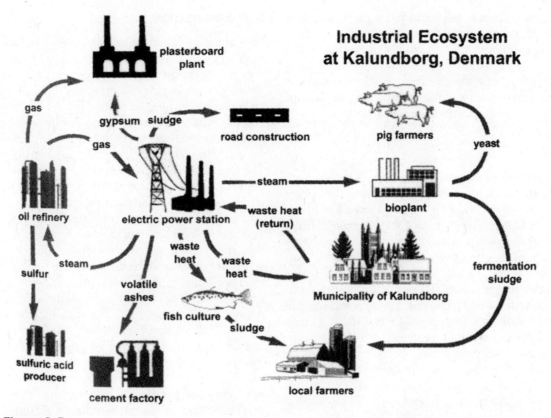

Figure 2–5.

Relationships of waste as food for other industrial processes are diagrammed for the Kalundborg industrial ecosystem in Denmark. (Kibert, Charles. Copyright © 2005, John Wiley & Sons, Inc. Reprinted with the permission of John Wiley & Sons, Inc.)

waste from one process is food for another, industrial ecosystems have started to develop where excess waste and energy from one industry serves as an input for another (Kibert et al. 2002). Referred to as industrial symbiosis, this incurs fewest impacts if the industries are colocated or at least within reasonable proximity. The Kalundborg eco-industrial park in Denmark is a good example of industrial symbiosis housing seven complementary industries. An electric power station provides waste heat to a fishery, volatile ashes to a cement factory, steam to an oil refinery and a bioplant, gypsum to a plasterboard plant, and sludge for road construction. The oil refinery provides gas to the electric power station, sulfur to a sulfuric acid producer, and gas to the plasterboard plant. The bioplant provides yeast to pig farmers and fermentation sludge to local farmers.

Construction Ecology

Within the goal of sustainable development, the building material production and construction industries ideally would shift their use of resources and fuels from nonrenewables to renewables, from waste production to reuse and recycling, from first-cost emphasis to life-cycle cost emphasis, and full-cost accounting where all costs such as waste, emissions, and pollution are factored into the cost of materials (Kibert et al. 2002). Construction ecology, an outgrowth of industrial ecology, is defined by Charles Kibert and coeditors of *Construction Ecology* as "a view of the construction industry based on natural ecology and industrial ecology for the purpose of shifting the construction industry and the materials and manufacturing industries supporting it onto a path much closer to the ideals of sustainability." They add "Construction ecology embraces a wide range of symbiotic, synergistic, built environment–natural environment relationships to include large-scale, bioregional, 'green infrastructure' in which natural systems provide energy and material flows for cities and towns and the human occupants provide nutrients for the supporting ecological systems (Kibert et al. 2002)."

BIOMIMICRY

Biomimicry, like industrial ecology, draws lessons from nature and views "the conscious emulation of life's genius as a survival strategy for the human race and a path to a sustainable future" (Benyus 2002). The core concept is that nature has already solved many of the problems that humans are struggling with, and that we can learn the solutions from nature. Biomimicry demonstrates direct applications of ecological concepts to industrial products, with the aim of creating strong, durable, and intelligent materials, with no waste and use of nonrenewable energy sources. An example with potential application to building materials is the epoxy produced by mussels' "feet" with "adhesive properties that rival any superglue on the market." Scientists believe that chemical and biological lessons can be drawn from this natural epoxy to develop natural, waterproof adhesives for application in several industries, including construction. This "glue" that mussels produce remains intact in seawater, is created at relatively low temperatures, and is environmentally safe (Biomimicry Institute).

PREVENTION PRINCIPLE

The prevention principle dictates that waste and pollution prevention or minimization in all phases of a product's life cycle should be given the highest priority (Azapagic et al. 2004). This principle is based on the notion of environmental legislation that preventing environmental harm is cheaper, easier, and less environmentally dangerous than reacting to environmental harm that has already been done. This view forms the basis for some nations' regulation of hazardous waste and pesticides. The prevention principle, an important aspect of industrial ecology, includes concepts of dematerialization, eco-efficiency, closed-loop systems, zero waste, cleaner production, zero emissions, and green chemistry.

DEMATERIALIZATION

The notion of dematerialization aims to reduce material flows with both improvements in resource and energy use by industry, and by more efficient use of the product by consumers (Kibert et al. 2002). Dematerialization in product design advocates use of material flow analysis or life-cycle analysis to examine all stages of a material or product's life cycle with the intent to minimize or eliminate waste, resource use, and energy use. The United Nations Environment Programme (UNEP) defines dematerialization as "the reduction of total material and energy throughput of any product and service, and thus the limitation of its environmental impact. This includes reduction of raw materials at the production stage, of energy and material inputs at the use stage, and of waste at the disposal stage." (UNEP 1999).

Dematerialization can improve a product's efficiency by saving, reusing, or recycling materials and products. Actions at every stage of the life cycle include resource savings in the material extraction phase, improved design of products (e.g., lighter weight or longer-lasting), innovations and efficiencies in the production process, use of renewable fuels in the manufacturing and transport phase, and reduction or reuse of waste and by-products either within the manufacturing process or in other processes.

Some argue that dematerialization is not much more than an attempt to increase profitability of a product by improving the efficiencies in manufacturing and lowering the costs of production (Kibert et al. 2002). And indeed, potential cost savings may be the way to make dematerialization happen in our market-based society. There are some concerns about dematerialization as this may encourage use of high-tech polymers, nano materials, or carbon composite materials, some of which may use less resources by weight but pose toxicity concerns, and be less durable and recyclable (Kibert et al. 2002).

FACTOR 4 AND FACTOR 10

Factor 4 and Factor 10, strategies developed to reduce resource use and support the idea of dematerialization, suggest that to live sustainably, we need to reduce resource use for products and services by one-quarter or one-tenth respectively. Factor 4 states that "natural resources can be used more efficiently in all domains of

Table 2–16 Characteristics of Ecological Systems as Compared with Industrial Systems

Strategies of Ecosystems in Nature	Current Industrial Practices	Industrial and Construction Ecology Goals
Waste from one species is food for another. True waste does not exist.[a]	Billions of tons of waste are generated through industrial processes each year. Beneficial uses are increasingly found for some of it either within or outside of the industrial process from which it resulted. Yet networks of waste recycling are not well established.[b]	Excess waste and energy from one manufacturer serves as an input for another manufacturing process, either within or outside the industry. The goal is closed-loop material systems eliminating waste and consumption of virgin resources.[b]
Renewable solar energy is the only source of power for ecosystems.[c]	Industrial systems operate by using stored solar energy in the form of fossil fuels. Fossil fuels are being consumed at a pace of 10,000 times their renewal rate. Nonrenewable resources, such as coal and natural gas, are the primary energy sources in the manufacturing industry.	Waste energy is captured from one process and used to power another.[c] Renewable energy sources such as biofuels and solar, wind, or geothermal power are utilized instead of fossil fuels.
Concentrated toxic materials are generated and used locally.[c]	Toxic materials are generally not reused; instead the large quantities that are generated are released to soil, air, and water or disposed of in landfills.	Toxic waste and by-products are minimized and/or captured and beneficially reused locally in other processes.[b]
Efficiency and productivity are in dynamic balance with resiliency. Emphasis on the first two qualities over the third creates brittle systems likely to crash.[c]	Manufacturing often emphasizes efficiency and productivity to the exclusion of resiliency and flexibility.[d]	Manufacturers alter processes with the aim of efficiency or material and energy use and maximization of productivity and profit. The two are not seen as mutually exclusive; instead, efficiency can lead to increased profit (and minimized environmental impact).
Ecosystems remain resilient in the face of change through a high biodiversity of species, organized in complex webs of relationships. The many relationships are maintained through self-organizing processes, not top-down control.[c]	Manufacturing is highly centralized and specialized with top-down control. Local manufacturers are being replaced by enterprises operating at larger scales (national or global).[d]	Manufacturers remain resilient and open to changes in product, process, and scale.[b]
In an ecosystem, each individual in a species acts independently, yet its activity patterns cooperatively mesh with the patterns of other species. Cooperation and competition are interlinked and held in balance.[c]	Competition is emphasized over cooperation, although industries do share technologies. Emphasis is on the competitive free market where the best product (often the one with the lowest first cost dominates) and the most efficient manufacturing practices will produce the strongest bottom line.[d]	Relationships are developed among industries that complement each other through industrial symbiosis.[b]

[a]Beynus 2002

[b]Azapagic et al. 2004

[c]Lowe 2002

[d]Graedel and Allenby 1996

daily life, either by generating more products, services and quality of life from the available resources, or by using less resources to maintain the same standard" (Weizsäcker et al. 1997). According to material scientists and industrial designers, the technology and knowledge currently exists to execute Factor 4 (Weizsäcker et al. 1997).

Factor 10, developed at the Wuppertal Institute for Climate and Energy, builds on Factor 4 with the idea of creating products and services with a drastically lower resource intensity than the conventional alternative. This idea aligns with the United Nations Environment Programme's (UNEP) goals as published in *Global Environment Outlook 2000*. The report concludes: "A tenfold reduction in resource consumption in the industrialized countries is a necessary long-term target if adequate resources are to be released for the needs of developing countries" (UNEP 1999).

DESIGN FOR ENVIRONMENT

Design for environment (DfE) is a proactive, front-loaded approach used in industrial design that mini-

mizes environmental impacts during the development of a product and its related processes. An aspect of industrial ecology, environmental thinking is integrated into the product design process by utilizing techniques of LCA to develop product and process engineering procedures considering the entire life cycle (Graedel and Allenby 1996). Balance of environmental, business, and technical considerations in product and process design is a major aspect of DfE. DfE includes design for disassembly (DfD), design for recycling (DfR), and design for reuse. Goals of DfE as stated in Graedel and Allenby's book *Design for Environment* are summarized in the table below.

ECO-EFFICIENCY

Closely aligned with the ideas of dematerialization, the concept of eco-efficiency involves creating more goods and services while using fewer resources and creating less waste and pollution. The term was coined by the World Business Council for Sustainable Development (WBCSD) in a 1992 publication called *Changing Course*. The WBCSD states that eco-efficiency is "achieved

Table 2–17 Goals of Design for Environment (DfE)

Every molecule that enters a specific manufacturing process should leave that process as part of a salable product.
Every erg of energy used in manufacture should produce a desired material transformation.
Industries should make minimum use of materials and energy in products, processes, and services.
Industries should choose abundant, nontoxic materials when designing products.
Industries should get most of the needed materials through recycling streams (theirs or those of others) rather than through raw materials extraction, even in the case of common materials.
Every process and product should be designed to preserve the embedded utility of the materials used. An efficient way to accomplish this goal is by designing modular equipment and by remanufacturing.
Every product should be designed so that it can be used to create other useful products at the end of its life.
Every industrial landholding or facility should be developed, constructed, or modified with attention to maintaining or improving local habitats and species diversity, and to minimizing impacts on local or regional resources.
Cooperative agreements should be developed with materials suppliers and customers for the purpose of minimizing packaging.

Source: Graedel and Allenby 1996

through the delivery of competitively priced goods and services that satisfy human needs and bring quality of life while progressively reducing environmental impacts of goods and resource intensity throughout the entire life-cycle to a level at least in line with the Earth's estimated carrying capacity" (1992).

CLOSED-LOOP SYSTEMS AND ZERO WASTE

The last two decades have seen the beginnings of a shift in the product manufacturing industry from linear production and consumption of materials and products to some cyclic manufacturing activities. An alternative to the one-time use and disposal of materials is to reuse materials and material by-products multiple times with the aim of creating closed-loop material systems that reduce or eliminate waste and pollution.

Cradle-to-cradle design, a product design philosophy developed by William McDonough and Michael Braungart and detailed in their 2002 book *Cradle to Cradle: Remaking the Way We Make Things,* builds on the ideas of eco-efficiency with the aim of closing material life-cycle loops and eliminating waste. This approach to sustainability models flows of industry on the integrated processes of nature's ecosystems where waste from one process is food (or feedstock) for another. Industrial systems, like natural systems, are closed-loop systems where every ingredient is safe and beneficial, rather than the current linear flows of resources often producing toxic by-products that are released to the environment.

The concept of zero waste, turning outputs from every resource use into the input for another use, is central to closed-loop material systems. Not just recycling, zero waste involves changes to production systems and product design where instead of planned obsolescence, products are designed for perpetual reuse or to be disassembled and component parts reused. Packaging is minimized and designed for reuse or recycling, and often returned to the manufacturer.

CLEANER PRODUCTION AND ZERO-EMISSIONS CONCEPTS

Cleaner production and zero-emissions concepts follow notions of closed-loop material systems by aiming for reductions in waste and emissions while maximizing material output. Cleaner production is a preventive goal that adapts production organization and technology to make the best possible use of materials and energy and avoid waste, wastewater generation, gaseous emissions, waste heat, and noise. Zero emissions is a goal to emit no waste products from engines, motors, or energy sources that pollute the environment, contribute to climate change, or pose human health risks. Zero emissions are most easily achieved through renewable energy sources such as solar power, wind power, tidal power, and geothermal power. However, carbon capture and storage technologies in development may also produce zero emissions.

GREEN CHEMISTRY

Green chemistry is a philosophy of chemical and material design that aims to increase performance while reducing or eliminating the use and generation of hazardous substances. Principles of green chemistry are summarized in Table 2–18.

THE NATURAL STEP FRAMEWORK

The Natural Step Framework proposes system conditions that can lead to the sustainability of the planet. The framework was developed by Karl-Henrik Robèrt in response to the 1987 Bruntland Report, *Our Common Future.* The four system conditions of the Natural Step leading to a sustainable society are summarized in Table 2–19.

INCREASED PRODUCER RESPONSIBILITY

Currently, producers bear limited responsibility for the environmental and human health impacts of the materials and products they produce. American industry functions in a culture of almost pure market response, minimal governmental intervention, a history of cheap resources, and low waste disposal costs. Producers are not asked to take responsibility for impacts of their products in use or disposal, and while hazardous emissions and waste are regulated, penalties for production are minimal.

The European Union has recently established policies requiring manufacturers to extend producer responsibility through all phases of their products' life cycle, taking

Table 2–18 Principles of Green Chemistry

Prevent waste: Design chemical syntheses to prevent waste, leaving no waste to treat or clean up.
Design safer chemicals and products: Design chemical products to be fully effective, yet have little or no toxicity.
Design less hazardous chemical syntheses: Design syntheses to use and generate substances with little or no toxicity to humans and the environment.
Use renewable feedstocks: Use raw materials and feedstocks that are renewable rather than depleting. Renewable feedstocks are often made from agricultural products or are the wastes of other processes; depleting feedstocks are made from fossil fuels (petroleum, natural gas, or coal) or are mined.
Use catalysts, not stoichiometric reagents: Minimize waste by using catalytic reactions. Catalysts are used in small amounts and can carry out a single reaction many times. They are preferable to stoichiometric reagents, which are used in excess and work only once.
Avoid chemical derivatives: Avoid using blocking or protecting groups or any temporary modifications if possible. Derivatives use additional reagents and generate waste.
Maximize atom economy: Design syntheses so that the final product contains the maximum proportion of the starting materials. There should be few, if any, wasted atoms.
Use safer solvents and reaction conditions: Avoid using solvents, separation agents, or other auxiliary chemicals. If these chemicals are necessary, use innocuous chemicals.
Increase energy efficiency: Run chemical reactions at ambient temperature and pressure whenever possible.
Design chemicals and products to degrade after use: Design chemical products to break down to innocuous substances after use so that they do not accumulate in the environment.
Analyze in real time to prevent pollution: Include in-process real-time monitoring and control during syntheses to minimize or eliminate the formation of by-products.
Minimize the potential for accidents: Design chemicals and their forms (solid, liquid, or gas) to minimize the potential for chemical accidents including explosions, fires, and releases to the environment.

Source: U.S. EPA "Green Chemistry"

Table 2–19 Four System Conditions of the Natural Step

Nature's functions and diversity are not systematically subject to increasing concentrations of substances extracted from the earth's crust.
Nature's functions and diversity are not systematically subject to increasing concentrations of substances produced by society.
Nature's functions and diversity are not systematically impoverished by physical displacement, overharvesting, or other forms of ecosystem manipulation.
People are not subject to conditions that systematically undermine their capacity to meet their needs.

Source: Robèrt 2002

greater responsibility for the waste and pollution they create. German industry is regulated by a strong regulatory framework that holds industry to a higher standard of materials use than the United States (Kibert et al. 2002).

EXTENDED PRODUCER RESPONSIBILITY (EPR)

The extended producer responsibility principle advocates that "waste producers should bear full 'cradle to grave' responsibility for any damage caused by the waste that they produce" (Azapagic 2004). Traditionally, the producer's responsibility for a product ends as it leaves the factory and there is no incentive for the producer to package the product with less material or to make the product durable and long-lasting. In fact, the concept of planned obsolescence ensures that the producer will need to make even more products, increasing sales and profits.

Extended producer responsibility asks the manufacturer of the product to be responsible for the entire life cycle of the product, including the take-back, disposal, and final recycling of the product (European Commission 2003). The intent is to encourage less waste and pollution by requiring manufacturers to plan, presumably more efficiently, the entire life cycle of their products in order to work toward a closed-loop manufacturing system. If the producers have to take a product back after its useful life, they are more likely to reuse or recycle it to save material costs rather than to landfill it. Also, if the producers are required to take back packaging, they are more likely to minimize the packaging in order to save transport costs back to the factory.

The emphasis in Europe on reduction of waste and pollution has resulted in legislation extending producer responsibility for some products through their entire life cycle. The EU has recently issued many directives on waste and EPR that member country governments will implement. The Directive on Packaging and Packaging Waste set targets for the recovery of packaging and required the setup of return, collection, and recovery systems. The Directive on End-of-Life Vehicles proposed several recovery, reuse, and recycling targets for vehicle manufacturers, including recovery and reuse of 85% by weight of vehicles by 2005 and 95% by 2015 (Azapagic et al. 2004).

There is some speculation that as EPR becomes more widespread, it may lead producers to form product service systems where they lease their products to the consumer. The producers would maintain, repair, and upgrade when necessary and take the original product back to refurbish it or reuse its parts. This has the benefits of involvement of the producers throughout the entire life cycle, producer care of the product as they are the product experts, and ease of replacement with a newer product without the extensive waste. An example of this that is currently in use is copy machines that are leased to offices, maintained by the manufacturer, and removed and replaced by the manufacturer when a new model is out. The old copy machine is dismantled and some components reused.

POLLUTER PAYS PRINCIPLE

The polluter pays principle, part of extended producer responsibility, shifts the cost responsibility of waste from the government to those who produce it. If the polluters bear the cost of dealing with the waste, particularly the more costly to dispose of toxic waste, they may reduce the amount of waste they produce or find ways to reuse or recycle it. This is also a principle in international environmental law where the polluting party pays for the damage done to the natural environment.

Currently, lack of regulation in the mining industry frees mining companies from "paying" for the waste they produce and any environmental burdens that result from their practices. Many mines are abandoned after use and mining companies go out of business, leaving large piles of waste, some of which has a toxic effect on surrounding ecosystems and water and air quality. If producers were required to pay for disposal of the waste they produce and cleanup of their pollution, the costs of virgin resources would be much higher, thereby encouraging the use of recycled or recovered materials.

In construction, the polluter pays principle is most commonly implemented with landfill taxes. In the United States, some municipalities require construction and demolition (C&D) debris to be disposed of in special landfills with higher fees. This encourages the "producer" of the waste, the owner, or the demo contractor as the owner's rep to recycle or reuse the waste rather than pay the high landfill fees. In other areas with very low landfill fees and no C&D waste restrictions, there is no penalty for the "polluters" to shift the waste burden to the municipality at their landfill.

PROXIMITY PRINCIPLE

The proximity principle advocates that waste should be disposed of or managed as close to the point of generation as possible. Current municipal solid waste (MSW) practices truck or ship waste hundreds, even thousands, of miles to distant landfills. This shifts the environmental and human health burden of waste to another location and reduces awareness of the impacts of the waste by those who created it. As long as the waste disappears, there is not much incentive to reduce it. On the other hand, if an urbanized region is required to dispose of its waste within the urban area, legislation and taxes might generate greater recycling markets or waste reduction measures. This principle aims for responsible self-sufficiency at a regional level, and while currently applied to waste management, it could just as easily apply to the material manufacture and use phases.

REFERENCES

Agency for Toxic Substances and Disease Registry (ATSDR). "ToxFAQs." U.S. Department of Health and Human Services, http://www.atsdr.cdc.gov/toxfaq.html (accessed between May 2006 and November 2007).

Allen, D. T. 2004. "An Industrial Ecology: Material Flows and Engineering Design." In *Sustainable Development in Practice*, eds. A. Azapagic, S. Perdan, and R. Clift. Chichester, England: John Wiley & Sons.

The Aluminum Association February 2003. "Aluminum: Industry Technology Roadmap." Washington, D.C.: The Aluminum Association, Inc.

Anastas, P., and J. Warner. 1998. *Green Chemistry: Theory and Practice*. New York: Oxford University Press.

Anink, D., Boonstra, C., and Mak, J. 1996. *Environmental Preference Method for Selection of Materials for Use in Construction and Refurbishment*. London: James & James Science Publishers.

Athena Sustainable Materials Institute. *Athena Environmental Impact Estimator*, version 3.0.3. Kutztown, ON, Canada: Athena Sustainable Materials Institute.

Ayers, Robert U. 2002. "Minimizing waste emissions from the built environment." In *Construction Ecology: Nature as the Basis for Green Building*, ed. C.J. Kibert. London: Routledge.

Azapagic, A., A. Emsley, and I. Hamerton, eds. 2003. *Polymers, the Environment and Sustainable Development*. Chichester, England: John Wiley & Sons.

Azapagic, A., S. Perdan, and R. Clift, eds. 2004. *Sustainable Development in Practice: Case Studies for Engineers and Scientists*. Chichester, England: John Wiley & Sons.

Benyus, J. M. 2002. *Biomimicry*. New York: Harper Collins.

Biomimicry Institute. "Mollusk Inspired Epoxy." http://biomimicryinstitute.org/case-studies/.

Comprehensive Environmental Response, Compensation, and Liability Act (CERCLA). 2005. CERCLA Priority List of Hazardous Substances. Agency for Toxic Substances and Disease Registry, Department of Health and Human Services. http://www.atsdr.cdc.gov/cercla/ (accessed February 14, 2006).

European Commission. 2003, December. "Chapter 4: Waste Management.", In *Handbook for the Implementation of EU Environmental Legislation*. Brussels: European Commission, Europa.

Food and Agriculture Organization of the United Nations (FAO). 2005. *Global Forest Resources Assessment 2005*. FAO Forestry Paper 147. Rome: Food and Agriculture Organization of the United Nations.

Graedel, T. E., and B. R. Allenby. 1996. *Design for Environment*. Upper Saddle River, NJ: Prentice Hall.

Gutowski, Timothy. 2004, December. "Design and Manufacturing for the Environment." In *The Handbook of Mechanical Engineering*. New York: Springer-Verlag.

Hammond, G. and Jones, C. 2006. "Inventory of Carbon and Energy", Version 1.5 Beta, Bath, UK: University of Bath, Department of Mechanical Engineering.

Healthy Building Network. *The Pharos Project*. http://www.pharosproject.net/wiki/ (accessed October 16, 2007).

International Lake Environment Committee (ILEC)/Lake Biwa Research Institute (LBRI), eds. 1988 "Interim Report on the Survey of the State of the World's Lakes. Volumes I–IV, 1988-1993". Nairobi: International Lake Environment Committee, Otsu, and United Nations Environment Programme.

Intergovernmental Panel on Climate Change (IPCC). 2001. *Climate Change 2001: Synthesis Report*. Ed. R.T. Watson and the Core Writing Team. Cambridge: Cambridge University Press.

Intergovernmental Panel on Climate Change (IPCC). 2007a. *Climate Change 2007: Impacts, Adaptation and Vulnerability. Contribution of Working Group II to the Fourth Assessment Report of the Intergovernmental Panel on Climate Change*. Ed. M. L. Parry, O. F. Canziani, J. P. Palutikof, P. J. van der Linden, and C. E. Hanson. Cambridge: Cambridge University Press.

Intergovernmental Panel on Climate Change (IPCC). 2007b. *Climate Change 2007: The Physical Science Basis. Contribution of Working Group I to the Fourth Assessment Report of the Intergovernmental Panel on Climate Change*. New York: Cambridge University Press.

International Aluminum Institute (IAI). 2007. http://www.world-aluminum.org.

Kapur, Amit, and Gregory Keoleian. "CSS Factsheets, U.S. Material Use." University of Michigan: Ann Arbor (2005): 1-2. CSS05-18.

Kibert, Charles, J. 2005. *Sustainable Construction: Green Building Design and Delivery*. Hoboken, NJ: John Wiley & Sons.

Kibert, C. J., J. Sendzimir, and B. Guy, eds. 2002. *Construction Ecology: Nature as the Basis for Green Building*. London: Spon Press.

Lowe, Ernest. 2002. "Forward." In *Construction Ecology: Nature as the Basis for Green Buildings*, ed. C.J. Kibert, J. Sendzimir, and B. Guy. London: Spon Press.

Marris, Emma, and Daemon Fairless. 2007. "Wind Farms' Deadly Reputation Hard to Shift." *Nature* 447(126) .

McDonough, William, and Michael Braungart. 2002. *Cradle to Cradle: Remaking the Way We Make Things*. New York: North Point Press.

Moll, S., S. Bringezu, and H. Schutz. 2005. *Resource Use in European Countries*. An Estimate of Materials and Waste Streams in the Community, Including Imports and Exports Using the Instrument of Material Flow Analysis. Wuppertal Report No. 1. Wuppertal Institute.

National Institute of Standards and Technology (NIST). *BEES 4.0: Building for Environmental and Economic Sustainability*. http://www.bfrl.nist.gov.

National Observatory of Athens. "Climate Change." http://www.climate.noa.gr/Emissions/CC_emissionsFCs.htm.

National Renewable Energy Laboratory (NREL). "U.S. Life-Cycle Inventory Database User Guide." U.S. Department of Energy, Office of Energy Efficiency & Renewable Energy. http://www.nrel.gov/ (accessed September 9, 2007).

North American Industry Classification System (NAICS). 2002. NAICS Codes and Titles. U.S. Census Bureau.

Portland Cement Association. http://www.cement.org/basics/cementindustry.asp.

Robèrt, Karl-Henrik. 2002. *The Natural Step Story: Seeding a Quiet Revolution*. Gabriola Island, British Columbia: New Society Publishers.

Roodman, D. M., and N. Lenssen. 1995, March. "A Building Revolution: How Ecology and Health Concerns Are Transforming Construction." *Worldwatch Paper 124*. Washington, DC: Worldwatch Institute.

Thomark, C. "Environmental Analysis of a Building with Reused Building Materials." *International Journal of Low Energy & Sustainable Building*. 2000. As cited in "Buildings and Climate Change." United Nations Environmental Programme (UNEP). 2007.

Thompson, J.W., and K. Sorvig. 2000. *Sustainable Landscape Construction: A Guide to Green Building Outdoors*. Washington, DC: Island Press.

United Nations Convention to Combat Desertification (UNCCD). http://www.unccd.int/ (accessed October 30, 2007).

United Nations Environment Programme (UNEP). *Global Environment Outlook 2000*. GEO Team. Division of Environmental Information, Assessment and Early Warning (DEIA & EW). UNEP, 1999.

United Nations Environment Programme (UNEP). "Convention on Biological Diversity." http://www.cbd.int/default.shtml.

U.S. Department of Energy (U.S. DOE). Energy Information Administration. "Natural Gas Issues and Trends 1998." 1998.

U.S. Department of Energy (U.S. DOE). Energy Information Adminstration. Office of Integrated Analysis and Forecasting. 2006. "Emissions of Greenhouse Gases in the United States 2005." U.S. DOE/EIA-0573.

US Department of Energy (US DOE) Energy Information Administration (EIA). 2007a "International Energy Outlook 2007". Report #:DOE/EIA-0484(2007), May 2007.

U.S. Department of Energy (U.S. DOE). Energy Information Administration. 2007b. *Net Generation by Energy Source by Type of Producer*. Washington, DC. Oct 2007.

U.S. Environmental Protection Agency (U.S. EPA). "Exposure and Human Health Reassessment of 2,3,7,8-Tetrachlorodibenzo-p-Dioxin (TCDD) and Related Compounds." National Center for Environmental Assessment: Research and Development. Washington DC, December 2003.

U.S. Environmental Protection Agency (U.S. EPA). Toxic Release Inventory (TRI). "TRI Explorer. Version 4.6." Chemical Report. 2005. http://www.epa.gov/triexplorer/.

U.S. Environmental Protection Agency (U.S. EPA). Office of Solid Waste. 2006a. "Muncipal Solid Waste in the United States: 2005 Facts and Figures-Executive Summary."

U.S. Environmental Protection Agency (U.S. EPA). 2006b. "Beneficial Reuse Sector Report." 2006 Sector Strategies Performance Report. Sector Programs, U.S. EPA.

U.S. Environmental Protection Agency (U.S. EPA). 2007a. Toxic Release Inventory (TRI). "2005 TRI Public Data Release Report." March 2007.

U.S. Environmental Protection Agency (U.S. EPA). Office of Policy, Economics, and Innovation. 2007b. *Energy Trends in Selected Manufacturing Sectors: Opportunities and Challenges for Environmentally Preferable Energy Outcomes*. Prepared by ICF International, March 2007.

U.S. Environmental Protection Agency (U.S. EPA). 2007c. *Inventory of U.S. Greenhouse Gas Emissions and Sinks, 1990-2005*. April 2007. Report EPA 430-R-07-002.

US Environmental Protection Agency (US EPA). 1998. "Characterization of Building-Related Construction and Demolition Debris in the United States", Report No. EPA530-R-98-010. Prepared by Franklin Associates for Office of Solid Waste, US EPA

U.S. Environmental Protection Agency (U.S. EPA). "Industrial Waste Management." http://www.epa.gov/epaoswer/non-hw/industd/tools.htm.

U.S. Environmental Protection Agency (U.S. EPA). "Green Chemistry" http://www.epa.gov/greenchemistry/

U.S. Environmental Protection Agency (U.S. EPA). "Climate Change: Greenhouse Gas Emissions." http://www.epa.gov/climatechange/emissions/.

U.S. Environmental Protection Agency (U.S. EPA). Air and Radiation. "What Are the Six Common Air Pollutants?" http://www.epa.gov/ttn/atw.

U.S. Geological Survey (USGS). "Radioactive Elements in Coal and Fly Ash: Abundance, Forms, and Environmental Significance." USGS Fact Sheet FS-163-97. October 1997.

U.S. Geological Survey (USGS). 2007. "Sand and Gravel, Construction." *2005 Minerals Yearbook*. Washington, DC: U.S. Geological Survey.

US Geological Survey (USGS). 1998. "Material Flow and Sustainability", USGS Fact Sheet FS-068-98. Washington, D.C.: US Geological Survey. June 1998.

Wackernagel, M,, and W. Rees. 1996. *Our Ecological Footprint.* Gabriola Island, British Columbia: New Society Publishers.

Wagner, L. A. *Materials in the Economy: Material Flows, Scarcity, and the Environment.* U.S. Geological Survey Circular 1221. Denver, February 2002.

Washington State Department of Ecology. "Multiyear PBT Chemical Action Plan Schedule." Department of Ecology Publication No. 07-07-016. March 2007.

Weizsäcker, Ernst Ulrich v., Amory Lovins, and Hunter L. Lovins. 1997. *Factor Four: Doubling Wealth—Halving Resource Use.* London: Earthscan.

World Business Council for Sustainable Development (WBCSD). 1992. http://www.wbscd.org/.

World Resource Assessment. 2005. *Millennium Ecosystem Assessment.* "Ecosystems and Human Well-Being." Washington, DC: Island Press.

World Resources Institute (WRI). 2000. "Weight of Nations: Material Outflows from Industrial Economies." Washington, DC: WRI.

chapter 3

Evaluating the Environmental and Human Health Impacts of Materials

aterials evaluation and selection may be one of the most confusing and controversial areas of sustainable site design, with multiple variables and many right and wrong answers. Other aspects of sustainable site design may be more easily quantified. For example, hydrological analysis can disclose the necessary dimensions and type of bioswale along a street to infiltrate and cleanse storm water, but it is difficult to know if the path along the bioswale should be constructed from asphalt pavement made 20 miles away that may release polycyclic aromatic hydrocarbons (PAHs) over time into the water in the swale, or decomposed granite with stone fragments from a quarry adjacent to a wetland 300 miles away stabilized with renewable plant-based binder produced 1,500 miles from the site.

"What are the impacts?" is the first question that must be asked in evaluating the environmental and human health impacts of a material or product. Taking a complete inventory of *all* environmental and human health impacts resulting from *all* inputs and outputs at *all* phases of a material's life cycle is a huge undertaking—some would call it endless. This practice, called a life-cycle inventory (LCI), is a complex process best undertaken by material scientists and life-cycle analysts. And an inventory of impacts takes a certain expertise to interpret and will not provide answers in comparing materials without some idea of their relative importance.

"What is the relative importance of the magnitude and risks of the impact compared to the other products impacts?" is the second question and is most critical in successful evaluation of materials. Determining how much importance to assign to a given environmental or human health impact is challenging, and different weightings can produce highly variable results. Some emphasize that using resources efficiently, reusing them in closed-loop cycles, and eliminating waste is of paramount importance (McDonough and Braungart 2002). Others claim that global climate change and reduction of carbon footprint is the most critical issue (Architecture 2030), and still others place greatest emphasis on reducing human health impacts of construction materials (Healthy Building Network).

Environmental and human health impacts associated with building material/product use can be minimized with careful attention to environmental and human health costs throughout their life cycle. This chapter will discuss techniques of evaluating materials, such as life-cycle assessment (LCA), sustainability assessment (SA), and embodied energy (EE) analysis. Current LCA tools such as the Athena Environmental Impact Estimator by the Athena Sustainable Materials Institute of Canada, the National Institute of Standards and Technology's Building for Environmental and Economic Sustainability (BEES), and general rating systems defining standards for green materials such as LEED and Green Globes are summarized. Establishment of environmental and human health priorities and weightings will also be discussed.

Techniques for Evaluating Materials and Products

LIFE-CYCLE ASSESSMENT (LCA)

Life-cycle assessment (LCA), also called life-cycle analysis, is a qualitative technique for the evaluation of environmental impacts of construction materials and products, services, and processes. It is the most comprehensive tool for evaluating the environmental and human health impacts of materials and products. However, it is also the most challenging, and clear answers are often elusive. LCA identifies and quantifies environmental impacts of a product for a given scope, usually cradle to gate (manufacturer's gate) or cradle to grave (use then disposal or reuse). All inputs (e.g., energy, water, and material resources) and outputs (e.g., emissions, effluents, and waste to air, water, and land) are quantified. The International Organization for Standardization (ISO) defines LCA as a compilation and evaluation of inputs, outputs, and the potential environmental impacts of a product throughout its life cycle (ISO 1996).

An LCA is comprised of four phases (ASTM 2005):

Goal and scope definition. During this phase the purpose of the LCA is defined to include questions to be answered, the level of detail to be achieved, the scope of analysis (e.g., cradle to gate or other), and priorities regarding the various environmental impacts possible throughout the life cycle.

Inventory analysis. This phase involves data collection on environmental inputs and outputs of the mate-

rial or product under study at all phases of its life cycle. The depth of information gathered will be consistent with the goal and scope of the study. The results of this phase are called life-cycle inventory (LCI). The detailed LCI tracking of all flows can be very complex. And it can involve data from multiple individual unit processes of the supply chain, all of which involve tens, and sometimes hundreds, of substances to track (Trusty and Horst n.d.).

LCI data for an individual product is expensive and challenging to obtain. Some manufacturers try to keep such proprietary data confidential. If data is available, it is usually for a generic product that may differ from the actual product. And where data exists for two products that are being compared, the parameters of the data likely differ. For example, one set of data may include LCI data for the fuel used to produce the energy in manufacture, while the other may not.

The U.S. LCI database is a public-private research partnership that provides LCI data for commonly used materials and processes. Some of the data is self-reported by manufacturers. Researchers can use the data for their LCA activities. However, its use and interpretation in LCAs may be outside the skill of designers instead, use of one of the LCA tools available, the Athena Impact Estimator or BEES, may offer more easily accessible information.

Impact assessment. This phase is an evaluation of the environmental impacts of the inputs and outputs identified in the inventory analysis phase. LCI data is characterized by its impact potentials, such as its global warming potential or its ozone depletion potential. These measures, called midpoint indicators, are a way to summarize and compare the large amounts of inventory data. However, there is still disagreement on the best methods of bringing the midpoint indicators together to assess end-point impacts (Trusty and Horst n.d.). Categories of impacts that may be considered are discussed in detail in chapter 2, but they are also included later in this chapter under the discussion of priorities.

Interpretation. This phase is an analysis of the impacts in relation to the goals and intended use of the LCA. Sometimes, weights are applied to the results depending on priorities of the stakeholders. Weighting and priorities of materials evaluation are discussed later in this chapter.

While guidelines for conducting an LCA have been established by the ISO and ASTM, LCA is a complex and time-consuming activity, and may be outside the time and skill constraints of many designers; thus it is often performed by professional life-cycle analysts. The complexity and level of detail gathered for an LCA will vary greatly depending on the skills of the rsesearcher, priorities of the project, intended use of information, material/product being studied, and resources available to complete the study. LCA outcomes can vary or be skewed depending on the weight given to each type of impact. For example, a product might have relatively low embodied energy yet produce by-products that are persistent bioaccumulative toxins (PBTs). If the results during interpretation are not weighted for this serious impact, the product may still appear to be a viable alternative.

LCA tools, such as BEES and the Athena Environmental Impact Estimator, that evaluate construction materials and building assemblies are in a constant state of development, adding more products all the time. These tools, developed for the construction fields, will be discussed in detail later in the chapter. And while they can be quite useful for some products, they are geared primarily to evaluating building products and whole assemblies, limiting their application for site construction materials.

SUSTAINABILITY ASSESSMENT (SA)

Where LCA information does not exist for a given material or product, some evaluation of the impacts can still be made using the less formal and scientific method of sustainability assessment. The sustainability assessment (SA) method involves a set of questions and instructions for the collection of pertinent data on environmental and human health impacts of a building material or product from cradle to gate or cradle to grave. Information is gathered in categories of product feedstock materials acquisition, manufacturing, installation and operational performance, end-of-life-recovery or disposal, and corporate policy. Information gathered is then evaluated based on the priorities and goals of the particular project (ASTM 2003).

The "Sustainability Assessment Questions," Table 3–2 lists questions to consider when performing an SA for a construction material or product. It has been adapted with permission from ASTM Standard E2/29 for use with site construction materials. The questions are not intended to produce one right answer for which product is best—that is nearly impossible given the potential complexity of information garnered. Also, different projects and clients will have differing priorities. Rather, the questions are designed to bring the major environmental impacts, hazards, and opportunities to light, and to assist with material/product selection. Information and answers to the questions can be obtained from a variety of sources, including manufacturers and distributors, government resources and standards, health risk fact sheets from government agencies (U.S. or international), material safety data sheets (MSDSs), and an ever-evolving group of print and Web-based resources. Each question is written so that "yes" answers are preferred. Not all of the questions will be applicable to all materials/products, and some may require additional questions not listed.

Table 3–1 International Standards for LCA and SA

Standard Number	Standard Title
ISO 14040	Life-Cycle Assessment: General Principles and Practices
ISO 14041	Life-Cycle Assessment: Goal and Definition/Scope and Inventory Assessment
ISO 14042	Life-Cycle Assessment: Impact Assessment
ISO 14043	Life-Cycle Assessment: Improvement Assessment
ASTM E1991	Standard Guide for Environmental Life-Cycle Assessment (LCA) of Building Materials/Products
ASTM E2129	Standard Practice for Data Collection for Sustainability Assessment of Building Products
ASTM E2114	Standard Terminology for Sustainability Relative to the Performance of Buildings

Table 3–2 Sustainability Assessment Questions

Sustainability Assessment Question	Considerations for Evaluation and Comments
1. Product Feedstock Materials and Acquisition	
1.1 Have efforts (such as mining management, site restoration, etc.) been made to minimize and/or avoid negative environmental impacts (such as releases of toxic chemicals or hazardous air pollutants, etc.) in obtaining raw materials for this product? If YES, describe these efforts.	Acquisition of feedstock materials should not involve clear-cutting, strip mining or dredging.
1.2 Are any raw materials for the product from endangered species, sensitive ecosystems, or habitats of endangered species? If YES, describe.	Refer to the IUCN Red List; the Convention on International Trade in Endangered Species (CITES); and the US Fish and Wildlife Service.
1.3 Is the product a recycled content product? If YES, indicate what percentage of the product is recycled and differentiate between pre-consumer and post-consumer recycled content.	If applicable the recycled content product should contain the percentage of recovered materials recommended by the U.S. EPA's Comprehensive Procurement Guidelines. Where not specified in the Guidelines, products with recycled content should have a minimum 25% post-consumer and 50% pre-consumer content.
1.4 Is the product 100% recyclable? If NO, please indicate what percentage of the product is recyclable.	
1.5 Is the product a biobased product (i.e. agricultural or forestry material)? If YES, please indicate the source. and biobased content percentage. If percentage refers to a component rather than the entire product, please specify.	Organic agriculture practices are preferred. Is the product designated under the USDA's Biobased Affirmative Procurement Program? If YES, does it meet or exceed the program's biobased content recommendations?
1.6 Is the product made from a renewable resource? If YES, indicate the renewable cycle time and what percentage of the product that resource represents.	A product can be considered renewable if it's use life is longer that the time it takes to renew the material. For instance, redwood lumber can be considered a renewable product if it is in use for over 25 years.
1.7 Are raw materials for 80% of the mass of the product mined/harvested/extracted or reclaimed within 150 miles of the site for a heavy product, 500 miles for a medium weight product or 1000 miles for a lightweight product?	Environmental impacts vary by transport method. Shipping by Rail and Boat is more fuel efficient than by truck or plane. Full loads and direct delivery methods are more fuel efficient.
2. Manufacturing	
2.1 Does the product have low embodied energy (less than 750 mj/ton)? If not, is it medium (less than 8000 mj/ton) or high?	Some materials such as steel, aluminum, and cement are relatively high embodied energy from primary processing. Use of recycled content will often reduce the embodied energy of a product.
2.2 Has the manufacturer taken steps to minimize the use of nonrenewable energy from the point at which raw materials are gathered to the point at which the final product is transported to the building site? If YES, describe these measures.	Manufacturers should be able to provide energy use information. Does the manufacturer engage in any voluntary industrial sector energy reduction programs with the US EPA, US DOE or others? Does the manufacturer purchase Green-E certified energy?

Table 3–2 Sustainability Assessment Questions *(Continued)*

Sustainability Assessment Question	Considerations for Evaluation and Comments
2.3 Is any of the waste produced in making this product reclaimed on-site? If YES, what percentage of the waste is reclaimed? Of the waste that is not reclaimed on-site, how is that waste handled?	Does the manufacturer recycle waste off-site into other manufacturing processes? Does the manufacturer engage in any supply chain or industrial ecology practices such as waste reuse or exchange with other manufacturers?
2.4 Does the process for manufacturing this product avoid the use of or by-product production of listed substances above the levels that would require reporting under the U.S. EPA's Toxics Release Inventory (TRI)? If NO, indicate how much of each substance is released per unit of product.	www.epa.gov/tri
2.5 Does the process for manufacturing the product avoid the addition or by-product production of substances listed in the National Toxicology Program's Report on Carcinogens or the International Agency for Research on Cancer (IARC) Group 1 or Group 2 carcinogens?	http://ntp.niehs.nih.gov/ http://www.iarc.fr/ If substances listed in the National Toxicology Program's Report on Carcinogens or IARC Group 1 or Group 2 are added directly in the manufacturing process or are reported by suppliers on Material Safety Data Sheets (MSDS), do the concentrations fall below levels required to be reported under federal regulations on the products' MSDS? If NO, indicate the substance, classification, and concentration per unit of product.
2.6 Does the process for manufacturing the product avoid the addition or by-product production of substances listed in the EPA's Persistant Bioaccumulative Toxin (PBT) list or the Stockholm Convention list of Persistent Organic Pollutants (POP)?	http://www.epa.gov/pbt/ http://www.pops.int/
2.7 Is any constituent, by-product, or process a hazard for workers during the manufacturing or fabrication process?	Are MSDS sheets required for manufacturing or fabrication workers? Does the manufacturing facility comply with OSHA requirements?
2.8 If water is used during the production process, have water conservation and/or recycling measures been initiated? If YES, describe the measures and what percentage of the total water usage they address.	When process water is released has it been cleansed, filtered, or treated to remove pollutants?
2.9 Has the manufacturer undertaken any recent improvements to limit negative environmental or human health impacts resulting from the manufacturing or fabrication processes? If YES, indicate when the action(s) was (were) taken and describe the benchmark against which the improvements are measured and the degree of improvement.	Has the manufacturer: Redesigned a production process to decrease greenhouse gas emissions? Redesigned a production process to decrease liquid effluents? Redesigned a production process to utilize less toxic materials? Substituted safer solvents in a production process? Instituted more stringent dust controls? Installed smoke-stack particulate collectors or gas scrubbers? Installed or improved in-plant solid and toxic waste reduction programs?

Continued

Table 3–2 Sustainability Assessment Questions *(Continued)*

Sustainability Assessment Question	Considerations for Evaluation and Comments
3. Installation and Operational Performance	
3.1 Is any component of the product an installation hazard for construction workers? If YES, describe steps that are taken to minimize these impacts.	Refer to MSDS sheets for information.
3.2 Does the product, in the specified condition of use, meet the requirements of South Coast Air Quality Management District Regulations or Greenseal's GS-11 for content of VOCs?	SCAQMD Rule 1113 and Rule 1168 http://www.scaqmd.gov/ http://www.greenseal.org/certification/standards.cfm
3.3 Describe the product's energy efficiency impacts during the use phase.	If applicable, does the product qualify for an EPA EnergyStar® rating or meet the energy efficiency recommendations of the DOE's Federal Energy Management Program? http://www.energystar.gov/
3.5 If applicable, does the product qualify for an EPA WaterSense® rating?	http://www.epa.gov/watersense/
3.6 Describe routine maintenance procedures for the product. Can the product be maintained without use of toxic cleaners, sealers, or coatings?	Does the manufacturer provide detailed instructions with the product upon delivery to the job site for the proper use and maintenance required in order to ensure that this product will last this long?
3.7 How long will the product last in the site construction if maintained properly with routine maintenance procedures?	Does the expected life of the product (or the warranty) meet or exceed the expected life of the built site? Does the manufacturer provide information on the service life of the product or encourage the use of professional guidelines to determine the service life of the product?
4. End-of-Life—Recovery or Disposal	
4.1 Can the product be easily removed from the installation and reused/recycled after its use?	Does the manufacturer facilitate ultimate deconstruction of the site (in which components are taken apart for reuse) by, for example, designing products for disassembly? If YES, describe. Refer to DfD strategies in chapter 4.
4.2 Is the material recyclable?	Do recycling facilities for the material or product exist within reasonable transport distances of the site? Some finishes or adhesives may render the product unrecyclable.
4.3 Is the product biodegradable or compostable?	Will the product break down into benign, organic components within a reasonable period?
4.4 If not recyclable, is the product non-hazardous to dispose of?	Does the material or product pose hazards in disposal either in landfills or incinerators? If landfilled, will chemicals from the material/product affect soil or groundwater? If incinerated, will harmful chemicals or particulates be released? Is it difficult to "scrub" any constituents (e.g., dioxins)? Has the EPA targeted any chemicals released during disposal for reduction?

Table 3–2 Sustainability Assessment Questions *(Continued)*

Sustainability Assessment Question	Considerations for Evaluation and Comments
5. Corporate Environmental Policy	
5.1 Does the manufacturer have a written environmental policy? If YES, obtain a copy.	Has the manufacturer interfaced with credible third-party product certification or evaluation systems (e.g., Greenspec, Green Seal, BEES, Cradle to Cradle certification)?
5.2 Is documentation available to support the product's environmental claims such as an LCA or participation in an accepted standard or benchmarking program?	If no, comment on the environmental impact of the product as a waste material. If yes, comment on how much of the product is actually reused or recycled at the end of the product's useful life.
5.3 Does the manufacturer have a reclamation program or any other program in place to facilitate the recycling or reuse of its product by accepting return of the product at the end of its useful life?	
5.4 Does the manufacturer have a program in place to reduce the amount of the product's packaging? If YES, describe.	
5.5 Does the manufacturer have a program in place to facilitate the return, reuse, recycling, or composting of the product's packaging? If YES, describe.	

Sources: Adapted from ASTM 2003; HBN Pharos Project; McGowan and Kruse 2003; Mendler, Odell, and Lazarus 2006; Thompson and Sorvig 2000; Center for Sustainable Building Research 2007.

Life-cycle assessment (LCA) and sustainability assessment (SA) differ from life-cycle costing (LCC) in that an LCA and SA deal with environmental and human health costs over the life of a material and LCC deals with the economic costs. They all consider the length of time that the product will be in use and what maintenance it will need during that time. While LCA is of primary importance to sustainable design, performing an LCC may also be helpful as it could demonstrate that higher first costs of a material will be recovered over the material's life. BEES allows for evaluation of both environmental and economic costs.

EMBODIED ENERGY ANALYSIS

The energy used during all stages of a material or product's life is known as *embodied energy* (EE). Embodied energy refers to the total energy consumed in raw material acquisition, manufacture, transport, and disposal of a building material/product. Like LCA, EE analyses can set different parameters of study. EE is commonly performed for either cradle to gate or cradle to cradle,

but it may also be performed just to evaluate one segment of the manufacturing process.

Minimally processed materials generally have a lower EE than those with extensive or multiple manufacturing processes. And if a product has high energy requirements in primary processing (e.g., stainless steel and aluminum), then it is likely that recycled-content percentages will be maximized to reduce the energy required to produce the material. If the product is complex (made from more than one material, such as a steel and wood bench), then the embodied energy of the bench includes all of the energy inputs from both the wood and steel components and the energy inputs to assemble them. It is challenging to quantify all the energy used to manufacture a product. Embodied energy figures for common site construction materials are provided from multiple sources in Appendix A.

Embodied carbon (EC), like EE, refers to the CO_2 released during a material or product's life cycle. Parameters of analyses will vary, but common ones are cradle to gate and cradle to cradle. Because fossil fuels are a primary source of energy during most phases of the material or product's life cycle, EC figures generally correspond to EE figures—if a product has a high EE, it will probably have a high EC. There are some exceptions to this. For example, aluminum has the highest EE of almost any construction material, yet EC is not correspondingly high because the primary power source for aluminum manufacture is relatively clean hydroelectric energy.

Embodied energy and embodied carbon analyses as a means of evaluating materials or products can be a useful step; however, they should not be the only factor in evaluating or comparing materials and products. Some limitations of EE and EC are as follows:

- Unlike life-cycle assessment (LCA), these methods do not directly consider the health or ecological impacts of construction materials or products.
- EE does not differentiate between sources of energy, and some sources, such as coal, pose greater environmental impacts than others, such as natural gas. Use of renewable sources of energy will be reflected in lower EC figures, but not in EE figures.
- EE and EC figures can vary widely, sometimes by as much as 100%, for a variety of reasons, such as parameters and techniques of analysis, country, distances of transport, manufacturing processes, fuel inputs, and recycled content.
- EE and EC figures are often stated by weight or volume of a material, yet as material densities vary, comparisons can be skewed. For example, EE figures for a ton of aluminum might be compared to a ton of steel. However, the weight of actual structures made from these materials, such as handrails, would differ substantially. By most estimates, the aluminum handrail would weigh one-third of the steel one.

Many embodied carbon analyses don't take into account other greenhouse gases released from the material's production. For instance, pig iron production and thermal processes used to create sinter and metallurgical coke release methane (CH_4), which is a far more powerful greenhouse gas than CO_2. Figures for EE and EC of common site construction materials can be found in Appendix A.

ESTABLISHING RISK PRIORITIES AND WEIGHTING EVALUATION RESULTS

Interpretations of LCA data, SA information, and EE and EC analyses can vary widely and are dependent on priorities and the moral and ethical perspectives of decision makers and project stakeholders. Some will find global climate change to be the most critical concern in evaluating construction materials, while others will focus on finding a material that minimizes human toxicity risks. Rarely is a material or product found to perform best under all priorities. And in fact, completely differing results can be produced from LCA analysis just by altering the parameters of the study or the relative weights of the impacts.

Determining the relative importance of the potential impacts of construction materials is not always clear. Environmental and human health organizations warn of so many different risks that it is difficult to know which are most critical. And some impacts may be critical in one region, but may only be minor in another.

To assist with prioritizing environmental policy, legislation, funding, and research, the EPA's Science Advisory Board (SAB) performed studies in 1987, 1990, and 2000 to assess scientists' perceptions of risks of various environmental and human health impacts. The studies compared thirty-one different problems in four classes and provided ranked lists of ecological risk, human welfare risk, cancer risk, and noncancer human health risk priorities (U.S. EPA 1990, 2000). Rankings were based on the following criteria (Graedel and Allenby 1996):

- The spatial scale of the impact, with large-scale impacts being considered worse than small-scale, local impacts.
- The severity of the hazard, including the damage potential of a material, how much material is involved, and how numerous is the exposed population (e.g., highly hazardous substances are of more concern than less hazardous substances).
- The degree of exposure, with well-sequestered substances less of a concern than easily mobilized substances.

- The penalty for being wrong—longer remediation or reversibility times being of more concern than shorter times.

All EPA reports discussed the considerable scientific uncertainty, methodological inadequacy, and insufficient data that have limited attempts to compare risks (U.S. EPA 2000). Incomplete data leave large gaps in our ability to evaluate materials. Results of the risk assessments are shown in Tables 3–3 and 3–4.

The Precautionary Principle

Some feel that chemicals or hazardous constituents should not be used until they are tested and deemed safe for use, while others argue that harm should be proven before use of the chemical should be banned. The precautionary principle is both a moral and political principle that states: "When an activity raises threats of harm to human health or the environment, precautionary measures should be taken even if some cause and effect relationships are not fully established scientifically. In this context the proponent of an activity, rather than the public, should bear the burden of proof. The process of applying the precautionary principle must be open, informed and democratic and must include potentially affected parties. It must also involve an examination of the full range of alternatives, including no action" (Wingspread 1998).

There are many interpretations of the precautionary principle that are invoked for different situations. The precautionary principle is increasingly invoked in legislation and directives in the EU and in a few situations in the United States. A summary of the 2000 EU Communication on the Precautionary Principle states: "The precautionary principle may be invoked where urgent measures are needed in the face of a possible danger to human, animal or plant health, or to protect the environment where scientific data do not permit a complete evaluation of the risk. It may not be used as a pretext for protectionist measures. This principle is applied mainly where there is a danger to public health. For example, it may be used to stop distribution or order withdrawal from the market of products likely to constitute a health hazard" (European Union 2000).

Table 3–3 Risks to the "Natural Ecology and Human Welfare"

Severity of Risk	Risk Impacts
Relatively high-risk problems	Global climate change
	Habitat alteration and destruction
	Species extinction and overall loss of biological diversity
	Stratospheric ozone depletion
Relatively medium-risk problems	Acid deposition
	Airborne toxics
	Herbicides/pesticides
	Toxics, nutrients, biochemical oxygen demand, and turbidity in surface waters
Relatively low-risk problems	Acid runoff to surface waters
	Groundwater pollution
	Oil spills
	Radionuclides
	Thermal pollution

Source: U.S.EPA 1990 as cited in Scorecard 2005

Table 3–4 Final Rankings of "Welfare Effects" Work Group

Severity of Risks	Risk Impacts
High effects	Criteria air pollutants from mobile and stationary sources (includes acid precipitation)
	Nonpoint source discharges to surface water
	Indirect point source discharges to surface water
	Discharges to estuaries, coastal waters, and oceans from all sources
	Carbon dioxide and global warming
	Substances suspected of depleting the stratospheric ozone layer (e.g., CFCs)
	Other air pollutants (includes fluorides, total reduced sulfur, substances not included in other problems that emit odors)
	Direct, point source discharges (e.g., industrial) to surface water
Medium effects	Hazardous waste sites—inactive (Superfund; groundwater and other media)
	Nonhazardous waste sites—municipal (groundwater and other media)
	Hazardous waste sites—active (includes hazardous waste tanks; groundwater and other media)
	Discharges to wetlands from all sources
	Other pesticide risks, including leaching and runoff of pesticides and agricultural chemicals, air deposition from spraying, etc.
	Biotechnology (environmental releases of genetically altered materials)
Low effects	Nonhazardous waste sites—industrial (includes utilities; groundwater and other media)
	Releases from storage tanks (includes product and petroleum tanks—above, on, and underground)
	Accidental releases—toxics (includes all media)
	Accidental releases—oil spills
	From drinking water as it arrives at the tap (includes chemicals, lead from pipes, biological contaminants, radiation, etc.)
	Radon—indoor air only
	Mining waste (includes oil and gas extraction wastes)
	Contaminated sludge (includes municipal and scrubber sludge)
	Hazardous/toxic air pollutants
Minor effects	Application of pesticides (risks to applicators, which includes workers who mix and load, as well as apply, and also to consumers who apply pesticides)
	Consumer product exposure
	Indoor air pollutants—other than radon
	New toxic chemicals
	Other groundwater contamination (includes septic systems, road salt, injection wells, etc.)
	Pesticide residues on foods eaten by humans and wildlife
	Radiation—other than indoor radon
	Worker exposure to chemicals

Source: U.S.EPA 1990 as cited in Scorecard 2005

Tools for LCA Information and Material Evaluation

Currently there are two LCA evaluation tools in use in North America for evaluating construction materials—the Environmental Impact Estimator, developed by the Athena Institute, and Building for Environmental and Economic Sustainability (BEES), developed by the National Institute of Standards and Technology (NIST). Both incorporate LCI data and weighted impacts to evaluate and compare building (and some site) assemblies. They are geared toward building materials and products, yet due to the overlap of materials between buildings and sites, they can be useful in a limited way for evaluating site construction materials.

BUILDING FOR ENVIRONMENTAL AND ECONOMIC SUSTAINABILITY (BEES)

The BEES system evaluates building material and product assemblies for their environmental and economic attributes. The BEES 4.0 Reference Guide explains the basic premise of the BEES system in the following way (Lippiatt 2007):

> The BEES (Building for Environmental and Economic Sustainability) version 4.0 software implements a rational, systematic technique for selecting environmentally-preferred, cost-effective building products. The technique is based on consensus standards and designed to be practical, flexible, and transparent. The Windows-based decision support software, aimed at designers, builders, and product manufacturers, includes actual environmental and economic performance data for over 230 building products across a range of functional applications. BEES measures the environmental performance of building products using the environmental life-cycle assessment approach specified in International Organization for Standardization (ISO) 14040 standards. All stages in the life of a product are analyzed: raw material acquisition, manufacture, transportation, installation, use, and waste management. Economic performance is measured using the ASTM International standard life-cycle cost method (E917),

which covers the costs of initial investment, replacement, operation, maintenance and repair, and disposal. Environmental and economic performance are combined into an overall performance measure using the ASTM standard for Multiattribute Decision Analysis (E1765). For the entire BEES analysis, building products are defined and classified based on the ASTM standard classification for building elements known as UNIFORMAT II (E1557).

BEES is a free tool that can be downloaded along with a reference guide detailing the assumptions and impacts of the materials and products studied. The reference guide is a valuable tool for understanding impacts of materials and their production processes even if the BEES tool is not used. Materials and products for evaluation are either "generic" products with typical attributes or they are manufacturer-provided LCAs for proprietary products.

Interpretation of BEES Results and Weighting of Impacts

To interpret BEES results, the user is offered the option of relative weighting of the various environmental impacts to synthesize environmental and economic performance of products. One can also define the percentage of emphasis on environmental versus economic impacts, with both totaling 100%. The BEES User Guide explains: "Few products are likely to dominate competing products in all BEES impact categories. Rather, one product may out-perform the competition relative to fossil fuel depletion and habitat alteration, fall short relative to global warming and acidification, and fall somewhere in the middle relative to indoor air quality and eutrophication. To compare the overall environmental performance of competing products, the performance scores for all impact categories may be synthesized" (Lippiatt 2007). Derivation of final performance scores is illustrated in Figure 3–1. The weighting of impact scores is optional. There are three weighting options:

Self-determined weights can be assigned if particular impacts are a priority for a user. For instance, if one is particularly concerned with global warming, a high weight could be assigned to that issue, keeping others

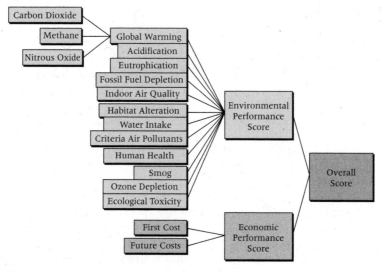

Figure 3–1.

This figure illustrates BEES criteria and BEES overall performance measure, synthesizing both environmental and economic criteria. A single score is derived using the technique of Multiattribute Decision Analysis (MADA) (Lippiatt 2007).

low. It should be noted that the weight or relative importance that is assigned to a particular LCA exercise can dramatically vary the results, often completely altering the recommended material or assembly. This is one of the major criticisms (and weaknesses) of LCA. One can adjust the priorities to achieve just about any result. Most of the time this is not used for "false" results, but it can be. It is recommended that one of the two following weighting schemes be used.

U.S. EPA Science Advisory Board (SAB). The studies discussed above from 1990 and 2000 determined the relative importance of a variety of environmental impacts based on the spatial scale of the impact, the severity of the hazard, the degree of exposure, and the penalty for being wrong (U.S. EPA 1990, 2000). The percentage weights assigned in BEES reflect the EPA SAB findings (see Table 3–5).

BEES Stakeholder Panel. In 2006, the National Institute of Standards and Technology (NIST) assembled a panel of volunteer stakeholders comprised of producers, users, and LCA experts "in order to promote balance and support a consensus process" (Lippiatt 2007). This panel determined the relative importance of impacts and created the "BEES Stakeholder Panel" weightings.

ATHENA ENVIRONMENTAL IMPACT ESTIMATOR AND ECOCALCULATOR

The Athena Sustainable Materials Institute is a nonprofit organization based in Ontario, Canada. Its self-stated premise and aims are as follows: "At the Athena Institute, we believe that better information and tools are critical to achieving a sustainable built environment. We also believe that a life cycle assessment (LCA) approach to sustainability is the only way to create a level playing field for the vast array of building materials in use. From our Canadian offices, and through our US affiliate, Athena Institute International, the not-for-profit Athena organization undertakes and directs innovative research and development activities that allow architects, engineers and others to factor environmental considerations into the design process from the conceptual stage onward" (Athena Sustainable Materials Institute).

The Athena Sustainable Materials Institute offers two tools for evaluating the impacts of building material assemblies and products:

Table 3–5 BEES Weighting of Impacts

Impact	EPA Science Advisory Board (SAB) Study (2000) Relative Importance Weight (%)	BEES Stakeholder Panel (2006) Relative Importance Weight (%)
Global warming	16	29
Acidification	5	3
Eutrophication	5	6
Fossil fuel depletion	5	10
Indoor air quality	11	3
Habitat alternation	16	6
Water intake	3	8
Criteria air pollutants	6	9
Smog	6	4
Ecological toxicity	11	7
Ozone depletion	5	2
Human health	11	13

Source: Lippiatt 2007

The Athena Environmental Impact Estimator (EIE), available for purchase, provides detailed LCA information for building assemblies, whole-building designs, and additional materials in the following impact areas:

- Embodied primary energy use
- Global warming potential
- Solid waste emissions
- Pollutants to air
- Pollutants to water
- Weighted resource use

Results can be summarized by assembly or life-cycle phase, and comparisons can be made with up to five different buildings or assemblies. The Institute estimates that the Estimator is capable of modeling 95% of all buildings in North America as it simulates over 1,000 different assembly combinations. The Estimator does not include operating energy simulation capability; however, users can enter results of a simulation in order to compute the fuel cycle burdens and factor them into the overall results. This tool offers the ability to examine impacts of some construction materials and products individually outside of their assemblies.

The Athena EcoCalculator for Assemblies offers LCA information for more than 400 common building assemblies based on detailed results from the Impact Estimator for Buildings. Because the assemblies are predetermined, it is less easy to adapt the results for use with site materials. The EcoCalculator is a free tool that can be downloaded from the Athena website (http://www.athenasmi.ca/tools/ecoCalculator/index.html). It was commissioned by the Green Building Initiative (GBI) and developed by the Athena Institute in association with the University of Minnesota and Morrison Hershfield Consulting Engineers for use with the Green Globes environmental assessment and rating system.

Standards, Labels, and Certification Systems

As more attention is paid to environmental and human health impacts of construction materials, a wide variety of standards, rating systems, regulations, labels, guidelines, and certification programs have been developed to guide specifiers in material and product selection.

They have been created by nonprofit organizations, government agencies, for-profit organizations, manufacturers, and trade associations. Certifications by neutral third-party organizations are generally preferable to certifications developed by trade organizations of manufacturers.

Criteria of standards and labels vary widely from addressing a single issue, such as recycled content or indoor air quality, to inclusion of a broad range of evaluation criteria. Below are detailed summaries and applicable credits from the LEED system and Green Globes. Then Table 3–9 follows, summarizing other standards and labels.

LEADERSHIP IN ENERGY AND ENVIRONMENTAL DESIGN (LEED)

The LEED™ (Leadership in Energy and Environmental Design) Green Building Rating System™ is a voluntary national standard for developing sustainable and high-performance buildings and sites. LEED is a product of the U.S. Green Building Council (USGBC), a national coalition of building industry professionals, contractors, policy makers, owners, and manufacturers. Their stated mission is "to promote buildings that are environmentally responsible, profitable and healthy places to live and work." Council members work in a committee-based, consensus-focused way to develop LEED products and resources, policy guidance, and educational and marketing tools to facilitate the adoption of green building. The council develops alliances with industry and research organizations, and federal, state, and local governments.

Table 3–6 LEED-NC Version 2.2 Credit Categories

Category
Sustainable Sites
Water Efficiency
Energy & Atmosphere
Materials & Resources
Indoor Environmental Quality
Innovation & Design Process

Source: USGBC 2005

Table 3–7 LEED NC Version 2.2 Certification Levels

Certification Level
Certified
Silver
Gold
Platinum

Source: USGBC 2005

The USGBC states that "LEED™ was created to: define 'green building' by establishing a common standard of measurement; promote integrated, whole-building design practices; recognize environmental leadership in the building industry; stimulate green competition; raise consumer awareness of green building benefits; and transform the building market" (USGBC 2005). USGBC members developed and continue to refine the system through a membership consensus process.

Registered projects can choose from a variety of sustainable strategies and earn points toward a certified project in the six categories listed in Table 3–7.

LEED standards are available or under development for projects with a building component in the following areas:

- LEED-NC, New Commercial Construction and Major Renovation Projects—LEED-NC, the original LEED system, is designed to guide high-performance commercial and institutional projects. It has also been applied to schools, multiunit residential buildings, manufacturing plants, laboratories, and other building types.
- LEED-EB, Existing Building Operations—This system is a set of performance standards for the sustainable operation of existing buildings. Criteria cover building operations and system upgrades where the majority of the building surfaces remain unchanged.
- LEED-CI, Commercial Interiors Projects—This system addresses the specifics of tenant spaces in office, retail, and institutional buildings.
- LEED-CS, Core and Shell Projects—This system covers core and shell project criteria such as structure, building envelope, and building-level systems.

Table 3–8 LEED-NC Version 2.2 Credits Related to Site Construction Materials and Products

Credit and Title	Requirements
MR Prerequisite 1: Storage & Collection of Recyclables	Provide an easily accessible area that serves the entire building and is dedicated to the collection and storage of nonhazardous materials for recycling, including (at a minimum) paper, corrugated cardboard, glass, plastics, and metals.
MR 2.1: Construction Waste Management: Divert 50% from Disposal	Recycle and/or salvage at least 50% of nonhazardous construction and demolition debris. Develop and implement a construction waste management plan that, at a minimum, identifies the materials to be diverted from disposal and whether the materials will be sorted on-site or commingled. Excavated soil and land-clearing debris do not contribute to this credit. Calculations can be done by weight or volume, but must be consistent throughout.
MR 2.2: Construction Waste Management: Divert 75% from Disposal	Recycle and/or salvage an additional 25% beyond MR Credit 2.1 (75% total) of nonhazardous construction and demolition debris. Excavated soil and land-clearing debris do not contribute to this credit. Calculations can be done by weight or volume, but must be consistent throughout.
MR 3.1: Materials Reuse: 5%	Use salvaged, refurbished, or reused materials such that the sum of these materials constitutes at least 5%, based on cost, of the total value of materials on the project.
MR 3.2: Materials Reuse: 10%	Use salvaged, refurbished, or reused materials for an additional 5% beyond MR Credit 3.1 (10% total, based on cost).
MR 4.1 Recycled Content: 10% (post-consumer + $\frac{1}{2}$ pre-consumer)	Use materials with recycled content such that the sum of post-consumer recycled content plus one-half of the pre-consumer content constitutes at least 10% (based on cost) of the total value of the materials in the project. The recycled content value of a material assembly shall be determined by weight. The recycled fraction of the assembly is then multiplied by the cost of assembly to determine the recycled content value.
MR 4.2 Recycled Content: 20% (post-consumer + $\frac{1}{2}$ pre-consumer)	Use materials with recycled content such that the sum of post-consumer recycled content plus one-half of the pre-consumer content constitutes an additional 10% (by weight) beyond MR Credit 4.1 (total of 20%, based on cost) of the total value of the materials in the project.
MR 5.1 Regional Materials: 10% Extracted, Processed, & Manufactured Regionally	Use building materials or products that have been extracted, harvested, or recovered, as well as manufactured, within 500 miles of the project site for a minimum of 10% (based on cost) of the total materials value.
MR 5.2 Regional Materials: 20% Extracted, Processed, & Manufactured Regionally	Use building materials or products that have been extracted, harvested, or recovered, as well as manufactured, within 500 miles of the project site for an additional 10% beyond MR Credit 5.1 (total of 20%, based on cost) of the total materials value.
MR 6 Rapidly Renewable Materials	Use rapidly renewable building materials and products (made from plants that are typically harvested within a ten-year cycle or shorter) for 2.5% of the total value of all building materials and products used in the project, based on cost.
MR 7 Certified Wood	Use a minimum of 50% of wood-based materials and products, which are certified in accordance with the Forest Stewardship Council's (FSC) Principles and Criteria, for wood building components.
EQ 4.1: Low-Emitting Materials: Adhesives & Sealants	All adhesives and sealants used on the interior of the building (defined as inside of the weatherproofing system and applied on-site) shall comply with the requirements of the following reference standards: ■ Adhesives, Sealants and Sealant Primers: South Coast Air Quality Management District (SCAQMD) Rule #1168. VOC limits are listed in the table below and correspond to an effective date of July 1, 2005, and rule amendment date of January 7, 2005. ■ Aerosol Adhesives: Green Seal Standard for Commercial Adhesives GS-36 requirements in effect on October 19, 2000.

Continued

Table 3–8 LEED-NC Version 2.2 Credits Related to Site Construction Materials and Products *(Continued)*

Credit and Title	Requirements

EQ 4.2: Low-Emitting Materials: Paints & Coatings	Paints and coatings used on the interior of the building (defined as inside of the weatherproofing system and applied on-site) shall comply with the following criteria:
	
	■ Architectural paints, coatings and primers applied to interior walls and ceilings: Do not exceed the VOC content limits established in Green Seal Standard GS-11, Paints, First Edition, May 20, 1993.
	  ● Flats: 50 g/L
	  ● Non-Flats: 150 g/L
	■ Anti-corrosive and anti-rust paints applied to interior ferrous metal substrates: Do not exceed the VOC content limit of 250 g/L established in Green Seal Standard GC-03, Anti-Corrosive Paints, Second Edition, January 7, 1997.
	■ Clear wood finishes, floor coatings, stains, and shellacs applied to interior elements: Do not exceed the VOC content limits established in South Coast Air Quality Management District (SCAQMD) Rule 1113, Architectural Coatings, rules in effect on January 1, 2004.
	  ● Clear wood finishes: varnish 350 g/L; lacquer 550 g/L
	  ● Floor coatings: 100 g/L
	  ● Sealers: waterproofing sealers 250 g/L; sanding sealers 275 g/L; all other sealers 200 g/L
	  ● Shellacs: Clear 730 g/L; pigmented 550 g/L
	  ● Stains: 250 g/L

EQ 4.4: Low-Emitting Materials: Composite Wood & Agrifiber Products	Composite wood and agrifiber products used on the interior of the building (defined as inside of the weatherproofing system) shall contain no added urea-formaldehyde resins. Laminating adhesives used to fabricate on-site and shop-applied composite wood and agrifiber assemblies shall contain no added urea-formaldehyde resins.
SS 7.1: Heat Island Effect: Non-Roof	OPTION 1 Provide any combination of the following strategies for 50% of the site hardscape (including roads, sidewalks, courtyards, and parking lots): ■ Shade (within 5 years of occupancy) ■ Paving materials with a Solar Reflectance Index (SRI) of at least 29 ■ Open grid pavement system OR OPTION 2 Place a minimum of 50% of parking spaces under cover (defined as under ground, under deck, under roof, or under a building). Any roof used to shade or cover parking must have an SRI of at least 29.

Source: USGBC 2005

■ LEED-H, Homes—This system covers homebuilding practices.
■ LEED-ND, Neighborhood Development—This system offers standards for neighborhood design that integrate the principles of green building and smart growth.

GREEN GLOBES

Green Globes, a tool of the Green Building Initiative (GBI), is a rating system for new building and site construction or existing building and site renovation. GBI's self-stated mission is "to accelerate the adoption of building practices that result in energy-efficient, healthier and environmentally sustainable buildings by promoting credible and practical green building approaches for residential and commercial construction" (GBI). Governance of the GBI is by a multistakeholder board comprised of equal numbers of representatives from industry, NGOs, construction companies, architectural firms, and academic institutions.

The Green Globes system encourages use of LCA data in making material decisions for building assemblies. Credit E.1.1 asks: "Have the following assemblies [used in foundations, floor, structural system, roof, and envelope assembly] been selected based on a life cycle assessment of their embodied energy and greenhouse gas emissions using the ATHENA 'Environmental Impact Estimator' or NIST BEES?" Up to 40 of 1,000 possible points for the entire system are awarded for this activity. Points are not currently offered for LCA data use for site construction materials.

Green Globes certification is evaluated by "independent third-party verifiers." GBI projects that score at least 35% of the 1,000 total points are eligible to receive a Green Globes rating. Levels of rating increase with point increases.

Table 3–9 Green Globes Credits Related to Site Construction Materials and Products

Credit and Title	Requirements
E.2.1 What proportion of building materials and components is reused?	Points are awarded where 1–10% or more of materials used are "reused." The Green Globes system will calculate this based on the percentage cost of reused materials versus the total cost of materials. (Note: Site materials can only contribute to a small portion of points.) Maximum points = 10 points
E.2.2 What proportion of building materials contains recycled post-consumer content? (Federal Recommended Recycled Content for Products Guidelines and EPA's List of Designated Products at minimum)	Points are awarded where 1–20% or more of the materials contain recycled content. The Green Globes system will calculate points awarded based on the percentage cost of recycled materials versus the total cost of materials. (Note: Site materials can only contribute to a small portion of points.) Maximum points = 10 points
E.2.3 What proportion of materials is bio-based products, such as green insulation, natural fibers, and natural structural materials?	Points are awarded where 1–20% or more of materials used are bio-based. The Green Globes system will calculate points awarded based on the percentage cost of bio-based materials versus the total cost of materials. (Note: Site materials can only contribute to a small portion of points.) Maximum points = 5 points
E.2.4 What proportion of solid lumber and timber panel products originates from sustainable sources that are third-party certified by the Sustainable Forestry Initiative (SFI), CSA Sustainable Forest Management (SFM), Forestry Stewardship Council (FSC), or American Tree Farm System (ATFS)?	Points are awarded where 1–100% of the wood used comes from third-party-certified acreage. The Green Globes system will calculate points awarded based on the percentage cost of certified wood products versus the total cost of wood products. Maximum points = 5 points
E.4.4 What proportion of the following materials is of standard size and fastened using fastening systems that allow for easy disassembly?	Points are awarded where 1–50% of the elements of the building an be disassembled. The Green Globes system will calculate cpoints awarded based on the stated percentage. Maximum points = 3 points

Continued

Table 3–9 Green Globes Credits Related to Site Construction Materials and Products *(Continued)*

Credit and Title	Requirements
E.5.1 What proportion by weight of construction, demolition, and renovation waste is diverted from landfill?	Points are awarded where 1–100% of waste is diverted. The Green Globes system will calculate points awarded based on the stated percentage. Maximum points = 6 points
E.5.3 Is there space for a recycling dumpster next to the general waste dumpster?	1 point
B.2.5 What percentage of hardscape has measures to mitigate the heat island effect (i.e., shading and/or high albedo paving)?	Points are awarded where 1–100% of hardscape has measures to avoid the heat island effect. The Green Globes system will calculate this based on the stated percentage of hardscape that is shaded with vegetation or surfaced with high albedo materials. Maximum points = 10 points or N/A
G.2.9 Are materials specified that are low-VOC-emitting and third-party environmentally certified, with the following VOC limits? (Note: This credit refers to interior materials, but could offer useful standards for exterior materials.)	Construction adhesives: the greater of 15% by weight or 200 grams/liter—*California Air Resources Board* 2 points Sealants and caulks: the greater of 4% by weight or 60 grams/liter—*California Air Resources Board* 2 points Contact adhesives: the greater of 80% by weight or 650 grams/liter—*California Air Resources Board* 2 points Paints: Interior latex coatings flat: 100 grams/liter Nonflat: 150 grams/liter Interior oil-based: 380 grams/liter EPA Environmentally Preferable Program 2 points Carpets: 50 grams/liter or no carpeting Carpet & Rug Institute's Green Label Plus program 2 points

Source: GBI

Table 3–10 Other Standards, Labels, and Certification Systems

Source	Description and Details Related to Construction Materials
OTHER GREEN PROJECT GUIDELINES	
The Living Building Challenge, Cascadia Chapter, US Green Building Council http://www.cascadiagbc.org/lbc	The Living Building Challenge was issued by the Cascadia Chapter of the US Green Building Council "to define the highest measure of sustainability possible in the built environment based on the best current thinking recognizing that 'true sustainability' is not yet possible. *The Living Building Challenge* is by definition difficult to obtain, and yet all facets of this tool have been attained in numerous projects around the world—just not all together. With this standard Cascadia hopes to encourage dialogue on where the building industry needs to head and engender support for the first pilot projects, until more and more living buildings emerge." The Challenge is composed of sixteen prerequisites in areas of site design, energy, materials, water, indoor environmental quality, beauty, and inspiration. Prerequisites that apply to materials are: ***Prerequisite Five***—Materials Red List

Table 3–10 Other Standards, Labels, and Certification Systems *(Continued)*

Source	Description and Details Related to Construction Materials
The Living Building Challenge, (Continued)	*The project cannot contain any of the following red list materials or chemicals:*
	No added formaldehyde; halogenated flame retardants; PVC (except electrical wiring); mercury; CFCs or HCFCs; neoprene (chloroprene); cadmium; chlorinated polyethylene and chlorosulfonated polyethylene; wood treatments containing creosote, arsenic, or pentachlorophenol; polyurethane; lead; phthalates
	Prerequisite Six—Construction Carbon Footprint
	The project must account for the embodied carbon footprint of its construction through a one-time carbon offset tied to the building's square footage and general construction type.
	Prerequisite Seven—Responsible Industry
	All wood must be FSC certified or from salvaged sources.
	Prerequisite Eight—Appropriate Materials/Services Radius
	Materials and services must adhere to the following weight/distance list:
	Ideas: 12,429.91 miles; Renewable energy technologies: 7,000 miles; Consultant travel: 1,500 miles; Lightweight materials: 1,000 miles; Medium-weight materials: 500 miles; Heavy materials: 250 miles
	Prerequisite Nine—Leadership in Construction Waste
	Construction waste must be diverted from landfills to the following levels:
	Metals: 95%; Paper and cardboard: 95%; Soil and biomass: 100%; Rigid foam, carpet, and insulation: 90%; All others—combined weighted average: 80%
National Association of Home Builders (NAHB) Model Green Home Building Guidelines www.nahb.org/gbg	NAHB's voluntary Model Green Home Building Guidelines were developed to consolidate several green homebuilding guidelines and are designed for individual builders use. Materials guidelines primarily focus on resource efficiency and waste reduction. Guidelines for material use reduction are written for building framing, but could be useful principles for reduction of site material use.
State of Minnesota Sustainable Building Guidelines (B3-MSBG) version 2.0 www.msbg.umn.edu	Focus on performance management, site and water, energy and atmosphere, indoor environmental quality, materials, and waste. All projects funded in whole or in part with Minnesota state bond money since 2004 are required to follow B3-MSBG guidelines. The Materials and Waste Required Guidelines are as follows: M.1 Life Cycle Assessment of Building Assemblies (Using Athena EIE data) M.2 Evaluation of Environmentally Preferable Materials M.3 Waste Reduction and Management
BuiltGreen www.builtgreen.net/	Built Green describes their program as "an environmentally-friendly, non-profit, residential building program of the Master Builders Association of King and Snohomish Counties, developed in partnership with King County, Snohomish County, and other agencies in Washington State. These guidelines provide consumers with easy-to-understand rating systems, which quantify environmentally friendly building practices for remodeling and new home construction, communities and multifamily development units." The self-certification checklist offers many benchmarks for sustainable material use and specification.

Continued

Table 3–10 Other Standards, Labels, and Certification Systems *(Continued)*

Source	Description and Details Related to Construction Materials
GREEN PRODUCT STANDARDS	
EPA Comprehensive Procurement Guidelines www.epa.gov/cpg	The Comprehensive Procurement Guideline (CPG) program is part of the EPA's continuing effort to promote the use of materials recovered from solid waste. Buying recycled-content products ensures that the materials collected in recycling programs will be used again in the manufacture of new products The CPG sets recycled-content guidelines for many site construction materials.
Greenseal www.greenseal.org/	Greenseal is a nonprofit organization that utilizes a science-based life-cycle approach to establish standards for and certify a variety of materials and coatings. Greenseal Standards related to site construction materials are: GS-03 Anti-Corrosive Paints GS-11 Paints GS-34 Degreasers GS-36 Commercial Adhesives GS-37 Industrial & Institutional Cleaners GS-39 Green Facilities Operation and Maintenance Criteria GS-42 Cleaning Services GS-43 Recycled Content Latex Paint Standard
South Coast Air Quality Management District **Rule 1113 Architectural Coatings** **Rule 1168 Adhesives and Sealants** http://www.aqmd.gov/rules/	VOC limits per liter for hundreds of architectural coating and adhesive and sealant types. Threshold limits are revised yearly. Commonly used coating limits for site construction materials are as follows: Flat paints: 50g VOC/liter Nonflat coatings: 50g VOC/liter Wood preservatives: 350g VOC/liter Waterproofing sealers: 100g VOC/liter Traffic coatings: 100g VOC/liter Concrete-curing compounds: 100g VOC/liter
PRODUCT CERTIFICATIONS[a]	
MBDC Cradle to Cradle (C2C) Certification www.mbdc.com/c2c/	C2C is a certification program for building products. Products can be certified as Silver, Gold, or Platinum products with a focus on chemical hazards, material reuse, recycled content and recyclability, energy use, water use, and social responsibility. Homogeneous materials or less complex products can be labeled as Technical/Biological Nutrients with Cradle to Cradle Certification. Certified products are listed by product type, company name, and certification rating on the MBDC website. C2C-certified site construction products include: wood treatments, concrete additives, athletic surfaces, coatings, and cleaners.
Scientific Certification Systems http://www.scscertified.com	SCS is a third-party provider of certification, auditing, and testing services, and standards for both environmental and social factors. The organization certifies reclaimed and recycled material content, biodegradability, FSC certification, and others.

Table 3–10 Other Standards, Labels, and Certification Systems *(Continued)*

Source	Description and Details Related to Construction Materials
EcoLogo, Environmental Choice http://www.ecologo.org/	EcoLogo is a third-party certification system established in 1998 by the Canadian government with over 250 products. Site construction products include: paints, wood preservatives, adhesives, release agents, sealants, and steel. The development of EcoLogo certification criteria is a multi-step process involving purchasers, environmental groups, industry, consumers and consumer groups, academia, government, and other interested groups. As a "Type I ecolabel" (as defined by the International Organization for Standardization in the standard ISO 14024), criteria are developed and evaluated using a life-cycle approach.
Energy Star http://www.energystar.gov/	Energy Star is a voluntary labeling system for energy efficiency of appliances, lighting, and heating and cooling equipment that is a joint program of the Department of Energy and the EPA. Thresholds are set to capture about one-quarter of the market for a given product or appliance. Manufacturers provide the program information on their product's energy efficiency.
WaterSense http://www.epa.gov/watersense/	This EPA program certifies water-efficient products that are independently tested prior to certification. Site construction products that are certified include irrigation systems and irrigation control technologies.
GREEN PRODUCT DIRECTORIES AND DATABASES	
EPA Environmentally Preferable Purchasing Program http://www.epa.gov/epp/	The US EPA's Environmentally Preferable Purchasing (EPP) program is designed to assist the Federal Government with green purchasing but it is also a useful tool for finding and evaluating information about green products and services.
EPA Comprehensive Procurement Guidelines http://www.epa.gov/cpg	The Comprehensive Procurement Guideline (CPG) program is part of the EPA's continuing effort to promote the use of materials recovered from solid waste. Buying recycled-content products ensures that the materials collected in recycling programs will be used again in the manufacture of new products The CPG sets recycled-content guidelines for many site construction materials.
California Integrated Waste Management Board (CIWMB) http://www.ciwmb.ca.gov/RCP/search.asp	The CIWMB's RCP Directory lists thousands of products containing recycled materials as well as information about the manufacturers, distributors, and reprocessors of these products. Some products are certified under the state's State Agency Buy Recycled Campaign (SABRC).
GreenSpec http://www.buildinggreen.com	GreenSpec is a subscription online and print directory of environmentally preferable product manufacturers by BuildingGreen, the publishers of *Environmental Building News*. The directory lists over 2,100 listings from more than 1,500 companies organized by the CSI MasterFormat structure. Online, the directory is searchable by green attribute (post- or pre-consumer recycled content, among others), CSI designation, LEED credit, or category.
Oikos Green Building Source http://oikos.com/	Library, gallery, and bookstore of green building products, which can be searched by category, topic, company, environmental benefit, and company type.
OTHER INFORMATION RESOURCES	
Whole Building Design Guide	The Whole Building Design Guide offers the Federal Green Construction Guide for Specifiers. The guide contains outline specs for many site construction materials and technologies.

Continued

Table 3–10 Other Standards, Labels, and Certification Systems *(Continued)*

Source	Description and Details Related to Construction Materials
Pharos Project www.pharosproject.net	The Pharos project is a materials evaluation system, database, and building product information site with a focus on environment and resources, health and pollution, and social and community sustainability of construction materials and products. The Pharos Project's self-stated mission is as follows: "The Pharos Project seeks to define a consumer-driven vision of truly green building materials and how they should be evaluated in harmony with principles of environmental health and justice." (http://www.pharosproject.net/about_pharos/index.php) The Pharos Lens: *Environment & Resources*: Water: net use, Energy: embodied, Energy: renewable, Materials: renewable *Health & Pollution*: User exposures, solid waste, water quality, air quality, climate change, toxic releases *Social & Community*: Occupational safety, consumer safety, fair compensation, equality, community, contributions, corporate practices
Material Safety Data Sheets (MSDS)	OSHA-required documents supplied by manufacturers of products containing hazardous chemicals. MSDSs contain information regarding potentially significant levels of airborne contaminants, storage and handling precautions, health effects, odor description, volatility, expected products of combustion, reactivity, and procedures for spill cleanup (WBDG 2007).

aForest certification programs are summarized in chapter 10.

References

Architecture 2030. http://www.architecture2030.org/

ASTM Standard E1991. 2005. "Standard Guide for Environmental Life-Cycle Assessment of Building Materials/Products" ASTM International, West Conshohocken, PA, <www.astm.org>.

ASTM Standard E2129. 2003. "Standard Practice for Data Collection for Sustainability Assessment of Building Products." West Conshohocken, PA: ASTM International. www.astm.org.

Athena Sustainable Materials Institute. Athena Environmental Impact Estimator. Version 3.0.3. Kutztown, ON: Athena Sustainable Materials Institute.

Center for Sustainable Building Research. 2007. *The State of Minnesota Sustainable Building Guidelines*. Center for Sustainable Building Research, College of Design, University of Minnesota.

European Union. Communication from the Commission of 2 February 2000. http://europa.eu/scadplus/leg/en/lvb/l32042.htm (accessed February 11, 2005).

Graedel, T. E., and Allenby, B. R. 1996. *Design for Environment*. Upper Saddle River, NJ: Prentice Hall.

Green Building Initiative (GBI). "Green Globes Design v.1—Post Construction Assessment." https://www.thegbi.org/gbi/.

Healthy Building Network (HBN). http://www.healthybuilding.net/

Healthy Building Network (HBN), Pharos Project. http://www.pharosproject.net/wiki/.

International Organization for Standardization (ISO). 1996. *Environmental Management—Life-cycle Assessment: Principles and Framework. Draft International Standard 14040*. Geneva, Switzerland: International Standards Organization.

Lippiatt, Barbara C. 2007. *BEES 4.0 Building for Environmental and Economic Sustainability Technical Manual and User Guide*. Gaithersburg, MD: National Institute of Standards and Technology.

McDonough, W., and M. Braungart. 2002. *Cradle to Cradle: Remaking the Way We Make Things*. New York: Melcher Media.

McGowan, Mary Rose, and Kelsey Kruse. 2003. *Interior Graphic Standards*. Hoboken, NJ: John Wiley & Sons.

Mendler, Sandra, William Odell, and Mary Ann Lazarus. 2006. *The HOK Guidebook to Sustainable Design*. Hoboken, NJ: John Wiley & Sons.

Scorecard, The Pollution Information Site. 2005. http://www.scorecard.org/comp-risk/report.tcl?US=US#Final%20Rankings%20of%20Welfare%20Effects%20Work%20Group (accessed August 23, 2007).

Thompson, J. William, and Kim Sorvig. 2000. *Sustainable Landscape Construction: A Guide to Green Building Outdoors.* Washington, DC: Island Press.

Trusty, W., and Horst, S. n.d. *Intergating LCA Tools in Green Building Rating Systems.* Ontario, Canada: Athena Sustainable Materials Institute.

U.S. Environmental Protection Agency (U.S. EPA). Science Advisory Board. 2000, August. *Toward Integrated Environmental Decision-Making.* EPA-SAB-EC-00–011, Washington, DC.

U.S. Environmental Protection Agency (U.S. EPA). Science Advisory Board. 1990, September. *Reducing Risk: Setting Priorities and Strategies for Environmental Protection,* SAB-EC-90–021. Washington, DC.

U.S. Green Building Council (USGBC). 2005. *LEED-NC for New Construction Reference Guide.* Version 2.2. 1st ed. Washington, DC: USGBC.

Wingspread Statement on the Precautionary Principle, January, 26, 1998.

4

Resource Reuse: Designing with and Specifying Reclaimed, Reprocessed, and Recycled-content Materials

As rapid growth in the built environment continues, so does the burgeoning waste crisis. Buildings constructed today are expected to last 30–50 years and the design life of concrete pavements is 30 years. It is likely that many new structures built today will become waste in little more than a generation. At this rate the problem of waste will continue to grow. The short life of new structures makes the disposal phase of a material a critical determinant in the selection of materials or products with lower environmental impacts. Extending the use phase of a structure is the best way to reduce the environmental impacts of new materials, but it is not always possible given constraints of land use, changing programs, and real estate markets. So, extending the life of materials through reuse or recycling can go a long way toward offsetting the environmental and human health impacts of their initial extraction, processing, and manufacture.

An increasingly common way to address the waste crisis and reduce use of natural resources is to "mine" the built environment for "raw" materials for reuse, ei-

ther whole or in recycled-content products. Deconstruction, reuse, and recycling of building materials is at an all-time high and markets to receive these materials are growing, but these activities are not without challenges. Costs of deconstruction are often higher than for demolition and without well-established recycling markets, the costs may be prohibitive. Even where established markets exist, time frames for building and site demolition may prohibit deconstruction activities. From the design end, reclaimed materials may not be available in the type or quantity needed. Codes may require regrading of reclaimed structural members. And recycled-content products may not be available, or may be at a cost premium in a particular region.

While some waste and resource consumption problems are outside a designer's control, decisions made about construction materials from early in the design phase can impact their performance across the life cycle. Specifying reclaimed or recycled-content materials that can be easily disassembled and reused or recycled again is a major strategy for reducing resource use of construction materials. And it can have large impacts, not just in resource conservation, but also in the related energy and pollution impacts from production of new materials. Some examples of this are as follows:

- A Swedish study of two buildings, one with a large proportion of recycled materials and the other with all new materials, found that the environmental impacts of the building with recycled materials were only about 55% of the one with new materials and that 12%–40% of energy was saved in material production (Thormark 2000).
- Impacts of the production of a relatively high embodied energy material such as aluminum can be offset substantially by its reuse in whole form. Even when it is recycled several times into new aluminum products, the initial energy and emissions will be reduced, as recycled aluminum products use only 5% of the energy and produce 5% of the emissions of aluminum made from virgin resources (International Aluminum Institute 2007).
- A compilation of embodied energy and embodied carbon figures of portland cement (PC) found that the substitution of ground granulated blast furnace slag (GGBFS), a by-product of iron making, for 64%–73% of the PC reduced embodied energy by 51% and embodied carbon by 66% (Hammond and Jones 2006).

This chapter discusses priorities and techniques for resource conservation and waste minimization, and the associated pollution impacts, by reclaiming, reusing, reprocessing, and recycling building materials. Subsequent "materials" chapters will discuss resource and pollution reduction specifics of individual site construction materials.

Closed-Loop Systems in Practice

The concept of waste is one that belongs to the throwaway society in which we live. Proponents of closed-loop systems advocate the elimination of waste by not producing it or by using it as "food" for new products and processes. Early efforts at recycling focused on what could be done with the mountain of waste that exists. While this can minimize the amount of waste that is landfilled and incinerated, it will not significantly ad-

dress the problem of excessive use of limited resources. Instead, a shift in the construction material production, design, and specification strategies can move the industry toward closed-loop design.

Many of the principles discussed in chapter 2 advocate some form of closed-loop material systems, yet closing loops is challenging in our current manufacturing culture, particularly in the manufacture of construction materials. In their book *Construction Ecology,* Kibert, Sendzimir, and Guy discuss the following challenges to closed-loop material systems (Kibert, Sendzimir, and Guy 2002):

- *The materials of products and construction components are challenging or sometimes impossible to recycle*—Composite materials, such as composite plastic lumber made from wood fiber and plastic, or lightweight metal composite with polymers, are essentially commingled materials that are rendered unrecyclable because they are impossible to separate. Other materials, particularly plastics such as polyvinyl chloride (PVC), are nonrecyclable because of their additives or widely varying composition.
- *Products and structures are not designed for disassembly*— Many products are comprised of multiple material components that are not easily separated for recycling or reuse (e.g., aluminum and plastic light fixture). In structures, metal welds, brick and mortar, and pneumatically driven nails are all examples of construction details that render disassembly very challenging without destroying the component materials or extremely high labor costs.
- *Demolition is more common than deconstruction*— Deconstruction is more expensive than demolition, and in most regions there is little financial incentive to deconstruct and reuse or recycle most materials.
- *In the United States, there are no requirements or incentives for manufacturers or producers to take back packaging or products*—Producers and distributors bear no responsibility for end-of-life impacts of their products or packaging; therefore they don't design with either reuse or recycling in mind.

A culture of market response, minimal governmental intervention, history of cheap resources, and low waste disposal costs all contribute to these challenges in closing material loops. Recycled-content or remanufactured

Table 4–1 Definitions of Key Terms Related to Resource Reuse

Term	Definition
Post-consumer materials	A material or finished product that has served its intended use and has been diverted or recovered from waste destined for disposal, having completed its life as a consumer item. Post-consumer materials are part of the broader category of recovered materials.[a]
Post-consumer content	Material from products that were used by consumers or businesses and would otherwise be discarded as waste. If a product is labeled "recycled content," the rest of the product material might have come from excess or damaged items generated during normal manufacturing processes and not collected through a local recycling program.[a]
Pre-consumer materials	Materials generated in manufacturing and converting processes, such as manufacturing scrap and trimmings/cuttings.[a]
Deconstruction	The dismantling of a building in such a manner that its component parts can be reused.[b] A process of carefully taking apart components of a building, possibly with some damage, with the intention of either reusing some of the components after refurbishment or reconditioning, or recycling the materials. It may be undertaken during refurbishment, when adapting a building for new use, or at the end if its life.[c]
Demolition	A term for both the name of the industry and the process of intentional dismantling and reduction of a building (or site) without necessarily preserving the integrity of its components or materials for the purpose of reuse or recycling.[c]
Design for disassembly (DfD)	DfD is the design of buildings or products to facilitate future change and the eventual dismantlement (in part or whole) for recovery of systems, components, and materials. This design process includes developing the assemblies, components, materials, construction techniques, and information and management systems to accomplish this goal.[d]
Recovered materials	Waste materials and by-products that have been recovered or diverted from solid waste, but not including materials and by-products generated from, and commonly reused within, an original manufacturing process.[a]
Reclaimed material	Material set aside from the waste stream for future reuse with minimal processing.[b]
Reuse	The use of reclaimed materials for their original purpose or related purposes.[b]
Reprocessed materials	Materials that are broken down or size reduced from their unit or standard size. Although downcycled, reprocessing materials uses less energy and produces less emissions than remanufacturing for recycling.[e]
Recycled-content products	A new product manufactured using reclaimed materials, scrap, or waste as feedstock. Usually incurs some environmental impacts such as energy use, emissions, and waste.[b] New product is usually substantially different than the recycled product (e.g., milk jugs recycled into plastic lumber). Recycled-content products are made from materials that would otherwise have been discarded. Items in this category are made totally or partially from material destined for disposal or recovered from industrial activities, such as aluminum soda cans or newspaper. Recycled-content products also can be items that are rebuilt or remanufactured from used products.[a]
Recyclable products	Recyclable products can be collected and remanufactured into new products after they've been used. These products do not necessarily contain recycled materials and only benefit the environment if people recycle them after use. Check with your local recycling program to determine which items are recyclable in your community.[a]

Continued

Table 4–1 Definitions of Key Terms Related to Resource Reuse *(Continued)*

Term	Definition
Precycling	The decision-making process consumers use to judge a purchase based on its waste implications. Criteria include whether a product is reusable, durable, and repairable; made from renewable or nonrenewable resources; overpackaged; or in a reusable container.[g]
Upcycling	Taking a low-grade material and turning it into a higher-grade material, often using human energy.[b]
Downcycling	Taking a high-grade material and turning it into a lower-grade material, often using fuel energy.[b] Reusing a product, component, or material for a purpose with lower performance requirements than it originally produced.[c]
Closed-loop recycling	A recycling process in which a manufactured product is recycled back into the same (or similar) product without significant deterioration of the quality of the product. Materials that can be recycled in this fashion include steel and other metals, as well as glass and some types of plastics (e.g., nylon carpet fiber).[h]
Source reduction	Any change in the design, manufacture, purchase, or use of materials or products (including packaging) to reduce their amount or toxicity before they become municipal solid waste. Source reduction also refers to the reuse of products or materials.
Product stewardship	Product stewardship is a product-centered approach to environmental protection. Also known as extended product responsibility (EPR), product stewardship calls on those in the product life cycle—manufacturers, retailers, users, and disposers—to share responsibility for reducing the environmental impacts of products.[f]
Municipal solid waste (MSW)	Waste generated in households, commercial establishments, institutions, and businesses. MSW includes used paper, discarded cans and bottles, food scraps, yard trimmings, and other items. Industrial process wastes, agricultural wastes, mining waste, and sewage sludge are not MSW.[f]
Construction and demolition waste (C&D waste)	Materials resulting from the construction, remodeling, repair, or demolition of buildings, bridges, pavements, and other structures.[g]
Industrial solid waste	Materials discarded from industrial operations or derived from manufacturing processes.[g]
Solid waste	Any garbage, refuse, or sludge from a wastewater treatment plant, water supply treatment plant, or air pollution control facility and other discarded material, including solid, liquid, semisolid, or contained gaseous material resulting from industrial, commercial, mining, and agricultural operations, and from community activities, but not including solid or dissolved materials in domestic sewage, or solid or dissolved materials in irrigation return flows or industrial discharges that are point sources subject to permit under 33 U.S.C. 1342, or source, special nuclear, or by-product materials as defined by the Atomic Energy Act of 1954, as amended.[g]
Virgin materials	Resources extracted from nature in their raw form, such as timber, stone, or metal ore.[f]
Resource recovery	A term describing the extraction and use of materials and energy from the waste stream. The term is sometimes used synonymously with energy recovery.[g]
Energy recovery	Conversion of waste to energy, generally through the combustion of processed or raw refuse to produce steam.
Waste-to-energy system (WTE)	A method of converting MSW into a usable form of energy, usually through combustion.

Table 4–1 Definitions of Key Terms Related to Resource Reuse *(Continued)*

Term	Definition
Hazardous waste	Waste material that exhibits a characteristic of hazardous waste as defined in RCRA (ignitability, corrosivity, reactivity, or toxicity), is listed specifically in RCRA 261.3 Subpart D, is a mixture of either, or is designated locally or by the state as hazardous or undesirable for handling as part of the municipal solid waste and would have to be treated as regulated hazardous waste if not from a household.[g]
Scrap	Discarded or rejected industrial waste material often suitable for recycling.[g]
Primary material	A material whose production has involved extraction from natural resources.[g]
Secondary material	A material that is used in place of a primary or raw material in manufacturing a product.[g]

[a]U.S. EPA "Glossary"

[b]Scottish Design Association (SEDA) 2005

[c]Addis 2006

[d]Hamer Center for Community Design 2006

[e]Sustainable Sites Initiative 2007

[f]U.S. EPA "Glossary: Solid Waste Management"

[g]U.S. EPA "Glossary: Municipal Solid Waste"

[h]Amatruda 2007

Table 4–2 Site Components, Products, and Materials and Their Potential for Closed-Loop Life Cycles

Categories of Components, Materials, or Products of Site Construction	Reuse or Recycling Potential
Products brought to site and installed with little or no modifications onsite. (e.g., light fixtures, pumps, controllers, irrigation systems)	Complete manufacturing and assembly is in control of manufacturer. And, while most are currently not, they can be designed for disassembly, remanufacturing, and reuse. These types of products hold very good potential for being part of a closed-loop system.
Products and components fabricated offsite, but assembled onsite (structural steel, precast concrete elements, guardrail panels, fence panels)	Structures comprised of these elements can be designed in such a way that they are easily dismantled and the components reused whole in other structures.
Materials and products that are mixed or processed off-site, but placed, cast, or finished onsite (cast in place concrete, asphalt pavement, aggregates)	These installations can be removed, usually not whole, but can be minimally reprocessed (e.g., crushed and graded) for reuse. With the exception of asphalt pavement and stabilized soil pavements, this practice usually results in downcycling.
Materials and products that are fabricated, finished, and processed onsite (e.g., dimensional lumber, plastic lumber, piping)	These materials and products can be challenging to deconstruct and reclaim. However, connections can be designed for disassembly (e.g., no glue or pneumatic nails, but bolts and screws). Recycling markets for some of these components are limited in some regions.
Products that are applied to structures onsite (e.g., paints, sealers, glues, mastics)	Very low to no reuse or recycling potential because of difficulties separating the materials and the low quantities.

Sources: Kibert et al. 2002; Addis 2006; SEDA 2005; King County; Guy and Shell

products need to compete with products made from virgin resources (Kibert et al. 2002).

THE RESOURCE EFFICIENCY HIERARCHY

All of the strategies—reduce, reuse, recycle—are not equal. Just diverting a waste material from the landfill is not always enough. While it is a step in the right direction, what is actually done with the diverted material will determine whether it is a large or small step. In resource conservation, as in other aspects of designing for sustainable sites, there are shades of green from light to dark.

Table 4–3 lists a hierarchy of waste reduction strategies that can work toward the ideal of a closed-loop life cycle of materials. The first strategy, prevention, is the "darkest green," as using no new material most often poses no impacts. While this is not always possible as new projects need to be built or existing projects must be modified, there are several strategies ranging from designing for deconstruction to reusing materials on-site to using recycled-content materials that follow.

The last strategies address the scenario of no possible reuse or recycling of a material. The concept of energy recovery recognizes that most products have an energy value that can be recovered to power another process. The energy value of plastics, for example, is nearly equal to the amount of energy used in their primary

EU Principles for Waste Management

As part of the EU waste management directive from 2003, the following principles guide individual countries' efforts at waste management and reduction (European Commission 2003):

WASTE MANAGEMENT HIERARCHY

Waste management strategies must aim primarily to prevent the generation of waste and to reduce its harmfulness. Where this is not possible, waste materials should be reused, recycled, recovered, or used as a source of energy. As a final resort, waste should be disposed of safely (e.g., by incineration or in landfill sites).

SELF-SUFFICIENCY AT COMMUNITY AND, IF POSSIBLE, AT MEMBER STATE LEVEL

Member states need to establish, in cooperation with other member states, an integrated and adequate network of waste disposal facilities.

PROXIMITY PRINCIPLE

Wastes should be disposed of as close to the source as possible.

PRECAUTIONARY PRINCIPLE

The lack of full scientific certainty should not be used as an excuse for failing to act. Where there is a credible risk to the environment or human health of acting or not acting with regard to waste, that which serves to provide a cost-effective response to the risk identified should be pursued.

PRODUCER RESPONSIBILITY

Economic operators, and particularly manufacturers of products, have to be involved in the objective to close the life cycle of substances, components, and products from their production throughout their useful life until they become waste.

POLLUTER PAYS

Those responsible for the generation of waste, and consequent adverse effects on the environment, should be required to pay the costs of avoiding or alleviating those adverse consequences. A clear example can be seen in the Landfill Directive 99/31/EC, Article 10.

BEST AVAILABLE TECHNIQUE NOT ENTAILING EXCESSIVE COST (BATNEEC)

Emissions from installations to the environment should be reduced as much as possible and in the most economically efficient way.

Table 4–3 Resource Efficiency Hierarchy in Decreasing Order of Preferability

REDUCE	
Prevent building and rebuilding— use no new material	Don't build or rebuild, and design sites for adaptability with open plans and multiuse spaces so the site and its structures do not require adaptation in a short period of time. Engage in scenario planning during the programming phase to envision multiple scenarios of site use.
	Design long-lasting structures with durable materials and details.
Reuse site structures in place, in whole form	Don't tear down and rebuild structures.
	Adapt and modify sites and site structures to new uses.
Use less material	Use durable materials that will last the life of the landscape and are reusable multiple times in other structures.
	Design to minimize construction waste such as "cutoffs," excessive finish waste, etc.
	Design smaller structures (e.g., smaller decks, thinner slabs and walls, flexible footings, cable balustrades rather than hollow steel tube rails).
	Use fewer elements.
	Specify smaller members (e.g., use 4 × 4 posts, not 6 × 6, unless structurally necessary).
	Expose structures as the finish (e.g., leave concrete walls exposed, don't coat with stucco or face with stone or brick).
Design for disassembly (DfD)	Designing sites with deconstruction and reuse of materials after their useful life in the current application can extend the lives of materials, save resources, and limit associated impacts of new material production. See Table 4–6 for principles of DfD.
REGENERATE	
Use materials from renewable resources	Use living materials (e.g., slope stabilization with plants, willow wattles, willow fences, and domes).
	Use biobased materials (e.g., jute, hemp, bamboo, strawbale, plant-based stabilizers, and form-release agents).
	Use renewable materials (e.g., wood if it is certified as sustainably grown and harvested).
	Look for renewable materials that can be reused, recycled, or composted.
RECLAIM and REUSE	
Reuse components whole and on-site	Employ deconstruction rather than demolition techniques to reclaim materials for reuse in other applications on the site.
	Storage facilities on-site should maintain the integrity of the material (e.g., recovered wood should be protected from moisture).
	Survey all potentially reusable materials prior to the design phase.
	Budget for additional labor required to make the components reusable.
	Use of reclaimed materials from the site can save money and add meaning and richness to a site design.

Continued

Table 4–3 Resource Efficiency Hierarchy in Decreasing Order of Preferability *(Continued)*

Reclaim components whole for use on other sites	Employ deconstruction rather than demolition techniques to reclaim materials for reuse first or recycling if not reusable in whole form.
	Store for use on other projects, distribute to salvage facilities, or place in online material exchanges.
	Budget for additional labor required to make the components reusable.
Use reclaimed materials from other sites	Use of reclaimed materials from other sites can save money and add meaning and richness to a site design.
	Source materials prior to the design phase to let the materials inspire the design and ensure type and quantity.
	Budget for additional labor required to make the components reusable.
REPROCESS and RECYCLE	
Reprocess existing structures and materials for use on-site	Although downcycled, reprocessing materials uses less energy and produces fewer emissions than remanufacturing for recycling.
	Bring crushing or other processing equipment to the site rather than hauling the materials to a reprocessing facility.
	Plan for processed material stockpiles during construction.
Reclaim on-site structures and distribute to off-site reprocessing facilities	Demolished concrete, asphalt, aggregate, wood, asphalt shingles, and glass can be taken to local reprocessing facilities where they will be stockpiled for use on other sites.
	Care should be taken to minimize haul distances.
Use reprocessed materials from other sites	Crushed concrete, tires, asphalt, glass, and other materials can be obtained from reprocessing facilities for use as aggregates in base and backfill applications as well as in new asphalt, concrete, and other pavements.
	Care should be taken to minimize haul distances.
Specify recyclable materials	By specifying materials with recycling potential, the chances that they will be recycled after the useful life of the site or structure are increased.
	Commonly recycled materials are clean wood (not pressure treated or coated with lead-based paint), metals (unless coatings prohibit), polyethylene-based plastics, concrete, asphalt, precast concrete products, and bricks.
	Avoid mixed material assemblies or products where materials are not easily separated.
Use recycled-content materials	With the exception of metals and some plastics, most recycled-content products are downcycled.
	Recycled content of a product should be at minimum 20% post-consumer material and 40% pre-consumer material.
	Refer to U.S. EPA Comprehensive Procurement Guidelines for recycled-content thresholds for site products.

Table 4–3 Resource Efficiency Hierarchy in Decreasing Order of Preferability *(Continued)*

Reclaim on-site materials and distribute to off-site recycling facilities	While reuse of reclaimed, deconstructed materials in whole form is preferable, there will be some materials that are not reusable, so sending the materials off-site to recycling facilities and secondary production processes can save resources for new products.
	Recycling can be challenging because the material composition is diverse or the assembly is comprised of mixed materials.
Facilitate on-site recycling with area for storage and collection of recyclables	Facilitate recycling over the life of the site with facilities for storage and collection of both organic and inorganic recyclables.
	Plan for these facilities in the site design process.
RECOVER	
Divert nonusable materials for energy recovery	Where materials can't be reclaimed or recycled, recovering their calorific value in waste-to-energy facilities with adequate pollution controls is preferable to disposal in a landfill.
	Energy recovery can be accomplished by either direct incineration in municipal waste incinerators to generate heat and electricity or directly in industrial production processes to replace other fuels (Azapagic et al. 2003). An example of this is waste tires burned to power cement kilns.
	Energy recovery is controversial because while it recovers energy from waste, pollution impacts can be substantial if not well controlled. High-efficiency pollution control equipment is a large capital investment that many facilities are not willing or able to make unless mandated by regulations.
DISPOSE	
Disposal of materials in controlled landfills	The least preferable option for waste is dispoal to landfills. If the waste can't be reclaimed, recycled, or energy recovered, it should be disposed of in an appropriately controlled landfill.

manufacture (Azapagic, Emsley, and Hamerton 2003). The "very light green" practice of energy recovery is far from the most efficient use of a material, but in many cases it may be preferable to landfill disposal.

Construction and Demolition Waste and Resource Reuse

Construction and demolition (C&D) debris is waste material that is produced in the process of construction, renovation, or demolition of the built environment. This includes buildings of all types (both residential and nonresidential) as well as roads and bridges and other site structures. Common components of C&D debris include concrete, asphalt pavement, wood, metals, gypsum wallboard, floor tile, and roofing materials. Land-clearing debris, such as stumps, rocks, and soil, are also included in some state definitions of C&D debris (U.S. EPA 1998). C&D debris is usually classified in four categories: building-related waste and construction, demolition, and renovation debris; roadway-related waste; bridge-related waste; land-clearing and inert debris waste (U.S. EPA 1998). Site hardscape demolition waste is usually placed into the building-related waste category.

In 1996, the most recent year for which data is available, 136 million tons of debris was created from building- (and site-) related construction and demolition activities in the United States. Of this, 43% came from residential sources and 57% from nonresidential sources. Building demolitions generated 48% of the debris, renovations generated 44%, and 8% was from new construction "cutoffs" and waste from the construction process (U.S. EPA 1998). Waste managed on-site is not included in these figures.

In 1996, and still today, landfilling is the most common management practice for C&D debris, with an estimated 30%–45% discarded in C&D landfills and 30–40% discarded in municipal solid waste (MSW) landfills or at nonpermitted landfills (U.S. EPA 1998). In 1996, it was estimated that 20%–30% of C&D debris was recovered for processing and recycling. This figure has likely grown as landfill tipping fees have increased, the number of landfills has decreased, and reuse and recycling markets have developed in the past decade.

Research by the EPA's Office of Solid Waste C&D Recycling group in 2003 estimated the material composition of building- (and site-) related C&D debris as shown in the table below.

WASTE REDUCTION MANDATES

Movement toward closing material loops in the solid waste industry has begun. As landfills in some regions reach capacity, and citizens oppose new ones, some states have placed stringent waste reduction mandates on their municipalities. Canada and California mandated goals of a 50% reduction in municipal solid waste by the year 2000, and many municipalities have reached or exceeded these goals. Some landfills now ban organic and other wastes. In Massachusetts, it is against regulations to send C&D waste to landfills. These mandates and ever-increasing landfill tipping fees have resulted in an increasing array of recycled products. In the construction field, the mandates have spurred the rapid growth of the building deconstruction field, the construction material salvage industry, and the reuse of reclaimed materials in new site and building projects.

DECONSTRUCTION VS. DEMOLITION

Growing concerns for resource use coupled with waste reduction mandates have led to increased recycling of construction and demolition debris. To facilitate this practice, the processes of dismantling a building or site have shifted from demolition to deconstruction. *Deconstruction* involves the dismantling of a building or site with the intention of reusing or recycling the components. In contrast, *demolition* reduces the building or site to debris without preserving the integrity of its components for reuse. Materials are commingled and usually landfilled. A good deconstruction contractor will be able to reclaim/recycle 75%–95% of the site and building if salvage or recycling markets are available nearby.

While deconstruction takes more time and incurs higher labor costs than demolition, recent studies indicate that it may be less expensive than paying landfill costs; and resale of the materials, either whole or ground, can generate additional income. Where the demo contractor is also responsible for the new construction, it may make economic sense to stockpile materials on- or

Table 4–4 Building-related C&D Debris Generation: Estimated Percentages by Material

Material and Component Content Examples	Estimated Percentage of Building-related C&D Debris Generated Annually (%)
Concrete and mixed rubble: concrete, asphalt, cinder blocks, rock, earth	40–50
Wood: forming and framing lumber, stumps, plywood, laminates, scraps	20–30
Drywall: Sheetrock, gypsum, plaster	5–15
Asphalt roofing	1–10
Metals: pipes, rebar, flashing, steel, aluminum, copper, brass, stainless steel	1–5
Bricks: bricks and decorative block	1–5
Plastics: vinyl siding, doors, windows, floor tile, pipes	1–5

Source: Sandler 2003

off-site. It is common for materials like concrete to be removed, crushed on-site, and stockpiled for backfill on the new construction. The table below summarizes both benefits and challenges of deconstruction.

DECONSTRUCTION STRATEGIES

The following strategies can maximize success of site deconstruction activities:

Conduct an inventory to identify all site and building components that can be removed and reused or recycled. This inventory should be conducted early in the design process to allow maximum opportunity to reuse structures and materials on-site. Determine the highest and best strategy for each component based on the resource efficiency hierarchy. For example, if asphalt can be removed and replaced on-site, this is a better option than trucking the asphalt to a remote recycling facility.

Obtain "as-built" plans of the building and site to be deconstructed. These plans may reveal structural members, subgrade structures, and other features that are not easily seen in the walk-through inventory.

Bring the contractor onto the project as soon as possible. Ideally, the general contractor can assist with the inventory of components for deconstruction and reuse in the schematic design phase if possible.

Table 4–5 Benefits and Challenges of Deconstruction

Benefits of Deconstruction	Comments
Reduced environmental and health impacts from raw material use, acquisition, manufacture, and processing of new materials[a]	Use of reclaimed or recycled materials will reduce virgin resource use, habitat destruction, energy use, and emissions from acquiring and manufacturing new materials.
Reduced landfill debris[a]	Reductions in material that must be landfilled can save costs of landfill tipping fees, which are substantial in some areas. In some cases the savings will pay for the increased labor costs of deconstruction. Additionally reducing landfill disposal preserves land and may reduce the possibility of any future problems associated with the landfill.[b]
Management of hazardous resources[c]	Deconstruction allows for management of hazardous materials, such as pressure treated-lumber, as they can be segregated and disposed of appropriately rather than commingled and landfilled, where they hold the potential to leach hazardous substances. In addition, when hazardous waste is commingled with nonhazardous waste, the entire load must then be treated as hazardous waste.[b]
Strengthens the salvage and recycling industry[a]	Growth in markets for reclaimed and recycled materials is directly related to the increase in deconstruction activities. The more deconstruction taking place, the stronger the markets for reused and recycled materials. This can result in job growth and benefits the local economy.[b]
Design opportunities with use of reclaimed materials (e.g., aesthetic, historic, symbolic)[a]	Reclaimed materials can add a layer of meaning to a project, revealing the cultural history of a place that is often difficult to achieve with mass-produced, internationally distributed, new materials. Reclaimed materials are sometimes unique and one of a kind.
Can achieve LEED credits	Deconstruction can contribute directly to achievement of two LEED credits: MR Credit 2.1: "Construction Waste Management: Divert 50% from Disposal" and "Divert 75% from Disposal." It can also help achieve several other credits in areas of "Materials Reuse" and "Regional Materials."
Can save costs of new materials[a,d]	Using reclaimed and reprocessed materials can often be cost effective, saving material acquisition expenses. Hauling and landfill expenses can be saved if materials are reused on-site.

Continued

Table 4–5 Benefits and Challenges of Deconstruction *(Continued)*

Challenges of Deconstruction	Comments
More time required for deconstructing[c]	As deconstruction involves careful dismantling of a structure, often by hand, versus knocking a structure down with bulldozers and excavators, it takes more time. This can be problematic if construction schedules are tight. If possible, begin deconstruction activities during the design and documentation processes. An added benefit may be the discovery of potentially reusable unknown structures in time to incorporate them into the design.
May cost more than demolition	The additional time for dismantling a building or site translates to higher labor costs. Cost is the single most prevalent reason that buildings and structures are not deconstructed.
Time required for cleaning, processing, and refurbishing	Cleaning, processing, and refurbishing materials can take time, which translates to added costs. Removal of connectors such as nails, screws, and joist hangers, as well as cleaning paints, mortar, sealants, and adhesives from materials, is necessary for their reuse.
Lack of space to stage and store reclaimed materials until they are reused[e]	Reclaimed materials from a deconstructed structure may need to be stored or stockpiled for a long period, sometimes more than a year, until they can be reused in new structures. Some construction sites may not have appropriate or secure space to store reclaimed materials. Storing materials offsite will likely incur costs of storage and transport. Additionally, weather sensitive materials such as wood must be stored in a location protected from the weather.
Increased worker safety/health risks[c]	Deconstructing structures such as retaining walls or buildings can pose hazards to workers, as structures can be weakened and fail during the deconstruction process. Also, materials for stripping paint, sealers, and adhesives can be hazardous to worker health.
Lack of well-established supply-demand chains[c]	Lack of salvage or recycling markets is the second most prevalent reason that project planners choose to demolish and not to deconstruct. In many regions markets for reclaimed or recycled materials are weak. This almost always corresponds to the cost of landfill tipping fees as there is a point at which it becomes more cost effective to deconstruct than to pay the landfill fees.
Inexperienced contractors[d]	In some areas, there are few contractors that are experienced with techniques of deconstruction. Demolition contractors are typically used to very different methods of removing buildings and may inflate the price due to the unknown aspects of the job. Look for contractors with deconstruction experience or put them in touch with remote deconstruction contractors to learn techniques.
Lack of standards for use of some recovered materials[c]	Lack of standards and established track records for some recovered materials will inhibit their use, decreasing the market for them. Recycled aggregates such as concrete rubble and waste tire chips are a good example of this. An increasing number of states have incorporated standards for their use in the past few years, and as a result, the market for natural aggregate substitutes has expanded quickly. Other recovered materials are relatively untested, and not widely collected or reused.
Buildings and sites are not designed to be deconstructed[c]	There is a high variability in assembly techniques. Connections such as pneumatically driven nails, welding, and adhesives make disassembly challenging, and materials can be ruined during efforts at removal.

[a]National Association of Home Builders
[b]Cochran
[c]Guy and Shell n.d.
[d]U.S. EPA C&D
[e]Schwab

Set the goal or deconstruction early in the design process and acquaint all consultants, contractors, and subs with the goal, techniques, and strategies. LEED points can be earned for diverting 50% or 75% of C&D debris from the landfill.

Write specifications for deconstruction and job-site waste management and include them in construction documents. Some government publications listed below offer model specification language to address the use of waste reduction techniques, reuse of construction waste material, salvage of construction and demolition waste for sale or reuse, and/or return of unused construction material to vendors.

Refer to the following resources for model waste specifications and techniques of designing for disassembly:

- *Federal Green Construction Guide for Specifiers,* Whole Building Design Guide, http://www.wbdg.org/design/greenspec.php
- *WasteSpec: Model specification for construction waste reduction, reuse, and recycling* (www.tjcog.dst.nc.us/cdwaste.htm). Triangle J Council of Governments
- *Design for Disassembly in the Built Environment: A guide to Closed-loop Design and Building.* City of Seattle, King County, Washington and Resource Venture Inc. Prepared by the Hamer Center for Community Design, The Pennsylvania State University
- California Integrated Waste Management Board C&D Waste Management Specifications http://www.ciwmb.ca.gov/ConDemo/Specs/
- King County Design Specifications and Waste Management Plans http://www.metrokc.gov/dnrp/swd/greenbuilding/construction-recycling/specifications-plans.asp

Sources for Locating C&D Reuse and Recycling Facilities

If the materials reclaimed from deconstruction will not be reused on-site, locating facilities to dispose of them can be a challenge in some areas. Generally, regions with waste reduction mandates or incentives will have adequate facilities and recycling centers to take reclaimed materials. The Pacific Northwest, California,

Massachusetts, and major East Coast cities all have good salvage and recycling infrastructure in place. However, these facilities may be few and far between in the Midwest and in central States (excluding Chicago), and more creative disposal methods must be undertaken, such as reuse on other sites, donation of materials to charitable organizations, or online materials exchanges.

Because of waste reduction mandates, some states and municipalities are heavily involved in facilitating the deconstruction industry and the creation of markets for the use of reclaimed or recycled materials. Most states run online databases listing salvage outlets, salvage dealers, recycling centers, and materials exchanges.

The California Integrated Waste Management Board's (CIWMB) construction and demolition recycling website (www.ciwmb.ca.gov) lists many reuse links and resources both within the state of California and nationally. They maintain extensive lists of non-profit, government-sponsored, and for-profit deconstruction firms, salvage dealers, salvage outlets, and materials exchanges (CIWMB).

King County, Washington, places particular emphasis on establishing markets for salvaged, recycled, and recycled-content materials, and assisting design and construction professionals in these areas. They offer numerous referrals to recycling providers, charitable organizations, national online materials exchanges, and salvage dealers in King County. The county maintains an online reusable building materials exchange for construction products (King County).

Other municipal programs with useful information on salvage and recycling resources are Austin, Texas; Oakland, Alameda County, Santa Monica, and San Jose, California; Portland, Oregon; and Triangle J Council of Governments in North Carolina.

The Building Materials Reuse Association (BMRA) offers a database by state of salvage outlets, deconstruction contractors, materials exchanges, and recycling facilities. The listings are limited to members of their organization. Also refer to state and municipal solid waste websites and the EPA C&D website (EPA C&D).

Some deconstruction contractors will vertically integrate reclaimed materials from the site into other jobs or into salvage stores that they own. Or reclaimed materials can be sold or dispersed directly from the site by bringing potential buyers to the site. See "Locating Reclaimed Materials" below.

DESIGNING FOR DISASSEMBLY

Designing for disassembly (DfD), also called designing for deconstruction, in the early phases of project design can facilitate deconstruction activities and reuse of materials after the useful life of the site or structure. In this way, the site or building being deconstructed is the resource for the next structure either on or off the site. This can help to ensure multiple-use phases for a material and promote closed-loop material life cycles.

DfD in construction has borrowed concepts developed in the consumer product design industries. The overall goal of DfD is to design a site, structure, building, or product in such a way as to "increase resource and economic efficiency and reduce pollution impacts in the adaptation and eventual removal of buildings [and sites], and to recover components and materials for reuse, remanufacturing and recycling" (Guy and Shell n.d.).

The list of principles and strategies for DfD in Table 4–6 was adapted for site DfD from two major sources:

Table 4–6 Principles and Strategies of Design for Disassembly

DfD Principles	Strategies for Site DfD
Design the site and structure for maximum flexibility and plan for adaptation of the site over time. Planning for change and differing occupancy patterns can ensure that a site or structure, as built, will last a long time.	Design a flexible spatial configuration. Design multiuse spaces to allow for flexible programming. Order extra materials or spare parts in small amounts so repairs/replacements can be made without removal of the entire structure.
Document materials and methods to facilitate deconstruction and disassembly after the useful life of the structure or site.	Documenting materials and methods of construction and developing a deconstruction plan either during construction documentation or shortly after construction will facilitate deconstruction efforts several decades later (hopefully) at the end of the structure's/site's life. The deconstruction plan can include the following: "As-built" drawings labeling connections and materials List of all components and materials in project, including all manufacturer contacts and warranties. Specifics on finishes and materials chemistries Specifics on connections and how to deconstruct them Information on hidden or subgrade materials Three-dimensional drawings showing disassembly of key connections Copies of the deconstruction plan should be given to the owner, designers, builders, and/or other stakeholders who may be involved with the project for its use life.
Specify materials and products with good reuse or recycling potential. When specifying materials for DfD, plan for reuse of materials before recycling of materials. Refer to the resource efficiency hierarchy list of priorities (Table 4–3).	Refer to Table 4–8 for easily removed, reused, and recycled materials. Avoid composite materials unless they are reusable in whole form. Specify simple products, not complicated assemblies that can reduce the likelihood of reuse or recycling. Specify materials and products from manufacturers with take-back programs in place. (Note: These are few and far between, but expected to increase.)

Table 4–6 Principles and Strategies of Design for Disassembly *(Continued)*

DfD Principles	Strategies for Site DfD
Specify materials that are durable, modular, and/or standardized to facilitate reuse many times. Materials that are standard sizes are more likely to be useful to another structure. If they are durable and carefully deconstructed they can be reused many times.	Interface with manufacturers to better understand the expected life of the product/material/finish and how the life can be extended. Research standard sizes of materials, structural bays, parking spaces, etc., and design with these in mind. Designing structures and modules of structures based on standard sizes will help ensure their viability in reuse. Where a component is not easily reusable, it should be recyclable.
Design connections that are accessible. Visually, physically, and ergonomically accessible connections will increase efficiency and avoid requirements for expensive equipment or extensive environmental health and safety precautions for workers.	Components should be readily accessible for disassembly and easily dismantled for repair and replacement of parts.
Detail connections that facilitate disassembly. Chemical connections can make materials difficult to separate and recycle. Too many types of connections can lengthen deconstruction time and require many different tools.	Chemical connections such as mortar, adhesives, and welds can make materials difficult to separate and recycle. And it can increase the likelihood that the material will be destroyed during attempts at deconstruction. Use of bolted, screwed, or hand-nailed connections can ease disassembly. Use of lime mortar can facilitate disassembly of brick walls. Using standard and limited connector palettes can also simplify deconstruction. Design joints to withstand repeated assembly and disassembly. Refer to Table 4–7 for an evaluation of connection alternatives for deconstruction.
Avoid finishes that can compromise the reuse or recyclability of the material. Some coatings and finishes are difficult to remove and can compromise the reusability or recyclability of a material.	Coatings such as paint or sealers can make it difficult to reuse deconstructed materials. While technically they can be reused, the chances of reuse are low due to the costs of cleaning the material. Some plastic-coated or electroplated metals are not recyclable.
Support the DfD process in the design process. Designing for deconstruction or disassembly can necessitate modifications to the traditional design process. If a design process that supports general principles of sustainable design is used, such as early goal setting and inclusion of all team members at the project inception, it may accommodate DfD design activities.	Design process techniques that can facilitate DfD are as follows: Allow extra time in the design process for full incorporation of DfD principles Involve the whole team and client with the idea of DfD in project goal setting and throughout the design process. Establish deconstruction targets and benchmarks to design for both the percentage of structure/site reused, but also the number of times a component can be reused. Brief and train contractors in DfD principles to ensure compliance with strategies. Budget for extra time spent on "as-builts" and deconstruction plan during C&D phase. Balance aesthetic concerns with disassembly goals. Provide an operating manual for the site and structure to ensure longevity. Maintain a formal connection with the project to periodically monitor the site and structure. The owner will need to be convinced of this as this is very nontraditional.

Adapted from sources: Hamer Center for Community Design 2006; SEDA 2005; NAHB; Addis 2006

Table 4–7 Evaluation of Connection Alternatives for Deconstruction

Type of Connection	Advantages	Disadvantages
Screw fixing	Easily removable	Limited reuse of both hole and screws
		Cost
Bolt fixing	Strong	Can seize up, making removal difficult
	Can be reused a number of times	Cost
Nail fixing	Speed of construction	Difficult to remove
	Cost	Removal usually destroys a key area of element
Friction	Keeps construction element whole during removal	Relatively undeveloped area
		Poor choice of fixings
		Structurally weaker
Mortar	Can be made to variety of strengths	Mostly cannot be reused, unless clay or lime
		Strength of mix often overspecified, making it difficult to separate bonded layers
Resin bonding	Strong and efficient	Virtually impossible to separate bonded layers
	Deal with awkward joints	Resin cannot be easily recycled or reused
Adhesives	Variety of strengths available to suit task	Adhesives cannot be easily recycled or reused; many are also impossible to separate
Riveted fixing	Speed of construction	Difficult to remove without destroying a key area of element

Source: SEDA 2005

Design and Detailing for Deconstruction, SEDA Design Guides for Scotland: No. 1 by Chris Morgan and Fionn Stevenson; and *Design for Disassembly in the Built Environment: A Guide to Closed-loop Design and Building* by Brad Guy and Nicholas Ciarimboli for the City of Seattle, King County, Washington, and Resource Venture, Inc.

Reclaimed and Reused Materials and Products

Using reclaimed materials, also called salvaged materials, in new site construction has many potential benefits. Materials are diverted from landfills, and virgin resources and energy that would have gone to manufacture new materials are conserved. From a design standpoint, reusing materials can add a layer of meaning to a project, revealing the cultural history of a place, which is often difficult to achieve with mass-produced, internationally distributed, new materials. Reclaimed materials are sometimes unique and one of a kind. Lastly, using reclaimed materials can often be cost effective, saving material acquisition expenses and demolition hauling and landfill expenses if obtained on-site.

Yet use of reclaimed materials is not without challenges. Perhaps the greatest challenge for designers is locating enough appropriate materials for a given application to the site to still gain an environmental benefit. Issues of storage, inventory, and limited markets are challenges facing the rapidly expanding salvage industry. Sometimes it is easier for salvage companies to grind up the materials and sell them immediately to manufacturers in reduced form for recycling rather than house the materials while waiting a few months for a buyer. Other challenges stem from refurbishing activities, such as paint stripping and nail pulling, that are required before the reclaimed material can be reused.

Table 4–8 Components and Materials for DfD

Relatively easy disassembly

Nonmortared unit pavers: concrete, brick, stone
Interlocking block retaining wall systems: no mortar
Low-impact foundation technology (LIFT)
Gravel trench foundations
Aggregates
Precast concrete elements

Disassembly requires some additional labor

Unit walls (e.g., brick, stone, CMU) with lime mortar
Unit paving (e.g., brick, stone, concrete units) with lime mortar
Untreated lumber
Plastic lumber
Metal structures with mechanical connections

Potentially reprocessed materials

Concrete slabs and walls
Asphalt pavement
Soil cement
Rammed earth
Aggregates
Recyclable construction materials
Metals: steel, aluminum, stainless steel, copper, iron
Wood (not pressure treated)
Some plastics: HDPE, LDPE, PE, PP, PS
Glass

Nonrecyclable construction materials and products

PVC products
Treated lumber
Some coated metals
Composite products (e.g., fiberglass, composite lumber)
Mixed-material assemblies that are not easily separated

Locating Reclaimed Materials

Reclaiming on-site structures and materials. Sourcing materials from on-site can be cost effective from both an economic and environmental point of view, as both landfill fees and material acquisition and transportation costs are saved. The discussion on site deconstruction above addresses techniques of evaluating the site for potential materials and structures to reclaim.

A growing number of projects, such as Latz+Partner's Landschaftspark Duisburg Nord in the Emscher region of Germany and Hargreaves Associates Waterfront Park in Louisville, Kentucky, have demonstrated the aesthetic benefits and cost savings of maintaining and adaptively reusing structures in whole form on a site. This practice necessitates a thorough site inventory prior to demolition and early in the design process while

Figure 4–1.

Recycled structures, products, and materials are incorporated into this plaza at the Menomonee River Valley Redevelopment by Wenk Associates. Concrete pipes salvaged on-site are used as benches, glass panels in the railings are made by local artist Catherine Lottes of Lucid Glass Industries using recycled glass from Miller Brewing Company, and the smokestack in the background references the site's previous industrial history. (Photo from Wenk Associates, Inc.)

existing structures can still be incorporated into the site design.

Even sites without such rich cultural histories can be a good source of materials to reuse, either in place or removed, stockpiled, and reconstructed. Buildings, pavement, landscape structures, site debris, and vegetation all are potential resources for reclaimed materials. Reusing materials and structures on-site will perhaps provide the greatest environmental savings, as little or no transportation energy is required. It may also be the most economical way of obtaining materials for new construction.

Many salvaged materials are located by word of mouth between designers, with contractors, and even with clients, especially municipal and developer clients. If the contractor is included in the project during schematic design, he or she may be able to procure reclaimed materials from other projects.

Obtaining materials from salvage stores. As the salvage industry grows, many nonprofit and for-profit salvage material stores, dealers, and exchanges are springing up around North America. Salvage stores, both nonprofit and for-profit, are more commonly found in areas of the country with a lot of deconstruction activity. The CIWMB; King County, Washington; Alameda County, California; and many other state solid waste websites list salvage store facilities. And salvage stores may be listed in the local phone book under "Building Materials— Used" or in the local trading paper. The drawback to obtaining reclaimed materials from salvage stores is that the inventory is constantly changing, so one will need to spend time going to see what they have, sometimes multiple times.

The Building Materials Reuse Association (BMRA) is a nonprofit group that represents companies and organizations involved in the acquisition and redistribution of used building materials and the deconstruction industry. It works toward improving the image of the industry, sponsor workshops and conferences, and lobby for national regulations requiring the use of salvaged materials. It lists salvage and reuse facilities by state on its website.

Obtaining materials from online salvage distributors and materials exchanges. There is an abundance of ma-

terials exchanges and salvage distributors on the Internet, with extensive listings for commonly used landscape materials. Exchanges vary by the scale of the inventory and the quantities of any given material available. Exchanges geared to residential projects will advertise one pallet of salvaged bricks, for example, while those geared to larger projects and broader areas might advertise 100 pallets of salvaged bricks. The term *exchange* is slightly misleading. While some are advertising free materials, many materials must be purchased.

The CIWMB lists materials exchanges across the country (www.ciwmb.ca.gov/Reuse/Links/Exchange .htm). The BMRA recommends the national materials exchange build.recycle.net. Recycler's World keeps an Information and Material Exchange Directory, which

Using Reclaimed Materials in the Landscape

- Let the materials inspire the design.
- Locate materials early in the design process to avoid major design revisions when materials are found.
- Maintain flexibility in the design until materials are found.
- Use materials with interesting "stories" or cultural significance to the project.
- At start of project, evaluate project sites and old buildings for materials to reuse.
- Hire demo contractors with experience in deconstruction and salvage.
- Require contractors to provide a plan for construction and demolition salvage and recycling.
- Use materials for their highest use—avoid "downcycling."
- Include appearance and environmental performance standards in the specifications.
- Get the contractor on board with using salvage early in the process.
- Avoid reuse of materials that are considered hazardous (eg. CCA treated lumber) or remove hazardous finishes (eg. lead paint) in a controlled manner

deals with all types of recycled and salvaged materials. It also sponsors a national materials exchange called the Recycler's Exchange, listed by commodity.

Larger quantities of materials can be found on what are often called industrial materials exchanges. These exchanges deal not only with salvaged materials, but also reprocessed/recycled materials and industrial by-products. King County runs the tristate Industrial Material Exchange (King County).

When locating reclaimed materials online, it is important to keep in mind that sourcing the materials needed on the other side of the country may not make environmental (or economic) sense as shipping energy and cost will be high. Designers must use their judgment as to an appropriate limit on the shipping distance with respect to the weight and volume of the material being purchased. Also, inventory of these exchanges is always changing, so some communication with the party listing the material should occur immediately.

Costs of Using Reclaimed Materials

While there are clear financial advantages to salvaging construction and demolition materials on-site, there can be hidden costs in reusing certain types of reclaimed materials. The cost of obtaining salvaged materials is often substantially less than if one purchased similar new materials, but it is the cost of refurbishing and installing the

Figure 4–2.
At the Olympic Sculpture Park in Seattle, Weiss/Manfredi reclaimed granite curbs from nearby sites and positioned them as ascending stairs from the park's valley district to the major Z-shaped path. (Weiss/Manfredi).

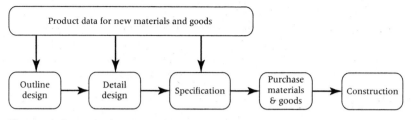

Figure 4–3. Specification process for new materials

reclaimed materials that may be higher. Reclaimed materials may have irregularities that make working with them more challenging, resulting in higher labor costs. They may need to be obtained from many different sources, not easily delivered to the job site like new materials. Contractors may be nervous about these "unknown" factors, so they may price the job higher to accommodate any extra labor, extra transport, or timing delays.

Another hidden cost of using salvage can be the required testing of reclaimed materials that are being used in structural or high-performance situations. When using salvaged wood in certain structural applications, inspectors will require that the wood be regraded. An existing grade mark on a piece of wood is usually not acceptable. Some mills or distributors will have wood regraded, but the price will increase. For large amounts of wood, independent graders can be hired.

Design Processes with Reclaimed Materials

Techniques of finding and using salvage can vary from traditional design and specification practices, and often require extra effort and ingenuity on the part of the designer. Finding appropriate types and quantities of materials can be the most challenging part of using reclaimed materials. There is often additional design time, resulting in more fee usage, involved in finding salvage and designing/specifying with it. A reclaimed material will not be found in a catalog with all specifications listed. Designers must often leave their office to go look at reclaimed materials in salvage stores or on job sites. The rapidly growing Internet materials exchange industry will facilitate locating salvaged materials, as a perusal of exchanges can be accomplished online.

Use of reclaimed materials may be easiest if the materials are sourced early in the design process, while

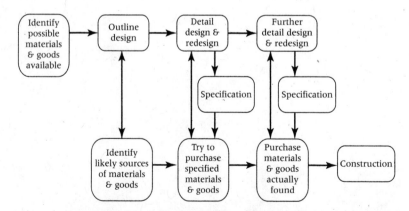

Figure 4–4. Specification process for reclaimed materials

These figures illustrate the difference in material and product specification techniques between use of reclaimed materials and new materials. Use of reclaimed materials necessitates identification and purchase of potential materials and products prior to and during the design process, rather than just prior to the construction phase. (Source: Addis 2006).

they can still influence the design of structures on the site. Some designers generate a design idea and then look for the reclaimed materials to support the idea, while others find materials first and let them inspire the design. In either case it is best if the design remains as flexible as possible until materials are found.

Specifications may also take more time as there is not standard specification language or details for most reclaimed materials. While it takes extra effort, it is very important to clearly document the performance and environmental requirements of reclaimed materials in clear specification language to avoid miscommunication, as reclaimed materials can contain irregularities not found in new materials.

Another issue when using reclaimed materials can be difficulty in finding the correct amount and size of the materials needed. Sometimes the lengths or sizes vary, and that can cause each piece to be unique. The lack of uniformity—each piece being different—makes it more time consuming for the contractor who will refurbish the materials. Figure 4–3 contrasts a typical design process when using new products and materials with a design process (Figure 4–4) that can facilitate use of reclaimed materials and products.

Recycled-content Materials and Products

Recycled-content building products may be the most commonly used "green" building materials. The market for them has rapidly grown, spurred by increased waste recycling efforts by consumers and industry, and supported by "buy recycled" programs at federal, state, and local agencies aimed at reducing solid waste disposal.

Recycling waste and specifying recycled-content products and materials can reduce use of virgin resources and divert materials from landfills. In many cases, use of waste material as feedstock for new products can also reduce energy use, waste, and emissions that would have resulted from the primary processing of new raw materials for the new product. However, waste product recycling, collection, and remanufacturing does pose environmental impacts—often greater than recovered material that is reused in whole form without remanufacturing. Collection and transportation of recovered materials uses fuel resources and produces emissions, and distances that recovered materials travel to recycling plants can be substantial. Remanufacturing a waste material into a new product uses energy and produces emissions as well.

Recycling often results in a downcycled material that is used for a lesser purpose and can never be reused for the original product. Examples of recycling for construction materials are waste tires that are chipped for use in rubberized asphalt or concrete that is crushed and used for base aggregate material. Neither recycled product will be used to form new products with as high a use as the original product. Exceptions to this are metals and some plastics. Steel, aluminum, copper, iron, and others can be recycled many times into products with as high a quality as those made with virgin materials. Plastic products made from HDPE can also be recycled several times.

When different waste materials are commingled and recycled into a composite material or product, the new product's recycling potential is severely limited. For instance, recycled plastic milk jugs and sawdust from lumber processing are combined into composite lumber. Composite lumber can be composed of up to 100% recycled materials; however, since two different materials have been commingled in the new composite lumber product, they can never be separated for recycling. The chances are good that after the use phase the composite lumber will be disposed of in a landfill or, at best, incinerated for energy recovery.

Reprocessed materials are those that are broken down or size reduced from their unit or standard size, although most are not sent back to the plant to be remanufactured into new products. "Wet" materials, such as concrete or asphalt, that are installed in flowable form and cure or dry in place are commonly reprocessed, then reused. Although reprocessing can result in downcycled materials, it often uses less energy and produces fewer emissions than remanufacturing products. In addition, it is increasingly common to reprocess materials and reuse materials on-site, saving energy and emissions incurred by transport of these heavy materials. Old asphalt pavement can be milled up, mixed with new binder, and relaid in place. Concrete pavement is often crushed on-site for use as aggregate base material, and branches from cleared trees are often chipped on-site for mulch.

STANDARDS FOR RECYCLED CONTENT

Most recycled materials contain some percentage of virgin materials and are usually defined by percentage of recycled content. A product with higher post-consumer recycled content is more preferable than a product with lower pre-consumer recycled content. However, in product advertising, recycled-content percentages are not always clearly stated, or if they are stated, distinctions are not always drawn between percentages of post-consumer and pre-consumer content. Careful review of the product literature or questioning of the manufacturer to determine content percentages is recommended. If clear answers are not forthcoming, or the manufacturer is not willing to certify the percentages, the recycled-content claims may be exaggerated.

Third-party certification of recycled content by independent agents can verify recycled content of materials and products. There is currently only one national independent certifying organization in the United States: Scientific Certification Systems. It offers a standard for material content called "Environmental Certification Program: Material Content" standard SCS-EC11–2004 (SCS). Other product certification systems such as Cradle to Cradle examine recycled content as one of many criteria in their certification systems.

EPA Comprehensive Procurement Guidelines

As a result of amendments to the Resource Conservation and Recovery Act (RCRA) of 1976, the EPA developed the Comprehensive Procurement Guidelines (CPGs) and issued Recovered Materials Advisory Notices (RMANs) to encourage federal purchasing agencies to buy recycled-content products. The CPGs and RMANs designate products that can be made with recovered materials and they recommend minimum post-consumer and total recycled-content percentages. The CPGs and RMANs cover a wide variety of products that may be purchased by federal agencies, including site construction materials and products. While the information is intended for federal agencies, it is a useful starting point when specifying recycled-content products (http://www.epa.gov/epaoswer/non-hw/procure/). The site construction products covered are listed in the table below. The CPG program also offers a database of

Table 4–9 EPA Comprehensive Procurement Guidelines for Site Construction Materials and Products

Recycled-content Site Construction Product	Recycled/Recovered Material	Percent Post-consumer Recycled Content	Percent Total Recycled Content
Parking stops	Plastic and/or rubber	100	100
Park benches and picnic tables	Plastics (single or commingled)	90–100	100
Bike racks	Steel[a]	16	25–30
	HDPE	100	100
Playground equipment	Plastic	90–100	100
	Plastic composites	50–75	95–100
	Steel[a]	16	25–30
		67	100
	Aluminum	25	25
Playground surfaces and running tracks	Rubber or plastic	90–100	90–100
Water hoses—garden	Rubber and/or plastic	60–65	60–65
Soaker hoses	Rubber and/or plastic	60–70	60–70
Plastic fencing	Plastic	60–100	90–100

Table 4–9 EPA Comprehensive Procurement Guidelines for Site Construction Materials and Products *(Continued)*

Recycled-content Site Construction Product	Recycled/Recovered Material	Percent Post-consumer Recycled Content	Percent Total Recycled Content
Plastic landscaping timbers and posts	HDPE	25–100	75–100
	Mixed plastics/sawdust	50	100
	HDPE/fiberglass	75	95
Patio blocks	Plastic or rubber blends	90–100	90–100
	Plastic or plastic blends	—	90–100
Nonpressure pipe	Steel[a]	16	25–30
		67	100
	HDPE	100	100
	PVC	5–15	25–100
Modular threshold ramps	Steel[a]	16	25
		67	100
	Aluminum	—	10
	Rubber	100	100
Cement/concrete with coal fly ash	Fly ash	—	20–30[b] (blended cement)
			15 (replacement admixture)
Cement/concrete with ground granulated blast furnace slag	Slag	—	70[c] (replacement % of portland cement)
Cement/concrete with cenospheres	Cenospheres	—	10
Cement/concrete with silica fume	Silica fume	—	5–10
Flowable fill	Coal fly ash or ferrous foundry sands	—	varies
Reprocessed latex paint[d]	Latex paint: white, off-white, and pastel colors	20	20
	Latex paint: gray, brown, earth tones, and other dark colors	50–99	50–99
Consolidated latex paint	Latex paint	100	100

[a]The recommended recovered materials content levels for steel in this table reflect the fact that the designated item is generally made from steel manufactured in a basic oxygen furnace (BOF). Steel from the BOF process contains 25%–30% total recovered steel, of which 16% is post-consumer steel. Steel from the EAF process contains a total of 100% recovered steel, of which 67% is post-consumer.

[b]Replacement rates of coal fly ash for cement in the production of blended cement generally do not exceed 20%–30%, although coal fly ash blended cements may range from 0% to 40% coal fly ash by weight, according to ASTM C595, for cement Types IP and I(PM). Fifteen percent is a more accepted rate when coal fly ash is used as a partial cement replacement as an admixture in concrete.

[c]According to ASTM C595, GGBF slag may replace up to 70% of the portland cement in some concrete mixtures. Most GGBF slag concrete mixtures contain between 25% and 50% GGBF slag by weight. The EPA recommends that procuring agencies refer, at a minimum, to ASTM C595 for the GGBF slag content appropriate for the intended use of the cement and concrete.

[d]The EPA's recommendations apply to reprocessed latex paints used for interior and exterior architectural applications such as wallboard, ceilings, and trim; gutter boards; and concrete, stucco, masonry, wood, and metal surfaces, and to consolidated latex paints used for covering graffiti, where color and consistency of performance are not primary concerns.

Source: U.S. EPA CPG

vendors who sell or distribute designated products that is searchable by product, material, or location (U.S. EPA CPG).

LEED and Recycled Content

Use of recycled-content materials and products can directly contribute to two LEED-NC Version 2.2 credits: MR Credit 4.1: Recycled Content: 10% (post-consumer + $1/2$ pre-consumer) and MR Credit 4.2: Recycled Content: 20% (post-consumer + $1/2$ pre-consumer). The credits require that the sum of the post-consumer recycled content plus one-half of the pre-consumer content is at least 10% or 20% (based on cost) of the total value of materials in the project. The recycled-content value of the material assembly is determined by weight (U.S. Green Building Council

2005). The U.S. Green Building Council does not require that materials and products with recycled content be third-party certified; however, it does define recycled content in accordance with the International Organization of Standards document ISO 14021.

RESOURCES FOR LOCATING RECYCLED-CONTENT MATERIALS

There are an ever-increasing number of databases and resources for locating materials and products with recycled content. While the listings below include national and a few state sources, it is important to note that using locally or regionally produced recycled-content products is preferable to using a heavy or bulky recycled-content product that has been trucked across

Table 4–10 Resources for Locating Recycled-content Materials

U.S. EPA Comprehensive Procurement Guideline (CPG) program database http://www.epa.gov/cpg	Database of vendors who sell or distribute CPG-designated products. Searchable by product, material, or location.
GreenSpec® Directory http://www.buildinggreen.com	A subscription online and print directory of environmentally preferable product manufacturers. The directory lists over 2,100 listings from more than 1,500 companies organized by the expanded CSI MasterFormat 2004 structure. Online, the directory is searchable by green attribute (post- or pre-consumer recycled content, among others), CSI designation, LEED credit, or category.
MBDC, Cradle to Cradle Certification http://www.c2ccertified.com/	Introduced in 2005 by McDonough Braungart Design Chemistry (MBDC), Cradle to Cradle design protocol outlines environmentally intelligent design criteria, which are the basis for Cradle to Cradle product certifications.
Oikos Green Building Source http://oikos.com/	Library, gallery, and bookstore of green building products, which can be searched by category, topic, company, environmental benefit, and company type.
RecyclingMarkets.net http://www.recyclingmarkets.net/	RecyclingMarkets.net is a subscription directory of more than 17,000 companies involved in the recycling process throughout the United States and Canada.
CIWMB Recycled Content Product Directory http://www.ciwmb.ca.gov/RCP/search.asp	The RCP Directory lists thousands of products containing recycled materials as well as information about the manufacturers, distributors, and reprocessors of these products. Some products are certified under the state's State Agency Buy Recycled Campaign (SABRC).
King County Environmental Purchasing Program http://www.metrokc.gov/procure/green/	This site describes the tools and techniques developed by King County, Washington, agencies for purchasing recycled products.

the country. Many of these databases offer vendors by state; however, this does not mean that the product was manufactured in the region.

REFERENCES

Addis, B. 2006. *Building with Reclaimed Components and Materials: A Design Handbook for Reuse and Recycling*. London: Earthscan.

Amatruda, John. 2007. "Evaluating and Selecting Green Products." In *The Whole Building Design Guide*. Washington, D.C.: National Institute of Building Sciences.

Azapagic, A., A. Emsley, and I. Hamerton. 2003. *Polymers: The Environment and Sustainable Development*. New York: John Wiley & Sons.

Building Green. 2007. "Green Spec Product Directory." www.buildinggreen.com.

Building Materials Reuse Association (BMRA). 2006. http://www.buildingreuse.org/.

Build.Recycle.Net. http://build.recycle.net/.

California Integrated Waste Management Board (CIWMB). *Recycled Content Products Directory*. http://www.ciwmb.ca.gov/RCP/.

California Integrated Waste Management Board. www.ciwmb.ca.gov/Reuse/Links/Building.htm (accessed November 1, 2007).

Cochran, Kimberly. Environmental Engineer, US EPA Office of Solid Waste. Personal communication, October 24, 2007.

European Commission. 2003, December. "Chapter 4: Waste Management." In *Handbook for the Implementation of EU Environmental Legislation*. European Commission, Europa.

Guy, Brad and Nicholas Ciarimboli. 2007. *Design for Disassembly in the Built Environment: A Guide to Closed-loop Design and Building*. Prepared by the Hamer Center for Community Design at the Pennsylvania State University for City of Seattle, King County, Washington, and Resource Venture.

Guy, B., and S. Shell. n.d. "Design for Deconstruction and Materials Reuse." https://www.denix.osd.mil/denix/Public/Library/Sustain/BDC/Documents/design_for_decon.pdf.

Hammond, G., and C. Jones. 2006. "Inventory of Carbon and Energy." Version 1.5 Beta. Bath, UK: University of Bath, Department of Mechanical Engineering.

International Aluminum Institute (IAI). 2007. http://www.world-aluminium.org/Sustainability/Recycling/.

Kibert, C. J., J. Sendzimir, and B. Guy, eds. 2002. *Construction Ecology: Nature as the Basis for Green Building*. London: Routledge.

King County, Washington. "Solid Waste Division: Reduce, Reuse, Recycle." http://www.metrokc.gov/dnrp/swd/exchange/building.asp (accessed September, 30, 2007).

National Association of Home Builders (NAHB) Research Center. "Deconstruction: Building Disassembly and Material Salvage." www.nahbrc.org/.

Oikos. 1996–2007. "REDI Guide Resources for Environmental Design Index." www.oikos.com/redi/.

Recycler's World. 2007, November 12, 2007. www.recycle.net/exch/index.html.

Recycling Markets.Net. 2001–2007. "Your Online Recycleing Database." www.recyclingmarkets.net.

Sandler, Ken. 2003, November. "Analyzing What's Recyclable in C&D Debris." Biocycle:51–54.

Schwab, Jean. GreenScapes Program Manager, US EPA Office of Solid Waste. Personal communication, October 24, 2007.

Scientific Certification Systems (SCS). "Environmental Certification Program: Material Content." Standard SCS-EC11–2004.

Scotland Environmental Design Association (SEDA). 2005. *Design and Detailing for Deconstruction*. Prepared by C. Morgan and F. Stevenson for SEDA Design Guides for Scotland: No. 1.

Sustainable Sites Initiative (SSI). "Standards & Guidelines Preliminary Report." Prepared for The Lady Bird Johnson Wildflower Center, American Society of Landscape Architects (ASLA), and the United States Botanic Garden. November 1, 2007.

Thormark, C. "Environmental Analysis of a Building with Reused Building Materials." *International Journal of Low Energy & Sustainable Building*. 2000 In] "Buildings and Climate Change." United Nations Environmental Programme (UNEP), 2007.

U.S. Environmental Protection Agency (U.S. EPA). 1998. "Characterization of Building-related Construction and Demolition Debris in the United States." Report No. EPA530-R-98–010. Prepared by Franklin Associates for Office of Solid Waste, U.S. EPA.

U.S. Environmental Protection Agency (U.S. EPA). "Comprehensive Procurement Guidelines." http://www.epa.gov/cpg

U.S. Environmental Protection Agency (U.S. EPA). "Construction and Demolition (C&D) Materials." http://www.epa.gov/cdmaterials

U.S. Environmental Protection Agency (U.S. EPA), "Construction & Demolition (C&D) Materials: Deconstruction and Reuse." http://www.epa.gov/epaoswer/non-hw/debris-new/reuse.htm.

U.S. Environmental Protection Agency (EPA). n.d. "Glossary: Decision Maker's Guide to Solid Waste Management. Vol. II." http://www.epa.gov/epaoswer/non-hw/muncpl/dmg2/glossary.pdf.

U.S. Green Building Council (USGBC). 2005. *LEED-NC for New Construction Reference Guide*. Version 2.2. 1st ed. Washington, DC: USGBC.

chapter 5 |

Concrete

Concrete is the most commonly used construction material in the world, and after water is the second most consumed product on the planet. Each year worldwide the concrete industry uses 1.6 billion tons of cement, 10 billion tons of rock and sand, and 1 billion tons of water. Every ton of cement produced requires 1.5 tons of limestone and fossil fuel energy inputs (Mehta 2002). And its use is expected to double in the next 30 years (EcoSmart Concrete). Concrete's popularity is due to the many advantages the material offers. It can be durable and high strength with the proper mix of cementitious and pozzolanic materials, admixtures, aggregates, and water. A high reflectance value can be achieved to aid in heat island reduction. It is generally locally available. It can be used without finishes, and, with the right mix, is resistant to weathering. It can be made porous to aid in storm water infiltration and groundwater recharge. And recycled materials can be incorporated into the mix, reducing consumption of raw materials and disposal of waste products.

The huge popularity of concrete also carries environmental costs, the most harmful of which is the high energy consumption and CO_2 release during the production of portland cement. While the resources for aggregate and cement are considered abundant, they are limited in some areas, and more importantly, mining and extraction of the raw materials results in habitat destruction, and air and water pollution. Also, many concrete structures today are not constructed to be durable, causing overuse of resources resulting from their premature replacement (Mehta 1998).

Several measures can be taken to minimize the environmental and human health impacts of concrete—and some can result in improved performance and durability of the concrete as well. Perhaps the most important strategy is to minimize the use of portland cement by substituting industrial by-products (e.g., fly ash, ground granulated blast furnace slag, or silica fume) or other cementitious materials for a portion of the mix. Recycled materials substituted for both coarse and fine natural aggregates will minimize use of nonrenewable materials and the environmental impacts of their excavation. Porous concrete can contribute to the sustainable function of a site by allowing for storm water infiltration, and light-colored concrete can minimize a pavement's contribution to the urban heat island (UHI) effect.

Concrete is produced from a mix of coarse and fine aggregates, cement—usually portland—water, air, and often admixtures (Portland Cement Assocation [PCA]). While the percentages shown in Table 5–1 represent a typical ratio of ingredients, concrete mixes are increasingly tailored to individual installations, and use of admixtures—materials added to impart specific properties to a concrete mix—is increasing. Some admixtures can reduce the amount of cement or water required and allow for beneficial use of cement and virgin aggregate substitutes. These custom mix designs can result in more durable concrete structures, saving long-term costs, resource use, and environmental impacts of new concrete.

Environmental Impacts of Concrete Components

PORTLAND CEMENT

Portland cement is the key ingredient in concrete, binding the aggregates together in a hard mass. However, it is also the ingredient in concrete that produces the greatest environmental burden. In 2006, more than 2 billion tons of portland cement were consumed worldwide, with 131 million metric tons (MMT) consumed in the United States. This is a 16% increase over 2002. Ninety-nine MMT of cement were produced in the United States and 32 MMT were imported, primarily from Canada, Thailand, China, and Venezuela (U.S. Geological Survey 2007).

A 2007 EPA report titled *Energy Trends in Selected Manufacturing Sectors: Opportunities and Challenges for Environmentally Preferable Energy Outcomes* shows the cement industry to be ranked eighth among manufacturing sectors for energy use and emissions released. The cement industry has the highest energy intensity per dollar value of output of any manufacturing sector. The energy consumption per dollar value of shipments in KBtus is 56.2—over twice that of the second-ranked iron and steel sector, with 27.8 (U.S. EPA 2007b).

Table 5–1 Typical Constituents of Concrete

Constituent	Average Percentage
Portland cement	9.3
Fly ash	1.7
Coarse aggregate	41
Fine aggregate	26
Water	16
Air	6

Source: Adapted from PCA

Table 5–2 Key Environmental Aspects of Cement Production

Air Emissions	NO_x, SO_x, Dust/Particulates
Use of waste as fuel	Stakeholder concerns over release of dioxins, other chlorinated hydrocarbons, and heavy metals
Local nuisance	Noise, vibration, dust, visual impact
Greenhouse gases	CO_2
Land use and biodiversity	Primarily associated with quarrying activities

Source: Marlowe and Mansfield 2002

A report by the World Business Council for Sustainable Development (WBCSD) Cement Sustainability Initiative (CSI), titled "Toward a Sustainable Cement Industry," characterized the following key environmental aspects of cement production, presented in table 5–2 above.

One hundred fourteen plants produce cement in thirty-seven states at locations with adequate supplies of the raw materials for cement. Major raw materials for cement include limestone, cement rock/marl, shale, and clay. These materials contain calcium oxide, silicon dioxide, aluminum oxide, and iron oxide in varying contents. Because these contents vary, the mixture of raw materials differs among cement plants and locations. Typical proportions of raw materials for 1 kg of portland cement are shown in the table on the following page. The total weight of inputs is greater than the portland cement output, as a large percentage of the weight of limestone is released as CO_2 (Lippiatt 2007).

Manufacture of portland cement is a four-step process, as outlined by the Portland Cement Association (PCA) below (2006):

- Virgin raw materials, including limestone and small amounts of sand and clay, come from a quarry, usually located near the cement manufacturing plant.
- The materials are carefully analyzed, combined, and blended, and then ground for further processing.
- The materials are heated in a very large kiln, which reaches temperatures of 1,870°C (3,400°F). The heat

Table 5–3 Portland Cement Constituents

Constituent	Mass of Inputs (kg)	Mass Fraction
Limestone	1.17	72.2%
Cement rock/marl	0.21	12.8%
Clay	0.06	3.7%
Shale	0.05	3.2%
Sand	0.04	2.5%
Slag	0.02	1.2%
Iron/iron ore	0.01	0.9%
Fly ash	0.01	0.8%
Bottom ash	0.01	0.6%
Foundry sand	0.004	0.2%
Slate	0.001	0.1%

Source: Lippiatt 2007

causes the materials to turn into a new, marble-sized substance called clinker.

■ Red-hot clinker is cooled and ground with a small amount of gypsum. The end result is a fine, gray powder called portland cement. This cement is so fine that one pound of cement powder contains 150 billion grains.

Portland cement is manufactured with one of the following processes: wet process, long dry process, dry process with preheater, or dry process with precalciner. The wet process is the oldest and most energy consumptive. Newly constructed plants and some that are retrofitted use the more energy-efficient dry processes of preheater or precalciner.

In addition to CO_2 release and energy use, mining of limestone, the major raw material in cement, can cause habitat destruction, increased runoff, and pollutant releases to air and water. Some limestone mining operations are abandoning open pit mining techniques in favor of underground mining. This technique may reduce some habitat and pollution impacts yet may increase cost.

Energy Use in Cement Production

The production of cement is an energy-intensive process using primarily fossil fuel sources. Cement composes about 10% of a typical concrete mix but accounts for 92% of its energy demand. Cement production requires the pyroprocessing of large quantities of raw materials in large kilns at high and sustained temperatures to produce clinker. An average of almost 5 million Btus is used per ton of clinker. In 2004, the cement sector consumed 422 trillion Btus of energy, almost 2% of total energy consumption by U.S. manufacturing (PCA 2006).

Coal is the primary energy source for cement production, followed by petroleum coke and purchased electricity, a high percentage of which is produced from coal. Low-cost waste fuels are also used, with fifteen plants in 2002 burning waste oil and forty plants burning scrap tires, solvents, unrecyclable plastics, and other waste materials. While some of these materials produce high energy, there are concerns about uncaptured emissions from their combustion. For example, combustion of chlorine-containing by-products may form and release dioxin compounds (Humphreys and Mahasenan 2002). Table 5–4 illustrates the breakdown of fuel sources for the four cement manufacturing processes. It also provides a weighted average with total energy of 4,798 kJ to produce one kilogram of cement (Medgar, Nisbet, and Van Geem 2006). Energy intensity of cement production fell by 7% between 2001 and 2004 and is expected to further decrease with improvements in production energy efficiency (U.S. EPA 2007a). The U.S. EPA recently launched the Energy Performance Indicator (EPI) program to assist cement plants in increasing their energy efficiency and recognize the top 25% most energy-efficient plants (U.S. EPA 2006).

Air Emissions from Cement Production

Emissions from portland cement manufacturing include carbon dioxide (CO_2), particulate matter, carbon monoxide (CO), sulfur oxides (SO_x), nitrogen oxides (NO_x), total hydrocarbons, and hydrogen chloride (HCl). Emissions vary by type of cement, compressive strength, and blended constituents.

CO_2 emissions. Worldwide, the cement sector is responsible for about 5% of all man-made emissions of CO_2, the primary greenhouse gas that drives global climate change (Humphreys and Mahasenan 2002). CO_2 emissions in the cement sector result from two causes:

Table 5–4 Energy Requirements for Portland Cement Manufacturing by Process Type

Energy source	Wet	Long Dry	Preheater	Precalciner	Average
	GJ/metric ton of cement				
Coal	3.165	2.780	3.064	2.658	**2.823**
Gasoline	0.0121	0.0017	0.0037	0.0034	**0.0046**
Liquefied petroleum gas	0	0.0011	0.0001	0.0004	**0.0004**
Middle distillates	0.0277	0.0258	0.0311	0.0526	**0.0412**
Natural gas	0.0786	0.203	0.143	0.276	**0.212**
Petroleum coke	1.145	1.850	0.488	0.471	**0.783**
Residual oil	0.0008	0.0023	0	0.0026	**0.0018**
Wastes	1.476	0.187	0.087	0.240	**0.412**
Electricity	0.495	0.541	0.540	0.517	**0.520**
Total	**6.400**	**5.591**	**4.357**	**4.220**	**4.798**

Source: Medgar et al. 2006

the chemical conversion from the calcination of limestone and other carbonate-containing feedstocks, and carbon-based fuel consumption. CO_2 from the chemical conversion is the second largest industrial (nonfuel-related) source of CO_2 in the United States, totaling 45.9 MMT in 2005 (U.S. EPA 2007a). Nearly 50 MMT were released the same year from fuel combustion for electricity and power to manufacturing equipment to produce cement (U.S. EPA 2007b). So the total CO_2 is slightly less than 1 ton of CO_2 released for each of the 99 million tons of cement produced in 2005.

The nonfuel release of CO_2 accounts for about 29% of nonfuel-related CO_2 emissions from manufacturing, second only to the iron and steel industry, which accounts for about 37% (U.S. EPA 2006a). It is currently impossible to convert limestone ($CaCO_3$) to calcium oxide (CaO) and then clinker without generating CO_2. This CO_2 is emitted to the atmosphere; however, research is under way on methods to sequester a portion of it (Humphreys and Mahasenan 2002).

A summary of the status of the worldwide cement industry on the issue of climate protection is shown in Table 5–5. It was generated by the WBCSD's Cement Sustainability Initiative (CSI) in a 2002 report. The report links climate protection measures of reduced energy use and CO_2 release to manufacturing cost savings.

Some methods that cement producers use to reduce CO_2 emissions are as follows:

- Use of the dry process, which uses as little as 830 kWh/ton of clinker to produce. The less efficient wet process uses 1,400–1,700 kWh/ton of clinker (Humphreys and Mahasenan 2002). In the United States, new plants use the dry process and some older plants have converted from wet to dry.
- Increasing use of blended cements that include materials such as fly ash or slag which do not need processing in the cement kiln.
- Use of alternative fuels and fuel-efficient processes.

Emissions of Criteria Air Pollutants (CAPs) Cement manufacturing releases three criteria air pollutants: particulate matter (PM), nitrogen oxides (NO_X), and sulfur dioxide (SO_2).

Sources of particulate matter (PM) are quarrying and crushing, raw material storage, grinding and blending (dry process only), clinker production, finish grinding, and packaging and loading. The largest emissions occur in the pyroprocessing systems. Some dust from the kiln, if the alkali content is not too high, is captured and recycled back into the kiln for clinker (U.S. EPA 1995).

Estimates of fugitive dust emissions released from Western European cement plants average about

Table 5–5 Cement Industry Status on the Issue of Climate Protection

Strengths	Opportunities
Some companies have demonstrated reduced average CO_2 released per ton of product. A standardized CO_2 inventory protocol has been developed by ten major cement companies, together with external stakeholders.	Energy efficiency improvement Use of alternative raw materials (e.g., fly ash and blast furnace slag) Use of alternative, low-carbon fuels Emission reduction credits CO_2 capture and sequestration or possible resale Trading schemes to reduce costs
Weaknesses	**Threats**
Heavy dependence on fossil energy Reliance on limestone-based cement Limited attention to the significant CO_2 reductions required Inadequate investment in R&D that would enable future cost-effective CO_2 reductions Intermittent engagement in climate policy activities without a clear long-term agenda	Large financial burdens Possibility of imposed technological controls Early retirement of plants and equipment Potential for the cement industry to be overlooked in the policy debate and disadvantaged by policies designed for larger polluters Loss of market share to competing materials that are less GHG intensive

Source: Humphreys and Mahasenan 2002

$50 mg/m^3$ (Humphreys and Mahasenan 2002). Near ground fugitive emissions will impact the local environment and air quality, and dust emissions from high stacks may travel over a very broad area, affecting air quality in entire regions. Fine particles of PM2.5 (particulate matter with a diameter less than or equal to 2.5 micronmeters) are the greatest cause for concern as they have the greatest negative impact on human health. They are difficult for the body to remove from the lungs and can lead to asthma and other respiratory problems. The EPA National Emissions Inventory (NEI) estimates that in 2002, the U.S. cement industry released 31,000 tons of PM10 and 13,000 tons of PM2.5 (U.S. EPA 2006a).

Nitrogen oxides (NO_x) are generated during fuel combustion, and as flame temperature increases, the amount of NO_x generated increases. Nitrogen oxides negatively affect air quality and contribute to the formation of ground-level ozone, leading to the urban heat island effect, reduced air quality, and human health impacts. Fuel type used to heat kilns will influence their temperature and subsequent NO_x release. Use of coal generates less NO_x than oil or natural gas, although combustion of coal releases more CO_2 and particulates. The NEI estimates that in 2002, the U.S. cement industry released 214,000 tons of NO_x. The cement sector accounts for 1% of all nonagricultural NO_x emissions. Through the use of various controls, the normalized quantity of NO_x emissions fell by 6% between 1996 and 2002 (U.S. EPA 2006a).

Sulfur dioxide (SO_2) emissions are generated from sulfur compounds in the raw materials and from fuel used in processing. The amount of sulfur varies by plant type and geographic location. The alkaline nature of the raw materials does some "self-scrubbing" by absorbing between 70% and 95% of SO_2. The NEI estimates that in 2002, the U.S. cement industry released 177,000 tons of NO_x, when normalized, down 9% from 1996 (U.S. EPA 2006a). SO_2 emissions contribute to reduced air quality, smog, acid rain, and aggravated respiratory problems (Humphreys and Mahasenan 2002).

Total emissions to air for one metric ton of cement production are shown in Table 5–6. These figures are from the PCA's 2006 Life-cycle Inventory of

Table 5–6 Total Emissions to Air from Cement Manufacture by Process Type

Emissions	Wet	Long Dry	Preheater	Precalciner	Average
	kg/Metric Ton of Cement				
Particulate matter, total	2.62	2.46	2.07	2.32	**2.35**
Particulate matter, PM10	0.324	0.288	0.266	0.299	**0.296**
Particulate matter, PM2.5	0.000099	0.000091	0.0000843	0.0000907	**0.0000911**
CO_2	1,100	1,010	852	874	**927**
SO_2	3.88	4.80	0.272	0.541	**1.66**
NO_x	3.58	2.94	2.35	2.10	**2.50**
VOC	0.0662	0.0186	0.013	0.0648	**0.0502**
CO	0.125	0.146	0.521	1.84	**1.10**
CH_4	0.0562	0.0111	0.00430	0.0525	**0.0395**
NH_3	0.00472	0.00479	0.00475	0.00476	**0.00476**
HCl	0.043	0.055	0.13	0.065	**0.070**
Hg	0.0000551	0.0000834	0.0000269	0.0000694	**0.0000624**
Dioxins and furans, TEQ	0.0000000950	0.000000550	0.00000000355	0.000000100	**0.000000149**

Source: Medgar et al. 2006

Portland Cement Production. Quantities are in kilograms/metric ton.

Emissions of Hazardous Air Pollutants (HAPs) The cement industry uses or produces a variety of chemicals in cement production and reports on their release through the EPA's Toxics Release Inventory (TRI). Emissions of HAPs also occur from fuel combustion. If fuel does not completely combust, carbon monoxide (CO) and VOCs are released. Emissions of metal compounds result from portland cement kilns.

In 2003, cement production facilities reported 450 million pounds of chemicals released, disposed of, or managed through treatment, energy recovery, or recycling. Three percent of this was disposed of or released to the environment, with 22% to land and 78% to air or water. Normalized releases increased 196% between 1994 and 2003. Releases in 2003 were primarily hydrochloric and sulfuric acids (51%); ammonia, manganese, and zinc (24%); and ethylene, benzene, and lead (14%; U.S. EPA 2006a).

When weighted for toxicity, the cement sector's normalized air and water releases increased by 218% from 1994 to 2003. Ninety-nine percent of toxicity weighted releases were sulfuric acid, manganese, lead, chromium, and hydrochloric acid (U.S. EPA 2006a).

Waste from Cement Production

The major waste material from cement manufacturing is cement kiln dust (CKD). An industry average of 38.6 kg of CKD is generated per metric ton of cement. Seventy-nine percent of this is landfilled and 21% is recycled (Medgar et al. 2006).

Water Use and Discharge in Cement Production

Water is used in cement production to suppress dust, to condition or cool kiln exhaust gases, to finish mills, and for noncontact cooling. About one ton of water is discharged in the production of one ton of cement. Effluents result from quarry dewatering, storm water runoff of facilities, CKD pile runoff, and landfill wells. Discharged water contains suspended solids, aluminum,

Table 5–7 Water Discharge from Cement Manufacture

Water Use, kg/Metric Ton of Cement	Average
Quarry dewatering	610
Storm runoff	304
CKD landfill well	1
CKD pile runoff	11
Other	80
Total	**1,007***

*Data do not add to total shown because of independent rounding.
Source: Medgar et al. 2006

phenolics, oil and grease, nitrates, dissolved organic compounds, chlorides, sulfates, ammonia, zinc, and pH (Medgar et al. 2006). The table above illustrates typical water discharge from one metric ton of cement production.

AGGREGATES

Mining and Processing

Coarse and fine aggregates in concrete make up between 60% and 75% of the concrete volume. Aggregates are either mined or manufactured. Some are by-products of industrial processes or post-consumer waste products. Natural fine aggregates are usually quarried natural sand and coarse aggregates are either quarried or manufactured from crushed stone. Sand and gravel are typically dug or dredged from a pit, river, or lake bottom. They usually require minimal processing. Crushed rock, a manufactured aggregate, is produced by crushing and screening quarry rock or larger-size gravel (Lippiatt 2007).

The primary impacts of aggregate extraction and processing are habitat alteration and fugitive dust. It is difficult to capture dust in operations of mining and blasting, quarry roads, loading and unloading, crushing, screening, and storage piles. Primary impacts of crushed rock, aside from mining impacts, stem from fugitive dust released during crushing and screening operations. Processing of aggregates, particularly the commonly used silica sand, releases particulates into the air that can cause eye and respiratory tract irritations in humans.

Mining, dredging, and extraction of sand and gravel alter plant and animal habitats and contribute to soil erosion and air and water pollution. Mining for sand and gravel near or in water bodies causes sedimentation and pollution in water and disrupts aquatic habitats. The operation of mining equipment consumes energy and releases emissions from internal combustion engines. Impacts from mining and quarrying aggregates are discussed in greater detail in the stone and aggregates chapter.

Energy to produce coarse and fine aggregates from crushed rock is estimated by the PCA's Life Cycle Inventory to be 35,440 kJ/metric ton. The energy to produce coarse and fine aggregate from uncrushed aggregate is 23,190 kJ/metric ton (Medgar, Nisbet, and

Greening the Cement Industry Worldwide

The Cement Sustainability Initiative (CSI) is a serious international effort by leading cement companies to reduce environmental and human health impacts of cement production while "increasing the business case for the pursuit of sustainable development" (WBCSD). The group of eighteen cement producers, accounting for 40% of global cement production, is organized under the World Business Council for Sustainable Development. The stated purpose of the initiative is to explore what sustainable development means for the cement industry and identify actions and facilitate steps companies can take, individually and as a group, to accelerate progress toward sustainable development (WBCSD).

To that end, the CSI developed a detailed "Agenda for Action" in 2002 and published a series of subsector reports examining the following issues they have identified as "critical": energy use and CO_2 management, responsible use of fuels and materials, employee health and safety, emissions reduction, impacts on land and local communities, and communications. They have prepared guidelines, protocols, and benchmarks for addressing these issues for distribution to industry stakeholders and policy makers (WBCSD).

Van Geem 2007). Energy sources are split evenly between diesel oil and electricity.

Fuel consumption and environmental impacts of fuel combustion for transportation of aggregates can be significant, as they are heavy and bulky materials. Using local or on-site materials for aggregate can minimize fuel use, resource consumption, and emissions.

CONCRETE PRODUCTION

About 75% of U.S. concrete is produced at ready mix plants. Raw materials are delivered to the plants by rail, barge, or truck. Fugitive particulate matter, primarily consisting of cement and pozzolan dust with some aggregate dust, is the primary environmental and human health concern at ready mix plants. Most sources of dust, with the exception of transfer of material to silos, are not easily contained and some dusts contain heavy metal particulates.

Water consumption and pollution are often overlooked impacts of concrete and cement production. Water requirements of concrete are quite large, with over 1 billion gallons used each year worldwide. Water consumption at ready mix plants is affected by the type of plant, the location of the plant, and the size of the plant. Average water consumption, not including batch water which is around 16% of volume of the mix, is 65 L/m^3 of concrete. Average water disposed of is 35 L/m^3 (Medgar et al. 2007).

Water pollution is a concern during all phases of concrete's life cycle; however, impacts are greatest at the concrete production phase. Water used to wash out equipment (including trucks) is high in pH and is toxic to fish and other aquatic life. At batch plants, wash water is often discharged into settling ponds for solids to settle out. Some local regulations require plants to treat the wash water before release. Other plants have developed closed-loop systems where both water and solids from the ponds are reused.

Minimal solid waste is created at ready mix plants as returned, unused concrete is recycled. Methods of recycling include curing and then crushing for use as fill or base aggregate, using hydration control or set-retarding agents to delay curing for reuse on another site, pouring unused material into precast forms, or reclaiming and reusing the slurry (Medgar et al. 2007).

Energy use and emissions of ready mix concrete vary widely by cement type and use of pozzolanic constituents such as fly ash, silica fume or slag. Mixes with lower cement content and higher percentages of other pozzolanic constituents have lower embodied energy and lower emissions. A Life-cycle Inventory by the Portland Cement Association of three different ready mixes supports this idea. One mix studied was a standard 28-day compressive strength, 3,000 psi ready mix with 100% portland cement. The second mix replaced 25% of the cement with fly ash, and the third replaced 50% of the portland cement with slag cement. Key findings are (Medgar et al. 2007):

- Embodied energy for the standard PCC mix is highest at 1.13 GJ/m^3 of concrete and is lowest for the 50% slag cement mix at 0.73 GJ/m^3.
- CO_2 emissions are highest for mix 1 at 211 kg/m^3 and lowest for mix 3 at 112 kg/m^3. CO_2 reductions are even more substantial for mixes 2 and 3 because of the additional savings of CO_2 release from calcination of limestone, which accounts for an average of 60% of CO_2 emissions from the production of cement.
- Particulate emissions from cement production account for 70% of the total and aggregate production for 30% of total particulate emissions for concrete. The use of fly ash and slag lowers total particulate emissions.

The material and energy inputs and GWP figures for a portland cement concrete roadway mix shown in Table 5–8 were assembled for a 2006 study by the Athena Institute. The study compared typical Canadian portland cement pavements and asphalt pavements. A summary of the study's findings is discussed in chapter 8. Figures shown in the table are for one cubic meter of 30–40 MPa portland cement based road concrete are shown by life-cycle phase. The mix includes 13% Fly Ash and 18% blast furnace slag substituted for portland cement—the weighted average for Canada.

TRANSPORTATION

Transportation of materials throughout the life cycle of concrete varies. Portland cement is manufactured in twenty-eight states, so transport distances are usually not extensive. Admixtures, slag, fly ash, and silica fume

Table 5–8 Material and Energy Inputs and Greenhouse Emissions per m³ of Portland Cement Based Road Concrete (Canada, Weighted Average)

	Cement Manufacture		Raw Materials Extraction and Processing		Raw Materials Transportation		Concrete Plant Processing		Total	
	input	output	input	output	input	output	input	output	input	output
Materials (t/m³)										
Cement	0.26686						0.26686			
Slag				0.04814			0.04814			
Fly ash							0.03500			
Coarse aggregate				1.10000			1.10000			
Fine aggregate				0.70000			0.70000			
Water							0.15000			
Concrete								2.30000		2.30000
GHG emissions (kg/m³ of concrete)										
CO_2	242.35			7.32		6.30		17.77		273.75
CH_4	0.0284			0.0090		0.0027		0.0224		0.0626
N_2O	0.00012			0.00002		0.0000007		0.000009		.0001567
Embodied primary energy (GJ/m³ of concrete)										
Embodied primary energy	1.3961		0.1002		0.0998		0.2619		1.8580	

Source: Athena Institute 2006

Table 5–9 Athena LCA of Concrete and CMU Walls

	Primary Energy Consumption (MJ)	Solid Waste (kg)	Air Pollution Index	Water Pollution Index	Global Warming Potential (kg)	Weighted Resource Use (kg)
Cast in place, 20 MPa, 25% fly ash	839	37	13	0	75	800
Cast in place, 20 MPa, 35% fly ash	788	37	12	0	67	789
Cast in place, 20 MPa, average fly ash	891	38	14	0	83	813
Concrete masonry blocks	737	30	11	0	60	98

Assumptions:

All figures based on 1 m²

All exterior wall types, with no opening area or windows

Poured in place concrete wall with reinforcing

Concrete thickness: 300 mm

Average fly ash is figured at 9%

Concrete block wall with every third core grouted and reinforced

Source: Athena Institute 2006

made in the last decade to lessen the waste burden through reuse of concrete debris. Concrete is estimated to account for 67% by weight of construction and demolition waste—the largest single component (U.S. EPA 1998). With rising landfill tipping fees, concrete waste is increasingly recycled into road base or clean fill. It is used to a much lesser extent for aggregate in new concrete. Broken slabs of concrete are used for low "dry stack" walls, either with or without mortar, and for paving "stones" in new pavements.

CONCRETE MASONRY UNITS AND PRECAST CONCRETE PRODUCTION

Concrete masonry units and precast concrete units are manufactured by placing no-slump concrete into molds, then removing and curing it in 24-hour cycles. Accelerated curing temperatures range from ambient to 90°C (190°F). The typical mix contains a higher percentage of

may have longer transport distances, but their quantities in the mix are limited. Because aggregates are so heavy, they are usually obtained within 100 miles of a ready mix plant, often even closer. Obtaining local aggregates will likely have the largest impact on reducing transport energy use and related emissions.

PLACEMENT AND USE

During mixing and placement, cement dust can have negative impacts on human health. In powder form or while wet, it is highly alkaline and can burn lungs, skin, and eyes. Gloves, masks, and protective eyewear should be used when working with cement.

END OF LIFE

Concrete waste from construction and demolition is an environmental concern, but great strides have been

Table 5–10 Mix Description and Summary PCA LCI results for CMU and Precast Concrete

Concrete Mix Description	CMU Mix, 100 CMUs Using 1 m³ Concrete	Precast Concrete, (70 MPa/ 10,000 psi), 1 m³
Cement	8.7%	18.8%
Silica fume	—	2.4%
Water	5.9%	5.7%
Coarse aggregate	25.9%	47.0%
Fine aggregate	59.3%	25.8%
LCI Data	**CMU Mix**	**Precast Concrete**
Embodied energy	1.32 GJ	3.79 GJ
CO_2 emissions	205.7 kg	573 kg
Particulate matter emissions	0.848 kg	1.92 kg
Total air emissions	316.4 kg	878.5 kg
Emissions to water	0.255 kg	0.715 kg
Emissions to land	57.25 kg	93.2 kg

Source: Adapted from Medgar et al. 2007

portland cement than ready mix concrete because the mix needs to cure quickly enough that molds can be removed and blocks cured within a 24-hour cycle. One cubic meter of concrete results in 131 8" × 8" × 16" CMU blocks and one cubic yard of concrete results in 100 blocks.

Table 5–10 illustrates typical mix proportions; embodied energy and emissions to air, land, and water from production of 100 CMUs (20-MPa/3,000 psi); and a cubic meter of precast concrete units (70-MPa/10,000 psi). Energy use and emissions are higher for the precast concrete because the mix uses over twice the cement of the CMU mix.

Use Concrete Efficiently

BUILD DURABLE STRUCTURES

Some sources claim that many exposed exterior concrete structures and pavements are not built to last their 30–40 year design life and are, on average, only in place for half that time (Mehta 1998). Premature failure can result in a great deal of resource use for structures that must be replaced before the end of their design life. The reduced durability may be the result of a variety of factors, including improper mix design, improper placement or curing, or overuse of deicing chemicals (Mehta 1998). Mixes tailored to specific installations; use of pozzolanic or cementitious industrial by-products such as fly ash, silica fume, or ground granulated blast furnace slag; or use of high-performance concrete can extend the life of concrete structures.

The development and increasing use of high-performance concrete (HPC) mixes can reduce the amount of energy-intensive cement, water, and/or aggregate used in concrete and result in a stronger, more durable structure. HPC is concrete that has a low water/cement (W/C) or water/binder (W/B) ratio, often made possible through the use of superplasticizers. It results in concrete of higher compressive strength (6,000 to 7,200 psi as opposed to the typical concrete mix's 2,200 to 3,600 psi). It is considered to be economical as structures can be smaller or thinner, use less concrete and reinforcing steel, and require less formwork. High-performance concrete has a low porosity, which makes it more resistant to freezing and thawing, sulfate and chloride-ion penetration, and other chemical attack. The life cycle of high-performance concrete has been estimated to be two to three times longer than that of usual concrete, and it can be recycled two to three times before it is transformed into road base aggregate (Aïtcin 2000).

DON'T OVERSIZE STRUCTURES (BUILD SMALL)

Designing smaller structures and thinner concrete sections can reduce the total amount of materials and resources used to make concrete. However, thinner sections of walls and paving may require increases in the amount and size of reinforcing needed, potentially negating any resource savings.

In cold climates, use of modular unit retaining wall systems set on a sand base can eliminate the need for extensive concrete footings for a cantilever retaining wall extending below the frostline. Use of pier foundation systems may use less concrete than spread footing foundation systems, and they are often formed with recycled cardboard sonotubes rather than the typical plywood formwork.

Minimize Environmental Impacts of Portland Cement

As a good portion of the environmental impacts of concrete stem from the production of portland cement, reducing the quantity used may be the most important step toward "greener" concrete. Strategies for minimizing the environmental impacts of cement are twofold: reduce use of cement in a concrete mix, and substitute appropriate alternatives, such as pozzolanic industrial by-products, for a portion of the cement in a concrete mix or in premixed blended cements.

USE LESS CEMENT IN A CONCRETE MIX

Less cement can be used by specifying a 56-day full-strength requirement instead of the traditional 28-day full-strength requirement. Research has shown that this results in a more durable structure (Aïtcin 2000). It also allows use of higher volumes of fly ash and other industrial by-product admixtures that slow curing of concrete. Cement and water can also be reduced with the use of high-performance concrete (Aïtcin 2000).

USE CEMENT SUBSTITUTES

Reductions in cement use in a concrete mix are most easily achieved through the substitution of other pozzolanic or hydraulic materials for portland cement. In 2000, the Portland Cement Association estimated that supplementary cementitious materials (SCMs) partially replaced or supplemented portland cement in 60% of modern concrete mixtures. This percentage is likely higher today as use of SCMs has gained greater acceptance in the market.

The most common SCMs are industrial by-products used individually or in some combination in a concrete mix. These include fly ash (both Class C and Class F), ground granulated blast furnace slag (GGBFS), and silica fume. Other SCMs are natural pozzolans such as calcined clay, calcined shale, and metakaolin. While substitution amounts vary by design requirements and substituting materials, it is estimated that a 30% reduction of portland cement use in mixes worldwide could reverse the rise in CO_2 emissions (Mehta 1998). Replacing 50% of cement with ground-granulated blast furnace slag (GGBFS) in a typical ready mix is estimated to save 34% of embodied energy (560,000 btu) and 46% of embodied CO_2 emissions (248 lb) per cubic yard of concrete (SCA 2006).

Other benefits of substituting some portion of SCMs for portland cement are reduced air emissions of concrete mixes, the reuse of industrial waste products, and improved performance of concrete.

SCMs' basic chemical components—silica, alumina, calcium, and iron—are similar to those of portland cement and work in two sometimes combined ways (Federal Highway Administration [FHWA] 2006). *Hydraulic* SCMs such as GGBF slags and some Class C fly ashes set and harden like portland cement when mixed with water. *Pozzolanic* materials, such as Class F fly ash or silica fume, require a source of calcium hydroxide, which is usually supplied by portland cement in the mix to react.

Pozzolans can produce stronger and more durable concrete in the end; however, they take longer to gain strength than concrete with portland cement. ASTM standard C618 defines a pozzolan as "a siliceous or siliceous and aluminous material, which in itself possesses little or no cementitious value but which will, in finely divided form and in the presence of moisture, chemically react with calcium hydroxide at ordinary temperatures to form compounds possessing cementitious properties" (ASTM 2005b). In addition to industrial by-products, other pozzolans are mined (e.g., diatomaceous earth or volcanic tuffs) and manufactured (e.g., metakaolin from calcined clay). ASTM C618 defines these pozzolans as Class N (see Tables 5–12 and 5–13).

Fly ash and ground granulated blast furnace slag are sometimes blended with cement during the cement manufacturing process, resulting in reduced CO_2 emissions, a reduction in energy consumption, and increased production capacity. Blended cements are discussed following this section on cement substitutes added during concrete mixing.

Fly Ash

Fly ash can be both a pozzolanic and a cementitious material. Its abundance and performance makes it the most commonly used industrial by-product substitute for portland cement, with use in about 50% of all ready mix concrete. Fly ash is a by-product from the combustion of coal, primarily from coal-fired power plants. It is the microscopic glass beads of ash that rise to the top of smokestacks and are captured with pollution control equipment. Fly ash contains high amounts of reactive silica and small amounts of iron, alumina, calcium,

Table 5–11 Standards for Supplementary Cementing Materials (SCMs)

Type of SCM	Specifications
Ground granulated blast furnace slag	ASTM C989/AASHTO M 302
Fly ash and natural pozzolans	ASTM C1240
Silica fume	ASTM C1240
Highly reactive pozzolans	AASHTO M 321
General Standards	ACI 318

Source: FHWA 2006

magnesium, sulfur, potassium, and sodium. With a specific gravity of 1.9 to 2.8, it is less dense than cement's specific gravity of 3.15. Particle sizes range from less than 1 m to more than 100 m, with 35 m the typical size. The color is either tan or gray (FHWA 2006).

ASTM C618 classifies two types of fly ash for use in concrete (2005b):

- **Class C fly ash,** produced by burning lignite or subbituminous coal, primarily in western states, is characterized by a calcium oxide (CaO) content between 8% and 30% (FHWA 2004). It is also sometimes defined by the sum of oxides of silica, alumina, and iron. The higher calcium content makes this type of fly ash a cementitious pozzolan that requires only water to hydrate and harden (King 2005). Class C fly ash is generally used in amounts of 15%–40% by mass of cementing material. Some Class C fly ashes can completely replace portland cement in a conventional mix. Laboratory experiments have shown that it offers excellent performance in short-term strength gain, long-term strength, and workability (Cross, Stephens, and Vollmer 2005); however, there has been limited application in the field.
- **Class F fly ash** results from burning anthracite and bituminous coal, and is the most abundant type of fly ash available worldwide (King 2005). Containing a relatively low amount of calcium, it is considered a normal pozzolan requiring cement hydration products to react with for hardening. Class F fly ash is generally used in amounts of 15%–25% by mass of cementing material.

Use of 15%–20% of fly ash in concrete is currently standard practice with many ready mix companies and is even mandated by some governmental agencies. However, several years of field and laboratory studies indicate that fly ash can be substituted for much higher percentages of cement, producing a higher quality concrete. High fly ash concrete (HFAC), also called high-volume fly ash (HVFA), is concrete where fly ash is used to replace 40% or more of the portland cement (Meyer 2005).

Effects of Fly Ash on Concrete

Fly ash substituted for cement can have a variety of effects on concrete in placement, finishing, and use. Fly ash affects fresh concrete like a superplasticizer with reduced water demand, reduced bleed water, increased workability, and continuing slump.

Increased workability. Fly ash reduces water demand and increases workability of fresh concrete because the small particles of fly ash pack voids between larger cement particles; their spherical shape acts like ball bearings; and they have an electrostatic effect on the cement particles, reducing clumping. These attributes make fly ash concrete easier to pump, work, consolidate, and place in complex forms (FHWA 2004).

Lower water demand results in less bleed water; however, it may be more difficult to know when the concrete is ready for finishing. In addition, fly ash concrete should be protected from premature drying, particularly paving with its high surface area, with limited exposure to sun, wind, and dry air. Protective measures might include covering the surface with plastic, spraying on a curing compound (look for low-VOC, natural, or nontoxic compounds), or pouring and finishing at night (King 2005).

Longer set times, but enhanced long-term strength. Use of fly ash will extend set and curing times of concrete. Fly ash delays both initial and final set times of concrete because there is less cement to hydrate quickly and the pozzolanic reaction takes longer, although this phenomenon is less pronounced with Class C fly ashes. Slower set times can be advantageous as there is more time to work and finish the concrete; however, in other instances, this may slow the removal of formwork. For final set, it may mean that the concrete won't meet 28-day strength requirements for a longer period. However, the concrete will continue to gain strength as the pozzolanic reaction continues, and can ultimately result in a higher compressive strength and far stronger concrete. Where possible, full-strength requirements should be changed from 28 to 56 days. Some sources say this will save a bag or more of cement per cubic yard (King 2005).

Where a concrete structure does need to gain strength more quickly (e.g., for retaining walls that need to be backfilled, or curbs with a slip form), initial strength gain can be achieved with accelerating admixtures, high early strength cement (type III), a high-grade pozzolan (e.g., silica fume), and/or water content reduction (King 2005).

Reduced thermal stress and cracking. Because fly ash concrete reduces the need for water in a mix to attain workability, there is less drying shrinkage and cracking from restraints such as rebar, welded-wire mesh, or formwork. The reduced cement and slower set times of HFAC will reduce the heat of hydration and the associated thermal shrinkage cracking from differential temperatures between the core and surface of a pour.

Reduced permeability. Reduced cracking, smaller particles, more tightly filled voids, and reduced clumping of fly ash concrete all contribute to a reduction in permeability. This results in concrete that is more durable and

more resistant to rebar corrosion and chemical attack than conventional concrete (FHWA 2006). Concrete with class F fly ash is also more resistant to sulfate attack and alkali silica reaction.

Vulnerability to deicing salts. There is some concern that concrete with fly ash will not hold up well to deicing salts, therefore ACI 318 and some building codes limit fly ash content to 25% for structures exposed to deicing chemicals. Early laboratory tests showed scaling from deicing salts to be a problem; however, field tests of fly ash concrete sidewalks repeatedly exposed to deicing salts and freeze-thaw cycles have not had problems. Some tests reveal that the use of curing compounds may help prevent problems, but testing continues (FHWA 2006).

Table 5–12 Effects of SCMs on Fresh Concrete Properties

| | Fly Ash | | GGBF Slag | Silica Fume | Natural Pozzolans | | |
	Class F	Class C			Calcined Shale	Calcined Clay	Metakaolin
Water requirements	Significantly reduced	Significantly reduced	Reduced	Significantly increased	No significant change	No significant change	Increased
Workability	Increased	Increased	Increased	Significantly reduced	Increased	Increased	Reduced
Bleeding and segregation	Reduced	Reduced	Effect varies	Significantly reduced	No significant change	No significant change	Reduced
Air content	Significantly reduced	Reduced	Reduced	Significantly reduced	No significant change	No significant change	Reduced
Heat of hydration	Reduced	Effect varies	Reduced	No significant change	Reduced	Reduced	Reduced
Setting time	Increased	Effect varies	Increased	No significant change	Increased	Increased	No significant change
Finishability	Increased	Increased	Increased	Effect varies	Increased	Increased	Increased
Pumpability	Increased	Increased	Increased	Increased	Increased	Increased	Increased
Plastic shrinkage and cracking	No significant change	No significant change	No significant change	Increased	No significant change	No significant change	No significant change

Source: FHWA 2006

Widely varying chemical composition. Class C and Class F fly ash vary among sources in carbon content, color, weatherability, and potential strength and rate of strength gain of the finished concrete. Mixes should be designed specifically for the type and characteristics of fly ash available, and supply sources should remain consistent across a project.

The color of the concrete resulting from use of fly ash varies by type. Class C fly ash will generally result in a buff-colored concrete, while Class F is shades of gray, from lighter than portland cement to medium gray.

It should be noted that some fly ashes will contain ash from other products sometimes burned with coal. This may reduce the effectiveness of the fly ash for use in concrete. Beneficiation techniques to amend and improve ash from cogenerated burning are being studied (King 2005). Properties, characteristics, and content of

fly ash should be well understood as the concrete mix is determined.

While fly ash is an abundant material, it can be in short supply in some localities as it is easier for some coal plants to landfill rather than transport it by rail to the concrete market. By some estimates, only about 16% of available fly ash is used in concrete for this reason (PATH).

Ground Granulated Blast Furnace Slag

Ground granulated blast furnace slag (GGBFS, or "slag") is the most like cement of all the mineral admixtures and least like a pozzolan (PATH). ASTM C125 Definition of Terms Relating to Concrete (2006) defines slag as "the non-metallic product consisting essentially of silicates and alumina, silicates of calcium and other bases that is developed in a molten condition simultaneously with iron in a blast furnace." GGBFS is slag that is

Table 5–13 Effects of SCMs on Hardened Concrete Properties

| | Fly Ash | | | | Natural Pozzolans | | |
	Class F	Class C	GGBF Slag	Silica Fume	Calcined Shale	Calcined Clay	Metakaolin
Early strength	Reduced	No significant change	Reduced	Significantly increased	Reduced	Reduced	Significantly increased
Long-term strength	Increased	Increased	Increased	Significantly increased	Increased	Increased	Significantly increased
Permeability	Reduced	Reduced	Reduced	Significantly reduced	Reduced	Reduced	Significantly reduced
Chloride ingress	Reduced	Reduced	Reduced	Significantly reduced	Reduced	Reduced	Significantly reduced
ASR	Significantly reduced	Effect varies	Significantly reduced	Reduced	Reduced	Reduced	Reduced
Sulfate resistance	Significantly increased	Effect varies	Significantly increased	Increased	Increased	Increased	Increased
Freezing and thawing	No significant change	No significant change	No significant change	No significant change	No significant change	No significant change	No significant change
Abrasion resistance	No significant change	No significant change	No significant change	No significant change	No significant change	No significant change	No significant change
Drying shrinkage	No significant change	No significant change	No significant change	No significant change	No significant change	No significant change	No significant change

Source: FHWA 2006

cooled quickly with a high water volume, forming glassy granules. These granules are then ground and processed for use in concrete or in premixed bags with cement. GGBFS is highly valued as a cement supplement and substitute, and can replace as much as 70%–80% of cement in some concrete mixes (U.S. EPA 2006b).

Use of GGBFS can improve workability, strength, and durability of concrete. It provides reduced chloride permeability and heat of hydration. It improves compressive and flexural strength (National Slag Association [NSA]). Concrete made with GGBFS can be effective in mitigating sulfate attack from arid soils, seawater, or wastewater. Through pozzolanic action, GGBFS can remove alkalinity of high-silica aggregates and high-alkali cement that can cause an alkali silica reaction (ASR), leading to internal expansion and crazing of concrete. Slag concrete is a lighter gray than most Class F fly ash concretes. As it cures it occasionally shows a blue-green mottling; however, this will disappear quickly.

Other forms of blast furnace slag are used as aggregate in concrete and for base and fill material. The National Slag Association estimates that construction-related applications use over 13 million tons annually in North America (NSA).

While slag is more readily available in steel-processing regions of the United States, it is imported to other areas because of its value for high-quality concrete. This shipping energy can make it slightly less energy saving than the more widely abundant fly ash. The ASTM standard specification for GGBFS use in concrete and mortars is ASTM C989.

Silica Fume

Silica fume, a by-product of silicon metal or ferrosilicon alloy production, is another industrial by-product that can replace a portion of cement. Silica fume's fine particle sizes (100 times smaller than cement particles), large surface area, and high SiO_2 content make it a very reactive pozzolan. Silica fume produces such a high-strength (some in excess of 15,000 psi) and durable concrete that it is often used in high-performance concrete applications or structures where top weathering performance and high strength are needed. The quality of silica fume for use in concrete is specified in ASTM C1240.

Silica fume concrete with low water content is highly resistant to penetration by chloride ions and helps block their migration to reinforcing steel. The small particle size requires the use of superplasticizers to improve workability without increasing the water content. Flatwork containing silica fume concrete generally requires less finishing effort and has greater freeze-thaw resistance than conventional concrete (Holland 2005).

Concrete with silica fume is relatively expensive because of the material cost, superplasticizers, and difficulty of handling the powdery fineness. If inhaled, it can have negative health effects, so it is often turned into slurry before use.

Rice Hull Ash

Rice hull ash, from the papery hulls covering rice grains, is another by-product that has potential to replace a portion of cement in concrete mix. The ash material is primarily silica and is a highly reactive pozzolan. Rice hulls are an abundant material as the world produces about 60 million tons annually. It has been tested for its applications in concrete, but it is not in widespread use (King 2005).

Metakaolin

Metakaolin, ground calcined kaolin clay, is a highly active natural pozzolan that can act as a cement substitute. Kaolin is a by-product of oil sands operations. ASTM C618 classifies it as a Class N "Natural Pozzolan." Metakaolin particles are almost ten times smaller than cement particles, resulting in a denser, more impervious concrete. This quality improves resistance to chemical attacks, sulphate, ASR expansion, and freeze-thaw cycles (Advanced Cement Technologies [ACT] 2007). Mechanical properties of concrete made with metakaolin, such as early-age compressive strength and flexural strength, are also improved. Metakaolin is available commercially under a variety of trade names. It is an equivalent substitute to silica fume for its high-performance concrete requirements (ACT 2007). Volcanic tuffs, pumicite, opaline cherts and shales, and diatomaceous earth are other natural pozzolans (King 2005).

Table 5–14 Cement Replacement Materials (SCMs) Added During Concrete Mixing at Batch Plant

	Cement Substitute %	Performance Benefits/ Value Added	Drawbacks/ Special Considerations
Fly ash Class C ASTM C618 By-product of lignite or subbituminous coal combustion, primarily from coal-fired power plants Has cementitious properties	15%–40% standard practice[a] 25% max for concrete subject to deicers[b] 50%+ is high fly ash concrete (HFAC)[c] Some lab and field experiments using 100%[c]	Increased workability Higher ultimate strength concrete More durable Requires less water Uses a waste by-product Reduced thermal stress and cracking Less drying shrinkage Reduced heat of hydration Reduced permeability Usually produces buff-colored concrete	Longer set times; may not meet 28-day strength requirements; formwork removal slowed. Reduced bleed water may make finishing timing unclear. HFAC should be protected from premature drying. Chemical composition of fly ash can vary among sources; design mixes to characteristics; keep sources consistent across project. Some fly ashes may contain ash from other products burned with coal.
Fly ash Class F ASTM C618 By-product of anthracite and bituminous coal combustion, primarily from coal-fired power plants Has pozzolanic properties	15%–25% standard practice[a] 25% max for concrete subject to deicers[b] 40%+ is high fly ash concrete (HFAC)[c]	Increased workability Higher ultimate strength More durable Requires less water Uses a waste by-product Resistant to sulfate attack and alkali silica reaction (ASR) Reduced thermal stress and cracking Less drying shrinkage Reduced heat of hydration Reduced permeability Resulting concrete color varies from lighter gray to medium gray	Longer set times; may not meet 28-day strength requirements; formwork removal is slowed. Reduced bleed water may make finishing timing unclear. HFAC should be protected from premature drying. Chemical composition of fly ash can vary among sources; design mixes to characteristics; keep sources consistent across project. Some fly ashes may contain ash from other products burned with coal.
Ground granulated blast furnace slag (GGBFS) and pelletized blast furnace slag (PBFS) ASTM C989 Coproduct of iron-making process	35%–80%[a] 50% max for concrete subject to deicers[b]	Improves paste to aggregate bond in concrete resulting in greater strength, reduced permeability, improved resistance to sulfate attack, and reduced ASR reaction Lighter in color than portland cement, aiding in increased reflectance of concrete pavement Improves concrete workability and pumpability	Initial hydration is slower. Rate of reaction increases with particle fineness. Higher dosages can be considered when providing for resistance to alkali silica reaction or reducing heat of hydration.

Continued

Table 5–14 Cement Replacement Materials (SCMs) Added During Concrete Mixing at Batch Plant *(Continued)*

	Cement Substitute %	Performance Benefits/ Value Added	Drawbacks/ Special Considerations
Silica fume ASTM C1240 By-product of silicon metal or ferrosilicon alloy production	10% max for concrete subject to deicers[b]	Fine particle sizes, large surface area, and high SiO_2 content make it a very reactive pozzolan. Produces a very high-strength, durable concrete Good weathering performance, highly resistant to penetration by chloride ions Good freeze-thaw resistance	Reduces workability Not typically used in pavements Relatively expensive because small particle size requires use of plasticizers to improve workability without increasing water content Precautions need to be taken in handling because of its fineness; sometimes sold as a slurry. High material cost Higher risk of plastic shrinkage
Rice hull ash AASHTO M321 Ash from papery hulls covering rice grains		Ash material is primarily silica and is a highly reactive pozzolan.	Abundant material, but not widely available In testing stages
Metakaolin, Class N pozzolans ASTM C618 Metakaolin is ground calcined clay. Other Class N pozzolans are volcanic tuffs, pumicite, opaline cherts and shales, and diatomaceous earth	Addressed in AASHTO M321 or ASTM C618	Small particle size results in a denser, more impervious concrete. Improved resistance to chemical attacks, sulfate, ASR expansion, and freeze-thaw cycles Higher compressive and flexural strength than standard concrete	Particles are 10 times smaller than typical portland cement, difficult to handle. Available under many different trade names

[a]FHWA 2006
[b]ACI 318 (2002) from FHWA Note: Percentages given for individual SCMs; total SCM content should not exceed 50% of cementitious material.
[c]King 2005

Blended Cements

Blended cements are mixtures of portland cement and other pozzolans like fly ash, silica fume, or GGBFS that are blended during the cement manufacturing process. Blended cements, preblended at the cement manufacturing facility, can offer efficiency and accuracy in mixes; however, they don't offer the opportunity to increase the amounts of cement substitutes. Blended cements are sold under the names in Table 5–15 as defined in ASTM C595–05 Standard Specification for Blended Hydraulic Cements.

Ground Limestone

ASTM C150 now permits ground limestone to be used in up to 5% of portland cement. The Portland Cement

Table 5–15 Blended Cements with SCMs

	Cement Substitute %	Performance Benefits/ Value Added	Special Considerations/ Drawbacks
Type I (PM) pozzolan-modified portland cement Intimate and uniform blend of portland or portland blast furnace slag cement and fine pozzolan (fly ash)	Less than 15%[a]	Relatively low use of fly ash, therefore both benefits and drawbacks are minimal. Some savings of energy and CO_2 release for cement production Slight increased workability Slightly higher ultimate strength concrete Slightly more durable Requires slightly less water	Relatively low use of fly ash, therefore both benefits and drawbacks are minimal. Slightly reduced bleed water The major drawback is that not enough fly ash is substituted for portland cement to gain any real environmental or performance benefits.
Type IP and Type P portland-pozzolan cement Intimate and uniform blend of portland or portland blast furnace slag cement and fine pozzolan (fly ash)	15%–40%[a] pozzolan content	Higher percentage of fly ash is used, gaining more environmental and performance benefits. However, this is not considered high-volume fly ash concrete. Some savings of energy and CO_2 release for cement production Increased workability Higher ultimate strength concrete More durable Requires less water Resistant to sulfate attack and alkali silica reaction (ASR) Reduced thermal stress and cracking Less drying shrinkage Reduced heat of hydration Reduced permeability	Slightly longer set times; may not meet 28-day strength requirements; formwork removal can be slowed. Reduced bleed water may make finishing timing unclear. Protect from premature drying. Higher volumes of fly ash could be used in some applications.
Type IS portland blast-furnace slag cement Intimate and uniform blend of portland cement and fine granulated blast furnace slag	25%–70%[a] slag content	Uses a good amount of a potential waste product and substantially reduces use of portland cement, reducing energy use and CO_2 release. Improves paste to aggregate bond in concrete, resulting in greater strength, reduced permeability, improved resistance to sulfate attack, and reduced ASR reaction.	Initial hydration is slower. Rate of reaction increases with particle fineness.

Table 5–15 Blended Cements with SCMs *(Continued)*

	Cement Substitute %	Performance Benefits/ Value Added	Special Considerations/ Drawbacks
Type IS portland blast-furnace slag cemen (cont'd.)		Lighter in color than portland cement, aiding in increased reflectance of concrete pavement	
Type I(SM) slag-modified portland cement Intimate and uniform blend of portland cement and fine granulated blast furnace slag	Less than 25%[a] slag content	Relatively low use of slag, therefore both benefits and drawbacks are less. Improves paste to aggregate bond in concrete, resulting in greater strength, reduced permeability, improved resistance to sulfate attack, and reduced ASR reaction. Lighter in color than portland cement, aiding in increased reflectance of concrete pavement	Relatively low use of slag, therefore both benefits and drawbacks are less. The major drawback is that not enough slag is substituted for portland cement to gain maximum environmental or performance benefits. Rate of reaction increases with particle fineness.
Type S slag cement Intimate and uniform blend of granulated blast furnace slag and portland cement or hydrated lime of both	At least 70%[a]	Uses a high amount of a potential waste product and substantially reduces use of portland cement, reducing energy use and CO_2 release. Improves paste to aggregate bond in concrete, resulting in greater strength, reduced permeability, improved resistance to sulfate attack, and reduced ASR reaction. Lighter in color than portland cement, aiding in increased reflectance of concrete pavement	Initial hydration is slower. Rate of reaction increases with particle fineness.

[a]ASTM 2005a

Sources: FHWA 2006; SCA; FHWA 2004; ASTM 2005a; King 2005

Association estimates that if an average of 2.5% ground limestone were used, environmental impacts would be reduced annually in the United States in the following amounts (PCA 2003):

- Reduction in raw materials use of 1.6 million tons
- Reduction in energy use of over 11.8 trillion Btus
- Reduction in carbon dioxide emissions of over 2.5 million tons
- Reduction of cement kiln dust of over 190,000 tons

Substitute Recycled Materials for Natural Aggregates in Concrete

Substituting recycled materials for virgin aggregates in concrete can have economic, environmental, and even aesthetic advantages. It has the dual benefit of reduced resource use and the associated mining impacts, and the diversion of waste materials from the landfill. Recycled materials can be less expensive than natural aggregates,

Table 5–16 Other Substitutes for Portland Cement Added During the Cement-Manufacturing Process

	Cement Substitute %	Performance Benefits/ Value Added	Special Considerations/ Drawbacks
Steel slag Coproduct of steel-making processes (NSA) Can be used as a raw feed in cement manufacture	8%–11%[a]	Use of steel slag as raw feed in a cement kiln saves energy and resources, reduces emissions, and improves production. Yield of cement clinker is higher than limestone's because it has already been calcined.	Steel slag is different from blast furnace slag and possesses different properties for different end uses. Availability limited to eastern and midwestern regions or where steel-processing operations are located
Foundry sand Good source of silica for cement manufacture By-product of metal casting	13%[b]	Concrete made from cement with some spent foundry sand can show slightly higher compressive strengths. Saves money for cement manufacturer, possibly for consumer Saves use of virgin resources	Foundry sand for cement manufacture must possess the following properties: minimum silica content of 80% low alkali level uniform particle size
Ground limestone Virgin material	5%[c]	Reduces energy use, CO_2 release, and resource use by cutting down on the material than needs to be calcined	ASTM C150 now allows up to 5% ground limestone in portland cement.

[a]SCA
[b]FHWA 2004
[c]ASTM 2007

especially if demolition materials such as concrete or brick can be crushed on or near the site and reused in new concrete. Concrete is easily recycled on-site by bringing in equipment to break, remove, and crush the old material. This practice also can save on landfill and transportation fees.

Other recycled products that can be used for coarse or fine aggregates in concrete are crushed blast furnace slag, brick, glass, foundry sand, granulated plastics, waste fiberglass, sintered sludge, mineralized wood shavings, and many others. While many of these recycled aggregates have been tested in concrete, only reclaimed concrete aggregate (RCA), blast furnace slag and glass have been widely applied in the field (PATH).

A primary limitation of using recycled materials as aggregates in concrete is the requirement of predictable and consistent performance. Standards for performance must be met and properties of recycled aggregates such as water absorption, specific gravity, and compressive strength can vary widely and will affect the concrete mix requirements (Khalaf and DeVenny 2004). Mixes may need to be adapted to accommodate variations in recycled aggregate properties. With use of any new aggregate, testing is necessary to account for variations in the aggregate's properties. Recycled aggregates should be free of constituents that may have a negative reaction with cement or may contain contaminants or debris. For example, some recycled aggregates may be contaminated with sulfate from contact with sulfate-rich soil or chloride ions from marine exposure (PATH).

Reclaimed Concrete Aggregate (RCA)

Reclaimed concrete can be used as both coarse and fine aggregate in new concrete structures, though it is more commonly used as a base or subbase for pavement structures or other fill applications. RCA in concrete has been used primarily in paving applications with limited use in other structures. Some sources do not recommend use of RCA for fine aggregate, while others limit the percentage to 30% of fines because of its high water demand (FHWA 2004, 2006). In addition to saving virgin resources and their related environmental impacts, use of RCA can save money, particularly where gravel, sand, and stone are less readily available, such as in urban areas.

Sources of RCA. Sources of recycled concrete are abundant. Recycling concrete structures on-site is the most energy-efficient and cost-effective use of reclaimed concrete aggregate, as transportation is virtually eliminated. Stone-crushing equipment can be brought to the site with recently developed measures to reduce noise and dust. The procedure for on-site concrete recycling involves 1) breaking and removing the old concrete; 2) crushing in primary and secondary crushers; 3) removing reinforcing steel, wire mesh, and other embedded items; 4) grading and washing; and 5) stockpiling the resulting coarse and fine aggregates. During this process, care should be taken to avoid contamination of the aggregate with dirt, gypsum board, asphalt, wood, and other foreign materials (FHWA 2006).

Precrushed concrete can be obtained from widespread concrete recycling centers. The real cost of this aggregate is in the transportation from the recycling source to the construction site; however, sources of recycled concrete and concrete-crushing facilities are increasingly more local than virgin aggregate mining sites.

As landfill tipping fees increase, concrete, being a relatively heavy and expensive material to landfill, will become ever more economically feasible to use as aggregate in concrete mixes or as base material. Some state DOTs recycle all concrete debris for this reason (FHWA 2004).

Another common source of RCA is fresh concrete that is returned to the originating concrete plant for reasons of oversupply or rejection. Some plants will allow it to cure, then crush it and reuse it as base aggregate on other jobs (FHWA 2006).

An economic benefit of recycling concrete is the value of the steel reinforcing that is removed during the concrete recycling process. When concrete is landfilled,

steel is not usually removed, yet when concrete is recycled, removed steel can be sold for scrap, bringing additional economic value to recycling efforts.

Properties of new concrete with RCA. Reclaimed concrete aggregate (RCA) for use in concrete can have slightly different properties than conventional natural aggregates. New concrete made with RCA has good workability, durability, and resistance to saturated freeze-thaw action. Permeability and carbonation has been found to be the same or better than conventional aggregate concrete.

Use of RCA in concrete can pose some challenges. RCA can be contaminated with dirt, debris, or other foreign materials; quality of RCA can fluctuate; and it must be graded to ensure a proper concrete mix (Meyer 2000). RCA has a lower specific gravity and higher absorption rate than most natural aggregates. This is a result of the higher absorption of porous mortar and hardened cement paste within the reclaimed concrete aggregate. Absorption increases as coarse particle size decreases. Coarse RCA has a water absorption rate of 5%–6% and fine RCA a water absorption rate of 9%–10%. Natural aggregates typically have an absorption rate of 1%–2% (FHWA 2006).

To overcome this, additional water may need to be added to the mix; however, prewetting the recycled aggregate can help decrease absorption of mix water. Superplasticizers or water-reducing agents may also address the absorption issue. Sometimes RCA can require use of more cement in a concrete mix, possibly negating the environmental benefits of RCA use.

The compressive strength of recycled concrete aggregate is related to the compressive strength of the original concrete and the water-cement ratio of the new concrete. Research has found that compressive strength values at 7 and 28 days are slightly lower than concrete with natural aggregates; however, this may not be significant in most applications (PATH). The modulus of elasticity decreases as the amount of recycled aggregate increases. With 100% RCA, the modulus of elasticity decreased 35% from the reference concrete. Drying shrinkage can also be increased with RCA, particularly with high use of fine RCA aggregates.

Standards vary by state and by use for recommended amounts of RCA in concrete. A 2004 Federal Highway

Administration survey of state transportation agencies found that eleven recycle concrete for use as a coarse aggregate in new concrete. Some have even incorporated 100% coarse RCA with only 30% RCA fine aggregates because of their water absorption and drying shrinkage (FHWA 2004).

Blast Furnace Slag

In addition to being ground and used as a cement substitute, blast furnace slag is also substituted for both coarse and fine aggregates in concrete. During the period of cooling and hardening from its molten state in iron making, slag can be cooled in many ways to produce different types of slag products.

Air-cooled blast furnace slag (ACBFS) crushes to more angular cubic shapes with a rougher texture and greater surface area than most natural aggregates; therefore it has a strong bond with portland cement. The angular shape of ACBFS and the high angle of internal friction result in improved aggregate interlock. It is lighter weight than conventional aggregates and water absorption is low. ACBFS is resistant to abrasion and weathering (NSA). The lower unit weight of ACBFS can reduce shipping costs and energy use.

Expanded slag is quickly cooled with water or steam, then crushed for use as a lightweight aggregate in concrete and concrete masonry units. It is also used as lightweight embankment fill. It shares many properties with air-cooled slag (NSA).

Pelletized slag is cooled with water and manipulated into droplets, or slag pellets, which cool quickly and rapidly solidify. Pelletized slag is used as lightweight aggregate in concrete and concrete masonry units. It is also ground for use in premixed slag cement mixes (NSA).

Recycled Waste Plastic

Recycled waste plastic can be used in both precast and poured-in-place concrete applications. Plastic aggregate is relatively new and not widely used or available. Some plastic aggregate suppliers mix recycled plastic and fly ash (RMRC 2001). Precast concrete blocks with mixed recycled plastic are produced in the Northeast. They are about half the weight of traditional CMUs. The Texas DOT has evaluated scrap plastics, including PVC, for use in concrete. Their standard specification allows substitution of recycled plastic for up to 10% of coarse aggregate and up to 10% of fine aggregate in a road mix (Texas DOT).

Mineralized Wood Fiber Shavings

Mineralized wood fiber shavings from wood processing are chemically treated and mineralized and used in concrete masonry products such as stay-in-place concrete wall forms, freestanding sound barriers, and concrete blocks. The blocks are lighter weight than traditional aggregate blocks.

Crushed Recycled Glass

Crushed recycled glass, also called cullet, can be used as either fine or coarse aggregate in concrete. While it is more widely substituted for sand in concrete, it is increasingly used in larger sizes to impart color and aesthetic properties to concrete and concrete products.

Use of glass aggregate in concrete can be challenging, as an alkali silica reaction (ASR) can occur between the alkali in cement and the silica in glass. This reaction creates a gel that swells in the presence of moisture, causing cracks and damage to the concrete. Research has been done on methods of avoiding an ASR, rendering use of glass in concrete viable. The following methods can avoid or substantially reduce expansions from ASR (Meyer 2000):

- Use of green glass aggregate, which causes little or no expansion of the concrete, and amber glass, which causes considerably less than clear glass
- Glass that is ground (to less than mesh size #50) and substituted for a portion of sand
- Additions of mineral admixtures such as metakaolin or fly ash
- Use of glass that can be coated with zirconium, although this may not be viable for post-consumer glass aggregate
- Use of ASR-resistant cements

While the above techniques offer ways to minimize ASR, concrete with glass aggregate is still used primarily in nonstructural applications such as sidewalks, paths, and nonstructural pads.

Use of glass aggregate in concrete offers some advantages beyond the obvious use of waste material.

Table 5–17 Substitutes for Natural Aggregate in Concrete

	Aggregate Substitute %	Performance Benefits/ Added Value	Special Considerations/ Drawbacks
Reclaimed concrete aggregate (RCA)	100% coarse[a] 30% fine[a]	RCA sources are abundant. Can save money Concrete with RCA has good workability, durability, and freeze-thaw resistance.	RCA absorbs more water than virgin aggregates. Absorption increases as particle size decreases. Prewetting RCA can offset some absorption. Modulus of elasticity may be lower. Drying shrinkage can increase with use of RCA fine aggregates.
Air-cooled blast furnace slag (ACBFS)		Angular shapes with rougher texture and greater surface area produce stronger bond with cement. Lighter weight, lower shipping costs Water absorption is low. Resistant to abrasion and weathering	Availability limited to eastern and midwest regions or where steel-processing operations are located
Expanded blast furnace slag (EBFS)		Angular shapes with rougher texture and greater surface area produce stronger bond with cement. Lighter weight, lower shipping costs, lighter weight CMUs Water absorption is low. Resistant to abrasion and weathering	Availability limited to eastern and midwestern regions or where steel-processing operations are located Primarily used for CMUs
Pelletized blast furnace slag (PBFS)		Angular shapes with rougher texture and greater surface area produce stronger bond with cement. Lighter weight, lower shipping costs, lighter weight structures Water absorption is low. Resistant to abrasion and weathering	Availability limited to eastern and midwestern regions or where steel-processing operations are located
Glass cullet		Uses a post-consumer waste material that might otherwise be landfilled	Supply consistency varies. Alkali silica reaction (ASR) can occur with coarse glass aggregate, less with fine aggregates.

Table 5–17 Substitutes for Natural Aggregate in Concrete *(Continued)*

	Aggregate Substitute %	Performance Benefits/ Added Value	Special Considerations/ Drawbacks
Tires/crumb rubber pellets	10% fines[b] <20% of total aggregate volume[h]	Uses a post-consumer waste material that might otherwise be landfilled Lightweight, produces lightweight structures and blocks	
Plastics Sometimes combined with other materials (e.g., synthetic lightweight aggregate [SLA] is mix of #3–7 plastics and fly ash)	10% coarse[c] 15% coarse[b]	Uses a post-consumer waste material that might otherwise be landfilled Lightweight aggregate, produces lightweight structures and blocks Increases deformation of concrete without failure. This may be a benefit in freeze-thaw or high expansion situations.[d]	Compressive strengths are generally lower than concrete made with virgin aggregates[b,d] In initial testing stages, not in widespread use
Crushed bricks	20% coarse[e]	Uses a post-consumer waste material that might otherwise be landfilled Colors of bricks can add visual qualities to the concrete. Produces a light- to medium-weight concrete	Concrete with crushed brick has a slightly lower, but still acceptable compressive strength.[e] Crushed brick aggregates that include fines should not be used as this will compromise the concrete's durability.[e] Crushed brick is more angular than round, so it will not pack as efficiently and will produce larger voids than typical virgin aggregates.[e] Crushed brick has a higher porosity than typical aggregates, absorbing more mix water and reducing workability. Saturation with water prior to mixing or adding water to the mix may address the problem. In order to avoid the decreased strength from added water, cement content may need to be higher.[e]

Continued

Table 5–17 Substitutes for Natural Aggregate in Concrete *(Continued)*

	Aggregate Substitute %	Performance Benefits/ Added Value	Special Considerations/ Drawbacks
Foundry sand *Core sand* has been processed to remove fines and organic materials. *Green sand* has usually not been processed to remove fines and organic materials such as clay and dust.	35%[f] 15%–50%[g] (Depends on quality of sand. Core sand can be 35%–50%.)	Uses a waste material that might be landfilled, saves virgin sand use	Sometimes slight decrease in compressive strength of concrete, but still structural grade Foundry sand is too fine for full substitution of fine aggregates. Foundry sand can be blended with other coarser fine aggregates. Foundry sand is black, so if too much is used, it will affect the color of the finished concrete. A substitution of 15% is estimated not to noticeably change the color.

[a]fHWA 2004, 7
[b]Texas DOT
[c]Khatib and Bayomy 1999
[d]Ghaly and Gill 2004
[e]Khalaf and DeVenny 2004
[f]Naik et al. 1992
[g]FHWA 2006

The glass has almost zero water absorption, rendering concrete made with glass aggregate more durable (if ASR is avoided). The hardness of glass gives the concrete more abrasion resistance, and in plastic form, the concrete is more flowable and easily placed without water-reducing admixtures. Very finely ground glass has pozzolanic qualities and can act as a partial cement replacement or filler in concrete (Meyer 2000). Glass aggregate can impart a variety of color qualities to the concrete when aggregate is exposed or when the surface of the concrete is ground.

Sources of recycled glass, primarily post-consumer glass bottles and post-industrial float glass cullet, vary widely across the country and may be abundant in some areas while scarce in others. Where consistent sources are available, use of glass cullet can be an economical and aesthetic replacement for natural sand or aggregates in concrete.

CONCRETE FORMWORK

Concrete formwork can use substantial resources if it is used once then torn off and discarded. Reuse of formwork can save resources and reduce material sent to landfills. Steel or plastic forms can be reused many times. Wood forms can be reused if form-release agents that don't damage the wood are used, such as those made from plant oils. Wood formwork from a reclaimed source will also save resources.

Earth forms can minimize use of resources and save cost of formwork materials. Footing width should be increased by 3 cm for each earth-form side. Concrete that will show above grade should be formed with formwork.

Fabric formwork systems can be a resource-saving method of forming concrete. Fabric forms, a relatively new technology, are composed of a polyethylene fabric held in place by a temporary minimal wood frame and reusable support stakes. Advantages of fabric forms (Fab-Form):

- Minimal resources are required for formwork.
- Fabric footing forms save resources as the top of a spread footing is rounded because of the flexibility of the fabric. Less concrete is used.
- Forms are lightweight and easily transported, using less energy. A 12.5-pound roll of fabric formwork will form the same footing as 900 pounds of lumber.
- Minimal wood is used and wood can be reused easily as it never comes in contact with concrete.
- The flexible nature of the fabric requires minimal grading and ground leveling.
- Structures supporting the fabric can be reused an indefinite number of times.
- Fabric forms can be left in place and can be biodegradable.

Disadvantages:

- Fabric formwork is a relatively new technology and contractors may resist its use, or they may not be willing to invest in the reusable metal support structures.
- Fabric forms can't be used to form the stem of walls, only applications below grade.

Form Release Agents

Many form release agents are petroleum based and contain VOCs, which can cause environmental and human health problems. Diesel fuels and waste oils are also used as they are inexpensive. When these products are sprayed on forms, they can release PCBs and heavy metals into the soil and air. Use of these form release agents can also prohibit reuse of forms. Plant-based form release agents using rapeseed oil, soybean oil, or vegetable oil are usually VOC free and allow reuse of forms (EBN 2004).

CONCRETE ADMIXTURES

Admixtures are materials other than cement, aggregate, or water added to a concrete mix to impart special properties during mixing, placement, curing, and/or use. They can alter workability, curing temperature range, set time, color, permeability, and many other proper-

ties. As concrete mixes are increasingly tailored to specific placement situations and structures, admixture use is growing. New admixtures are being developed and existing admixtures are being refined.

While some may pose toxicity risks to humans and the environment, admixtures can also enhance the "green" qualities of a given concrete mix. They are sometimes necessary to aid use of cement and virgin aggregate substitutes. Other admixtures can ensure long life for a concrete structure, conserving resources over the life of a landscape.

The environmental and human health risks of admixtures are not well documented, partly because so many admixtures are proprietary and manufacturers will not release lists of actual chemicals used. Some admixtures can cause skin, eye, or lung irritation in placement or they may pose toxicity risks to surface and ground waters. Others contain toxic heavy metals, such as chrome, lead, and cobalt, and other harmful chemicals. When specifying an admixture, material safety data sheets should be examined and where chemical names are stated, cross-referenced with toxics inventories at the U.S. EPA and international organizations. Potential health and environmental risks should be weighed against benefits of increased durability or high recycled-content concrete mixes. Admixtures can be classified into the categories below.

Retarding Admixtures

Retarding admixtures slow the hydration of cement, which lengthens the set time of the concrete. Retarders are used in hot weather to overcome the accelerating effects of the hotter ambient air, or if a concrete structure is a large mass that may have a higher heat of hydration. ASTM C494 defines type B as retarding admixtures and type D as both retarding and water reducing. Type D may result in concrete with greater compressive strength because of the lower water-to-cement ratio.

Retarding admixtures can help with the disposal problem of leftover partial loads of concrete. Excess concrete not used in a pour is often landfilled, or used to make simple concrete blocks or structures. But retarding admixtures can be added before curing to extend a partial load of unused concrete for one or two days, then reactivate it for use in another structure (Spiegel and Meadows 2006).

Most retarding admixtures are relatively benign sucrose-based chemicals added in small amounts (EBN 1993). Retarding admixtures are composed of both organic and inorganic agents. Organic retardants include unrefined calcium, sodium, salts of lignosulfonic acids, NH_4, hydrocarboxylic acids, and carbohydrates. Inorganic retardants include oxides of lead and zinc, magnesium salts, phosphates, fluorates, and borates (PATH).

Accelerating Admixtures

Accelerating admixtures shorten the set time of concrete. This can allow pouring in cold weather, early surface finishing, early removal of forms, and sometimes early load application. Accelerating admixtures are sometimes used to counteract the slower set time of cement substitutes such as fly ash, GGBFS, or silica fume. Type and proportion of accelerating admixtures should be chosen carefully as they can cause and increase drying shrinkage. Use of accelerating and freeze-preventing admixtures can be minimized by scheduling work in appropriate temperatures and seasons (Thompson and Sorvig 2000).

Calcium chloride is a common ingredient of accelerating admixtures. While it can be an eye, skin, and lung irritant, it is relatively benign. Calcium chloride accelerating admixtures can cause corrosion of reinforcing steel. Some sources recommend avoidance of accelerating admixtures with calcium chloride.

Superplasticizers

Superplasticizers, also known as plasticizers, are "high-range" water reducers that allow large water reductions and increase flowability of concrete without slowing set time or increasing air entrainment. Superplasticizers may be necessary with use of some cement and aggregate substitutes. In arid regions, use of superplasticizers and other water reducers can save water (Thompson and Sorvig 2000).

Some superplasticizers can include chemicals such as sulfonated melamine-formaldehyde and sulfonated naphthalene formaldehyde condensates, which can pose both human and environmental health risks (EBN 1993). There is a new generation of superplasticizers based on polycarboxylic esthers. Ground and surface water pollution is a particular concern with some superplasticizers (PATH).

Water-reducing Admixtures

Water-reducing admixtures require less water to make concrete with an equal slump, or to increase the slump of concrete at the same water content. Changing the amount of water in a mix can change the initial set time. Water-reducing admixtures are primarily used for hot weather placement of concrete or to improve pumpability. Some cement substitutes, such as fly ash, act as water reducers, producing a more durable concrete.

Air-entraining Admixtures

Air-entraining admixtures improve concrete's workability and resistance to freeze-thaw conditions by entraining small air bubbles in the concrete (PATH). In exterior structures repeatedly exposed to freeze-thaw cycles, use of air-entraining admixtures can result in a more durable structure. Air-entraining chemicals can include various types of inorganic salts, which are relatively benign. However, they can also include chemicals of more concern, such as alkylbenzene sulphonates and methyl-ester-derived cocamide diethanolamine (EBN 1993).

Other Admixtures

Bonding admixtures are used to join new concrete to old concrete structures. They can include polyvinyl chlorides and acetates, acrylics, and butadiene-styrene copolymers, all of which pose a range of health risks. Waterproofing admixtures are used to decrease water penetration into concrete pores. These include soaps, butyl stearate, mineral oil, and asphalt emulsions. Some may contain VOCs and other hazardous chemicals. Coloring agents are considered admixtures and are discussed in a separate section below.

CONCRETE FINISHES

Making concrete decorative through the use of coloring agents or surface finishes can save resources, eliminating the need to cover the concrete structure with brick or stone veneer. However, some pigments and

Table 5–18 Greener alternatives for Concrete Products

Concrete products	SCAQMD VOC limits	Green alternatives
Curing agents	100 g/l (350 g/l for roads and bridges)	Biobased materials, low-solvent, low-VOC (50 g/l or less), water-based, or a combination of above
Water-repelling admixtures	100 g/l	Some products react with cement to provide a seal without VOC-emitting solvents; biobased material, low-solvent content, or low-VOC content (50 g/l or less); (Some can be more effective than surface applied.)
Surface applied waterproofing	100 g/l	Some products react with cement to provide a seal without VOC-emitting solvents; biobased material, low-solvent content, or low-VOC content (50 g/l or less); water-dispersed polyester polymers.
Concrete pigments		Natural iron oxide products, some are recovered from abandoned coal mine drainage; recycled-glass powder fines from post-consumer bottle glass and post-industrial float glass cullet—color effect is somewhat different from other pigments.
Concrete cleaning agents		Biodegradable, biobased materials; some are citrus based; water-soluble.
Form release agents Typically are petroleum based. Can contain heavy metals. Can be a major source of VOCs, and can lead to soil contamination and human health risks		Biodegradable, biobased, nonpetroleum or water based alternatives are available; Many made with agricultural crops and biodegradable, and have less than 60 grams per liter VOC.

Sources: BuildingGreen; SCAQMD; Thompson and Sorvig 2000

finishes can pose toxicity risks to humans and the environment.

Integral and surface-applied concrete coloring agents use little extra material and can provide a finished look to a concrete slab, eliminating the need for additional veneer materials. Some manufacturers estimate that a colored finish on concrete is about one-third the cost of a stone or brick veneer.

Some coloring agents contain heavy metals, such as chrome, lead and cobalt, and toxic chemicals (Berge 2000). Material safety data sheets (MSDSs) for a product should be carefully reviewed for human health and toxicity impacts before the product is specified. MSDSs should be cross-referenced with toxics inventories at the U.S. EPA, Agency for Toxic Substances and Disease

Registry (ATSDR), and National Institute for Occupational Safety and Health (NIOSH).

Methods of applying color to concrete are as follows:

Integral color is a colored pigment that is added in either powder or liquid form during the concrete-mixing process. This results in a color application that extends through the entire thickness of the concrete structure. If the concrete chips, the color is still visible in the chip, lending durability to the color and the structure.

Some mineral-based pigments are made from recycled and reclaimed steel and iron. Others are made from natural clay. A natural iron oxide pigment recovered from abandoned coal mine drainage producing earth-toned pigments is available. Recycled glass fines from post-consumer or post-industrial processes are an alternative coloring agent that provides a slightly different effect than pigments. Integral color pigments will fade with exposure to UV rays, so structures should be sealed with nontoxic water-based sealers periodically if color intensity is a priority.

Surface-applied coatings are applied in powder or paste form to the surface of a concrete structure as part of the finishing process. They are made from cement-modified acrylic resins and/or epoxy-based polymers and a blend of fine aggregates. This coating system can provide a wide range of colors and textures. Some surface-applied coatings are designed to harden the surface of concrete. Surface strength may be increased up to 7,500 psi, possibly resulting in increased durability of the structure (PATH).

Concrete stains are formulated to chemically react with the concrete's lime content to produce a colored surface. The stains lightly etch and bond color penetrating into a thin outer layer of concrete. Perhaps the greatest benefit of concrete stains is their ability to give new life to old structures that might otherwise be removed, allowing old structures to be reused and saving resources. Many chemical stains are water soluble, but they may contain acids that can produce some negative health effects.

The lower permeability of high fly ash concrete (HFAC) may mean that concrete stains will not penetrate as deeply; however, the lighter color of the concrete may make colors look more vivid.

CONCRETE CURING COMPOUNDS

Curing compounds are used on the surface of newly poured concrete to protect the surface during curing of the concrete. Some curing compounds release VOCs. Refer to California's South Coast Air Quality Management District (SCAQMD) guidelines for appropriate VOC levels in curing compounds. Some water-based compounds will release lower levels of VOCs. Some curing compounds are made from renewable biobased resources such as soy and other plant-based formulations.

CONCRETE SEALERS

Concrete sealers and stains can contain VOCs and other hazardous chemicals. While this is less of a human health concern in exterior applications, VOCs negatively impact air quality, contribute to ground-level ozone and pollution, and runoff-carrying compounds can negatively affect water and soil quality. Water-based sealers containing less than 100 g/1 VOCs and free of hazardous chemicals should be specified. Biobased, VOC-free sealers, such as those made from soybean oil, are available for exterior applications but may require more frequent application. Biobased or water-based concrete cleaners are also available.

REINFORCING

Adequate reinforcing in concrete structures will ensure their durability. Therefore, reinforcing is an important component to minimize the environmental impacts of concrete structures by ensuring a long use phase.

Steel Reinforcing

Steel, either welded wire mesh or reinforcing bar, is the primary material used to reinforce concrete. However, steel manufacture has some serious environmental impacts, discussed in greater detail in chapter 12. In addition to high energy use, steel manufacture emits hazardous air pollutants such as CO, SO_2, NO_x, CO_2, and VOCs. Emission levels of hazardous air pollutants (HAPs) are federally regulated and manufacturers have installed various pollution control equipment; however, emissions still occur at reduced levels. Steel is a commonly recycled material with a recycling rate of 80%, and rebar with 95%–100% recycled content is widely available.

While steel can support durable concrete, it can also pose a threat to the durability with its potential to corrode. If water permeates the concrete extensively, it can corrode and compromise the performance of the reinforcing and the aesthetics of the concrete with rust.

Synthetic Fiber Reinforcing

Synthetic fiber reinforcing is a relatively new type of reinforcing for nonstructural concrete applications, yet it offers some potential advantages in certain applications.

Synthetic fiber reinforcing—usually nylon, glass, steel, or polypropylene—prevents cracks in concrete before they happen, whereas welded wire mesh works after cracks occur (PATH). Prevention of cracking improves concrete's impermeability, and increases its long-term weatherability, strength, and impact resistance. Synthetic fiber reinforcing has been shown to reduce shrinkage cracking as well.

Synthetic fiber reinforcing, sometimes made from recycled materials, is added to the concrete during mixing. And while synthetic fiber–reinforced concrete costs more, labor costs of placing rebar or welded wire mesh (WWM) are eliminated. ASTM C1116 provides a specification for fibrous reinforcement.

Porous Concrete

A significant environmental impact of concrete paving during the use phase is its impermeability to storm water runoff. Large areas of impermeable surfaces in urban areas contribute to high quantities of storm water contained in drainage systems and piped into overburdened surface water bodies carrying high concentrations of pollutants. Paving, usually concrete or asphalt, is a major contributor to this increase in runoff; however, both concrete and asphalt paving can be made porous.

Porous concrete is concrete with uniformly graded course aggregate, usually No. 89 or No. 8 with no fines. The uniformly sized aggregate creates pore spaces between 11% and 21% of the mix for water to flow through the pavement. The typical porous pavement is six inches thick with a minimum subbase of four inches of open graded aggregate. This can support a 2,000 psi load. Thickening the slab and subbase may support heavier loads. A thickened subbase will also accommodate soft subgrade and/or provide greater storm water storage for slower percolating soils (Ferguson 2005). Refer to Table 5–19 for properties of porous concrete pavements.

Precast Concrete Products

Precast concrete products can offer advantages over poured-in-place structures in certain applications. They eliminate waste, as unused units can be returned to the supplier or reused in other installations. They are available in a wide range of decorative colors and textures, so the structure can also be the finish, conserving resources. Segmental retaining wall blocks and concrete unit pavers can be reused whole in other structures if no mortar is used. Segmental retaining walls are designed to move slightly with freeze-thaw cycles, so they don't require a footing down to the frostline, also conserving resources.

Like poured-in-place concrete, precast products incorporate a wide variety of recycled materials as aggregates. However, they require a high early strength because forms must be quickly reused, so use of slower curing cement substitutes is limited.

Nanotechnology and Concrete

Nanotechnology, the manipulation of matter at the billionth of a meter, holds some promising innovations for improving the environmental performance of concrete, cements, admixtures, and coatings. It should be noted that environmental and human health impacts of nanoparticles are relatively unknown, unregulated, and may pose some risks. Concerns are inhalation or skin absorption of nanoparticles during manufacture, use, disposal, or incineration (Korthals Altes 2008).

Figure 5–1.
Open pores of porous concrete, with filter fabric below to prevent migration of soil up into pores. (Photo by Meg Calkins)

Table 5–19 Properties of Porous Concrete Pavement

Phase	Advantages/Drawbacks as Compared with Standard Impermeable Concrete Pavement	Special Considerations
Pavement design	Cost of porous paving is higher than standard concrete paving because it requires a special mixture with special installation requirements, placed by specialized personnel. However, if porous paving is an integral part of a site's storm water management system, the added cost of porous paving can be offset by reduced storm water infrastructure costs. Steel reinforcing is not recommended, as water migrating through pore spaces will corrode reinforcing in most situations. Polymer fiber reinforcing is a relatively new technology and may be a better reinforcing as contact with water will not reduce its effectiveness. It is mixed directly into concrete.	Porous concrete is a relatively new technology; however, intensive field testing in certain areas, specifically Florida and the Pacific Northwest, is proving its effectiveness. Grade surrounding landscape so that water does not flow onto or across the porous pavement installation to minimize potential clogging of pore spaces with sediments and debris in runoff. To prevent edge cracking of a porous concrete slab, the subbase can be extended beyond the edge of the slab and/or the slab can be thickened at its edge. Requirements for control and expansion joints in porous concrete are similar to requirements in a standard concrete slab; however, control joints can be spaced slightly farther apart (20 feet versus 15 feet).
Mix design	Requires more portland cement than standard concrete There are concerns about using fly ash as a cement substitute in porous concrete, as it slows set times, potentially allowing water to evaporate through voids, causing inadequate curing and weaknesses.	Testing of mix design and infiltration capacity of subgrade before placement will ensure maximized infiltration. No. 67 aggregate can be used, offering larger pore spaces for water to move through, but it results in a coarser surface that may not be appropriate for all uses. It has less compressive strength, but less internal shrinkage and internal cracking than No. 89. Air-entraining admixtures may improve porous concrete's resistance to freeze-thaw conditions, sulfate soil, and seawater. It may also improve the workability. While the proportioning of ingredients in porous concrete is project specific, it is recommended that cement not be less than 600 pounds per cubic yard in a typical No. 89 mix. Cement quantities for pervious pavement range from 450–700 pounds per cubic yard. Water in a mix must be limited so it does not drain down, leaving the top layers with no paste and clogging the bottom. Porous concrete should have virtually zero slump.
Placement	In placement, porous concrete does not flow and must be raked into place; however, it requires no surface finishing after initial set. After placement it should be rolled, but not compacted or vibrated.	Surface infiltration rate can be reduced with excessive finishing or improper mixtures. Porous concrete is a relatively new technology and experienced contractors may be hard to find.

Table 5–19 Properties of Porous Concrete Pavement *(Continued)*

Phase	Advantages/Drawbacks as Compared with Standard Impermeable Concrete Pavement	Special Considerations
Placement (cont'd.)	Porous concrete placement should be done by experienced installers.	Soil below porous concrete and subbase should not be compacted more than 95%.
Curing	Porous concrete shrinkage during curing is less than standard concrete because of uniformly sized aggregate, which offers more stone-to-stone contact and interlock with less cement between.	Porous concrete should be covered immediately after rolling to prevent evaporation of water from the mix. Sheeting should remain for a few days.
Use/performance	Can aid infiltration of storm water with as much as 55 to hundreds of inches per hour of surface infiltration rate Can cleanse storm water, improving water quality by reducing organic carbon, phosphorus, and some metals through microbial growth attached to the concrete in the pore spaces Reduces driving noise Offers increased traction for vehicles driving on it Porous concrete made with No. 89 aggregate is usually around 2,000 psi. This is acceptable for most parking lot or light traffic road paving, but not the standard 3,500 psi of traditional concrete pavement. Thicknesses above the standard 6 inches can withstand greater loads.	Porous concrete made with No. 89 aggregate produces a smooth enough surface for bicycles and wheelchairs, but not in-line skates or possibly narrow high heels. Porous concrete is relatively untested in climates with freeze-thaw conditions. Porous concrete performance in Florida and other southern states is well proven. It is gaining use in the Pacific Northwest and parts of California. In cold climates, there are concerns about water freezing and expanding in pore spaces, or penetration of deicing chemicals leading to pavement failure. Research and testing of porous pavement in freeze-thaw situations is ongoing.
Maintenance	Is relatively low maintenance compared with other porous pavements. In areas where organic debris or sand is washed onto the pavement, porous pavements may require periodic pressure washing.	Snowplows should not be used on porous concrete. Or the blade should be set $1/2"$ higher than the pavement surface.

Ferguson 2005; Cahill, Adams, and Marm 2005; Maher et al. 2005; Pervious Concrete 2007

Some examples of potential nanotechnology applications in concrete are as follows (Elvin 2007; Korthals Altes 2008):

■ Grinding portland cement into nanoparticles has been shown to result in concrete with a fourfold increase in compressive strength. This finding could lead to concrete that uses significantly reduced amounts of portland cement.

■ The addition of nanoparticles of silica (SiO_2), titanium dioxide (TiO_2), and iron oxide (Fe_2O_3) to cement can improve cement's mechanical properties, such as increases in compressive and flexural strength. These additions could also lead to substantial reductions in cement use. Nano-silica can create denser packing of particles and reduce water penetration. It allows for greater amounts of fly ash in the mix without slowing curing speed.

■ Nanoparticles of titanium dioxide both in the concrete mix and surface-applied sealers can impart self-cleaning properties to concrete—and some can even reduce airborne pollutants. Some titanium dioxide molecules

Figure 5–2.

The Indiana Redi Mix Concrete Association trained contractors in placement of porous concrete for pavement at the Merry Lea Environmental Learning Center of Goshen College, a LEED Platinum Project. (Photo © Conservation Design Forum, 2008. All rights reserved www.cdfinc.com)

Figure 5–3.

SvR designed Washington's first porous concrete street in Seattle's High Point neighborhood as part of a community-wide natural drainage system. The porous concrete is six inches thick and the subgrade reservoir overflows to an adjacent bioswale. (Photo by SvR Design Company)

Figure 5–4.
SvR designed four-inch-thick porous concrete sidewalks throughout Seattle's High Point neighborhood. (Photo by SvR Design Company)

Figure 5–5.
The parking lot at Wenk Associates' Denver office is constructed from precast interlocking unit pavers with crushed, graded recycled concrete "gravel"-filled voids to allow infiltration of storm water. This allows tree planting in the pavement, as air and water will make their way to the roots. Pavers can be lifted out as the tree trunk grows. (Design by Wenk Associates, Inc. Photo by Meg Calkins)

Figure 5–6.
This strip of porous unit pavers divides the asphalt driving lanes on a "skinny street" in Seattle's New Columbia community by Mithun. While the asphalt pavement is not porous, it is graded to drain to the paver strip, where it can infiltrate into a gravel reservoir below the pavement. (Photo copyright Mithun, from Juan Hernandez)

Table 5–20 ASTM Standards Related to This Chapter

C33	Standard Specification for Concrete Aggregates
C125	Standard Terminology Related to Concrete and Concrete Aggregates
C150	Standard Specification for Portland Cement
C260	Standard Specification for Air-entraining Admixtures for Concrete
C330	Standard Specification for Lightweight Aggregates for Structural Concrete
C494/C494M	Standard Specification for Chemical Admixtures for Concrete
C595	Standard Specification for Blended Hydraulic Cements
C618	Standard Specification for Coal Fly Ash and Raw or Calcined Natural Pozzolan for Use in Concrete
C989	Standard Specification for Ground Granulated Blast Furnace Slag for Use in Concrete and Mortars
C1116	Standard Specification for Fiber-Reinforced Concrete and Shotcrete
C1157	Standard Performance Specification for Hydraulic Cement
C1240	Standard Specification for Silica Fume Used in Cementitious Mixtures

have photocatalytic properties. They release an electric charge when absorbing sunlight that forms reactive radicals, which oxidize nearby organic (and some inorganic) substances. Cement products with TiO_2 nanoparticles are formulated to be self-cleaning and/or to remove nitrogen oxide pollution from the surrounding air. These surface layers are available in panels, pavers, and cementitious plaster, as well as paint-on concrete sealants. In tests, a nano TiO_2 surface product applied to road surfaces was found to reduce the nitrogen oxide levels on the road by up to 60%.

- Carbon nanotubes, microscopic cylinders of graphite, called grapheme, are strong, flexible, and electrically and thermally conductive materials that can improve compressive and flexural strength of concrete, and adherence with mix elements.
- Nanofiber reinforcement, including carbon nanotubes, holds potential to strengthen concrete, possibly eliminating the need for conventional steel reinforcing in concrete. Nanofiber reinforcement, made from carbon, steel, or polymers, adds randomly oriented fibers in lengths ranging from nanometers to micrometers to increase concrete's tensile strength. Because of the fibers' ability to conduct electricity, they could also allow for heating of bridges and pavements, or self-monitoring for cracks.
- Nanosensors can be integrated into concrete to collect performance data such as stresses, reinforcing corrosion, pH levels, moisture, temperature, density, shrinkage, and curing. "Smart aggregates" are microelectromechanical devices cast directly into concrete buildings or roads and can monitor traffic volumes, road conditions, loads, and seismic activity.

REFERENCES

Advanced Cement Technologies (ACT). 2007. "Technical Bulletin, 10.1.07-Concrete Compressive Strength." http://www.metakaolin.com/.

Aïtcin, Pierre-Claude. 2000. "Cements of yesterday and today, concrete of tomorrow." *Cement and Concrete Research* 30(2000): 1349–59.

ASTM Standard C595. 2005a. "Standard Specification for Blended Hydraulic Cements." West Conshohocken, PA: ASTM International. www.astm.org.

ASTM Standard C618. 2005b. "Standard Specification for Coal Fly Ash and Raw or Calcined Natural Pozzolan for Use in Concrete." West Conshohocken, PA: ASTM International. www.astm.org.

ASTM Standard C125. 2006. "Standard Terminology Relating to Concrete and Concrete Aggregates." West Conshohocken, PA: ASTM International. www.astm.org.

ASTM Standard C150. 2007. "Standard Specification for Portland Cement." West Conshohocken, PA: ASTM International. www.astm.org.

Athena Sustainable Materials Institute. *Athena Environmental Impact Estimator.* Version 3.0.3. Kutztown, ON: Athena Sustainable Materials Institute.

Athena Sustainable Materials Institute. 2006. "A Life Cycle Perspective on Concrete and Asphalt Roadways: Embodied Primary Energy and Global Warming Potential." Submitted to Cement Association of Canada. Ottawa, ON: Athena Sustainable Materials Institute.

Austin Energy Green Building Program. 2007. *Sustainable Building Sourcebook.* Austin Energy. http://austinenergy.com/Energy%20Efficiency/Programs/Green%20Building/Sourcebook/earthConstruction.htm.

Berge, Bjørn. 2000. *The Ecology of Building Materials.* Oxford: Architectural Press.

BuildingGreen. *GreenSpec Directory Online.* Brattleboro, VT: BuildingGreen, Inc. http://www.buildinggreen.com (accessed November 11, 2007).

Cahill, Thomas, Michele Adams, and Courtney Marm. 2005. "Stormwater management with porous pavements." *Government Engineering,* March–April:14–19.

Cross, Doug, Jerry Stephens, and Jason Vollmer. 2005. "Structural Applications of 100% Fly Ash Concrete." http://www.flyash.info/2005/131cro.pdf (accessed December 12, 2005).

Demkin, J., ed. 1998. "Materials Report 05410: Concrete." In *Environmental Resource Guide.* New York: John Wiley & Sons.

EcoSmart Foundation. EcoSmart Concrete. http://www.ecosmartconcrete.com/enviro_cement.cfm (accessed June 7, 2007).

Elvin, G. A. 2007, June. "Nanotechnology for Green Building." Green Technology Forum. http://www.greentechforum.net/.

Environmental Building News (EBN). 2004. "A Green Release Agent for Concrete Forms." In *Environmental Building News.* Brattleboro, Vermont: Building Green. Vol. 6:1.

Environmental Building News (EBN). 1993."Cement and Concrete: Environmental Considerations." In *Environmental Building News.* Brattleboro, Vermont: Building Green. Vol. 2:2.

Fab-Form <http://www.fab-form.com/products/green/fastfoot_green.html>

Federal Highway Administration (FHWA). 2004, September. "Transportation Applications of Recycled Concrete Aggregate." *FHWA State of the Practice National Review.* U.S. Department of Transportation.

Federal Highway Administration (FHWA). 2006, December. *Integrated Materials and Construction Practices for Concrete Pavement: A State-of-the-Practice Manual,* FHWA HIF–07–004. Authors: Peter C. Taylor, Steven H. Kosmatka, Gerald F. Voigt, et al. Ames, IA: National Concrete Pavement Technology Center/Center for Transportation Research and Education, Iowa State University.

Ferguson, Bruce. 2005. *Porous Pavements.* Boca Raton, FL: CRC Press.

Ghaly, A.M. and Gill, M.S. (2004) "Compression and Deformation Performance of Concrete Containing Postconsumer Plastics" *Journal of Materials in Civil Engineering,* Volume 16, Issue 4, pp. 289–296 (July/August 2004)

Hammond, G., and C. Jones. 2006. "Inventory of Carbon and Energy." Version 1.5 Beta Bath, UK: University of Bath, Department of Mechanical Engineering.

Holland, Terrance C. 2005. *Silica Fume User's Manual.* Lovettsville, VA: Silica Fume Association, and Washington, DC: Federal Highway Association.

Humphreys, K., and M. Mahasenan. 2002, March. *Substudy 8: Climate Change—Toward a Sustainable Cement Industry.* An Independent Study Commissioned by the World Business Council for Sustainable Development (WBCSD).

Khalaf, F. M., and A. S. DeVenny. 2004. "Recycling of demolished masonry rubble as coarse aggregate in concrete: Review." *Journal of Materials in Civil Engineering* 16(4): 331–40.

Khatib, Z. K., and F. M. Bayomy. 1999. "Rubberized portland cement concrete." *Journal of Materials in Civil Engineering* 11(3): 206–13.

King, Bruce P.E. 2005. *Making Better Concrete.* San Rafael, CA: Green Building Press.

Korthals, Altes, Tristan. 2008. "Is Nano a No-No? Nanotechnology Advances in Buildings." *Environmental Building News.* Brattleboro, VT: Building Green. Volume 17:3.

Lippiatt, Barbara C. 2007. *BEES 4.0 Building for Environmental and Economic Sustainability Technical Manual and User Guide.* Gaithersburg, MD: National Institute of Standards and Technology.

Maher, M., C. Marshall, F. Harrison, and K. Baumgaertner. 2005. *Context Sensitive Roadway Surfacing Selection Guide.* Lakewood, CO: Federal Highway Administration, Central Federal Lands Highway Division.

Marlowe, I., and D. Mansfield. 2002, December. *Substudy 10: Environment, Health & Safety Performance Improvement.* An independent study commissioned by the World Business Council for Sustainable Development (WBCSD).

Medgar, L. M., M. A. Nisbet, and M. G. Van Geem. 2006. "Life Cycle Inventory of Portland Cement Manufacture." PCA R&D Serial No. 2095b, prepared for the Portland Cement Association (PCA), Skokie, Illinois.

Medgar, L. M., M. A. Nisbet, and M. G. Van Geem. 2007. "Life Cycle Inventory of Portland Cement Concrete." PCA R&D Serial No. 3011, prepared for the Portland Cement Association (PCA), Skokie, Illinois.

Mehta, P. K. 1998. The role of fly ash in sustainable development. *Concrete, Fly Ash and the Environment Proceedings,* December 8, 1998. pp. 13–25.

Mehta, P. K. 2002. "Greening of the Concrete Industry for Sustainable Development," *Concrete International,* Vol. 24, No. 7, July 2002, pp. 23–28.

Meyer, C. 2000. "Concrete Materials Research at Columbia University." Concrete Materials Research Laboratory. http://www.civil.columbia.edu/meyer/pdffiles/glass.pdf.

Meyer, C. 2005. "Concrete as a Green Building Material." Invited Lecture, Proceedings of the Third Int. Conference on Construction Materials, ConMat'05, Vancouver, BC, August 22–25, 2005.

Naik, T. R., Parikh, D.M., and M.P. Tharaniyil. "Utilization of Used Foundry Sand as Construction Materials." Report No. CBU-1992–23, Center of By-Product Utilization, Department of Civil Engineering and Mechanics, University of Wisconsin, Milwaukee (June 1992).

National Slag Association (NSA). http://www.nationalslag.org/.

Partnership for Advancing Technology in Housing (PATH). "Concrete Aggregate Substitutes: Alternative Aggregate Materials." PATH: Toolbase Resources. <http://www.toolbase.org/Construction-Methods/Concrete-Construction/concrete-aggregate-substitutes> (accessed November 4, 2006).

Pervious Concrete. <http://www.perviouspavement.org/> (accessed March 20, 2007)

Portland Cement Association (PCA) Newsroom. 2003. "Cement Formulation Change Promises Improved Emission Performance." Press release November 13, 2003. Skokie, IL: Portland Cement Association.

Portland Cement Association (PCA). "Concrete Thinking for a Sustainable World." Skokie, IL: Portland Cement Association. http://www.cement.org/concretethinking/ (accessed April 14, 2006).

Recycled Materials Resource Center (RMRC). "Synthetic Lightweight Aggregate for Highway Construction." Prepared by GEI Consultants, Inc. Durham, NH: The Recycled Materials Resource Center, July 2001, Project 99288–2.

Recycled Materials Resource Center. http://www.rmrc.unh.edu/Partners/UserGuide/index.htm.

Slag Cement Association (SCA). 2006. "Slag Cement and LEED." Sugar Land, Texas: Slag Cement Association, 2006 No.28.

South Coast Air Quality Management District (SCAQMD). "Rule 1113, Architectural Coatings." Amended July 13,

2007. California South Coast Air Quality Management District.

Spiegel, Ross and Dru Meadows. 2006. *Green Building Materials.* Hoboken, NJ: John Wiley & Sons.

Texas Department of Transportation (DOT). www.dot.state.tx.us/.

Thompson, J. W., and K. Sorvig. 2000. *Sustainable Landscape Construction: A Guide to Green Building Outdoors.* Washington, DC: Island Press.

U.S. Environmental Protection Agency (U.S. EPA). 1995. "Chapter 11: Mineral Products Industry, Section 11.6.6 Portland Cement Manufacturing." *AP 42,* 5th ed. Clearinghouse for Inventories and Emissions Factors, Technology Transfer Network, U.S. EPA.

U.S. Environmental Protection Agency (U.S. EPA). 1998. "Characterization of Building-related Construction and Demolition Debris in the United States." Report No. EPA530-R-98-010. Prepared by Franklin Associates for Office of Solid Waste, U.S. EPA.

U.S. Environmental Protection Agency (U.S. EPA). 2006a. "Cement Industry." *2006 Sector Strategies Performance Report.* Sector Programs, U.S. EPA.

U.S. Environmental Protection Agency (U.S. EPA). 2006b. "Cement and Concrete." Comprehensive Procurement Guidelines. http://www.epa.gov/cpg/products/cement. htm.

U.S. Environmental Protection Agency (U.S. EPA). 2007a. "Inventory of U.S. Greenhouse Gas Emissions and Sinks, 1990–2005." April 2007. Report EPA 430-R-07–002.

U.S. Environmental Protection Agency (U.S. EPA). Office of Policy, Economics and Innovation. 2007b. *Energy Trends in Selected Manufacturing Sectors: Opportunities and Challenges for Environmentally Preferable Energy Outcomes.* Prepared by ICF International, March 2007.

U.S. Geological Survey (USGS). 2007. "Cement." In *2005 Minerals Yearbook.* Washington, DC: USGS.

U.S. Green Building Council (USGBC). 2005. *LEED-NC for New Construction Reference Guide.* Version 2.2 1st ed. Washington, DC: USGBC.

World Business Council for Sustainable Development (WBCSD). "Cement Sustainability Initiative." http://www. wbcsdcement.org.

chapter **6**

Earthen Materials

Earth construction building methods have been in use worldwide, both in buildings and site structures, for thousands of years. The adobe walls of Jericho, dating to 8300 BC; parts of the Great Wall of China over 2,000 years ago; and some of the oldest historic structures in the western United States are of earth construction, having survived for hundreds of years (McHenry 1984). And while earth structures are currently not widely used in the United States outside the Southwest, it is estimated that 40% of the world population lives in earth structures (Houben and Guillard 1994). Many feel that with the end of inexpensive oil, there will be a movement back to lower embodied energy construction techniques and use of local materials (Piepkorn 2005).

Earth construction offers many environmental and aesthetic advantages. The raw materials for earth construction, primarily soil and sand, are inexpensive, and often can be found on or near the project site, saving transport energy costs as well. The materials are minimally processed and coupled with minimal transport, result in relatively low embodied energy. Most earth materials are nontoxic and nonpolluting. Earth buildings perform very well thermally, with the thick walls moderating temperature extremes and acting as thermal mass for storing heat gain from sunlight. After a structure's useful life, the materials can either be returned to the earth or reused easily in a new earth structure.

But earth construction is not without challenges, many of which stem from the lack of its use in modern construction. Codes only minimally address earth construction methods, if at all—structural performance of some methods is not well documented, structural engineers are not trained to design earth structures, and contractors skilled in earth construction are not easily found in many parts of the United States. Public perceptions of earth construction limit its viability to the southwestern United States, although many methods are appropriate for areas of temperature extremes and even heavy rainfall. And there is a perception that earth structures are not as structurally sound as concrete or wood frame construction, although many adobe structures have survived earthquakes in California that other buildings haven't.

Materials for Earth Construction

The materials for earth construction vary slightly by construction type, but all incorporate soil with some percentage of clay, and water. The soil is minimally processed, if at all, and is used efficiently as any waste can be returned to the earth or used in other structures. For instance, any leftover soil from a rammed earth wall or building can be used to make soil cement paving for

Table 6–1 Embodied Energy and Carbon for Earth Materials (1 Metric Ton)

Earth Material (1 metric ton)	Embodied Energy (MJ)	Embodied Carbon (kg CO$_2$)	Comments
Soil cement	850	140	Quantity of cement not specified
Rammed earth	450	24	No cement
Lime (hydrated)	5,300	1,290	

Source: Adapted from Hammond and Jones 2006 (All data is for materials used in the UK. Data was collected from UK and EU sources and worldwide averages. Values may vary from U.S. figures but are useful for comparisons among materials.)

paths on-site, or if it does not contain cement, it can be used as soil in other site applications.

Soil used in earth construction is locally obtained, often from the site, and the type of earth construction used is often determined by the suitability of local soils. Southwestern soils are ideally suited for adobe block, and the dry climate easily permits the ten dry days required for curing of the blocks.

Soils

Soil mixes for earth construction vary by application and performance requirements. They may be locally occurring soils or engineered mixes of different soils. Good sources of soils can be on-site horizons (not topsoil), alluvial deposits, soil from other construction excavations, or by-products of gravel and sand quarrying.

Types of soil available and climatic and site conditions are critical considerations when determining whether to build earth structures, and which type to build. Properties of the soil that will be used in the earth structure may be the most critical factor and must be well understood to determine the appropriate mix. Desirable properties for soil construction are

Table 6–2 Embodied Energy of Block Materials

Block Material (1 unit)	Embodied Energy (MJ)	Size of Unit
Adobe block	2.64	10" × 4" × 14"
Concrete block (1 block)	30.6	8" × 8" × 16"
Common brick	14.3	2$\frac{1}{2}$" × 4" × 8"

Source: Adapted from McHenry 1984

strength, low moisture absorption, limited shrink/swell reaction, and high resistance to chemical attack (SBS).

The following soils discussion contains information drawn from two sources addressing soil suitability for earth construction: *The Handbook for Building Homes of Earth* (1980) and *Earth Construction: A Comprehensive Guide* (1994). Properties of soil for earth construction fall into four main categories:

Particle size distribution, also referred to as texture, is the percentage of different grain sizes within the soil. Soils with a high percentage of coarse grains may weaken earth structures by crumbling and will need to be amended with fine materials. Soils with too many fine grains (e.g., clayey soils) may need the addition of sand to become useful.

Plasticity refers to a soil's ability to deform without cracking or disintegrating. It is important in earth construction because it reveals the ease of shaping the soil and the sensitivity of the soil to variations in humidity.

Compactibility defines a soil's potential to reduce its porosity and decrease its void ratio. The higher the density achieved, the more porosity is reduced and the less water can penetrate it.

Cohesion is the ability of a soil's grains to remain together when a tensile force is placed on the material. Cohesion is dependent on the adhesive or cementing properties of its coarse mortar (clay, silt, or fine sand).

Table 6-3 Unified Soil Classification (USC) System from ASTM D2487

Major Divisions			Group Symbol	Typical Names
Course-grained soils More than 50% retained on the 0.075 mm (No. 200) sieve	**Gravels** 50% or more of coarse fraction retained on the 4.75 mm (No. 4) sieve	Clean gravels	GW	Well-graded gravels and gravel-sand mixtures, little or no fines
			GP	Poorly graded gravels and gravel-sand mixtures, little or no fines
		Gravels with fines	GM	Silty gravels, gravel-and-clay mixtures
			GC	Clayey gravels, gravel-sand-clay mixtures
	Sands 50% or more of coarse fraction passes the 4.75 mm (No. 4) sieve	Clean sands	SW	Well-graded sands and gravelly sands, little or no fines
			SP	Poorly graded sands and gravelly sands, little or no fines
		Sands with fines	SM	Silty sands, sand-silt mixtures
			SC	Clayey sands, sand-clay mixtures
Fine-grained soils More than 50% passes the 0.075 mm (No. 200) sieve	**Silts and clays** Liquid limit 50% or less		ML	Inorganic silts, very fine sands, rock four, silty or clayey fine sands
			CL	Inorganic clays of low to medium plasticity, gravelly/sandy/silty/lean clays
			OL	Organic silts and organic silty clays of low plasticity
	Silts and clays Liquid limit greater than 50%		MH	Inorganic silts and organic silty clays of low plasticity
			CH	Inorganic clays of high plasticity, fat clays
			OH	Organic clays of medium to high plasticity
Highly organic soils			PT	Peat, muck, and other highly organic soils

Prefix: G = Gravel, S = Sand, M = Silt, C = Clay, O = Organic, PT = Peat
Suffix: W = Well Graded, P = Poorly Graded, M = Silty, L = Clay, H = Clay
Source: ASTM Standard D2487 2006

The main groups of soils that offer potential use in earth construction are silt, clay, sand, and gravel soils. They are a mix of binder soils such as clay, silt, clay-silt combination, or loam mixed with temper soils of sand (particle sizes of 0.5 mm to 2 mm) and gravel (particle sizes greater than 2 mm) (see Table 6–3). Straw, hair, and chaff are organic tempers added for fibrous bonding and reduction of cracking during the curing process. The following discusses these soil components as they relate to earth construction:

Clay, when wetted, is the sticky material that bonds the soil particles together. It is inorganic soil with particle sizes less than 0.005 mm with high to very high dry strength, and medium to high plasticity (ASTM 2005a). The best types of soils for earth structures are those characterized as "clayey sands." Adobes and mud plasters are made with 8%–15% clay, and earth mixtures with over 30% clay content are subject to excessive cracking (Moquin 2000).

Some clay soils, such as montmorillonites or bentonitic soil, are highly expansive when wet and when dry can shrink and crack. They are unsuitable for earth construction unless they are modified with sand (Austin Energy 2007). Other clays such as kaolinite, laterites, and illite do not swell and crack and can be appropriate for earth construction.

Sand, an inorganic soil, consists of fine grains of rocks, primarily quartz ranging in size from 0.05 mm to 2 mm. Sand is characterized by its high strength and lack of particle porosity. Clayey sands can be suitable for earth construction.

Silt is inorganic soil particles ranging from 0.005 mm to 0.05 mm that are characterized by low dry strength, low plasticity, and softening when wet. When wet and compressed, silt particles hold together, but when frozen and wet, they tend to swell and lose strength. Soils with high silt content should be stabilized with emulsified asphalt, cement, or other stabilizers when used in earth construction.

Gravel is inorganic soil with sizes greater than 2 mm. It is characterized by its relatively high compressive strength, resistance to freeze-thaw movement, and lack of particle porosity. Gravel is used in earth construction, for gravel trench foundations, and for levels of earthbag construction that are just above or below grade. Clayey gravel soils with small gravel particles can be suitable for earth construction. Larger particles can be sifted out prior to mixing.

Organic soils such as loam are characterized by their dark color, spongy texture when wet, decaying smell, and acidic pH (5.5 or less). These soils should be avoided in earth construction mixes.

Soil Testing

It is critically important to test soils for suitability of use in an earth structure. Tests will reveal a soil's stability, permeability, plasticity, cohesion, compactibility, expansiveness, durability, abrasiveness, and material content (SBS). Soil requirements vary among earth construction types and structures. There are a variety of soil tests—some of which can be performed on-site, others in labs—that should be performed to determine traits and necessary amendments of a potential soil.

Soil testing for earth structures should be performed in the following three phases:

Soil property testing can be performed first informally on-site (if on-site materials will be used), then in a soil-testing laboratory. Testing should be conducted early in the design process to determine the feasibility of the soil and the earth construction system. There are several on-site tests that can be performed to determine potential usefulness of soil.

The "shake test, testing the basic composition of a soil, involves filling a glass jar half full with soil, then adding water to fill the jar, shaking until all particles are suspended. Particles will fall to the bottom in order of weight: first stones, then sand, then silt. Clay will stay in suspension and organic matter will float to the top" (Smith 2000).

Once composition of soil is determined, a sample should be sent to a lab for testing. While there are numerous soil engineering classifications, Houben and Guillaud (1994) recommend that the Engineering Geology Classification is the best suited to earth construction. Soils are classified by grain size distribution, plasticity, compactibility, cohesion, and quantity of organic matter.

Construction mix testing determines the correct mix and moisture content for a given soil and application. Sample mixes are made and shaped into forms that are dropped, measured, or deformed in some way to test the mix proportions. Numerous soil mix tests for earth construction are well detailed in Houben and Guillard (1994), Norton (1997), and Minke (2006). It is important to note that tests and results will vary depending on the application or construction method.

Table 6–4 Standards and Codes for Earth Construction

Codes	
Part 4 2003	New Mexico Earthen Building Materials Code *Title 14 Housing and Construction, Chapter 7 Building Codes General*, State of New Mexico
ASTM standards	
E2392	Standard Guide for Design of Earth Wall Building Systems
D4609	Standard Guide for Evaluating Effectiveness of Chemicals for Soil Stabilization
D5239	Standard Practice for Characterizing Fly Ash for Use in Soil Stabilization
D653	Standard Terminology Relating to Soil, Rock, and Contained Fluids
C618	Standard Specification for Coal Fly Ash and Raw or Calcined Natural Pozzolan for Use in Concrete
C977	Revision of Standard Specification for Quicklime and Hydrated Lime for Soil Stabilization
D559	Test Methods for Wetting and Drying Compacted Soil-Cement Mixtures
D560	Test Methods for Freezing and Thawing Compacted Soil-Cement Mixtures
D698	Standard Test Methods for Laboratory Compaction Characteristics of Soil Using Standard Effort (12,400 ft-lbf/ft^3 [600 kN-m/m^3])
AASHTO standards	
M147	Materials for Aggregate and Soil-Aggregate Subbase, Base, and Surface Courses
TF28–1	Guidelines and Guide Specifications for Using Pozzolanic Stabilized Mixture (Base Course or Subbase) and Fly Ash for In-place Subgrade Soil Modifications

Quality control testing tests samples of blocks or wall or paving sections for performance under various stresses and impacts. Compressive strength, modulus of rupture, resistance to water erosion, and absorption are important properties to test (Norton 1997). The Uniform Building Code (UBC) standard for wall compressive strength for buildings is 960 psi (Austin Energy 2007). ASTM offers some standards for testing at the quality control phase. They are listed in the table above along with other standards pertaining to earth construction.

Structural Considerations for Earth Construction

Structural considerations for earth structures vary widely with the type of application, performance requirements, construction method, and climatic and seismic conditions of the site. Most sources of information on structural design of earth structures address building structures, not retaining walls, freestanding walls, and pavements. Therefore some information provided in this section has been adapted or interpreted for use in landscape structures. With the exception of earthbag construction, there is little mention of structural design of earth retaining walls.

There exists a large body of literature on structural considerations for soil cement and stabilized soil bases for pavements. However, little attention is given to the use of soil cement as a wearing course in pavement design. Because structural considerations of soil cement vary so widely from earth wall systems, they will be discussed primarily in the soil cement section of this chapter.

IMPROVING SOILS FOR EARTH CONSTRUCTION

Soils for earth construction typically must be able to attain compressive strengths between 200 and 800 pounds per square inch (psi). By some codes, 300 psi is considered to be the minimum allowed for adobe (State of New Mexico 2003; King 2000; McHenry 1984). Some conditions to which the earth structure will be subjected necessitate that soil be stabilized. And some soils deemed unsuitable for earth construction can be altered with stabilizers to make them appropriate. Stabilization can be mechanical (e.g., compacting), physical (e.g., addition of fibers or minerals), or chemical (e.g., cement, lime, or asphalt emulsions) (Houben and Guillard 1994). Table 6–5 summarizes six methods of soil stabilization for earth construction.

It is important to note that some modifications such as cementation, stabilization, and waterproofing will decrease or eliminate the possibility of an earthen struc-ture being recycled quickly to living soil (Sorvig 2007). However, the demolished structure could be reworked into a new earthen structure.

FOUNDATIONS FOR EARTH STRUCTURES

Foundations for earth structures should ensure that the loads of the structure (often quite considerable given the weight of compacted soil) are transferred to soil capable of supporting the structure. Foundations also serve to hold the earth material above prolonged contact with water from soil moisture and runoff.

In temperate climates, impervious materials, such as concrete, concrete block, stone, or fired brick should be

Table 6–5 Methods of Soil Stabilization for Earth Construction

Densification	Usually accomplished through grinding and compaction and elimination of air, creating a dense soil medium that blocks pores and capillarity.
Reinforcement	Addition of materials either fibrous or mineral, such as straw, synthetic hair strands, sand, or gravel, can increase a soil's resistance to tension, thermal expansion, and drying/cracking.
Cementation	Introduces a new matrix to the soil that consolidates it by filling voids and coats the grains with an insoluble binder. Portland cement is the primary matrix used; however, class C fly ash, sodium silicates, resins, and adhesives have been used. Cementation involves chemical reactions where the main activity takes place within the stabilizer and with the sandy part of the soil. Cement is fairly inexpensive, but uses significant energy inputs and releases greenhouse gases and other pollutants in production, so use of other cementitious materials such as Class C fly ash may be desirable.
Linkages	The addition of a new matrix to cause a pozzolanic reaction that binds the clay particles together, producing a stable bond. ASTM standard C618 (2005) defines a pozzolan as "a siliceous or siliceous and aluminous material, which in itself possesses little or no cementitious value but which will, in finely divided form and in the presence of moisture, chemically react with calcium hydroxide at ordinary temperatures to form compounds possessing cementitious properties." Typical materials used for this in earth construction are hydrated lime and fly ash, to a lesser degree. Lime is inexpensive and readily available, but like many pozzolanic materials, it can pose hazards to workers from breathing in lime dust. Other pozzolanic materials that are potential stabilizers for earth construction are industrial by-products such as fly ash, ground granulated blast furnace slag, and silica fume. Other pozzolans are mined (e.g., diatomaceous earth or volcanic tuffs) and manufactured (e.g., metakaolin from calcined clay). These pozzolans are defined as Class N. Like the use of pozzolans in concrete, the reaction proceeds slowly. Addition of cement, lime, or pozzolanic materials can increase the compressive strength of earth materials to 1,000–2,000 psi or more.
Imperviousness	Stabilization techniques help reduce water erosion and shrink swell by limiting or eliminating water absorption. This method, using bitumen (naturally occurring) or low percentages of asphalt (2%–4%), fills voids, pores, and cracks and surrounds soils with a waterproof film.
Waterproofing	Waterproofing eliminates a soil's absorption of water by coating particles and filling pore spaces with a waterproofing compound such as emulsified asphalt.

Sources: Minke 2006; King 2000; Houben and Guillard 1994; Sorvig 1995, 2007

used for foundations for earth structures to minimize water penetration to the structure above. Rammed earth tires can also be used, as tires are not prone to decay in the presence of moisture.

In arid climates with short duration rainstorms, earth foundations can be used in conjunction with compacted ground next to the structure to minimize infiltration near the foundation (Minke 2006, Norton 1997).

Earth foundations, stabilized with lime, cement, pozzolanic materials, or asphalt, are sometimes used for earth structures, particularly in freeze-thaw climates or seismic zones. Foundations with lime and some pozzolans will take time to cure and should be constructed several months ahead of the wall structure.

Like concrete or concrete block wall structures, foundations for earth structures must resist forces from earth cycles of freezing and thawing. This usually requires extension of the footing below the frostline, which in some climates can be a considerable distance. In most cases, foundations extend out from the width of the wall at a 60° angle (Norton 1997).

An alternative foundation system, the gravel-sand trench, acts as an isolation layer between soil movement and the structure and is a shallow alternative that may be appropriate for low walls. A concrete bond beam is sometimes used in conjunction with the gravel-sand trench when modular earth materials such as adobe or compressed earth blocks are used. The gravel-sand trench foundation is said to be one of the most seismically resistant foundations, as it performs as a type of isolation system (Minke 2006; Moquin 2000).

Earth structures will often benefit from stabilization of the lower levels of the wall with asphalt or other waterproofing to protect against moisture penetration. For instance, in adobe construction, it is common to use stabilized adobe (asphalt added) for the first few courses of block above grade. Traditionally, these first courses were often stone (Sorvig 2007). Rammed earth tires or earthbags will not need a stabilized layer as they are resistant to decay by virtue of their permanent "formwork" (tires or plastic sacks).

REINFORCING FOR EARTH STRUCTURES

Design of earth structures in seismic zones does not typically incorporate steel reinforcing, unless required by code. Instead, the primary method of stabilization of earth structures is the addition of portland cement or other strengthening additives.

Reinforcing steel does not bond to unstabilized earth mixes as it does to wet concrete, and the two materials have different coefficients of expansion. Reinforcing steel in rammed earth or cob construction will get in the way of tamping and compacting efforts during construction. And the penetration of rebar from a concrete footing into a rammed earth wall may weaken it with more points for cracks to occur (Beatty 1994). Therefore, steel reinforcing used in concrete foundations should not extend more than a few inches into rammed earth walls.

Pneumatically impacted stabilized earth (PISE) is an exception to this. Steel reinforcing is commonly used as it provides a structure that can support the sprayed earth and to which it can attach.

Earth Construction Methods

ADOBE BRICKS

Adobe bricks, the most common method of earth construction worldwide, are formed and air-dried bricks made from clay and sand, and sometimes straw or stabilizing additives. These bricks are primarily laid in a running bond using clay-based mortar. They are also used to form arches and domes. Stabilized adobe bricks containing emulsified asphalt for waterproofing have also been used as pavers (Sorvig 1995).

Adobe structures offer many benefits. Clay soil suitable for adobe is found in many locations throughout the world, making it a local material, saving transportation energy and costs. Many building sites contain soil that is suitable for adobe bricks and portable brick-making equipment is available to travel to sites. Adobe is relatively simple to produce, and like brick is easily laid by hand. Because bricks are not fired, it is a relatively low embodied energy product. And when an adobe structure is no longer in use, it can be returned to the soil.

Sizes of adobe blocks vary by region and manufacturer. Modern adobe walls are usually one adobe brick thick (10"–16"). The standard New Mexico adobe is

Table 6–6 Earth Construction Methods for Site Walls

Type, Compressive Strength, and Applications	Mix and Material Proportions	Notes
Unstabilized adobe Unfired masonry units made of soil, water, and straw without admixtures[a] 430–580 psi[b] Freestanding walls	Suitable soil mixes vary widely. Average mix of soils:[d] Coarse sand: 23% Fine sand: 30% Silt: 32% Clay: 15% Water, sometimes straw	Maximum particle size recommended is $1/4$ Must cure in sun for 10–14 days before use Suitable for low-height retaining walls if blocks are keyed or interlock
Stabilized adobe Unfired masonry units made of soil, water, and straw to which admixtures, such as emulsified asphalt or cement, are added during the manufacturing process to help limit water absorption and increase durability[a] 430–580 psi[b] Low retaining walls Freestanding walls	Average mix of soils:[d] Coarse sand: 23% Fine sand: 30% Silt: 32% Clay: 15% Water, sometimes straw 3–4% asphalt emulsion for "semi-stabilized" 4–6% asphalt emulsion for "stabilized"[d]	Maximum particle size recommended is $1/4$" Must cure in sun for 10–14 days before use Suitable for low-height retaining walls if blocks are keyed or interlock
Pressed block or compressed earth block A construction system that consists of walls made from earth materials formed in a block mold by the compacting of lightly moistened earth into a hardened mass[a] 1,100 psi if unstabilized[b] 3,000 psi if stabilized[b] Low retaining walls Freestanding walls	"Unstabilized" is 30% clay content soil, 6%–8% water[b] "Semi-stabilized" contains 2%–5% portland cement or pozzolanic materials by weight[b] "Stabilized" contains 5%–10% portland cement or pozzolanic materials by weight[b]	Can be laid immediately after being formed. Will take days to fully cure. Suitable for low-height retaining walls if blocks are keyed or interlock
Rammed earth A construction system that consists of walls made from moist, sandy soil or stabilized soil that is tamped into forms[a] 450–800 psi[c] Low retaining walls Freestanding walls	Mixes vary widely. 15%–18% dimensionally stable clay[c] 35% silt 50% sand Sometimes 3%–8% portland cement, lime, or fly ash[e] Contains less water than other earth construction types	Suitable in many climates More time consuming to construct than adobe

Table 6–6 Earth Construction Methods for Site Walls *(Continued)*

Type, Compressive Strength, and Applications	Mix and Material Proportions	Notes
Pneumatically impacted stabilized earth (PISE) A modified version of rammed earth construction where an earth mixture is sprayed onto one-sided formwork with high-pressure air delivery This method, similar to dry mix shotcrete or gunnite delivery of concrete for swimming pool walls, was developed by David Easton to increase speed of earth construction, allowing trained crews to complete up to 1,200 square feet of eighteen-inch-thick wall per day (Rammed Earth Works). Freestanding walls	Proprietary mix of soil and cement	While construction time is shorter, PISE requires more costly equipment than rammed earth construction and a six-to-eight-person crew. After PISE is shot against the one-sided forms, excess material is shaved and smoothed to produce a plumb wall. The PISE method was recently developed in California and is not yet widely in use. Efforts to refine formwork construction, mix design, and construction techniques are ongoing with the intent to make the cost of PISE construction competitive with standard methods of home building (Rammed Earth Works).
Cast earth A construction system utilizing a slurry containing soil, calcined gypsum, and water which is poured into forms similar to those used for cast-in-place concrete[a] The chemical reaction between calcined gypsum (better known as plaster of paris) and water causes cast earth to cure very rapidly, so set-retarding admixtures are used to allow time for placement. 600–700 psi Low retaining walls Freestanding walls	Soil (15%–40% clay), calcined gypsum (15%), water, set retarder, sometimes iron oxide pigments for aesthetic purposes[f] A wide range of soils is appropriate for cast earth construction. The mix is not dependent on the soil's natural cohesiveness as the calcined gypsum is cementitious. The presence of gypsum can counteract the tendency of some clays to expand and shrink with changing moisture content.[f]	Currently this is a proprietary system in limited use. The quick-curing and relatively high compressive wet strength of the material (50 psi) means that formwork can be removed almost immediately.[f] Like other earth walls, cast earth should be protected from water penetration with a surface treatment such as cement plaster, mud plaster, or silicone water repellents. While the addition of integral asphalt emulsion is feasible with this technology, the manufacturer does not recommend use of asphalt for health and aesthetic reasons. Experiments are ongoing with another type of integral waterproofing material.[f]
Cob A construction system utilizing moist earth material balls stacked on top of one another and packed into place to form monolithic walls. Reinforcing is often provided with organic fibrous materials such as straw and twigs.[a] Freestanding walls	Soil with 5%–25% clay content 10% long fiber (eight to sixteen inches) straw	

Continued

Table 6–6 Earth Construction Methods for Site Walls *(Continued)*

Type, Compressive Strength, and Applications	Mix and Material Proportions	Notes
Earthbags Earthbags are plastic or textile bags filled with soil and sometimes sand or gravel, laid in courses, and tamped solid. Low retaining walls Freestanding walls	Soil mix can vary widely as bags act as formwork until soil is set. Cement, lime, or fly ash is sometimes added for increased strength. 100% gravel, no soil, is sometimes used in bags in lower courses.	Excellent in retaining walls
Rammed earth tires Reclaimed tires are filled with a damp soil mix, like rammed earth, and tightly packed using sledgehammers or a pneumatic tamper. Filled tires are stacked in a running bond pattern. Low retaining walls Freestanding walls	Soil mix can vary widely as tires act as permanent formwork; soil composition is less critical than with other earth construction systems.	Tires should be stacked with a batter for retaining walls. Stability depends on dead weight of tires filled with rammed earth, which is about 300–400 pounds per tire.

[a]ASTM Standard E2392 2005
[b]Demkin 1998
[c]McHenry 1984
[d]Moquin 2000
[e]Austin Energy 2007
[f]Cast Earth

4" × 10" × 14", and in Arizona they are typically 4" × 12" × 16" (Moquin 2000). And if adobe bricks are self-manufactured, sizes can vary widely. Because the large bricks are air dried, they are usually produced in thicknesses of four inches or less.

There are three types of adobe brick produced in the United States today:

Traditional adobe brick is a mix of sand, silt, clay, and straw (for fibrous bonding). Adobe is susceptible to moisture, so structures of traditional bricks exposed to weather will need to have a waterproof finish applied, and bricks should not come in direct contact with the ground.

Semi-stabilized adobe brick contains 3%–4% asphalt emulsion in addition to the traditional ingredients. The addition of asphalt emulsion will result in adobe bricks that are waterproof and can be used in grade-level base courses. They will still need to be finished with cement stucco or clay mud plasters.

Stabilized adobe brick contains 4%–6% asphalt emulsion. As a result, adobe bricks resist water penetration with an absorption rate under prolonged water exposure of 0.5%–3%, lower than 8% for standard concrete and 8%–12% for fired brick. The resistance to water and wind erosion of stabilized bricks means that they can be left exposed with no finish material applied. Sandier soil requires less asphalt emulsion than soils with higher clay content (Moquin 2000). Use of too much asphalt emulsion will result in a weakened block as the soil particles become too lubricated.

Because water entering unstabilized adobe bricks will cause them to disintegrate, there is a common

Figure 6–1.
Adobe blocks can be formed on the construction site, often from on-site soil if appropriate, at the rate of 1,000 bricks per day. (Photo by Quentin Wilson)

Figure 6–2.
Adobe blocks with straw reinforcing in a demonstration display. (Photo by Quentin Wilson)

misperception that adobe structures are only suitable in dry climates; however, adobe is used in locations such as England, France, Central America, and China, and soil suitable for adobe is found in these areas (Moquin 2000). The incorporation of stabilizers such as asphalt and/or plastering and roof overhangs will allow an adobe structure to resist the erosional forces of rain.

The primary reasons that adobe is not used in regions of the United States other than the Southwest have to do with building codes and manufacturer locations. U.S. building code addresses adobe (as unreinforced masonry); however, it requires vertical reinforcing in all zones with seismicity greater than 1 (this includes most of the western United States). And the code has resulted in nonuse of adobe construction in regions, such as California, that are noted for their historic adobe structures (Moquin 2000).

Some experts feel as if this code treats adobe construction like concrete by requiring strength-based measures and ignoring the unique way that adobe performs. They argue for stability-based measures such as surface skins and wider walls (Moquin 2000).

New Mexico's adobe code, requiring no vertical reinforcing, has served as a model for other state codes. Many feel that it better acknowledges the nature of the material by requiring thickened walls (16" minimum) in seismic areas. Also, surface skins for adobe structures comprised of chicken wire netting or vinyl straps have been found to perform well by preventing out-of-plane failure with simulated lateral forces of earthquakes (State of New Mexico 2003).

COMPRESSED EARTH BLOCKS

Compressed earth blocks are soil, water, and sometimes cement, pressed into block molds with a high-pressure or hydraulic press. They are quite similar to adobe blocks but stronger, more dense, and uniform as a result of compression of the mix during manufacture.

They can be manufactured on-site with a portable block-making machine. Some mobile industrial machines can manufacture as many as 800 blocks per hour, while small mechanical hand presses produce less, but are less expensive. Once compressed, soil blocks can be laid immediately and will continue to cure for several days.

Soil for compressed earth blocks is around 30% clay with 6% water added. Blocks can be stabilized with cement or pozzolanic cement substitutes. A semi-stabilized block will contain 2%–5% portland cement by weight and a fully stabilized block contains 5%–10% portland cement by weight. Compressive strength of unstabilized blocks is around 1,100 psi and 3,000 psi for fully stabilized blocks (Nelson 2007).

Compressed earth blocks come in a variety of sizes, depending on the orientation of the press (horizontal or vertical), the soil's compatibility, and the manufacturer's standards. Blocks from a vertical press are often 10" × 14" with a nominal height of three inches. This type of block requires use of cement or clay mortar. Blocks from a horizontal press are often 4" × 14" with a variable length from two to twelve inches. Some contain holes or grooves for reinforcing

and others are available in interlocking shapes that do not require mortar but can be stacked clean (Nelson 2007).

RAMMED EARTH

Rammed earth construction, also called *pisé de terre*, consists of moist, sandy soil lifts in formwork tamped solid to form walls. Rammed earth construction shares the benefits of low embodied energy, local materials, high thermal mass, low resource use, recyclability, and longevity with other earth construction systems. It offers an advantage over adobe as rammed earth is produced simultaneously as it is built and does not require at least ten consecutive dry days to cure as do adobe bricks. Also, the monolithic properties of rammed earth differ from adobe bricks and mortar, which can be susceptible to water penetration in wet climates (Easton 2000).

Soil mixes for rammed earth vary; however, the mix is different from other earth construction techniques as it contains less water. Soil mixes generally contain 15% dimensionally stable clay, 35% silt, and 50% sand (both coarse and fine aggregate) (Austin Energy 2007). Many contemporary rammed earth mixes contain 3%–8% portland cement, lime, or fly ash for additional strength and durability.

The New Mexico Adobe and Rammed Earth Building code recommends that rammed earth structures achieve 200–300 psi full strength (2003). Tests in North Dakota have shown that with an addition of 5% portland cement and 5% lignite fly ash, strengths of 462 psi can be achieved. A mix of 10% portland cement and 10% lignite fly ash achieved a strength of 788 psi (Pflughoeft-Hassett et al. 2000).

Rammed earth construction is a labor-intensive construction method as compared to other earth building systems. Rammed earth soil mixes must be screened and pulverized to break up clumps and make certain of a uniform mix. Transporting soil mixes to the forms, sometimes quite vertically for upper layers, can be demanding. Soil mixes are dry, not liquid like concrete. Soil mixes can be passed up to the top of forms in buckets; however, on large jobs, a front-end loader is often used (Austin Energy 2007).

Soil mixes, placed in six-to-eight-inch lifts, are rammed either manually or mechanically. Manual

Table 6–7 Adobe Walls: Design and Specification Considerations

Primary detailing considerations with adobe construction have to do with control of moisture and prevention of erosion of the structure.
Structures should be sited on higher ground and away from standing water or poorly drained areas.
Drainage should be directed away from the structure to keep water away from the base and lower courses of the structure. They should also be sited out of range of lawn sprinklers and irrigation.
Adobe blocks can be used in low retaining walls. Reinforcing measures should be incorporated into high retaining walls. Backs of retaining walls should be coated with emulsified asphalt.
When using unstabilized adobe, wall caps with overhangs and waterproof foundations should be used.
Stabilized or semi-stabilized bricks should be used for the first three courses above grade. If mud mortar is used, it should also be fully stabilized for these courses as well.
Adobe bricks need to air cure for 10–14 days, so for bricks made on-site, construction sequencing plans should accommodate this as well as set aside a space to place the bricks while they are air drying.
Protection from direct sun for the first five days and protection from rain during the entire drying process are critical to adequate curing of adobe bricks. Production estimates are 300–400 bricks per day for a crew of two people with minimal equipment. Production will increase with a plaster mixer and gang forms.
Typical mortar joints range in width from $1/2$" to 1". Mortar for adobe bricks should be applied to the full surface of the block, as opposed to the ribbon method of brick masonry, for best compressive strength.
Mortar can be mixed from the same soil mix and water as the blocks, and/or cement or asphalt emulsion can be added for additional stabilization; however some sources warn that hard mortar may accelerate damage to softer adobe bricks.
Unstabilized and semi-stabilized adobe structures require a mud or cement plaster finish coat.
Foundations for adobe structures will vary with seismic and climatic conditions of the site, height and forces on structures, and cost considerations. Modern adobe building walls are usually built on concrete footings and stem walls. However, for lower walls in areas where frost heave is not a concern, adobe can be laid directly on a well-compacted gravel and sand trench foundation, with or without a concrete grade beam. Some engineers view the gravel trench foundation as a form of base isolation for seismic performance. Other foundations are made from stone with mud mortar to hold the adobe away from soil moisture.
Adobe walls should not be taller than eight times their width.
Gates in walls should not be anchored to the adobe. Instead, they should be self-supporting structures.
Lintels over openings in adobe walls should extend at least 20 inches beyond the edge of the opening.
Adobe mud plaster requires periodic reapplication every 1–3 years. Cement stucco on wire mesh attached to the adobe is a more permanent, if higher embodied energy, finish.

Sources: Minke 2006; State of New Mexico 2003; McHenry 1984; Moquin 2000; Sorvig 1995

Figure 6–3.
An adobe block structure with earth-based mortar. Construction is crude, as the structure will be plastered upon completion. (Photo by Quentin Wilson)

Figure 6–4.
TerraBuilt's portable Green Machine can produce tongue-and-groove compressed earth blocks on a construction site at a rate of four or five per minute. The bricks are 92% subsoil (potentially from on-site) and 8% cement with a compressive strength of 2,240 psi. (Photo from TerraBuilt Corporation International)

ramming is accomplished with a shaped tool with a long handle and flat head of wood or metal called a rammer. Mechanical ramming uses pneumatic ramming machines that are designed specifically for rammed earth construction.

Engineering rammed earth structures can be challenging, as the Uniform Building Code (UBC) does not cover earth structures, and engineers are not trained to design them; however, the body of research on structural performance of rammed earth is growing. In California, engineers currently use the "working stress method of analysis" to design rammed earth and PISE structures. A compressive strength of 800–1,200 psi is assumed and steel reinforcing is designed along concrete guidelines for this compressive strength (Minke 2006; Easton 2000).

Thicknesses and stabilization of rammed earth vary by location, climate, and structural requirements. Thicker building walls will resist the extremes of climate and be able to carry roof loads with lower strength rammed earth walls. In the southwestern United States, rammed earth building walls are commonly twenty-

Figure 6–5.
A rammed earth wall is compacted by a pneumatic tamper during a Rammit Yourself workshop in Oracle, Arizona. Walls are formed and tamped in "lifts" of soil. The snapties keep removable forms from spreading apart as earth is packed within them. (Photo by Rammed Earth Solar Homes Inc.)

ever, as the construction process is time consuming and labor is expensive, construction costs can ultimately be higher than concrete or concrete masonry structures. In an effort to reduce construction time and labor costs of rammed earth, a construction technique called pneumatically impacted stabilized earth (PISE) has been developed that sprays rammed earth mixes into formwork. The construction costs of this technique can be lower than those of rammed earth.

COB

Cob, a mix of clay, sand, and straw, is one of the simplest forms of earth construction as it is hand-formed into monolithic walls, requiring no formwork, ramming, or machinery. Cob lumps or loaves (*cob* is an Old English word for loaf) are packed and layered by hand in lifts that dry in place to form walls. This hand-packing method allows an opportunity to incorporate sculptural, irregular, and curved forms that can integrate with landforms on-site. Many proponents of cob remind us that curved walls are more structurally stable than rectilinear walls meeting at right angles (Smith 2000).

Cob offers the usual benefits of earth construction; however, because of the wide variety of appropriate soils for this construction method, on-site soil is commonly used. Cob has lower embodied energy than other earth systems (which are already lower than many materials), as it does not require machinery to mix or place or manufactured stabilizing additives such as cement or asphalt. If natural earth or lime-based plasters are used, complex manufactured chemicals can be completely avoided, and the structure can return to the soil after its useful life. Cob proponents also point to the opportunity for engaging nonexperienced builders such as project stakeholders or community members in the construction process (Austin Energy 2007).

Cob construction was used for centuries in the British Isles, the Middle East, equatorial Africa, parts of East Asia, and the American Southwest. In the American Southwest it is called coursed adobe. Cob was the predominant residential building material in many parts of the UK until the rise of inexpensive brick in the mid-1800s.

four inches thick with 5% cement stabilization. In Australia's temperate climate, wall thicknesses are often twelve inches with 10% cement (Easton 2000).

There are a wide variety of formwork systems for rammed earth construction, from those that allow construction of large wall sections at one time to formwork that is repositioned frequently to form small portions of walls. Repositionable formwork can save resources and construction time. With any system, formwork construction and repositioning is the most time-consuming part of rammed earth construction (see Table 6–8).

Material costs for rammed earth structures can be quite low, particularly if on-site soil is used. How-

Table 6–8 Rammed Earth Walls: Design and Specification Considerations

In seismic areas, rammed earth walls may require vertical and horizontal reinforcing steel. In low seismic risk areas reinforcing may not be necessary.
Foundations for rammed earth are usually reinforced concrete and should extend far enough above grade to ensure that the walls will never contact standing water.
Formwork for rammed earth construction must be stable enough to withstand the pressure and vibration from the ramming process. Small, simple forms may be the simplest to manage. Since forms are moved along the structure as it is formed, ease of assembly and dismantling should be considered when forms are designed.
If cement is used, the earth mixture must be prepared and placed/rammed in small batches as the cement will begin to cure as soon as it is mixed with water.
Rammed earth mixes are usually drier than other types of earth construction. Keeping moisture levels low will prevent the mix from shrinking and cracking as it dries. However, if it is too dry, it may crumble.
Soil should be placed in six-to-eight-inch lifts and compacted to approximately half this height.
Rammed earth construction waste can be used to form soil cement in pathway and paving applications.

Sources: State of New Mexico 2003; Minke 2006; Easton 2000; Norton 1997; Sorvig 1995

Figure 6–6.

A soil and cement mixture is sprayed through equipment similar to a shotcrete blower onto one-sided formwork to form walls of the Camp Arroyo Bathhouse by Siegel & Strain Architects. (Photo from Siegel & Strain Architects)

Figure 6–7.
The walls of the Camp Arroyo bathhouse, designed by Siegel & Strain Architects, are PISE, a pneumatically sprayed earth construction system developed by David Easton. The walls used soil from the site that was stabilized with cement. They are variable in thickness, from eight to fourteen inches, and finished with stucco. (Photo from Siegel & Strain Architects)

English cob was made from clay-based subsoil mixed with straw, water, and sometimes sand or crushed flint or shale. Clay contents ranged from 3% to 20%, with an average of 6%. This stiff mixture was shoveled with a cob fork onto a stone foundation, then stomped and compacted by workers on the 20–36-inch-wide walls. Modern cob building in England has largely followed historic techniques, with 24-inch average width walls, but mixing sometimes utilizes a tractor rather than human feet or oxen. The soil is sometimes amended with sand or crushed shale to reduce shrinkage or cracking (Smith 2000).

Oregon cob is a technique of modern cob construction sometimes used in the United States. This method forms the stiff cob into loaves that are tossed from person to person, then to a worker on top of the wall where it is packed either by hand or by foot stomping. As wall heights increase, this method can be easier than lifting the cob mix up by pitchfork.

Oregon cob is also distinguished by more attention to precise mix proportions, using a relatively high proportion of sand and about 10% long-fiber straw. Oregon cob walls are between 12 and 20 inches thick with an eight-inch average thickness for nonload-bearing partitions.

Cob can be placed in three different ways, sometimes all used in the same wall (Smith 2000):

Pisé (not to be confused with *pisé de terre* or PISE sprayed earth) is larger patties of cob either packed by hand or garden fork, then trod upon. Human weight causes the fresh cob to stick to the older layers. A cobber's thumb can improve adhesion where feet have missed and a wooden paddle is used to pat and smooth the wall edges. This method is best used for low, wide walls.

Gaab-cob, using a loose, moist mix, is applied to the wall in large handfuls or forkfuls, then worked in by hand using either fingers or a cobber's thumb.

Cob loaves involve kneading the mix into loaves that are tossed up to a builder on top of the wall. The kneading compresses the mixture, giving it a workable consistency to be pressed onto the wall.

While cob was used centuries ago, the cob revival is still relatively young, and much research must be done to determine structural performance under different conditions and with different cob wall types.

MODULAR CONTAINED EARTH

Rammed Earth Tires

Rammed earth tire construction, ideal for retaining walls, is a system of permanent formwork (tires) for rammed earth. Reclaimed tires are filled with a damp soil mix, like rammed earth, and tightly packed using sledgehammers or a pneumatic tamper. Filled tires are stacked in a running bond pattern.

Benefits of this construction system include use of a waste material, low cost (labor is most of the cost, as tires are usually free but for transport), good retaining performance, ease of construction by unskilled workers, and resistance to decay. The major challenge is the difficulty and awkwardness of shoveling and pounding earth into the inside of each tire (Sorvig 2007).

While the soil mix is often similar to a rammed earth mix, soil can be stabilized with cement or left unstabilized. Each tire, filled and compacted individually and in

Table 6–9 Cob Walls: Design and Specification Considerations

Soils with a high proportion of organic matter, silt, or fine sand can be difficult to work with.
Cob walls should be protected from prolonged soaking by water. While cob is able to absorb water and then dry out, too much water will make the straw rot. Water running down the face of the wall will erode the surface. Cob walls should be held up off grade on stone or concrete foundations. Wall caps extending beyond the face of the wall will shed water away from the cob.
Clay content should be between 5% and 25% of soil.
Straw should be 8–16" strands of strong-fibered grain straw (e.g., wheat, barley, oat, rice).
Foundations for cob walls are generally stone, rubble, or concrete; however, alternative materials are soil cement, brick, rammed earth tires, or rammed earthbags.
Plasters made from "breathable" materials are recommended for cob walls so moisture that finds its way into the wall can escape easily. Lime-sand plasters or earth plasters are recommended. Cement-based stucco can shorten the life of cob structures as it may trap moisture and hide the damage.
A hot area of the site at least eight feet in diameter should be dedicated to tarp mixing of the cob.
In seismic zones, a cob wall's center of mass should be kept as low as possible. A wall taper of 5% minimum is recommended. Walls should be a minimum of ten to twelve inches at the top.
Curved walls will increase the stability of a cob structure.
Walls can be thickened at points of high stress (e.g., ends of walls, corners).

Sources: Minke 2006; Smith 2000; Norton 1997

Figure 6–8.
Rammed earth tire retaining walls use a waste material (tires) as permanent formwork for rammed earth. As the soil is contained and compacted within the tires, it does not require any additional stabilization additives such as cement. (Photo from www.earthship.com)

place, will accommodate about three to four wheelbarrows of soil when compacted and will weigh more than 300 pounds (Reynolds 2000).

The structural performance of rammed earth tires is dependent on the deadweight of the structure and the high coefficient of lateral friction between the running bonds of tires (Reynolds 2000). In a retaining wall application, tires can be staggered back toward the slope in a batter for additional resistance. Voids between the tires can be packed with mud or concrete and then cement or mud plaster can be applied to the surface with chicken wire if desired.

As soil is contained within tires that will not decay in contact with water, rammed earth tires make good foundation systems for other types of earth construction such as rammed earth, adobe, or cob. Field tests have shown that rammed earth tires are more flexible than adobe and rammed earth walls without losing

Figure 6–9.
Earthbag construction, also called superadobe, is a modular construction system of soil-filled plastic or textile bags. Earthbags are used here to construct a wall and vault structure. Plastic earthbags can be vulnerable to degradation by solar exposure, so most building structures are finished with stucco. (Photo from Khalili/Cal-Earth; Design: Architect Nader Khalili; Location: Cal-Earth Institute & Hesperia; Erosion control of Lakeshore)

strength, making them ideal for freeze-thaw soil cycles (Reynolds 2000).

Earthbags

Earthbags, also called superadobe, are plastic or textile bags filled with soil and sometimes sand or gravel, laid in courses, and tamped solid. This construction technique, considered to be a variation of rammed earth construction, is used to construct foundations, walls, domes, and arches.

Earthbag construction is distinguished from rammed earth and adobe in the following ways (Kennedy 2000):

■ Because bags contain the soil, virtually any soil type (except highly organic) can be used, increasing the chances of using material from on-site.

■ The technique requires few skills, so project stakeholders or community members with no construction experience can assist with the building process.

■ It requires few tools and no earth-moving equipment.

■ Curvilinear forms are easily executed.

■ Bags are placed wet and more can be added without waiting for them to dry. This makes the earthbag construction faster than adobe or rammed earth.

■ While earthbag construction for buildings and walls is a relatively new construction method, they have historically been used as a fast-assembly relief method for erosion control, flood control, military bunkers, and retaining walls.

Earthbags may be the most appropriate earth construction system for retaining walls. Used in this way, bags should be set with a slight batter and compacted at a slight angle toward the earth bank for stability. Barbed wire should be placed between courses, and as with any retaining wall, drainage behind the wall should be accommodated.

Two types of bags can be used for earthbag construction (Cal-Earth):

Hessian (burlap) bags are a natural woven fabric that is biodegradable. These bags can be used if the soil inside is compactible and not sand, as the bags will hold the soil together until it dries, but not for the life of the structure.

Figure 6–10.
Earthbags can also be filled with sand. They are used here to stabilize a lake edge. (Photo from Khalili/Cal-Earth; Design: Architect Nader Khalili; Location: Cal-Earth Institute & Hesperia; Superadobe/Earthbag construction training course)

Polypropylene bags, the more common material for earthbags, are made from woven threads of plastic. These come in presized bags or in tube form on a roll. Long tube bags can be used to form continuous layers of earthbags called "super adobe." These long layers simplify curved wall construction and make very stable walls. Polypropylene bags will deteriorate if exposed to UV rays, so they must be plastered or covered in some way.

The choice of bag type is directly related to the soil type. Generally, the weaker the soil mix, the stronger the bag that should be used. Stronger soil mixes can use weaker bags as they won't need the bags for stabilization once the soil has set (Kennedy 2000). Recycled polypropylene seed or feed sacks can be used for earthbag construction.

Bag-to-bag connections are critical to the wall's stability, relying on compressive weight of soil and barbed wire. Four-point barbed wire is often used to prevent slipping between bag layers, with a single strand used for twelve-inch-wide bags and two parallel strands used for sixteen-inch-wide or greater walls (Cal-Earth).

The ideal mix for earthbag construction is sand and clay soil, similar to adobe, that is wet, then placed in bags, laid, and then tamped flat. Cement, lime, or fly ash is sometimes added in small amounts to form soil cement mix in the bags (Cal-Earth).

Gravel is sometimes used for lower courses and foundations that might be in contact with water. This prevents the rise of water into the structure. Earthbags filled with gravel are also used as foundations for straw bale or adobe walls. Foundations for earthbag walls are generally a rubble trench with lower bags filled with gravel.

Figure 6–11.
Stability of stacked earthbag walls relies on the weight of the soil-filled bags and sometimes four-point barbed wire between the bags, which can prevent lateral slippage. (Photo from www.davidsheen.com)

Finishes and Weatherproofing for Earth Structures

Like stone, earth structures are slightly porous. While they can be very durable, the surface of the structure is vulnerable to weather extremes such as rain, wind, and freeze-thaw cycles. In arid climates, waterproofing or wall finishes may not be necessary, but in temperate climates earth structures will almost always need additional protection.

Finishes and stabilizers can provide many benefits to earth structures. They can waterproof structures; provide resistance to surface wear from rain washing, strong winds, or abrasion; reduce maintenance; ease surface cleaning; and improve appearance (Norton 1997). Yet in some cases they may pose the greatest environmental impacts of the structure as they can involve constituents such as cement and lime with relatively high embodied energy and pollution impacts. They may place the environmental impact of the earth structure on a par with precast concrete block walls.

Holding the earth structure above finished grade on a waterproof foundation, use of a waterproof barrier between the foundation and wall, and a wall cap or overhang will go a long way toward weatherproofing earth walls; however, added protection in the form of integral stabilizers, sealers, or finishes may be necessary (Houben and Guillard 1994).

Surface finishes used for aesthetic purposes can improve the rough appearance of the earth wall and add color or texture to the wall. Some may prefer the look of earth construction, particularly the unique striations of rammed earth lifts. In this case, clear sealers or cement can be used for stabilization and weather protection.

Weatherproofing finishes can be natural or synthetic plasters; facing, such as tile or stone; impregnation with organic or inorganic coatings; or integral stabilizers such as asphalt or cement.

Stabilized finishes such as cement stucco are more permanent; however, they may be incompatible with earth structures that do not contain cement stabilization. They will have a different coefficient of expansion than the earth structure, causing cracking and water penetration. They can hide internal water damage to the structure of the wall. Also, they may not adhere well to the earth structure and are not "breathable" (Minke 2006; McHenry 1984) (see Table 6–10 below).

Table 6–10 Stabilizers and Finishes for Earth Construction

Type	Components	Performance Comments
INTEGRAL STABILIZERS	Integral stabilizers are added to the structure's soil mix prior to placement. They can serve as both waterproofing and strengthening agents for earth structures.	
Emulsified asphalt	Petroleum product containing emulsifiers and sometimes solvents	Look for products with low- or no-VOCs or hazardous constituents.
Cementitious or pozzolanic substances	Includes portland cement, hydrated lime, fly ash, silica fume, ground granulated blast furnace slag, or other Class N pozzolans in various amounts	Use cement substitutes for a portion of the cement where possible.
Natural stabilizers	Organic materials (e.g., agave juice, opuntia cactus juice, gum arabic, cowpats, tree resins, and many others) can be added to soil mixtures to stabilize earth walls and paving[a] Ingredients vary widely with availability to traditional earth builders.	Agave, cactus juice, and tree resin stabilizers are commercially available in the United States. In addition to their use in earth structures, many can be mixed with soils to form mud plaster finishes. Agave and cactus juices are poisonous and can harm eyes.
Synthetic stabilizers and soil plasters	Many chemical stabilizers can be added to soil mixes to stabilize earth walls and paving. These include polyvinyl acetate, PVC, acrylics, sodium silicate, betonite, casein glues, paraffin, etc.[a]	Some synthetic stabilizers such as vinyl chloride or polyvinyl acetate may be toxic or contain high levels of VOCs. In addition to their use in earth structures, many can be mixed with soils to form mud plaster finishes.
PLASTERS AND STUCCO	Plasters are applied to the surface of earth walls. They provide a wearing layer that is affected first by erosion and is easily replaced when required. Mix proportions are critical and should be tested on a section of the wall prior to full application. Plasters must be flexible enough to match the flexibility of the earth structure on which they are placed. For example, cement-based plasters are suitable for cement-stabilized earth structures; however, they will be too rigid for unstabilized structures and can crack from different rates of expansion of the two materials. Plasters for unstabilized structures should be "breathable," allowing for passage of air and water vapor.[a] A roughened surface of the soil structure will improve adherence of plasters. Plasters should be applied with at least two layers.[a]	

Table 6–10 Stabilizers and Finishes for Earth Construction *(Continued)*

Type	Components	Performance Comments
Basic mud plaster	Breathable plaster that is one part clay (often native soil) to three parts sand with straw chopped into short lengths. Clay coats the particles of sand, silt, and straw and binds them together.[b] Manure can be used, with one part manure to five parts soil. $1/2$"–1" thick Can be applied in single or multiple layers; finish layer can be made without straw. 10% clay, 40% silt, 50% sand, 12 parts soil, 1.5 parts cow dung, 1.5 parts straw, and 0.25–0.5 part water[d]	In rainy climates, mud plaster should be stabilized with cement, asphalt, lime, or pozzolans[a] (see next six items) or sealed with a protective but breathable coating.[c] Adheres very well to earth walls Suitable for unstabilized walls Too much clay will crack Cracks and chips in mud plasters will have to be repaired annually. Clay offers a variety of colors specific to a particular place. No uniformity of material—some experimentation is usually needed to obtain a suitable texture.[c]
Cement/soil plasters	Use in proportions between 1:10 and 1:8 cement and soil. Soil should be sandy.	Use on walls stabilized with cement. Soil-based plasters have better adhesion than sand-based plasters.
Cement/sand plasters	Applied in three 4–6 mm layers First coat has a low cement content (1 part cement to 15 parts sand), increasing with each layer to 1:8. For cement-stabilized walls the proportion should be between 1:6 and 1:9. This will help the plastering adhere to the wall.[b]	Suited to earth structures that are stabilized with cement or asphalt Could have adhesion problems with unstabilized earth structures Not breathable like mud plasters or lime plasters Cracking, but not adhesion, will be improved with use of chicken wire.[a]
Stucco (also called masonry cement)	Similar to cement-sand plaster, but dries more slowly and is more workable.	Very commonly used and widely available
Cement/lime/sand plasters	Commonly used in proportions of 1:2:9 or 1:3:12, cement, lime, and sand[a] (although lime can compose 25% to 50% of the mix).[b]	Suitable for use on cement- or lime-stabilized surfaces Select mix intended for above-grade use and plastering (rather than bricklaying); look for higher percentage of lime in the mix for lower environmental impact.[c]
Lime plaster	Two types: hydrated lime and hydraulic lime (different curing processes; hydrated lime is more common) Look for hydraulic lime or "Type S" hydrated lime for plaster or masonry use; avoid agricultural lime.	These plasterings are more flexible than cement-based ones.[a] Breathable Used extensively in human history
Pozzolana with sand or soil plasters	This is a mixture of pozzolans (e.g., burnt clay, fly ash, burnt rice husks, and volcanic ash), lime, and sand or soil. Mix proportions will vary depending on the silica content of the pozzolan. Use a weaker mix for unstabilized soil structures.	These plasterings are more flexible than cement-based ones.[a] Some industrial by-products, such as fly ash, are pozzolans.

Continued

Table 6–10 Stabilizers and Finishes for Earth Construction *(Continued)*

Type	Components	Performance Comments
Bitumen/soil plasters	Mix of 3%–10% of emulsified asphalt mixed with basic mud plaster. High clay content soils will require more asphalt than sandy soils. Apply in two thin coats for a total thickness of 10–20 mm.[b] A variation of this is to paint asphalt emulsion directly on the wall, then coat it with sand.	Avoid use of cutback asphalt, as it contains high amounts of VOCs. Requires regular maintenance This may be a more efficient use of asphalt than impregnating the entire wall thickness with asphalt. This plaster will darken the surface of the wall, as asphalt is black.
Sump oil/soil	A mix of sandy soil with 7% sump oil, a by-product of metalworking operations. Applied in two thin coats.	May contain additives and/or contaminants from metalworking or from engine wear.[e]
Natural stabilizer and soil plasters	Organic materials (e.g., agave juice, opuntia cactus juice, gum arabic, cowpats, tree resins, and many others) can be combined with soil for a stabilized mud plaster.[a] Ingredients vary widely with availability to traditional earth builders.	Agave, cactus juice, and tree resin stabilizers are commercially available in the United States. These can be used in mud plaster or integrally mixed into earth walls and paving. Agave and cactus juices are poisonous and can harm eyes.
Synthetic stabilizer and soil plasters	Many chemical stabilizers can be mixed with soil for a stabilized mud plaster. These include polyvinyl acetate, vinyl chloride, acrylics, sodium silicate, betonite, casein glues, paraffin, etc.[a]	Some synthetic stabilizers such as vinyl chloride or polyvinyl acetate may be toxic or contain high levels of VOCs. In addition to their use in mud plaster, many can be integrally mixed into earth walls and paving.
FACING MATERIALS		
Brick facing	Fired brick facing can be laid to interlock with a mud brick (adobe) structure. This will provide the best adherence to the wall structure as the facing becomes part of the structure. Another method uses masonry ties that are embedded in mortar joints between adobes that can tie the bricks on.	Using mud brick/adobe for most of the wall and fired brick for facing will save embodied energy. Fired brick must be the same dimensions as the adobe brick for the interlocking to work. If they are different sizes, masonry ties may be the best method.
Tile facing	Fired clay tiles can be used as facing for earth structures; however, adherence can be challenging. There is no chemical bond between grout and earth structures, so an interlocking layer of tile laid perpendicular and embedded within the wall will need to be laid every 500 mm.	The tile face may separate from the earth wall as adherence is not a chemical, but a mechanical bond. Moisture may be trapped behind the tile and damage the wall.
SLURRIES, SEALANTS, AND PAINTS	Slurries are brushed or sprayed on wetted stabilized earth walls in multiple coats. Paints are brushed or sprayed on dry earth structures to form a thin protective film. This film can be opaque and tinted or transparent. Sealants are brushed on and penetrate the surface of the structure to harden and waterproof the structure.	

Table 6–10 Stabilizers and Finishes for Earth Construction *(Continued)*

Type	Components	Performance Comments
Cement and lime slurries	Cement and lime are mixed with water in a ratio of 6:1:1, water, cement, and lime. This slurry is brushed onto walls like paint. Addition of fine sand can give a gritty texture and improves water resistance.[b]	Slurries may flake off and need to be recoated every few years.[a]
Bitumen washes	Emulsified asphalt can be brushed on the surface of a very dry earth structure, making it less permeable to water[a]	This is an inexpensive treatment. The wash is black and can result in an unappealing appearance on walls. This can be slightly remedied by dusting on clean sand after application of asphalt.[a] Black surface may be desirable on paving for traffic striping. The surface can also be painted with asphalt paint. There may be some health and environmental risks from PAHs and other compounds washing off the surface.
Plant juices	Plant-based sealers are available that are made from juice of the agave plant or cacti.[a]	This type of sealer will need to be reapplied every few years.
Earth slurries	Earth slurry, a mix of soil and water, is more appropriate for interior applications; however, lime, cement, or emulsified asphalt can be added for use in exterior applications.[a]	
Surface water repellents	Surface water repellents made from polymers or silicones in solvent or water-based solutions are often used to finish plasterings, rather than the body of an earth structure, as they will not penetrate large cracks.[a]	Impregnation is critical to success.[a]
Resin-based film-forming impregnation treatments	Resin-based treatment that penetrates earth structure	Impregnation is critical to success.[a] Permeability to water vapor should be maintained
Waterproofing coatings	Usually resins in an organic solution or water	Impregnation is critical to success.[a] Limited by cracks Risk of blistering sometimes unpredictable

[a]Houben and Guillaud 1994
[b]Norton 1997
[c]Magwood, Mack, and Thierren 2005
[d]Moquin 2000
[e]Sorvig 2007

Soil-based Pavements and Substructures

The last sixty years of site construction have seen a strong movement toward highly engineered asphalt and concrete pavements—"built to last." However, time has shown that these pavements may not last as long as planned, they can produce negative environmental effects such as increased storm water runoff or the urban heat island effect, and their sheer volume and stark colors can aesthetically disrupt a site design. This trend toward exclusive use of asphalt and concrete for pavements has forgotten some very durable, low resource use, aesthetically appropriate soil pavement technologies. Many CCC and WPA soil cement projects from the 1930s are still in good functional shape today (Sorvig 2007).

Use of stabilized soil pavements can offer environmental, economic, and aesthetic benefits to a site design. Their primary ingredient is on-site soil, often from the location where the pavement will be placed. This can save the purchase costs of new, frequently virgin, resources and the energy and expense of transporting these heavy materials to the site. Stabilized soil pavements, primarily the color of the native soil, can integrate with the landscape and produce an informal, yet structurally sound, accessible paved surface. Lastly, because many stabilized soil pavements are mixed in place requiring minimal formwork, their construction is relatively nonintrusive to sensitive sites.

Recently, the increased attention paid to "context-sensitive" design has moved into pavement, road, and highway design, bringing stabilized soil pavements and bases back into limited use. Research and testing of soil-stabilized pavements, primarily soil cement, has been increasing, resulting in increased confidence in this family of pavements and pavement bases. The Central Federal Lands Highway Division of the Federal Highway Administration has produced a comprehensive manual for a broad variety of pavement types called *Context Sensitive Roadway Surfacing Selection Guide* (Maher et al. 2005). In addition to more standard pavement technologies, the guide provides thorough design and construction information for many methods of stabilizing soil for pavement surfaces and base courses.

SOIL CEMENT

Soil cement is the most well-used soil stabilization technique for road bases, and to a much lesser degree, road surfaces. It is a mixture of native soil, a small amount of cement (3%–10%) and water, often mixed in place and then rolled for compaction. The water serves the purpose of hydrating the cement and increasing compaction of the soil mixture (Portland Cement Association [PCA] 1995). Soil cement, like rammed earth and compressed earth block, relies on cement for stabilization, and is a compacted soil mix.

Nearly any soil can be used for soil cement pavements and bases; however, the type of soil and its intended use will determine the amount of cement required in the mix (PCA 1995):

Well-graded sandy and gravelly soils with 10%–35% nonplastic fines usually require the least amount of cement for adequate hardening. These soils are defined as containing 55% or more material less than 4.75 mm and 37% less than 2 mm.

Sandy materials deficient in fines can make good soil cement; however, they will require more cement and greater care to avoid crushing during compaction.

Silty and clayey soils can make good soil cement; however, these soils will require more cement and should not be placed in wet conditions. Soils with high clay content may be difficult or costly to adequately pulverize, so sometimes use of better soil materials from nearby can keep costs low.

Like other earth construction methods, soil should be tested for appropriateness and to determine the most effective mix and quantity of cement required. ASTM and AASHTO have developed standard tests, listed in Table 6–15, for maximum density and moisture content for soil cement mixes and required cement amounts determined by laboratory wet-dry and freeze-thaw tests. In some areas, locally developed tests are used.

Most soil cement applications, laboratory and field tests, and road standards specify portland cement Types I and II; however, blended cements such as Type IP can potentially be used. Other cementitious materials, such as Class C fly ash alone or a percentage of Class F fly ash with cement, may also hold potential for stabilizing soils, but their use and testing is not well publicized (Maher et al. 2005).

Where soil cement is used as a base course, the type and thickness of the wearing course will vary with traffic volume and local conditions. Generally a soil cement– stabilized base requires less thickness in a surface course. In many applications, such as low-traffic parking lots, paths, driveways, and low-volume roads, a thin layer of bituminous material, such as chip seal ($1/4"-3/8"$) or microsurfacing ($1/2"-1"$) can be

Table 6–11 Soil Cement with Cementitious and Pozzolanic Materials

Soil Cement Type and Purpose	Materials	Comments
Soil cement pavement (SCP) Cement-stabilized soil pavement suitable for light traffic (e.g., low-traffic parking lots) and bicycle and pedestrian paths	Sandy soils with some silt and clay are best suited to the application and require the least cement.[a] However, nearly any combination of sand, silt, clay, gravel, or crushed stone can be used. Waste materials such as cinders, fly ash, foundry sands, and screenings from gravel pits and quarries can be incorporated; however, as the soil cement is the finished wearing surface, attention should be given to color and texture.[c] Organic soils are unsuitable.[a] 4%–10% cement,* mixed in place depending on soil type 3%–6% cement,* plant mixed Fly ash– or lime-stabilized soil is not recommended for a surfacing material.[b]	Can be a finished pavement for light traffic applications, saving import of material resources and associated costs Can crack under heavy traffic loads or in areas prone to frost heave[b] Creates an aesthetically pleasing, yet stable, accessible surface that can integrate with the surrounding landscape Low embodied energy Mixing in place will minimize site disruption. Very durable if well mixed and compacted Easily patched, unlike concrete paving[a] Uses a greater percentage of material (soil) from on-site, minimizes imported paving material. However, energy savings of transport can be negated with use of portland cement, a relatively high embodied energy material.
Cement-treated base (CTB) Strong, frost-resistant base layer for roads and pavements achieving seven-day unconfined compressive strengths of 300–800 psi[b]	Nearly any combination of sand, silt, clay, gravel, or crushed stone. Also waste material such as cinders, fly ash, foundry sands, and screenings from gravel pits and quarries.[c] 4%–10% cement, mixed in place depending on soil type[d] 3%–6% cement, plant mixed[d]	Can be finished with a thin asphalt surface application such as chip seal ($1/4"-3/8"$), microsurfacing ($1/4"-1"$), or a thin asphalt course ($1/2"-1"$) for low-to-medium-traffic road, parking, or pathway applications, saving resources. Standard asphalt or concrete overlays are used for heavier traffic and highway applications. Can reduce the required base thickness for a given application, saving resources Uses a greater percentage of material (soil) from on-site; minimizes imported material such as aggregate for traditional bases. However, energy savings of transport can be negated with use of portland cement, a relatively high embodied energy material. Not appropriate in areas prone to heavy frost heave[b] Soils with high clay content should be well pulverized prior to application of cement.

Continued

Table 6–11 Soil Cement with Cementitious and Pozzolanic Materials *(Continued)*

Soil Cement Type and Purpose	Materials	Comments
Fly ash–treated base Strong, frost-resistant base layer for roads and pavements achieving seven-day unconfined compressive strengths of 100–510 psi[b]	Nearly any combination of sand, silt, clay, gravel, or crushed stone. Also waste material such as cinders, fly ash, foundry sands, and screenings from gravel pits and quarries.[c] 10%–20% fly ash, mixed in place depending on soil type and fly ash type[b] Class C fly ash, self-cementing, can be mixed with soil to perform similarly to portland cement. Class F fly ash, a pozzolan, requires an activation agent such as portland cement or lime to create cementitious bonds within the soil.	Can be finished with a thin asphalt surface application such as chip seal ($1/4"$ –$3/8"$), microsurfacing ($1/4"$ –1"), or a thin asphalt course ($1/2"$ –1") for low-to-medium-traffic road, parking, or pathway applications, saving resources. Standard asphalt or concrete overlays are used for heavier traffic and highway applications. Can reduce the required base thickness for a given application, saving resources Uses a greater percentage of material (soil) from on-site; minimizes imported material such as aggregate for traditional bases. Uses a waste material (fly ash) Not appropriate in areas prone to heavy frost heave[b] Soils with high clay content should be well pulverized prior to application of cement. Leaching of fly ash from base is a concern as fly ash often contains heavy metals. Test fly ash for composition prior to use.
Lime-modified soil Quicklime or hydrated lime added to soil to stabilize clay soils and submarginal base materials. Pozzolanic reaction causes cementitious bonds to form over a long period.[b] 100–400 psi[b]	Clayey soils with moderate to high plasticity (plasticity index greater than 15).[b] Pozzolanic reaction will not work as well with silts and granular materials. Not recommended for soils with high sulfate contents (> 0.3%). 2%–3% by weight quicklime or hydrated lime for soil modification[b] 5%–6% by weight for soil stabilization[b]	Lime reacts with water in the soil and reduces the water content. An ion exchange with the lime and clay changes soil structure and reduces plasticity. Increases soil workability, strength, and stiffness[b] Rarely used as surfacing material Quicklime can pose worker safety issues with inhalation and heat of chemical reaction. Hydrated lime is safer to work with. Lime can leach from soils and raise pH of adjacent aquatic waters.
Cement-modified soil (CMS) Improves engineering properties and workability of soft, plastic, and/or difficult-to-compact silt and clay soils by addition of small amount of cement[d]	Cohesive soils, silt/clay/sand mixtures 3%–5% cement[e]	Reduces plasticity index, improves bearing strength, and makes a good construction platform for pavements Less susceptible to water Allows use of any on-site soil, rather than importing better fill material, saving money and fuel use

[a]Sorvig 1995

[b]Maher et al. 2005

[c]Halstead 2005

[d]PCA 2005

[e]Cement substitutes such as fly ash, GGBF slag, lime, or blended cements may be used with testing.

Table 6–12 Soil Cement Paving Surfaces: Design and Specification Considerations

Primary detailing considerations with soil cement for paving surfaces have to do with preventing the deterioration of the paving surface.
The mix formula should be carefully adjusted for the soil type based on a soil analysis.
Care should be given to thorough mixing of cement and soil to avoid erosion of poorly consolidated patches. Removing soil and mixing in a cement mixer or pug mill will ensure even mixing; however, this technique will add labor and equipment costs to the project. Tilling/spreading/mixing machines, which control the rate of cement release and tilling, can be effective, but widths of these machines may be too wide for pathways.
Soil cement thickness will vary from four to ten inches depending on soil type and expected loads.
Soil cement should be adequately compacted to the full depth of mixing with asphalt compacters or grass rollers.
Soil cement pavements should have minimal cross-slopes to prevent erosion of the surface.
Adjacent surfaces should drain away from the soil cement pavement, not across it.
As soil cement is more flexible than standard concrete, expansion and control joints are not necessary.

Sources: Maher et al. 2005; PCA 1995; Sorvig 1995

overlayed. For lightly traveled streets, a double surface treatment about 3/4" thick can be used (PCA 1995). A full two-to-four-inch asphalt installation is not necessary for most applications except medium-to-high-volume roadways.

OTHER SOIL STABILIZATION METHODS FOR PAVEMENTS

While soil cement is the most common soil stabilization method for paving, there are numerous other soil

Table 6–13 Stabilizers for Soil Pavements

Soil Cement Type and Purpose	Materials	Comments
Tree resin emulsions Stabilizers derived from tree resins (mostly pine, spruce, and fir) combined with other additives. Can be mixed into soil or sprayed on. 5–10 years life expectancy for soil stabilization	Mixed with 1"–2" native soils for dust suppression, 4"–8" for soil stabilization, and/or 2" graded aggregates (less than 10 mm) Silty sands with fines content between 5% and 30% and 8 plasticity index are best. Emulsions provide little or no improvement for soils with plasticity over 30.	Can be used for pavement bases or very low- to low-traffic surfaces Performance varies among manufacturers and products. Can be used in all climates, but best in arid or moderate precipitation conditions Can become slippery when wet if soils are used Surfaces can be damaged by snowplows Can increase compressive strength of soils by 25% to 75%. Can be three times as strong as hot-mix asphalt. Tree resins are a by-product of the pulp and paper industry.

Continued

Table 6–13 Stabilizers for Soil Pavements *(Continued)*

Soil Cement Type and Purpose	Materials	Comments
Bituminous binder, asphalt-stabilized soil, and organic petroleum emulsions These products use adhesive properties of the asphalt component to bind soil particles together for stabilization and dust suppression. Most are sprayed on, but some can be mixed in. 5–9 years life expectancy for soil stabilization	Work on soil types with up to 30% clay fines and a plasticity index of less than 10. Penetration depth decreases as amount of fines increases, so low-viscosity mixes should be used on soils with fines. Mixed with 1"–2" native soils for dust suppression, 4"–6" for soil stabilization, and/or 2" graded aggregates (less than 10 mm)	Can be used for pavement bases or very low- to low-traffic surfaces Performance varies among manufacturers and products. Can be damaged by snowplows Avoid cutback asphalts, as they release hydrocarbon emissions during evaporation and can be a health, environmental, and fire hazard. Use emulsified asphalts with low or no solvents and polycyclic aromatic hydrocarbons (PAHs). Can be used in all climates Requires a 24-hour period of dry weather after installation Changes appearance of soil to dark brown or dark gray Recyclability of asphalt-stabilized soil is limited to base applications. Less easily "returned to the earth" than other unstabilized earth materials.
Synthetic polymer emulsions Primarily acrylic or acetate polymers for dust control or soil stabilization, often by-products of the adhesive or paint industries. Varying proprietary formulations. Polymers cause a chemical bond to form between soil particles, resulting in a dense, water-resistant road surface. Applied with a mixed-in method for soil stabilization. 5–10 years life expectancy for soil stabilization	Can be used on most soils and/or graded aggregates. Different products are suitable for different soil types. Mixed with 1"–2" native soils for dust suppression, 4"–8" for soil stabilization, and/or 2" graded aggregates (less than 10 mm) Silty sands with fines content between 5% and 20% and 8 plasticity index are best. More polymer required for gravel mixes with less than 2% fines. Compressive strength can range from 800 to 2,200 psi.	Can be used for pavement bases or very low to low-traffic surfaces Performance varies among manufacturers and products. Can be used in all climates Requires a 48-hour period of dry weather after installation Can become slippery when wet if soils are used Surfaces can be damaged by snowplows Polymers are a petroleum product involving some environmental and human health impacts in manufacture. Some emulsions contain VOCs.

Table 6–13 Stabilizers for Soil Pavements *(Continued)*

Soil Cement Type and Purpose	Materials	Comments
Electrolyte emulsions/stabilizers, ionic stabilizers, sulfonated oils, and electrochemical stabilizers Contain chemicals that affect the electrobonding characteristics of soils and replace water molecules within the soil structure. Soil stabilizer or dust palliative. 3–5 years life expectancy; however, some applications have been in place for 15 or more years. Can be sprayed on or mixed in (most common).	Mixed with 1"–2" native soils for dust suppression, 4"–8" for soil stabilization Can increase soil strength by 30%–50%.	Can be used for pavement bases or very low- to low-traffic surfaces Performance varies among manufacturers and products. Electrolyte products are often by-products or intermediate products of manufacturing processes. Sulfonated D-limonene and sulfonated naphthalene, primary components, can have toxic impacts to both human and environmental health in concentrated form. When diluted, impacts are minimal.
Enzymatic emulsions Contain enzymes (protein molecules) that form a cementing bond by reacting with soil particles. Soil stabilizer or dust palliative 5–7 years life expectancy; however, some applications have been in place for 12 or more years. Can be sprayed on or mixed in (most common).	They work on a variety of soils as long as a minimum amount of clay molecules are present (greater than 10%) and the plasticity index is greater than 8. They work best on soils with 12%–24% clay content, with plasticity index between 8 and 35, and when soil moisture content is 2%–3% below optimum for compaction. Mixed with 1"–2" native soils for dust suppression, 4"–8" for soil stabilization. Can increase soil strength by 30%–300%.	Can be used for pavement bases or very low- to low-traffic surfaces Performance varies among manufacturers and products. Can become slippery when wet when used on soils with high clay content (20%–30%) Enzyme materials are often by-products of food-processing and manufacturing industries. Not as commonly used as other products Once diluted, typically biodegradable and nontoxic.
Fiber reinforcement Used to stabilize clays, sands, and sandy gravel soils with metallic, polypropylene, glass, wire, cellophane, hemp, or straw fibers. The soil mix is then placed and compacted. This can increase the stiffness, shear strength, and bearing capacity of the soil by 30%–100%. Life expectancy varies with fiber and soil type. Average is 4–6 years.	Fiber application rates are 0.1% to 0.5% by weight Different fibers are suited for different soils. Fines content up to 10% are preferred for granular surfacings that are reinforced with polypropylene fibers.	Used as a base stabilization method. Used as a surface course in very low traffic areas. Wet or cold climates will lead to more deterioration of surfaces as they soften with moisture and thaw. Use of dust-suppressant methods in conjunction with fiber reinforcing is recommended. Yearly maintenance, regrading, and dust suppression is required. Use of biobased fiber materials will allow easy reuse of road material. Reduces erosion, but erosion of soil may affect adjacent aquatic environments. Fibers are visible in surface applications.

Source: Adapted from Maher et al. 2005

Table 6–14 Stabilized Soil Paving: Design and Specification Considerations

Primary detailing considerations with stabilized soil for paving surfaces have to do with preventing the deterioration of the paving surface.
Sharp sandy soils will interlock better than round sandy soils.
A heavy lawn roller should be used to compact the stabilized soil to the full mix depth.
Stabilized paths should be contained with an edge restraint.
Stabilized pavements should have minimal cross-slopes to prevent erosion of the surface.
Adjacent surfaces should drain away from the stabilized pavement.
As stabilized soil pavement is more flexible than standard concrete, expansion and control joints are not necessary.

Sources: Maher et al. 2005; Sorvig 1995

stabilization applications, ranging from natural plant resin–based emulsions to bituminous stabilizers. Some of these stabilizers, in the right conditions with certain soils, can produce strong, durable, soil-based pavements. Others are best used as stabilized pavement bases with a bituminous surface layer. Many of these stabilizers are lower embodied energy than portland cement. Many of these formulations are proprietary products with varying ingredients. They should be examined for VOCs, HAPs, and toxic by-products (see Table 6–13).

Figure 6–12.
A desired historic dirt road look is achieved with stabilized soil for Battle Road in the Minute Man National Park in Massachusetts. The stabilizer used allows for support of fire trucks and accommodates bikes and wheelchairs without rutting. (Photo from Carol R. Johnson Associates)

Table 6–15 ASTM and AASHTO Standards Related to Soil Cement

ASTM standards	
D558	Standard Test Methods for Moisture-Density (Unit Weight) Relations of Soil-Cement Mixtures
D559	Standard Test Methods for Wetting and Drying Compacted Soil-Cement Mixtures
D560	Standard Test Methods for Freezing and Thawing Compacted Soil-Cement Mixtures
D806	Standard Test Method for Cement Content of Hardened Soil-Cement Mixtures
AASHTO standards	
T134	Standard Method of Test for Moisture-Density Relations of Soil-Cement Mixtures
T135	Standard Method of Test for Wetting-and-Drying Test of Compacted Soil-Cement Mixtures
T136	Standard Method of Test for Freezing-and-Thawing Tests of Compacted Soil-Cement Mixtures

Building with Earth Materials

While earth structures are the oldest construction system, earth construction, with the exception of soil cement road bases, is perceived as a very "alternative" building material in site and architectural construction. And it is misperceived by many engineers, designers, code officials, contractors, and clients, limiting its use. However, rising fuel prices coupled with environmental and human health concerns of building materials are causing a reexamination of traditional earth construction technologies. And new technologies such as PISE (sprayed earth), cast earth, and soil cement use modern construction techniques or materials to bring earth construction more in line with current construction practices.

But as earth construction gains marginal ground in the building industry, it faces many challenges, some of which inhibit its use. Modern structural engineers are not trained in earth structure design and there is a perception that earth structures are not durable. Consequently most are not comfortable designing earth structures, and many building codes do not directly address earth construction, so the onus can be on the designer, contractor, or engineer to test the earth construction system to make sure it complies with code requirements.

As earth construction gains popularity in certain regions, structural testing is being performed and select structural engineers are gaining comfort with earth building, which in turn may satisfy some code officials. ASTM and other standards organizations have developed various standard tests for soil mix performance in wet-dry and freeze-thaw situations. However, the lack of experienced engineers, code officials, and contractors may currently be the largest obstacle to earth building in many areas.

The exception to this is soil cement and other stabilized base technologies. AASHTO and ASTM standards address testing of soil mixes for soil cement, and these tests can be applied to some other stabilization methods as well. Many state DOTs have standards for use of soil cement in paving bases and soil stabilization methods for low-volume rural roads. Use of stabilized soil as a surface course is less common, but may grow with the current emphasis on context-sensitive design combined with rising fuel costs.

Building material costs for earth structures can be lower than for other materials, particularly if the soil material is derived from the site. However, many earth construction methods such as rammed earth, adobe (if manufactured on-site), and cob are labor intensive, causing labor costs to be higher.

Construction by owners, project stakeholders, or community members can substantially lower costs, and many earth construction methods can be executed by relatively unskilled workers with some guidance from experts. Using community members and project stakeholders in construction can also encourage "ownership" of the built landscape and increase the likelihood that it will be appropriately cared for during the life of the site.

Perhaps the strongest aesthetic argument for use of earth materials in construction is the potential of the built structure to blend with the natural landscape. The color of local soil can integrate with the site better than black asphalt or gray concrete. Varying striations of rammed earth or colors of adobe can result in attractive walls that require no finish if stabilized and reflect the varied nature of the soil. Soil cement parking lots in natural areas can rest lightly within the scenic landscape.

REFERENCES

ASTM Standard E2392. 2005a. "Standard Guide for Design of Earthen Wall Building Systems." West Conshohocken, PA: ASTM International, www.astm.org.

ASTM Standard C618. 2005b. "Standard Specification for Coal Fly Ash and Raw or Calcined Natural Pozzolan for Use in Concrete." West Conshohocken, PA: ASTM International, www.astm.org.

ASTM Standard D2487. 2006. "Standard Practice for Classification of Soils for Engineering Purposes (Unified Soil Classification System)," ASTM International, West Conshohocken, PA, www.astm.org.

Austin Energy. *Earth Building: A Factsheet from Austin Energy's Green Building Program.* http://www.austinenergy.com/Energy%20Efficiency/Programs/Green%20Building/Resources/Fact%20Sheets/EarthBuilding.pdf (accessed October 19, 2007).

Austin Energy Green Building Program. 2007. *Sustainable Building Sourcebook.* http://austinenergy.com/Energy%20Efficiency/Programs/Green%20Building/Sourcebook/earthConstruction.htm

Cast Earth. www.castearth.com (accessed April 30, 2007).

Cal-Earth, The California Institute of Earth Architecture. "Eco-Dome." http://www.calearth.org/EcoDome.htm

Beatty, Russell. "Garden Earthworks" in *Pacific Horticulture.* Berkeley, CA: Vol. 55, No. 1 Spring 1994.

Easton, D. 2000. "Rammed Earth." *Alternative Construction: Contemporary Natural Building Methods.* Ed. L. Elizabeth, and C. Adams. New York: Wiley.

Demkin, J., ed. 1998. "Materials Report 04210: Brick and Mortar." In *Environmental Resource Guide.* New York: John Wiley and Sons.

Halstead, G. 2005. "Soil Cement for Commercial Sites." Skokie, IL: Portland Cement Association.

Hammond, G., and C. Jones. 2006. "Inventory of Carbon and Energy." Version 1.5 Beta. Bath, UK: University of Bath, Department of Mechanical Engineering. http://www.bath.ac.uk/mech-eng/sert/embodied/

Houben, H., and H. Guillard. 1994. *Earth Construction: A Comprehensive Guide.* London: Intermediate Technology Publications.

Kennedy, J. 2000. "Modular Contained Earth." *Alternative Construction: Contemporary Natural Building Methods.* Ed. L. Elizabeth and C. Adams. New York: Wiley.

King, B. 2000. "Structural Properties of Alternative Building Materials." In *Alternative Construction: Contemporary Natural Building Methods.* Ed. L. Elizabeth and C. Adams. New York: Wiley.

Magwood, C., P. Mack, and T. Thierren. 2005. *More Straw Bale Building: A Complete Guide to Designing and Building with Straw.* Gabriola Island, British Columbia: New Society Publishers.

Maher, M., C. Marshall, F. Harrison, and K. Baumgaertner. 2005. *Context Sensitive Roadway Surfacing Selection Guide.* Lakewood, CO: Federal Highway Administration, Central Federal Lands Highway Division.

McHenry, P. G. 1984. *Adobe and Rammed Earth Buildings.* Tucson, AZ: University of Arizona Press.

Minke, G. 2006. *Technology of Sustainable Architecture.* Basel; Boston: Birkhauser-Publishers for Architecture.

Moquin, M. 2000. "Adobe." In *Alternative Construction: Contemporary Natural Building Methods.* Ed. L. Elizabeth and C. Adams. New York: Wiley.

Nelson, Wayne. "Compressed Earth Blocks". Natural Building Colloquium <http://www.networkearth.org/naturalbuilding/ceb.html> (accessed 3 November 20).

Norton, John. 1997. *Building with Earth: A Handbook.* 2nd ed. London: Intermediate Technology Publications.

Pflughoeft-Hassett, D. F., B. A. Dockter, D. J. Hassett, K. E. Eylands, and L. L. Hamre. 2000, September. "Use of Bottom Ash and Fly Ash in Rammed-Earth Construction." University of North Dakota Energy and Environmental Research Center. http://www.undeerc.org/carrc/Assets/RammedEarth.pdf.

Piepkorn, Mark. 2005. "The Natural Building Movement." *Environmental Building News,* May.

Portland Cement Association (PCA). 1995. *Soil Cement Construction Handbook, Engineering Bulletin.* Skokie, IL: Portland Cement Association.

Portland Cement Association (PCA). 2005. "Soil-Cement Technology for Pavements: Different Techniques for Different Applications." Skokie, IL: Portland Cement Association.

Rammed Earth Works. http://rammedearthworks.com/p.i.s.e.html (accessed March 5, 2007).

Reynolds, M. 2000. *Alternative Construction: Contemporary Natural Building Methods.* Ed. L. Elizabeth and C. Adams. New York: Wiley.

Smith, M. 2000. "Cob." *Alternative Construction: Contemporary Natural Building Methods*. Ed. L. Elizabeth and C. Adams. New York: Wiley.

Sorvig, Kim. Personal communication. November 7, 2007.

Sorvig, K. 1995. "Earth-Building in Landscape Architecture." *Landscape Architecture*, February: 28–32.

State of New Mexico. 2003. "Part 4 2003 New Mexico Earthen Building Materials Code" *Title 14 Housing and Construction, Chapter 7 Building Codes General*, State of New Mexico.

Wolfskill, L., W. Dunlap, and B. Callaway. 1980. *Handbook for Building Homes of Earth*. Washington, DC: Peace Corps.

chapter 7

Brick Masonry

Introduction

Clay bricks are known for their durability, and when used in a well-built structure, they can last for hundreds of years with little maintenance. While bricks have a relatively high embodied energy, this can be offset by their durability. And bricks can be used over and over again in many different structures, often outlasting the life of a landscape and giving new life to another.

Clay bricks require from 150% to 400% more energy to produce than concrete paving bricks or CMUs, but the primary fuel source for bricks is cleaner-burning natural gas while the primary fuel source for production of portland cement for use in concrete products is coal (U.S. EPA 2007a). Additionally, less waste and emissions are generated in brick manufacture than in the production of portland cement, which releases almost one ton of CO_2 for every ton produced.

Bricks are made primarily from clay and shale, abundant nontoxic natural resources found in many locations around the world. Some solid wastes are incorporated into brick as well, as high firing temperatures neutralize and encapsulate wastes.

There are three main types of clay bricks produced:

Extruded bricks, also called stiff mud bricks, are the most common type of brick produced today, with about 90% of brick being produced by this method. Water,

about 10%–15%, is mixed with the clay and then is sent through a de-airing chamber that maintains a vacuum of 15–19 in. of mercury, removing air holes and bubbles (Brick Industry Association [BIA] 2006c). Then the stiff clay mix is extruded through a die where textures or surface coatings are added and it is sliced into brick shapes by wires. Holes and perforations are added. The bricks are hardened by drying 20–40 hours at 50–150°C before firing.

Molded bricks, also called soft mud bricks, are a mix of raw wet clay and 25%–30% sand to reduce shrinkage. It is pressed into steel molds with a hydraulic press and then fired at 900–1,000°C.

Dry press brick production methods are similar to soft mud bricks, yet a much thicker and dryer (up to 10% water) clay mix is used. The clay mix is pressed into steel molds under pressures ranging from 500 psi to 1,500 psi. This produces a more accurate, sharper-edged brick than soft mud bricks.

BRICK PRODUCTION

In 2002, the most recent year for which data are available, 8.1 billion bricks were sold. Eighty-one percent were used in residential construction, 16% in commercial/industrial or institutional construction, and 2.9% for non-building uses, primarily landscape structures (BIA 2007d).

Table 7–1 Brick Production and Consumption by Region

	Production	**Consumption**
New England	0.7%	1.3%
Middle Atlantic	5.1%	6.4%
East North Central	8.2%	15.6%
West North Central	4.4%	3.9%
South Atlantic	38.7%	33.7%
East South Central	19.7%	15.5%
West South Central	19.5%	20.5%
Mountain	3.5%	2.0%
Pacific	0.2%	0.6%

Source: BIA 2007d

Like so many industries, the brick industry is moving toward consolidation of manufacturing and increasing scales of production. Sixty years ago there were thousands of brick manufacturers with nearly 3,000 brick plants in operation. Now there are 83 manufacturers operating 204 plants. The plants are located in forty-one states, producing a wide variety of clay products such as face brick, paving brick, glazed brick, and tile (BIA 2007d). The table above illustrates brick production and consumption in U.S. regions in 2002.

The closing of so many brick plants means that bricks are transported longer distances from the plant to the jobsite. The BIA estimates that the average brick travels 200 miles from the cradle to its use phase, and now the primary means of transport is by truck rather than by train, as it had historically been (BIA 2007d).

On a positive note, the transition from smaller, family-owned brick companies to larger, publicly held companies has spurred improvements and efficiencies in brick production techniques. The capital investment of improved, energy-efficient production processes and pollution controls is more easily achieved by larger companies, and great strides have been taken to improve environmental performance of brick manufacturing.

Environmental and Human Health Impacts of Clay Brick

RAW MATERIALS

Natural raw materials. The primary raw materials of clay bricks are surface clays and shale with moisture

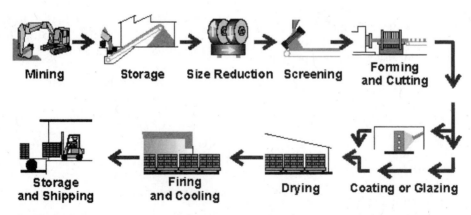

Figure 7–1.

The brick manufacturing process consists of six general phases: mining and storage of raw materials, preparing raw materials, forming the brick, drying, firing and cooling, and dehacking and storing finished products. (Source and Photo from *Technical Notes on Brick Construction 9,* "Manufacturing of Brick," Brick Industry Association, Reston, VA, December, 2006.)

contents between 3% and 15%. Clay is an abundant fine-grained material composed of clay minerals with varying amounts of feldspar, quartz, and other impurities such as iron oxides. Shale is a laminated sedimentary rock of consolidated clay, mud, or silt. In 2005, 24.5 million tons of clay and shale were used to produce brick and related clay products (U.S. Geological Survey 2007). Most clay and shale quarries are located adjacent to or within a few miles of the brick manufacturing facility to minimize transport costs.

Recycling within the brick manufacturing process. Waste is minimal and is often reused within the brick manufacturing process. The Brick Industry Association (BIA) estimates that about 80% of manufacturers either reuse their own fired waste material or convert it into other products (BIA 2007b). Unfired clay waste from manufacturing is returned to the mixers. To a lesser degree, waste from firing, called grog, is ground and then added into the mix, although it is more commonly sold for use in landscape mulch and aggregate base applications. Dust captured from pollution control equipment, primarily wet scrubbers, in brick manufacturing facilities is recycled back into the mix.

Use of recycled raw materials from other sources. With the growing trend toward beneficial reuse of industrial and consumer waste products, an increasing amount of recycled materials and by-products are used as raw materials in brick manufacture. The BIA estimates that almost 50% of manufacturers incorporate some kind of waste into their bricks (BIA 2007b). The high firing temperatures are said to neutralize, burn off, or encapsulate any toxins in the recycled materials, rendering the brick nontoxic.

Some brick manufacturers have begun to work in conjunction with other stone or metal mining operations to obtain the clay materials they remove as overburden or by-products of their mining activities (Brick Development Association [BDA]). While this can minimize disturbance to habitats and ecosystems, it could result in longer raw material transport distances.

Bottom ash from coal-fired power plants is the most widely used recycled material from other industrial processes. The BEES Reference Guide estimates that an average replacement of clay or shale with bottom ash is 0.8%, although some companies use much higher amounts (Lippiatt 2007). Bottom ash can reduce drying and firing shrinkage of bricks and it can act as a moderate flux, reducing energy use in firing (Coal Ash Research Center 2007). Petroleum-contaminated soils are incorporated into brick. When fired at the high temperatures required to produce brick, the hydrocarbons are burned off.

Fly ash, sewage sludge, waste treatment incinerator ash, recycled iron oxides, metallurgical wastes, papermaking sludge, rice husk, slag, and recycled glass are also incorporated into bricks (Demkin 1998b).

The average recycled content of bricks ranges from 5% to 30%; however, a very limited number claim 100% recycled content through use of "recycled" clay quarry by-products. The primary material for these bricks is clay waste from nonclay mining activities, with no new clay mined for these bricks (California Integrated Waste Management Board).

A recently developed brick is made from 100% fly ash, air-entraining agents, and water. Coal fly ash is a fine particle by-product of coal-fired power plants. Each year about 25 million tons of fly ash is incorporated into building materials, primarily concrete, but 45 million tons is disposed of in landfills. Fly ash bricks can incorporate this waste material, requiring no clay and the associated mining impacts (National Science Foundation [NSF] 2007).

Fly ash bricks solidify in molds under 4,000 psi pressure as opposed to being fired at high temperatures like clay bricks. This results in substantial energy and cost savings, yet produces bricks with a compressive strength of concrete. These bricks are expected to be introduced to the market in late 2008 (NSF 2007).

Some brick manufacturers are reluctant to incorporate large amounts of recycled content into their bricks for supply and quality reasons. Manufacturers need to adapt their mix for any recycled content they use, and if they can't be assured of a steady supply of the recycled material, they may have to change their mix often. This can inhibit consistency of quality and color between brick batches. Some solid wastes can burn out during firing of the brick, leaving small voids that can be vulnerable to water (BDA).

Some manufacturers incorporate additives in the mix to control quality or color. Barium carbonate is added to prevent sulfates from rising to the surface of the brick. Surface treatments such as manganese dioxide, iron oxide, and iron chromite are applied to the unfired surface of formed bricks to impart color or texture. Chronic exposure to manganese dioxide can cause problems of the central nervous system and the respiratory tract (Agency for Toxic Substances and Disease Registry [ATSDR] 2003b).

RAW MATERIALS ACQUISITION: MINING AND EXTRACTION

Clay and shale are mined in open-pit surface mines. Mining activity incurs similar environmental impacts as aggregate mining; however, mines may not be as deep and nearly all clay and shale material that is mined is usable, producing far less waste material than stone or metal mining (Demkin 1998b).

However, surface mining incurs substantial land disturbance and impacts to the habitat in and around the quarry site. Vegetation and soil overburden are removed to expose the clay deposits underneath, resulting in a loss of habitat on the mine area. Habitats around the mine are affected by the soil erosion from the mine site, which can increase turbidity in surrounding waterways and pose other impacts to the waterways. Reclamation of clay pits is commonly performed with an estimated 90% of brick companies engaging in some form of reclamation (BIA 2007b).

Dust and particulates are released from extraction. While these emissions are largely nontoxic, their small size can pose a risk to workers as they can enter the lungs and are not easily removed by the body. Airborne dust particulates can also enter surface waters, degrading water quality (Demkin 1998a).

MANUFACTURING

Clay, shale, and other brick components are crushed, graded, screened, and mixed and then extruded or molded to form "green" bricks. They are then dried and fired under intense heat where the mineralogical structure of the material changes and solidifies into a semivitreous state.

Energy Use

The primary environmental impact of brick manufacture is the amount of fuel and energy used for firing and drying brick. Formed and stacked bricks are sent through a pre-dryer and then a dryer chamber that is heated to between 100°F and 400°F. The heat source for some dryers is captured exhaust heat from the cooling zone of the kiln. Other kilns heat dryers with gas or other fuels (U.S. EPA 1997).

Firing of bricks can take 15–50 hours, depending on kiln type and brick specs. Bricks with greater compressive strength and lower absorption, such as weather-resistant brick pavers, are fired longer or at higher temperatures (BIA 2006c). Most kilns are tunnel kilns, but vertical downdraft periodic kilns are increasing in use due to efficiencies created by rising heat drawn up over the bricks. Firing of bricks can be divided into the five rough stages shown in Table 7–2 (BIA 2006c).

Flashing is the technique of creating a reduced atmosphere in a kiln by adding uncombusted fuel or other materials. This modifies the color of the brick (EPA 1997). Other bricks are coated with sand, affecting both the color and the texture.

Natural gas is the most common fuel used for firing brick. Coal and sawdust are also commonly used as burn-off fuel. Based on figures from the BIA, the U.S. Life-cycle Inventory (LCI) database states that brick manufacturing requires an average of 1,974 ft^3 of natural gas and 45 kWh of grid electricity per ton of brick produced (Lippiatt 2007). Natural gas is a cleaner fuel source than the typically used coal; however, it is a more limited resource (see Table 7–3).

Advances in brick manufacturing technology and energy-monitoring programs can reduce the energy use of brick production. Computer-controlled kilns allow heat recycling, and advances in burner technology and

Table 7–2 Brick Firing Stages

Stage	Firing Temperature
Final drying (evaporating free water)	up to 400°F
Dehydration	300°F–1,800°F
Oxidation	1,000°F–1,800°F
Vitrification	1,600°F–2,400°F
Flashing or reduction firing	varies

Source: BIA 2006c

the installation of variable-speed motors can better match energy consumption to the task (BDA).

Alternative fuel sources are used by some manufacturers to heat brick kilns. Waste is burned for energy recovery; however, regulations require pollution control equipment that can be a significant capital expenditure. Some companies are experimenting with capturing landfill gases or other methane sources for fuel. A new brick manufacturing plant in Alabama was built in 2006 adjacent to a landfill that is currently satisfying 40% of the kilns' needs and is projected to satisfy 100% by 2016 as the landfill grows. The plant estimates that it will reduce greenhouse gas emissions by 62,000 metric tons of carbon dioxide equivalent per year (U.S. EPA 2007b).

Emissions and Pollution Control

Emissions from brick manufacture result from raw material processing, raw material composition, and fuel combustion. Emissions include particulate matter

Table 7–3 Embodied Energy and Carbon for Bricks and Mortars

Product (1 Metric Ton)	Embodied Energy (MJ)	Embodied Carbon (kg CO₂)
Engineering bricks	8,200	850
Brick, general	3,000	200
Tile	9,000	430
Precast concrete	2,000	215
Mortar (1:3 cement-sand mix)	1,520	228
Mortar (1:1/2:4 1/2 cement/lime/ sand mix)	1,640	251
Mortar (1:2:9 cement/ lime/sand mix)	1,330	198

Source: Adapted from Hammond and Jones 2006 (All data is for materials used in the UK. Data was collected from UK and EU sources and worldwide averages. Values may vary from U.S. figures but are useful for comparisons among materials.)

(PM10 and PM2.5), sulfur dioxide (SO_2), sulfur trioxide (SO_3), nitrogen oxides (NO_x), carbon monoxide (CO), carbon dioxide (CO_2), metals, methane, ethane, VOCs, HAPs, hydrochloric acid (HCl), and fluoride compounds (U.S. EPA 1997).

Particulate matter (PM10 and PM2.5) is the primary type of emission resulting from raw material grinding, drying, and screening operations. Most manufacturers either wet the material or capture a certain percentage of this dust in pollution control equipment, although some is released. Some captured material is reused as raw material for new bricks. Other sources of particulate matter are sawdust dryers from sawdust-fired kilns, coal-crushing systems for coal-fired kilns, and fugitive dust sources such as storage piles and unpaved roads (U.S. EPA 1997).

Combustion products emitted from fuel combustion, primarily natural gas, in kilns and dryers include SO_2, NO_x, CO, CO_2, VOCs, methane, and particulates. Environmental and health effects of these pollutants are discussed in chapter 2. Brick dryers that are heated with waste heat from kilns are not usually a source of combustion emissions (U.S. EPA 1997).

Hydrogen fluoride (HF) and other fluoride compounds are the emissions of greatest concern of the additional pollutants and emissions resulting from the raw material composition of clay and shale. Fluorine is present in brick's raw materials at concentrations of 0.01%–0.06%. Upon firing, the fluorine forms HF and other fluorine compounds. Emissions vary with the fluorine content and pollution control equipment. Health effects of HF include eye, nose, and respiratory irritation, pulmonary edema, laryngeal and bronchial spasms, and eye and skin burns (ATSDR 2003a). Chlorine to a lesser degree is present in raw materials and on firing becomes hydrogen chloride with similar health effects to HF.

Acid precipitation is the primary environmental effect of fluorine and chlorine. This can result in tree and crop damage, metal corrosion, and surface water acidification (Demkin 1998b). Fluorine can't be destroyed in the environment; it can only change its form. It forms salts with minerals in soil and will accumulate in plants and animals (ATSDR 2003a).

Sulfur dioxide (SO₂) emissions result from clay, shale, or other additives that sometimes contain sulfur compounds. Manufacturers using low-sulfur raw materials will have lower SO_2 emissions.

Nitrogen oxide (NOₓ) emissions result from brick manufacturing at a rate of about 0.35 lb/ton. The majority of these results from fossil fuel combustion; however, some nitrogen is present in clay raw materials and is "liberated" during firing (Sanders and Brosnan 2007).

Crystalline silica, contained in clay, is commonly called silica dust. Crystalline silica can cause eye and respiratory tract irritations, or even more severe conditions, in humans. It can lead to the development of silicosis, and in extreme exposures to lung cancer, pulmonary tuberculosis, and airway diseases in mining, processing, and construction workers (National Institute for Occupational Safety and Health [NIOSH] 2002).

Brick manufacturers minimize emissions with pollution controls such as scrubbers, filtering systems, vacuums, additives, and water mists (BIA 2006c). Fluorine emissions control is a major concern of the industry and some plants employ dry scrubbers using limestone as an absorption medium to control HF emissions. Control efficiencies of 95% have been reported with this type of equipment (U.S. EPA 1997) (see Table 7–4).

Water Use

Water is used in brick manufacturing, but little wastewater is released as much of the water evaporates from heat or is reused. Water is stored for recirculation or reuse (BIA 2006c).

TRANSPORTATION

Deposits of clay and shale are commonly found throughout the world. They are mined commercially in forty-one states; however, not all deposits are suitable for all applications. The BIA estimates that shipping of the average brick load from manufacturer to construction site is about 200 miles. Most clay and shale quarries are located adjacent to or within a few miles of the brick manufacturing facility to minimize transport costs (BIA).

Bricks, like concrete and stone, are heavy materials requiring substantial energy and costs to transport.

Table 7–4 Athena Institute Life-Cycle Comparison of Clay Bricks and Concrete Masonry Bricks (One metric ton)

	Clay Brick (natural gas fired, Canadian average)	Concrete Masonry Brick[a] (Toronto average)
Embodied Energy (MJ/ton)		
	4,584	1,855
Processing Emissions		
CO_2	232.254 kg/ton	180 kg/ton
SO_2	260.465 g/ton	50.418 g/ton
NO_x	287.798 g/ton	543.489 g/ton
TOC	77.500 g/ton	—
CH_4	36.726 g/ton	8.280 g/ton
VOC	51.916 g/ton	30.919 g/ton
CO	745.452 g/ton	187.786 g/ton
TPM (total particulate matter)	590.530 g/ton	329.763 g/ton
HF	190.000 g/ton	—
HCl	105.000 g/ton	—
Water Effluent Loads (average)[b]		
pH	7.83	8.15
TSS (Total suspended solids)	214.672 g/ton	61.634 g/ton
DOC (Dissolved Organic Compounds)	4.237 g/ton	1.981 g/ton
oil & grease	—	1.565 g/ton
Ammonium, -ia	0.604 g/ton	0.288 g/ton
phenolics	0.001 g/ton	0.0045 g/ton
cyanide	0.002 g/ton	—
sulfur compounds	158.837 g/ton	112.296 g/ton
iron	5.975 g/ton	
non-ferrous metals		
aluminum	6.150 g/ton	0.287 g/ton
copper	0.006 g/ton	—
zinc	0.060 g/ton	0.000 g/ton
Solid Waste (processing only)		
	11.352 kg/ton	3.455 kg/ton

[a]Figures for concrete masonry brick originally published for one cubic meter of material. In conversion to metric tons the assumed density of concrete masonry brick is 1,436 kg/m³.

[b]Effluent for concrete brick is expressed as a weighted average while effluent from clay brick is expressed as an average.

Source: Athena Institute 1998

Therefore it is important that bricks be obtained from the closest possible source. Energy used in transport, particularly by less efficient trucks, can be greater than energy used in manufacture if the manufacturer is located too far from the site.

Manufacturers should be questioned as to the production location of the particular bricks specified, as different types of bricks are often produced in different plants. In addition, the corporate office location of the brick manufacturer can be very different from the plant that produces the bricks.

While it is desirable to purchase bricks from a manufacturer who takes steps to minimize the environmental impacts of their brick manufacture through use of recycled content, pollution controls, or use of alternative fuels, if they are located thousands of miles from the project site, the transport impacts can negate any of the other environmental benefits.

Specifying Bricks from Manufacturers Who Minimize Manufacturing Impacts

As evidenced in the discussion of raw material acquisition and brick manufacturing above, brick producers use recycled raw materials in addition to clay and shale, and they employ a wide range of manufacturing techniques resulting in varying environmental impacts. It is possible to specify bricks with less environmental impact by asking questions of the manufacturers and suppliers.

Questions to ask of manufacturers:

- Do you incorporate recycled materials into your bricks (e.g., bottom ash, coal fly ash, sewage sludge, petroleum-contaminated soils, waste treatment incinerator ash, recycled iron oxides, metallurgical wastes, papermaking sludge, rice husk, slag, recycled glass, or others)? What percentage of the specific brick being specified is recycled content?

- Are any manufacturing wastes reused in new bricks or other applications?

- What steps does your plant take to reduce energy use in firing and drying brick (e.g., vertical shaft kilns, computer-controlled kilns and dryers, recycling kiln heat for use in dryers, variable-speed motors to match energy consumption to the task)?

- Do you burn waste for fuel? What type of pollution controls do you employ for the waste you burn?

- What is the energy source for the dryers and kilns (e.g., natural gas is better than coal-fired power)? Does the plant use alternative energy sources (e.g., methane gas sources, wind, hydroelectric energy)?

- What type of pollution controls do you employ to reduce fluorine and chlorine emissions? To reduce dust emissions?

- What quarry remediation efforts are made after a quarry is closed (e.g., reforestation, planting of native species, stabilization of soils, grading to match surrounding topography and drainage patterns)?

- What steps are taken to protect the environment during mining (e.g., dust suppression in mining areas and on transport roads, soil stabilization efforts, topsoil stockpiling, and runoff control)? Is the mine in or near a sensitive ecosystem or habitat?

- Is the quarry associated with other mining operations potentially using quarry waste or soil removed for deeper mining?

- Is water recycled in the brick manufacturing process? Is wastewater treated prior to release?

- How far from the manufacturing facility is the clay or shale mined? How far from the project site is the brick manufactured (e.g., less than 200 miles preferred as brick is so heavy)?

- Does the manufacturer have a take-back program for bricks after their useful life?

- Can extra bricks be returned to the distributor after construction is complete? Does the distributor take back brick pallets or other packaging?

CONSTRUCTION AND USE

Installation of brick structures can use less energy than comparable concrete or asphalt structures, as bricks are usually hand laid. Waste generated during the installation phase is estimated to be about 5% of the materials per square foot (Lippiatt 2007). Design of brick structures that require excessive cutting of bricks can produce more brick waste. Waste is typically landfilled; however, construction and demolition recycling specifications can require recycling of brick waste.

Dust from cutting bricks can irritate lungs and eyes. Prolonged inhalation of iron oxide dust can produce siderosis, a benign lung disease resulting from deposition of iron in lung tissue. Material safety data sheets (MSDSs) for brick recommend that goggles, gloves, and respirators be worn during brick cutting. Chronic exposure to manganese dioxide, used to create brown bricks, can cause problems of the central nervous system and the respiratory tract (ATSDR 2003b; Demkin 1998b).

Human health impacts of crystalline silica dust are discussed above.

Reducing the Environmental Impacts of Brick Structures

DESIGN BRICK STRUCTURES TO MINIMIZE ENVIRONMENTAL IMPACTS ON-SITE

Bricks and mortar arc inert and will not off-gas, leach, or contaminate a site while in use. However, brick structures can impact the health of sites in other ways. Rigid or semirigid brick pavements are impervious surfaces, increasing storm water runoff, concentrating pollutants, and sterilizing soil underneath through lack of air and water. Even flexible sand-set brick pavements with 1/8-inch sand-swept joints are too narrow to allow a significant amount of water to infiltrate the pavement, as joints quickly become filled with dirt and dust.

Table 7–5 Comparison of Wall Cladding Materials Using the Athena Environmental Impact Estimator

	Metric (Modular) Brick (1m²)[a]	Ontario (Standard) Brick (1m²)[b]	Concrete Brick (1m²)[c]	Split-faced Concrete Block (1m²)[d]	Stucco over Metal Mesh (1m²)[e]
Primary energy consumption (MJ)	1,229	1,393	337	535	60
Solid waste (kg)	10	11	2	2	0
Air pollution index	20	23	5	9	1
Water pollution index	0	0	0	0	0
Global warming potential (kg)	65	74	23	41	6
Weighted resource use (kg)	112	128	188	329	33

[a]Metric (Modular) Clay Brick:
Length = 190 mm (8.25"); width = 102 mm (4"); height = 60 mm (2.4") cored. Coverage: 75 bricks/m².
Note these figures do not include the impacts of the concrete or CMU wall structure to which these bricks are attached. If used as a double wythe wall, figures should be doubled.

[b]Ontario (Standard) Clay Brick:
Length = 213 mm (7.6"); width = 90mm (3.5"); height = 57 mm (2.3") cored. Coverage: 64.5 bricks/m².
Note these figures do not include the impacts of the concrete or CMU wall structure to which these bricks are attached. If used as a double wythe wall, figures should be doubled.

[c]Concrete Brick:
Length = 200 mm (8"); width = 100 mm (4"); height = 100 mm (4") cored. Coverage: 50 bricks/m².
Note these figures do not include the impacts of the concrete or CMU wall structure to which these bricks are attached. If used as a double wythe wall, figures should be doubled.

[d]Split-faced Concrete Blocks:
Architectural block length = 400 mm (16"); width = 200 mm (8"); height = 200 mm (8") cored. Coverage: 12.5 blocks/m².

[e]Stucco over Metal Mesh:
Figures for stucco over metal mesh do not include the impacts of the concrete or CMU wall structure to which this stucco is applied.

Source: Athena Sustainable Materials Institute

Clay brick pavements can be specially designed as porous pavements for pedestrian and light vehicular traffic applications. While no known porous clay brick paving systems exist, bricks can be laid in a variety of patterns with use of plastic spacers that can encourage water to flow through gravel-filled joints and voids between the bricks (Ferguson 2005). Shallower pavement slopes, 2% or less, will allow storm water enough time to infiltrate the joints.

Use of manufactured plastic spacers will widen the joints between bricks while offering some stability and interlock of the clay brick units. Plastic spacers can create joint sizes from $3/8$ inch to two inches and when filled with open-graded aggregates can create a porous pavement. Because interlock of clay brick pavements with spacers is not as strong as with concrete pavers designed for porous paving applications, porous brick pavements should only be specified in pedestrian and light vehicular applications. Interlock can be increased through use of herringbone patterns (see Figure 7–2).

Use of vegetation in the joints between bricks does not allow for much infiltration of water. The vegetation can act as a dam, prohibiting water from entering the joints, and once in the joints, soil housing the vegetation does not infiltrate water as quickly, leading to greater water runoff (Ferguson 2005).

If bricks must be set on sand on a concrete slab, weep holes can be specified every twelve inches in the slab with spacers between bricks. If the slab is placed on an open-graded aggregate base, some water will permeate the paving installation.

USE LESS MATERIAL IN BRICK STRUCTURES

Brick structures can be designed in many ways, some of which use more material than others. It is important to consider the expected life of the landscape, the traffic or loads bearing on the structure, and the climatic conditions to which the structure will be subjected to determine just how the structure should be constructed. And it is also important that structures meeting these needs be designed to minimize material use, particularly those materials with high embodied energy or pollution impacts. There can be a tendency among designers to use details without considering how a durable structure might be designed using less material.

Using Less Material in Brick Walls

Single-wythe walls can use fewer bricks and materials than double wythe or brick veneer walls. Single-wythe walls are not stable or able to resist wind loads without curves or angles in the wall. The structural concept of serpentine, chevron, or staggered walls is similar to that of corrugated metals in that the opposing curves of the wall serve to stiffen the thin wall.

Single-wythe freestanding serpentine walls, if constructed with the proper radii for the height of the wall, can produce structurally sound freestanding walls. For serpentine walls up to four feet in height, the radii of the tangential curves of the wall should not exceed twice the overall height of the wall above finished grade. The depth of curvature should be no less than half the height of the wall above grade (BIA 1994) (see Figure 7–3).

Single-wythe chevron walls are similar to serpentine walls and should be designed with chevron angles, spacing, and geometric principles of serpentine walls.

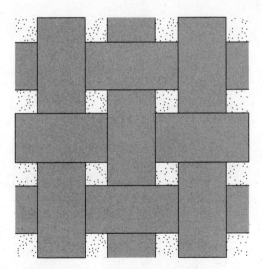

Figure 7–2.
This brick paving pattern allows for gravel-filled voids that can allow storm water to infiltrate. (Source: POROUS PAVEMENTS by Bruce Ferguson. Copyright 2005 by Taylor & Francis Group LLC – Books. Reproduced with permission of Taylor & Francis Group LLC – Books in the format Tradebook via Copyright Clearance Center; Illustration by John Wiley & Sons)

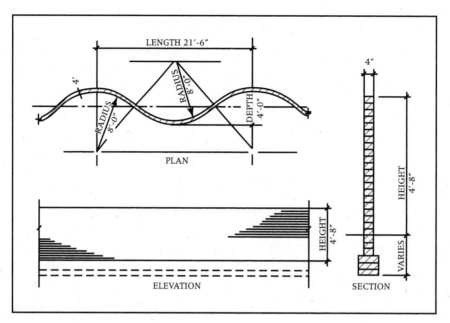

Figure 7–3.
The serpentine wall can save resources, as fewer bricks are used in a single wythe than in a double wythe or a brick-faced CMU wall. The relationship of radii to length of curve is shown for a structurally sound four foot eight inch–high wall. (Source: *Technical Notes on Brick Construction 29A*, "Brick in Landscape Architecture—Garden Walls," Brick Industry Association, Reston, VA, January, 1999; Illustration by John Wiley & Sons)

Single-wythe staggered walls rely on the wall turning a right angle periodically for stability. Single-wythe walls up to seven feet high must be offset at least eight inches every six feet or less (Jewell 1983). Comparable serpentine and chevron walls provide greater wind resistance.

Pier and panel walls consist of intervals of panels spanning between and braced by piers or pilasters. Panels can be either single or double wythe; however, single-wythe panels will require fewer bricks, minimizing both environmental and economic costs. The piers in a pier and panel system share dead loads of the panels and live loads, such as wind, bearing on the panels. Bonding between the panel and pier, usually reinforcing, is critical for resistance to horizontal forces (Cervelli-Schach 2007). Because panels are thin, they are less appropriate in situations where high lateral loads, such as wind loads, are expected or in areas of expansive soils.

The finished dimension of a pier should be at least twice the panel thickness. Therefore a four-inch-thick panel requires at least an eight-inch pier. The unsupported height for piers should not be greater than ten times their least cross-sectional dimension, or four times for unfilled hollow masonry units (Landphair and Klatt 1988). Twelve-inch-square piers are common for four-inch panel walls that are eighty inches or above. Figure 7–4 shows the three possible relationships of pier to panel.

The BIA recommends the footing for a pier and panel wall to be poured-in-place concrete piers under the brick piers in undisturbed soil extending down into stable soil. Footings should extend below the frost line.

Other sources recommend use of a grade beam spanning between concrete pier foundations or even a continuous spread footing (Cervelli-Schach 2007). Both of these methods will use more material than the pier foundation recommended by the BIA; however, special

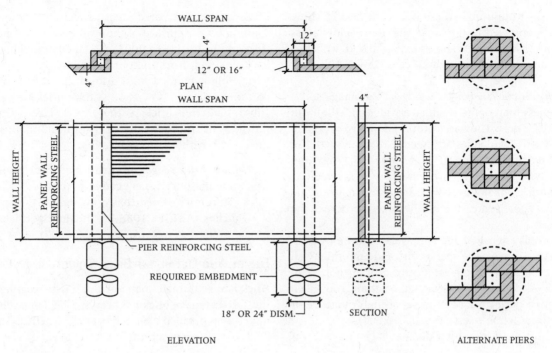

WALL SPAN

4"

12"

12" OR 16"

4"

PLAN

WALL SPAN

WALL HEIGHT

PANEL WALL REINFORCING STEEL

PIER REINFORCING STEEL

REQUIRED EMBEDMENT

18" OR 24" DISM.

ELEVATION

4"

PANEL WALL REINFORCING STEEL

WALL HEIGHT

SECTION

ALTERNATE PIERS

Figure 7–4.
This pier and panel wall minimizes resource use with a single-wythe panel (which can be perforated) and footings only under the piers. The wall panel is reinforced with steel in the mortar joints and under the panel, which is tied into the piers (Source: *Technical Notes on Brick Construction 29A,* "Brick in Landscape Architecture—Garden Walls," Brick Industry Association, Reston, VA, January, 1999; Illustration by John Wiley & Sons)

conditions such as expansive soils or unusual loading can necessitate their use.

Perforated freestanding brick walls can use fewer bricks and offer the added benefits of air and light access while creating a perceptual, if not visual, barrier. Most perforated walls are a variation on the pier and panel design, with perforated areas in the panels spanning between regularly spaced piers.

Like pier and panel walls, perforated brick walls are subject to wind loads. The wind load is not as great due to perforations in the surfaces of the panels, but it is still considered the same due to the trade-off of reduced wall weight (Jewell 1983). While structural requirements will vary by wind load and other conditions, the general height rule for perforated wall panels is that panels under seven feet high can be one wythe thick and panels over seven feet must be two or three wythe thick (Jewell 1983).

Other types of single-wythe perforated walls are staggered walls, chevron walls, or serpentine walls. These types of walls rely on "corrugation" for stability and do not require intermittent piers. See the discussion above of these types of solid panel walls for more information.

Perforated walls that are double wythe can be designed similarly to a standard double-wythe wall with a continuous spread footing. Perforating the wall will use less brick than a solid wall. However, the continuous spread footing may use more foundation material than a pier and panel design in colder climates with freeze-thaw activity and lower frost lines. The height of straight double-wythe walls should be less than or equal to three-fourths of the thickness squared ($h \leq {}^3/_4 T^2$; BIA 1999).

Perforated brick walls can leave joints vulnerable to water penetration and should be detailed in such a manner as to minimize these opportunities. Flashing should be inserted in the horizontal joint below areas where a vertical mortar joint is exposed, both in perforations and in wall tops without caps (Jewell 1983).

Cavity and hollow bonded walls, both drainage walls, can use less material to produce a wider wall than can solid brick walls. They are comprised of two wythe of brick, if two good sides are needed, or one wythe of brick and one wythe of CMU if only one "fair" side is required, with a two- to four-inch cavity in between. A header brick (for hollow bonded walls) or masonry tie (for cavity walls) ties the wythe together across the cavity.

The walls are called drainage walls because water is conducted through the open cavity and out of the wall with flashing and weep holes located near the bottom of the wall. Aside from using less material than grout-filled walls, they perform well in areas of high moisture or freeze-thaw action (Cervelli-Schach 2007).

Masonry ties for cavity walls should be either galvanized or copper-coated steel to resist corrosion and staining on the surface of the wall from water passing through the wall (BIA 2003). Metal ties should be kept back one inch from the outside surface of the mortar joint. Hollow bonded walls using a shiner and rowlock pattern with a 4" × 4" × 12" utility brick tie can use substantially less brick, as the 4" × 8" face is exposed on the wall and the wall can be a substantial twelve-inch width with a four-inch cavity.

Thinner brick veneer units can use fewer resources. Anchored masonry veneer can be as thin as $2\,^5/_8$ inches thick. Thin brick veneer has a maximum thickness of $1\,^3/_4$ inches (ASTM C1088 2007). Hollow brick units can be utilized as well (ASTM C652 2007).

DESIGN AND DETAIL THE BRICK STRUCTURE TO LAST

Brick is very durable material and resists weathering if the correct type of brick has been specified and the brick structure is detailed well. Some brick structures such as walls have been in service for over 100 years. The BEES

Table 7–6 Design and Specification Considerations for Preventing Moisture in Brick Walls

Wall caps with overhangs should be placed on the top course of the wall to protect inner cavity and mortar joints of the wall. Slope caps to drain at least 2%.
Use of flashing and drip kerfs under caps will help prevent water from entering the wall under caps.
Drainage-type walls (e.g., cavity walls or veneer walls with air spaces) will allow water that penetrates the wall to freely drain through and out weep holes.
In areas of high acid rain, use of silicone water-repellent surface treatments can preserve the brick and joint longevity. Note that many sealers contain VOCs and other toxic constituents.
Mortar joints should be designed to quickly shed water, and joints that result in "shelves" on which water can stand should be avoided.
Joints should be well tooled for compaction of mortar and resistance to water penetration.
Use of chamfered bricks below recessed bricks can help shed water from joints.
Use concave, V-shaped, or weathered joints.
Avoid raked, weeping, or struck joints, as they can allow standing water that may penetrate the joint.
Avoid flush joints as they are not tooled for compaction and may allow water to penetrate.
Avoid extruded joints, as they can host water and are subject to water penetration and breakage.
Use flashing in the horizontal mortar joint under an exposed vertical joint.

Sources: BIA 1999; Cervelli-Schach 2007

model assumes a 200-year useful life for a brick wall (Lipiatt 2007). Detailing of the structure with durability in mind can help the structure meet its full potential life.

Brick Walls

The durability and life span of a brick wall are largely determined by its ability to resist moisture penetration. If water is allowed to penetrate the interior of the wall, it can lead to premature failure. Research and experience has shown that most masonry structures fail at joints; therefore careful detailing of joints and mortar is critical. Water penetration is the primary way that joints can fail. Efflorescence—salt deposits on the surface of the wall from water moving through the structure—while not in and of itself harmful to the structure of the wall, is an indication that water has penetrated a brick wall. The measures summarized in Table 7–6 will reduce the chance of moisture penetration in brick walls, prolonging the life of the structure.

Careful use of control and expansion joints in long brick walls can ensure longevity of the structure. A 100-foot-long brick wall can expand or contract about 0.43 inch for every 100-degree temperature change. Rigid restraint of the wall structure can produce cracking and failures as wall materials expand and contract with heat and cold. The BIA recommends use of control joints in brick walls every twenty to thirty-five feet, and at points of stress and weakness such as level changes, openings, and between panels and columns. It also recommends use of expansion joints every twenty-five to thirty feet (BIA 1999).

Well-designed and constructed brick walls resist water penetration and do not require water repellents or external coatings. Coatings can be used around copings, parapets, and sills; however, care should be taken to specify nontoxic, low-VOC products. Only water repellents such as siloxanes and silanes that allow water evaporation and passage of water vapor should be used. Film-forming coatings should not be used in exterior brick applications (BIA 2002).

Brick Pavements

There is a popular misconception that rigid, mortar-set brick pavements are stronger and more durable than flexible brick pavements. However, this is not the case

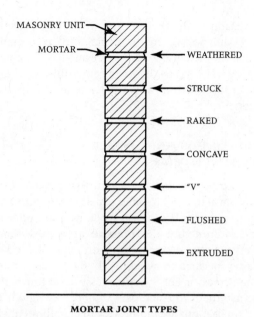

MORTAR JOINT TYPES

Figure 7–5.

Mortar joints in brick walls should be designed to shed water quickly to minimize the chance of water penetration into the wall. Use of concave, V-shaped, or weathered joints will shed water most effectively while struck, raked, and extruded joints provide ledges that may allow for water to pool and make its way into the wall cavity. Flush joints place the transition from brick to mortar in a position where it is more exposed to the elements increasing the chance of water penetration (Source: Hopper, Leonard, ed. Copyright © 2006, John Wiley & Sons, Inc. Reprinted with the permission of John Wiley & Sons, Inc.)

as rigid, mortar-set pavements are more likely to fail completely and require replacement sooner. They are subject to more freeze-thaw stresses, and when brick or mortar joints do crack, they are very difficult to spot repair. With large amounts of cracking the entire installation is usually removed and replaced. Brick pavers set on a sand bed on well-compacted aggregate are much more easily repaired if shrinking or swelling soil causes pavement displacement. Rigid, mortared brick pavements are only recommended for light vehicular traffic, whereas sand-set brick pavers on an asphalt or concrete base can accommodate heavy traffic volumes (BIA 2007a) (see Table 7–7).

Semirigid pavements of sand-set brick on concrete or asphalt will allow for easy replacement of the brick pavers, but they use a large amount of material (e.g., concrete and asphalt), resulting in excessive use of resources and posing environmental impacts in manufacture. Use of a dense graded aggregate base stabilized with portland cement or other cementitious binders may offer just as strong and stable a base with less use of material.

MINIMIZE ENVIRONMENTAL IMPACTS FROM CEMENT MORTAR

Mortar, composing about 17% of the surface of a brick wall, is critical to the durability of a brick structure. The two important traits of masonry mortar are bonding ability and durability. Compressive strength is important, but the lowest compressive strength for the load should be specified to avoid overly rigid mortar joints that may crack or fail or exert pressure on bricks that may cause them to crack (BIA 2006b). As rigid brick paving applications are more likely to be saturated with water, a more durable mortar should be used. Sand-set pavements are more durable.

Brick and stone mortar is a mix of dry ingredients including portland cement, mortar cement, masonry cement, and/or hydrated lime mixed with sand. Portland cement is the primary ingredient in many masonry mortars. Environmental impacts of portland cement manufacture include high embodied energy and substantial release of CO_2. They are discussed in greater detail in chapter 5. Masonry cement is comprised of 50%–75% clinker from portland cement kilns mixed with limestone, clays, gypsum, retarders, and air-entraining agents (EBN 2002).

Minimizing use of portland cement in masonry mortars can reduce the impacts incurred in manufacture. Current practice substitutes fly ash, a by-product of coal combustion, for about 25% of the portland cement in masonry cement mixes, primarily for cost-saving reasons. At least one masonry cement product substitutes Type C fly ash for 100% of the portland cement. Fly ash composes about 85% of the mix, with the remaining ingredients being mineral products such as gypsums and clays. Admixtures are incorporated for plasticity and to slow set time for setting the bricks. The fly ash mortar is currently available in Types N, S, and M (EBN 2002).

Other blended hydraulic cements, such as blast furnace slag cement, portland-pozzolan cement, and slag cement, can be substituted for portland cement in mortar mixes. These hydraulic cements should meet the property specifications of ASTM C270 Specification for Mortar Unit Masonry (BIA 2006b).

Pigments to impart color to mortar can contain metal oxides and other organic constituents. Colors containing cadmium, lithopone, zinc chromate, and lead chromate can pose toxicity risks and should be avoided.

Alternatives to cement mortars exist, but are far less used. Lime mortars were used as far back as 4000 BC in Ancient Egypt and up until the twentieth century. Lime putty, composed of slaked quicklime, is mixed with water and sand to form lime mortar. Lime mortars are nonhydraulic and set slowly through reaction with carbon dioxide in the air. Pozzolanic materials such as calcined clay or brick dust can be added to the mortar mix to speed hardening. Hydraulic lime mortars, used as a dry powder, will harden more quickly upon contact with water (BIA 2006b).

Lime mortars are softer than cement mortars and are most commonly used to repair historic masonry structures that were constructed with lime mortar. The softness of lime mortars offers flexibility to the brick structure, more easily accommodating slight shifts in the ground or changing conditions. Lime mortars should be used with softer bricks in light or nonload-bearing applications. Lime mortar is breathable, allowing moisture to move through it and evaporate from its surface. Minor moisture trapped in a brick wall with lime mortar can easily escape (BIA 2006b).

MAINTENANCE AND REPAIRS

Brick is a very low-maintenance material and most brick structures require little maintenance if well designed and detailed. Other components in brick structures, such as caps, copings, flashing, weep holes, seals, and joints, may be less durable than brick and require some maintenance and repair. Copings and metal flashing are expected to last from 20–75 years. Mortar is expected to last over 25 years (BIA 2005). Brick structures should be inspected every year for signs of moisture penetration or other necessary repairs. In addition, the maintenance and repair activities discussed below can increase the life of brick

Table 7–7 Comparison of Brick Pavement Types

Clay Pavers On:	Advantages	Disadvantages
Sand Setting Bed on Aggregate Base	Most durable Cost-effective Easy access to repair underground utilities Good as overlay to existing asphalt or concrete pavement Allows use of semiskilled labor Can be designed as permeable pavement	Intensive cleaning may erode joint sand May require a thicker base
Sand Setting Bed on Asphalt Base	Good as overlay to existing asphalt pavement	Intensive cleaning may erode joint sand
Sand Setting Bed on Cement-treated Aggregate Base	Good over poor soils or in small, confined areas Good as overlay to existing concrete pavement	Intensive cleaning may erode joint sand
Sand Setting Bed on Concrete Base	Good over poor soils or in small, confined areas Good as overlay to existing concrete pavement	Intensive cleaning may erode joint sand Requires good drainage above base Susceptible to greater offset with subgrade movement
Bituminous Setting Bed on Asphalt Base	Reduced horizontal movement and uplift Enhanced water penetration resistance	Repairs are more difficult and expensive. Little tolerance for paver thickness variations or inaccurate base elevations
Bituminous Setting on Concrete Base	Reduced horizontal movement and uplift Enhanced water penetration resistance Good over poor soils or in small, confined areas	Repairs can be more difficult and expensive than sand settings. Little tolerance for paver thickness variations or inaccurate base elevations
Mortar Setting Bed Bonded to Concrete Base	Greater tolerance for paver thickness variations or inaccurate base elevations Can be used on steeper slopes and with greater vehicle speeds Drainage occurs on the surface	Movement joints must align through entire paving system Least cost-effective Mortar joint maintenance required Repairs are the most difficult and expensive.
Mortar Setting Bed Unbonded to Concrete Base	Greater tolerance for paver thickness variations or inaccurate base elevations Movement joints in setting bed and base are not required to align. Preferred when used over elevated structural slab	Bond break must be used to avoid stresses caused by horizontal movement between layers. Least cost-effective Mortar joint maintenance required Repairs are most difficult and expensive.

Source: BIA 2007a

Table 7–8 Design and Specification Considerations for Flexible Brick Pavements

Specifying bricks with appropriate strength and weather resistance is critical to the longevity of a brick pavement.
Bricks used in vehicular or heavy pavement applications such as streets or crosswalks should be thicker paving bricks (minimum $2^5/_8$").
Material use can be minimized by using thinner bricks in residential pedestrian applications ($1^1/_2$" thick) or commercial pedestrian traffic, driveway, and parking lot applications ($2^1/_4$" thick).
Herringbone patterns are more stable because of the interlock.
Slope the pavement a minimum of 2%.
Edge restraints for pavements subjected to vehicular traffic should be concrete or stone curbs, or steel angles connected to a concrete base.
Edge restraints in pedestrian applications can be concrete, stone, steel, aluminum, or plastic headers.
Well-designed and constructed brick pavements do not require water repellents or external coatings. Unlike colored concrete "brick" pavers, the color of clay brick pavers will not fade with exposure to sun, snow, or foot traffic, and does not require sealing if the appropriate weathering grade is used. Sealers can decrease the slip resistance of the pavement.
Light-duty flexible brick pavers should comply with ASTM C902 Standard Specification for Pedestrian and Light Traffic Paving Brick.
Heavy-duty vehicular applications of flexible brick pavers should comply with ASTM C1272 Standard Specification for Heavy Vehicular Paving Brick.
Sand should be used for the setting bed that complies with ASTM C33 Standard Specification for Concrete Aggregates.
Sand in joints can be stabilized to preserve the application; however, avoid stabilizers with high VOC contents and toxic constituents.

Sources: BIA 2007a, 2007c

structures. Table 7–9 summarizes key maintenance and repair strategies for brick walls, and Table 7–10 summarizes key strategies for brick pavements.

END OF LIFE: REUSE, RECYCLING OR DISPOSAL

Bricks can easily outlast the life of a site structure and if properly detailed, the bricks can be reclaimed and reused multiple times. Late-nineteenth-century street bricks found all over the eastern half of the United States are an enduring example of this, as many have been repeatedly reused in new pedestrian paving applications. Others have been re-leveled and remain as functional streets today—over a century later.

Use of mortar, or not, is usually the determining factor in the reuse of bricks. While it is technically feasible to separate mortar from bricks when reclaiming them

for reuse, it is a labor-intensive job and cement mortar can be stronger than the brick itself, resulting in a high "casualty" rate. Lime mortar, used in brick structures prior to the mid-twentieth century, is softer and much easier to remove from bricks. Where removal of cement mortar is not feasible, reclaimed bricks with mortar fragments can be crushed for reuse as base or fill material.

If a brick structure is designed with disassembly in mind, avoiding use of mortar is the simplest way to ensure that the bricks can be reused. In pavement applications, this is relatively simple as brick patterns (such as herringbone) and edge restraints will hold sand-set bricks in place. Longevity of the installation is an added benefit, as the pavement is easily repaired if an individual brick is broken or settling occurs. Conversely, broken bricks, cracked mortar joints, or settling of mortared brick pavements often results in

Table 7–9 Maintenance and Repair Considerations for Brick Walls

Repointing of some brick wall mortar joints can be expected after 25 years.
Efflorescence is water soluble and can be easily removed with brushing or natural weathering. However, efflorescence is a sign that water has penetrated the wall cavity or joints and may indicate a larger problem. Proprietary cleaners can be used for stubborn stains, but care should be taken to find cleaners with low toxicity, or spill, rinsing, and runoff control measures should be taken.
Sealants in joints should be repaired when they become brittle or loose.
Hairline cracks in mortar joints should be repaired to keep moisture out of the wall.
Plants such as ivy should be periodically removed from the wall and joints damaged by suckers repaired.
Spalled bricks should be removed and replaced.
"Retrofit" anchors can be installed where existing masonry anchors have failed.
Cleaning of brick walls should employ the gentlest effective cleaner to avoid damage to both the bricks and to human health and the environment around the brick wall. Muriatic or other acid solutions should be avoided. Look for nontoxic, low-VOC cleaners and test on an inconspicuous part of the wall prior to use.
The gentlest cleaning method is hand cleaning by bucket and brush. Pressurized water cleaning and abrasive blasting can be used, but care should be taken not to damage brick or mortar joints. Pressurized water cleaning can carry potentially toxic cleaners into the surrounding environment.
The BIA Technical Notes 20 on Cleaning Brickwork offers detailed advice for cleaning brick structures and for removing specific stains.

Sources: BIA 2002, 2005, 2006a

Table 7–10 Maintenance and Repair Considerations for Brick Pavements

Sand-set brick pavers can be lifted out and re-leveled as required. Bases of flexible pavements can be easily repaired as well.
Repair of mortared brick pavements can be more complicated and can involve reconstruction of some or all of the pavement application.
Metal blades on snow removal equipment should be rubber tipped or mounted on rollers, and the blade edge should be set at an appropriate clearance height above the brick to minimize chipping.
Chemicals containing rock salt to melt ice should not be applied to the brick pavement, as they may cause efflorescence. Clean sand can be used on icy areas.
Efflorescence caused by soluble salts will usually be worn away by traffic.
Most coatings are not recommended for exterior pavements, as they can reduce the slip resistance of brick. Coatings used to prevent joint sand displacement should be applied to the joint only. Care should be taken to select a nontoxic, low-VOC coating.
Some repointing may be required with rigid brick pavements. The BIA suggests use of type S mortar.

Sources: BIA 2002, 2005, 2006a, 2007a

Table 7–11 Design and Specification Considerations When Using Salvaged Brick

As bricks placed with portland cement mortar absorb some cementitious particles prior to curing, salvaged bricks, even if well cleaned, may have traces of mortar that can compromise the bond with new mortar.
Early 20th century firing techniques produced bricks with highly variable durability, strength, and absorption characteristics. Design of the new structure should accommodate these potential irregularities.
Size and uniformity of historic bricks may be more variable than modern bricks.
Labor costs may be higher when using salvaged brick, as placement may not be as fast and cleaning of bricks prior to placement may be required.
National building codes require a 50% reduction in working stresses from those of new masonry when using salvaged bricks.
Salvaged brick may have a more worn or rugged appearance.

Source: BIA 1988

removal of the entire application, as repair of small areas is difficult.

It is more challenging to avoid mortar in brick wall applications; however, new interlocking clay masonry wall products are entering the market. Interlocking concrete masonry units are another alternative. Where mortar is used, specifying lime mortar will make reuse easier.

Salvaged Bricks

Use of salvaged bricks can reduce resource use, energy consumption, and pollution to manufacture new bricks; and they can offer historic aesthetic qualities to a site structure. Yet preparing used bricks for reuse can incur higher labor costs, and irregularities in the bricks can make precision in construction challenging. Table 7–11 summarizes design and specification considerations when using salvaged brick.

REFERENCES

Agency for Toxic Substances and Disease Registry (ATSDR). 2003a. "ToxFAQs for Fluorine, Hydrogen Fluoride, and Fluorides." Atlanta: U.S. Department of Health and Human Services.

Agency for Toxic Substances and Disease Registry (ATSDR). 2003b. "ToxFAQs for Manganese Dioxide." Department of Health and Human Services.

ASTM Standard C652. 2007. "Specification for Hollow Brick." West Conshohocken, PA: ASTM International. www.astm.org.

ASTM Standard C1088. 2007. "Specification for Thin Brick Veneer Units Made from Clay and Shale." West Conshohocken, PA: ASTM International. www.astm.org.

Athena Sustainable Materials Institute. *Athena Environmental Impact Estimator*, version 3.0.3. Kutztown, Ontario, Canada: Athena Sustainable Materials Institute.

Athena Sustainable Materials Institute. 1998. "Life Cycle Analysis of Brick and Mortar Products." Prepared by Venta, Glaser & Associates, Ottawa, Canada.

Brick Development Association (BDA). "Innovations in Brick." http://www.brick.org.uk/ (accessed July 20, 2007).

Brick Industry Association (BIA). 1988. "Salvaged Brick." In *Technical Notes on Brick Construction*, May 1988, Number 15. Reston, VA: Brick Industry Association.

Brick Industry Association (BIA). 1994. "Brick in Landscape Architecture—Pedestrian Applications." In *Technical Notes on Brick Construction*, July 1994, Number 29. Reston, VA: Brick Industry Association.

Brick Industry Association (BIA). 1999. "Brick in Landscape Architecture—Garden Walls." In *Technical Notes on Brick Construction*, January 1999, Number 29A. Reston, VA: Brick Industry Association.

Brick Industry Association (BIA). 2002. "Colorless Coatings for Brick Masonry." In *Technical Notes on Brick Construction*, June 2002, Number 6A. Reston, VA: Brick Industry Association.

Brick Industry Association (BIA). 2003. "Wall Ties for Brick Masonry." In *Technical Notes on Brick Construction*, May 2003, Number 44B. Reston, VA: Brick Industry Association.

Brick Industry Association (BIA). 2005. "Maintenance of Brick Masonry." In *Technical Notes on Brick Construction*, December 2005, Number 46. Reston, VA: Brick Industry Association.

Brick Industry Association (BIA). 2006a. "Cleaning Brickwork." In *Technical Notes on Brick Construction*, June 2006, Number 20. Reston, VA: Brick Industry Association.

Brick Industry Association (BIA). 2006b. "Mortars for Brickwork: Selection and Quality Assurance." In *Technical Notes on Brick Construction*, October 2006, Number 8B. Reston, VA: Brick Industry Association.

Brick Industry Association (BIA). 2006c. "Manufacturing of Brick." In *Technical Notes on Brick Construction*, December 2006, Number 9. Reston, VA: Brick Industry Association.

Brick Industry Association (BIA). 2007a. "Paving Systems Using Clay Pavers." In *Technical Notes on Brick Construction*, March 2007, Number 14. Reston, VA: Brick Industry Association.

Brick Industry Association (BIA). 2007b. "Sustainability and Brick." In *Technical Notes on Brick Construction*, September 2007, Number 48. Reston, VA: Brick Industry Association.

Brick Industry Association (BIA). 2007c. "Paving Systems Using Clay Pavers on a Sand Setting Bed." In *Technical Notes on Brick Construction*, October 2007, Number 14A. Reston, VA: Brick Industry Association.

Brick Industry Association (BIA). 2007d. "Brick Overview." http://www.brickinfo.org/html/biaoverview.html (accessed July 3, 2007).

California Integrated Waste Management Board. *Recycled Content Products Directory*.

Cervelli-Schach, J. 2007. "Freestanding and Retaining Walls." In *Landscape Architectural Graphic Standards*, ed. L. Hopper. Hoboken, NJ: John Wiley & Sons, pp. 495–500.

Coal Ash Research Center. "The Buyers Guide to Coal Ash Containing Products—Masonry." Grand Forks, ND: University of North Dakota, Energy & Environmental Research Center. http://www.undeerc.org/carrc/Buyers Guide/default.asp (accessed June 23, 2007).

Demkin, J., ed. 1998a. "Material Report 03100: Concrete." In *Environmental Resource Guide*. (ERG) American Institute of Architects. New York: John Wiley & Sons.

Demkin, J., ed. 1998b. "Material Report 04210: Brick and Mortar." In *Environmental Resource Guide (ERG)*. American Institute of Architects. New York: John Wiley & Sons.

Environmental Building News. 2002. "Masonry Cement without the Portland." In *Environmental Building News*. Brattleboro, VT: Building Green. Volume 11, Number 4:7.

Ferguson, Bruce. 2005. *Porous Pavements*. Boca Raton, FL: CRC Press.

Hammond, G. and C. Jones. 2006. "Inventory of Carbon and Energy." Version 1.5 Beta. Bath, UK: University of Bath, Department of Mechanical Engineering. http://www.bath.ac.uk/mech-eng/sert/embodied/

Jewell, L. 1983. "Perforated Brick Walls." *Landscape Architecture*. Washington, DC: American Society of Landscape Architects 73(3): 8–90.

Landphair, H., and F. Klatt. 1988. *Landscape Architecture Construction*. 3rd ed. Upper Saddle River, NJ: Prentice Hall.

Lippiatt, Barbara C. 2007. *BEES 4.0 Building for Environmental and Economic Sustainability Technical Manual and User Guide*. Washington D.C.: National Institute of Standards and Technology.

National Institute for Occupational Safety and Health (NIOSH). April 2002. *NIOSH Hazard Review: Health Effects of Occupational Exposure to Respirable Crystalline Silica*. Publication np. 2002–129. http://www.cdc.gov/niosh/topics/silica/.

National Science Foundation (NSF). 2007. "Follow the Green Brick Road? Bricks Made from Ccoal-fired Power Plant Waste Pass Safety Test." National Science Foundation press release 07–058. http://www.nsf.gov/news/news_summ.jsp?cntn_id=109594&org=ENG (accessed June 24, 2007).

Sanders, J., and D. Brosnan. 2007. "Nitrogen Emissions from Raw Materials." *Brickyard Road*, April, p. 18.

U.S. Environmental Protection Agency (U.S. EPA). 1997. "Chapter 11: Mineral Products Industry, Section 11.3 Brick and Structural Clay Product Manufacturing," *AP 42*, 5th ed. Clearinghouse for Inventories and Emissions Factors, Technology Transfer Network, U.S. EPA.

U.S. Environmental Protection Agency (U.S. EPA), Office of Policy, Economics, and Innovation. 2007a. *Energy Trends in Selected Manufacturing Sectors: Opportunities and Challenges for Environmentally Preferable Energy Outcomes*. Fairfax, VA: ICF International, March.

U.S. Environmental Protection Agency (U.S. EPA). 2007b. "Landfill Gas Fuels New Brick Plant." Press release October 20, 2006. U.S. Environmental Protection Agency Newsroom. http://yosemite.epa.gov/opa/admpress.nsf/8822edaadaba0243852572a000656841/7b9993ed70ea068a8525720d004fe20c!OpenDocument (accessed June 29, 2007).

U.S. Geological Survey. 2007. "Clay and Shale." In *2005 Minerals Yearbook*. Washington, DC: U.S. Geological Survey.

8

Asphalt Pavement

Asphalt pavement, formally called asphalt concrete pavement, is aggregate bound with asphalt cement. It is the most commonly used site and road construction material, used on 90% of new roads. It is inexpensive, flexible, easily placed without formwork, and durable. In addition, a wide range of surface finishes or overlays can be applied to fit almost any design setting and extend the pavement's life cycle without removal of the full paving section.

The main environmental and human health impacts from asphalt pavements include use of nonrenewable petroleum and aggregate resources, potentially hazardous air emissions and fumes from mixing and placement, impermeable surfaces of asphalt pavement concentrating runoff quantities and nonpoint source (NPS) pollutants, and contributions to the urban heat island (UHI) effect resulting from asphalt pavement's dark surface.

Total pavement surfaces in the United States cover an estimated 34,500 square miles, an area roughly equal to the state of Illinois, and since a good portion are constructed from asphalt, the above impacts can be significant. Greening the use of this material through use of cooler placement temperatures, recycled content in the binder, recycled aggregates, and porous pavement installations could make great inroads in construction of sustainable sites.

ASPHALT BASICS

Asphalt pavement is composed of coarse and fine aggregates, and asphalt cement that binds the aggregates together. Asphalt cement is a coproduct of petroleum production, composed of heavy hydrocarbons after lighter fractions of crude oil have been extracted. It is a good adhesive, waterproofing agent, and preservative.

Proportions and mix temperatures of aggregates, binder, and sometimes additives vary by installation, ambient temperature, and expected intensity of use. Typically aggregates compose 60–90% of the mix, with asphalt cement and sometimes emulsifiers (for cold mixes) or water as the remainder. Hot-mix asphalt pavement (HMA) is the most common type, with all aggregates and asphalt cement heated at the asphalt plant to temperatures ranging from 250°F to 350°F and then delivered and placed on-site immediately.

Constituents of a typical asphalt installation are shown in Table 8–1, including the tack coat, which is an asphalt emulsion that is sprayed on the aggregate base layer to increase adhesion for the asphalt surface layer. A typical asphalt mix would likely contain a percentage of recycled asphalt pavement (RAP), reducing virgin aggregate use by 15% and asphalt binder use by 1% (Lippiatt 2007).

Two types of asphalt pavement are placed at ambient temperatures. They are cold-mix (also called emulsified asphalt) and cutback asphalt. Cold-mix asphalt pavement is a mix of aggregate and an asphalt emulsion, water, and/or diluent. This emulsion consists of about two-thirds asphalt cement and water containing an emulsifying agent such as soap or detergents to enable mixing. Asphalt emulsion can be sprayed on the aggregate and mixed in place, travel plant mixed, or be pug mill mixed at the aggregate source. There are many grades of emulsion for different applications, set times, and traffic loads. Some emulsified asphalts can contain up to 12% petroleum distillates, so ingredients should be checked carefully. There are a few cold patch products that are low-VOC, incorporate recycled content, and rely on compaction, not evaporation, to harden (King County Environmental Purchasing Program 2001).

Cutback asphalt concrete is aggregate mixed with asphalt binder composed of asphalt cement blended with different solvents, depending on the cutback use. While some cutback binders are billed as "rapid cure" because of the solvents used, their use is diminishing as they contain VOCs, hydrocarbons, and other chemicals hazardous to humans and the environment.

Table 8–1 Typical Hot-Mix Asphalt Constituents

Constituent	Percentage of Layer (Mass)	Percentage of Components (Mass)
Hot-Mix Asphalt	99.5%	—
Aggregate		81%
Asphalt binder		4%
RAP		15%
Tack Coat	0.5%	—
Asphalt		66%
Water		33%
Emulsifier		1.1%
HCl		0.2%

Source: Lippiatt 2007

Environmental and Human Health Impacts of Asphalt Pavements

Asphalt paving can pose both environmental and human health risks in production, placement, and use. The most serious environmental impacts occur during extraction and refining of the asphalt binder, and to a lesser degree during mixing and placement. About three-quarters of the embodied energy of asphalt pavement is feedstock energy (Athena Institute 2006). Impacts also occur with mining and processing of aggregates and fuel use in transport during all phases of the life cycle. In use, the imperviousness of asphalt paving can contribute to increased storm water runoff and concentrations of NPS pollution. And as most asphalt surfaces are black or dark gray, they retain solar radiation and then release that energy as heat. This release of thermal energy potentially contributes to the urban heat island effect and associated air pollution.

Approximately 500 million tons of HMA were produced in the United States in 2004 at an estimated 3,600 asphalt plants, 2,300 of which are batch plants and 1,300 are drum plants (U.S. EPA 2005). An average batch plat produces approximately 100,000 HMA tons annually and a drum mix plant produces approximately 200,000 HMA tons annually. Natural gas is used to produce 70–90% of HMA (U.S. EPA 2005).

RAW MATERIALS ACQUISITION

Asphalt Binder
Crude oil is produced by drilling into porous rock, generally thousands of feet below ground. Crude oil drilling and extraction can produce both toxic and nontoxic by-products that pollute waters, sediment, and air. And petroleum processing and distillation releases hydrocarbons, VOCs, and mercaptans, affecting air quality, and wastewater containing emulsified and free oils, sulfides, ammonia, phenols, heavy metals, and suspended and dissolved solids. This can lead to increased biochemical oxygen demands (BODs), eutrophication, environmental poisoning, and consumption of toxics by wildlife (Demkin 1998).

Aggregates
Coarse and fine aggregates compose an average of 85% of asphalt pavement by volume and 94% by weight

(Newcomb 2007). While the resources for aggregate are considered abundant, mining and extraction of the raw materials causes many environmental impacts. Mining contributes to habitat loss, soil erosion, and air and water pollution. Mining and processing equipment use nonrenewable fossil fuels as does transport of heavy aggregates. Detailed impacts of aggregate mining and processing are discussed in chapter 9.

PRODUCTION OF ASPHALT CEMENT

Air and water emissions from petroleum refining and production of asphalt binder vary widely by facility and chemical constituents in the petroleum. Air emissions include hydrocarbons, sulfur oxides, particulates, and other hazardous air pollutants (HAPs) in addition to fuel-related emissions such as CO_2. Water emissions include dissolved and suspended solids, phenols, oils, acids, and trace amounts of heavy metals (Franklin Associates 2001).

PRODUCTION, TRANSPORT, AND PLACEMENT OF ASPHALT CONCRETE

Energy Use

Production of hot-mix asphalt requires energy to heat the aggregate and binder to temperatures ranging from 250°F to 350°F while mixing at the plant, and to keep it heated as it is transported to the site and during place-

ment. Embodied energy and GWP figures shown in table 8–2 were derived from a 2006 study by the Athena Institute for Canadian roadway pavements. The figures, based on Canadian average mixes for arterial roadways and highways, compare concrete pavement and asphalt pavement with no recycled asphalt pavement (RAP) and 20% RAP. The figures illustrate the higher primary embodied energy of one cubic meter of asphalt concrete, largely due to the feedstock portion. Use of 20% RAP reduces the primary energy use by about 16%. The GWP of one cubic meter of portland cement concrete is higher, but would likely be offset by its longer expected lifecycle (Athena Institute 2006).

Emissions and Fumes

Heating, mixing, and placement of asphalt concrete releases emissions and fumes, affecting air quality and posing human health risks. It is generally accepted that emissions and fumes increase as the temperature of the mix increases. Yet the extent of impacts and risks is a very controversial topic, as results of health risk studies conflict, and estimates of emissions from asphalt plants are criticized as inaccurate (Center for Health, Environment and Justice n.d.).

Air emissions from heating, mixing, storing, and transporting hot-mix asphalt were estimated by the U.S. EPA's Office of Air Quality Planning and Standards in a

Table 8–2 Embodied Energy and Embodied Carbon Comparison of One Cubic Meter of Asphalt Concrete and Portland Cement Concrete Pavement Mixes

Impact	Units	Asphalt Concrete, 0% RAP	Asphalt Concrete, 20% RAP	Portland Cement Concrete, 13% Fly Ash 18% Blast Furnace Slag[a]
Primary energy	GJ/m³	7.613	6.410	1.858
Feedstock portion		5.610	4.488	
GHG emissions	kg			
Carbon Dioxide (CO_2)		135	130	272.2
Methane (CH_4)		0.323	0.296	0.425
Nitrous Oxide (N_2O)		0.0002	0.0002	0.0002
GWP (kg CO_2 equiv.)		142	137	282

[a]Average Canada 30 Mp mix

Adapted from source: Athena Institute 2006

December 2000 report titled "Hot Mix Asphalt Plants Emission Assessment Report" (U.S. EPA 2000). The report states: "The Particulate Matter emissions associated with HMA production include criteria pollutants (coarse and fine particulates), hazardous air pollutant (HAP) metals, and HAP organic compounds. The gaseous emissions associated with HMA production include the criteria pollutants sulfur dioxide (SO_2), nitrogen oxides (NO_x), carbon monoxide (CO), and volatile organic compounds (VOCs), as well as HAP organic compounds" (U.S. EPA 2000). Emissions of total HAPs from a typical plant range from 0.4 tons per year to 1 ton per year dependent upon plant design and fuel used.

By measuring emissions for typical hot-mix asphalt facilities and determining that there were no facilities with emissions of any HAP greater than 10 tons/year or a combination totaling more than 25 tons, the EPA removed hot-mix asphalt plants from the "Categories of Sources of Hazardous Air Pollutants" list to be regulated (Federal Register 2002). The average totals are reduced because of the numerous asphalt plants, with 3,600 estimated in 2005. Table 8–3 shows estimated emissions from an average asphalt plant. They do not include emissions that occur during transport or placement of HMA. These figures were developed and published in the EPA report mentioned above (U.S. EPA 2000).

Human Health Impacts

Uncaptured emissions and fumes from heating asphalt binders can pose irritation symptoms and other health impacts during plant mixing and placement of asphalt pavement, yet the degree of exposure and the severity of the impacts are still debated. And it is complicated by varying production temperatures. Below are excerpts from a 2000 National Institute for Occupational Safety and Health (NIOSH) report entitled "Hazard Review: Health Effects of Occupational Exposure to Asphalt." It is important to note that the statements below pertain to both asphalt roofing and asphalt pavement. Hazardous fumes and risks to asphalt roofing workers have been found to be greater, as asphalt roofing materials are placed at higher temperatures. The report states (NIOSH 2000):

■ The complex chemical composition of asphalt makes it difficult to identify the specific component(s) re-

Table 8–3 Emissions from Typical HMA Facilities

Pollutant	Drum Mix HMA Facility, Gas Fired, Pounds per Year	Batch Mix HMA Facility, Gas Fired, Pounds per Year
Criteria Air Pollutants (CAPs)		
Particulate matter less than 10 micrometers (PM10)	31,000	10,700
Volatile organic compounds (VOCs)	10,000	1,500
Carbon monoxide (CO)	28,000	41,000
Sulfur dioxide (SO_2)	710	480
Nitrogen oxides (NO_x)	5,800	2,900
Total CAPs	**75,510**	**56,580**
Hazardous Air Pollutants (HAPs)		
Polycyclic aromatic hydrocarbons (PAHs)	50	13
Phenol	0.80	0.40
Volatile HAPs	1,200	760
Metal HAPs	16	1.4
Total HAPs	**1300**	**770**

Source: Adapted from U.S. EPA 2000

sponsible for adverse health effects observed in exposed workers. Known carcinogens have been found in asphalt fumes generated at worksites. Observations of acute irritation in workers from airborne and dermal exposures to asphalt fumes and aerosols and the potential for chronic health effects, including cancer, warrant continued diligence in the control of exposures.

■ The exact chemical composition of asphalt depends on the chemical complexity of the original crude petroleum and the manufacturing processes. The proportions of the chemicals that constitute asphalt (mainly aliphatic compounds, cyclic alkanes, aromatic hydrocarbons, and heterocyclic compounds containing nitrogen, oxygen, and sulfur atoms) can vary because of significant differences in crude pe-

Table 8–4 Emissions from One Metric Ton of Hot-Mix Asphalt Pavement Production

	Road Asphalt (per metric ton of material)
Atmospheric Emissions	
CO_2	307 kg
SO_x	3.95 kg
NO_x	962 g
VOCs (non-methane)	6.99 kg
CO	823 g
HCl	4.39 g
Methane	663 g
Metals	29.6 mg
Particulates	181 g
Benzene	1.25 mg
Waterborne Wastes	
Acid (H^+)	1.12 mg
TSS (Total suspended solids)	132 g
Dissolved solids	5.39 kg
Phenol	79.6 mg
Phosphate	573 mg
Sulphate	168 g
Cyanide	301 μg
Iron	3.74 g
Zinc	99.5 mg
Oil	122 g
Solid Wastes	
Solid waste	22.9 kg

Adapted from source: Athena Sustainable Materials Institute 2001

troleum from various oil fields and even from various locations within the same oil field. The chemical composition of vapors and fumes from asphalt products is variable and depends on the crude petroleum source, type of asphalt, temperature and extent of mixing during the manufacturing process, and temperature and extent of mixing during laboratory generation or field operation (e.g., paving of roofing.

■ Asphalt fumes generated at high temperatures are more likely to generate carcinogenic PAHs and therefore are potentially more hazardous than fumes generated at lower temperatures.

■ Studies of workers exposed to asphalt fumes have repeatedly found irritation of the serous membranes of the conjunctivae (eye irritation) and the mucous membranes of the upper respiratory tract (nasal and throat irritation). These health effects, which have been best described in asphalt road pavers, typically appear to be mild and transitory.

■ Symptoms of nausea, stomach pain, decreased appetite, headaches, and fatigue have been commonly reported among workers exposed to asphalt. These nonspecific symptoms also require further investigation to clarify and establish the nature of any causal relationships with asphalt fume exposure.

■ Reports of acute lower respiratory tract symptoms (i.e., coughing, wheezing, shortness of breath) and changes in pulmonary function (e.g., bronchial lability) among exposed workers are of particular concern. Results from recent studies indicated that some workers experienced lower respiratory tract symptoms (and in one case, significant changes in pulmonary function) during relatively low exposures to asphalt fumes, such as those found during open-air highway paving (0.075 to 0.48 mg/m^3 total particulates and 0.07 to 0.24 mg/m^3 benzene-soluble particulates, mean range exposures). Present data are insufficient to determine the causal relationship between asphalt fume exposures and lower respiratory symptoms or changes in pulmonary function.

■ Overall, the epidemiologic evidence for an association between lung cancer and exposure to asphalt in paving is inconclusive at this time. The collective data currently available from studies on paving asphalt provide insufficient evidence for an association between lung cancer and exposure to asphalt fumes during paving. The available data, however, do not preclude a carcinogenic risk from asphalt fumes generated during paving operations.

While the severity of these health effects is not always agreed upon, the asphalt industry has made huge strides toward reducing worker exposure during asphalt heating and placement. Responding to an earlier NIOSH report with the same conclusions, a joint 1997 effort by NIOSH, the Asphalt Institute (AI), the National Asphalt

Pavement Association (NAPA), some state associations, labor unions, and other federal agencies developed new controls that have resulted in substantial reductions in fumes and emissions. Reductions are achieved using engineering controls, cooler mixes, worker education, and respiratory protection in processing plants and in placement operations. The Asphalt Pavement Environmental Council published "Best Management Practices to Minimize Emissions during HMA Construction" in 2000, listing practices for minimizing and controlling fumes, emissions, and odors during mixing and placement.

USE AND MAINTENANCE

Asphalt pavements can affect air, water, and soil health surrounding the installation in the following ways:

- New asphalt can contain measurable levels of VOCs, polycyclic aromatic hydrocarbons (PAHs), and heavy metals. Typical releases of these compounds to air, water, and soil as the asphalt pavement cures, ages, and weathers have not been well quantified.
- Asphalt pavements, like many other pavement types, form impermeable surfaces that prevent storm water from infiltrating the soil below. This results in high quantities of runoff carrying high concentrations of NPS pollutants into storm sewers and structures. Porous asphalt pavements that address this issue are discussed later in the chapter.
- Conventional black asphalt pavement absorbs rather than reflects the sun's radiation, resulting in increased temperature of pavement surfaces and nighttime ambient air. The surface temperature of asphalt pavement can be up to 50 degrees higher than a reflective white surface, making the pavement uncomfortable to occupy (Lawrence Berkeley National Laboratory 1999), but the converse is also noted—reflective surfaces increase the daytime air temperature above a pavement as compared to dark pavements. This phenomenon, along with other dark surfaces such as roofing, is one contributor to the urban heat island (UHI) effect. Highly reflective pavements can also increase ground-level UV radiation (Howard Marks, personal communication, November 8, 2007).
- Asphalt pavements are a major source of carbon sequestration during use. The Energy Information Ad-

ministration's Inventory of Emissions of Greenhouse Gases in the United States estimates that asphalt sequestered 100 million metric tons (MMT) of CO_2 equivalents in 2005, up from 88.5 MMT in 1990 (U.S. EPA 2007).

While asphalt pavement installations can have a 15–20 year life span, they will require patching and periodic resurfacing. Impacts vary by surfacing type and are addressed later in this chapter, as are techniques to prolong the life of an asphalt pavement installation.

END OF LIFE

End-of-life impacts of asphalt are minimal, as most asphalt that is removed is either recycled directly back into new asphalt pavement on-site or is hauled to an asphalt plant for recycling. Asphalt recycling is discussed later in the chapter.

Athena Institute Comparison of Asphalt and Portland Cement Roadways

The table at right illustrates results of a 2006 LCA comparison of typical Canadian highway and roadway materials by the Athena Sustainable Materials Institute. The study compared primary embodied energy and global warming potential (GWP) of asphalt concrete and portland cement concrete arterial highway pavements. Impacts for one kilometer of two-lane roadway, including shoulders, were quantified for several highway types and material mixes. Pavement types shown in the table below are for a typical Canadian arterial roadway using flexible asphalt concrete pavement with a California Bearing Ratio (CBR) of 3 and a rigid portland cement concrete pavement with 13% fly ash and 18% blast furnace slag (Canadian averages). Two types of asphalt concrete were studied— 0% RAP and 20% RAP.

The results of the Athena Institute's comparison illustrate that over a 50 year life-cycle, the concrete pavement has substantially lower embodied energy and a similar global warming potential to asphalt concrete pavement.

Table 8–5 Comparison of Primary Embodied Energy and GWP of Asphalt Pavement and Portland Cement concrete on Canadian Arterial Highways (per 2 lane kilometer including both shoulders)

Impact	Flexible Asphalt Concrete (California Bearing Ratio 3) 0% RAP	Flexible Asphalt Concrete (California Bearing Ratio 3) 20% RAP	Rigid Portland Cement Concrete 13% Fly Ash 18% Blast Furnace Slag
Initial Construction			
Embodied Energy (GJ)	14,049	12,645	6,319
—feedstock portion	9,287	8,037	1,790
GWP (metric tons)	355	299	554
Rehabilitation			
Embodied Energy (GJ)	10,630	10,195	NA
—feedstock portion	7,833	7,446	NA
GWP (metric tons)	200	182	NA
Totals (50-year life cycle)			
Embodied Energy (GJ)	24,679	22,840	6,319
—feedstock portion	17,120	15,483	1,790
GWP (metric tons)	555	425	554

Adapted from source: Athena 2006

Strategies for Minimizing the Impacts of Asphalt Paving

LOWER THE MIX TEMPERATURES

Reducing the temperatures at which asphalt is mixed and placed can address some of the environmental and human health impacts of traditional hot-mix asphalt. Potential construction and performance benefits of lowering the production and placement temperatures of asphalt mixes are as follows (Newcomb 2005):

- Energy savings
- Reduced emissions
- Decreased fumes
- Reduced aging of the asphalt binder
- Decreased wear of equipment
- Reduced draindown of asphalt

Warm-mix Asphalt

Lowering mix temperatures will reduce asphalt air emissions and fumes, greenhouse gas releases, and re-source consumption from fuel combustion to heat the asphalt. Warm-mix asphalt, with reductions of 50 to 100 degrees in mix temperatures, is achieved through use of asphalt emulsions, foam processes, or additives that increase the workability of the asphalt at lower temperatures. Research has shown that lowering mix temperatures from an average 300°F to just over 200°F and use of an asphalt emulsion will result in fuel cost savings of 50%. There is also a reduction in fumes, greenhouse gases, and air emissions, with no reduction in pavement performance.

Table 8–6 Placement Temperature Ranges of Asphalt Pavement Types

Type of Asphalt Pavement	Temperature Range
Hot-mix asphalt[a]	275°F–325°F
Warm-mix asphalt[b]	200°F–275°F
Cold-mix asphalt[a]	±60°F

[a]NAPA
[b]Newcomb 2005

Currently, there are four different processes of warm-mix asphalt, some proprietary, that are being used. They are as follows (Newcomb 2005):

- The *foam process* injects cold water into the warm asphalt cement, causing a foaming reaction and reducing the stiffness of the mix and increasing workability. This allows for placement at lower temperatures (around 230°F). Techniques of injection vary by manufacturer.
- The *mineral additive* type is a proprietary process using zeolite, a fine crystalline hydrated aluminum silicate added in small concentration to the mix. Like foamed asphalt, it increases workability, reducing the laydown temperatures. This method allows for temperatures of 250°F–295°F.
- *Organic additives*, paraffins and low molecular weight ester compounds, are used to modify the behavior

of asphalt by lowering the viscosity while maintaining stiffness. Compaction can begin at temperatures of 250°F.

- A *chemically modified binder* allows placement and compaction temperatures of as low as 140°F. As the product is proprietary, the exact chemicals employed are not known, leaving questions about the types and quantity of emissions that result from heating the chemicals. However, emissions are lower than typical HMA (Dave Newcomb, personal communication, November 8, 2007).

While warm-mix asphalt pavement is still in experimental stages in North America, it is slightly better used in Europe due to the EU's more stringent greenhouse gas reduction mandates. As fuel costs escalate, the U.S. asphalt industry experts expect an increase in warm-mix technologies (Newcomb 2005).

Figure 8–1.
Reducing the temperature at which asphalt pavement is placed can reduce emissions and energy use. Two trucks are side by side, with one containing typical hot-mix asphalt and the other warm-mix. Emissions are visibly greater from the hot-mix truck. (Photo from the National Asphalt Pavement Association)

Cold-mix Asphalt

Cold-mix asphalt using an asphalt emulsion mixed at ambient temperatures is another option to save fuel and reduce hydrocarbon emissions and fumes. Asphalt emulsions with high-VOC and/or solvent contents should be avoided. Primary applications of cold-mix are road patching, cold in-place asphalt recycling, and chip and slurry seals. Cold-mix is less commonly used in new asphalt paving applications except at locations remote from hot-mix plants. Most cold-mix is mixed in place, in a traveling plant on-site, or in a pug mill at the aggregate source. There are costs involved in mobile mixing equipment, so cold-mix is often cost prohibitive for smaller projects. In urban areas there is not always room for the equipment and material stockpiles, and some roads can't be closed for the amount of time required to place and cure the cold-mix pavement.

While cold-mix pavement is more pliable in placement than hot-mix asphalt pavement, facilitating compaction and reducing cracking potential, it cures more slowly and is less applicable in situations where the road must reopen quickly. An FHWA pavement guide states that cold-mix is "useful in applications where distortion due to frost or poor subgrade conditions may be a problem . . . and it is considered to be 'self-healing' under solar heat and traffic" (Maher et al. 2005). On low-volume roads a cold-mix binder course can be expected to last as long as a typical hot-mix installation (fifteen to twenty years) if a thin-wearing course of HMA, or chip or slurry seal is applied over the top.

USE LESS ASPHALT BINDER

Using less asphalt binder will reduce hot-mix asphalt emissions and fumes. Placing the asphalt installation on an aggregate base course instead of directly on grade will allow a thinner asphalt section, resulting in less binder use. While the same amount of binder is used in the asphalt pavement paving course, the paving thickness will be reduced with the structural stability of the aggregate base. Generally, thickening the aggregate course will allow a thinner asphalt course, and in some applications such as paths and sidewalks, a thin, half-inch chip seal course is all that is required over a stable aggregate base. Care should be taken to not thin the asphalt section to the point that it does not last the full

expected life, resulting in greater use of material resources.

Foamed or expanded asphalt is sometimes used in base stabilization to provide improved structural capacity prior to surfacing with hot-mix asphalt. Foamed asphalt is a method of combining hot asphalt binder with recycled or new aggregate that uses substantially less asphalt binder material (2%–4% versus the typical 5%–10%; Maher et al. 2005). The process of heating the asphalt and then mixing in cold water causes the binder to expand to ten times the normal size. When the foamed binder is mixed with aggregate, it coats the aggregate with tiny particles, resulting in a very well-mixed material with less binder used. While there is a savings on binder material, foamed asphalt requires approximately 16% higher temperatures.

USE RECYCLED AGGREGATES

Many pre- and post-consumer waste materials can be used for aggregate, mineral filler, and granular base in an asphalt installation, saving virgin resources and related mining and processing impacts. While reclaimed asphalt is the most commonly recycled material used in new asphalt, other potential aggregates include tires, roofing shingles, glass, slag, and concrete. Refer to Table 8–7 for a comprehensive list of waste materials that may be appropriate for use in asphalt paving applications.

Use of recycled material in asphalt can result in cost savings, both directly, with some recycled materials available for only the cost of transport; or indirectly, by saving on landfill fees. Many states are requiring that a percentage of aggregate be recycled material in their standard mixes. This is spurred in large part by the growing waste crisis, particularly in California and East Coast states, and the cost savings of using recycled, often free materials.

Availability of recycled materials will vary by region, and as the transport costs of heavy materials for aggregate can be high, it makes the most financial and environmental sense to use locally available recycled materials in asphalt paving mixes.

Use of recycled aggregates can have some limitations. Occasionally, impurities or unknown ingredients can reduce the new pavement's strength and durability. There is also concern that reclaimed asphalt may have

Table 8–7 Recycled Materials Appropriate for Use in Asphalt Pavements

Application	Recycled Material	Application	Recycled Material
Asphalt Pavement		Asphalt cement modifier	Roofing shingle scrap
Mineral filler	Asphalt plant dust		Scrap tires
	Sewage sludge ash		Plastic
	Cement kiln dust	**Granular Base**	
	Lime kiln dust	Granular base materials	Blast furnace slag
	Coal fly ash		Coal bottom ash
Asphalt aggregate (hot mix)	Blast furnace slag		Coal boiler slag
	Coal bottom ash		Combustor ash
	Coal boiler slag		Foundry slag
	Foundry sand		Mineral processing wastes
	Mineral processing wastes		Municipal solid waste
	Municipal solid waste ash		Nonferrous slag
	Nonferrous slag		Petroleum-contaminated soils
	Petroleum-contaminated soils		Reclaimed asphalt pavement
	Reclaimed asphalt pavement		Reclaimed concrete
	Roofing shingle scrap		Steel slag
	Scrap tires		Waste glass
	Steel slag		Reclaimed tires
	Waste glass	**Stabilized Base**	
Seal coat or surface treatment aggregate	Blast furnace slag	Stabilized base or subbase aggregate	Coal bottom ash
	Coal boiler slag		Coal boiler slag
	Steel slag		Petroleum-contaminated soils
			Reclaimed asphalt pavement

Source: Recycled Materials Resource Center (RMRC)

unknown contaminants or heavy metals. Some states, such as Washington, require testing of reclaimed asphalt for some projects. Finally, some reclaimed materials are more porous than natural aggregates and can require increased asphalt binder.

Reclaimed Asphalt

Perhaps the most widespread and abundant material that can be recycled into new asphalt paving applications is reclaimed asphalt pavement. The Asphalt Recycling and Reclaiming Association (ARRA) estimates that 80% of demolished asphalt is recycled, primarily in new asphalt paving and base applications (ARRA 2001). This

results in huge cost savings as much less new material must be purchased and fuel costs for processing and hauling the material from quarries and refineries to the asphalt plant are eliminated. There are several methods of using reclaimed asphalt with varying environmental, economic, and performance issues.

Cold in-place recycling (CIR), the least energy intensive, involves milling up an existing asphalt installation (not the base aggregate) and mixing the reclaimed material with an emulsified asphalt and recycling agent to restore the properties of the asphalt binder. This mix is then placed back down as a base/binder course with a new thin hot-mix, chip seal, or slurry seal surface over it. Since CIR does not require preheating, the FHA estimates a total energy savings of 40%–50% (Maher et al. 2005). Transport energy is also minimal. Because the CIR installation takes one to two weeks to fully cure before the surface coat can be applied, this is not a good application for roads that need to reopen quickly.

Hot in-place recycling (HIPR) involves heating and softening the existing asphalt pavement, scarifying or milling it, adding a rejuvenating agent, and placing and compacting it with traditional hot-mix equipment. In most installations, a surface layer of new hot-mix or chip seal is applied. A disadvantage is that significant heat is generated and energy consumed during the HIR process, and with increased heat comes increased emissions. Also there is no opportunity to make significant changes to the mix.

Recycled asphalt pavement (RAP) is cold-milled asphalt from old pavements that is transported to an asphalt plant, crushed, and mixed with virgin asphalt binder and aggregate. The percentage of RAP in new asphalt is dependent on the plant's technology, the RAP aggregate gradation, physical properties of the binder, and regulations on gaseous emissions. Substitution rates in batch plants are 10%–30% and in drum plants up to 50% (New York City Department of Design and Construction and Design Trust for Public Space [DDC NYC and DTPS] 2005).

Recycled hot-mix may require slightly higher mix temperatures than virgin hot-mixes, using more energy and producing higher emissions. The required temperature is dependent partially on how wet the aggregates are. In addition, fuel is used hauling the materials from the old site, to the plant, and to the new site. For large jobs, a portable asphalt plant brought to the site can be used to eliminate this impact. However, there may be impacts associated with this, such as dust, noise, and uncontrolled emissions. Some agencies will not allow recycled hot-mix to be used as a surface course, especially where the source of the recycled material is not known, because there is no way to control the exact properties of the mix that are critical to a pavement's wearing course. However, performance tests are being developed that would allow RAP to be used if the final mix passes the test (Newcomb 2007).

Full depth reclamation. While the above recycling techniques only remove the asphalt layers full depth reclamation (FDR) removes and pulverizes asphalt and underlying base materials into a new stabilized base. This base only requires a very thin layer of hot-mix, chip seal, or slurry seal. The FDR base is stabilized with the addition of a small amount of new asphalt binder or cementitious materials such as portland cement, lime, kiln dust, or fly ash (a pre-consumer waste material from coal combustion). Or mechanical stabilization methods such as compacting may be used instead of binders. FDR can save substantial amounts of material, energy, and transportation costs.

Recycled Tire Aggregate

With nearly 300 million discarded in the United States each year, tires are an abundant waste product for recycling into rubberized asphalt concrete (RAC). The sheer volume, coupled with health and environmental concerns of burning tire dumps and groundwater contamination from tires in landfills, is spurring the development of construction applications with tires. And while waste tires have been available across the United States for years, tire-chipping facilities are only recently considered to be widespread. In paving, RAC is the most common application being used for asphalt surface courses and chip and slurry seals. However, chipped tires are also used in asphalt base course applications and as asphalt modifiers.

There are three distinct methods of integrating crumb rubber made by chipping discarded tires into asphalt pavement (Turner Fairbank Highway Research Center [TFHRC]).

- *Asphalt rubber (AR) or "wet process"* (the most common way) involves blending the crumb rubber particles ranging in size from #30 to #100 sieve with hot asphalt cement before it is mixed with the aggregates. It is defined as "a blend of asphalt cement, reclaimed tire rubber, and certain additives in which the rubber content is at least 15% by weight of the total blend and has reacted in the hot asphalt cement

Metered injection of water and emulsion

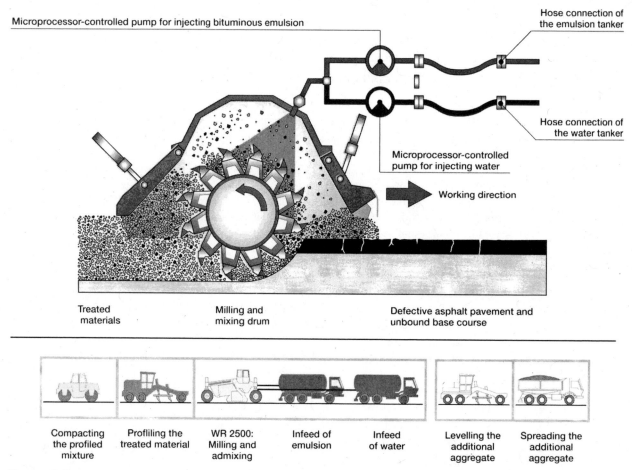

Microprocessor-controlled pump for injecting bituminous emulsion

Hose connection of the emulsion tanker

Hose connection of the water tanker

Microprocessor-controlled pump for injecting water

Working direction

Treated materials

Milling and mixing drum

Defective asphalt pavement and unbound base course

| Compacting the profiled mixture | Profiling the treated material | WR 2500: Milling and admixing | Infeed of emulsion | Infeed of water | Levelling the additional aggregate | Spreading the additional aggregate |

Figure 8–2.

Use of foamed bitumen for cold in-place recycling of asphalt pavement allows for energy- and fuel-efficient pavement recycling. (Photo from Wirtgen International, Inc.)

sufficiently to cause swelling of the rubber particles." Arizona, California, and Texas commonly use 18%–25% rubber in their asphalt rubber mixes.

■ **The "dry process"** mixes the rubber particles ranging in size from one-fourth inch down to #20 sieve with the aggregate before it is blended with the asphalt cement.

■ **"Terminal blend"** (also called the refinery process) is a patented process where crumb rubber is digested into the asphalt cement at the refinery.

When RAC is used as a surfacing layer, it is called asphalt rubber hot-mix resurfacing (ARHM). When ARHM is placed on an existing asphalt installation that has substantial reflective cracking, a minimum thickness of $1\frac{1}{2}$ inches is recommended (Maher et al. 2005). This is one-half inch less than typical nonrubberized hot mix surface layers. Asphalt rubber is also used in stress-absorbing membranes, a thinner layer over an existing basically sound roadway, and chip and slurry seals with hot or cold applications.

Pioneered thirty years ago in Phoenix, these surfacing methods are increasingly used on Arizona, Texas, and California highways and some surface streets. A typical two-inch surface layer of RAC will use 2,000 tires per lane mile. But perhaps the greatest environmental benefit of RAC pavements is a substantially increased life, with one study by the University of Illinois concluding that these pavements will last up to three times as long as conventional asphalt. Other benefits include greater wet traction and skid resistance, substantially reduced noise, and resistance to reflective cracking, rutting, and shoving (CIWMB 2006).

Asphalt rubber may cost more than conventional asphalt. California's Integrated Waste Management Board estimates that a one-inch thickness of asphalt rubber costs roughly $2.50 per square yard compared to $1.35 per square yard for conventional asphalt (CIWMB 2006). The return on the investment will come with decreased maintenance, use of less virgin material, and longer pavement surface life.

The federal government has funded an emission-testing program at seven U.S. sites. Initial reports find that emissions are no greater for RAC than for conventional AC (NIOSH 2001). However, RAC is not easily compacted at temperatures under 290°F, and emissions for all types of asphalt increase with higher temperatures.

While RAC applications are most cost effective in large-scale applications such as roads, highways, and large parking lots, a proprietary product made with reclaimed tire chips is a porous paving system for parking lots, sidewalks, and trails. It is poured in place (by certified installers) and is an impact-absorbing, slip-resistant surface that promotes storm water infiltration. Installed over a drainage layer like all porous paving, it is a blend of 3/8-inch tire chips, half-inch aggregate, and a proprietary single-component, moisture-cured urethane. The product comes in a range of colors.

Tires as aggregate base material. Tire chips are also used in aggregate base courses for asphalt and other types of paving. They are cost effective, lightweight, and structurally sound, yet concerns remain about the effect of uncoated tire chips on water quality. Tests by the University of Maine found the accumulation of metals to be acceptable under secondary drinking water standards; however, they did detect some volatile organic com-

pounds for tires used in structures below the water table. Tire chips provide greater water permeability and several times the insulation value of natural aggregates where frost penetration is an issue (Spiegel and Meadows 2006).

Industrial By-products

Many industrial by-products can be used as coarse or fine aggregates or mineral filler in asphalt pavements. Refer to Table 8–7 above for the wide variety of potential industrial wastes that can be used and to chapter 9, "Aggregates and Stone," for discussion of the qualities and sources of these materials. The Turner Fairbank Highway Research Center has published *User Guidelines for Waste and By-product Materials in Pavement Construction*, providing detailed specification information on them (TFHRC 2004). As disposal costs rise and waste reduction mandates increase, markets for exchange of industrial by-products are increasing, as is research on their beneficial reuse in pavement applications. Common industrial by-products used in asphalt pavements are discussed below.

Air-cooled blast furnace slag (ACBFS), often called just slag, is a by-product of iron manufacture and can be crushed and screened for use as coarse aggregate in asphalt paving. ACBFS is readily available, and often less

Figure 8–3.
Rubberized asphalt concrete (RAC) is used for asphalt surface courses and chip and slurry seals. A typical two-inch surface layer of RAC will use 2,000 tires per lane mile and can result in a quieter, more durable road surface. (Photo from Asphalt Rubber Association)

expensive than virgin aggregate in steel-processing regions. It weighs less than conventional aggregate and improves pavement stability. It also provides additional resistance to rutting and stripping. As ACBFS is more porous than many conventional aggregates, it may absorb up to 3% additional asphalt binder. Only ferrous metal slags should be used, as nonferrous slags, such as air-cooled granulated copper, nickel, and phosphorus, are vitreous and result in poor skid resistance (TFHRC 2004).

Mineral processing wastes, or ore tailings, are waste rock derived from ore processing. These can also be used as coarse aggregate. The ore tailings are often trap rock or granite and perform very well as aggregate in asphalt pavements.

Foundry sand is uniformly sized, high-quality silica sand or lake sand that is used to form molds for both ferrous and nonferrous metal castings. Foundry sand is used as a substitute for fine aggregate in asphalt paving mixes in the range of 8%–25%. Higher percentages can be used if it is well cleaned of metal impurities, clays, and organic material. Approximately 85%–95% of foundry sand is between #30 and #100 sieve sizes. The particle shape is subangular to rounded (TFHRC 2004). There is some concern about the presence of phenols in foundry sand and leaching from stockpiles into soil and water. Sand for reuse as fine aggregate should be tested for phenol content.

Recycled Plastics

Post-consumer recycled plastics can be used as aggregate or an asphalt cement additive in asphalt pavement. Both technologies are relatively new and are proprietary, yet offer a good reuse opportunity for the 1,050,000 tons of plastics that are recycled each year in the United States (American Chemistry Council).

Treated recycled plastic aggregate (TRPA) uses chemically treated chipped and shredded plastics for aggregates in asphalt. One proprietary technology uses all types of plastics, reducing the need for separation of commingled plastics. Plastic chips are chemically treated to enhance bonding of asphalt cement. The treatment process releases small amounts of ozone; however, air-borne dust from conventional aggregate processing is reduced with substitution of plastic. Preliminary tests show that asphalt with plastic aggregate is less susceptible to cracking, rutting, and surface degradation than conventional asphalt. The first costs of asphalt made with recycled plastics are slightly higher than conventional asphalt; however, the life cycle is expected to be 25%–30% longer for much the same flexibility reasons as RAC (TFHRC 2004).

Recycled plastic is also used as an *asphalt cement polymer modifier.* Proprietary products use recycled low-density polyethylene resin obtained from trash bags and sandwich bags in asphalt cement. The recycled plastic is made palletized and added to asphalt cement at percentages of 4%–7% by weight of binder. It performs in much the same way as other polymer-modified binders (Maher et al. 2005).

Glasphalt

Glass cullet can be used as coarse and fine aggregate in asphalt. Consistent supplies of glass will determine the feasibility and cost value of cullet's use. In some regions where virgin aggregates are scarce, glass can be a cost-effective alternative. Glasphalt can have aesthetic benefits as the asphalt binder wears away, exposing some glass; however, there are concerns about exposed glass cracking under impacts from sharp objects (DDC NYC and DTPS 2005). In addition, the use of glass cullet may decrease the feasibility of standard asphalt surface milling and replacement techniques. Worker health and safety may be at risk with fine glass particles.

Use of recycled glass cullet as a base material may be more feasible, as it compacts well yet is still quite permeable. As aesthetics are not a concern in a base course, mixed-color cullet can be used.

MINIMIZE ASPHALT PAVEMENT'S CONTRIBUTION TO URBAN HEAT ISLANDS

Conventional black asphalt pavement absorbs rather than reflects the sun's radiation, resulting in increased temperature of pavement surfaces and nighttime ambient air. The surface temperature of asphalt pavement can be up to 50 degrees higher than a reflective white surface (Pomerantz et al. 2000), making the pavement uncomfortable to occupy, but the converse is also noted—reflective surfaces increase the daytime air temperature above a pavement as compared to dark pavements (Margaret Cervarich, personal communication, November 8, 2007). The nighttime phenomenon, along with other dark surfaces such as roofing, is one contributor to the urban heat island (UHI) effect. The UHI effect can adversely affect air quality by trapping pollutants at ground level with ground-level ozone and with higher ambient air temperatures, and increased energy demands, which in turn contribute to global warming.

Design of the urban landscape, including choices of pavement materials, can have a tremendous impact on the intensification or mitigation of the UHI effect. LBNL studies of four urban areas (Sacramento, Chicago, Salt Lake City, and Houston) estimate that pavement (roads, parking lots, and sidewalks) composes between 29% and 45% of land cover, while roofs make up 20%–25%. Vegetation covers just 20%–37% (Pomerantz et al. 2000). Clearly, pavement and planting design play a major role in causing (or mitigating) the urban heat island effect.

While use of reflective materials may be the best-known approach to mitigating pavements' contribution the UHI effect, multiple strategies can be employed to work together, and it is important to remember that not all strategies will be appropriate for every situation and location. Porous paving or composite pavement struc-

tures can also minimize heat storage. One must examine all aspects of thermal diffusivity, including heat storage capacity, thermal conductivity, etc., based on the function of the material and diurnal impacts from urban morphology and meteorology.

Use High-albedo Paving Materials

While it is not the only one, increased surface reflectance of pavement materials may be the most straightforward heat island reduction strategy, reducing absorption and reradiation of solar heat. Solar reflectance, or albedo, refers to a material's ability to reflect the visible, infrared, and ultraviolet wavelengths of sunlight. An albedo of 0.0 indicates total absorption of solar radiation and a 1.0 value represents total reflectivity. Generally, albedo is associated with color, with lighter colors being more reflective. Emittance, a material's ability to release absorbed heat, is indicated on a scale of 0 to 1 or 0% to 100%.

The Solar Reflectance Index (SRI) combines albedo and emittance into a single value expressed as a fraction (0.0 to 1.0) or percentage. A source for SRI data on basic paving materials is SS credit 7.1 of the U.S. Green Building Council's LEED for New Construction Version 2.2 (2005). The reference guide states that new asphalt has an SRI of 0, meaning that all solar radiation is absorbed, while new white portland cement concrete has an SRI of 86. Other pavement types generally range between these values, with a 35 SRI for new gray concrete. The LEED credit requires an SRI of at least 29 for 50% of the paving. While the guide only covers new and weathered asphalt and concrete, ASTM Standard E1980 defines calculation methods for SRI measurement of any material. A new ASTM standard is under development that will define the thermal diffusivity and SRI for many types and structures of paving.

Weathering of pavements can substantially alter albedo and SRI values. The albedo of new asphalt pavement is 0.04 because of the black asphalt binder coating the aggregate. Over the years, black asphalt oxidizes and lightens in color, and aggregate is exposed as traffic wears away the surface coat of black binder. The albedo increases to an average of 0.12 or even higher (Lawrence Berkeley National Laboratory 1999). This value varies with the color of the aggregate, with lighter aggregates increasing the albedo of the pavement.

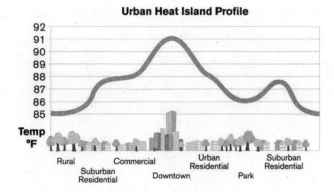

Figure 8–4.

Temperatures can be as much as 8% higher in urban areas than in adjacent rural areas due to relative lack of vegetative cover and heat-absorbing hard surfaces such as pavement and roofs. (Illustration from U.S. EPA Heat Island Reduction Initiative)

While lighter pavement colors may help mitigate UHI effects, they may not be desirable from an aesthetic or functional standpoint. Appearance of asphalt pavement is important to property owners, and they may want to seal or coat the asphalt to maintain darker hues for clear striping and a well-maintained image. White concrete and high-albedo surfaces reflect UV radiation that can cause glare, which may be uncomfortable to pedestrians (including increasing ground-level UV radiation), and even potentially limiting to visibility.

In addition, dark-colored paving is useful for melting ice and snow in cold climates. And if light-colored pavement is used, ecologically toxic deicing chemicals may be required to do the job. White concrete can also result in increased light pollution if fixtures are aimed directly at the paving, although it may result in reduced site lighting requirements, reducing energy use.

Lighter-colored surfaces with integral pigments or colored surfaces such as microsurfaces, white topping, or chip seals with light aggregate will increase the SRI of an asphalt pavement. Chip seal with light aggregate can increase the albedo of asphalt to 0.35 (DDC NYC and DTPS 2005). Research by the Lawrence Berkeley National Laboratory Heat Island Group found that high-albedo-coated asphalt was cooler, with a surface temperature of 88°F compared with 123°F on an adjacent area of conventional asphalt (Lawrence Berkeley National Laboratory 1999). Nanosurface coatings that change the optical characteristics of a surface are being developed along with engineered feedstocks and other techniques for mitigating the UHI effect (Jay Golden, personal communication, November 2006).

Alter the Pavement Composition

Thickness and conductivity of pavement will affect its contributions to the UHI effect. Thinner pavements will heat faster during the day, but cool quickly at night. Pavements that conduct heat quickly from the surface to the cooler base will retain less heat. These factors are quite complex and are the subject of ongoing research at Arizona State University's SMART program. The program has been experimenting with a composite paving of a rubberized asphalt surface course (made with recycled tires) over a concrete base. They have found that it has a lower nighttime temperature than adjacent concrete pavements. Other benefits include reduced tire

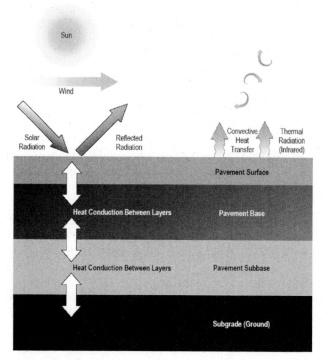

Figure 8–5.

This schematic pavement section demonstrates heat-related processes of reflectivity, conductivity, and emissivity that can contribute to the urban heat island effect. (Illustration from U.S. EPA 2005)

pavement noise and use of recycled materials (Jay Golden, personal communication, November 2006).

Make Paving Permeable

Permeable or porous paving cools pavement through evaporation and percolation of water, and in some instances, convective airflow through the voids, cooling base layers and soil under paving. Turf-based porous paving can also cool air through evapotranspiration. Another option to achieve LEED NC credit 7.1 is the use of a turf-based, open-grid paving system for 50% of site pavement.

Permeable paving systems used to mitigate the UHI effect can assist with Clean Water Act compliance by infiltrating and cleansing storm water, and reducing thermal pollution from runoff heating as it moves across paving. These storm water performance benefits may also result in reduced costs for pipes and other infrastructure.

While porous paving is not appropriate in all conditions, research has shown that some cooling benefits can be achieved with an open-graded asphalt friction course on a standard asphalt or concrete base (U.S. EPA 2005). Additional benefits of this include reduced tire noise and increased traction during rain, as standing surface water is virtually eliminated (see Table 8–8).

Shade Pavement

Like porous paving, shading pavement with trees has many benefits beyond mitigation of the UHI effect. Vegetation cools the air, absorbing carbon dioxide and producing oxygen; offers habitat; and improves the aesthetic qualities of a place. And shading asphalt will retard oxidation of the binder, prolonging the

Impacts of the Urban Heat Island Effect

Ten of the hottest years on record have been in the last fourteen years. Numerous cities in the West set all-time high temperature records in the summer of 2005 (Gore 2006). Scientists attribute this phenomenon to a combination of global climate change (Intergovernmental Panel on Climate Change 2007) and the urban heat island (UHI) effect. Contributors to the UHI effect include dark roofing and paving materials and lack of vegetative cover in urban areas to shade paving and buildings and cool the air. The EPA Heat Island Reduction Initiative defines the UHI effect as "a measurable increase in ambient air temperatures resulting primarily from the replacement of vegetation with buildings, roads, and other heat absorbing infrastructure" (U.S. EPA "Heat Island Effect"). Pavement and roofing materials often have very low reflectivity, or albedo (the measure of a surface's ability to reflect solar radiation). So they absorb much of the solar radiation contacting them, which heats up the materials, and then reradiates the heat, elevating surrounding ambient air temperatures.

The Lawrence Berkeley National Laboratory (LBNL) estimates that the heat island effect can elevate temperatures as much as 8% above those of adjacent suburban and rural areas. And air quality research in Los Angeles has demonstrated that for every one-degree rise in summer temperatures, smog formation can increase by 3%. Cities can be five to ten degrees warmer than the surrounding countryside on hot days, requiring increased energy for air conditioning.

The urban heat island effect can result in negative impacts on both environmental and human health. Hotter air in cities can cause an increase in the formation of ground-level ozone, the primary ingredient in smog. Smog is created from air pollutants like volatile organic compounds (VOCs) and nitrogen oxides (NO_x) when they are mixed with sunlight and heat. The rate of this reaction increases as temperatures increase over 70°F. A rise in ground-level ozone, a criteria air pollutant, above the one-hour standard of 120 parts per billion can push an urban area into "nonattainment" of the National Ambient Air Quality Standards (NAAQS) established by the Clean Air Act. When an urban area is classified as a "nonattainment region," it is penalized by a withdrawal of federal transportation funds and industries are subject to higher criteria air pollutant emissions offset rates.

High concentrations of ground level ozone and smog can cause an increase in asthma and other respiratory problems with children and the elderly at exceptionally high risk. Additionally, the UHI effect intensifies and lengthens heat waves, increasing risk of heat exhaustion and heat stroke.

A direct environmental and economic impact of the UHI effect is increased energy use for air conditioning of buildings in hotter urban areas. And while urban heat islands don't directly cause global warming, the burning of fossil fuels to produce electricity to cool buildings does. The EPA estimates that $41 billion is spent on air conditioning in the United States each year. And peak air conditioning loads in large cities increase 1%–2% for every one-degree Fahrenheit increase in temperature. And anywhere between 3% and 8% of the current electrical demand is a direct outcome of the UHI effect. One benefit of the UHI effect is that winter heating demand will be slightly reduced; however, most researchers agree that in most U.S. cities, the negative summer impacts outweigh the winter gains.

pavement life, possibly recouping some of the costs of the tree planting.

Shading pavement to mitigate the UHI effect may be most effective in parking lots, as new street trees tend not to shade road pavement for several years, if at all. The City of Davis Municipal Code requires that all new parking lots be planted to shade 50% of the lot in fifteen years (City of Davis 2007). Similarly, LEED NC 2.2 credit 7.1 asks that projects shade 50% of paving within five years of occupancy (U.S. Green Building Council [USGBC] 2005).

If the parking lot is graded to drain into planting islands containing appropriate bioswale plantings, this HIR strategy can also infiltrate and cleanse storm water. Porous pavement, another dual-purpose strategy, will help promote healthier trees as more water will find its way through the paving to root systems.

Urban geometry has an effect on the shading of pavement, as careful placement of buildings can shade paved surfaces at critical sun times. However, if buildings are too close together, as in a downtown area, they can produce an "urban canyon" that reduces nighttime radiational cooling as release of long-wave radiation requires access to the sky.

Also, in areas with severe winters, dark asphalt helps to absorb heat and melt snow, so light-colored surfaces may not be appropriate, but deciduous shade trees will cool pavement in the summer and allow solar access in the winter.

EXTEND THE LIFE OF ASPHALT PAVEMENTS

Advancements in pavement design and the techniques of milling and recycling in the last few decades have resulted in the potential for asphalt pavements to last longer with lower life-cycle costs and impacts than previous installations. "Perpetual pavements" or long-lasting pavements are increasingly used on roads and highways. The basic idea is that the pavement is built to last 50 years without requiring major structural rehabilitation or reconstruction. Instead the surface layers are engineered such that any distress that occurs is confined to the upper surface layer. Regular periodic maintenance is performed on the surface to detect and repair surface rutting and cracking before they impact the structural integrity of the asphalt pavement. Milling and

replacement of the surface layer is performed every 15–20 years. The surface layer that is milled up is either reconditioned and replaced or taken to an asphalt plant for recycling into new asphalt pavement (Washington Asphalt Pavement Association [WAPA] 2002).

The structural concept of perpetual pavements utilizes a thick HMA pavement over a strong foundation (California Bearing Ratio of 5% or larger). The HMA pavement is composed of three layers, each designed to resist specific stresses (Transportation Research Board 2001):

The HMA base layer is designed to resist fatigue cracking. There are two approaches to the design of this layer. The pavement thickness can be made large enough so the tensile strain at the bottom is insignificant, or an extra-flexible HMA can be made by increasing the asphalt content.

The intermediate layer is designed to carry most of the traffic load, necessitating stability and durability. Stability is achieved by stone-on-stone contact with coarse aggregate.

The wearing surface, the top layer, is designed to resist surface-initiated distresses such as top cracking and rutting. This surface can use asphalt rubber binder.

The resulting pavement is quite a bit thicker than traditional asphalt installations, yet given its extended life cycle it will likely use fewer resources in the long run.

Preventative maintenance is the key to long-lasting and perpetual pavements. A study by the Wisconsin Department of Transportation of preventative maintenance programs in Arizona, Montana, and Pennsylvania found a cost savings of $4–$10 in rehabilitation costs with every dollar spent on preventative maintenance. The study also concluded that the earlier the preventative maintenance was conducted, the lower the costs (WIDOT 2003).

"GREEN" ASPHALT'S SURFACE TREATMENT

A major environmental benefit to the longevity of asphalt paving is the fact that a thin surface course can be replaced at shorter intervals with minimal use of

Table 8–8 Cool Pavement Alternatives

Paving Type	UHI Issues	Other Benefits/Drawbacks
Gray portland cement concrete (PCC)	SRI 35[a] Surface reflectivity is affected by color of cement and color of aggregate.[b] Meets LEED NC 2.2 SS Credit 7.1 min. SRI of 29[a]	Durable, long life Can incorporate a wide variety of recycled materials Fly ash varies widely in color, so look for sources of lighter ash. More expensive than asphalt paving[c]
Concrete (mix of slag cement and portland cement)	Lighter color than standard gray PCC[c] Meets LEED NC 2.2 SS Credit 7.1 min. SRI of 29 Lighter-colored aggregate will further lighten.	Durable, long life Incorporates recycled materials Improves workability and performance (e.g., strength, chemical resistance)[c]
Exposed aggregate PCC	SRI depends on color of aggregate Can meet LEED NC 2.2 SS Credit 7.1 min. SRI of 29	Can incorporate a wide variety of recycled materials Not suitable in all applications[c]
White PCC	SRI new 86, weathered 45[a] Meets LEED NC 2.2 SS Credit 7.1 min. SRI of 29	More expensive than gray PCC May cause glare; less suitable for high-pedestrian spaces Can show dirt and oil more than gray PCC[c]
Porous concrete	Surface reflectivity is affected by color of cement and color of aggregate. Can meet LEED NC 2.2 SS Credit 7.1 min. SRI of 29 Water and, in some cases, air filtering through pavement cools it.	Reduces storm water runoff Reduces thermal pollution of storm water Not appropriate in all applications (e.g., truck traffic, high speeds) Snow removal can't use sand or it will clog the pores. Needs some ongoing maintenance[c]
Asphalt	SRI new 0, weathered 6[a] Does not meet LEED NC 2.2 SS Credit 7.1 min. SRI of 29 Ongoing research at ASU on nanocoatings and engineered feedstocks may increase surface reflectance.[d]	Less expensive than concrete Long installation life with resurfacing periodically required Can incorporate recycled materials[c]
Whitetopping (4–6 in.), ultra-thin whitetopping (UTW; 2–4 in.; concrete applied over milled asphalt pavement)	Provides SRI of concrete on an asphalt base Meets LEED NC 2.2 SS Credit 7.1 min. SRI of 29	UTW gaining widespread use, but relatively new techniques still being refined[c] Can incorporate recycled materials

Continued

Table 8–8 Cool Pavement Alternatives *(Continued)*

Paving Type	UHI Issues	Other Benefits/Drawbacks
Synthetic binder concrete pavement (graded aggregate mixed with clear, amber-colored hot-mixed polymer modified synthetic binder)	Clear binder allows for lighter colors. Color is determined primarily by the aggregate.[c] Can meet LEED NC 2.2 SS Credit 7.1 min. SRI of 29	More expensive than standard asphalt Relatively new product Can incorporate recycled materials Requires clean asphalt mixing and placing equipment[c]
Resin-modified pavement (open-graded asphalt with voids filled with latex rubber–modified cement grout)	Can meet LEED NC 2.2 SS Credit 7.1 min. SRI of 29	Lower cost than PCC Limited to less than 40 mph roads and 5% slopes[c] Relatively new in United States (common in France), so experienced contractors may be hard to find. Can incorporate recycled materials
Light aggregate in asphalt (e.g., limestone)	Will start as very low SRI like traditional asphalt, but as binder wears away, aggregate color will dominate surface color[b] Can meet LEED NC 2.2 SS Credit 7.1 minimum SRI of 29 dependent on binder type and aggregate reflectivity	Light aggregates are not always locally available, and economic and environmental costs to transport light aggregate long distances are high.
Chip seal with light aggregate	Aggregate color will determine surface color. Can meet LEED NC 2.2 SS Credit 7.1 minimum SRI of 29 dependent on binder type and aggregate reflectivity	Light aggregates are not always locally available, and economic and environmental costs to transport light aggregate long distances are high. For applications with light traffic volumes[c]
Traditional asphalt pavement with surface "shot-blasting" abrasion (see Figure 8–6)	Can meet LEED NC 2.2 SS Credit 7.1 minimum SRI of 29 dependent on binder type and aggregate reflectivity	Removes asphalt binder from surface and exposes aggregate. Can be used for decorative purposes as well.
Microsurfacing (slurry seal surface treatment that is a polymer-modified emulsified asphalt with dense graded fines)	Can be tinted with light colors to increase reflectance of pavement surface[c] Can meet LEED NC 2.2 SS Credit 7.1 min. SRI of 29	Experienced contractors may be hard to find. Cold-mix results in lower energy requirements than other asphalt products.
Porous asphalt	Water and, in some cases, air filtering through pavement cools it.[d] LEED credit does not currently acknowledge the HIR benefits of this technology.	Reduces storm water runoff Reduces thermal pollution of storm water Not appropriate in all applications (e.g., truck traffic, high speeds) Snow removal can't use sand or it will clog the pores. Needs some ongoing maintenance[c]

Table 8–8 Cool Pavement Alternatives *(Continued)*

Paving Type	UHI Issues	Other Benefits/Drawbacks
Rubberized asphalt friction course on asphalt or concrete base	ASU research has found cooler night surface temps than adjacent PCC concrete; further studies in progress.[d] LEED credit does not currently acknowledge the HIR benefits of this technology.	Reduces tire noise Reduces splash and skid potential during rain events
Plastic and masonry modular porous pavement systems	LEED NC 2.2 SS Credit 7.1 requires that system be less than 50% impervious and open cells contain vegetation.[a] Open cells containing light aggregate don't currently qualify for LEED credit.	Suitable for parking lots, driveways, and pedestrian paving, but not most roadways.[c]

[a]USGBC 2005

[b]U.S. EPA 2005

[c]Maher et al 2005

[d]Jay Golden, personal communication, November 2006

Figure 8–6.
Asphalt pavement can be abraded with shot blasting to remove the black asphalt from the surface. This process exposes the aggregate in the asphalt pavement and if it is a light-colored aggregate, the surface will be lightened and reflect more solar radiation, reducing the pavement's contribution to the urban heat island effect. (Photo from Blastrac)

material while the larger paving installation can remain in place for several years. The asphalt surfacing options table (Table 8–9) lists environmental considerations, typical thicknesses, and performance considerations for a wide range of asphalt surfaces.

When selecting a surface application for asphalt pavement with the intent of minimizing environmental impacts, consideration should be given to longevity, application temperature, incorporation of recycled material, and surface color/reflectivity.

Table 8–9 Asphalt Pavement Surface Course Materials

Type of Seal, Thickness, and Life Expectancy	Uses/Limitations	Environmental Issues	Performance/ Aesthetic Issues
PAVEMENT SURFACING; PREVENTATIVE MAINTENANCE, MINOR CRACKS, IRREGULARITIES, SKID RESISTANCE			
Cape seal $3/8$"–$3/4$" thick 7–15 years	Slurry seal or microsurfacing on top of a chip seal Slurry fills voids in chip seal. Can be used over new or existing hot-mix or over aggregate base only with low to medium traffic	Reduces asphalt use if cape seal is applied to an aggregate base only Emulsified application means cooler temps, less fumes, and less energy. Light colors will increase reflectance of pavement.	Microsurfacing can be colored. Microsurfacing has polymers that make pavement more flexible, with less aging in placement.
Chip seal $1/4$"–$3/8$" thick 3–7 years	Single-size crushed aggregate and binder layer. Can be used over new or existing hot-mix or over aggregate base only with low to medium traffic Not for heavy truck traffic or >8% grades Can be hot, cutback, or emulsified application	Reduces asphalt use if chip seal is applied to an aggregate base only Emulsified application means cooler temps, less fumes, and less energy. Avoid cutback asphalt as it's high in VOCs. Light-colored aggregates will increase reflectance of pavement.	Color of aggregate will determine surface color unless chips are precoated with asphalt binder. Fog seal can be used to improve bonding of chips to road surface, but it creates a black surface.
Multiple chip seals $1^1/2$" thick 4–8 years	Double- or triple-chip seals are two or three layers of chip seal with successively reduced aggregate sizes and thicknesses. Not for heavy truck traffic or >8% grades Can be hot, cutback, or emulsified application	Reduces asphalt use if chip seals are applied to an aggregate base only Emulsified application means cooler temps, less fumes, and less energy. Avoid cutback asphalt as it's high in VOCs. Light-colored aggregates will increase reflectance of pavement.	Color of aggregate will determine surface color unless chips are precoated with asphalt binder. Fog seal can be used to improve bonding of chips to road surface, but it creates a black surface.
Microsurfacing $3/8$"–$3/4$" thick 5–8 years	Enhanced slurry seal is made of polymer-modified emulsified asphalt, crushed fine aggregate, mineral filler or additives, and water.	Emulsified application means cooler temps, less fumes,and less energy. Light colors will increase reflectance of pavement.	Can use an almost clear binder that can be pigmented or used with colored aggregate Smooth surface is good for bike/recreational trails.

Table 8–9 Asphalt Pavement Surface Course Materials *(Continued)*

Type of Seal, Thickness, and Life Expectancy	Uses/Limitations	Environmental Issues	Performance/ Aesthetic Issues
Open-graded friction course (OGFC) $3/4$" thick 8–12 years	Porous hot-mix asphalt concrete wearing course Contains little sand or dust, with 15%–25% air voids Water drains through surface and across cross slope into drainage ditch or structure.	OGFC is only porous on the surface course; binder course is impermeable Hot-mix asphalt binder uses energy, generates heat, and produces emissions and fumes.	Good friction; reduces splash, spray, and hydroplaning Less susceptible to deformation Can freeze more quickly because water is in pores
Ultra-thin white topping (UTW) 2"–4" thick Life expectancy not known	Thin overlay of high-strength, fiber-reinforced concrete on asphalt paving	Light color of concrete will increase reflectance of pavement. Concrete surface may last longer than another asphalt-based surface treatment, using fewer resources. Concrete is high in embodied energy.	Louder tire noise No rutting
Otta seal $1/2$"–$3/4$" thick 4–8 years, single 8–15 years, double	Graded aggregate placed on a relatively thick binder course of HMA, cutback, or emulsified asphalt, then rolled. Can do two applications for a double Otta seal.	Local aggregates that might not meet high-quality paving aggregates can be used, saving transport energy. Light-colored aggregates will increase reflectance of pavement. Dust can be a problem during application.	Only for low-traffic applications Color is determined by color of aggregate.
Sand seal $1/8$"–$3/8$" thick 2–6 years	Bituminous binding agent is sprayed on; then sand is rolled onto it. Can be used over new or existing hot-mix or over aggregate base only with low traffic Not for heavy truck traffic or >8% grades Can be hot, cutback, or emulsified application	Reduces asphalt use if sand seal is applied to an aggregate base only Emulsified application means cooler temps, less fumes, and less energy. Avoid cutback asphalt as it's high in VOCs. Light-colored aggregates will increase reflectance of pavement. Silica dust can be a health risk during construction.	Usually a dark color as asphalt binder dominates the finished color Not used in some parts of the country

Continued

Table 8–9 Asphalt Pavement Surface Course Materials *(Continued)*

Type of Seal, Thickness, and Life Expectancy	Uses/Limitations	Environmental Issues	Performance/ Aesthetic Issues
PAVEMENT SURFACING; PREVENTATIVE MAINTENANCE, MINOR CRACKS, IRREGULARITIES, SKID RESISTANCE			
Slurry seal $1/8"$–$3/8"$ thick 3–8 years	Cold-mix thin surface treatment of a mix of emulsified asphalt, dense-graded crushed fine aggregate, mineral filler, and water	Use of light binder will increase reflectance of paving surface. Cold-mix saves energy and emissions.	Can use an almost clear binder that can be pigmented or used with colored aggregate Can be damaged by snow removal equipment Has a smooth texture, less skid resistance for roads
Ultra thin friction course $3/8"$–$3/4"$ 10–12 years	Thin layer of gap-graded, coarse aggregate hot-mix bound to the existing pavement	Hot-mix application generates heat and some emissions and uses energy. Can extend life of an existing paving installation, saving resources Dark color can contribute to the heat island effect.	Used to rejuvenate pavement and repair minor irregularities
PREVENTATIVE MAINTENANCE AND COLOR RESTORATION			
Scrub seal Minimal thickness 2–6 years	This asphalt surface treatment consists of spraying emulsified asphalt onto an existing pavement and dragging a broom across to work it into surface cracks, then spreading fine aggregate into cracks.	Emulsified application means cooler temps, less fumes, and less energy. Extends life of pavement with little material use Black color can contribute to the heat island effect.	Can be damaged by snow removal equipment
Fog seal Minimal thickness 1–3 years	Light application of emulsified asphalt diluted with water Common maintenance treatment	Emulsified application means cooler temps, less fumes, and less energy. Extends life of pavement with little material use Black color can contribute to the heat island effect.	Sometimes reduces skid resistance Fog seals are black unless pigment is added.

Source: Adapted from Maher et al. 2005

As with any pavement, surface color of asphalt will affect heat absorption, retention, and reflectivity of the pavement, and as most asphalt surfaces are black or dark gray, they can contribute to the heat island effect in urban areas. Therefore, in areas where this is a concern, lighter-colored surfaces with integral pigments, or colored surfaces such as microsurfaces, white topping, or chip seals with light aggregate should be considered. Aggregate color largely determines the overall color of the pavement as asphalt binder wears away and fades, so use of light-colored aggregates in any hot-mix asphalt pavement will help minimize heat absorption.

Avoid Sealants for Asphalt Pavements

Asphalt parking lot sealants impact water quality through storm water runoff carrying toxic pollutants to water bodies. And with the average parking lot being resealed every three years, toxicity of sealers is a major issue.

There are two major kinds of parking lot sealants: asphalt based and coal-tar based. Both types of sealers contain volatile organic compounds (VOCs) and polycyclic aromatic hydrocarbons (PAHs), a family of environmental contaminant chemicals created from the incomplete combustion of hydrocarbons. PAHs adhere to surfaces, such as sand, soil, or living tissues, and are not easily dissolved by water. These characteristics make them effective sealers, especially those that are tar-based with 20%–35% PAHs; however, it also means that they can negatively impact soil, sediments, and living organisms. Asphalt-based sealers typically contain about 5% PAHs. PAHs have been linked to reproductive effects in wildlife and cancers in humans.

Therefore, the best strategy may be to not seal asphalt, but to let it fade and then resurface it every seven to ten years. Low-VOC asphalt-based sealers exist and will minimize air and water pollution, but they still contain PAHs.

Make Asphalt Porous

A major environmental impact of asphalt pavement—and most other types of paving as well—is a virtually impermeable surface, resulting in large concentrations of storm water runoff and nonpoint source pollutants, and unhealthy soil below from lack of water and air. In urban watersheds, pavements compose around two-thirds of the impermeable surfaces, causing two-thirds of the storm water runoff and almost all of the hydrocarbon pollution (Ferguson 2005). Porous pavements can offer a solution to these impacts by infiltrating storm water near where it falls. Porous asphalt is an open-graded asphalt course with 14%–18% air voids over the top of an aggregate filter course and aggregate base reservoir. Aside from the absence of fines and mineral dust, porous asphalt mixes are similar to standard hot-mixes and can be mixed and placed with the same equipment; however, an experienced contractor should place it. On installations with high use, such as streets or parking lots,

Figure 8–7.
The contrast between impermeable and porous asphalt is illustrated. Porous asphalt in the background eliminates standing water by draining storm water through to an underlying reservoir, then to treatment in water quality swales at the edge of the pavement. (Photo from Cahill Associates)

specifications should require that the contractor test the mix using open-graded asphalt highway testing procedures (Cahill, Adams, and Marm 2005).

Many types of pavements are potentially appropriate to be constructed with porous asphalt, such as the following:

- parking lots
- walking paths and sidewalks

- bike lanes
- on-street parking areas and road shoulders
- low-volume roads
- alleys and service areas
- fire truck access lanes

Components of Porous Asphalt Pavements

The porous asphalt layer is open-graded asphalt concrete that is two to four inches thick for light applications. Heavier applications, such as city streets and highways, will warrant thicknesses of four to seven inches (NAPA 2004). Binder coats the aggregate particles in a thin film. The proportions of a porous asphalt mix will vary by expected traffic volume, climate, rainfall, and aggregate characteristics.

Binder quantities will vary by application; however, there must be enough binder to form a thick enough layer to reduce degradation by oxidation, but not so much that it drains down and clogs pores (Ferguson 2005). Drain-down of binder can be a problem where the heat of the sun softens asphalt cement, which carries dust and dirt from the surface down into a cooler part of the asphalt pavement where it hardens and clogs pores. Recent techniques to reduce drain-down include use of polymer modifiers (e.g., styrene-butylene styrene [SBS]), high asphalt content, mineral or cellulose fibers, and larger open aggregate gradations (Ferguson 2005). Rubberized asphalt cement containing recycled tire crumbs can be used in porous pavement applications.

Aggregate for porous asphalt is an open-graded mix (a relatively consistent size of aggregates) that relies on stone-to-stone contact to form the pavement structure, supporting loads while offering pores through which water can move. Aggregate sizes will vary between installations. A half-inch open-graded aggregate mix is recommended by many sources (Cahill et al. 2005; Ferguson 2005; NAPA 2004), but some are now using a $3/4$" mix to reduce clogging potential (Ferguson 2005). Minimal fine aggregates are used, and then only to form a matrix with the binder for greater cohesiveness. Table 8–10 illustrates a typical aggregate gradation specification by Cahill Associates, one of the pioneering engineering firms of porous asphalt paving.

The top filter course, also called a choker course, is an approximately two-inch-thick course of half-inch

Table 8–10 Standard Porous Asphalt Aggregate Gradation[a]

U.S. Standard Sieve Size	Percent of Aggregate Passing
$3/4$" (19.1mm)	100
$1/2$" (12.7mm)	85–100
3/8" (9.5mm)	70–90
#4 (4.75mm)	10–20
#8 (2.36mm)	5–10
#30 (600 μm)	2–5

[a]Asphalt cement is 5.75%–6.0% by weight.
Source: Cahill Associates, personal communication, February 22, 2008

crushed stone aggregate that protects the reservoir course pores from clogging by smaller aggregates in the asphalt pavement layer, and it protects the reservoir from disturbance during placement of the asphalt (NAPA 2004). It provides some filtration, but primarily provides a firm paving platform.

The reservoir course is a base course of crushed, open-graded stone that acts as a stable base for the pavement and a storage reservoir for water while it infiltrates into the soil below. The depth of the reservoir varies and is determined by the required water storage volume, structural capacity of the aggregate and soil, and frost depth. Reservoir courses can also be designed to accommodate rainfall from nearby roofs and other impermeable surfaces. The minimum thickness is eight inches, but it is recommended to be at least eighteen inches (Cahill et al. 2005). Recommended aggregate sizes range from $1^1/2$ inches to three inches with a No. 2 AASHTO gradation. This results in approximately 40% voids for storage of $3^1/2$ inches in a nine-inch-deep section. A No. 5 AASHTO gradation with smaller aggregates may offer some cost savings, but the depth of aggregate will increase with a 75% reduction in storage capacity (NAPA 2004).

A filter fabric layer will prevent migration of soil fines below the reservoir into the voids of the reservoir. It will also provide some stability for the aggregate courses. Soil beneath the fabric should be undisturbed, with care taken to avoid compaction by equipment or

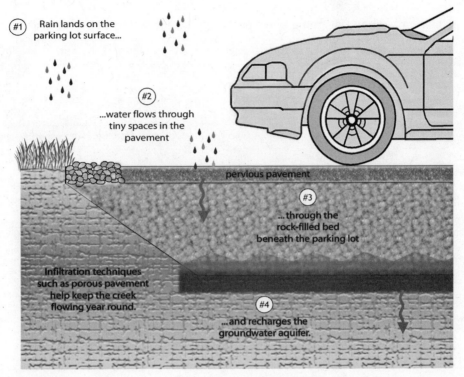

Figure 8–8.

This typical porous asphalt cross-section illustrates the pervious asphalt layer, the rock-filled storage reservoir, and flow into the soil under the reservoir to recharge groundwater. Where soil is inappropriate for infiltration or large amounts of pollutants are anticipated, water can be directed through perforated pipe and a liner to planted water quality swales at the edge of the pavement. (Photo from Cahill Associates, C. Marm)

Labels in figure:
- #1 Rain lands on the parking lot surface...
- #2 ...water flows through tiny spaces in the pavement
- pervious pavement
- #3 ...through the rock-filled bed beneath the parking lot
- Infiltration techniques such as porous pavement help keep the creek flowing year round.
- #4 ...and recharges the groundwater aquifer.

Table 8–11 Filter and Reservoir Course Aggregate Gradations

U.S. Standard Sieve Size	Percent of Aggregate Passing	
Top and Bottom Filter Courses		
1/2"		100
3/8"		0–5
Reservoir Course (AASHTO Gradation No. 2)		
3"		100
2 1/2"		90–100
2"		35–70
1 1/2"		0–15
3/4"	0–5	
#100		0–2

Source: NAPA 2004

material storage, affecting permeability (U.S. EPA 1999).

Costs of porous asphalt can be comparable or less than standard asphalt paving if the costs of paving and storm water management are evaluated as an entire system. If the porous asphalt is used to infiltrate storm water, downstream storm water management facilities can be reduced or eliminated, saving the cost of those structures. While porous asphalt pavements may not remove pollutants as effectively as plant-based BMPs (e.g., bioswales) prior to their reaching the soil layer, they do remove some pollutants. The aggregate in the filter course and reservoir course allows bacteria to grow that breaks down and reduces surface pollutants such as hydrocarbons (Ferguson 2005). This phenomenon in conjunction with the soil mantle will remove many pollutants except for solutes such as nitrate (Cahill et al. 2005). In situations with large

Table 8–12 Considerations When Designing and Specifying Porous Asphalt Pavements

Soil and hydrological analysis should be performed to determine suitability of porous asphalt pavement.
All aggregates should be clean and washed and have a minimum of 95% double-fractured faces.
Asphalt binder temperatures may need to be higher than in conventional mixes to accommodate a stiffer binder that can reduce drain-down.
Use of polymer-modified asphalts, asphalt rubber, and/or fibers can reduce drain-down and increase performance.
Consider use of conventional asphalt pavement in high-traffic portions of roads or parking lots, as infiltration rates of porous asphalt can be reduced where vehicles brake or turn repeatedly.
Use of porous asphalt near potential sources of pollution (e.g., gas stations, truck stops, and industrial sites) should be avoided to prevent soil and groundwater contamination.
Bottoms of reservoirs should be several feet above the water table or bedrock so water can filter through the soil mantle, removing pollutants.
Depth of gravel reservoirs should be sized by infiltration rate of soil and by expected rainfall quantities. Reservoir should be designed to completely drain within 72 hours.
Other storm water BMPs, such as bioswales at the edge of pavements, can be used in conjunction with porous asphalt pavement where expected pollutant or water loads may be high. The bioswales may filter pollutants more effectively than the porous asphalt.
Use of a geotextile below a reservoir will reduce sediment migration into the aggregate reservoir.
Compaction of porous asphalt should be performed with only moderate-weight rollers to avoid crushing of aggregate or clogging of pores.
Pavements should be closed to traffic for 24 hours after placement.
Porous asphalt should not be used in applications with greater than 6% slopes, heavy truck traffic, or areas with potential for large chemical spills.
On sloped sites, the bottom of the infiltration bed should be flat to maximize infiltration.
Use of filter strips and slopes away from the porous pavement will minimize potential clogging of pores by dust, sediments, and leaf litter. Use of porous pavement should be avoided on exceptionally windy sites.
The color of aggregate used in porous asphalt will determine the pavement color as the binder wears from the surface and the aggregate becomes more exposed over time.

Sources: Cahill et al. 2005; DDC NYC and DTPS 2005; Ferguson 2005; NAPA 2004

amounts of pollutants or risky types such as heavy metals, water that drains through the pavement can be stored in beds and discharged slowly into vegetated swales where it is more thoroughly cleansed.

In addition to storm water infiltration benefits, porous asphalt fosters healthier trees in urban situations, allowing air and water to the root zones. It also can help reduce the heat island effect, as the mass of a pavement installation can affect the amount of heat it retains and porous asphalt has less mass than standard asphalt. An unexpected benefit is that the natural drain-down of water in winter minimizes ice formation.

Table 8–13 Considerations When Maintaining Porous Asphalt Pavement

Periodic high-pressure washing and vacuuming will maintain infiltration capacity of pavement. Frequency will vary by site conditions and traffic. Analysis of sediments removed can help establish a vacuuming schedule.
Avoid use of sand for deicing and winter traction. Sand will clog pores. If necessary, deicing chemicals should be used instead. The dark asphalt color may melt snow and ice more quickly than light-colored pavements.
Care should be taken when snowplowing porous asphalt. Blades should be lifted a half inch above the surface on skid-plates.
Posting of signs at porous asphalt sites can alert maintenance personnel of the need to keep sediment and debris off the pavement surface. They may also prevent application of sealants as standard maintenance.

Sources: Cahill et al. 2005; DDC NYC and DTPS 2005; Ferguson 2005; and NAPA 2004.

Where ice does form, sand should not be applied since it will clog the pores; instead, deicing salts can be used, or the darker color of the pavement may melt the ice without use of deicing applications. The National Asphalt Pavement Association (NAPA) is a strong advocate of porous paving and has developed a useful publication called *Porous Asphalt Pavements, Design Construction and Maintenance Guide. (2004)*. The document, containing specs for porous asphalt paving, can be purchased from the NAPA website. Also, the book *Porous Pavements* (2005), by Bruce Ferguson, devotes a lengthy chapter to porous asphalt and is a very good source for those specifying porous asphalt pavements.

PAVE LESS

Reducing road width and parking lot size, necessitating less use of paving material, will make the largest impact

water quality treatment swale

porous asphalt

Figure 8–9.
A system of porous asphalt pavement, subsurface storage, and water quality swales to capture and treat runoff was used by Cahill Associates for the Mustang Lot at the Ford Motor Company's Rouge River Complex in Michigan. (Photo from Cahill Associates)

on attempts to green asphalt use. Reductions in sizes of parking spaces and drive aisles will reduce paving expanses, especially where there are a large number of spaces. Allowing the front end of cars to overhang low planting strips or porous stone storm water capture trenches can reduce asphalt pavement expanses. Reducing road widths will reduce impermeable paved surfaces and benefit the walkability of streets by slowing traffic.

Strategies for reducing pavement sizes are as follows:

- Reduce parking space sizes (e.g., depth of spaces, width of spaces), and use 30% compact spaces (DDC NYC and DTPS 2005).
- Reduce width of drive aisles.
- Reduce the number of parking spaces by using shared parking strategies with other business.
- Base parking space counts on average needs rather than peak needs. Use grasspave overflow parking for peak needs.

- Implement planted medians in wide expanses of pavements (e.g., cul de sacs and fire truck turn-arounds).
- Consider shared driveways.
- Use turning lanes and shoulders only when required.
- Reduce the width of vehicle lanes through lowering design speeds and traffic-calming measures.

Alternatives to Asphalt Paving

SYNTHETIC BINDER CONCRETE PAVEMENT

Synthetic binder concrete pavement, also called rustic pavement, is a hot-mix material much like asphalt, but with a mostly clear polymer-modified synthetic binder. The clear, amber-colored binder, composed of a petroleum hydrocarbon resin, is mixed with colored coarse, fine, and mineral aggregates at a hot-mix plant, then

---

Key Strategies: Asphalt for Sustainable Sites

- Encourage contractors to lower hot-mix temperatures and employ worker safety and engineering controls to limit fumes and emissions.

- Avoid cutback asphalt binders completely and use low-VOC emulsified binders with minimal diluents and solvents.

- Use less asphalt with thinner sections, and increased structural aggregate base courses made from recycled/reclaimed materials where applicable.

- Substitute a portion of the aggregates with recycled materials such as reclaimed asphalt, tire rubber, glass, slag, crushed concrete, roofing shingles, and industrial or mineral by-products.

- Use porous asphalt where appropriate to encourage storm water infiltration.

- To address the heat island effect, increase surface reflectivity with use of light-colored aggregate chip seals or light surfacing such as pigmented microsurfacing or slurry seal, white topping, or other high-albedo asphalt coating.

- Porous or open-graded asphalt pavement will cool pavements as well. Asphalt pavement reflectivity can be increased by "shot-blasting," a technique for abrading the surface binder.

- Maximize the life of the paving with preventative maintenance such as resurfacing and repairs.

- Use low- or no-VOC products in sealants, coatings, and traffic striping. Traffic markings could be thermoplastic reflectorized with recycled glass, high-build acrylic coatings, or paints with low levels of aromatic compounds and other restricted chemicals.

- Avoid use of sealants where possible, or when necessary, use asphalt-based sealants. Do not use tar-based sealants.

- Pave less. Reduce parking lot sizes by designing multiuse lots requiring fewer spaces, and reduce size of stalls and drive aisles. Where appropriate, use "skinny streets" or reduce road length and width.

placed using traditional asphalt techniques and machinery. The color of the aggregates largely defines the color of the finished paving; however, pigments can be added at the mixing plant to further modify the color of the installation. Smaller quantities of pigments are required than for traditional asphalt because the binder is mostly clear, as opposed to the very dark asphalt binder, which requires a lot of pigment to mask the dark gray color.

Because of the high cost of the binder (estimated at seven times the cost of standard asphalt binder), synthetic binder concrete pavement is usually placed as a thin half-inch to one-inch surface treatment over standard asphalt base course. However, it can be placed

Table 8–14 Alternatives to Asphalt Paving

Alternative Material	Cost,[a] Expected Life Span, and Traffic Volume	Environmental Considerations	Aesthetic/ Performance Considerations	Comments
Portland cement concrete pavement	$100–$135/yd. 30–40 years Very low to high	High embodied energy and CO_2 release of cement processing Potential for high recycled content Light colors can minimize the heat island effect. Durable, long lasting Can be made porous	Wide variety of finishes available Good performance	Refer to chapter 5 for more information.
Synthetic binder concrete pavement Petroleum hydrocarbon resin binder heated and mixed with coarse and fine aggregates and mineral filler, usually used as a $1/2$"–1" surface course	$120–$160/ton 15–20 years, although new product so not installed for long Very low to high	Unknown environmental and human health impacts Low temps mean less energy and presumably lower emissions and fumes.	Wide variety of potential colors Performs like HMA paving Requirements for clean mixing and placing equipment can be limiting. Color is affected by all aggregates and mineral fines.	New product, not widely tested
Resin-modified pavement Open-graded asphalt concrete with 25%–35% voids filled with latex rubber–modified cement grout, usually used as a $1/2$"–2" surface over 2" HMA	$10/yd. (2" thick) 15–25 years Very low to high traffic, but low speed due to low skid resistance	Unknown environmental and human health impacts of grout Grout contains fly-ash, an industrial by-product. Light-colored RMP can minimize the heat island effect.	Good abrasion resistance, good fuel resistance Low maintenance Lighter colored surface than standard HMA	Low use in United States, better used in Europe

Continued

Table 8–14 Alternatives to Asphalt Paving *(Continued)*

Alternative Material	Cost,[a] Expected Life Span, and Traffic Volume	Environmental Considerations	Aesthetic/ Performance Considerations	Comments
Stabilized surfacings There are a variety of stabilizers and dust suppressants that, when mixed with soil and/or aggregates, result in a flexible paving for low-volume traffic applications such as parking lots, private drives, trails, or informal pedestrian spaces.	Costs vary. Life spans vary. Very low to low traffic	See chapters 6 and 9 for environmental costs and benefits of individual stabilizers.	See chapters 6 and 9 for performance and aesthetic issues of individual stabilizers.	Stabilizing materials include the following: Chlorides Clay binders Electrolyte emulsions Enzymatic emulsions Lignosulfonates Organic petroleum-based emulsions Synthetic polymer emulsions Tree resin emulsions

[a]All prices are installed, from August 2005.

Source: Adapted from Maher et al. 2005

directly over a prepared, well-compacted subgrade of native materials. Required thicknesses will vary with design loads and stability of the base/subgrade provided. The thickness of the synthetic binder lift should be a minimum of three times the maximum aggregate size (Maher et al. 2005).

Synthetic binder concrete pavement is a very new material that has not been extensively studied for environmental or human health impacts. The environmental impacts of synthetic binders can be considered similar to standard asphalt binders, as they are both petroleum-based materials. However, the synthetic binder is a proprietary material, so all additives and processes are not known. Some environmental and human health considerations are as follows:

- The addition of polymers could have an additional negative impact on the health of workers during mixing, heating, and placement.

- Embodied energy for heating the synthetic binder will be lower, as the mix is heated at 260°F–285°F as opposed to 270°F–325°F for standard hot-mix asphalt.
- Lower temperatures generally result in lower emissions and fumes.
- As traditional asphalt has a relatively low solar reflectance index, synthetic binder concrete pavement in a light color could minimize the heat island impacts of asphalt pavement. The light color will be most easily achieved through use of light-colored aggregates.

Because of the relative newness of synthetic binders, it may be difficult to find experienced contractors or contractors willing to take the steps necessary for the application. While the techniques of placement are similar to standard asphalt, all equipment must be cleaned (or new) prior to mixing, and the plant dedicated exclusively to the mix; otherwise asphalt residue will re-

Table 8–15 Some Organizations Performing or Sponsoring Research on Asphalt Pavements

Organization	Contact Information
Federal Highway Administration Turner-Fairbank Highway Research Center	http://www.tfhrc.gov
Transportation Research Board	http://www.trb.org/
National Asphalt Pavement Association	http://www.hot-mix.org
	www.warmmixasphalt.com
National Center for Asphalt Technology	http://www.eng.auburn.edu/center/ncat
Recycled Materials Resource Center	http://www.rmrc.unh.edu/
Rubberized Asphalt Concrete Technology Center (RACTC)	http://www.rubberizedasphalt.org/
EPA Heat Island Reduction Initiative (HIRI)	www.epa.gov/heatisland
The National Center of Excellence, Sustainable Materials and Renewable Technologies (SMART) Solutions for Energy and Climate, Arizona State University	www.asusmart.com
Lawrence Berkeley National Laboratory Heat Island Group	http://eetd.lbl.gov/HeatIsland/
Federation of Canadian Municipalities and National Research Council	http://www.infraguide.ca
The National Center for Pavement Preservation	http://www.pavementpreservation.org
Foundation for Pavement Preservation	http://fp2.org
Washington State Department of Transportation, State Materials Laboratory	http://www.wsdot.wa.gov/biz/mats/

sult in black streaks in the application. This requirement will likely increase the cost of the material and pose some logistical and scheduling constraints on contractors (Maher et al. 2005).

The Future of Asphalt

Asphalt will likely continue to be the material of choice for roadways, highways, and parking lots. And while there are environmental and human health impacts from the use of asphalt, there are many new formulations and technologies on the horizon that can minimize its environmental impacts. Recycled aggregates, porous installations, and coatings to decrease solar absorption will all reduce impacts. Attention to reducing emissions and fumes through cooler mixes and pollution controls can further minimize health risks.

Research on technologies to improve the performance of asphalt paving continues to be strong, and with time, performance of installations will show the valid-ity of some new technologies. Table 8–15 lists some agencies and organizations engaging in or funding asphalt pavement research.

REFERENCES

American Chemistry Council. http://www.americanchemistry.com/plastics/doc.asp?CID=1581&DID=6011 (accessed August 8, 2007).

Asphalt Recycling and Reclaiming Association (ARRA). 2001. *Basic Asphalt Recycling Manual.* Annapolis: Asphalt Recycling and Reclaiming Association, FHWA. http://www.arra.org/.

Athena Sustainable Materials Institute. 2006. "A Life Cycle Perspective on Concrete and Asphalt Roadways: Embodied Primary Energy and Global Warming Potential." Submitted to Cement Association of Canada. Merrickville, ON: Athena Sustainable Materials Institute.

Athena Sustainable Materials Institute. 2001. "A Life Cycle Inventory for Road and Roofing Asphalt." Ottawa, ON: Franklin Associates.

Cahill, Thomas, Michele Adams, and Courtney Marm. "Stormwater Management with Porous Pavements." *Government Engineering* March–April 2005:14–19.

California Integrated Waste Management Board (CIWMB) [Formerly Rubberized Asphalt Technology Center]. "Rubberized Asphalt." http://www.ciwmb.ca.gov/tires/RAC/ (accessed August 26, 2006).

City of Davis, California. 2007. "Municipal Code 37.0.0" http://www.ci.davis.ca.us/cmo/citycode/chapter.cfm?chapter=37.

Demkin, J., ed. 1998. "Application 10 Plumbing Pipe." In *Environmental Resource Guide*. New York: John Wiley & Sons.

Federal Highway Administration (FHWA), U.S. Department of Transportation. 2005. "Highway Statistics 2005." Tables HM-53, HM-60. http://www.fhwa.dot.gov/policy/ohim/hs05/roadway_extent.htm.

Federal Register. "National Emissions Standards for Hazardous Air Pollutants: Revision of Source Category List Under Section 112 of the Clean Air Act." *Federal Register* 67, no. 29, (February 12, 2002). AD-FRL-7142–8 RIN 2080-A182.

Ferguson, Bruce. 2005. *Porous Pavements.* Boca Raton, FL: CRC Press.

Gore, Al. 2006. *An Inconvenient Truth: The Planetary Emergency of Global Warming and What We Can Do about It.* New York: Rodale.

Intergovernmental Panel on Climate Change. 2007. *Climate Change 2007: Impacts, Adaptation and Vulnerability.* Contribution of Working Group II to the Fourth Assessment Report of the Intergovernmental Panel on Climate Change, ed. M.L. Parry, O.F. Canziani, J. P. Palutikof, P. J. van der Linden, and C. E.Hanson. Cambridge: Cambridge University Press.

Lawrence Berkeley National Laboratory. "Pavement Albedo at Night." Heat Island Group. http://eetd.lbl.gov/heatisland/Pavements/Albedo/Night.html (accessed June 24, 2007)

Lawrence Berkeley National Laboratory. Heat Island Group. 1999. http://eetd.lbl.gov/HeatIsland/Pavements/Overview/Pavements99–03.html.

Lippiatt, Barbara C. 2007. *BEES 4.0 Building for Environmental and Economic Sustainability Technical Manual and User Guide.* Gaithersburg, MD: National Institute of Standards and Technology.

Maher, M., C. Marshall, F. Harrison, and K. Baumgaertner. 2005. *Context Sensitive Roadway Surfacing Selection Guide.* Lakewood, CO: Federal Highway Administration, Central Federal Lands Highway Division.

National Asphalt Pavement Association (NAPA). http://www.hotmix.org/ (accessed May 8, 2006)

National Asphalt Pavement Association (NAPA). 2004. *Porous Asphalt Pavements, Design Construction and Maintenance Guide.* Lanham, MD:National Asphalt Pavement Association.

National Institute for Occupational Safety and Health (NIOSH). 2000, December. *Hazard Review: Health Effects of Occupational Exposure to Asphalt, Publication no. 2001–110.*

National Institute for Occupational Safety and Health (NIOSH). 2001. "NIOSH Health Hazard Evaluation Report: Crumb-Rubber Modified Asphalt Paving: Occupational Exposures and Acute Health Effects." HETA # 2001–0536–2864.

National Institute of Standards and Technology (NIST). *BEES 4.0: Building for Environmental and Economic Sustainability.* http://www.bfrl.nist.gov.

Newcomb, Dave. 2005. "Warm Mix: The Wave of the Future?" *Hot Mix Asphalt Technology* July/August: 33–36.

New York City Department of Design and Construction (NYC DDC) and Design Trust for Public Space (DTPS). 2005. *High Performance Infrastructure Guidelines: Best Practices for the Public Right-of-Way.* New York: New York City Department of Design and Construction and Design Trust for Public Space.

Pomerantz, M., B. Pon, H. Akbari and S. Change. 2000 "The Effect of Pavements' Temperatures on Air Temperatures in Large Cities." Report No. LBNL-43442. Berkeley: Lawrence Berkeley National Labratory. <http://eetd.lbl.gov/HeatIsland/PUBS/2000/43442rep.pdf>.

Recycled Materials Resource Center (RMRC). http://www.rmrc.unh.edu/Partners/UserGuide/index.htm.

Spiegel, Ross and Meadows, D. 2006. *Green Building Materials.* Hoboken, NJ: John Wiley & Sons.

Transportation Research Board. 2001. "Perpetual Bituminous Pavements.". Transportation Research Circular No. 503. Washington, DC: Transportation Research Board, National Research Council.

Turner Fairbank Highway Research Center (TFHRC). 2004. *User Guidelines for Waste and By-product Materials in Pavement Construction.* McLean, VA: Turner Fairbank Highway Research Center, Federal Highway Administration. http://www.tfhrc.gov/hnr20/recycle/waste/begin.htm.

U.S. Environmental Protection Agency (EPA). 1999, September. "Stormwater Technology Fact Sheet." EPA 832-F-99–023.

U.S. Environmental Protection Agency (EPA). 2000, December. "Hot Mix Asphalt Plants Emission Assessment Report." Report EPA-454/R-00–019. http://www.epa.gov/ttn/chief/ap42/ch11/related/ea-report.pdf.

U.S. Environmental Protection Agency (EPA). 2005. *Cool Pavement Report. EPA Cool Pavements Study Task 5, Draft Report.* Prepared for U.S. EPA Heat Island Reduction Initiative. Prepared by Cambridge Systematics.

U.S. Environmental Protection Agency (EPA). 2007, April. "Inventory of U.S. Greenhouse Gas Emissions and Sinks, 1990–2005." Report EPA 430-R-07–002.

U.S. Environmental Protection Agency (EPA). "Heat Island Effect." http://www.epa.gov/heatisland/ (accessed June 6, 2006).

U.S. Green Building Council (USGBC). 2005. *LEED-NC for New Construction Reference Guide, Version 2.2.* 1st ed. Washington, DC: USGBC.

Washington Asphalt Pavement Association (WAPA). 2002. "WAPA Asphalt Pavement Guide." http://www.asphaltwa. com/wapa_web/modules/06_structural_design/06_perpetual.htm.

Wisconsin Department of Transportation (WIDOT). 2003. "Pavement Preventive Maintenance." *Transportation Synthesis Report,* prepared for Bureau of Highway Operations by CTC & Associates, WisDOT RD&T Program. Madison: Wisconsin Department of Transportation.

Figures CP1–CP3 Wenk Associates used a process of "selective subtraction" to reveal structures from an abandoned 1930s wastewater treatment plant in Denver's Northside Park. They estimate that reuse of the existing structures for new peristyles, loggia, and sculptural elements reduced demolition costs by 30%. (Photos from Wenk Associates, Inc.)

Figures CP4–CP5 Concrete panels cut and removed from exterior building walls in a remodel were reused as site walls by artist Linda Weisong and Greenworks. The concrete panels define spaces in the landscape, reference the history of the building, and reduce waste materials from the remodel. Holes cut in the concrete panels focus views. (Photo from Greenworks, PC)

Figure CP6 At the Olympic Sculpture Garden in Seattle, Weiss/Manfredi reclaimed granite curbs from nearby sites and positioned them as ascending stairs from the park's valley district to the major Z-shaped path. (Weiss/Manfredi).

Figure CP7 Mithun upended a salvaged concrete pipe for a cistern to catch roof runoff at Islandwood's Learning Studio on Bainbridge Island, Washington. The project earned a Gold LEED Rating. (Photo copyright Mithun, from Roger Williams)

Figure CP8 In keeping with the site's history as an industrial facility of Union Oil of California, concrete walls and structures at the Olympic Sculpture Park contain fly ash, an industrial by-product of coal combustion. (Photo from Paul Warchol)

Figure CP9 Throughout the park, fly ash was used in both cast-in-place concrete and pre-cast concrete. (Photo from Bruce C. Moore)

Figure CP10 Concrete with 70% ground granulated blast furnace slag substituted for portland cement is used by EHDD Architecture for concrete pavement and the rainwater sluice, making sustainability part of the learning landscape at the LEED Platinum Chartwell School in Seaside, California. (Photo by Michael David Rose)

Figure CP11 This stabilized rammed earth wall designed by Arkin Tilt Architects at the Hidden Villa Youth Hostel and Camp in Los Altos Hills, California, incorporates tailings from a local gravel quarry, along with sand and portland cement. Different color sands, cements, and pigments create the look of strata. Volunteers directed by seasoned earth builder Herman Bojarsky collaborated to construct this thermal mass wall, located between the hostel dining room and kitchen. (Photo from Arkin Tilt Architects)

Figure CP-12 A series of sculptural soil cement drop structures with wetlands in between, designed by Wenk Associates in collaboration with civil engineers, transformed the heavily eroded Shop Creek drainage basin into a healthy and vibrant ecosystem. (Photo from Wenk Associates, Inc.)

Figure CP-13 Soil cement drop structures at Shop Creek, designed to allow access to the water, are constructed from a mix of on-site soil and cement. The native soil color of the structures helps to blend the sculptural structures within the natural landscape. (Photo from Wenk Associates, Inc.)

Figure CP-14 Bricks at Leger Wanaselja Architects Dwight Way remodel in Berkeley, California, were salvaged from a demolished building, cleaned of mortar, and sand set in a paving application. In keeping with the project's strong emphasis on reclaimed and recycled materials, the concrete work is 50% fly ash substituted for portland cement. The designers estimate that their use of 100 yards of fly ash concrete kept about 30,000 pounds of CO_2 out of the atmosphere.

Figure CP-15 Glass cullet can be used in both course and fine aggregate in asphalt pavement, and when used in the surface course, it can lend aesthetic qualities to the pavement installation. Feasibility of cullet use is dependent on a consistent supply. (Photo from the Cambridge Arts Council)

Figure CP-16 Local aggregate was used in this asphalt road in Zion National Park in Utah, saving fossil fuel use in transport and aesthetically blending the road into the landscape. (Photo from Dmitrii Zagorodnov)

Figure CP-17 Crushed oyster shell paving at the Confluence Project, commemorating the journey of Lewis and Clark, by Maya Lin and Greenworks was obtained from nearby Oysterville, Washington, the Pacific Northwest hub of oyster production. This reused material from a local industrial waste product was crushed to a spec equivalent to one-quarter inch minus stone and installed four inches thick in the Totem Circle. (Photo from Greenworks, PC)

Figure CP-18 WRT specified concrete fines from a nearby demolished airport runway in place of natural decomposed granite paving at the Windsor, California, Town Green. (Photo from WRT Design)

Figure CP-19 Local Glen Rose limestone was used in structures designed by Robert Jackson & Michael McElhaney Architects at Westcave Preserve Environmental Learning Center. It is a stone that underlies most of the Texas hill country and has been used in structures there for hundreds of years. An owner of a local quarry donated dozens of large fossils that were embedded in the walls for "fossil hunts" for visiting schoolchildren. (Photo from Robert Jackson & Michael McElhaney Architects)

Figures CP-20–CP-22 The limestone wall at the Peggy Notebaert Nature Museum in Chicago was designed by Conservation Design Forum and Perkins + Will to represent nearby Kankakee River limestone cliffs. The locally obtained limestone saves transport energy expenditures and aesthetically references the native landscape. The wall is planted with native plants and irrigated from a roof scupper and an underground rainwater cistern. (Photos from Conservation Design Forum, www.cdfinc.com)

Figures CP-23–CP-24
At Hargreaves Associates Chrissy Field in San Francisco, stabilized aggregate paths cut across open fields, referencing alignments of historic runways, and skirt along the beach. The decomposed granite was chosen to blend seamlessly with the color of the sand beach at the water's edge and is stabilized with a nontoxic solution derived from plant by-product materials. The fill for the elevated "airfield" was obtained from excavation for the marsh. (Photos from Hargreaves Associates)

Figures CP-25 Over 2500 linear feet of "Stone" walls at the Steel Indian School Park in central Phoenix by Ten Eyck Landscape Architects, Inc. are constructed of broken concrete foundation slabs from demolished buildings of a former Indian School. The entry garden, pictured, is bound by the walls and a concrete cistern.

Figure CP-26 A viewing blind at Northside Park in Denver by Wenk Associates is constructed from reused pieces of "staplestone" from runways at Denver's decommissioned Stapleton Airport. (Photo from Wenk Associates, Inc.)

Figure CP-27 The wood columns and framing lumber for structures designed by Siegel & Strain Architects at the Angelo Reserve Science Center in Mendocino County, California, are milled from Douglas fir trees that fell on-site. They were milled and dried on-site, reducing transportation energy use. (Photo from Siegel & Strain Architects)

Figure CP-28 The entry columns and bench in this remodeled Bay Area home designed by Leger Wanaselja Architects are fashioned from two California oak trees on the property that died during the design phase. The owner had the trees milled and dried and then used the wood throughout the house. The concrete entry porch floor is 50% fly ash content. (Photo from Leger Wanaselja Architects)

Figure CP-29 Columns at the Islandwood Art Studio are fashioned from Douglas firs felled for solar meadows around buildings at the learning center. Other wood on the structures is local, FSC-certified sustainably harvested wood from Pacific Northwest forests. (Photo copyright Mithun, from Roger Williams)

Figure CP-30 Burned (but not charred) trees from the 1991 Oakland Hills fire were used as posts in a trellis carport structure designed by Leger Wanaselja Architects for a rebuilt home in the burn zone. Two sides of the posts are left in their rough, treelike state to reveal their history.

Figure CP31 Benches and backdrop at Sidwell Friends School in Washington, DC, overlooking the courtyard were constructed of red cedar reclaimed from old wine caskets. Greenheart decking was salvaged from well-preserved harbor pilings. The project earned a LEED Platinum rating (Photo from Andropogon Associates).

Figure CP32 A 100% recycled-content steel arbor at the Government Canyon State Natural Area Visitor's Center in Texas by Lake Flato Architects is left unfinished to weather naturally without use of potentially toxic metal coatings. (Photo from Lake Flato Architects)

Figures CP-33–CP-34 Three tons of reclaimed street signs were reused as fencing and railings at Leger Wanaselja's Dwight Way remodel in Berkeley. Refurbished car hatchbacks are also used as fencing. Reuse of reclaimed metal products whole saves substantial resources and emissions, as metal products are so energy and pollution intensive (Photo from Leger Wanaselja Architects).

Figures CP-35–CP-37 The undulating wall at Tanner Springs Park in Portland, constructed from reclaimed railroad rails, connects the current park site to its history. Atelier Dreiseitl and Greenworks intended the wall to represent the "skin" of the city being pulled back to expose the original wetland site prior to the railroad, industry, and the current mixed-use neighborhood. (Photo from Greenworks, PC

Figure CP-38] The entry to one of Leger Wanaselja's Adeline Street remodels in Berkeley incorporates reclaimed car hatchback awnings, a truck tailgate bench, and old water heaters from the building as roof rainwater cisterns. (Photo from Leger Wanaselja Architects)

Figure CP-40 At Boston's South Beach Boardwalk, Carol R. Johnson Associates used 100% recycled HDPE decking and a high recycled content composite lumber decking support structure. Use of plastic and composite lumber allows the boardwalk to get periodically wet without the decay risk of untreated wood. (Photo from Carol R. Johnson Associates)

Figure CP-39 These plastic rain barrels capture and hold roof runoff for reuse in Marcus de la Fleur's home garden. The containers are reclaimed soap barrels from a nearby carwash that have been painted. (Photo from Marcus de la Fleur)

chapter 9

Aggregates and Stone

Stone and aggregates can be low-impact building materials when quarried locally, selected carefully, minimally processed, and used appropriately to form durable structures. While natural stone resources are abundant in most regions, waste products from both post-consumer and post-industrial processes are increasingly substituted for natural aggregates, particularly in urban areas or regions distant from natural aggregates quarries. The use of recycled aggregates holds potential to go a long way toward addressing the growing waste crisis, as aggregates are pervasive materials in the construction of structural bases and backfill, and in concrete and asphalt.

Aggregates, natural or recycled, are an integral component of many sustainable site structures such as porous pavements, other storm water structures, gravel pavement surfacing, and structural soil. Aggregates are both a structural and drainage medium in porous pavements. Crushed stone, or even recycled aggregates, can be used as an alternative surfacing material to concrete or asphalt pavement for paths, parking areas, driveways, and even low-traffic roads. Local stone, or even broken concrete, can be used to construct dry stack walls, gabions, and sand-set stone or broken concrete can be used in paving. Without the use of mortar these materials can be reused multiple times in new structures or new applications after the useful life of the structure.

Most aggregates and stone products are quarried and used locally due to the high economic costs of transporting a heavy material. This also helps to limit the environmental costs of fuel use in transport. The exception to this is dimension stone, specified for its aesthetic qualities, durability, and solidity, which is often imported from places such as Italy, Turkey, China, or Mexico. Even stone that is quarried in the United States is sometimes shipped overseas for shaping and finishing, then shipped back for use in a U.S. project.

Throughout this chapter, the term *aggregates* is the generic term used to refer to hard granular materials in the size range of 0.2 mm to 20 mm, such as gravel, sand, and crushed stone as well as recycled materials. Where applicable, the specific type of aggregate will be identified. This chapter addresses aggregates used in all applications except as constituents in concrete, asphalt pavement mixes, or bricks, which are discussed in their respective chapters. Table 6–3 in chapter 6 defines gravel and soils according to the Unified Soil Classification System by ASTM D2487 "Standard Practice for Classification of Soils for Engineering Purposes" (2006).

AGGREGATE AND STONE USE

By weight, aggregates such as crushed stone, sand, gravel, and recycled materials are the most used building material in construction. They are the largest

235

Table 9–1 Natural Aggregate and Stone Products

Stone Materials	Quantity Harvested, Geographic Production, Types and Uses
Sand and gravel Naturally occurring sands and aggregates	In 2006, there were 1.28 billion tons of sand and gravel produced in the United States by 6,000 operations in 50 states. Sand and gravel operations are located in every state, with the majority—521 million tons (41%)—produced in the western United States. Forty-five percent of this was used as concrete aggregates, 22% for road base, coverings, and stabilization, 14% as construction fill, 12% for asphalt pavement, 2% for plaster and gunite sands, 1% for concrete products such as blocks, bricks, and pipes; and the remaining 4% for filtration, railroad ballast, roofing granules, snow and ice control, and other uses.
Crushed stone Crushed stone particles resulting from mechanical crushing and grading operations Crushed stone tends to be more angular than sand and gravel due to the crushing process. This creates greater interlock than many rounded sands and gravels.	In 2006, there were 1.67 billion tons of crushed stone harvested, 85% of which was used for construction purposes. There are 3,200 quarries and 85 underground mines. The majority of crushed stone is mined in open-pit facilities, with only 6% obtained from underground mines. Only five dredging operations produce crushed stone in the United States. Crushed stone is produced in every state except Delaware; however, the majority of crushed stone is produced in the more densely populated eastern United States. In 2006, 70% was limestone, 16% granite, 8% traprock, and the remaining 6% was sandstone, quartzite, marble, and other stones.
Expanded shale, clay, and slate (ESCS) Manufactured substitutes for crushed stone, sand, and gravel are sintered or expanded shale, clay, or slate.	These strong yet lightweight aggregates are produced by firing lumps of clay, shale, or slate at high temperatures in a kiln. Air pockets in the material are formed by hot gases expanding the material to nearly two times its original size. The ceramic material is then crushed, resulting in hard, porous particles with rough surfaces. Use of ESCS in porous paving applications can add an additional 10% water storage capacity to the gravel reservoir since the particles are so porous. ESCS is primarily used as a lightweight aggregate in large concrete structures such as bridges and tall buildings (to reduce weight) and in horticultural planting media, as it possesses good aerating and water- and nutrient-holding capabilities. The high firing temperatures of ESCS mean that the embodied energy of this type of aggregate is relatively high, yet some energy use may be offset by its lighter weight in transport.
Dimension stone Defined by the USGS as natural rock material that is quarried for the purpose of obtaining blocks or slabs that meet specifications by size and shape	Approximately 1.5 million tons of dimension stone was produced in 34 states in the United States in 2006 at an estimated value of $275 million. The United States is the world's largest market for dimension stone, so imported stone is a much larger segment of the market with a value of $2.5 billion, an increase of 15% over 2005. Stone was imported from Italy (25%), Turkey (20%), China (9%), and Mexico (9%), incurring substantial environmental and energy costs in transportation. By weight, stone produced was limestone (38%), granite (27%), marble (14%), sandstone (13%), and others (8%).

Sources: Ferguson 2005; USGS 2007b, 2007c, 2007d

component of concrete and asphalt, and they are used for base or fill material for structures, for setting beds for paving units, as the key structural component in porous pavements and structural soil, and in gravel pavements. An estimate of aggregate use found that the average 1,500 square-foot new home used 114 tons of aggregate and if that home's proportional share of new streets, sidewalks, schools, municipal projects, and shopping centers was included, total aggregate use per home increases to approximately 328 tons (U.S. EPA 1995).

Consumption of natural aggregates in the United States reached the highest level ever in 2006, totaling 2.9 billion metric tons (U.S. Geological Survey 2007b). The U.S. Geological Survey (USGS) collects data yearly from crushed stone, dimension stone, and sand and gravel producers, and it is summarized in Table 9–1.

Environmental and Human Health Impacts of Natural Stone and Aggregates

Stone is one of the most accessible and abundant natural resources of the earth. The USGS estimates that stone resources worldwide are abundant; however, stone supplies are limited in some geographic areas and metropolitan regions.

Of concern to the stone industry are increasing environmental and land use regulations that prohibit quarries and dredging operations near many metropolitan areas or riparian ecosystems. Sand and gravel operations are usually associated with river channels, river floodplains, and offshore or glacial deposits, all of which may have environmental restrictions placed on them prohibiting dredging and excavation of sand and gravel. Thus, new quarries and acquisition sites are expected to locate greater distances from metropolitan areas.

This shortage has resulted in the transportation of natural aggregates across increasingly greater distances, incurring substantial energy and economic costs. As fuel prices increase, use of recycled aggregates is becoming financially desirable. And supplies of recycled aggregates, primarily from portland cement concrete and asphalt concrete, are highest in metropolitan areas due to

a combination of high construction and demolition (C&D) activity and a growing lack of landfill space.

The primary environmental stressors of stone and natural aggregates are related to habitat alteration and generation of waste. And while impacts of energy use and toxic emissions from stone processing are minimal compared to concrete and metals, mining and stone finishing operations can substantially affect ecosystems on and around quarry and fabrication sites. Large quantities of waste result from quarrying operations.

On the whole, the mining industry is one of the least regulated of any industry. Consequently, some quarry sites are abandoned with huge waste piles, little control of disposal of toxic wastes, and minimal attempts to restore the site's pre-mining habitat. Most mining and beneficiation wastes are categorized by the EPA as "special wastes" and were exempted by the Mining Waste Exclusion from federal hazardous waste regulations under Subtitle C of the Resource Conservation and Recovery Act (RCRA).

MATERIALS ACQUISITION: MINING AND EXTRACTION

The greatest environmental impacts from stone and aggregate materials occur during the materials acquisition phase. Sources of mineral aggregates are rock quarries, alluvial gravel deposits, and surface formations such as broken rock or caliche. Minerals extraction for stone products and aggregates occurs either by open-pit or surface mining or underground mining. Currently over 90% of stone is mined in surface quarries; however, underground mining, though more expensive, is increasing due to extraction efficiencies and increasingly stringent environmental regulations in some areas.

Surface mining incurs impacts to the habitat in and around the quarry site. Vegetation and soil and rock overburden are removed to expose the stone deposits underneath, resulting in a loss of habitat in the mine area. Habitats around the mine are affected by soil erosion, increased turbidity, and other impacts to surrounding waterways. Efforts to restore habitats on closed quarry sites are inconsistent and not always well regulated or enforced. Also, some mining companies go out of business, leaving quarry and waste pile sites unrestored.

Waste

Surface mining generates large quantities of waste, as overburden removal can be substantial and inferior stone materials are encountered in the first layers of stone. Overburden waste can be particularly substantial for dimension stone extraction since high-quality rock can start tens, even hundreds, of feet below the surface. Some inferior materials encountered when quarrying dimension stone can be sold for crushed stone aggregate; however, other tailings, often in great amounts, are left at the quarry and sometimes used to fill in old quarry sites. Some waste from quarrying operations can contain minerals that react with air and water to produce metal ions that can contaminate nearby water bodies.

Quarrying of stone can generate waste during excavation and fabrication processes. Some estimates state that 45%–80% of granite and 15%–20% of limestone will be wasted—this does not include overburden waste (Demkin 1998b). This discarded stone can be a potential source of material for applications that don't require as uniform a size or appearance, such as landscape walls. This can often be purchased directly from the quarry at minimal cost, with transportation the major expense (Bruce Ferguson, personal communication, September 9, 2007).

Sand and gravel quarrying tend to require less overburden removal, as sand and gravel deposits are often associated with waterways; however those sensitive ecosystems can be negatively impacted by mining and dredging operations.

Underground mining, which involves sinking a shaft through overburden to reach a good stone deposit, tends to incur fewer environmental and habitat impacts to the quarry site since surface disturbance is kept to a minimum. Tailings are often left inside the mine, decreasing waste brought to the surface. Limestone mining is increasingly done underground as equipment technologies have improved yield and reduced costs, and mining can be performed year-round (U.S. EPA 1995).

In addition to solid mine spoils and tailings, waste from mining and processing includes dusts from ex-

Figure 9–1.
A virgin aggregate quarry at the Luck Stone Aggregate Plant in Fairfax, Virginia. (Photo from FHWA 2004a)

Table 9–2 Waste Materials from Quarrying and Processing Operations

Primary	Subprocesses	Air Emissions	Process Waste Water	Other Waste Generated
Minerals extraction	Loading, conveying, off-road haulage, unloading	Particulates, exhaust from vehicles and machinery	Surface runoff, groundwater seepage	Overburden (e.g., soil, rock)
Minerals transportation	Loading, conveying, off-road haulage, unloading	Particulates, exhaust from vehicles and machinery	Water for transportation of ore to process plant	
Minerals processing	Crushing, grinding, screening, washing, drying, calcining, floating	Particulates, exhaust from machinery	Transport water, ore and product wash water, dust suppression water, classification water, heavy media separation water, flotation water, solution water, air emissions control equipment water, equipment and floor washdown water	Tailings

Source: U.S. EPA 1995

traction, cleaning, screening, cutting, and crushing materials into appropriate sizes. It is estimated that an average of 0.1 lb. of dust emissions is released for every ton of stone processed (Demkin 1998c). While these emissions are largely nontoxic, their small size can pose a risk to workers, as they can enter the lungs and are not easily removed. Airborne dust particulates can also enter surface waters, degrading water quality.

Air emissions result from fuel use for drilling, blasting, sawing, and cutting; however, these are substantially less than materials such as cement and metals (see Table 9–2). Correspondingly, energy use is also less. It is estimated that 150 MJ are used to produce 1,000 kg of aggregate and 100 MJ are used to produce 1,000 kg of sand. Table 9–3 below illustrates embodied energy and embodied carbon for common stone products.

Table 9–3 Embodied Energy and Embodied Carbon of Aggregate and Stone Products

Product	Embodied Energy (MJ/metric ton)	Embodied Carbon (kg CO_2/metric ton)
Aggregate[a]	150	8
Granular base (50/50 fine and coarse aggregate)[b]	90	7.2
Stone/gravel chippings[a]	300	16
Local granite[a]	5,900	317
Imported granite[a]	13,900	747
Limestone[a]	240	12
Sand[a]	100	5.3

[a]Hammond and Jones, 2006. Data is for United Kingdom stone and aggregates, used in the UK. Values are assumed to be similar to North American figures; however, in this study the imported granite is from Australia.

[b]Athena Sustainable Materials Institute 2006.

Mine Reclamation

Mine reclamation and restoration efforts vary widely by quarry and local regulations. Some restoration attempts are made with varying degrees of success depending on local and state regulations. The National Stone, Sand and Gravel Association recognizes this problem and is taking steps to educate quarrying companies and the public about quarry restoration techniques (NSSGA).

STONE PROCESSING

Processing, also called beneficiation, of stone products can incur environmental and human health impacts, the greatest of which are the production of large amounts of wastes and the potential for these wastes to contaminate surrounding environments and water resources.

To produce aggregates, stone and gravel are mechanically crushed and/or ground to reduce the size of rock fragments and to produce angular particles. Then the fragments are screened. Washing of gravel is sometimes performed to remove unwanted material. This can use substantial amounts of water and result in processing sludge (U.S. EPA 1995).

Processes used to remove mineral impurities can also contaminate nearby waterways. Flotation, a wet method, involves placing minerals in an acidic or basic bath of chemicals such as sulfuric acid, ammonia, and hydrofluoric acid. Wastewater from these processes can pose toxic impacts to surrounding environments.

Tailings, solid waste resulting from processing operations, can contain minerals that react with air and water to produce metal ions that can contaminate nearby water resources. In addition, acid runoff and windblown dust from large waste piles can pose risks of adverse health effects, and degradation of water and land resources. Large water impounds of processing wastes can be unstable, posing additional risks.

Mining and processing of aggregates, particularly the commonly used silica sand, release particulates into the air that can cause eye and respiratory tract irritations, or even more severe conditions, in humans. Crystalline silica, commonly called silica dust, is an extremely prevalent compound associated with gravel, sand, and stone quarrying and processing. It can lead to the development of silicosis, and in extreme exposures to lung cancer, pulmonary tuberculosis, and airway diseases in mining, processing, and construction workers (National Institute for Occupational Safety and Health [NIOSH] 2002).

Impacts from processing dimension stone are different from aggregate processing. Excavated rock is sawed to the desired size. Water, sometimes large amounts, is used to cool the saws. Particulates and dust are carried away in the water. Natural and synthetic abrasives are used to finish the stone. Natural abrasives include iron oxide, silica, garnet, and diamond dust. Synthetic abrasives include silicon carbide, boron carbide, and fused alumina. These abrasives can pose health risks to workers from inhalation if protective measures are not employed (U.S. EPA 2004).

Acid washes are used to finish some stone such as limestone and marble. While acids vary, in the United States hydrochloric acid is primarily used (Chacon 1999). Hydrochloric acid, both the mist and solution, can have a corrosive effect on human tissue with the potential to damage respiratory organs, skin, eyes, and intestines (U.S. EPA n.d.) (see Table 9–4).

TRANSPORTATION IMPACTS

The environmental impacts of transporting heavy and bulky stone and aggregates can be significant. The majority of all U.S. extracted stone products are transported by truck, a far less fuel-efficient and high-polluting form of transport than train transport. About 82% of operations report that they transport their materials from the quarry to the processing plant, and then to the distributor, by truck. The remainder is transported by rail or waterway. In 2005, quarries reported that a significant amount, 13.2% of sand and gravel and 6.1% of crushed stone, was used at or near the production site, most likely for cement or asphalt production (USGS 2007b).

Many quarries have facilities for crushing, screening, and grading crushed stone, gravel, and sand near the quarry. Dimension stone fabricating plants are also located near or on quarry sites. This saves the costs of transporting material that will be trimmed off as waste, and also saves energy.

By value, 90% of dimension stone used in the United States is imported from locations all over the

Table 9–4 Potential Pollution during Stone Processing

Stone Product	Potential Pollution
Granite	Dust containing silica can impact worker health and air quality.
	Abrasives for worked stone can pose worker health risks.
	Tailings, solid waste resulting from processing operations, can contain minerals that react with air and water to produce metal ions that can contaminate nearby water resources.
Limestone	Dust containing lime but no silica
	Abrasives for worked stone can pose worker health risks.
	Hydrochloric acid washes can impact workers and ecosystems.
	Tailings, solid waste resulting from processing operations, can contain minerals that react with air and water to produce metal ions that can contaminate nearby water resources.
Sandstone	Dust containing silica can impact worker health and air quality.
	Tailings, solid waste resulting from processing operations, can contain minerals that react with air and water to produce metal ions that can contaminate nearby water resources.
Slate	Dust containing silica can impact worker health and air quality.
Sand	Processes used to remove mineral impurities can also contaminate nearby waterways.
	Dust containing silica can impact worker health and air quality.

Sources: Chacon 1999; NIOSH 2002; U.S. EPA 1995, 2004, n.d.

world. While transport to the United States is by ship, once within the country, the stone is transported primarily by truck and to a lesser degree by rail. It is not unusual for stone to be extracted in the United States and shipped to Italy to be cut and finished, then shipped back for use in the United States.

Use of local or on-site materials for aggregate can minimize fuel use costs, resource consumption, and emissions. One New England study found that the cost of transporting a truckload of aggregates 56 km exceeded the cost of the aggregate materials (Willburn and Goonan 1998). This single fact alone explains the increasing use of certain C&D wastes and industrial byproducts as natural aggregate substitutes, as sources of these materials are more likely to be found near urbanized areas. Refer to chapter 2 for energy use and emissions resulting from transportation of heavy materials.

IMPACTS IN CONSTRUCTION AND USE

Stone and aggregates pose minimal potential environmental and human health impacts during the construction and use phases. Silica dust from sand can cause silicosis in construction workers, and airborne dust and particles from gravel dumping can also be an inhalation hazard.

In the use phase, aggregates in exposed gravel applications can pose some impacts. Poorly graded or compacted materials or materials improperly selected for their application can be highly susceptible to erosion, leading to sediment loading of waterways, reduced water quality, and impacts on aquatic species. Buffer zones between the paved area and bodies of water along with proper maintenance or use of stabilizers can control this problem, although leaching or runoff of some stabilizers can affect water quality as well. See the gravel paving stabilizers table (Table 9–13) for information on these risks.

Plant quality can be impacted by dust generated from untreated gravel surfaces. The dust can cover the leaves, reducing the amount of sunlight that is received by the plant. Studies of cropland adjacent to gravel roads have shown that dust can result in reduced crop output. Dust from gravel surfaces can also have a long-term impact on air quality (Maher et al. 2005). Specifying aggregate materials that have been sorted to eliminate fine particles will help to minimize dust. Dust suppression products can be used to minimize these problems; however, some can affect water quality.

Some recycled materials substituted for natural aggregates can pose environmental and human health risks. These risks are discussed by material in the next section. Testing of recycled aggregates should be performed either by the supplier or, if not, by the contractor or the specifier, to determine the type and quantity of any hazardous constituents. Recycled materials and aggregates that will be encapsulated in concrete are less likely to off-gas or leach than are those used in base applications. Special consideration should be given to the toxic risks of recycled aggregate used in porous pavement and drainage situations, as water will constantly pass through it with greater potential for leaching.

Aggregates from Recycled Materials and Industrial By-products

Pre- and post-consumer recycled materials and industrial by-products are increasingly substituted for crushed stone, sand, and gravel in a wide variety of applications. Reclaimed portland cement concrete (PCC), reclaimed asphalt concrete (RAC), and iron and steel slags are the most common recycled substitutes for natural aggregates. Other recycled materials and by-products are foundry sand, glass cullet, crushed bricks, quarry by-products, scrap tires, and mineral processing wastes. Substituting recycled materials for virgin aggregate provides the dual benefits of reduced resource use and associated mining impacts, and the diversion of waste materials from the landfill. The following section will discuss recycled aggregates for use in base, fill, and other engineering applications. For discussion on the use of these recycled materials as aggregates in concrete and asphalt, refer to chapters 5 and 8.

Many road-building agencies are turning to use of recycled aggregates for a percentage of their base and fill materials needs. Use of recycled materials for aggregate saves them money on both material disposal and new construction costs. The California Integrated Waste Management Board estimates that cost savings can range from $3 to $10 per ton, and up to $53,000 per lane mile (CIWMB). An even greater savings can result from bringing removal, crushing, and grinding equipment to the job site and recycling the material on-site.

Percentages of recycled aggregates allowed in standard DOT specs vary widely, but on the whole, allowable percentages are increasing as more pavements with recycled aggregates are in place and performing well. California Department of Transportation (Caltrans) standard specification allows up to 50% recycled aggregate for Class 1 road bases and 100% of reclaimed asphalt concrete, portland cement concrete, or glass for Class 2, and 3 subbases (Caltrans 2007).

With use of any new aggregate, testing is necessary to account for variations in the aggregate's properties. For example, some recycled concrete aggregates may be contaminated with sulfate from contact with sulfate-rich soil or chloride ions from marine exposure (PATH).

Sources of recycled materials for use in aggregate applications vary widely by region and over time. Many urban areas have seen rapid growth in the recycled aggregate industry due to a combination of sand and gravel quarries locating farther from metropolitan areas because of land costs and environmental regulations, and growing C&D and post-industrial waste due to limited landfill space in these regions. Conversely, the recycled aggregate market in rural areas can be virtually nonexistent due to the relatively low cost of virgin aggregates and landfill space.

Perhaps the most limiting factor in use of recycled aggregate materials is the need for a consistent supply and quality. Markets change and shift due to a number of factors, meaning that specifiers may opt to use a natural aggregate with known performance over a recycled aggregate that may not be currently available or may be variable in quality.

Construction and demolition (C&D) waste sources Supplies of natural aggregate substitutes, primarily portland cement concrete and asphalt concrete, are plentiful in major cities with a lot of construction activity. In some of these areas the flow of waste concrete and asphalt to the landfill has been virtually stopped by recycling (Willburn and Goonan 1998). Some asphalt pavement is milled and relaid as base material or new asphalt in place; however, most recycled C&D material is broken and recovered; transported to a collection

Table 9–5 Benefits and Limitations of Recycled Aggregates

Benefits of Recycled Aggregates
Reduces use of nonrenewable resources
Reduces habitat impacts from quarrying natural aggregates
Reduces pressure on landfills
Can reduce transportation costs and impacts if regionally available
Can offer cost savings over natural aggregates
Decreases the embodied energy of pavements and aggregate applications
Can improve aggregate installation and/or pavement strength and durability
Strengthens the market for recycled-material technologies

Potential Limitations of Recycled Aggregates
Supplies may be limited or inconsistent in some regions.
Quality assurance and quality control (QAQC) can be challenging to implement; quality can vary widely.
Impurities in recycled materials can result in reduced stability, strength, and durability of mix.
Inconsistent qualities of recycled materials can require quality control testing.
Some reclaimed materials or industrial by-products may contain contaminants such as heavy metals or high lime contents that can pose hazards to the environment around the installation.
Leaching of pollutants, toxins, heavy metals, and/or alkaline into soils and groundwater can occur. Where this is a concern, mechanistic leaching tests should be performed.
Some materials may result in more dust generation than natural aggregates and may pose hazards to workers or vegetation around the site.

Sources: Eighmy and Holtz 2000; Federal Highway Administration [FHWA] 2004a; Partnership for Advancing Technology in Housing [PATH]; Turner Fairbank Highway Research Center [TFHRC]

point; processed by crushing, screening, and separating; and then sold for use as aggregate. If the material will be reused in on-site applications, processing can be accomplished using mobile crushing and grading plants. This will save transportation costs and impacts.

Some natural aggregate producers also produce and supply recycled aggregates recovered from C&D debris using their crushing, grading, and cleaning equipment to recycle these recovered materials into new aggregate for construction. Cement concrete is primarily recycled at these facilities, while asphalt is primarily recycled at construction sites. While sand and gravel producers and crushed stone producers only process and sell a small fraction of the total amount of cement concrete and asphalt recycled for aggregate, they recycled 5.65 million tons of asphalt and 8.5 million tons of cement concrete in 2005. A majority of the concrete processed and sold

by natural aggregate producers was recycled in Illinois and California, and Florida and California facilities recycled the most asphalt (USGS 2007b).

Industrial by-product sources Recycled industrial by-product sources are most often place specific as well. For instance, slag is most available in regions with iron and steel manufacturing, and is not cost effective to truck long distances for use as aggregate.

Post-consumer waste sources Supplies of post-consumer recycled products such as tires and waste glass are variable by location and time. And if a supply is not consistent, distributors will not process, crush, and grade the material, so it is challenging to meet exact specifications. For glass, recycling policies and procedures can change, leaving an industry without a consistent supply of material; then the price of the recycled material may not be competitive with natural aggregates. While waste tires exist everywhere there are cars, landfill fees may not be high enough in some regions to warrant tire-recycling operations.

RECLAIMED CONCRETE

Reclaimed concrete aggregate (RCA) is the most commonly used recycled material for the base or subbase of pavement structures. To a lesser degree, it is also used as both coarse and fine aggregate in new concrete structures. A Federal Highway Administration study in 2004 found that 38 state transportation agencies use some percentage of recycled concrete for aggregates (FHWA 2004a). The highest consumers were Texas, Virginia, Michigan, Minnesota, Utah, and California.

Sources of RCA are abundant, particularly in urban areas. Recycling concrete structures on-site is the most energy-efficient and cost-effective use of reclaimed concrete aggregate, as transportation is virtually eliminated. Stone-crushing equipment can be brought to the site

with recently developed measures to reduce noise and dust. The procedure for on-site concrete recycling involves the following: 1) breaking and removing the old concrete; 2) crushing in primary and secondary crushers; 3) removal of reinforcing steel, wire mesh, and other embedded items; 4) grading and washing; and 5) stockpiling the resulting coarse and fine aggregates. During this process, care should be taken to avoid contamination of the aggregate with dirt, gypsum board, asphalt, wood, and other foreign materials (PATH).

If there are no concrete structures being removed from the project site, precrushed concrete can be obtained from widespread concrete recycling centers, often for a nominal price. The real cost of this aggregate is in the transportation from the recycling source to the construction site; however, sources of recycled concrete and concrete-crushing facilities are increasingly more local than virgin aggregate mining sites (FHWA 2004a).

As landfill tipping fees increase, concrete, being a relatively heavy and expensive material to landfill, will become ever more economically feasible to use as aggregate in concrete mixes or base material. Some

Table 9–6 Recycled Aggregates and Their Potential Applications

	Granular Base	Embankment or Fill	Stabilized Base	Stabilized Base, Cementitious	Flowable Fill
Reclaimed concrete	x	x			
Reclaimed asphalt pavement	x	x			
Blast furnace slag	x				
Steel slag	x				
Waste glass	x				
Crushed brick	x	x			
Scrap tires		x			
Foundry sand	x				x
Mineral processing wastes	x	x			
Quarry fines	x				x
Municipal solid waste ash	x				
Coal boiler slag	x		x		
Nonferrous slags	x	x			
Coal bottom ash			x		
Combustor ash	x				

Source: Adapted from TFHRC

Figure 9–2.
Graded recycled concrete aggregate at the Luck Stone Aggregate Plant. It is increasingly common for aggregate plants to recycle concrete, as they have the crushing and grading facilities in place. (Photo from FHWA 2004a)

state DOTs recycle all concrete debris for this reason (FHWA 2004a).

Another common source of RCA is fresh concrete that is returned to the originating concrete plant for reasons of oversupply or rejection. Some plants will allow it to cure, then crush it and reuse it on other jobs (*Environmental Building News* 1993).

RECLAIMED ASPHALT

Reclaimed asphalt from roads, parking lots, and other asphalt concrete pavements is a substitute for natural aggregates, yet it is more commonly recycled into new asphalt concrete pavements. A 2001 report by the Asphalt Recycling and Reclaiming Association (ARRA) estimates that 80% of old asphalt is recycled, primarily in new asphalt paving and base applications. This results in huge cost savings, as much less new material must be purchased and fuel costs for processing and hauling the

Figure 9–3.
Portable crushing, grinding, and grading equipment can be brought to a demolition site to crush concrete slabs for reuse as aggregate base material in new site structures, saving cost and energy use of transport off-site. Dust and noise from crushing can be a negative aspect of this process. (Photo from HMH/RUBBLE MASTER Austria, www.rubblemaster.com)

Table 9–7 Benefits and Limitations of RCA in Base and Subbase Applications

Benefits of Using Recycled Concrete Aggregate (RCA)
The angularity of RCA can increase structural stability of the base, resulting in improved load-carrying capacity.
RCA can stabilize soft, wet soils, as it is more porous and absorptive than many virgin aggregates (New York City Department of Design and Construction and Design Trust for Public Space [NYC DDC and DTPS] 2005).
RCA aggregates generally have a lower fines content, so they are more permeable and drainage through the base is better than with conventional gravel.
RCA can save construction costs of $3 to $10 per ton or more. Greater cost savings can be achieved with the use of crushing equipment on-site.
Some re-cementing action can occur, as the recycled concrete is wet in the new application, lending additional strength to the base. The RCA should be in a saturated state as it is compacted to aid in migration of fines through the mix.

Potential Limitations of and Considerations for Using Recycled Concrete Aggregate (RCA)
RCA is not always available in standard graded mixes, so if it is to be used in an application, such as porous pavements, where gradation is critical, some additional grading may be required.
The compressive strength of recycled concrete aggregate is related to the compressive strength of the original concrete and the water-cement ratio of the new concrete.
Alkaline leachate can occur if free lime or unhydrated cement is present in the RCA. This could affect the pH of surrounding soil and water, potentially harming plants or aquatic organisms.
Leachates can clog pores or geotextiles adjacent to the installation.
Fugitive dust of crushed concrete can irritate workers' respiratory tracts, and it can also affect surrounding plants and waterways. Wetting the concrete during crushing and placement will minimize dust.
Re-cementing can be irregular and may not be desirable in some applications of aggregate.

Sources: NYC DDC and DTPS 2005; FHWA 2004a; PATH 2006

material from quarries and refineries to the asphalt plant are eliminated (ARRA 2001).

Sources of recycled asphalt pavement (RAP) are abundant, particularly in urban areas. RAP for use in base aggregate applications can be obtained on-site from a practice called full-depth reclamation (FDR). FDR removes and pulverizes asphalt and underlying base materials into a new stabilized base. Off-site sources of RAP for aggregate bases are hot-mix asphalt plants, asphalt recycling facilities, and RAP distributors.

Applications of RAP not recycled into new asphalt pavement are base, subbase, stabilized base, or fill materials. For granular bases and subbases, RAP is crushed, screened, and blended with conventional granular aggregate or reclaimed concrete. Blending RAP is necessary to attain bearing strengths for most unbound load-bearing applications. By itself, RAP may result in lower bearing capacities than conventional aggregates (TFHRC).

Stabilized bases using RAP can be achieved with the addition of a small amount of new asphalt binder or cementitious materials such as portland cement, lime, kiln dust, or fly ash (a waste material from coal combustion). Mechanical stabilization methods such as compacting may be used instead of binders. For new asphalt pavements, bases constructed from stabilized RAP can sometimes require only a very thin layer of hot-mix, chip seal, or slurry seal for a surface course.

The Portland Cement Association (PCA) estimates savings of FDR stabilized by portland cement for a mile of 24 foot-wide road base, six inches deep (see Table 9–8).

IRON AND STEEL SLAG

Ferrous slags are co-products of iron and steel production that can be used as coarse and fine aggregate in

Table 9–8 Comparison of Full-depth Reclamation and New Aggregate Base

	Full-depth Reclamation (FDR)	New Pavement Base
Number of trucks needed	12	180
New roadway material	330 metric tons	5,000 metric tons
Material landfilled	0 m³	2,100 m³
Diesel fuel consumed	1,900 liters	11,400 liters

Source: Adapted from PCA 2005

many applications. U.S. sales of iron and steel slags totaled 21.6 million metric tons in 2006, an increase of 8.8% from 2002. The estimated annual world production of blast furnace slag is about 200–240 million tons, and steel slag output is 115–180 million tons (USGS 2007a). Many slags are competitively priced with natural aggregates and can offer some performance advantages in certain applications.

The ASTM C125 "Definition of Terms Relating to Concrete" (2006) defines iron blast furnace slag as "the non-metallic product consisting essentially of silicates and alumino silicates of calcium and other bases that is developed in a molten condition simultaneously with iron in a blast furnace." Slag can be cooled in many ways to produce different types of slag products: air-cooled, granulated, and pelletized (or expanded) slag.

Air-cooled blast furnace slag (ACBFS), often just called "slag," is formed by allowing molten slag to cool slowly under ambient conditions. It can be crushed and

Table 9–9 Benefits and Limitations of RAP in Asphalt and Base Applications

Benefits of Recycled Asphalt Pavement (RAP)
RAP bases can allow use of less paving surface course material. For new asphalt pavements, bases constructed from RAP can sometimes require only a very thin layer of hot-mix, chip seal, or slurry seal for a surface course if they are stabilized with asphalt binders or are well compacted mechanically.
When properly crushed and screened, recycled asphalt pavement makes a very stable base or subbase, as the asphalt residue binds the aggregate together, resulting in a better bearing capacity over time.
RAP aggregates generally have a lower fines content, so they are more permeable and drainage through the base is better than conventional dense-graded gravel.

Potential Limitations of and Considerations for Using Recycled Asphalt Pavement (RAP)
Properties of RAP can vary widely according to properties of the reclaimed asphalt pavement and the repairs, patching, crack sealing, or surface layers that were applied. Testing of RAP should be performed in critical base applications.
RAP requires a higher moisture content in base placement than conventional aggregates.
Milling up, grinding, or pulverizing reclaimed asphalt may generate undesirable fines.
The adhesive qualities of the asphalt binder that make for a stable base may make placement and grading of the base challenging.
The base must be adequately compacted to avoid post-construction compacting, which could lead to pavement failure.
Asphalt cement can contain small amounts of polycyclic aromatic hydrocarbons that may leach into soil or water near the pavement application.

Sources: NYC DDC and DTPS 2005; PATH; TFHRC

screened for use as coarse aggregate in pavement bases, backfill, asphalt or concrete paving, and as feed in cement kilns. It is often less expensive than natural aggregates in iron- and steel-processing regions. ACBFS is hard and dense yet has a vesicular texture and weighs less than conventional aggregate. It crushes to more angular cubic shapes with a rougher texture and greater surface area than most natural aggregates; therefore it has a strong bond with portland cement and good interlock in base applications. Water absorption is low and it is resistant to abrasion and weathering (National Slag Association). The lower unit weight of ACBFS can reduce shipping costs and energy use. It is the most commonly used form of blast furnace slag, with 8.4 million tons sold in 2005.

Ground granulated blast furnace slag (GGBFS) is formed by quick water quenching of molten slag to form sand-size particles of glass with moderate hydraulic cementitious properties. The particles are ground and then over 90% are used as a portland cement substitute in concrete. In 2005, 4.5 million tons were sold.

Pelletized or expanded slag is cooled through a water jet that leads to rapid steam generation, which results in

a vesicular texture with very low density and light weight. Pelletized slags are primarily used for lightweight concrete aggregates but can be ground for a supplementary cementitious material.

Steel slag, a by-product of steel production, is also used in some aggregate applications yet has slightly different properties than blast furnace slags. Steel slag is used for aggregates in asphalt pavement, fill, and pavement bases, but it is prone to expansion, which prohibits use in concrete mixes or applications that will not tolerate some expansion. In 2005, 8.7 million tons were sold in the United States (USGS 2007a).

The long-term availability of air-cooled blast furnace slags is not assured, as the number of operating blast furnaces is declining, and improvements are being made in processing technologies. Also, older stockpiles of blast furnace slag are being depleted as their beneficial use increases. Steel slag supplies are expected to continue at or above present rates. The market for GGBFS is expected to grow because it offers valuable performance advantages for concrete; however, imports of GGBFS may grow since only a few operations in the United States use granulation cooling techniques (USGS 2007a) (see Table 9–10).

Table 9–10 Sales of Ferrous Slags in the United States by Use in 2005[a]

Use	Blast Furnace Slag[b]		Steel
	Air-cooled	Granulated	Steel slag[c]
Ready-mixed concrete	16.1	—	—
Concrete products	5.2	—	—
Asphaltic concrete	16.7	—	15.6
Road bases and surfaces	34.0	—	53.0
Fill	11.1	—	10.5
Cementitious material	—	90.5	—
Clinker raw material	4.4	—	6.9
Miscellaneous[d]	9.0	—	2.3
Other or unspecified	3.5	9.5	11.7

[a]Data contain a large component of estimates and are reliable to no more than two significant digits.
[b]Excludes expanded or pelletized slag: this material is generally sold as a lightweight aggregate.
[c]Steel slag use is based on the 77% of total tonnage sold in 2004 and the 100% of total tonnage sold in 2005 for which usage data were provided.
[d]Reported as used for railroad ballast, roofing, mineral wool, or soil conditioner.
Source: USGS 2007a

Waste Glass

Waste glass can be a coarse or fine aggregate substitute. Color-sorted crushed glass, called cullet, is most often marketed as a raw material for new glass container manufacture; however, this is limited by the high cost of collection and hand sorting. Other waste glass is commingled, crushed, and used as aggregate or in other applications.

Glass composed 5.2% of the total municipal solid waste stream by weight in 2005, but it was only 3% of the recovered materials stream. The EPA estimates that 2.76 million tons of glass were recycled in 2005 and 10 million tons were landfilled. This is a recycling rate of 21% (EPA 2006).

Consistent supplies of glass will determine the feasibility and cost of use. In some regions where natural aggregates are scarce, glass can be a cost-effective alternative. Glass aggregate used in surface applications can impart a variety of color qualities and some reflectance. Worker health and safety may be at risk with fine glass particles.

The quality of crushed glass can vary widely, possibly containing dirt, paper, and plastics. Gradations and sizes available vary widely by recycling facility. Some glass may need additional crushing and screening. Recycled asphalt pavement processing equipment has been used for this.

When waste glass is crushed to the size of sand, it exhibits properties of natural sand. Recycled glass is angular, compacts well, and yet is still quite permeable. It has almost no water absorption and is quite hard. It is easily flowable and placed. As aesthetics are not a concern in a base course, mixed-color cullet can be used (TFHRC).

Sources of recycled glass, primarily post-consumer glass bottles and post-industrial float glass cullet, vary widely across the country and may be abundant in some areas while scarce in others. Where consistent sources are available, use of glass cullet can be an economical and aesthetic replacement for natural sand or aggregates.

Glass has been incorporated into some municipal roadway specifications as aggregate for granular bases, fill, and asphalt. Glass has also been used as an aggregate in concrete; however, some glass can cause an expansive alkali-silica reaction (TFHRC).

Waste Tires

Of the 299 million scrap tires generated in 2005, an estimated 259 million, or 87%, were recovered for beneficial uses such as rubberized asphalt, fill, surfacing, or energy recovery. Over 49 million scrap tires were processed into crumb rubber for "civil engineering" applications in 2005 and an additional 37 million were used in ground rubber applications (Rubber Manufacturers Association 2006). Where available, they can be low-cost gravel, aggregate, and stone substitutes, lightweight fill, embankment material, base material, drainage layers for landfills, septic tank leach fields, rubberized asphalt pavement, playground surfacing, and mulch. Waste tires are processed into a variety of sizes and forms depending on the applications.

Tire shreds are four to eighteen inches long and four to nine inches wide with some exposure of steel belt fragments at the edges. *Tire chips* are produced in a secondary process resulting in half-inch to three-inch pieces (Maher et al. 2005). Both tire shreds and tire chips are used in lightweight fill applications and as subbases for pavements. They are usually wrapped in geotextiles for containment. They are primarily available from tire shredder operators.

A major benefit of using tire chips and shreds as a substitute for soil, gravel, and stone is their lower unit weight. The in-place weight of tire shreds is 45–58 pounds per cubic foot compared to 125 pounds per cubic foot for soil (Maher et al. 2005). This can substantially reduce transportation costs and increase ease of placement. The permeability of tire shred fill, 1.5 to 15 centimeters per second depending on the void ratio, equals that of clean gravel. The low compacted density combined with the free-draining character of tire shreds can result in increased stability for embankments or subbases built on weak soils, and reduced lateral pressures when used as backfill for retaining walls (Northeast Waste Management Officials' Association [NEWMOA] 2001).

Tire shreds and chips perform favorably as compared to gravel and granular soils with respect to thermal characteristics. In subgrade applications, tires can reduce the depth of penetration compared with that of granular soil (NEWMOA 2001).

Consolidation over time can be a concern with use of tire shreds and chips. They can typically compact between 10% and 15% of the height of the layer. The Northeast Waste Management Officials' Association recommends that a minimum of three feet of compacted soil should separate the tire shred installation and the base of any pavement above. Another way to deal with consolidation is to mix tire shreds, 40% by weight, and soil (NEWMOA 2001).

Ground rubber is waste tires chipped and ground with steel belt fragments removed by a magnetic separator. Synthetic fabric reinforcing remains. Ground rubber particles range in size from 19 mm down to 0.85 mm (No. 20 sieve). Ground rubber is used as an aggregate substitute in walkways, playground surfacing, equestrian areas, and mulch. Ground rubber particles are regularly shaped and cubical with a comparatively low surface area (Maher et al. 2005). They resist degradation and compaction, making them useful for porous applications and for playgrounds where impact absorption is important (Sorvig 2005).

Crumb rubber consists of particle sizes ranging from 4.75 mm (No. 4 sieve) to less than 0.075 mm (No. 200 sieve). Smaller particles in this range are used primarily as an asphalt modifier, while large particles are used as fine aggregate in asphalt pavement. This is discussed in greater detail in chapter 8.

Environmental and Human Health Concerns of Recycled Tire Use

Recycled tires can be nonreactive under normal environmental conditions. The principal chemical component of tires is a blend of natural and synthetic rubber. Additional components include carbon black, sulfur, polymers, oil, paraffins, pigments, fabrics, and bead or belt materials (Maher et al. 2005).

There are some environmental and human health concerns with use of tire shreds and chips. They can produce leachate exceeding secondary drinking water standards for iron and manganese. Field studies have documented release of low levels of a limited number of volatile organic compounds when placed below the water table, although the levels were below primary drinking water standards and there was limited downgradient migration of organic constituents. Above the water table, studies have shown negligible releases of organics (Transportation Research Board 1996).

Leaching of toxic chemicals is less of a concern for ground tires as steel reinforcing has been removed. However, ground tires should be washed to remove surface contaminants before processing.

In the nineties there were some problems with heating and smoldering of tire shreds in major fill applications, and it still can be a risk; however, the following design specifications can minimize the potential for heating (NEWMOA 2001):

- Limit the thickness of tire shred installations to ten feet.
- Use larger treads.
- Limit the presence of organic soil, fine rubber particles, and exposed steel belts.
- Limit access of the tire shred layer to air and water with a substantial layer of soil over the top.

Table 9–11 Constituents of Tires

Constituent	Passenger Tires	Truck Tires
Natural rubber	14%	27%
Synthetic rubber	27%	14%
Carbon black	28%	28%
Steel	14%–15%	14%–15%
Fabric, fillers, accelerators, antiozonants, etc.	16%–17%	16%–17%
Average weight, new	25 lb.	120 lb.
Average weight, scrap	20 lb.	100 lb.

Source: Rubber Manufacturers Association 2008

FOUNDRY SAND

Foundry sand is clean, uniformly sized, high-quality silica sand or lake sand that is used to form molds for both ferrous and nonferrous metal castings. The Foundry Institute estimates that metal casters use and reuse about 100 million tons of sand multiple times each year, with 10–15 million tons of spent sand available for other beneficial use. Typically it takes one ton of sand to produce each ton of iron or steel cast (TFHRC).

Foundry sand can accumulate metal debris and some mold and core material. It can also contain some leachable contaminants such as heavy metals and phenols that are absorbed by the sand during casting operations. The presence of heavy metals is of greater concern in sand from nonferrous metal foundries. Spent foundry sand from brass and bronze foundries may contain cadmium, lead, copper, nickel, and zinc (TFHRC). *Core sand* has been processed to remove fines and organic materials. *Green sand* has usually not been processed to remove fines and organic materials such as clay and dust. But most foundry sand is screened to separate oversized materials.

With about 85%–95% between 0.6 mm and 0.15 mm sieve sizes (No. 30 and No. 100), foundry sand is too fine for full substitution of fine aggregates. Foundry sand can be blended with other coarser fine aggregates. Foundry sand has low absorption and is nonplastic. Foundry sand is black, so if used in a surface application, it will be a different aesthetic than natural sand. Foundry sand can be obtained directly from foundries or from centralized distributors, most of which are located in midwestern states and Pennsylvania (FHWA 2004b).

CRUSHED BRICK AND CRUSHED VITRIFIED CLAY

Crushed brick and crushed vitrified clay are chipped, deformed, and rejected products from plants that produce brick or vitrified clay products. They can make quite a strong, inert, angular aggregate, yet they are not often available in graded masses; instead they may be sold as "crusher run." As sources of crushed brick are brick and vitrified clay manufacturers, this material is not available in all locations (TFHRC).

MINERAL PROCESSING WASTES

Mineral processing wastes are generated during the extraction and beneficiation of ores and minerals. As discussed in chapter 11, the mining and processing of mineral ores result in large quantities of wastes that can be reused in other applications and industries. In addition, there are substantial accumulations of mineral processing wastes from past years. Mineral processing wastes can be divided into the following categories:

Waste rock is produced in large quantities from surface mining operations such as open-pit copper, phosphate, uranium, iron, and taconite mines. It is also generated from underground mining to a much lesser extent. Waste rock is removed during mining operations with overburden. Waste rock is generated in a wide range of sizes from very large boulders to fine sand-size particles and dust. A wide range of types of rock are generated. Some waste rock may be suitable for use as granular base, flowable fill, and engineered fill or embankment. Some could also be used as coarse and fine aggregates in concrete or asphalt paving. Ore tailings are often trap rock or granite and perform very well as aggregate.

Mill tailings are mostly extremely fine particles, from sand-size down to silt-clay, that are rejected from grinding, screening, or processing the raw material. They are usually uniform in size and are angular with a high percentage of fines. Mill tailings are usually slurried, where they become partially dewatered. Coarse mill tailings may be suitable for use as granular base, flowable fill, and engineered fill or embankment. Some could also be used as coarse and fine aggregates in concrete or asphalt paving. Mill tailings of quartz, feldspars, carbonates, oxides, ferromagnesian minerals, magnetite, and pyrite have been used in the manufacture of bricks and as a source of pozzolanic material.

Coal refuse is rejected material that results from the preparation and washing of coal. The material is usually varying amounts of slate, shale, sandstone, siltstone, and clay minerals. Coal refuse ranges in size from 100 mm (four inches) to 2 mm (No. 10 sieve). Fine coal refuse is less than 2 mm and is usually in slurry form.

Seven hundred thousand short tons of coal refuse was recovered in 2006, primarily in coal-producing states (National Mining Association).

Large quantities of mineral processing wastes have been used in highway production, as they can be near the mines where the waste is created. The mining industry also makes use of their wastes to build mining roads, dikes, impoundments, and mine backfill. Yet this uses only a small percentage of the actual waste generated.

Some mineral processing wastes have limited use in aggregate applications because they have a high impurity content and could leach trace metals and/or generate acids that could contaminate the environment around the structure in which they are used.

The feasibility of using waste rock depends on its parent rock and the mineral waste processing operations. Waste rock should be tested before use as an aggregate. Some environmental concerns are acid leachate from sulfide-based metallic ores, low-level radiation from uranium host rock, or radon gas generation from uranium and phosphate rocks. Traces of cyanide used for leaching additional ore from rock may also contaminate waste rock. Mill tailings from gold mining can contain cyanide, and tailings from uranium processing may be radioactive. Both should not be used in aggregate applications. Coal refuse often contains some sulfur-bearing minerals such as pyrite and marcasite that could result in an acid leachate.

QUARRY BY-PRODUCTS

Quarry by-products result from blasting, crushing, washing, screening, and stockpiling crushed stone for aggregates. These by-products have various applications as coarse and fine aggregates in construction. A 1993 report estimated that 159 million metric tons of quarry by-products was generated yearly, primarily from crushed stone operations. As the total production of crushed stone, sand, and gravel was 1.1 billion metric tons in 1993, this is 14.5% of production (Tepordei 1993). There are three types of quarry by-products: screenings, pond fines, and baghouse fines. A large portion of quarry by-products are not used and most are disposed of at the quarry source; how-ever, they can have beneficial use in other applications (TFHRC).

Screenings are the finer fraction of crushed stone that accumulates after primary and secondary crushing and separation on a 4.75 mm (No. 4) sieve. The size distribution and particle shape vary by type of parent rock, crushing equipment, and type of quarry, but they are a damp, silty, sand-size material with an average 5%–10% moisture content. They range in particle size from 3.2 mm (1/8 inch) to finer than 0.075 mm (No. 200 sieve). Screenings are available at most quarries, especially limestone quarries. Screenings are used as a natural aggregate substitute in granular bases, concrete, flowable fill, and asphalt paving.

Settling pond fines result from the washing of crushed stone. They are the fines that settle to the bottom of the settling ponds. They are also sometimes called pond clay. They must be dewatered before they can be considered for use. A final moisture content of 20%–30% can be achieved. Pond fines are a fine-grained slurry with 90%–95% of the particles finer than 0.15 mm (No. 100 sieve) and 80% finer than 0.075 (No. 200 sieve). They can replace fines in flowable fill mixes.

Baghouse fines are captured dusts generated during crushing in dry quarry operations. They are a fine, dry powder (finer than 0.05, No. 270 sieve) that is used for mineral filler in asphalt paving or in flowable fill. Dry quarry operations are primarily located in the western states.

NONFERROUS SLAGS

Nonferrous slags are vitreous, air-cooled, granulated by-products of copper, nickel, and phosphorus processing. They can be substituted for natural aggregates in base and subbase applications (TFHRC).

MUNICIPAL SOLID WASTE COMBUSTOR BOTTOM ASH

Bottom ash, also called grate ash, is the ash fraction that remains on the grate at the completion of the municipal solid waste (MSW) incineration cycle. It is similar in appearance to porous, grayish, silty sand. It consists primarily of glass, ceramics, and ferrous and nonferrous metals and minerals. It also contains small amounts of unburned organic material (TFHRC).

MSW combustor ash has been used as a granular base material in Europe for two decades, but it is rarely used in the United States because standard practice of ash disposal does not separate bottom ash from other MSW combustor ashes, making it difficult to obtain. Bottom ash composes about 75%–80% of the combined ash stream.

In base applications, MSW bottom ash is screened to less than 25 to 38 mm and metal is removed. As with other types of ash, leaching of hazardous constituents can be a concern, and testing is recommended (TFHRC).

COAL BOILER SLAG AND COAL BOTTOM ASH

Coal boiler slag and coal bottom ash are the incombustible by-products collected from the bottom of furnaces that burn coal for the generation of steam. They are coarse, granular materials that can be used in a variety of applications, including as aggregate base material. The type of product produced, either coal boiler slag or coal bottom ash, depends on the type of furnace used to burn the coal.

Bottom ash is a dark gray material that is angular with a very porous surface texture. Particles range in size from a fine gravel to a very fine sand with small percentages of silt-clay-size particles. The ash is usually well graded, although it should be tested where gradation is critical. Boiler slags are predominantly single sized within a range of 5.0 to 0.5 mm (No. 4 to No. 40 sieve). They have a smooth surface texture, but if gas is trapped in the slag as it is quenched, it can become porous (TFHRC).

Bottom ash and boiler slags are composed primarily of silica, alumina, and iron, with small percentages of calcium, sulfates, magnesium, and other compounds. Their composition is determined by the source of coal. When used in base, backfill, or embankment applications, they can potentially corrode any metal structures that they contact.

Sources of bottom ash and boiler slags are ash marketing firms or local hauling contractors. Most electric utility companies do not sell the ash they produce, although as the ash is increasingly reused in beneficial applications, this may change.

Use of Stone, Aggregates, and Recycled Materials for Lower-impact Site Structures

Natural stone, aggregates, and recycled and reclaimed materials can be used to create lower-impact site structures than those resulting from the more commonly used asphalt, concrete, and concrete block. Site and roadway construction since World War II has taken the approach of highly engineered pavements and walls designed for rigidity, high traffic, extreme use (even when they will be lightly used), and ease of standardized construction and material specification. However, these materials use large amounts of resources and energy and release emissions and toxins during production. The resulting structures can produce negative environmental effects, such as increased storm water runoff with high concentrations of nonpoint source pollution, and contributions to the urban heat island effect.

Use of natural or recycled stone and aggregate structures, such as dry stack walls, gabion structures, gravel pavements, porous aggregate pavements, or gravel trench foundations, can minimize some of these impacts. They can be durable, reusable, permeable, and less resource- and energy-intensive alternatives to concrete, asphalt, and concrete block in appropriate applications.

When designing low-impact structures from stone, aggregates, or recycled materials, consideration should be given to appropriateness of intended use, durability of both the structure and the material used, use of local sources, and the reusability or recyclability of the materials after the useful life of the structure.

Specify Durable and Appropriate Materials
Durability of aggregates and dimension stone will ensure longevity of the installation. It is important to consider the environmental and use conditions to which the installation will be subjected. Granite, hard sandstone, hard limestone, and traprock make durable, abrasion-resistant aggregates. Granite, bluestone, and

sandstone are durable paving stones. Some stone, such as soft sandstone, may wear easily and will not be durable in high-traffic paving applications. Other stone, such as some limestone or marble, can be affected by water, causing it to crush or deteriorate. Limestone is also absorbent and will stain easily, so it is often not appropriate for cut stone pavements. Slate is subject to spalling from water penetration, which can freeze, expand, and loosen the stone layers.

Use Less Material

Stone structures should be designed in such a way as to not use unnecessary amounts of material. For instance, most dimension stone veneer for walls and stairs need not be more than 3/4" to two inches thick. Thicker veneer is often used on stair treads to impart a solid look to the stairs, but in parts of the structure where stone thicknesses are not visible, thickness of stone should be minimized.

Use of concrete wall spread footings extending below the frost line can use substantial amounts of material.

Use of wall structures such as segmental retaining blocks, dry-laid stone, or broken concrete that can accommodate minor movement may allow use of shallower gravel trench foundations in some applications.

Design for Disassembly

Structures made of stone or recycled materials, such as dry stack walls or sand-set stone paving, can theoretically be reused over and over again. If mortar is not used, disassembly and reuse of the materials is relatively simple. Where mortar is used, it is unlikely that it will be removed for reuse of the whole stone in another structure; however, the stone may be crushed and reused in an aggregate application. Stone or recycled concrete "stones," called urbanite, used in dry stack walls with minimal mortar may be reusable whole if mortar is held back from the face of the wall and used sparingly. Sand-set stone or urbanite paving on sand can be easily re-leveled during use and reclaimed for reuse after the useful life of the structure. Gabions offer ease of disassembly, as steel cages are easily cut to remove and reclaim stones.

Figure 9–4.

Stairs, walkways, and outdoor classroom walls leading into the LEED Platinum Sidwell Friends School courtyard, designed by Andropogon Associates, were constructed from reclaimed stones from a railroad bridge, recycled flagstone from Washington, DC, sidewalks, and slabs from an abandoned stone quarry. The gravel in the foreground is from a local source of river stones. A recycled granite millstone is reused as the overflow structure of the underground rainwater cistern. (Photo from Andropogon Associates)

Source Stone and Aggregate Materials Locally

As some of the largest impacts of stone use are the energy used and emissions released in transportation, use of locally quarried and worked stone can minimize these impacts. In urban areas or regions of heavy manufacturing, construction and demolition or post-industrial waste can make good aggregate or stone substitutes. See the discussion of aggregate sources above.

If local stones of rubble-size waste materials are available, but are not suitable for constructing walls, consider using the material in gabion cages, which rely on the weight of the stone material for stability but not the interlock of stones. Stones or rubble are contained within the steel cages.

AGGREGATE PAVEMENTS

While aggregate is a key constituent in base courses and fill for site structures, as well as the largest portion of concrete or asphalt pavements, used alone, gravel pavements can be a lower-impact alternative in appropriate applications. They can use less material than other pavements, as no other materials such as concrete, asphalt, or brick are laid over the aggregate base. Gravel has much lower embodied energy and produces fewer emissions and toxic impacts than these materials as well. Gravel pavements are permeable to water in varying degrees, and an open-graded, angular gravel installation can be one of the most quickly draining and low-cost forms of porous paving (Ferguson 2005).

Gravel pavements, simple to install and maintain, can be used in pedestrian walkways and paths, plazas, driveways, and light-use parking stalls. They can be unbound, relying on compaction and interlock among particles for stability, or they can be bound with a stabilizer or placed in stabilizing structures (see Table 9–13).

Because of gravel displacement, dust, safety issues, and ride quality, unbound gravel pavements are not appropriate in vehicular applications with greater than very low traffic volumes (<200–250 Average Annual Daily Traffic (AADT)) or where vehicles will move or turn rapidly or often (Maher et al. 2005). Gravel pavement can be used in the parking stall portion of parking lots, while the drive aisles can be asphalt or concrete pavements that better accommodate higher traffic volumes.

Bound pavements with added stabilizers or stabilizing structures can accommodate traffic volumes of up to 400 vehicle trips per day or greater. Stabilizing additives are discussed later in the chapter.

Gravel pavements rely on interlock of particles and compaction and packing of particles for their structural stability. Angular particles will interlock and compact better than round particles; therefore round particles should be crushed to produce at least one planar face. This will allow the particles to resist rotating and shifting.

Open-graded aggregates are a single size or a narrow range of sizes with air voids between the particles where water can be held or drain through. Only a minimal percentage of small particles exist in open-graded mixes, and dust is minimal.

Dense-graded aggregates contain a wide range of particle sizes. Dense-graded aggregates compact well, are stable, and can make good gravel pavements; however, the aggregate mass has low porosity and permeability, as the smaller particles tend to fill the voids of the larger particles. Fines contents should not exceed 15% (Maher et al. 2005). Dense-graded aggregate pavements can release dust with vehicular traffic and may require periodic applications of dust suppressants.

Dense-graded aggregates can be negatively impacted by freezing conditions, as water can be held in the pores with little space for it to expand as it freezes. Some will soften under moist conditions from thaw and rain.

Snowplows can be used with gravel pavements if runner or roller attachments are used that keep equipment blades at least a half inch above the surface. Sand should not be used as an ice-control device on open-graded pavements because it could clog the pores, inhibiting permeability of the pavement.

Weeds can grow in aggregate pavements, particularly in dense-graded pavements that will retain moisture and provide small particles between which to root. Higher traffic areas of the pavement will suppress weeds; however, other areas may require periodic weeding. Open-graded aggregates are less hospitable to weeds, as the open voids don't hold moisture and there is less rooting media. Gravel pavements can be accessible routes if small gradations of gravel are used (e.g.,

ASTM numbers 89 or 10) and the installation is even, well compacted, and maintained (Ferguson 2005).

Gravel and crushed stone are most commonly used for aggregate pavements; however, some post-consumer and industrial by-products could technically be used as well. Recycled aggregates must possess the same properties of suitable natural aggregates for pavements such as angularity, dense or open gradation, and durability and resistance to abrasion. Blast furnace slag, steel slag, waste glass, crushed concrete, and brick can all be used for aggregate surface paving applications. However, research on use and performance of recycled products in aggregate surface paving applications is quite limited.

Environmental Impacts of Aggregate Pavements

While aggregate pavements offer many environmental benefits, they can pose some impacts as well. Dust stirred by vehicular traffic on unbound, nondurable, or dense-graded pavements can impact the health of plants adjacent to the roadway by covering the leaves and reducing the amount of sunlight that reaches them. Aquatic species can be affected by sediment loading from the dust carried in air or runoff into the water (Maher et al. 2005).

Leaching concerns of heavy metals and harmful chemicals from slag aggregate, and alkalinity from recycled concrete, could be exacerbated by water flow thorough these materials, particularly in porous aggregate applications (Maher et al. 2005).

Porous Aggregate Pavement

Aggregates are a key component in porous pavement assemblies used as both a water-holding and filtering reservoir, and a structural base. They can also be used as the surface course of certain porous pavements, resulting in a low-cost, highly permeable pavement. Unbound aggregate pavements can perform well in conditions where the pavement may be slightly displaced by swelling subgrade soil, growth of tree roots, or winter freezing, as it is loose and easy to re-level (Ferguson 2005).

Porous aggregate surfaces are comprised of open-graded (single-sized), angular, and durable aggregates. The total porosity of void spaces in an open-graded aggregate installation will vary between 30% and 40% and can increase if the aggregate particles are porous. Typically rounded particles will have less void space (and less porosity), and angular particles will have more total void space. The typical void size will vary with the size of the aggregate and can be up to one-fifth the size of the aggregate (Ferguson 2005).

Gradation of particles is critical to successful performance of porous aggregate surfaces (and in other porous pavement applications as well). Gradations must be clearly specified, as some suppliers may provide dense-graded mixes when no grading is specified. Ferguson recommends use of open-graded ASTM numbers 57, 67, 78, 89, or 10 for porous aggregate applications. Larger sizes such as 57, 67, and 78 will have more rapid permeability and little susceptibility to clogging. Smaller sizes 89 and 10 produce smoother surfaces that are easier to walk on and are universally accessible. Aggregates should be clean of small soil particles and debris that might clog the pores.

Aggregates for porous pavement and surfacing applications should have good bearing strength and durability. Bearing strength is a combination of the resistance of the particles to crushing and the ability of the particles to form a strong interlock. A strong interlock is critical for open-graded installations, as the strength of the installation depends on the interlock of particles. Dense-graded installations rely on a combination of interlock and packing. Angular aggregates will form a better interlock than rounded aggregates.

Durability of aggregates is particularly critical to porous aggregate surfacing applications, as less durable aggregates may wear poorly and produce dust that can clog the voids. Specification of gradation and durability is also important when using recycled aggregates in porous aggregate surfacing applications. Locating open-graded recycled aggregates may be challenging since most are crushed and dense graded, or not even graded at all. For example, recycled concrete may be crushed and sold as "crusher run" aggregate for use in pavement bases and fills where less exact aggregate gradations and a greater presence of fines are tolerable so special sorting and grading may not be required. Where recycled materials are sold for use in concrete or asphalt pavement, more accurate or open gradations may be more easily sourced.

The subgrade under a porous aggregate surfacing application is usually not compacted so the soil's permeability and root habitat can be preserved. The unbound open-graded aggregate can adapt to some movement of softer soil. The aggregate material is compacted in lifts to resist displacement and rutting. Geotextiles can be used to separate the subgrade and aggregate to prevent aggregate from migrating into soil or soil into aggregate and clogging the voids (Ferguson 2005) (see Table 9–12).

Small quantities of stabilizers are sometimes used in porous aggregate surfacing to minimize displacement of particles. The stabilizers have been developed for use in dense-graded gravel pavements that are not intended to be porous; therefore they may limit the permeability of an aggregate surface. Stabilizers are made from resins, organic psyllium, or polymers. Stabilizers with fine particles such as clay are not appropriate since they can clog voids, substantially reducing porosity of the installation. Portland cement used in small amounts will form a light version of porous concrete.

Porous aggregate surfaces in low-traffic settings are low maintenance. Gravel can be displaced with sharp vehicular turns, but it is easily raked back into place. If aggregate is lost, it is easily supplemented with additional open-graded aggregate.

Sloping sites can inhibit the use of porous aggregate surfaces, and an upper limit of 3% slope is recommended. Dense-graded and stabilized gravel surfaces can accommodate greater slopes but are not as permeable.

For more detailed information on porous aggregates and the uses of aggregates in porous pavements, refer to Bruce Ferguson's *Porous Pavements* (2005). It discusses in great detail properties and performance expectations, and provides good case study information.

Porous Aggregate Base Courses and Reservoirs

Aggregate is a critical component of any porous paving application, handling both structural loads and water conveyance and storage. Like porous aggregate surface paving, aggregate masses must be open graded and clean. Relatively large particles are used for base reservoirs, as they are not the surface course and will hold more water. Ferguson recommends ASTM gradation No. 57 with a porosity of 30%–40% and a California Bearing Ratio of 40–50 for pedestrian and light vehicular loads and 80 for heavy vehicular loads (Ferguson 2005).

Blending sand into open-graded aggregates can enhance the filtration of water passing through the reservoir and assist rooting of trees, yet it may reduce porosity and permeability (Maher et al. 2005).

Stabilized Aggregate/Gravel Pavements

Aggregate pavements can be stabilized with binders or structures to minimize movement of aggregates under impacts from traffic or environmental conditions, to accommodate higher vehicle speeds and more trips per day, and to increase the life span of an aggregate

Table 9–12 Design and Specification Considerations of Porous Aggregate Pavement Surfaces

Angular aggregate mixes will interlock better than round aggregate mixes.
Use open-graded ASTM numbers 89 and 10 to produce smoother surfaces that are easier to walk on and are accessible.
Use open-graded ASTM numbers 57, 67, or 78 for rapid permeability and less susceptibility to clogging.
Aggregates should be clean of small soil particles and debris that might clog the pores.
Specify strong and durable aggregates that will not produce dust, which might clog pores.
Consider blending sand into open-graded mixes to enhance the filtration of storm water and tree growth.
Use recycled materials for aggregate where applicable.
If stabilizers are used, avoid dust based as they may clog pores and reduce or eliminate permeability.

Sources: TFHRC; Ferguson 2005; Maher et al. 2005; NYC DDC 2005

pavement. Unbound gravel road pavements can typically lose up to one inch of thickness per year, and even with regular maintenance must be reconstructed, replenished, or regraded every six to ten years. Use of stabilizers can increase pavement life spans and decrease gravel loss, displacement, and maintenance (Maher et al. 2005).

It is important to note that use of stabilizing agents mixed into aggregate pavements can reduce the permeability of the pavement by varying degrees. Stabilizing structures will minimally reduce the permeability of gravel pavements. Aggregate pavements can be stabilized in areas of heaviest traffic and unstabilized around trees to allow root access to water. Transitions from bound to unbound aggregates can often be made without visibility (Ferguson 2005).

The table below summarizes a wide variety of stabilizers and dust suppressants that when mixed with aggregates create varying degrees of pavement stabilization. While most are for low or very low traffic volumes (defined as 200–400 vehicles per day and less than 200 vehicle trips per day, respectively), they can be useful alternatives to concrete or asphalt for many applications, such as parking lots, private drives, trails, or informal pedestrian spaces (Maher et al. 2005).

Table 9–13 Stabilizers for Gravel and Decomposed Granite Pavements

Stabilizer[a]	Life Span,[b] Traffic Volume, Strength (SLC)[c]	Environmental Considerations[d]	Performance/Aesthetic Considerations
Tree resin emulsions Stabilizers derived from tree resins (mostly pine, spruce, and fir) combined with other additives. Other products use by-products derived from plants such as plantago (Indian wheat). Can be mixed into dense-graded aggregates or sprayed on	5–10 years or more Very low to low traffic volume 0.10–0.30. Some can be three times as strong as hot-mix asphalt.	Tree resins are a coproduct of the pulp and paper industry. Formulations vary by manufacturer; however, they are generally nontoxic. Reduces permeability of pavement, sometimes substantially	Mixed 1"–2" for dust suppression, 4"–8" for graded aggregates (less than 10 mm) Fines content between 5% and 30% and 8 plasticity index are best. Performance varies among manufacturers and products. Can be used in all climates, but best in arid or moderate precipitation conditions Pug mill mixing is recommended for use with aggregates. Emulsion is brown and darkens aggregate slightly.
Lignosulfonates Derived from lignin that binds cellulose fibers together in trees. When used for pavements, they have cementitious properties and draw moisture from the air through hydroscopic processes to keep the pavement moist.	3–5 years Very low to low traffic volume 0.08–0.14. Increases compressive strength and load-bearing capacity of pavement	By-product of the pulp and paper industry Spills, runoff, or leaching into surface waters can lower dissolved oxygen levels, possibly resulting in fish kills or groundwater concentrations of iron, sulfur compounds, or other pollutants.	Mixed 1"–2" for dust suppression, 4"–8" for graded aggregates (less than 10 mm) Most cost effective for mixes with 8%–30% fines and a plasticity index of greater than 8 Will leach from more open-graded or sandy mixes Work best in arid to moderate precipitation areas

Table 9–13 Stabilizers for Gravel and Decomposed Granite Pavements *(Continued)*

Stabilizer[a]	Life Span,[b] Traffic Volume, Strength (SLC)[c]	Environmental Considerations[d]	Performance/Aesthetic Considerations
Synthetic polymer emulsions Primarily acrylic or acetate polymers for dust control and/or aggregate stabilization, often by-products of the adhesive or paint industries Polymers cause a chemical bond to form between soil and aggregate particles, resulting in a dense, water-resistant road surface.	5–10 years Very low to low traffic volume 0.05–0.20 Compressive strength can range from 800 to 2,200 psi.	Polymers are a petroleum product involving some environmental and human health impacts in manufacture. Some emulsions contain VOCs.	Can be used for pavement bases or very low to low traffic surfaces Performance varies among manufacturers and products. Mixed with 1"–2" native soils for dust suppression, 4"–8" for graded aggregates (less than 10 mm) Fines content between 5% and 20% and 8 plasticity index are best. More polymer required for gravel mixes with less than 2% fines. Varying proprietary formulations Can be used in all climates
Clay additives Also called clay filler, bentonite, and montmorillonite Composed of montmorillonite, a naturally occurring, highly plastic clay mineral that, when mixed with water, will stabilize aggregate particles. It also reduces dust generation.	2–4 years, with localized repair every 3–6 months Very low to low traffic volume 0.10–0.14	Very low embodied energy. Natural materials—nontoxic, nonhazardous, noncorrosive Can contain a small amount of crystalline silica dust, which can be an inhalation hazard for workers Can damage adjacent vegetation during application	Susceptible to adverse, wet weather conditions. Wet and/or cold climates will require more frequent repair. Effectiveness is affected by aggregate mineralogy. Adheres well to limestone. Material is mined in the northwestern United States and Mississippi.
Organic petroleum-based emulsions These products use adhesive properties of the asphalt component to bind aggregates together for stabilization and dust suppression. Most are sprayed on, but some can be mixed in.	5–9 years Very low to low traffic volume 0.10–0.25	Avoid cutback asphalts, as they release hydrocarbon emissions during evaporation and can be a health, an environmental, and a fire hazard. Use emulsified asphalts with low or no solvents and polycyclic aromatic hydrocarbons (PAHs). Recyclability of asphalt-stabilized aggregates is limited to base applications.	Change appearance of soil to dark brown or dark gray Work on soil types with up to 30% clay fines and a plasticity index of less than 10. Mixed with 1"–2" native soils for dust suppression, 4"–6" for graded aggregates (less than 10 mm) Penetration depth decreases as amount of fines increases, so low-viscosity mixes should be used on soils with fines. Performance varies among manufacturers and products. Can be used in all climates

Continued

Table 9–13 Stabilizers for Gravel and Decomposed Granite Pavements *(Continued)*

Stabilizer[a]	Life Span,[b] Traffic Volume, Strength (SLC)[c]	Environmental Considerations[d]	Performance/Aesthetic Considerations
Electrolyte emulsions Contain chemicals that affect the electrobonding characteristics of soils and replace water molecules within the soil structure Soil stabilizer or dust palliative Can be sprayed on or mixed in (most common)	3–5 years; however, some applications have been in place for 15 or more years. Very low to low traffic volume 0.08–0.14	Electrolyte products are often by-products or intermediate products of manufacturing processes. Sulfonated D-limonene and sulfonated naphthalene, primary components, can have toxic impacts to both human and environmental health in concentrated form. When diluted, impacts are minimal.	Primarily used as dust suppressant Performance varies among manufacturers and products.
Enzymatic emulsions Contains enzymes (protein molecules) that form a cementing bond by reacting with soil particles Soil stabilizer or dust palliative Can be sprayed on or mixed in (most common)	5–7 years; however, some applications have been in place for 12 or more years. Very low to low traffic volume 0.08–0.14 Can increase strength by 30%–300%	Enzyme materials are often by-products of the food processing and manufacturing industries. Once diluted, typically biodegradable and nontoxic	Primarily used as dust suppressant Performance varies among manufacturers and products. Can become slippery when wet when used on soils with high clay contents (20%–30%) Work best on mixes with 12%–24% clay content, a plasticity index between 8 and 35 and when soil moisture content is 2%–3% below optimum for compaction
Chlorides, Liquid or solid compounds containing chloride salts that, when mixed with aggregates or unstabilized material, reduce dust generation. They also facilitate compaction and promote soil stabilization. Chlorides are obtained from natural brine deposits or are by-products of other manufacturing processes.	3–12 months Very low traffic: the higher the traffic the more frequent the application SLC—n/a	Typically sprayed on, and exposure during application can cause skin and eye irritation. Chlorides act as a defoliant, and overspray can impact adjacent vegetation and aquatic systems. Leaching over life of installation can affect water quality. A 25-foot buffer zone is recommended between pavement and water. Should not be used in shallow groundwater areas.	Very common dust palliative Not effective in arid or extremely wet climates Can corrode steel and aluminum alloys Use with well-graded, engineered aggregates. The more chlorides used, the more stable the installation. Chlorides don't affect the color of installation. Color is determined by aggregates.

Table 9–13 Stabilizers for Gravel and Decomposed Granite Pavements *(Continued)*

Stabilizer[a]	Life Span,[b] Traffic Volume, Strength (SLC)[c]	Environmental Considerations[d]	Performance/Aesthetic Considerations
Cellular confinement Contains aggregate in a cellular structure made from plastic or concrete. Dense-graded mixes can also be used.	15–20 years Very low to medium traffic volume 0.35 with granular infill	Can reduce the required aggregate thickness, using less material Energy use and emissions in manufacture of grids can be high for concrete and, to a lesser degree, plastic. Some are made with recycled plastic.	Typically covered with gravel, dense-graded, or other wearing surface Maximum particle size of 2 inches. Less than 10% fines content Cellular structure improves load distribution of pavement. Some will work for emergency access applications. Expansion joints are required for plastic structures, as they can expand in heat. Plastic structures are flexible and can adapt to swelling or freezing soils. Concrete structure use in cold climates can lead to more frequent maintenance and deterioration.

[a]Refer to individual product manufacturer's specifications for complete details.
[b]Life span will vary by climatic and use conditions.
[c]Structural Layer Coefficient.
[d]Many of these formulations are proprietary products with varying ingredients. Product literature should be examined for volatile organic compounds (VOCs), Polycyclic Aromatic Hydrocarbons (PAHs), heavy metals and other toxic chemicals.
Sources: Maher et al. 2005; TFHRC; Sorvig 2005; Ferguson 2005

Table 9–14 Design and Specification Considerations of Stabilized Aggregate Pavement Surfaces

Primary detailing considerations have to do with prevention of erosion of the paving surface.
Angular aggregate mixes will interlock better than round aggregate mixes.
Stabilized pavement should be contained with an edge restraint.
Stabilized pavements should have minimal cross-slopes to prevent erosion of the surface.
Adjacent surfaces should drain away from the stabilized pavement.
Expansion and control joints are not necessary.
Aggregate mix and type should closely follow the product manufacturer's recommended sizes and gradations to ensure stability and prevent erosion.
Specify local aggregate where appropriate.

Sources: Maher et al. 2005; NYC DDC 2005; Ferguson 2005; Sorvig 2005; Sorvig 1994; TFHRC

Structural Soils

Structural soils, made up of crushed stone, clay loam, and a hydrogel stabilizing agent, form a structural base for pavements while allowing for root penetration to support tree growth. A major problem in the establishment of trees in urban areas is the lack of adequate soil volume, moisture retention, nutrients, or oxygen for tree roots. Soils under pavements are typically heavily compacted to meet the load-bearing requirements of the pavement above; thus the tree can't develop a strong root system for adequate health. These conditions result in premature tree death after an average of seven to ten years, versus the 50 years that the same tree could be expected to live in better conditions (Bassuk et al. 1998).

Structural soils offer a hospitable environment for tree roots, fostering healthy urban trees and a structural pavement base. Components of a structural soil application are as follows (Bassuk and Trowbridge 2006):

The pavement surface can be a typical four- to six-inch pavement installation of concrete, asphalt, dimension stone, unit pavers, etc. It can be rigid, semirigid, or flexible.

The opening for the tree should be large enough to accommodate a forty-year-old tree. Ideally the porous

Figure 9–5.
Children approach the Islandwood Dining Hall on a stabilized path mixed in place with on-site soil and gravel as designed by Berger Partnership. (Photo copyright Mithun, from Roger Williams)

Figure 9–6.
Decomposed granite paving at Hoboken's South Waterfront Park by Arnold Associates is stabilized for pedestrian and light vehicular traffic and seamlessly transitions to unstabilized decomposed granite around trees to allow water and air penetration to tree roots. (Project: Hoboken South Waterfront; Designers: Arnold/Wilday Joint Venture; Image copyright: Arnold Associates)

area around the tree would be 8 × 8 and a good sand loam can be used to surround the root system with structural soil under the surrounding pavement (Bassuk and Trowbridge 2006). Unit pavers with half-inch spacers can be placed in the 8 × 8 area to allow air and water penetration but accommodate pedestrians. Pavers can be removed as the tree's buttress roots grow to meet them.

A conventional base course under the pavement can be installed to meet normal regional pavement specifications for the application. A geotextile can be used to separate this conventional base from the structural soil underneath (Bassuk et al. 1998).

The structural soil base is composed of gap-graded structural soil materials in the following typical proportions: narrowly graded crushed stone (100), clay loam (20), hydrogel (0.03), and a potassium propenoate-propenamide copolymer (an agricultural hydrogel) (Bassuk and Trowbridge 2006). The angular crushed stone forms a lattice, with the clay loam partially filling the voids. The hydrogel acts as a tackifier to prevent separation of the stone and soil during mixing and installation. The minimum depth for the structural soil base is 24 inches with an ideal of 36 inches (Bassuk et al. 1998).

Trees used for structural soil applications should be alkaline-tolerant and drought-tolerant species. Stone

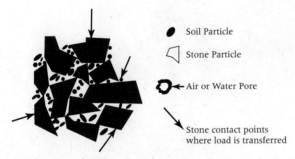

Figure 9–7.
Structural soils, developed by Cornell's Urban Horticulture Institute, are composed of an open-graded aggregate that forms a structural base for paving, and voids filled with soil allow tree roots water and air penetration below a pavement. (Image from Urban Horticulture Institute; Redrawn by John Wiley & Sons)

used in the structural soil mix will influence the pH of the soil, with limestone aggregates producing the highest alkalinity at about 8.0. Even granite and other aggregates will eventually raise the pH of the structural soil (Bassuk and Trowbridge 2006).

DRY-LAID STONE OR RECLAIMED CONCRETE WALLS

Dry-laid stone walls can be low-impact structures in areas where local stone is available and appropriate for use. Mortar can be used in the interior for strengthening, but use of mortar can make repairs more complicated and it will not allow the wall to move and settle slightly. Mud mortar will offer some stability yet is easily cleaned from stones if the wall is deconstructed and the stone reclaimed. Some masons stress the importance of allowing the wall to settle slightly in the first year as a way of gaining stronger interlock between the stones (see Figure 9–8).

Reclaimed concrete paving or walls without reinforcing, also called urbanite, can be a good substitute for natural stone in dry-laid walls, as it is strong and durable and often can be obtained at no cost besides transport. Urbanite from demolished walls offers ease of construction as both faces are formed to be flat and parallel, lending uniformity to the new structure. Paving offers the benefit of at least one flat side from the pavement surface, and the bottom of the broken slab may also be relatively flat. Foundations for dry-laid walls can be either gravel or poured-in-place concrete. See the discussion of foundations below.

GRAVEL TRENCH, RUBBLE, AND STONE FOUNDATIONS FOR WALLS

Gravel trench, rubble, or stone foundations for walls can be a low-impact alternative to poured-in-place concrete spread footings. Prior to the widespread use of concrete, they were one of the primary foundation and footing construction systems for buildings and walls, some of which have survived earthquakes and extreme weather, and are still in good condition today.

These types of foundations perform best in wall applications that will tolerate slight movement, such as dry-laid stone or urbanite, unmortared segmental retaining blocks, or unit-based earthen structures. They are constructed on similar principles as pavement bases

Table 9–15 Design and Specification Considerations of Structural Soils

Crushed stone should be narrowly graded from $3/4$"–$1^1/_2$". It should be highly angular with no fines. Stone can be limestone, granite, or other stone that can meet the necessary bearing capacity of the pavement application.
The structural soil mix should be compacted to regional standards, usually not less than 95% Proctor Density with a minimum California Bearing Ratio of greater than or equal to 50.
The subgrade should be excavated to parallel the finished grade, and adequate drainage should occur around the tree base.
The soil should be a loam to heavy clay loam with a minimum of 20% clay. Organic matter should compose about 5% to aid in nutrient and water holding.
Structural soil should be installed in six-inch lifts.
Underdrainage conforming to regional standards should be installed under the structural soil.
At minimum, a continuous running trench parallel to the curb, eight feet wide and three feet deep, is adequate for continuous street tree planting.
Testing for ideal moisture density relationships should be performed to determine the ratio of soil to stone. A starting point is 18%–22% soil by weight. Research has shown a loss of bearing capacity when too much soil fills the voids between stones.

Sources: Adapted from Bassuk et al. 1998; Bassuk and Trowbridge 2006

Figure 9–8.
Mud mortar is used in stone walls that have endured for centuries at the Quarai Mission in Salinas Pueblo Missions National Monument in New Mexico. (Photo by Quentin Wilson)

Figure 9–9.
"Staplestone," concrete salvaged from demolished runways at Denver's former Stapleton Airport, is a popular "stone" wall building material, as chunks are large (up to two feet thick) and free of steel reinforcing. (Photo from David Amalong)

in that they keep moisture away from the structure and provide a stable structural base on which to build. Gravel trench, rubble, or stone foundations should be designed with the same considerations as standard foundations with the exceptions noted below.

Gravel trench foundations, also called sand and gravel foundations, are a well-compacted mix of open-graded coarse gravel and sand. The proportions are approximately three parts gravel to two parts sand (McHenry 1984). The main goal is to provide a well-drained, structurally sound base that transfers the wall load to stable soil beneath. The open-graded gravel and sand mix will allow water to percolate quickly through the foundation into the soil below, avoiding the risk of frost heave. Some gravel is wrapped in a geotextile to prevent migration of gravel and sand into the subsoil.

Gravel trench foundations require well-drained soil with adequate percolation to avoid water buildup in heavy rains. If the soil is stable, but not well drained, the trench may be graded to a drainage structure. Expansive clay soils may not be suitable for gravel trench foundations.

Gravel and sand, or recycled aggregates (such as broken concrete, crushed brick, or slag), used in gravel

trench foundations should have sufficient compressive strength to bear the weight of the wall and other anticipated loads, and they should be minimally absorptive and resistant to degradation by water (McHenry 1984). Some structural engineers point out the similarities between gravel trench foundations and the earthquake structural system of base-isolation, a method of separating a building from the earth to allow it to move independently of ground movement in earthquakes. Similarly, gravel trench foundations can also minimize the transfer of ground motion into a wall structure (Moquin 2000).

Rubble trench foundations can be similar to gravel trench or stone foundations, depending on the type of rubble used and how it is placed. Rubble is larger than gravel, with minimum size for rubble of three to twelve inches (Texas DOT). If it is combined with sand and compacted, treatment is similar to a gravel trench foundation. If the rubble is carefully hand placed for interlock, then it can be treated as a stone foundation with use of mortar or dry-laid stone laying techniques.

Stone foundations can be either dry laid surrounded with gravel, or laid with mortar. If mortar is used, it should not be relied upon for holding the stones in place or for supporting the load above. Most sources recommend that the stones should be laid in such a way that the foundation will work as a dry-laid foundation even when mortar is used (Houben and Guillard 1994; Vivian 1976). The trench should be backfilled with gravel and spaces between stones filled with gravel to ensure good drainage. Urbanite can be used as a foundation material as well, particularly if both sides are relatively smooth. In colder climates, the footing may need to extend to below the frost line, although some sources claim that a gravel footing on well-drained soil need not (Houben and Guillard 1994; McHenry 1984).

GABION WALLS

Gabions are wire mesh or welded-wire containers filled with hard stone or rubble three to eight inches in diameter. They are primarily stacked walls used for stream bank erosion control; however, they are increasingly used for a low-impact yet stable retaining wall or foundation. Gabion walls, a type of gravity retaining wall, rely on the deadweight of the stone for stability. The wire mesh contains and stabilizes the stones, allowing use of stone or rubble that would individually be too small to withstand the erosive force of the stream (Freeman and Fischenich 2000). Unlike rigid structures, the gabions conform to ground movement and over time, their strength and stability can increase as silt and vegetation fill the interstitial voids, reinforcing the structure.

Gabion containers are usually steel welded-wire mesh or double-twist hexagonal mesh. The steel can be coated or left to rust. Most steel is either galvanized or coated with a proprietary zinc coating. In wet applications, the steel can be coated with a PVC coating. While durable, PVC can pose human health impacts in production and disposal. See the full discussion in chapter 12. Some gabions are made from Tensar or other heavy-duty plastic mesh (Freeman and Fischenich 2000). Gabion cages are fastened together with use of metal spiral, ring binders, or other methods specific to the manufacturer.

There are three basic gabion forms: gabion baskets, gabion mattresses, and sack gabions.

Gabion baskets, also called gabion cages, are $1\frac{1}{2}$ to three-feet deep. These are the most common type used in steeper stream bank walls and retaining walls. They are primarily sold in three-feet-long by three-feet-deep modular cells. A standard gabion consists of two cells resulting in a six-foot length; however, lengths from three feet to 24 feet are available. Internal cell walls of wire mesh, three feet on center, stabilize the external framework during loading (Gourley 2001).

Gabion mattresses are shallower with available heights ranging from three inches to $1\frac{1}{2}$ feet. These are designed to protect the bed or the banks of a stream against erosion. Gabion mattresses can also be stacked to form thick walls.

Sack gabions are mesh sacks filled with rock material. They are not commonly used in the United States (Freeman and Fischenich 2000).

Figure 9–10.

Figure 9–11.

Woven wire gabions form benches and retaining walls throughout a series of gardens by Nate Cormier and Paulo Pellegrino at the offices of FUPAM, a foundation supporting the research of faculty at the architecture school of the University of São Paulo. This gravel garden acts as a simple rain garden. The boardwalk, of sustainably harvested teak from a FUPAM research project, links three gardens and tops the gabion benches. (Photos by Nate Cormier)

Figure 9–12.

Gabion walls at the Kresge Foundation are constructed with broken concrete from a demolished parking lot on-site. The rock on exposed faces of the gabions is granite for a finished look. Gabion cages are galvanized steel. Parking bays are porous unit pavers. (Photo © Conservation Design Forum, 2008. All rights reserved. www.cdfinc.com)

Gabion structures are ideal for incorporating C&D and post-industrial waste products, as the containment of the wire cages means that shape and structural interlock of the rubble is less important than in dry-laid or mortared wall applications. Waste materials should be tested for leaching potential in structures near sensitive ecosystems.

Gabion walls can be detailed such that decorative stone is used in a layer of cages that will be visible, and nonvisible cages can be filled with more utilitarian stone or recycled material.

Gabion retaining walls usually are laid in a stepped formation with a widening of the structure in lower levels. A base-to-height ratio of 0.6:1 is recommended

Table 9–16 Select ASTM and AASHTO Standards Related to Aggregates and Stone

ASTM C88	Standard Test Method for Soundness of Aggregates by Use of Sodium Sulfate or Magnesium Sulfate
ASTM C131	Standard Test Method for Resistance to Degradation of Small-Size Coarse Aggregate by Abrasion and Impact in the Los Angeles Machine
ASTM C136	Standard Test Method for Sieve Analysis of Fine and Coarse Aggregates
ASTM C330	Standard Specification for Lightweight Aggregates for Structural Concrete
ASTM C535	Standard Test Method for Resistance to Degradation of Large-Size Coarse Aggregate by Abrasion and Impact in the Los Angeles Machine
ASTM D448	Standard Classification for Sizes of Aggregate for Road and Bridge Construction
ASTM D1883	Standard Test Method for CBR (California Bearing Ratio) of Laboratory-Compacted Soils
ASTM D2487	Standard Practice for Classification of Soils for Engineering Purposes (Unified Soil Classification System)
ASTM D2940	Standard Specification for Graded Aggregate Material for Bases or Subbases for Highways or Airports
ASTM D4791	Standard Test Method for Flat Particles, Elongated Particles, or Flat and Elongated Particles in Coarse Aggregate
ASTM D5084	Standard Test Methods for Measurement of Hydraulic Conductivity of Saturated Porous Materials Using a Flexible Wall Permeameter
ASTM D6270	Standard Practice for Use of Scrap Tires in Civil Engineering Applications
ASTM D6913	Standard Test Methods for Particle-Size Distribution (Gradation) of Soils Using Sieve Analysis
ASTM E11	Standard Specification for Wire Cloth and Sieves for Testing Purposes
ASTM E2277	Standard Guide for Design and Construction of Coal Ash Structural Fills
AASHTO M146	Standard Specification for Terms Relating to Subgrade, Soil Aggregate, and Fill Materials
AASHTO M147	Standard Specification for Materials for Aggregate and Soil-Aggregate Subbase, Base, and Surface Course
AASHTO T27	Sieve Analysis of Fine and Coarse Aggregates
AASHTO T88	Standard Method of Test for Particle Size Analysis of Soils
AASHTO T307	Standard Method of Test for Determining the Resilient Modulus of Soil and Aggregate Materials

(Dines and Brown 1999). Or sometimes the entire cage is tilted to achieve the batter.

Gabion walls are freely draining and require no weep holes or drainage structures. Geotextiles can be used behind the wall if the migration of soil particles into the voids between stones is not desirable. Voids between stones in battered or stepped gabion walls can be filled with soil and even plant plugs to encourage plant growth.

Foundations for gabion retaining walls can be compacted gravel, or they can even bear directly on soil subgrade. Gabions can accommodate substantial differential settlement without compromising the structure (Gourley 2001).

RESOURCES

Turner Fairbank Highway Research Center http://www.tfhrc.gov/

Context Sensitive Roadway Surfacing Guide http://www.cflhd.gov/techDevelopment/

Construction Materials Recycling Association http://www.cdrecycling.org/

California Integrated Waste Management Board www.ciwmb.ca.gov

Recycler's World www.recycle.net

Used Building Materials Association www.ubma.org

Scrap Tire Management Council http://www.energyjustice.net/tires/files/scrapchn.html

Institute of Scrap Recycling Industries www.isri.org

Rubber Association of Canada www.rubberassociation.ca

Rubber Manufacturers Association www.rma.org

Tire Industry Association www.tireindustry.org

REFERENCES

Asphalt Recycling and Reclaiming Association (ARRA). 2001. *Basic Asphalt Recycling Manual.* Annapolis: Asphalt Recycling and Reclaiming Association, FHWA, http://www.arra.org/

ASTM Standard C125. 2006. "Standard Terminology Relating to Concrete and Concrete Aggregates." West Conshohocken, PA: ASTM International, www.astm.org.

ASTM Standard D 2487. 2006. "Standard Practice for Classification of Soils for Engineering Purposes (Unified Soil Classification System)." West Conshohocken, PA: ASTM International, www.astm.org.

Athena Sustainable Materials Institute. 2006. "A Life Cycle Perspective on Concrete and Asphalt Roadways: Embodied Primary Energy and Global Warming Potential." Submitted to Cement Association of Canada. Merrickville, ON: Athena Sustainable Materials Institute.

Bassuk, N. L., J. Grabosky, P. J. Trowbridge, and J. Urban. 1998. "Structural Soil: An Innovative Medium under Pavement That Improves Tree Vigor." In *American Society of Landscape Architects Annual Meeting Proceedings.* http://www.hort.cornell.edu/uhi/outreach/csc/article.html (accessed September 21, 2007).

Bassuk, N. L., and P. J. Trowbridge. 2006. "Soils: Urban or Disturbed." In *Landscape Architectural Graphic Standards,* ed. L. J. Hopper. Hoboken, NJ: John Wiley & Sons, pp. 646–52.

California Department of Transportation (Caltrans). 2007. "Amendments to May 2006 Standard Specifications." Sacramento, CA: Caltrans, August 17, 2007.

California Integrated Waste Management Board (CIWMB). *Green Roads.* http://www.zerowaste.ca.gov/RCM/pdf/Folder.pdf (accessed June 20, 2007).

Chacon, M. 1999. *Architectural Stone: Fabrication, Installation and Selection.* New York: John Wiley & Sons.

Demkin, J., ed. 1998a. "Material Report 03100 Concrete." In *Environmental Resource Guide.* New York: John Wiley & Sons, p. 12.

Demkin, J., ed. 1998b. "Material Report 04450 Stone Veneer." In *Environmental Resource Guide.* New York: John Wiley & Sons, p. 17.

Demkin, J., ed. 1998c. "Material Report 09200 Plaster and Lath." In *Environmental Resource Guide.* New York: John Wiley & Sons, p. 8.

Dines, N. T., and K. D. Brown. 1999. *Timesaver Standards Site Construction Details Manual.* New York: McGraw Hill, pp. 340–41.

Eighmy, T. T., and K. Holtz. 2000. "Scanning European Advances in the Use of Recycled Materials in Highway Construction." U.S. Department of Transportation, Federal Highway Administration. *Public Roads* 64(1): 34–40.

Environmental Building News. (EBN) 1993, "Cement and Concrete: Environmental Considerations" In *Environmental Building News,* Braffleboro, Vermont: Building Green, Vol 6:1.

Federal Highway Administration (FHWA). 2004a, September. "Transportation Applications of Recycled Concrete Aggregate." *FHWA State of the Practice National Review.* U.S. Department of Transportation.

Federal Highway Administration (FHWA). 2004b. "Foundry Sand Facts for Civil Engineers." U.S. Department of Transportation, FHWA-IF-04–004.

Ferguson, Bruce. 2005. *Porous Pavements.* Boca Raton, FL: CRC Press.

Freeman, G. E., and J. C. Fischenich. 2000. "Gabions for Streambank Erosion Control." EMRRP Technical Notes Collection (ERDC TN-EMRRP-SR-22), U.S. Army Engineer Research and Development Center, Vicksburg, MS.

Gourley, E. 2001. "Too Hip to Be Square." *Landscape Architecture* 89:24–26.

Hammond, G., and C. Jones. 2006. "Inventory of Carbon and Energy." Version 1.5 Beta. Bath, UK: University of Bath, Department of Mechanical Engineering.

Houben, H., and H. Guillard. 1994. *Earth Construction: A Comprehensive Guide.* London: Intermediate Technology Publications.

Maher, M., C. Marshall, F. Harrison, and K. Baumgaertner. 2005. *Context Sensitive Roadway Surfacing Selection Guide.* Lakewood, CO: Federal Highway Administration, Central Federal Lands Highway Division.

McHenry, P. G. 1984. *Adobe and Rammed Earth Buildings.* Tucson: University of Arizona Press.

Moquin, M. 2000. *Alternative Construction: Contemporary Natural Building Methods.* Ed. L. Elizabeth and C. Adams. New York: Wiley.

National Institute for Occupational Safety and Health (NIOSH). 2002, April. *NIOSH Hazard Review: Health Effects of Occupational Exposure to Respirable Crystalline Silica.* Publication np. 2002–129. http://www.cdc.gov/niosh/topics/silica/.

National Mining Association. "Facts at a Glance." Washington, DC: National Mining Association. http://www.nma.org/pdf/c_facts_glance.pdf.

National Slag Association. http://www.nationalslag.org/.

National Stone, Sand and Gravel Association (NSSGA). http://www.nssga.org/.

New York City Department of Design and Construction (NYC DDC) and Design Trust for Public Space (DTPS). 2005. *High Performance Infrastructure Guidelines: Best Practices for the Public Right-of-Way.* New York: NYC DDC and DTPS.

Northeast Waste Management Officials' Association (NEWMOA). "NEWMOA Fact Sheet: Beneficial Use of Tire Shreds as Lightweight Fill." NEWMOA, April 6, 2001.

Partnership for Advancing Technology in Housing (PATH). "Concrete Aggregate Substitutes: Alternative Aggregate Materials" PATH: Toolbase Resources. http://www.toolbase.org/Construction-Methods/Concrete-Construction/concrete-aggregate-substitutes (accessed November 4, 2006).

Portland Cement Association (PCA). 2005. "Full-Depth Reclamation (FDR): Recycling Roads Saves Money and Natural Resources." Skokie, IL: Portland Cement Association.

Rubber Manufacturers Association (RMA). 2006. "Scrap Tire Markets in the United States -2005 Edition." Adapted from Figure 2 (*2005 U.S. Scrap Tire Disposition*), Table 4 (*2005 US Scrap Tire Market Summary*); pg. 18. Washington D.C.: RMA.

Rubber Manufacturers Association (RMA) http://www.rma.org/scrap_tires/scrap_tire_markets/scrap_tire_characteristics/ (Accessed April 7, 2008)

Scrap Tire Management Council, Rubber Manufacturer's Association. "Scrap Tire Characteristics." http://www.energyjustice.net/tires/files/scrapchn.html (accessed February 9, 2007).

Sorvig, K. 2005. "Soft Porous Surfacing." In *Porous Pavements,* ed. B. Ferguson. Boca Raton, FL: CRC Press.

Sorvig, K. 1994. "The Path Less Traveled." *Landscape Architecture* 84:12, 32.

Tepordei, Valentin V. 1993. "Crushed Stone." In *Bureau of Mines/Minerals Yearbook 1993* (pp. 1107–47). http://digicoll.library.wisc.edu/EcoNatRes/ (accessed October 27, 2007, in Ecology and Natural Resource Collection of University of Wisconsin Digital Collections).

Texas Department of Transportation. "Soil and Bedrock Classification." http://www.dot.state.tx.us/services/bridge/geo_soil_class.htm#classification (accessed October 27, 2007).

Thompson, J. W., and K. Sorvig. 2000. *Sustainable Landscape Construction: A Guide to Green Building Outdoors.* Washington, DC: Island Press.

Transportation Research Board. 1996, August. "Water Quality Effects of Using Tire Chips below the Groundwater Table, Transportation Research Record No. 1619, Final Technical Report 94–1." Washington, DC: Transportation Research Board.

Turner Fairbank Highway Research Center (TFHRC). *User Guidelines for Waste and By-product Materials in Pavement Construction.* Turner Fairbank Highway Research Center, Federal Highway Administration. http://www.tfhrc.gov/hnr20/recycle/waste/begin.htm.

U.S. Environmental Protection Agency, Office of Compliance. 1995, September. "Profile of the Metal Mining Industry." EPA Office of Compliance Sector Notebook Project, EPA/310-R-95–008.

U.S. Environmental Protection Agency, Office of Solid Waste. 2006, October. "Municipal Solid Waste in the United States: Facts and Figures." EPA530-R-06–011.

U.S. Environmental Protection Agency (U.S. EPA) Technology Transfer Network. 2004. "Chapter 11: Mineral Products Industry, Section 11.19.2 Crushed Stone Processing and Pulverized Mineral Processing" *AP 42,* Fifth Edition. Clearinghouse for Inventories and Emissions Factors, Technology Transfer Network, U.S. EPA.

U.S. Environmental Protection Agency (U.S. EPA) Technology Transfer Network. "Health Effects Notebook for Hazardous Air Pollutants, Hydrogen Chloride" http://www.epa.gov/ttn/atw/hlthef/hydrochl.html (accessed August 10, 2007).

U.S. Geological Survey (USGS). 2007a. "Iron and Steel Slag." *2005 Minerals Yearbook.* Washington, DC: U.S. Geological Survey.

U.S. Geological Survey (USGS). 2007b. "Sand and Gravel, Construction." *2005 Minerals Yearbook.* Washington, DC: U.S. Geological Survey.

U.S. Geological Survey (USGS). 2007c. "Stone, Crushed." *2005 Minerals Yearbook.* Washington, DC: U.S. Geological Survey.

U.S. Geological Survey (USGS). 2007d. "Stone, Dimension." *2005 Minerals Yearbook.* Washington, DC: U.S. Geological Survey.

Vivian, J. 1976. *Building Stone Walls.* Pownal, VT: Storey Communications.

Willburn, D. R., and T. G. Goonan. 1998. *Aggregates from Natural and Recycled Sources—Economic Assessments for Construction Applications—A Material Flow Analysis.* Denver, CO: U.S. Geological Survey.

chapter **10**

Wood and Wood Products

Wood has been used for centuries as a building material in forested regions. It is easily worked, structurally strong, and warm and inviting to touch. A renewable resource, grown primarily with solar energy inputs, wood sequesters carbon, even after harvest and processing into lumber products. But until recently, modern use of wood in construction has been dominated by largely unsustainable practices. Standard softwood harvesting techniques clear large expanses of forests, destroying habitats. Many Southeastern and Pacific Northwest tree plantations are monoculture forests with little habitat value and liberal use of pesticides and fertilizers. Sensitive rain forests are cut and indigenous people displaced for valuable decay-resistant species that are shipped around the world. Preservative treatments inject heavy metals and other insecticides into wood that may leach into soil and/or affect human health in use or disposal. And wood finishes can off-gas VOCs, negatively affecting air quality and contributing to human respiratory problems.

These issues have resulted in wood's being viewed as a somewhat unsustainable material, yet along with the general shift in the building industry toward environmental awareness and "greener" practices, opportunities are increasing to specify sustainable wood in construction. Sustainable forest management and harvesting practices monitored by forest certification pro-

grams are rapidly growing, reclaimed wood for reuse is increasingly available, and less-toxic wood preservative treatments and finishes are being developed. Engineered wood utilizing wood processing wastes and smaller lumber units is increasingly available for exterior applications with low-toxicity binders. And, like any building material, strategies to use wood efficiently, minimize waste, and build durable structures can also contribute to sustainable use of wood. If properly specified, wood can be one of the more sustainable construction materials.

Environmental and Human Health Impacts of Wood Use

Forests offer a wide variety of environmental benefits, from habitats to carbon sequestration to air purification. They also offer recreational and aesthetic value for communities. Yet these benefits are often in conflict with a forest's value for wood product production. While global and local impacts of wood harvesting can be substantial, especially with some current unsustainable forest management practices, there are potential benefits of wood use in construction as compared with fossil fuel–intensive alternatives such as steel and concrete, particularly as they relate to issues of global warming.

The *Inventory of U.S. Greenhouse Gas Emissions and Sinks: 1990–2005* estimates that approximately 33% (303 million hectares) of U.S. land area is forested. Seventy-nine percent of the 250 million hectares of forested area in the contiguous 48 states is classified as timberland, meaning they meet minimum levels of productivity. Forestlands in the United States declined rapidly over the settlement of North America; however, since 1980, average annual fluctuations either up or down have been around 0.1% due to reforestation efforts and protection measures. A net increase of 2% has been recorded between 1987 and 2002 with reforestation efforts in the Northeast and Pacific Northwest. However, less than 4% of old-growth forests remain (U.S. EPA 2007a).

Worldwide, loss of old-growth forests, rain forests, and other forestland is a larger concern. The World Resources Institute estimates that we have lost 80% of the world's ancient forests, and only 36% are primary forests (largely undisturbed by direct human activities). Plantation forests, seeded with fast-growing species for commercial use and far less robust as habitat, account for 3% of the world's forested areas (Food and Agriculture Organization of the United Nations 2005). A large percentage of harvested forests are not revegetated; instead they are converted to other land uses. Many rain forests are converted to crop or plantation lands after harvest. With the worldwide adoption of forest certification systems, sustainably managed forest area is increasing, but it is still less than 2% of world forests. One certifying organization, the Forest Stewardship Council (FSC), reports that certified forest area reached 68 million hectares in the beginning of 2006, a 45% increase in one year (FSC).

WOOD PRODUCTS, CARBON, AND GLOBAL WARMING

As global climate change concerns escalate, there is increasing study of the earth's carbon cycle, in which forests play a major role. Forests and vegetation contribute to balancing the carbon cycle between the biosphere and atmosphere by storing up carbon in relatively long carbon pools (some up to hundreds of years). Forests remove carbon from the atmosphere through the photosynthesis process of converting carbon dioxide into carbohydrates and releasing oxygen. This process is most productive in newer forests where rapid tree growth occurs. Trees harvested for lumber can sequester carbon in the wood products, and if the forest is replanted, additional carbon sinks are added to the carbon cycle (Consortium for Research on Renewable Industrial Materials [CORRIM] 2005).

Deforestation contributes directly to global warming by creating an imbalance in the carbon cycle with the removal of trees that could sequester carbon. It is estimated that 20% of human-caused carbon dioxide emissions are caused by deforestation, third only to petroleum then coal combustion (IPCC 2000).

The *Inventory of U.S. Greenhouse Gas Emissions and Sinks: 1990–2005* estimates that forests and harvested wood accounted for a net carbon sequestration of 698.7 Tg CO_2 equivalents in 2005. They estimate that forests (including vegetation, soils, and harvested wood) offset about 11.56% of total U.S. greenhouse gas emissions in 2005. This has increased 14% since 1990, due primarily to increased carbon density per area more than an increase in forestland. This increased density is due to improved management practices and an increase in fertilizer use, which causes greater carbon sequestration in quickly growing trees. The carbon sequestration from increased fertilizer use comes at a price of increased N_2O emissions from forest soils, which were more than five times higher in 2005 than in 1990. This increase in fertilized area primarily occurred on pine plantations in southeastern U.S. forests (U.S. EPA 2007b). A calculation tool has been developed to estimate carbon stored in forest products in use. The tool, currently in peer review, can be found on the National Council for Air and Stream Improvement (NCASI) website.

HARVESTING IMPACTS

In addition to the potential global warming impacts from loss of forests, a primary concern of wood use in construction is the habitat destruction and the associated impacts to ecosystems resulting from wood harvest. The magnitude of these impacts across the earth is quite substantial.

Logging operations can cause loss of habitat, soil erosion and compaction, pollutant runoff, and loss of species diversity. Increased runoff volume from deforested land can carry topsoil and pollutants into surface

Lumber Use for Carbon Sequestration: An Argument in Favor of Wood over Steel and Concrete

Some scientists make the argument in favor of using wood products over nonrenewable alternatives such as steel and concrete for the following reasons (CORRIM 2005):

- Trees remove carbon from the atmosphere, and a portion of the carbon remains fixed in wood products throughout their lives. Approximately 1.84 kg (4.06 lb.) of carbon dioxide is taken up from the atmosphere per kilogram of harvested wood (oven-dry weight; Lippiatt 2007). In the wood product, carbon is emitted over time as the product decays or combusts. If timber is burned, the CO_2 is emitted quickly; if the timber is used in deck lumber, the carbon will be released very slowly over decades as the lumber decays.

- Wood waste can be used to generate clean energy in biomass or cogeneration facilities. Bioenergy, unlike energy obtained from fossil fuels, is considered to be carbon neutral.

- Currently wood residuals such as bark generate the majority of energy used in wood processing, reducing the need to burn fossil fuels and the associated carbon release into the atmosphere. Fossil fuels are the primary energy source in steel and concrete manufacture.

- Forests can be regenerated, resulting in additional trees that remove more carbon from the air.

Research by the thirteen-member school research institution Consortium for Research on Renewable Industrial Materials (CORRIM 2005), located at the University of Washington, compared the use of wood, steel, and concrete in residential home construction. The study found a net negative carbon emission for a typical wood frame house over its entire life cycle, including emissions from manufacturing, construction and demolition, maintenance, and heating and cooling. The subtotal of the emission sources for the house was 434 metric tons of CO_2 and the offsets from forest sequestration and wood product storage subtotaled 489 metric tons, resulting in a net reduction of 55 metric tons of CO_2. In contrast, the steel frame home resulted in 185 metric tons of CO_2 emissions over its life cycle. Comparison of wood frame walls and steel stud walls in the study found that the steel walls require 43% more energy, resulting in 150% more global warming potential than wood. Production of the steel studs resulted in 60% more air emissions and 870% more water pollution than the wood studs for the same wall (CORRIM 2005).

Another research study by CORRIM found that different methods of forest management can maximize forest sequestration. For example, growing wood on shorter rotations as opposed to longer intervals between harvesting can sequester more total carbon over time. Trapping carbon in wood products capitalizes on young trees' rapid growth and ability to sequester carbon. It also decreases reliance on more fossil fuel–intensive construction materials such as steel and concrete (CORRIM 2005). It is important to note that the above discussion relates only to the carbon sequestration value of forests and wood products. It does not account for the habitat, soil, and water impacts of wood harvesting.

waters, causing reduced light penetration, increased turbidity, increased biochemical oxygen demand (BOD), and deoxygenation. These stressors can result in a loss of faunal diversity and possible fish kill (Demkin 1998). The EPA has estimated that erosion from clear-cut forests can be as much as 12,000 tons per square mile per year. This is 500 times the erosion rate of undisturbed forests.

Destruction of habitats for logging extends beyond the area of cutting with compaction of soil and vegetation removal for logging roads. Air pollution from logging trucks and machinery can damage adjacent forests, water bodies, and wildlife.

Solid waste, including tree limbs, treetops, broken and inferior logs, and stumps, is generated during harvesting operations. Some of this waste is removed for pulping, wood chips, fuel, or firewood; however, it is considered a good forestry practice to leave these elements to decay, adding nutrients and humic materials to the forest soil. In some tropical rain forests, organic material is embedded in the trees themselves and with removal, the soil can become hard and nearly sterile (Thompson and Sorvig 2000).

While wood is considered a renewable resource, some current forest practices such as clear-cutting do not allow true renewal of the resource. The main detriment to renewal of wood is the time it takes to replace the forests (and associated ecosystems), yet the demand for wood is so great that harvesting outpaces renewal. And longer rotation management is not often economically viable. Sixty billion board feet of virgin lumber is used each year in construction, and wood use in the landscape is outpacing the housing market's annual growth rate with an estimated three million new decks built each year (Imhoff 2005).

Clear-cutting techniques and reforestation with a single species is the most common forestry management practice, resulting in monoculture forests that are reharvested within a relatively short cycle. These reforestation efforts don't provide for a healthy level of species diversity of either flora or fauna (CORRIM 2005). Quick harvesting limits the available size and quality of lumber and results in a decline in forest health, often allowing invasive species to move in. Also, these monoculture plantation forests are more susceptible to attack from insects and pests, and can require more extensive management techniques such as use of pesticides and herbicides that can damage soil fertility and water quality.

Negative social impacts and human rights abuses can occur with conventional forestry practices, particularly in developing countries. It is estimated that at least 50 million indigenous people depend on Indonesia's forests for subsistence, yet they are being harvested at alarming rates. In 2003, 88% of the logging that took place in the forests was illegal. In the Amazon, an estimated 20 million people depend on and live in the forest, and 80% of the logging occurs illegally. The Amazon has one of the highest rates of forest destruction in the world (Greenpeace 2004).

The movement toward sustainable forestry practices is rapidly growing as negative impacts of traditional harvesting techniques are increasingly recognized by designers, specifiers and policy makers. Sustainable management of forests, sometimes called ecoforestry, uses selective harvesting to maintain the biological diversity of a forest and, in some cases, attempts to balance often competing environmental, social, and economic needs.

Sustainable forestry practices can ensure the benefits of carbon sequestration and promote relatively healthy habitats and ecosystems. It is possible to manage forests in such a way that supports wood yield and maintains ecosystem health. A 1999 study by EcoIndicator 99 found that a mixed broadleaf forest reduces species diversity by 10% versus a 91% reduction in conventionally farmed agriculture land. Mixed evergreen forests were not included in the study; however, it is assumed that species diversity would be similar to that of a broadleaf forest (Wilson 2006).

A 2004 study notes an improvement in overall forest health in the Pacific Northwest resulting from thinning alternatives in addition to preservation and protection policies, and to a lesser degree longer rotations. The study found an increase in understory reinitiation and more complex old forest structures (CORRIM 2005).

Some organizations, such as the Forest Stewardship Council, certify sustainable forest management practices (see certified wood discussion below). Table 10–1, developed by the Ecoforestry Institute, illustrates some differences between conventional and ecoforestry practices.

TRANSPORTATION IMPACTS

Today, lumber trade is a global market. In the quest for naturally decay- and insect-resistant, durable species for use in exterior applications, tropical hardwoods are imported from Southeast Asia, Central and South America, Australia, and Africa. The global lumber trade often results in transportation of lumber over thousands of miles from logging sites to mills and then to distribution centers. Within the United States, lumber from the Pacific Northwest and the Southeast is distributed nationwide and globally.

Fossil fuels used in transport of lumber products can have a substantial impact on CO_2 release and global

Table 10–1 Comparison of Industrial Forestry and Ecoforestry

Industrial Forestry	Ecoforestry
Trees are seen as products.	Forests are ecological communities.
Short-term production goals	Long-term sustainability
Agricultural production model	Forest ecosystem model
Trees are the only cash crop.	Diverse forest products and services
Trees' survival dependent on humans	Self-sustaining, self-maintaining, and self-renewing
Chemicals	No chemicals
Clear-cuts	Harvesting surplus wood and selective removal
Same-age stands of trees	All ages of trees
Monoculture of single or few species	All species of trees
Simplified ecosystem	Natural biodiversity and complexity
Capital intensive and corporate based	Labor intensive and locally based
Redesigning nature	Accepting nature's design
Life span: 60–100 years	Life span: millennia
Loss of the sacred	Sense of the sacred and mysterious
Older traditions and aboriginal knowledge are outdated.	Older traditions and aboriginal knowledge are sources of wisdom.

Source: Drengson and Taylor 1997

warming; therefore, transportation distances should be minimized when possible. Use of local wood can save transportation energy and costs, and sometimes use of local species will reduce reliance on commonly harvested species. Table 10–2 lists major sources of softwood by U.S. region.

Locally harvested and sourced wood can contribute to the achievement of LEED-NC v. 2.2 Materials and Resources Credits 5.1 and 5.2: Regional Materials. The credit requires that 10% or 20% (respectively) of materials by cost be harvested, processed and sourced within 500 miles of the project site (U.S. Green Building Council 2005).

MANUFACTURING IMPACTS: LUMBER

The environmental and human health impacts stemming from lumber production are fewer than those posed by production of the other structural materials, concrete and steel. They can be further minimized by specification of certified or reclaimed lumber.

Energy Use

Lumber, being relatively minimally processed, has a lower embodied energy as compared to other structural materials such as concrete and steel. Engineered wood products require more energy to produce than standard lumber, yet still less than the other materials. Fuel use in forestry includes electricity for greenhouse seedling growth, gasoline for chain saws, diesel fuel for mechanical harvesting equipment, and fertilizers (Lippiatt 2007). Milling processes that consume fuel are sawing, planing, kiln drying, and movement of stock around the plant. As with any product, long transportation distances can increase the embodied energy of lumber products.

Kiln drying, to lower the moisture content of lumber, is the most energy-consumptive process of lumber manufacture. The process, taking between 24 and 48 hours, uses about 90% of the thermal energy and 25% of the total energy of a typical mill. Advances in kiln technology and moisture sensors have reduced kiln energy use in recent years. A report by the Athena

Table 10–2 Major Resources of Softwoods According to Region

Western	Northern	Southern
Incense cedar	Northern white cedar	Atlantic white cedar
Port Orford cedar	Balsam fir	Bald cypress
Douglas fir	Eastern hemlock	Fraser fir
White firs	Fraser fir	Southern pine
Western hemlock	Jack pine	Eastern red cedar
Western larch	Red pine	
Lodgepole pine	Eastern white pine	
Ponderosa pine	Eastern red cedar	
Sugar pine	Eastern spruces	
Western white pine	Tamarack	
Western red cedar		
Redwood		
Engelmann spruce		
Sitka spruce		
Yellow cedar		

Source: Forest Products Laboratory (FPL) 1999

Sustainable Materials Institute finds that 2,795 MJ are required to produce 1,000 board feet of dry lumber and 1,138 MJ are used to produce green lumber, a difference of 60% (Athena Sustainable Materials Institute 2000). Air emissions related to energy consumption are correspondingly higher as well (see Table 10–4).

Alkaline copper quaternary–treated (ACQ) lumber uses approximately 35% more energy to produce than untreated lumber (Lippiatt 2007). Sources of energy vary by mill; however, industry-wide more than half of the energy is provided by "hogged" waste fuel (bark, sawdust, planar shavings, and fiber fines) and pulping liquors (chemicals and other burnable substances dissolved from wood in the pulping process; U.S. EPA 2007a). Other fuel sources are natural gas for boilers, and propane and diesel for forklifts and log haulers.

The wood products industry uses combined heat and power (CHP), with more than 65% of the industry's needs met through cogeneration processes. Thermal energy, primarily steam, is used for heating, evaporation, sawing, and drying. Electricity is used to power processing equipment (U.S. EPA 2007a) (see Table 10–3).

Air Emissions

Air emissions from lumber production occur primarily (79%) from the combustion of fossil fuels. CO_2 generated from biofuels (hogged wood fuel) is considered environmentally impact-neutral by the EPA; however, other criteria air pollutants (CAPs) result from its combustion (Lippiatt 2007).

Table 10–3 Fuel Sources for the Wood Product Industry

Fuel Source	Percentage
Net electricity	19
Natural gas	15
Fuel oil	3
Liquified petroleum gas (LPG) and Natural gas liquids (NGL)	1
Other (primarily biomass)	61

Source: U.S. EPA 2007a

Water Use and Emissions

The primary use of water in lumber processing is to cool saw blades. Because the heat of friction vaporizes the water, it can't be captured and reused. The greatest water impacts during lumber production stem from the application of preservative treatments for wood in exterior use. Common preservatives contain heavy metals and toxins, and wastewater from the treatment process can pose risks to workers and aquatic environments around lumber processing plants. Most wood preserving facilities take steps to minimize release of preservatives into the environment by recycling process water and reusing chemicals. However, accidental spills and other uncontrolled disposals can be an issue. Types of preservative treatments and their risks are discussed in greater detail later in the chapter.

Solid Waste Generation

Methods of milling lumber offer varying efficiencies for lumber yield and generation of sawmill waste. Plain-sawn lumber, sawn tangential to the grain, yields more lumber from a tree than quarter-sawn wood, which is sawn radially from the pith. However, quarter-sawn lumber is less susceptible to cups, surface-checks, and splits in seasoning and use. This may ultimately yield a longer use life and less waste.

Waste generated at sawmills (e.g., bark, sawdust, and trimmings) is often burned for fuel to power lumber-drying kilns. The resulting final waste product is wood ash, which is either disposed of in landfills or used in other products such as adhesives. Some mills separate wood chips for use in paper, engineered wood products, and mulch.

Waste generated in the mining of preservative compounds such as metals can be substantial. For instance, copper mining waste and overburden to obtain copper for copper-based preservative treatments can be substantial, with 400 tons of material mined to yield 1 ton of copper (Gutowski 2004). Some mine tailings can

Table 10–4 Wood Product Comparison Table from the Athena Environmental Impact Estimator[a]

Wood Product Type	Primary Energy Consumption (MJ)	Solid Waste (kg)	Air Pollution Index	Water Pollution Index	Global Warming Potential (kg)	Weighted Resource Use (kg)
Softwood lumber (small dimension, green)[b] (1 m^3)	1,230	6	12	0	73	1,262
Softwood lumber (small dimension, kiln dried)[b] (1 m^3)	5,079	18	25	0	96	1,971
Softwood lumber (large dimension, green)[c] (1 m^3)	1,089	20	11	0	56	1,237
Softwood lumber (large dimension, kiln dried)[c] (1 m^3)	5,213	18	25	0	99	2,023
Glulam beams (1 m^3)	7,542	24	59	1	279	2,608
Parallel strand lumber (1 m^3)	11,293	109	83	0	333	3,855
Laminated veneer lumber (1 m^3)	6,284	23	36	2	158	2,275
Softwood plywood[d] (1 m^2)	66	0	0	0	1	19
Oriented strand board[e] (1 m^2)	132	1	5	0	4	30

[a]All nonsheet material units are one cubic meter (1 m^3) or 0.612 Mbfm. All sheet material units are one square meter (1 m^2), $^3/_4$" thickness. This is a cradle to grave analysis for a typical U.S. installation.

[b]Small-dimension softwood lumber, kiln dried and green: m^3. All lumber products 2 × 6 (38 × 140 mm) and smaller are defined as small-dimension lumber.

[c]Large-dimension softwood lumber, kiln dried and green: m^3. All lumber products 2 × 8 (38 × 184 mm) and larger are defined as large-dimension lumber.

[d]Softwood plywood: m^2 on a 9 mm ($^3/_8$") thickness basis

[e]Oriented strand board: m^2 on a 9 mm ($^3/_8$") thickness basis

Source: Adapted from Athena Environmental Impact Estimator version 3.0.3

have toxic impacts on surrounding water bodies. For more information on metal mining impacts, refer to chapter 11.

MANUFACTURING IMPACTS: ENGINEERED WOOD PRODUCTS

As larger wood members are increasingly expensive and difficult to locate, engineered wood has gained widespread use in exterior applications. Engineered wood can offer many environmental advantages, primarily through the incorporation of small wood members and/or wood waste. Engineered wood products use lower-grade tree species and smaller-diameter trees that are more rapidly renewable. Wood is used more efficiently than in conventional lumber and a higher percentage of the wood fiber ends up in the product.

Human and environmental health impacts of engineered wood products stem primarily from the binders. The most common binders contain formaldehyde, a known carcinogen (International Agency for Research on Cancer [IARC]) and an irritant to the eyes and mucous membranes (Agency for Toxic Substances and Disease Registry [ATSDR]). Phenol formaldehyde is the type used in binders of exterior-grade wood products. Urea formaldehyde, a higher off-gassing VOC, is not used in exterior-grade products. In addition to health concerns, there is a risk of wastewater contamination from binder manufacture and wood product manufacturing facilities. The wastewater can contain small amounts of formaldehyde and phenol monomers.

A formaldehyde-free polyurethane-type binder called polymeric diphenyl methylene diisocyanate (PMDI or MDI) is used in some laminated strand lumber (LDL), medium-density fiberboard (MDF), oriented strand board (OSB), and straw particleboard products. Use in exterior engineered wood products may increase as it is a waterproof binder. While there are less off-gassing concerns with PMDI, there are concerns about worker health through exposure to uncured MDI during manufacturing (Environmental Building News [EBN] 2007). Most engineered wood approved for use in exterior applications exposed to the elements is pressure treated. The most common preservative used is alkaline copper quaternary (ACQ).

Embodied energy of engineered wood products is substantially higher than traditional "green" softwood lumber and slightly higher than kiln-dried softwood lumber. Of all engineered nonsheet materials, parallel strand lumber requires the highest amount of energy, about 11,000 MJ to produce one cubic meter. Oriented strand board (OSB) is about two times as energy intensive to produce as an equal amount of softwood plywood (Athena Environmental Impact Estimator, version 3.0.3) (see Table 10–4).

Glued laminated timbers (called glulams) are the most common engineered wood product used in exterior applications. Glulams are composed of individual layers of solid wood joined together with glue to form a large wood member. Environmental advantages of glulams are as follows: they are made from smaller pieces of wood, so smaller-diameter trees can be used and wood waste is reduced; very large wood member sizes can be achieved without threat to old-growth forests; they can be made from fast-growing, underutilized wood species; and they can be sized to specific structural needs, reducing wood waste.

Engineered board products such as plywood, oriented strand board, and strawboard can be used in concrete formwork, but most, with the exception of pressure-treated plywood and marine grade plywood, are not recommended for permanent exterior applications. Many engineered board products use wood and agricultural wastes.

CONSTRUCTION, USE, AND MAINTENANCE IMPACTS

Major environmental impacts of wood in construction stem from wood waste as board lengths are trimmed to fit. The BEES 4.0 User Guide estimates that an average of 5% of the product is lost to waste during construction (Lippiatt 2007). Unnecessary waste can be created if the structure was not dimensioned with standard board lengths in mind. Wood waste is often landfilled or incinerated, producing some air quality impacts, particularly if the wood is pressure treated. Wood scraps can be recycled or composted, but if they are pressure treated or contain glues, adhesives, or paints they should not be recycled or incinerated.

Health impacts for construction workers, particularly when building with treated wood, are a concern.

BEES 4.0 Comparison of Wood, Treated Wood, and Steel Framing

The table below compares environmental and human health impacts of wood, pressure treated wood, and steel framing materials. The data is from BEES version 4.0. Basic information about BEES is discussed in detail in chapter 3.

While steel and wood stud framing are not generally used in site structures, the comparison of the materials offers a useful, if limited, snapshot comparison of lumber, treated lumber, and cold-rolled steel products. Ideally, BEES would offer a comparison between wood decking, plastic lumber decking, and composite decking, or a comparison between wood structural lumber and composite structural lumber; however, it currently does not. See the section on plastic lumber in chapter 12 for a BEES 4.0 comparison of cedar and vinyl siding that can offer a rough comparison snapshot of wood and vinyl decking materials.

Table 10–5 Comparison of Wood and Steel Light Framing from BEES[a]

Impact	Units	Wood Framing Treated with ACQ (1 ft^2, 2 × 6 studs 16" OC)	Wood Framing, Untreated (1 ft^2, 2 × 6 studs 16" OC)	Steel Framing (1 ft^2, 33 mil cold-rolled 2 × 4 studs 20" OC)
Embodied energy (both feedstock energy and fuel energy)	MJ/1 ft^2 (megajoules)	7.85	1.87	9.05
Acidification	mg H+ equivalents	141.49	47.70	144.49
Criteria air pollutants	micro DALY (disability-adjusted life years)	0.05	0.02	0.02
Ecological toxicity	g 2,4-D (2,4-dichlorophenoxy-acetic acid) equivalents	1.27	0.96	7.75
Eutrophication	g N (nitrogen) equivalents	0.17	0.10	0.14
Fossil fuel depletion	MJ (megajoules)	0.29	0.19	0.60
Global warming	g CO_2 equivalents	198.71	132.83	564.22
Habitat alteration	Threatened and endangered species/unit	0.00	0.00	0.00
Indoor air quality	g VOC	0.00	0.00	0.00
Ozone depletion	g CFC-11 equivalents	0.00	0.00	0.00
Smog	g NO_x equivalents	1.57	0.93	1.86
Water intake	liters	0.68	0.51	4.36
Human health, all	g C_7H_8 (toluene) equivalents	48,770.68	44,447.29	405,766.23
Economic performance	Present value $	2.67	2.68	3.03
Overall performance	**Weighted score (EPA weights)***	**10.80**	**9.00**	**80.30**

*Note: In all values, including overall performance, lower values are better.

[a]Assumptions (see BEES User Guide [Lippiatt 2007]) pp.119–44 for more detailed information on assumptions):

Only framing materials are accounted for, not full wall assemblies.

Framing unit is one square foot of stud wall.

All products are transported 500 miles to site.

Wood framing is 2 × 4 studs at 16" OC.

The data for wood framing is based on a composite forest management scenario of Pacific Northwest and Southeastern U.S. wood species.

Preservative treatment for treated wood framing is alkaline copper quaternary (ACQ).

Steel framing is 33 mil cold-rolled galvanized steel studs placed 24" OC.

Fasteners for wood framing are steel nails and for steel framing are steel screws.

The service life for all framing materials is 75 years.

Recycling is assumed for steel at the end of life; landfill disposal is assumed for wood framing.

Source: National Institute of Standards and Technology

Precautions such as dust masks, protective eyewear, gloves, and laundering of affected clothing should be taken to minimize sawdust exposure to the heavy metals and toxins in many wood preservatives. In use and maintenance, toxicity impacts from wood stains, sealers, and cleaners can be a concern.

RECYCLING, REUSE, OR DISPOSAL

After the use phase, the majority of lumber is disposed of in a landfill, as it is often commingled with other demolition debris and is crushed beyond the potential for reuse. Wood is reasonably biodegradable, especially if it has not been treated, and decomposition will return carbon to the soil. However, this may not be the best end-of-use strategy. Reclaiming and reusing wood will extend the use life into a new project. And deconstruction of wood structures with the intent to reuse wood members can reduce landfill and new material costs. Where untreated wood can't be reclaimed and reused whole, it can be recycled into other wood products such as mulch or composite lumber.

Treated lumber poses a large disposal problem. Disposal of chromated copper arsenate–treated (CCA) wood from demolished structures is a growing concern as an estimated 60 billion cubic board feet of CCA-treated lumber that has been installed since the 1970s will need to be disposed of in the near future. And while the EPA phase-out of CCA-treated lumber does not mandate removal of CCA-treated structures, some owners have chosen to remove them due to health concerns. Other structures installed several years ago are nearing the end of their useful life (FPLa). The EPA-approved Consumer Fact Sheet on CCA suggests landfill or incineration disposal methods, yet there are strong concerns about the toxic impacts of CCA disposal in these ways.

Currently, the EPA regulations do not ask builders to separate their CCA waste from municipal waste or construction and demolition recycling streams. However, disposing of CCA-treated wood in landfills is a concern not only from the standpoint of landfill space consumption, but also because of the potential for leaching of the highly toxic copper, chromium, and/or arsenic. Incineration causes the arsenic to become airborne, eventually depositing on soil or surface waters, and ash from incineration contains arsenic, chromium, and copper.

Recycling of CCA-treated lumber is currently not a safe option because of the toxic heavy metal preservatives as well. Construction and demolition recycling facilities attempt to separate CCA-treated wood from other wood that is sent to them; however, pressure-treated and untreated wood are easily confused. Research has shown that CCA-treated wood is inadvertently processed with other wood into landscape and agricultural mulch, potentially spreading the chemicals back on soil. Accidental use of CCA wood in energy recovery incineration is also a concern, as captured ash containing CCA's toxic heavy metals is sometimes spread in agricultural fields (FPLa). Other copper-based wood preservatives pose some of the same risks to water and soil health.

Research is being performed on methods to remediate CCA-treated wood so it can be recycled safely. Two methods of separating the heavy metals from the wood are being tested. The first method uses anaerobic pyrolysis to remove the chemicals. This involves reducing the mass of wood fiber and extracting the chemicals for reuse. The reduced mass of wood can then be more easily landfilled and the chemicals can be reused in other applications. The second method extracts residual metals using supercritical fluid-ionic liquid, allowing the lumber to be reused in its entirety (FPLb).

Strategies for Design and Specification of Sustainable Lumber

USE WOOD RESOURCES EFFICIENTLY

Using wood efficiently will reduce the environmental impacts of wood use. Principles of resource-efficient building can be applied to wood structure design and detailing. While wood is theoretically a renewable resource, it may not be if members and structures are oversized, structures are not designed to last, wood is wasted, or disassembly and reuse are not considered in design.

Use Lowest Quality Grade of Wood for Application
There is tremendous pressure placed on forests for top-grade lumber, as forests produce only limited quantities of it. If lower appearance or quality grades, or a range of

grades of lumber are specified for appropriate applications, then the harvested trees can be used much more efficiently. For example, clear heart redwood shouldn't be specified unless flawless appearance is tantamount to the design concept. Knots and irregularities are part of the natural appearance of wood, and often the visual differences between premium and lower grades are barely noticeable. Lower appearance grades should be used especially where the wood is not visible, as long as the structural quality is not compromised. And lowest adequate structural grades should be used where possible.

Researching and specifying the quality grades that are most readily available from sustainably managed forests will lower the impact on forests. It may also increase the likelihood of obtaining FSC-certified lumber, and can result in cost savings (FSC 2005).

Use Lumber from Less Common Species to Reduce Pressure on Forests

Broadening the species market for wood will help reduce pressure on forests. Some trees in a forest are cut and then left to rot as the lumber companies determine that the market demand is minimal. Using these less widely available species can broaden the market and help decrease reliance on just a few species that are overproduced, often in monoculture plantations (Spiegel and Meadows 2006).

Lumber with a high number of grain lines (e.g., fifteen lines per inch or greater) may have come from old-growth trees from temperate ancient forests and should be avoided.

Build Small

An important way to conserve wood resources is to build smaller wood structures. Along with increases in house sizes, deck sizes have also grown to sometimes underutilized broad expanses and multiple levels. Decks should be designed to accommodate the anticipated uses but not be oversized. A deck can be sized for small gatherings and paired with a stone or recycled concrete patio for larger gatherings. Fences are often sized higher than necessary or made solid when a more open design would still minimize visual access or contain a pet. A fence with openings will encourage more air circulation and let in dappled light.

Wood members are often oversized, as span table recommendations already allow for a margin of error. It is not necessary to "size up" from the table's stated lumber size for a given application and span. A common oversized specification is the use of 6 × 6 posts when 4 × 4 posts are structurally appropriate. Many designers feel that 6 × 6 posts present a more "solid" look—yet they use 50% more wood. Thinner posts can look substantial if the structure on top is designed proportionately well.

Large wood members are often obtained from old-growth or mature trees. For example, 2 × 10s and 2 × 12s are typically milled from trees that are eighteen inches in diameter or larger. If large members are necessary because of long spans, they can be "built up" from smaller lumber sizes taken from younger trees. For example, two 2 × 8s can often be used in place of a 4 × 8 or three 2 × 8s instead of a 4 × 10.

In addition to reducing wood resource use, using less material or smaller member sizes can result in substantial cost savings. Prices increase exponentially for large solid lumber sizes, as they are increasingly hard to find. And glulaminated timbers are becoming more cost competitive for exterior use.

Design Details and Ornament Simply

Unnecessary use of wood for extreme overhangs, decoration, or appliqué should be avoided. Simple design and good craftsmanship can be elegant and will also save wood resources and costs.

Build a Durable Structure, but Don't Overdo Preservative Treatments

In order for wood to be a truly renewable resource, wood structures should be in use longer than the growth cycle of wood of comparable size and quality. It takes a redwood 30 years to reach a size where it can yield 2 × 10s. Preservative treatments, lumber types, details, and connections should be chosen with durability of the wood structure in mind. Preservative treatments should be chosen to achieve a durable structure, but as toxicity of preservatives generally increases with effectiveness, care should be taken to not overpreserve. For example, posts in ground contact may be treated with ACQ preservative, while decking could be redwood or treated with less harsh chemicals such as well-fixed borates or sodium silicate. Or posts could be held above grade on post bases to eliminate the need for ground contact strength preservatives.

Design to Reduce Wood Waste

Wood waste can be minimized by careful design of structures and by salvaging, reusing, and recycling dem- olition materials. Wood structures should be designed with standard board dimensions in mind to minimize trimming waste. For example, a concrete stair riser height of $5^1/_2$" will allow a 1×6 form board to be used. A riser height of six inches will require a 1×8 board to be ripped down to 6 inches, wasting wood. In a deck, a span of nine feet nine inches will allow use of a

Figure 10–1.
A parking arbor in Asperg, Germany, uses smaller wood members to provide enclosure. Small lumber sizes and built-up members can be derived from younger trees, shortening the renewability period for wood products. (Photo from Meg Calkins)

Strategies for Building a Longer-lasting Deck

Decks vary widely in their life span, some lasting only a few years before repairs are necessary and others lasting a few decades. While many conventional framing principles for houses are used for decks, decks don't have the protection from elements that houses do with sheathing, siding, and roofing. Details, connections, and protective treatments play a large role in the durability of a deck. The strategies for building a longer-lasting deck are drawn from two publications: "Details for a Lasting Deck," published in 1997 *Fine Homebuilding* (Falk and Williams 1996) and an FPL publication called "The Finish Line: The Bark-side/Pith-side Debate" (Williams and Knaebe 1995).

MAKE DURABLE CONNECTIONS, AS THIS IS WHERE MANY DECKS FAIL:

- Joists and beams should bear directly on posts if possible.
- Treat notches, cuts, screw holes, and bolt holes with brush-on preservative.
- Avoid connecting a deck directly to a house, as this opens the house to moisture and can trap moisture between the deck and house wall. Where decks are attached to a house wall, add spacers to allow the connection to dry.
- Use fasteners that are resistant to corrosion. Stainless steel fasteners are most resistant, yet expensive. Fasteners made of mild steel are often coated with protective metal coatings such as zinc or zinc/cadmium. These galvanized coatings vary in thickness and when they are chipped, corrosion can occur. Heavy-coated fasteners should be used. Hot-dipped fasteners generally have the thickest coatings and give the best corrosion resistance of galvanized fasteners.
- Some fasteners, particularly aluminum ones, can rapidly corrode when attached to wood treated with the new generation of copper-based preservatives. See the manufacturer's literature for the best type of fasteners for a particular preservative treatment.

- Stainless steel nails, bolts, and screws can be substantially more expensive but will be the most durable, particularly in wet or salty environments.
- Pay close attention to the holding capacity of fasteners. Smooth shank nails should be avoided, as years of wet and dry wood can cause their withdrawal resistance to fail. Screws or deformed shank nails are recommended for deck boards.
- Three-inch minimum nails or screws should be used to nail deck boards to joists.
- Washers should be used under both the bolt head and the nut to protect the wood.

USE A PROTECTIVE FINISH TO PREVENT DISCOLORATION, CHECKING, AND MILDEW EVEN WITH PRESERVATIVE-TREATED WOOD:

- Use penetrating finishes such as water repellents, water-repellent preservatives, and semitransparent penetrating stains. Avoid film-forming finishes for deck surfaces.
- Use finishes with mild or natural mildewcides.
- Pigmented finishes will protect both the wood and the finish from UV damage.
- Apply finishes around two months after completion of construction. This can vary depending on the moisture content of the wood at construction, but a year is too long to wait with any preventive treatment.
- Apply the second coat of penetrating stain before the first coat is dry to ensure that both coats soak into the wood.
- Reapply finishes annually or semiannually.

PLACE DECK BOARDS WITH THE BARK SIDE UP AND PITH SIDE DOWN FOR THE FOLLOWING REASONS:

- Cupping can result from shrinking of the top and swelling of the bottom of wood caused by moisture and drying in the sun.

Continued

- Vertical-grained lumber may cup less than flat-grained lumber. But it can cup when the top of a piece of lumber has dried faster than the bottom.

- The pith side of lumber is more prone to shelling (a severe type of raised grain).

- Pressure treatment does not penetrate heartwood as well and the pith side of lumber may contain more heartwood than the bark side.

- Exceptions to this rule do exist and if the pith side is clearly better, it should be placed up.

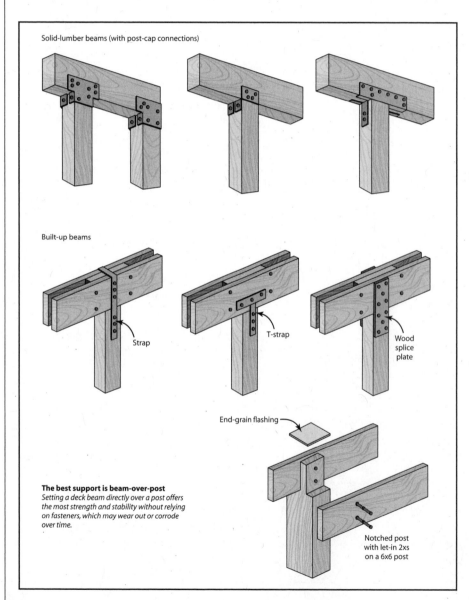

Solid-lumber beams (with post-cap connections)

Built-up beams

Strap

T-strap

Wood splice plate

End-grain flashing

The best support is beam-over-post
Setting a deck beam directly over a post offers the most strength and stability without relying on fasteners, which may wear out or corrode over time.

Notched post with let-in 2xs on a 6x6 post

Figure 10–2.

Durable connections can ensure that a wood structure lasts long enough for new wood to be grown. Setting a deck beam directly on a post offers the most stability without relying on fasteners, which can corrode or wear out over time. (Source: Drawings by Vince Babak, *Fine Homebuilding Magazine* © 1996, The Taunton Press, Inc.; Redrawn by John Wiley & Sons)

ten-foot-long length of lumber with only a small end trim, whereas a span of ten feet six inches will require a twelve-foot length and eighteen inches of wood waste.

Build for Disassembly

Structures should be designed for eventual disassembly so the wood can be reclaimed and reused in another structure. Screws and bolt connections as opposed to glued or pneumatically nailed connections will facilitate disassembly. Glue or nail connections can result in broken members or frayed ends during deconstruction. See chapter 4 for a detailed discussion of design for disassembly (DfD) strategies.

Use Engineered Wood Products to Reduce Pressure on Forests

Engineered wood products can be considered a "green" product if they avoid use of formaldehyde binders and the wood used is Forest Stewardship Council (FSC) certified. An increasing number of engineered wood products, particularly glulams, are available with FSC certification. Products with MDI binders are preferable to those containing formaldehyde. Some binders are newly available that are partially produced from soybeans. Products made with these binders contain phenol formaldehyde in lesser amounts or none at all (EBN 2007).

In an effort to reduce virgin timber use in engineered wood products, the Composite Panel Association (CPA) offers an Environmentally Preferable Product certification program (CPA). A product can be CPA certified if it contains 100% recycled or recovered content and it meets the ANSI standard A208.2–2002 limiting formaldehyde emissions.

USE CERTIFIED WOOD

Use of certified lumber and wood products can ensure that the wood comes from companies practicing sustainable forest management and harvesting. Some certification systems also require sustainable social and economic practices as well. Globally, there are multiple forest certification systems with varying priorities and standards. There are five systems in use in the United States and Canada summarized in Table 10–6. The Forest Steward-

ship Council (FSC) is the only one that currently has the support of the U.S. Green Building Council, the World Wildlife Fund, Greenpeace, and the Rainforest Action Network. FSC principles, standards, and practices are discussed in detail below. The Sustainable Forestry Initiative (SFI), a certification system created by the American Forest and Paper Association, is growing, yet many environmental organizations argue that the environmental and social standards are not as rigorous as the FSC's (Imhoff 2005) (see Table 10–6).

The Forest Stewardship Council

The Forest Stewardship Council (FSC), an international organization created in 1993, certifies environmentally and socially responsible forestry management practices, and forest products resulting from the operations. They have established principles and criteria for responsible management of forests. Their stated mission is to "promote environmentally appropriate, socially beneficial, and economically viable management of the world's forests" (FSC).

Environmentally appropriate forest management ensures that the harvest of timber and nontimber products maintains the forest's biodiversity, productivity, and ecological processes.

Socially beneficial forest management helps both local people and society at large to enjoy long-term benefits and also provides strong incentives to local people to sustain the forest resources and adhere to long-term management plans.

Economically viable forest management means that forest operations are structured and managed so as to be sufficiently profitable, without generating financial profit at the expense of the forest resources, the ecosystem, or affected communities (FSC).

The FSC accredits and monitors independent third-party auditors who certify forest managers and forest product producers to FSC standards. The two types of certification are the following (Miller and Campbell 2006):

Forest management (FM) certification applies to actual forests. Parcels can receive certification if their

Table 10–6 Comparison of Forest Certification Systems

Criteria	American Tree Farm Systems	Canadian Standards Association	Forest Stewardship Council	Program for Endorsement of Forest Certification Schemes	Sustainable Forestry Initiative
The Basics					
Basics of company participation	Voluntary	Voluntary	Voluntary	Voluntary	Voluntary
Scope	Private, nonindustrial forests in the United States	Focuses on all forest types in Canada	Focuses on all forest types throughout the world	PEFC is a mutual recognition body that endorses national systems throughout the world.	Primarily focused on large-scale forests in the United States and Canada
Number of participants	88,000 certified tree farmers in 46 states	There are 26 companies in Canada with 85 forest management certificates. There are 31 companies with 61 Chain of Custody certificates.	There are 862 Forest Management certificates and 6,683 Chain of Custody certificates in 83 countries.	PEFC Council formally endorsed 22 national systems. These cover 1,121 forest management certificates and 3,123 Chain of Custody certificates.	In the United States and Canada, there are 219 program participants.
Total land area	24 million acres in the United States	205,185,992 acres in Canada	234,287,410 acres globally 80,692,524 acres in North America	494 million acres globally	133,039,968 acres in Canada and the United States
Governance: Managing the System					
Oversight	National operating committee and individual state committees	A 27-member Board of Directors	The General Assembly consists of all FSC members who fall into three chambers: economic, social, and environmental. The Board of Directors consists of nine individuals, with three representing each chamber.	A General Assembly and a Board of Directors consisting of a chairman, two vice chairmen, and between two and ten members.	The 15-member Board of Directors manages the standards setting, fiber tracking, labeling, and certification process.

Table 10–6 Comparison of Forest Certification Systems *(Continued)*

Criteria	American Tree Farm Systems	Canadian Standards Association	Forest Stewardship Council	Program for Endorsement of Forest Certification Schemes	Sustainable Forestry Initiative
Representation	Tree Farmers and forestry professionals	Academic, government, industry, and consulting sectors	Academic, government, industry, and consulting sectors	The General Assembly consists of representatives from the 33 member countries reflecting major interest parties supporting PEFC, geographical distribution of members, and a gender balance.	Evenly split among SFI program participants, the conservation and environmental community, and the broader forest community.
Standardization: Developing the Standard					
Development	Set by independent standards review panel consisting of academia, environmental organizations, forest industry, forest owners, professional logging community, and government.	Set by a technical committee with representatives from academia, government, industry, and general interest groups.	Set by national and regional standards working groups with representation open to businesses, environmental groups, auditors, individuals, and government.	PEFC national governing bodies coordinate the setting process, which is set by invited parties including forest owners, industry, nongovernmental groups, unions, and retailers.	Set by the Board of Directors and implemented by the Resources Committee with two-thirds of representation from academic, government, and conservation organizations and the rest from the forest products industry.
Scope	Environmental and silvicultural issues	Environmental, silvicultural, social, and economic issues	Environmental, silvicultural, social, and economic issues	Environmental, silvicultural, social, and economic issues	Environmental, silvicultural, social, and economic issues
Public input	Subject to 60-day public review	Subject to 60-day public review	Subject to 60-day public review	The final draft of a system is subject to 60 days of public consultation as the minimum.	Subject to public review
Approval	American Forest Foundation Board of Trustees	Standards Council of Canada	National Board and FSC International Secretariat	PEFC Council assesses for purpose of endorsement	Board of Directors
Updating	Every five years	Every five years	Every five years	Every five years	Every five years

Continued

Table 10–6 Comparison of Forest Certification Systems *(Continued)*

Criteria	American Tree Farm Systems	Canadian Standards Association	Forest Stewardship Council	Program for Endorsement of Forest Certification Schemes	Sustainable Forestry Initiative
Product Tracking and Claims					
Material tracking	None	Chain of Custody tracks products from forest through each stage of manufacturing and distribution.	Chain of Custody tracks products from forest through each stage of manufacturing and distribution.	Chain of Custody tracks products from forest through each stage of manufacturing and distribution.	Participants required to have auditable monitoring system to account for all wood flows. Participants can also have Chain of Custody certification to track products from forest through each stage of manufacturing and distribution.

Source: Adapted from Metafore

forest management practices meet the FSC's principles and any regional criteria that may exist. This certification is performed by an FSC-accredited independent third-party auditor. Audits of forest parcels are performed annually.

Chain-of-custody (COC) certification applies to the supply chain through which the FSC harvested wood travels until it reaches the consumer (see Figure 10–3). COC certification is awarded to manufacturers, distributors, and suppliers through audits that verify the tracking of all FSC materials back to the certified forest source (FSC) COC certification can be applied to any product from lumber to paper to furniture. Certified products will have the FSC logo printed on them or on their packaging.

FSC's COC Standard, FSC-STD-40–004, contains three labels for Chain-of-Custody Certified materials:

- FSC *Pure* products are made from wood or wood fiber originating from an FSC-certified forest.

- FSC *Recycled* products contain 100% wood fiber that is post-consumer recycled. This standard currently applies primarily to paper products; however, it holds potential to apply to wood building products made from post-consumer recycled wood.
- FSC *Mixed* products contain some combination of post-consumer recycled content, pre-consumer recycled content, wood from FSC-certified forests and/or FSC-controlled wood.

FSC-controlled wood is wood that avoids the most controversial wood sources but is not from FSC-certified forests. The FSC Controlled Wood Standard states that wood should not be harvested illegally, in violation of traditional and civil rights, in forests in which high conservation values are threatened by management activities, from areas being converted from forests and other wooded ecosystems to plantations or nonforest uses, or from forest management units in which genetically modified trees are planted (FSC 2006).

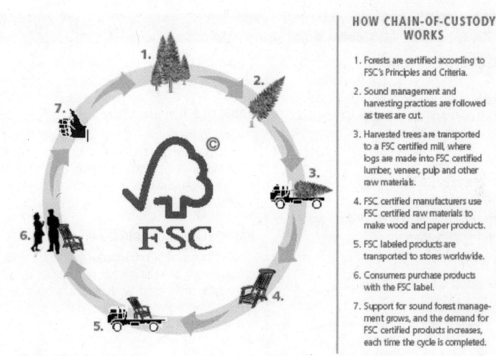

HOW CHAIN-OF-CUSTODY WORKS

1. Forests are certified according to FSC's Principles and Criteria.

2. Sound management and harvesting practices are followed as trees are cut.

3. Harvested trees are transported to a FSC certified mill, where logs are made into FSC certified lumber, veneer, pulp and other raw materials.

4. FSC certified manufacturers use FSC certified raw materials to make wood and paper products.

5. FSC labeled products are transported to stores worldwide.

6. Consumers purchase products with the FSC label.

7. Support for sound forest management grows, and the demand for FSC certified products increases, each time the cycle is completed.

Figure 10–3.
The Forest Stewardship Council's Chain of Custody tracks wood and wood products through the entire supply chain, ensuring that products are truly sustainably harvested and processed. (Source: © 1996 Forest Stewardship Council A.C.)

Quality of FSC Lumber. Some distributors maintain that some FSC lumber is a higher-quality product than conventionally harvested lumber, as FSC forests are on a longer rotation cycle than today's rapidly grown plantation trees. Older trees have a clearer, tighter, straighter grain with fewer knots than new plantation-grown trees that are harvested every few decades.

Sourcing and costs of FSC-certified lumber. Availability of FSC-certified wood is limited in some regions of the United States. This can result in increased costs and longer lead times for acquiring the wood. Currently costs of FSC-certified lumber are equal to or higher than uncertified lumber; however, as FSC lumber gains widespread use costs will likely lower (Miller and Campbell 2006). Recent commitments from some major home improvement chains and growing use of the LEED system will likely improve availability and lower costs (see Figure 10–4).

The U.S. Green Building Council's (USGBC) LEED systems award one point for use of FSC-certified wood. The credit requires that a project use a minimum of 50% FSC-certified wood by cost. At this time the USGBC does not recognize any other certification systems.

The FSC has certified nine inspection organizations around the world. Two are located in the United States, the nonprofit Rainforest Alliance's SmartWood program and the for-profit Scientific Certification Systems. Both organizations provide up-to-date lists of FSC-certified wood suppliers across the country.

The Forest Certification Resource Center provides a search tool that identifies manufacturers, distributors, importers, and retailers certified under the FSC, the Sustainable Forestry Initiative (SFI), and the Canadian Standards Association (CSA). The database is searchable by product, location, and certification system (Forest Certification Resource Center).

Forest Stewardship Council Principles of Forest Management

PRINCIPLE 1: COMPLIANCE WITH LAWS AND FSC PRINCIPLES

Forest management shall respect all applicable laws of the country in which they occur, and international treaties and agreements to which the country is a signatory, and comply with all FSC Principles and Criteria.

PRINCIPLE 2: TENURE AND USE RIGHTS AND RESPONSIBILITIES

Long-term tenure and use rights to the land and forest resources shall be clearly defined, documented, and legally established.

PRINCIPLE 3: INDIGENOUS PEOPLE'S RIGHTS

The legal and customary rights of indigenous peoples to own, use, and manage their lands, territories, and resources shall be recognized and respected.

PRINCIPLE 4: COMMUNITY RELATIONS AND WORKERS' RIGHTS

Forest management operations shall maintain or enhance the long-term social and economic well-being of forest workers and local communities.

PRINCIPLE 5: BENEFITS FROM THE FOREST

Forest management operations shall encourage the efficient use of the forest's multiple products and services to ensure economic viability and a wide range of environmental and social benefits.

PRINCIPLE 6: ENVIRONMENTAL IMPACT

Forest management shall conserve biological diversity and its associated values, water resources, soils, and unique and fragile ecosystems and landscapes, and, by so doing, maintain the ecological functions and the integrity of the forest.

PRINCIPLE 7: MANAGEMENT PLAN

A management plan—appropriate to the scale and intensity of the operations—shall be written, implemented, and kept up to date. The long-term objectives of management, and the means of achieving them, shall be clearly stated.

PRINCIPLE 8: MONITORING AND ASSESSMENT

Monitoring shall be conducted—appropriate to the scale and intensity of forest management—to assess the condition of the forest, yields of forest products, chain of custody, management activities, and their social and environmental impacts.

PRINCIPLE 9: MAINTENANCE OF HIGH CONSERVATION VALUE FORESTS

Management activities in high conservation value forests shall maintain or enhance the attributes which define such forests. Decisions regarding high conservation value forests shall always be considered in the context of a precautionary approach.

PRINCIPLE 10: PLANTATIONS

Plantations shall be planned and managed in accordance with Principles and Criteria 1–9, and Principle 10 and its Criteria. While plantations can provide an array of social and economic benefits, and can contribute to satisfying the world's needs for forest products, they should complement the management of, reduce pressures on, and promote the restoration and conservation of natural forests.

Use Reclaimed Wood

According to the EPA, 12.7 million tons of wood waste was generated from construction and demolition in 2000 (U.S. EPA 2005). Markets for wood waste recovery are growing rapidly; however, the largest quantity of wood waste is downcycled into mulch and fuel applications. These applications are convenient for contractors because they allow for machine-driven building demolition, rather than the more time-consuming deconstruction techniques

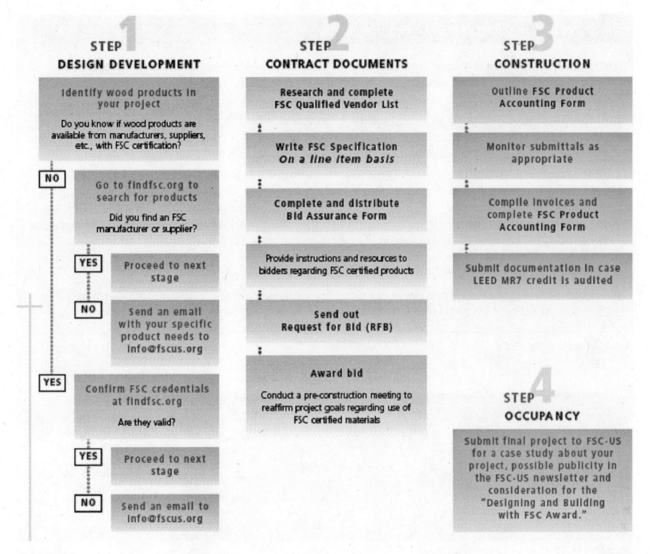

STEP 1 — DESIGN DEVELOPMENT

Identify wood products in your project

Do you know if wood products are available from manufacturers, suppliers, etc., with FSC certification?

NO → Go to findfsc.org to search for products

Did you find an FSC manufacturer or supplier?

YES → Proceed to next stage

NO → Send an email with your specific product needs to info@fscus.org

YES → Confirm FSC credentials at findfsc.org

Are they valid?

YES → Proceed to next stage

NO → Send an email to info@fscus.org

STEP 2 — CONTRACT DOCUMENTS

Research and complete FSC Qualified Vendor List

Write FSC Specification *On a line item basis*

Complete and distribute Bid Assurance Form

Provide instructions and resources to bidders regarding FSC certified products

Send out Request for Bid (RFB)

Award bid

Conduct a pre-construction meeting to reaffirm project goals regarding use of FSC certified materials

STEP 3 — CONSTRUCTION

Outline FSC Product Accounting Form

Monitor submittals as appropriate

Compile invoices and complete FSC Product Accounting Form

Submit documentation in case LEED MR7 credit is audited

STEP 4 — OCCUPANCY

Submit final project to FSC-US for a case study about your project, possible publicity in the FSC-US newsletter and consideration for the "Designing and Building with FSC Award."

Figure 10–4.
The Forest Stewardship Council publication *Designing and Building with FSC* offers questions designed to assist specifiers with locating and specifying FSC products. The publication offers detailed spec language as well. (Source: © 1996 Forest Stewardship Council A.C.)

necessary for reclaiming whole timbers. However, the market for reclaimed wood is growing as virgin lumber quality and sizes from second-growth sources decline.

Benefits of Building with Reclaimed Wood

Using reclaimed wood for landscape structures has many benefits. It reduces pressure on forests, keeps good material out of landfills, can be higher quality and larger members than virgin lumber, and can offer unique character to a new structure.

Reclaimed lumber can be of higher quality than the limited variety and quality of newly harvested wood that is found in lumberyards today. Much of the wood reclaimed from deconstructed buildings was cut from

Designing with and Specifying FSC-certified Wood

- Work with FSC-US or the FSC chapter for the country in which the project is located early in the project to determine appropriate and available types of wood for the project.

- During the design phase, contact suppliers to determine availability of wood species, products, sizes, and quantities needed for the project.

- Provide bidders with a list of certified vendors. "FSC Certified Bid Assurance Form" and "FSC Qualified Vendor List" are forms that can be used to assist contractors in finding FSC suppliers and ensure provision of certified wood. These forms can be located in the publication *Designing and Building with FSC* (FSC 2005).

- Availability of wood may change over the life of the project. Consider having the owner prepurchase and store wood. The items can then be supplied to the contractor as "furnished by owner, installed by contractor (FOIC)." Be sure that wood is stored in a moisture condition similar to the one in which it will be installed.

- If possible, specify FSC-certified wood from local sources.

- In contract documents, specify that wood should come from FSC-certified sources and require chain-of-custody documentation. If possible, employ a line-item strategy that is based on research for availability of lumber, rather than a blanket spec requiring FSC certification. This may ensure better success with contractors being able to find the required wood.

- If appropriate, use detailed specification language from the FSC publication *Designing and Building with FSC*.

Source: Adapted from FSC 2005

Figure 10–5.
At this Napa Valley home of rammed and sprayed earth construction, designed by Arkin Tilt Architects, the carport and garbage/propane tank enclosures are sheathed in a "corncrib" application of salvaged Port Orford cedar boards. This ventilated design is particularly welcome in this location. This material is also used on the tower stair rail; the stair treads are salvaged 3 × 12 redwood from wine tank bottoms. (Photo: Anni Tilt and David Arkin, AIA, Arkin Tilt Architects)

old-growth forests and is far denser, stronger, closer grained, and more free of structural defects than the wood that is grown and quickly harvested today. Many older buildings used large solid wood structural members, not even available today, which are ideal for long span landscape structures such as large trellis structures or decks. Some older wood structures were built from local or unique, decay-resistant wood species such as heart cypress, heart redwood, or Port Orford cedar, which are no longer available at many lumberyards. Lastly, some reclaimed wood contains ornamentation or hand-created detail that would be expensive to duplicate today.

Despite these advantages, reclaimed lumber remains a relatively untapped resource in North America, although the industry is growing with increasing state and local waste reduction mandates. SmartWood Rediscovered, a group dedicated to the reuse and source certification of wood, and part of the Rainforest Alliance, estimates that billions of board feet of reusable wood exist across the United States and Canada. They estimate that an old warehouse with one million board feet of reusable lumber can offset the need to harvest 1,000 acres of forest (Rainforest Alliance).

Sources of Reclaimed Wood

Reclaimed wood for reuse in landscapes and buildings can come from a variety of sources.

Architectural salvage sources are buildings, decks, bridges, and tanks. The most common buildings to be deconstructed are warehouses, military facilities, and industrial buildings because larger structural members are used and are not usually covered with a lot of finishes such as lath and plaster, which can make the wood difficult to get at during the deconstruction process. Most of the cost of architecturally reclaimed wood comes from the labor required to deconstruct the buildings and to "clean" the wood of nails and other fasteners. Transport across long distances can add additional costs.

A concern of architecturally salavaged painted wood is contamination from lead paint on the wood. Some reclaimed wood painted with lead-based paint may

Table 10–7 Benefits and Challenges of Reclaimed Wood Use

Benefits
Reduces use of virgin wood and pressure on forests
Extends the life cycle of existing building materials
Can offer performance advantages: larger size, density, dryness, better strength, decay resistance
Unique species and coloration of wood not found in lumberyards
Can provide unique design inspiration, add aesthetic character, or tell a story
Can be sourced regionally
Costs, especially from job site salvage, can be lower than virgin wood
Possible reduction in transportation costs and impacts

Challenges
Can require additional labor in sorting, milling, or carpentry
May require replacing and surfacing if appearance is a priority
Costs can be higher, especially if additional working of wood is required.
Lumber may need to be regraded if used in a structural application.
Sourcing wood can be challenging, particularly in some regions.
Potential contamination with lead paint or persistent pesticides, such as chromium, arsenic or chlordane (Wilson 2007).

actually qualify as hazardous waste under the EPA's Resource Conservation and Recovery Act. If a waste product contains lead at a concentration of 5mg/L or higher, it is illegal to give or sell the wood. It is considered hazardous and must be disposed of per Federal Regulations. However, if the paint is removed it may be that the wood can be sold. If the lead level of reclaimed painted wood is lower than the threshold, the wood can be shaved or planed to remove the lead paint for reuse, but the paint shavings must be disposed of in a method that meets Federal Regulations. Residential situations may be exempt from these regulations under the "household hazardous waste exclusion" (Falk 2002).

Job site salvage can offer a way of remembering the history and continuing the life of a building site. Job site salvage involves reuse of wood from structures on-site, such as an old deck structure for a new deck or a new retaining wall with timbers from an old wall on-site. Often the wood from a structure is still good, but design needs have changed, hence the new structure. Contractors are understandably nervous about this practice, as it can be hard to find new wood to match the old if additional wood is needed. In addition, there are usually labor costs involved with taking apart and cleaning the wood.

There are health and safety concerns with use of reclaimed pressure treated lumber—of which there is a large supply from Penta-treated railroad ties to CCA-treated decking (Falk and McKeever 2004). The Southern Forest Products Association estimates production of a total volume of 102 million cubic feet of CCA-treated southern pine alone since 1970, and the Forest Service estimates that 1.7 million cubic meters of CCA-treated lumber is removed each year from decks alone. In addition, with the recent CCA phase out, many existing CCA structures are expected to be demolished in the next few years (Falk and McKeever 2004). This will create an abundant suppy of potentially recyclable material, yet the safety concerns with milling, working, and reusing the material are real. And until new techniques of extracting the preservatives are in commercial use this reclaimed lumber should not be reused, but disposed of in controlled landfills.

Trees cleared for a building site can be a source of reclaimed wood. An on-site portable sawmill can be used to mill felled trees, saving resources, fuel use, and cost of transport. Portable sawmills offer advantages over traditional mills in that they are more fuel efficient and waste less wood because they use a narrower kerf. Some sources estimate that portable sawmills produce 30% more usable lumber than traditional sawmills, and the wood waste that is produced is returned to the soil. Portable sawmills can make it cost effective to saw less desirable or lower-grade species that are selectively thinned from small woodlots (Chappel 1998).

When reclaimed on-site wood is milled with a portable sawmill, it should be stored in a covered condition with similar humidity levels to the situation in which it will be used to avoid shrinkage after the structure is built. This may present the biggest challenge to this practice, as covered storage may not always be available on-site. There also may not be enough time for the wood to dry between cutting and use; however, local sawmills may offer use of their drying kilns for a fee.

Horticultural salvage, lumber from fallen or taken-down trees, comes from orchards, woodlots, and neighborhood trees. Some estimate that nearly 3.8 billion board feet of urban trees are landfilled, incinerated, chipped, or left to rot each year—an amount equal to 30% of U.S. annual hardwood lumber production (New Life Millworks). Many large street, yard, and orchard trees are taken down each year due to lightning strikes, development, nuisance, or life-cycle reasons. Many are very large hardwoods or fruit trees that have the potential to yield large, unique pieces of lumber. Traditionally these trees are chipped for mulch; however, the practice of milling them for lumber has grown enough in the past few years that the cost of taking down a tree may be offset when the arborist sells it to a mill for use as lumber. Portable sawmills are cost-effective ways to mill the lumber on-site (Chappel 1998).

River bottom salvage is the practice of salvaging "sinker" and "runaway" logs from river bottoms. A significant percentage of the virgin forest cypress and yellow pine logs harvested in the Southeast between 1860 and 1920 sank to the bottom of the rivers that were used to transport them to mills. Others bounded into inaccessible areas after felling. Many of these old-growth logs are still

Figure 10–6.

Figure 10–7.

At the Merry Lea Environmental Learning Center in Goshen, Indiana, logs from small trees cleared for the center's buildings are stacked and bolted to form an entry fence structure. (Photo © Conservation Design Forum, 2008. All rights reserved. www.cdfinc.com)

well preserved, as they were completely submerged in water, and are being reclaimed and sold. However, there are environmental concerns about methods used to reclaim this wood since sensitive aquatic or terrestrial habitats can be disturbed by placement of logs and impacts from the equipment used for the harvest.

Standing underwater timber salvage is the practice of harvesting timber from forests submerged by the construction of dams. An estimated 300 million trees potentially producing 100 billion board feet of lumber is currently submerged behind 45,000 dams around the world (EBN 2006). A Canadian Company is pioneering the practice with harvesting equipment developed for minimal environmental impact, energy use and worker safety risk. Harvesting equipment hovers above the bottom of the water body leaving habitat and root structures intact. Branches and wood debris are often returned to the submerged forest floor (EBN 2006).

While this harvesting practice is considered to have less environmental impact than terrestrial logging, processing of lumber does require greater energy expenditure to kiln dry the saturated lumber.

The Rainforest Alliance's SmartWood program audits sources of reclaimed wood in an effort to ensure that it was salvaged in a manner that was environmentally and socially sound. Reclaimed wood certified by this program is labeled "SmartWood Rediscovered." A chain of custody should accompany this certified wood.

DESIGNING WITH RECLAIMED WOOD

Reclaimed wood can offer unique design opportunities based on species, size, and character of wood members. However, finding specific member sizes and species of reclaimed wood after the design phase can be a challenge, as availability of standard sizes and types is inconsistent. If reclaimed lumber is located and purchased in the conceptual design phase, the design of the structure can be inspired by the characteristics of the reclaimed materials.

Reclaimed wood does not look new. And while it can be planed and sanded to improve the surface appearance, it often has bolt holes, fastener marks, stains, and blemishes left from its previous application. This can enrich the character of the wood, but clients should be made aware that the wood may have these irregularities.

Wherever possible, reclaimed wood should be reused whole, rather than ripped into smaller members. The value of reclaimed lumber is the opportunity to use larger members that can't easily be found in virgin lumberyards, so if a structure using reclaimed wood calls for smaller members, leave the large ones for a project where they can be used in whole form and their salvage potential for the next structure will not be reduced.

Reclaimed wood that is structurally sound but not visually acceptable can be used in temporary applications such as formwork and scaffolding, or in structural applications that won't be visible.

SPECIFYING RECLAIMED WOOD

Specifying reclaimed wood is different from specifying virgin lumber, particularly if the wood has not been

Figure 10–8.
This fence at a Bay Area property designed by Leger Wanaselja Architects is constructed from reclaimed redwood window trim from the house remodel. Boards are placed and nailed in an artful pattern to take advantage of the short lengths. (Photo from Leger Wanaselja Architects)

sourced prior to the design and written specification documents. It is challenging to specify the exact type, size, surfacing, and grade of wood and expect that the contractor will be able to locate it. Instead, appearance, decay resistance, and size specifications can be given, and the species type left open-ended to ensure best results. Or the design can be based on wood that is available or has already been acquired.

When using reclaimed wood in a structural application (e.g., deck structures), some inspectors will require that the wood be regraded. An existing grade mark on a piece of reused wood is usually not acceptable to inspectors. If graded wood is required, some mills or distributors will have it graded on request; however, the price of the wood may increase to pay the cost of grading. Graders can also be hired by a builder for $250–$400 per day. Grades are given for the entire batch of reclaimed wood, rather than for individual lumber pieces. The grade is based on the situation in which the wood will be used. The USDA Forest Products Lab in Madison, Wisconsin, is working on grading standards for reclaimed wood with the hope that the process will become more like grading new wood and thereby reduce the cost impact of its use.

Figure 10–9.
Deck boards for this Bay Area remodel by Leger Wanaselja Architects were salvaged from the old deck structure, planed, and oiled. Nearly all wood on the project was either salvaged on- or off-site or is FSC certified. (Photo from Leger Wanaselja Architects)

CONSTRUCTING WITH RECLAIMED WOOD

If reclaimed wood has not been cleaned, surfaced, and dimensioned to current standards, building with it can take extra time and effort. Reclaimed wood, not always in current standard sizes, may need to be trimmed or routed to work with standard wood connectors, or connection designs will need to be altered to fit wood sizes. Reclaimed wood can be drier than virgin wood and may split when nailing. Drilled and bolted connections should be specified.

WHEN USING RECLAIMED WOOD:

- Let the materials inspire the design.
- Source and reserve the wood before design work is complete to avoid design revisions and/or procurement delays.
- Specify wood from local sources when possible to avoid the resource consumption of extensive trucking.
- Include appearance standards in specifications.
- Keep big wood members whole when possible, rather than ripping them down, so they can be reclaimed again.
- Request a chain of custody for any questionably sourced wood.
- Make sure clients are aware of nail holes and other age marks from previous use.
- Make sure there is some extra wood in order—it may be difficult to find more of the same later.
- Use less pristine wood for rougher applications like concrete formwork.
- Have wood in structural situations regraded if code requires it.
- Specify drilled and bolted connections rather than nailed, as reclaimed wood is drier than "green" wood and may split.
- Be sure to preserve wood that is not naturally rot resistant.
- Use adequate protection for workers who strip wood with lead-based paint, or cut wood treated with toxic preservatives.

LOCATING/SOURCING RECLAIMED WOOD

Despite opportunities for using reclaimed wood to enrich the design of landscape structures, specifying it in

Distribution sources for reclaimed wood vary widely across the United States. Most reclaimed wood is found at sources without wide distribution networks or large inventories, making the specification of reclaimed lumber a hit-or-miss situation and a time-consuming, if ultimately rewarding, job. However, the combination of growing recycling mandates, numerous military base deconstruction activities, and increasing demand from designers, builders, and clients, means that distribution of reclaimed wood is an evolving and growing industry.

Figure 10–10.
This fence near the entrance arbor of the Mary, Star of the Sea Church in Gualala, California, designed by Arkin Tilt Architects, is constructed of salvaged redwood split rails, formerly sheep fencing on coastal ranches. This material is decades old and is probably good for many more, if kept vertical. (Photo from Anni Tilt and David Arkin, AIA, Arkin Tilt Architects)

a biddable construction document set is sometimes a challenge. Locating reclaimed lumber to meet the designer's specifications after construction documents are complete can be difficult. Instead, sourcing and obtaining the wood during the design process will ensure the best results. The specs can be written for the wood to be "supplied by owner, installed by contractor." Slightly more wood than is needed should be obtained in case of defects or changes during construction. Additional wood of the same type may be unavailable a few months later.

If project conditions don't allow for sourcing and purchase of reclaimed wood during the design phase, a list of suppliers of reclaimed wood can be included in the specifications. Also, some suppliers may let a designer "tag" the wood, much like one would tag plant material, and then write the source and price into the bid documents.

Figure 10–11.
Tree branches from trees felled to create solar meadows at Islandwood on Bainbridge Island were used to form balustrades along stairs and rails of remote site structures. Use of small tree branches, a material that is usually waste burned for wood-processing energy, is an efficient use of wood and the remaining tree bark can protect the wood from decay. (Design by Mithun; Photo by Meg Calkins)

The reclaimed lumber market is usually strongest in areas where waste reduction mandates keep demolition debris from landfills. However, these mandates do not guarantee a strong salvage market, as some demolition contractors find it easier to take reclaimed lumber to recycling facilities that chip the wood for mulch.

Some sources of reclaimed lumber are as follows:

The project site can be an inexpensive source for reclaimed wood, as there are no transport, storage, or landfill costs. The major expenses are labor costs of deconstructing structures and cleaning the wood of nails. It may pay to hire a reclamation specialist or have the demolition contractor walk through the site with the designer to identify potential materials to salvage.

Salvage yards can be valuable sources of larger quantities of reclaimed wood. Often they will broker wood salvage transactions, but the price will reflect their efforts to locate, transport, store, clean, and regrade the wood.

Figure 10–12.
Trees felled on-site at the Cambridge Fresh Pond were used to make "brush barriers"—temporary barriers to keep pedestrians out of newly planted areas. The brush barriers will decompose as the vegetation matures. Carol R. Johnson Associates used all parts of felled trees for log benches and staked logs for slope stabilization. (Photo from Carol R. Johnson Associates)

Biodeterioration and Weathering of Wood in Exterior Use

Wood is vulnerable to biological organisms such as fungi, insects, and marine borers and to weathering from sun, wind, snow, temperature extremes, and water. Properties of wood such as density, grain characteristics (presence of early wood or late wood), texture (hardwood or soft-wood), presence of heartwood or sapwood, and natural extractives, resins, and oils will all affect the weathering ability of wood.

Decay of wood is caused by fungi, microscopic organisms that eat the organic material of wood. The growth of these organisms is dependent on the presence of moisture, air, and mild temperatures. While air-dried wood will have a moisture content of 20%, decay accelerates when the moisture content of wood is above 30%, which is the fiber saturation point (FPL 1999).

Heartwood, the inner column of a tree that is naturally impregnated with extractives, pitch, oils, and other natural preservatives, is less susceptible to decay from fungus attack than is the outer sapwood. In some species the heartwood is so decay resistant that the wood does not require preservative treatment, only finishing. However, it should be noted that the sapwood of these species is not as decay resistant as the heartwood.

Sunlight (UV rays) will degrade the surface of wood through decomposition of lignin, the material in wood that bonds the cellulose fibers together. Changes in moisture content result in microscopic checks and cracks from the different shrink-swell rates of earlywood and latewood. As surface cracks and deformities enlarge, moisture is held longer and fungi can become established.

Insects, primarily termites and marine borers, can also damage wood in both exterior and interior environments. Therefore many preservative treatments contain insecticides as well as fungicides.

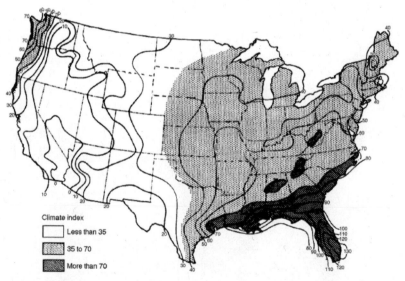

Figure 10–13.
This map illustrates the Forest Products Laboratory's climate index for wood decay hazard. Higher numbers indicate greater decay hazard and will require stronger preservative treatments or decay-resistant wood in exterior applications. (Source: Forest Products Laboratory 1999)

Small-scale sources of reclaimed wood are home-owner roadside displays, local dumps (get there at the right time), and local newspaper trade ads. These sources may yield some valuable finds, but they are not reliable sources for large orders or biddable projects.

Online materials exchanges are an increasing source of reclaimed lumber. Care should be taken to not obtain materials far from the project site, as transport energy will negate any resource savings from the use of reclaimed wood.

Other demolition sites and contractors can yield reclaimed wood, although the typical practice is to demolish a structure, splintering the wood, and then send the wood to be chipped for mulch. Many contractors find this more cost effective than salvaging wood, as less time is required for demolition than deconstruction. However, if the contractors are offered money for reclaiming materials, they may be willing to deconstruct portions of a project.

Specify Decay-Resistant Woods

Some tree species are naturally resistant to decay, making them good choices for lumber use in exterior applications. The same tannins that allow these trees to survive in rain forests and damp environments make them decay-resistant lumber. In most species, it is the heartwood, the darker inner column of wood in a tree, that is most decay resistant. As the individual cells of a tree die, they are impregnated with extractives, pitch, oil, and other extraneous materials that provide the resistance to decay and insects. It is important to note that sapwood is usually not decay resistant.

Old-growth trees of decay-resistant species most effectively resist decay-producing fungi and insects. However, lumber from old-growth trees should not be specified, as the few old-growth forests that remain are critical to local and global ecosystem health. Young-growth wood, grown and harvested more quickly before the heartwood is well developed, contains a higher percentage of sapwood, resulting in wood with less decay resistance. For example, the Forest Products Laboratory's *Wood Handbook* classifies old-growth redwood as "resistant or very resistant" and young-growth redwood as "moderately resistant" (FPL 1999).

Many tropical hardwoods from Central America, Asia, and Africa are highly resistant to decay and insects. These woods (e.g., teak, Ipe, *Mahogany* spp., and many others) are used primarily in exterior furniture and decking. While they are very durable in exterior applications, many are unsustainably harvested from rain forests and other sensitive habitats. Therefore, only Forest Stewardship Council–certified tropical hardwoods should be specified to ensure sustainable growth and harvesting practices (see Table 10–8).

Even decay-resistant woods are subject to the biological processes of weathering. Mildew can grow and sunlight's UV rays can degrade the surface of the wood. Therefore, to ensure maximum life of a wood structure, finishes such as nontoxic water repellants or penetrating stains should be regularly applied. See the wood finishes table (Table 10–12) for more information on effectiveness, standards, and toxicity issues of protective wood finishes.

Balance Wood Preservation Needs with the Strength (and Toxicity) of Preservatives

While wood is a strong and durable material, in exterior use it is vulnerable to weathering and attack by fungi and insects. Therefore, with the exception of decay-resistant species, if wood is expected to last more than a few years, it must be treated or preserved to inhibit decay and weathering (FPL 1999).

But while extending the life of wood structures will save habitats and resources, the often toxic chemicals of wood preservatives can place a different burden on the environment and affect human health in production, construction, use, and disposal phases. Generally, the more toxic the preservative, the more effective it is (although new preservative technologies may change this). Therefore, preservative and finishing strategies should be carefully chosen for the conditions in which the wood will be used. Stronger preservative treatments should be used for wood that is in ground contact than for wood that will be regularly coated with penetrating stains, paint, or other finishes.

Wood preservatives are pesticides, regulated by the EPA, that are designed to kill the organisms and insects

Table 10–8 Decay-Resistant Woods

Type of Wood	Decay Resistance[a]	Color[a] HW (Heartwood) SW (Sapwood)	Primary Geographic Region[b]	Notes
Domestic (U.S.) Wood Species				
Redwood *(Sequoia sempervirens)* FSC-certified available	Resistant to decay and insects Young-growth redwood is "moderately resistant."	HW light cherry to dark mahogany SW almost white	CA National market	Avoid use of lumber from old-growth trees. "Construction heartwood" is primarily from young-growth timber. "Construction Common grade" contains sapwood and may not resist decay. Reclaimed redwood lumber, often from old-growth trees, is available in some regions.
Western red cedar *(Thuja plicata)* FSC-certified available	Resistant to decay and insects	HW reddish or pinkish brown to dull brown SW almost white	WA, OR, ID, MT National market	Relatively expensive Limited availability
White cedar, northern and Atlantic *(Thuja occidentalis* and *Chamaecyparis thyoides)*	Resistant to decay	HW light brown SW white	Eastern U.S., lumber production in ME and Great Lakes	Widely available
Incense cedar *(Calocedrus decurrens)*	Resistant to decay	HW light brown, tinged red SW white, cream	CA, OR, NV	Low-quality lumber because disintegrated wood occurs while tree is living. Use for rough construction. Low cost
Bald cypress *(Taxodium distichum)* Also known as southern cypress, red cypress, yellow cypress, white cypress	Resistant to decay and insects (comparable to CCA-treated lumber) Young growth is "moderately decay resistant."	HW light yellow brown to red brown to chocolate brown SW white	Southern states and South Atlantic	Not widely available for exterior use Reclaimed cypress is available in limited areas www.cypressinfo.org
Black locust *(Robinia pseudoacacia)*	Very high decay resistance	HW greenish yellow to dark brown SW cream	TN, KY, WV, VA	Very hard, strong Not widely available

Table 10–8 Decay-Resistant Woods *(Continued)*

Type of Wood	Decay Resistance[a]	Color[a] HW (Heartwood) SW (Sapwood)	Primary Geographic Region[b]	Notes
Imported Wood Species				
Ipe (genus *Tabebuia*) Also known as Surinam greenheart, Lapacho, Pau d'arco FSC-certified available	Very high decay and insect resistance	HW light to dark olive brown SW yellow gray	Latin America	Hard, high density Difficult to machine, must be predrilled Very durable Specify only FSC-certified ipe. Harvesting of uncertified wood often destroys sensitive ecosystems. Listed by IUCN as vulnerable[b]
Jarrah *(Eucalyptus marginata)* FSC-certified available	Very high decay and insect resistance	HW pink to dark red SW pale	Australia coastal belt	Strong, heavy, hard Difficult to machine, must be predrilled
Teak *(Tectona grandis* and *T. philippinensis)* FSC-certified available	Old growth has very high decay and insect resistance. Young growth is moderately resistant.	HW yellow brown to dark brown SW light yellow	Southeast Asia, India	Specify only FSC-certified teak. Harvesting of uncertified wood often destroys sensitive ecosystems. *T. philippinensis* listed by IUCN as endangered.[b]
Mahogany, American *(Swietenia macrophylla)* Also called Honduran mahogany FSC-certified has limited availability.	Both hardwood and sapwood are resistant to decay and insects, with moderate termite resistance.	HW pale pink to dark red brown	Southern Mexico down to Bolivia	Specify only FSC-certified American mahogany. Listed by IUCN as vulnerable.[b] Harvesting of uncertified wood often destroys sensitive ecosystems. FSC-certified mahogany market is very limited.
Mahogany, African *(Khaya ivorensis)* FSC-certified has limited availability.	Moderately resistant to decay and insects	HW pale pink to dark brown	West central Africa	Specify only FSC-certified African mahogany. Harvesting of uncertified wood often destroys sensitive ecosystems. Listed by IUCN as vulnerable.[b] FSC-certified mahogany market is very limited.

Continued

Table 10–8 Decay-Resistant Woods *(Continued)*

Type of Wood	Decay Resistance[a]	Color[a] HW (Heartwood) SW (Sapwood)	Primary Geographic Region[b]	Notes
Imported Wood Species (continued)				
Meranti (*Shorea* sp.) Also known as Philippine mahogany Lauan and Meranti groups	Moderately resistant to decay and insects	Varies widely Dark red is used for decking.	Southeast Asia	More than half of the *Shorea* species are listed by IUCN as critically endangered, endangered or vulnerable.[b] Specify only FSC-certified Meranti. Harvesting of uncertified often destroys sensitive ecosystems Has coarser texture than American mahogany

[a]FPL 1999

[b]International Union for Conservation of Nature and Natural Resources 2006

Figure 10–14.

Ipe deck boards are extremely hard and dense, making them highly decay resistant, but necessitating screw connections that must be predrilled. (Photo from Meg Calkins)

that can eat wood. In many cases, the preservatives themselves are only available to licensed or certified applicators. While there is increasing focus on the environmental and human health effects of preservative treatments, this must be balanced by the effectiveness of the treatments. This section will address the wide range of existing and emerging wood preservative treatments.

It should be noted that the wood preservative industry is currently in a state of change. Since the EPA's 2003 voluntary phaseout of chromated copper arsenate–treated (CCA) wood for most uses, new "second generation" copper-based preservative treatments have entered the market. While these treatments, such as ACQ and copper azole, pose fewer human health risks, they still pose risks to aquatic organisms and questions about their stability in lumber have arisen. A "third generation" of wood preservatives, moving away from the use of metals, is entering the U.S. market in limited distribution from other countries or is in development in the United States. Some third-generation preservatives use nanosize particles to disperse and fix the preservative in the wood fibers.

Wood preservatives are divided into two classes. Waterborne preservatives are applied to wood in water solutions. Oilborne preservatives are applied in petroleum-based, volatile oil, or solvent-based solutions. Some active ingredients can be used in either water- or oilborne solutions.

Most wood preservative treatments are applied with a pressure process to embed the preserving chemicals as far into the wood cells as possible. The Forest Products Laboratory defines treated wood as "wood that has been pressure treated with a preservative to improve the resistance of wood to destruction from fungi, insects and marine borers" (FPL 1999). It is also possible to apply wood finishes such as penetrating stain or paint directly to the wood structure; however, most sources recommend that wood used in exterior applications be pressure treated first.

Pressure treatments only penetrate wood to a certain depth, so all field cuts of pressure-treated lumber should be treated with brushed-on preservatives such as copper naphthenate, zinc naphthenate, tributyltin oxide, or other less toxic wood sealers. Copper naphthenate is a reaction of copper salts and naphthenic acid from petroleum refining by-products. According to the Forest Products Laboratory's *Wood Handbook* (FPL 1999), it is not a restricted-use pesticide, but should be handled as an industrial pesticide and safety precautions taken. Less toxic, low-VOC, and/or plant-based wood sealers can be used to treat end cuts; however, the cuts should be retreated every few years.

WATERBORNE WOOD PRESERVATIVES: COPPER-BASED TREATMENTS

Chromated Copper Arsenate (CCA)

CCA is a highly effective treatment for wood used in exterior applications. It is classified as an inorganic arsenical wood preservative. Both a fungicide and an insecticide, it poses toxicity risks to humans and the environment, but the severity of risks and degrees of exposure are not always clear. Human health risks can occur during installation with inhalation of sawdust from cutting, and in use with hand and body contact. Chromium, a heavy metal and persistent bioaccumulative toxin (PBT) that fixes the copper preservative in the wood, can leach into soil and groundwater. Arsenic is a carcinogen and in high dosages is a lethal poison (ATSDR). While most CCA is well fixed in wood, leaching of the highly toxic chemicals through skin and ground contact is a concern. CCA poses a high risk to

aquatic environments, as all three substances are toxic to aquatic species.

At the end of 2003, the EPA called for a voluntary phaseout of CCA as a preservative in most wood products intended for residential use or where direct contact with humans is likely. Landscape applications where CCA is no longer used include decks, play structures, picnic tables, fences, etc. CCA remains in use for extreme moisture situations such as marine pilings (despite aquatic toxicity), piers, guardrails, soundwalls, and utility poles. At the time of this writing, the EPA has undertaken a "Probabilistic Risk Assessment" report slated for release in 2008 of CCA and children's playgrounds. At this point, CCA may possibly be reregistered for wider use (U.S. EPA "Pesticides: Topical and Chemical Fact Sheets"). Disposal issues of CCA-treated lumber are discussed earlier in the chapter.

Second-generation Copper-based Wood Treatments

With the 2003 CCA phaseout, a new generation of copper-based preservatives that do not contain arsenic or chromium are now in widespread use in the United States under a variety of product names.

Ammoniacal copper quaternary (ACQ) is a water-based wood preservative that is both a fungicide and an insecticide, with active ingredients of copper oxide (varies from 62% to 71%) and quaternary ammonium compound (quat 29%–38%; FPL 2007). There are several variations in use called ACQ-B, ACQ-C, and ACQ-D, all with varying compatibility with different wood species. In all, the copper oxide acts primarily as the fungicide and insecticide, and the quat or other chemicals as co-biocides for copper-tolerant bacteria (American Wood Preserver's Association).

Copper azole (CBA-A and CA-B) is a similar, recently developed preservative that relies on amine copper with co-biocides to protect wood from decay and insect attack. CBA-A contains 49% copper, 49% boric acid, and 2% tebuconazole. In moist conditions, the boric acid diffuses through the wood offering additional protection, but it can also leach from the wood. While it is environmentally benign, it may reduce the effectiveness of the preservative treatment. CA-B contains 96% copper and 4% tebuconazole (FPL 2007).

These copper-based preservatives, marketed under many different names and containing varying amounts of recycled copper, are considered to be environmentally preferable to CCA; however, they are not without toxic impacts. While the ingredients are less toxic than the arsenic and chromium of CCA-treated lumber, they contain a higher percentage of copper, which is toxic to aquatic organisms and can cause a range of health effects in humans, from respiratory irritation to liver and kidney damage (ATSDR). The high amounts of copper in these new preservatives still pose disposal concerns similar to CCA. While they don't contain arsenic or chromium, copper is a concern in groundwater contamination, as it is highly toxic to aquatic species and can also impact humans. Researchers at the Forest Products Lab are investigating biological methods to separate and recycle both the copper and the wood (FPL 2005). Environmental impacts from copper mining include habitat disruption, water contamination, and excessive waste generation.

Copper-based treatments are more prone to leaching than CCA-treated wood, as they do not contain chromium, the ingredient in CCA that bonds the copper to the wood. Small amounts of both copper and quat can leach into soil and groundwater surrounding the structure. In addition to the environmental risks, leaching of the protective chemicals may also render the treatment less effective against fungi and insects (Korthals Altes 2006).

While copper-based treated lumber is marketed as a comparable substitute to CCA-treated lumber, warranties of most products do not cover as long a life as CCA, or as many applications. Some companies only warrant their products in deck applications, not ground contact situations. Others don't warrant use of the product in structural applications or foundation systems.

Construction techniques with copper-based treatments vary slightly from CCA as well. Testing has shown that high copper content can cause metal fasteners to corrode or oxidize, potentially reducing their effectiveness (Austin Energy 2007). Recommended fasteners for copper-treated lumber are hot-dipped galvanized fasteners (ASTM A153 2005) and connectors (ASTM A653/A653M 2007), or 304 or 316 stainless steel. The treatment manufacturer can provide infor-

mation on recommended fastener types for their preservative formulation.

Micronized copper preservatives. While ACQ and copper azole are in the mainstream U.S. lumber market, other copper-based treatments have been recently developed. One formulation uses finely ground copper in suspension in water instead of the typical toxic monoethanolamine (MEA) solution. Manufacturers claim that the leaching and fastener corrosivity problems of traditional copper-based treatments are nearly eliminated because the copper adheres better to the wood without the MEA solution. Micronized copper also may allow 40–50% less copper to be used in an effective treatment (EBN 2008) (see Table 10–10).

WATERBORNE PRESERVATIVES: ALTERNATIVES TO COPPER-BASED WOOD PRESERVATIVE TREATMENTS

Concerns about the high quantities of copper in the new copper-based preservative treatments are beginning to bring them under greater scrutiny. This may lead to environmental restrictions in the future, particularly as new options come on the market (Advanced Housing Research Center 2004). Alternative wood treatments that move away from the use of heavy metals and solvents are in various stages of development. Some may offer promising wood preservation while posing few or no environmental and human health risks.

Sodium Silicate

Micro-manufactured sodium silicate treatment for wood is a promising new, durable, non-toxic development in wood preservation. Sodium silicate is a very old method of preservative treatment for wood; however, in past forms it has been water-soluble with a white powder residue, making it inappropriate for exterior uses exposed to moisture. The recent development of a micro manufacturing heat treatment process for a proprietary formula of sodium silicate converts the material to a microscopic layer of insoluble glass that, according to the manufacturers, crystallizes in the wood's cell structures, infusing and protecting them. This renders the wood inaccessible to insects and fungi without toxic metals and pesticides (Korthals Altes 2006).

If the sodium silicate treatment can be made insoluble to water, it will be an excellent wood preservative treatment, as it is nontoxic and the material is abundant. Currently, lumber treated with sodium silicate has very limited distribution and, while it has performed well in tests, it lacks a long-term track record. Because the primary material, sodium silicate, is relatively inexpensive compared to copper, lumber treated with sodium silicate is competitive in price with the better established copper-based treatments, and as use increases the price is expected to drop further (Korthals Altes 2006).

Borates

Borates are sodium salts, such as sodium octaborate, sodium tetraborate, and sodium pentaborate, that are dissolved in water. They are an effective wood treatment against fungi and insects, yet they pose low toxicity to mammals (FPL 2007).

Currently they are not an effective treatment for exterior use where the wood will come in contact with liquid water, as they are prone to leaching from wood in the presence of moisture, rendering them ineffective. New products in limited use combine a two-treatment process of pressure treatment with borates and a polymer binder that manufacturers claim fixes the borates into the wood. Borates are a colorless and odorless, low-toxicity wood treatment that accepts paint much better than copper-based treatments, so if the new two-step process holds up to manufacturers' claims, it may become a viable preservative treatment in aboveground exterior applications (Korthals Altes 2006).

Waterborne Organic Preservatives

A new waterborne wood treatment technology that is entering U.S. markets uses three organic (carbon-based) nonmetallic biocides. The biocides, tebuconazole, propiconazole, and imidacloprid, have been used in growing food crops and are already approved for use by the EPA (Korthals Altes 2007).

Wood preserved with this treatment is rated for above ground exterior uses such as decking, fence boards, beams, and joists, but not ground contact uses. The biocides will break down and degrade to carbon over time. Certain combinations of biocides and an added water repellant will help extend the biocides'

useful life to ensure preservation of wood for a reasonable time. The product has been tested over five years, but the manufacturers offer a limited lifetime warranty. In soil the biocides' expected life is between a month and a few years. Lumber with this treatment is not corrosive to fasteners as the copper-based treatments can be, and it can be painted immediately (Arch Chemicals).

Other Solvent-borne Organic Preservatives

Solvent-borne organic wood preservatives, often called light organic solvent preservatives (LOSPs), are carbon-based solutions rather than inorganic preservatives (e.g., arsenic, copper, or chromium). It is important to note that the term *organic* does not mean nontoxic; in fact, because most organics are water soluble, they are delivered into the wood in solvents and release relatively high levels of VOCs.

Because these preservatives are introduced to the wood in a solvent rather than in water, which causes the wood to swell, they result in dimensionally stable, readily paintable lumber that is primarily used in millwork. Some LOSP treatments are being introduced for aboveground exterior applications. With increasing air quality standards limiting VOC release, LOSPs may never gain widespread use in the United States. In addition to the human health impacts of VOCs, leaching of the organic biocides that make these treatments effective is a concern for the health of environments surrounding the wood structure and in disposal environments (Austin Energy 2007).

Toxic impacts of organic preservatives vary depending on the formula. Active ingredients of individual formulas can be researched on the hazardous chemical and carcinogen listings referenced in chapter 2.

Chemical Modification

Chemical modification of wood, as reported in *Environmental Building News,* "involves bonding a simple chemical with a reactive part of a cell wall polymer . . . reducing moisture retention and increasing dimensional stability and resistance to fungal decay." (Korthals Altes 2006). There are two main chemical modification techniques: acetylation, using acetic acid, the main chemical in vinegar, and furfurylation, using furfuryl, a plant-derived alcohol. While chemically modified wood is not appropriate for exterior structural and ground contact applications, it may soon enter U.S. decking markets from northern Europe.

Acetylated wood is not termite resistant, but the dry wood is less hospitable to termites. Furfurylation in high levels does offer termite protection; however, the process is expensive and makes the wood much heavier (Korthals Altes 2006).

Thermally Modified Wood

Thermal modification is a new chemical-free wood preservation technology that exposes wood to extreme heat and steam to change the composition of the sugars that support growth of mold and fungus and feed insects into non-edible substances. In a controlled environment the wood is exposed to temperatures up to 480 degrees F and steam is injected into the wood. While this process is more energy intensive than standard pressure treatments, it is chemical free and may be worth the added energy load. Thermally modified wood can be used in aboveground contact uses and in freshwater and saltwater immersion applications. This proprietary wood treatment is approved for European Structural Standards. It is in limited distribution in the United States (PureWood).

OILBORNE PRESERVATIVES

Coal tar creosote and pentachlorophenol (penta or PCP) are the most common oilborne preservatives currently in use. Both pose well-documented health and environmental risks, even greater than CCA, yet they still make up about 10% of all new treated wood used in North America (Korthals Altes 2006). Their occurrence is likely higher in reclaimed wood, and use of reclaimed railroad ties and telephone poles is common in landscape applications.

Creosote is a dark, oil-based preservative made by distilling coal tar after high-temperature carbonization of coal. It is a very effective preservative, as it is toxic to wood-destroying organisms, relatively insoluble in water, and highly permanent in a variety of tough conditions. It also penetrates deeply into wood.

Pentachlorophenol (penta or PCP) is a synthetic fungicide that is delivered to wood in a petroleum-based solution. Penta is an organochloride that is highly toxic to wood-destroying organisms (and to humans). Penta

is less fixed in wood than creosote, so leaching of the toxic chemicals into the soil and groundwater is a concern.

The EPA has classified both creosote and penta as "restricted use pesticides" because of their toxicity. The restricted use classification means that only certified pesticide handlers can apply it; however, use of creosote- or penta-treated lumber is not federally restricted (although it may be by some municipalities).

Penta is a chlorinated hydrocarbon that is known to the State of California to cause cancer. It also bioaccumulates in fatty tissue, moving up the food chain. Short-term health effects from exposure to penta can include damage to the central nervous system, and long-term effects can include reproductive problems, damage to the liver and kidneys, and cancer. Penta poses severe environmental hazards as

Tips for Specifying Lumber with Preservative Treatments

- Use the minimal preservative treatment applicable to the situation in which the wood will be used (e.g., for ground contact use a stronger preservative than for an arbor joist).

- Some applications may be mild enough that field-applied wood preservative finishes such as penetrating stains can be used on non-pressure-treated lumber.

- Avoid pressure treatments that contain PBTs, known carcinogens, or priority toxins. Refer to the lists discussed in chapter 2.

- Use BMP-certified (Best Management Practices) treated wood or decay-resistant wood in aquatic or sensitive environments (see page 316).

- Avoid inhalation of treated wood sawdust. Wash hands and clothes after use. Use protective eyewear.

- Consider most treated wood toxic waste. Write into construction and demolition specifications that treated wood waste should not be recycled or incinerated, but disposed of in commercial or hazardous waste landfills.

Table 10–9 EPA-approved Consumer Information Sheets for Three Groups of Preservative-Treated Wood

Inorganic Arsenicals (CCA)	Pentachlorophenol	Creosote
Use Site Precautions Wood pressure-treated with waterborne arsenical preservatives may be used inside residences as long as all sawdust and construction debris are cleaned up and disposed of after construction. Do not use treated wood under circumstances where the preservative may become a component of food or animal feed. Examples of such sites would be structures or containers for storing silage or food. Do not use treated wood for cutting boards or countertops. Only treated wood that is visibly clean and free of surface residue should be used for patios, decks, and walkways. Do not use treated wood for construction of those portions of beehives that may come into contact with the honey. Treated wood should not be used where it may come into direct or indirect contact with public drinking water, except for uses involving incidental contact such as docks and bridges.	Logs treated with pentachlorophenol should not be used for log homes. Wood treated with pentachlorophenol should not be used where it will be in frequent or prolonged contact with bare skin (for example, chairs and other outdoor furniture) unless an effective sealer has been applied. Pentachlorophenol-treated wood should not be used in residential, industrial, or commercial interiors except for laminated beams or building components that are in ground contact and are subject to decay or insect infestation and where two coats of an appropriate sealer are applied. Sealers may be applied at the installation site. Urethane, shellac, latex epoxy enamel, and varnish are acceptable sealers for pentachlorophenol-treated wood. Wood treated with pentachlorophenol should not be used in the interiors of farm buildings where there may be direct contact with domestic animals or livestock that may crib (bite) or lick the wood. In interiors of farm buildings where domestic animals or livestock are unlikely to crib (bite) or lick the wood, pentachlorophenol-treated wood may be used for building components that are in ground contact and are subject to decay or insect infestation and where two coats of an appropriate sealer are applied. Sealers may be applied at the installation site. Do not use pentachlorophenol-treated wood for farrowing or brooding facilities. Do not use treated wood under circumstances where the preservative may become a component of food or animal feed. Examples of such sites would be structures or containers for storing silage or food.	Wood treated with creosote should not be used where it will be in frequent or prolonged contact with bare skin (for example, chairs and other outdoor furniture) unless an effective sealer has been applied. Creosote-treated wood should not be used in residential interiors. Creosote-treated wood in interiors of industrial buildings should be used only for industrial building components that are in ground contact and are subject to decay or insect infestation and for wood-block flooring. For such uses, two coats of an appropriate sealer must be applied. Sealers may be applied at the installation site. Wood treated with creosote should not be used in the interiors of farm buildings where there may be direct contact with domestic animals or livestock that may crib (bite) or lick the wood. In interiors of farm buildings where domestic animals or livestock are unlikely to crib (bite) or lick the wood, creosote-treated wood may be used for building components that are in ground contact and are subject to decay or insect infestation and two coats of an effective sealer are applied. Sealers may be applied at the installation site. Coal tar pitch and coal tar pitch emulsion are effective sealers for creosote-treated wood-block flooring. Urethane, epoxy, and shellac are acceptable sealers for all creosote-treated wood. Do not use creosote-treated wood for farrowing or brooding facilities. Do not use treated wood under circumstances where the preservative may become a component of food or animal feed. Examples of such use would be structures or containers for storing silage or food.

Continued

Table 10–9 EPA-approved Consumer Information Sheets for Three Groups of Preservative-Treated Wood *(Continued)*

Inorganic Arsenicals	Pentachlorophenol	Creosote
Use Site Precautions (Cont'd.)		
	Do not use treated wood for cutting boards or countertops. Only treated wood that is visibly clean and free of surface residue should be used for patios, decks, and walkways.	Do not use treated wood for cutting boards or countertops. Only treated wood that is visibly clean and free of surface residues should be used for patios, decks, and walkways.
	Do not use treated wood for construction of those portions of beehives that may come into contact with the honey.	Do not use treated wood for construction of those portions of beehives that may come into contact with the honey.
	Pentachlorophenol-treated wood should not be used where it may come into direct or indirect contact with public drinking water, except for uses involving incidental contact such as docks and bridges.	Creosote-treated wood should not be used where it may come into direct or indirect contact with public drinking water, except for uses involving incidental contact such as docks and bridges.
	Do not use pentachlorophenol-treated wood where it may come into direct or indirect contact with drinking water for domestic animals or livestock, except for uses involving incidental contact such as docks and bridges.	Do not use creosote-treated wood where it may come into direct or indirect contact with drinking water for domestic animals or livestock, except for uses involving incidental contact such as docks and bridges.

Source: FPL 1999

Table 10–10 Wood Preservative Treatment Summary Table

Type	Availability	Applications	Toxicity	Relative Cost	Notes
ACQ and copper azole	Widely available	All uses, including ground contact	Less toxic than CCA; more toxic to aquatic organisms	Low to medium	Corrosive to some fasteners
Sodium silicate	Available in mid- and eastern U.S. markets as of August 2006	Deck construction (code compliance currently varies)	Nontoxic	Low to medium	Look for results of durability tests.
Borates	Stocked primarily in areas with Formosan termite problems	Currently most applicable for interior framing, sheathing, and in termite-prone areas	Low mammalian toxicity	Low to medium	Newer products are being developed for exterior applications.

Table 10–10 Wood Preservative Treatment Summary Table *(Continued)*

Type	Availability	Applications	Toxicity	Relative Cost	Notes
Waterborne organic preservatives	All-organic formulations are being introduced to the market.	All aboveground uses	Toxicity concerns; however, some pesticides are used in the food industry (specifics depend on formulation).	Medium to high	Some performance concerns (specifics depend on formulation) New formulas offer good potential heavy metal alternatives.
Light organic solvent preservatives (LOSPs)	Available in Oceania; beginning to enter North America	Most effective in painted wood, but above ground exterior formulas are being developed.	Variety of concerns depending on formulation; high-VOC emissions	High	Don't cause wood to swell like waterborne preservatives
Chemically modified wood	No current U.S. production	Potential includes decking	Nontoxic; VOC emission concerns	Medium to high	
Thermally modified wood	Limited U.S. production	Decking, pilings in water	Non-toxic, higher embodied energy	Medium to high	
Naturally resistant woods	Tropical hardwoods are available; highly resistant domestic softwoods are available but are not abundant.	Heartwood is decay resistant, but sapwood of most species is not. Uses depends on species and grade of wood	Nontoxic	High	Performance varies depending on age of tree. Sustainable forestry concerns Use FSC-certified wood.
CCA (chromated copper arsenate)	Voluntary phaseout in 2003 Currently less available	Pilings, phone poles, industrial applications	Toxic, but relatively well fixed in wood. Avoid use.	Low	EPA has phased out for residential markets. Sealers for chemical fixing are being tested for other applications. Refer to EPA-approved Consumer Fact Sheets.

Continued

Table 10–10 Wood Preservative Treatment Summary Table *(Continued)*

Type	Availability	Applications	Toxicity	Relative Cost	Notes
Creosote	Limited availability	Pilings, phone poles, industrial applications	Highly toxic Easily leached Avoid use.		Finishes can't be applied to oily surfaces. Refer to EPA-approved Consumer Fact Sheets.
Pentachloro-phenol (penta or PCP)	Limited availability	Pilings, phone poles, industrial applications	Highly toxic Less fixed in wood Leaching concerns Avoid use.		Refer to EPA-approved Consumer Fact Sheets.

Source: Adapted from Korthals Altes 2006

Table 10–11 Potential Environmental and Human Health Impacts of Select Chemicals Used in Wood Preservatives[a]

Preservative Compound	Potential Human Health Effects	Potential Environmental Impacts
Copper	Copper is on the 2005 CERCLA Priority List of Hazardous Substances (at #177).[b] Low levels of copper are essential for maintaining good health. High levels can cause harmful effects such as irritation of the nose, mouth, and eyes; vomiting; diarrhea; stomach cramps; and nausea. Very high doses of copper can cause damage to the liver and kidneys, and can even cause death.[b]	Copper has been found in at least 906 of the 1,647 National Priority List Sites identified by the Environmental Protection Agency. Copper released into the environment usually attaches to particles made of organic matter, clay, soil, or sand. Copper does not break down in the environment. Copper compounds can break down and release free copper into the air, water, and foods. Copper is highly toxic to aquatic organisms.
Chromium	Chromium is on the 2005 CERCLA Priority List of Hazardous Substances (at #77).[b] Ingesting large amounts of chromium(VI) can cause stomach upsets and ulcers, convulsions, kidney and liver damage, and even death. Skin contact with certain chromium(VI) compounds can cause skin ulcers.	Chromium has been found at 1,036 of the 1,591 National Priority List sites identified by the Environmental Protection Agency. In air, chromium compounds are present mostly as fine dust particles that eventually settle over land and water. Chromium can strongly attach to soil and only a small amount can dissolve in water and move deeper in the soil to underground water. Fish do not accumulate much chromium in their bodies from water.

Table 10–11 Potential Environmental and Human Health Impacts of Select Chemicals Used in Wood Preservatives[a] *(Continued)*

Preservative Compound	Potential Human Health Effects	Potential Environmental Impacts
	The World Health Organization (WHO) has determined that chromium(VI) is a human carcinogen. The Department of Health and Human Services (DHHS) has determined that certain chromium(VI) compounds are known to cause cancer in humans. The EPA has determined that chromium(VI) in air is a human carcinogen.	
Arsenic	Arsenic is at the top of the list of the 2005 CERCLA Priority List of Hazardous Substances (at #1).[b] Arsenic is a known human carcinogen.	EPA pesticides re-registration http://www.epa.gov/oppad001/reregistration/cca/health_safety.htm
Boron and compounds (boron acid)	There is little information on the health effects of long-term exposure to boron. Most of the studies are on short-term exposures. Breathing moderate levels of boron can result in irritation of the nose, throat, and eyes. Reproductive effects, such as low sperm count, were seen in men exposed to boron over the long term. Animal studies have shown effects on the lungs from breathing high levels of boron. Ingesting large amounts of boron over short periods of time can harm the stomach, intestines, liver, kidney, and brain. Animal studies of ingestion of boron found effects on the testes in male animals. Birth defects were also seen in the offspring of female animals exposed during pregnancy. We don't know what the effects are in people from skin contact with boron. Animal studies have found skin irritation when boron was applied directly to the skin.	No information is available on how long boron remains in air, water, or soil. Boron does not appear to accumulate in fish or other organisms in water. Boron accumulates in plants and is found in foods, mainly fruits and vegetables.
Sodium silicate	Sodium silicate is a relatively benign chemical. If inhaled, it can cause irritation of the respiratory tract. It can irritate skin and if ingested cause vomiting.	Sodium silicate is an alkaline solution.

Continued

Table 10–11 Potential Environmental and Human Health Impacts of Select Chemicals Used in Wood Preservatives[a] *(Continued)*

Preservative Compound	Potential Human Health Effects	Potential Environmental Impacts
Imidacloprid	Imidacloprid is a relatively new, systemic insecticide chemically related to the tobacco toxin nicotine. Like nicotine, it acts on the nervous system. Worldwide, it is considered to be one of the insecticides used in the largest volume. It has a wide diversity of uses: in agriculture, on turf, on pets, for household pests (and now in lumber preservative treatments).	Imidacloprid is acutely toxic to some bird species, including sparrows, quail, canaries, and pigeons. Partridges have been poisoned and killed by agricultural use of imidacloprid. It has also caused eggshell thinning. The growth and size of shrimp are affected by imidacloprid concentrations of less than one part per billion (ppb). Shrimp and crustaceans are killed by concentrations of less than 60 ppb. Imidacloprid is persistent. In a field test in Minnesota, the concentration of imidacloprid did not decrease for a year following treatment. It is also mobile in soil, so it is considered by the U.S. Environmental Protection Agency to be a potential water contaminant.
	Symptoms of exposure to imidacloprid include apathy, labored breathing, incoordination, emaciation, and convulsions. Longer-term exposures cause reduced ability to gain weight and thyroid lesions.	
	In studies of how imidacloprid affects reproduction, exposure of pregnant laboratory animals resulted in more frequent miscarriages and smaller offspring.	
	An agricultural imidacloprid product increased the incidence of a kind of genetic damage called DNA adducts.	
	The development of resistance to imidacloprid by pest insects is a significant concern. In Michigan potato fields, the Colorado potato beetle developed resistance to imidacloprid after just two years of use.	
Pentachlorophenol (penta)	Penta is on the 2005 CERCLA Priority List of Hazardous Substances (at #45).[b] Short-term health effects from exposure to penta include damage to the central nervous system, and long-term effects include reproductive problems, damage to the liver and kidneys, and cancer.[c]	This substance has been found in at least 313 of the 1,585 National Priorities List sites identified by the Environmental Protection Agency. Pentachlorophenol can be found in the air, water, and soil. It enters the environment through evaporation from treated wood surfaces, industrial spills, and disposal at uncontrolled hazardous waste sites.
	Some studies have found an increase in cancer risk in workers exposed to high levels of technical grade pentachlorophenol for a long time, but other studies have not found this. Increases in liver, adrenal gland, and nasal tumors have been found in laboratory animals exposed to high doses of pentachlorophenol.	Pentachlorophenol is broken down by sunlight, other chemicals, and microorganisms to other chemicals within a couple of days to months.
		Pentachlorophenol is found in fish and other foods, but tissue levels are usually low.

Table 10–11 Potential Environmental and Human Health Impacts of Select Chemicals Used in Wood Preservatives[a] *(Continued)*

Preservative Compound	Potential Human Health Effects	Potential Environmental Impacts
	The EPA has determined that pentachlorophenol is a probable human carcinogen and the International Agency for Research on Cancer (IARC) considers it possibly carcinogenic to humans.	
Creosote	Coal tar creosote is on the 2005 CERCLA Priority List of Hazardous Substances (at #23).[b] Creosote is a mixture of many chemicals. Eating food or drinking water with high levels of creosote may cause burning in the mouth and throat, and stomach pain. Long-term contact with creosote has been associated with increased risk of contracting cancer. Breathing creosotes can cause irritation of the respiratory tract and skin, and with long term exposure, creosote is considered a carcinogen	Creosote has been found in at least 46 of the 1,613 National Priorities List sites identified by the Environmental Protection Agency (EPA). Coal tar creosote is released to water and soil mainly as a result of its use in the wood preservation industry. Components of creosote that do not dissolve in water will remain in place in a tar-like mass. Some components of coal tar creosote dissolve in water and may move through the soil to groundwater. Once in groundwater, it may take years for it to break down. Coal tar creosote can build up in plants and animals.

[a]This table discusses documented health and environmental risks of preservative compounds. Actual severity of health and environmental impacts will vary with exposure concentrations.

[b]ATSDR

[c]U.S. EPA "Ground Water & Drinking Water Consumer Fact Sheets"

well. The EPA's Toxic Chemical Release Inventory states that 100,000 pounds of penta was released to the environment between 1987 and 1993, primarily from wood-preserving industries (U.S. EPA "Ground Water & Drinking Water"). It enters the environment from treatment facilities and through evaporation or leaching from wood in use or in disposal (ATSDR). It takes a long time to break down in the environment and it can contaminate drinking water, aquatic environments, and soil.

The U.S. Department of Health and Human Services Agency for Toxic Substances and Disease Registry states that breathing creosotes can cause irritation of the respiratory tract and skin, and with long-term exposure, creosote is considered a carcinogen. Creosote enters the environment and can move through the soil to groundwater. It takes a long time to break down and, like penta, can build up in plants and animals (ATSDR).

The EPA requires that information on safe handling, use, and disposal be provided by suppliers for creosote, penta, and inorganic arsenical-treated wood (CCA and others). The EPA-approved consumer information sheets are summarized in *Wood Handbook* (FPL 1999), excerpted in the table below. While the information sheets advocate disposal in landfills, federal agencies such as Health and Human Services and the EPA express concern about the potential for leaching of toxic chemicals from creosote- and penta-treated wood (see Table 10–9).

Preservative-Treated Lumber for Marine and Other Sensitive Environments

Preservative-treated wood is widely used to construct piers, docks, boardwalks, and decks in aquatic environments. Yet many common wood preservatives pose toxic risks to aquatic species and water quality in these environments. This problem is made especially complex by the constant presence of moisture around the wood structure, necessitating well-preserved wood. (Note: Wood that is completely submerged in water will not decay as fungi need oxygen to survive. An example of this is the piers supporting buildings in Venice, Italy, that have survived for hundreds of years submerged below the water.)

The Western Wood Preservers Institute (WWPI), Wood Preservation Canada (WPC), the Southern Pressure Treaters Association (SPTA), and the Timber Piling Council (TPC) have joined to respond to these issues by developing and encouraging use of a set of standards called *Best Management Practices (BMPs) for the Use of Treated Wood in Aquatic and Sensitive Environments.* This standard focuses on minimizing environmental exposure to preservatives while ensuring the longevity of wood structures in these environments. The BMPs' stated goal is to "place enough preservative into a product to provide the needed level of protection while also minimizing use of the preservative above the required minimum to reduce the amount potentially available for movement into the environment." The BMPs address specific techniques for individual preservative treatments and focus on post-treatment methods of fixing the preservatives permanently in the wood. The BMPs are regularly updated as new treatments and techniques are developed.

The group has developed a third-party certification system for the BMPs. Wood treated in compliance with the BMPs will be documented by a "BMP" mark on the wood or a certification letter accompanying the wood. Some manufacturers treat all their wood according to the BMP guidelines, and others just some.

Specifications for use of preservative-treated wood in aquatic or sensitive environments should require BMP compliance, or alternative materials such as plastic lumber should be used. However, BMP-treated wood is for use in continuously moist situations and may contain more preservatives than are necessary in a lower moisture application. Also, the BMP document emphasizes that not all aquatic environments are alike. Fast-flowing water will require a different preservative treatment than stagnant, brackish water. The BMP document defines applicability of common wood treatments (WWPI et al. 2006).

It is important to note that recently developed micromanufacture sodium silicate or thermally modified wood may become the least harmful preservative treatments for marine uses as they are benign formulations. They are currently in development or limited use for use in docks and marine pilings.

THE FUTURE OF TREATED WOOD

While chemicals used for treatment vary widely, many share a common challenge: getting them into the small pore spaces of wood can be difficult, yet it has everything to do with the effectiveness of the preservative. A nanotechnology technique where 100 nanometer plastic beads containing a wood preservative (currently copper based) that is dispersed into the wood with water is in experimental and preliminary use phases. This nanoscale application disperses copper preservatives further into wood cells than current treatment techniques. The researchers working on this technique note that it could be used with other less toxic wood preservatives as well. There are concerns with some nanoparticles and research has not yet proven their safety.

Increasingly stringent air quality regulations in parts of the United States limit volatile organic compound (VOC) levels of wood preservatives. California's South Coast Air Quality Management District (SCAQMD) Rule 1113, Architectural Coatings (2006), sets a VOC limit of 350 g/L for wood preservatives. While this is not a nationwide standard, California is a huge market so many preservative manufacturers are adopting, or may adopt, their formulations accordingly. Look for labeling that states, "meets California air quality standards" or similar.

One of the most significant developments in pressure treating wood is micro-manufactured sodium silicate. According to Alex Wilson of Building Green, newly developed sodium silicate preservative treatments may be the most promising new development in wood preservation, potentially rendering all other treatments irrelevant (Wilson 2007). Wood products treated with this preservative method have been rated for various uses such as decking, with new ratings for playground equipment, deck structures, docks and marine pilings in progress (Timber Treatment Technologies). Thermally modified wood is another promising treatment technology using heat and steam to transform wood sugars into inedible substances for microorganisms that cause decay.

Use Natural and Low-VOC Wood Finishes

The primary function of wood finishes in exterior applications is to protect wood from weathering. Unfinished wood surfaces are roughened by photo degradation and surface cracking, eroding slowly and changing color over time. Even pressure-treated and decay-resistant wood will weather, reducing the life span of the wood structure. Other functions of wood finishes are to achieve a specific color/appearance and provide a cleanable surface.

Types of Wood Finishes for Exterior Applications

Penetrating finishes are stains, oils, and sealants that penetrate a wood's surface and don't cure to a hard film like film finishes. Most are oil based, although water-based penetrating finishes are gaining availability with increasing air quality and health concerns about many oil-based products.

Penetrating finishes for exterior use include the following:

- penetrating stains—oil based and some water based
- water repellents
- water-repellent preservatives
- water- and latex-based semitransparent stains

- oil finishes such as tung oil and linseed oil (Green Seal 2005)

Film or coating finishes are coatings and sealants that cure hard and form a thin film on wood but do not penetrate the surface. Films and coatings in extreme exterior or wear conditions may bubble, chip, and/or peel as wood expands and contracts. Denser woods have a higher rate of expansion and contraction, and are therefore more likely to cause film or coating finishes to fail than less dense woods. These finishes are often inappropriate for exterior surfaces that will experience foot traffic such as decks and boardwalks. Films and coatings for exterior use are as follows:

- paint—oil based and latex
- varnish
- lacquer
- solid-color stains

Most finishes are either solvent- or water-based petroleum products. Some combine natural oils such as linseed (flax) oil or tung oil with distillates that are petroleum derivatives. Others, such as polyurethane and latex paints, are synthetic.

Water-based formulations generally contain fewer solvents (and associated health and environmental risks) than oil-based formulas; however, they may still contain biocides and other harmful chemicals. Water-based formulations may raise the grain and offer only moderate resistance to water and heat (Green Seal 2005).

Components of Wood Finishes

Pigments or dyes are used in wood finishes to color and hide flaws in the wood. Some pigments are made from heavy metals.

Resins are either natural or synthetic components of wood finishes that are film forming. They are also called binders (in stains and paints), as they bind pigments to the wood surface and determine the finish's durability, hardness, flexibility, and resistance to water, stains, and solvents. Acrylics, vinyls (some contain phthalates), alkyds, epoxies, cellulosics, and oils are all considered resins.

Solvents and/or thinners maintain the finish in liquid form by dissolving the resins. Thinners reduce the viscosity of the liquid. Some finishes use both solvents and thinners. Typically organic solvents are used in wood finishes such as alcohols, ketones, glycol ethers, petroleum distillates (mineral spirits), toluene, xylenes, naphtha, and turpentine. In waterborne coatings, the solvent is usually glycol ether with water as the thinner.

Various additives are used in small amounts to modify drying time or act as fungicides, biocides, or thickeners.

Human and Environmental Health Risks of Wood Finishes

Like wood preservatives, many wood finishes contain chemicals and compounds that are potentially harmful to human health and the environment. And generally the more toxic the ingredients, the more effective protection the finish provides for the wood. However, in response to increasingly stringent air quality regulations, less toxic, low-VOC finishes are increasingly available (Green Seal 2005).

Most wood finishes contain volatile organic compounds (VOCs) that evaporate as the finish dries and/or cures often over a long period of time (FPL 1999). Finishes can also contain other hazardous chemicals and heavy metals that pose risks to construction workers, site users, and air quality in the region. Additional hazards occur in manufacture and disposal. Material safety data sheets (MSDSs) identify potentially hazardous ingredients in finishes; however, they are only required to identify ingredients that make up 1% or more of product content and/or are known carcinogens. U.S. federal lists of known carcinogens may not be as stringent and comprehensive as international lists. See the International Agency for Research on Cancer's Monographs on the Evaluation of Carcinogenic Risks to Humans (IARC) for a comprehensive listing of known and suspected carcinogens. The U.S. Department of Health and Human Services Agency for Toxic Substances and Disease Registry provides fact sheets on numerous toxic compounds, some of which are found in wood finishes (ATSDR). Some hazardous substances are also discussed in Appendix B of this book.

Some higher-toxicity wood finish formulations are being replaced by finishes with low or no VOCs and/or natural ingredients. In some cases manufacturers are turning back to older wood-finishing methods for "greener" formulas.

No- or Low-VOC Finishes

Finish manufacturers are responding to tightening federal and state air quality regulations with no- or low-VOC formulations. Often this means water-based formulations, which some claim do not penetrate as well as oils; instead they form more of a film finish and offer less moisture protection. To overcome this problem, some no- or low-VOC finishes may need to be reapplied more often than their higher VOC counterparts. Applying two coats may improve the durability of the finish (Green Seal 2005).

Many penetrating finishes, such as semitransparent stains, have a low solids content (pigments, oils, and polymers), resulting in a very low amount of allowable VOCs. VOC limits are based on solids contents. In response to this issue, some are being reformulated with a higher solids content, reactive diluents, and/or new types of solvents.

Natural Finishes

Natural finishes, sometimes also low VOC, are made with rapidly renewable materials such as seed oils (e.g., linseed oil from the flax plant or tung oil from the tung oil tree [*Aleurites* sp.]), tree resins, citrus peel extracts, essential oils, inert mineral fillers, tree and bee waxes, and natural pigments. Some finishes with plant oils contain toxic ingredients to improve drying time, so ingredient lists should be read carefully.

Regulations and Standards for Wood Finishes

As a result of the 1990 Clean Air Act, the EPA and many states have enacted legislation limiting VOC levels in architectural coatings to protect outdoor air quality. Other organizations committed to both indoor and outdoor air quality issues also offer standards and product listings for wood finishes.

The Wood Handbook (FPL 1999) states a concern that some traditional wood finishes—such as oil-based semitransparent stains, oil- and alkyd-based primers and topcoats, solvent-borne water repellents and

Table 10–12 Wood Finishes for Exterior Applications

Type of Finish	Applications, Performance, and Notes	Typical Ingredients/ Low-VOC, and/or Plant-based Alternatives	Recommended VOC Limit/Standard
Water repellents (WR) and water-repellent preservatives (WRP)[a] Also called waterproofing sealers Coatings formulated for the primary purpose of preventing penetration by water 6-month–2-year life span[a]	Oil-based repellents are penetrating. Some waterborne finishes are penetrating, but others form only a thin film. Oils (e.g., paraffin, linseed) do not dry; they just get absorbed by the wood. Drying usually takes several days. Can be lightly pigmented. Added pigment increases service life of wood as pigment blocks UV rays.	Typically formulated with organic solvents such as mineral spirits or turpentine, although lower VOC waterborne formulations are increasingly available. Some contain polymers. WRs also contain a sealer such as linseed oil, paraffin oil, or varnish and a water repellent such as paraffin wax. WRPs contain a mildewcide or fungicide that can be toxic—see product's MSDSs. Some plant oil formulations with earth pigments are available.	100 g/L SCAQMD Rule 1113 Architectural Coatings[a]
Semitransparent penetrating stains Water-repellent preservative solutions that contain dyes or pigments. They soak into and become part of wood. They are more durable than WRPs because the pigment protects wood from UV degradation. 3–8-year life span[a]	Water-based and oil-based stains are available. Latex is used for solid-color applications but should not be exposed to direct sunlight. Higher pigment concentrations block more UV, but some pigments contain heavy metals and VOCs.	Oil-based stains may offer best protection for exterior use, although lower VOC water-based oil-alkyd modified formulations are newly available for decks. Some are made from nonpetroleum products, often plant-based materials. Newer formulations have higher solids content.	100 g/L SCAQMD Rule 1113 Architectural Coatings[a]
Oils (e.g., linseed and tung oil) Penetrating finishes that cure by absorbing oxygen from the air. However, since they are natural oils, they are food for mildew, so they should be formulated with a mildewcide when used in an exterior application. 1–2-year life span	Oils are durable, water resistant, and soak into wood but require several coats and take a long time to dry.	Plant-based linseed and tung oils are nontoxic; however, many are formulated with petroleum distillates or heavy metals to assist in drying. Some natural oils, called polymerized oils, have been heat treated to increase gloss and hardness and reduce curing time.	

Continued

Table 10–12 Wood Finishes for Exterior Applications *(Continued)*

Type of Finish	Applications, Performance, and Notes	Typical Ingredients/ Low-VOC, and/or Plant-based Alternatives	Recommended VOC Limit/Standard
Clear wood finishes Clear and semi-transparent coatings, including lacquers and varnishes, that provide a transparent or translucent solid film (SCAQMD 2007) 2–3-year life span[a]	Clear wood finishes are not appropriate for exterior surfaces that will experience foot traffic, as they may chip and peel (e.g., decks). There is some concern that water-based formulations are not as durable as oil based; however, these new formulations are being continuously improved.	Most polyurethanes use petroleum-based solvents. A new generation of water-based polyurethanes is available. They still contain VOCs, but in lesser amounts. The VOCs they contain are less-toxic aliphatic hydrocarbons instead of the traditional aromatic hydrocarbons, some of which are known carcinogens.	Varnish and Lacquer 275 g/L SCAQMD Rule 1113 Architectural Coatings[a]
Paints and solid-color stains Film-forming finishes that are available in oil or water based (latex or acrylic) Provide wood protection by blocking UV rays and excluding moisture 7–10-year life span[a]	Paints and solid-color stains are appropriate for vertical exterior surfaces, but not for horizontal surfaces that will experience foot traffic, as they may chip and peel (e.g., decks).	Many no- or low-VOC paints are available. Some have higher solids content and cover better low-VOC stain-resistant primers are available. Exterior paints often contain biocides: look for "low biocide" formulations. Avoid paints with polyvinyl acetate (PVA).	Paint non-lat 50 g/L Flat 100 g/L (50 g/L in 2008) SCAQMD Rule 1113 Architectural Coatings[b] Green Seal GS-11 standard (addresses VOC and toxic ingredients).[b]

[a]FPL 1999
[b]SCAQMD 2007
[c]Green Seal 1993

solvent-borne water-repellent preservatives—may no longer be available since they have higher VOC levels than the regulations in some states allow. This is particularly a concern for exterior applications, as these are primary finishes for decks.

U.S. EPA National Volatile Organic Compound Emission Standards for Architectural Coatings. The U.S. EPA established emissions standards for VOCs in architectural coatings in 1998. The standards establish a maximum amount of VOCs that can be released for a given amount of solids (e.g., binder, pigments), commonly expressed as grams per liter (g/L). Maximum amounts vary for different types of finishes.

The action states: "This final rule is based on the Administrator's determination that VOC emissions from

the use of architectural coatings have the potential to cause or contribute to ozone levels that violate the national ambient air quality standards (NAAQS) for ozone. Ozone is a major component of smog, which causes negative health and environmental impacts when present in high concentrations at ground level. The final rule is estimated to reduce VOC emissions by 103,000 megagrams per year (Mg/yr) (113,500 tons per year[tpy]) by requiring manufacturers and importers to limit the VOC content of architectural coatings."

South Coast Air Quality Management District. California's South Coast Air Quality Management District (SCAQMD) developed more stringent regulations in Rule 1113 limiting VOC content of architectural coatings, including wood preservatives and finishes. For ex-

When Specifying Finishes:

- Obtain and review material safety data sheets (MSDSs) from the finish manufacturer that list hazardous ingredients and environmental and human health precautions. Note that MSDSs only identify hazardous ingredients that make up 1% or more of the formulation and/or are carcinogens.

- Look for "no-VOC" or "low-VOC" products. VOC content is stated on the product label, and SCAQMD-recommended thresholds are stated by product type in the chart above.

- Avoid products with labels stating "Danger" or "Poison." These are typically dangerous during use. Products with "Warning" or "Caution" on the label pose a moderate or slight health risk.

- Purchase the exact amount needed to minimize storage and disposal hazards.

- Carefully read labels. Avoid products that warn of neurotoxic effects (e.g., "may affect brain or nervous system").

- Look for labels that reference California's Proposition 65 warning of chemicals that may cause cancer, birth defects, or reproductive problems. While manufacturers are not required to state their compliance outside of California, some leave it on products that will go to other states. An example of a California Proposition 65 label may be as follows: "WARNING: This product contains a chemical known to the State of California to cause cancer and birth defects or other reproductive harm."

- Look for products listed in *Green Seal's Choose Green Report: Wood Finishes and Stains* or in *GreenSpec* Building Green's product database (BuildingGreen).

ample, Rule 1113 limits VOC content for nonflat paints to 50 g/L in 2006 while the EPA's limit for nonflat coatings is 380 g/L. While the SCAQMD VOC limits only apply to regions in California, they have become a standard for those dedicated to minimizing air quality problems in both interior and exterior applications. As a result, some companies are formulating their finishes to comply with the SCAQMD Rule 1113 limits shown in Table 10–13.

The SCAQMD standards are based on evaluations of VOC levels of available and effective products. As new developments are made in products with low-VOC contents, the maximum allowable amounts are annually adjusted.

The Future of Wood Use in Site Applications

The future of wood use as a site construction material looks good, but quite different from the recent past. Growing concerns about the health of ecosystems and humans have resulted in efforts and opportunities to "green" wood specifications. Specifying lumber that has been clear-cut and impregnated with toxic preservatives may soon be a thing of the past. Forests that are certified as sustainably managed are increasing in acreage as the green building market grows. Every day brings more certified wood products to the market in expanding regions.

Third-generation preservative technologies such as sodium silicates and thermally modified wood offer good potential for preservation of exterior wood use. These technologies are not yet in widespread use, nor have they been in use for the decades that will reveal their true performance, but they avoid the use of heavy metals and toxins, and their testing has shown good potential.

NANOTECHNOLOGY AND WOOD

New nanomaterials in development may revolutionize wood's environmental performance in exterior situations. Nanotechnology is defined as the manipulation of matter measuring 100 nanometers or less. This quickly growing area of material science may offer some opportunities for new wood preservatives, finishes, adhesives, and engineered wood products. It is important to note, however that there are concerns of unknown human and environmental health impacts of nanomaterials.

A report by the American Forest and Paper Association's Agenda 2020 technology initiative titled

Table 10–13 EPA and SCAQMD VOC Limits in Grams of VOC per Liter of Coating[a]

Coating Category	EPA VOC Limit (gVOC/ liter coating)	SCAQMD VOC Limit (gVOC/ liter coating)
Stains		100
-Clear and semi-transparent	550	
-Opaque	350	
-Low solids	120[b]	
Flat coatings		50
-Exterior	250	
-Interior	250	
Non-flat coatings		50
-Exterior	380	
-Interior	380	
-High gloss		50
Pretreatment wash primers	780	420
Primers and undercoaters	350	
Quick-dry coatings		
-Enamels	450	
-Primers, sealers, and undercoaters	450	100
Sealers (including interior clear wood sealers)	400	100
Recycled coatings		250
Shellacs		
-Clear	730	730
-Opaque	550	550
Stain controllers	720	
Clear wood finishes		275
-Varnish		275
-Sanding sealers		275
-Lacquer		275
Clear Brushing Lacquer		275
Wood preservatives		
-Below ground wood preservatives	550	350
-Clear and semitransparent	550	350
-Opaque	350	350
-Low solids	120	

[a]Unless otherwise specified, limits are expressed in grams of VOC per liter of coating thinned to the manufacturer's maximum recommendation excluding the volume of any water, exempt compounds, or colorant added to tint bases.

[b]Units are grams of VOC per liter (pounds of VOC per gallon) of coating, including water and exempt compounds, thinned to the maximum thinning recommended by the manufacturer. Sources: U.S. EPA 1998; SCAQMD 2007

Nanotechnology for the Forest Products Industry: Vision and Technology Roadmap lays out some products and technologies in use, in development, or on the horizon. Nanotechnology may be used to do the following (American Forest & Paper Association 2005; Elvin 2007):

- create photochemical "factories" mimicking the operation of a plant cell by harnessing or reproducing the carbon sequestration potential that trees offer with photosynthesis
- produce "intelligent" products with nanosensors for measuring moisture levels, attack by wood-decaying

fungi, chemical emissions, forces, loads, temperature, etc.

- create coatings and impregnation materials to preserve wood fibers from attack by fungus and insects, protect wood from weathering, clean the surface of mold, protect wood from fire, or increase the insulation value of wood
- create lighter weight products from less material that are as strong as their heavier counterparts with fewer energy requirements
- produce building blocks for wood products with substantially enhanced properties beyond standard wood materials

While some of the technologies mentioned above are a long way from the market, already the following products are available in a limited capacity (American Forest & Paper Association 2005; Elvin 2007):

- Nanoscale UV absorbers are added to protective coatings to protect wood from UV radiation that can degrade the surface. A product made from zinc oxide is a nontoxic yet effective material. The small particle size allows the coating to remain transparent.
- Researchers at the School of Forest Resources and Environmental Science at Michigan Technological University have developed a preservative that is an organic insecticide and fungicide embedded in 100 nanometer plastic beads. The beads are suspended in water as they are dispersed through the wood under pressure. Their nano size allows them to move completely within the wood fibers.
- An antimicrobial sealant made of nanoscale cross-linked polymers encapsulates mold spores that may have settled on wood fibers and prevents further growth. The sealant bonds to wood fibers, eliminating mold's nutrient sources.
- Another nanosealant forms a molecular bond with the wood fibers, completely encapsulating each while still allowing the wood to breathe.
- Wood/plastic composite material has been developed that uses carbon nanofibers and nanoclays to improve stiffness and other mechanical properties. One material technology is bamboo fiber–reinforced polypropylene composites.

Conclusion

This chapter has laid out options for using wood for sustainable sites. But in today's market, a good portion of the wood sold for exterior applications can't be considered a truly "green" material. "Friends of the Earth" summarizes the opinion of some environmental groups, stating: "The rate of the world's consumption of wood is unsustainable"; even though it is a theoretically renewable resource, it is being used at a rate faster than its renewal (Friends of the Earth). And many wood structures, particularly in the landscape, are used for less time than it takes to regenerate the wood. (It takes around 35 years to grow a tree large enough to mill a 2×12 board). Other organizations like the Forest Stewardship Council foresee the potential for wood to be sustainably grown to meet the world's demand for it. All are in agreement that forests, even young ones, offer critical "lungs" for the planet.

One of the greatest environmental benefits of well-managed forests is in their potential as carbon "sinks." The CORRIM study discussed earlier in the chapter found that a wood frame house constructed in Minnesota actually resulted in a net reduction of CO_2 emissions as opposed to production of emissions that occurs to varying degrees with just about any other building material. And a Dutch study of wood use in residential construction concluded that CO_2 emissions could be reduced by 50% if an increased amount of wood was used in residential construction (Goverse et al. 2001). Wood holds the potential to be a truly sustainable and renewable building material in the future.

Wood use in the landscape offers more challenges than in interior applications, as some techniques to protect it from decay can be toxic. Generally, the more effective the preservation treatment the more risks to humans and the environment. However, with growing concerns for human and environmental health, new preservative and finish treatments newly marketed or in development may make preserved wood in landscape applications a good choice.

So specifying reclaimed, sustainably harvested, or engineered wood products and lumber with nontoxic or low-toxicity preservatives and finishes is a good idea. Where certified or low-toxicity preserved wood is not available or is cost prohibitive, alternative materials such as plastic lumber may have fewer environmental impacts in some situations.

REFERENCES

Advanced Housing Research Center. 2004. "Research in Progress: Environmentally Benign Wood Preservation without Heavy Metals." Report: RIP 4723-001. Madison, WI: Forest Products Laboratory.

Agency for Toxic Substances and Disease Registry (ATSDR). "ToxFAQs." U.S. Department of Health and Human Services. http://www.atsdr.cdc.gov/toxfaq.html (accessed between May 2006 and November 2007).

American Forest & Paper Association, TAPPI, U.S. Department of Agriculture Forest Service, U.S. Department of Energy. 2005. *Nanotechnology for the Forest Products Industry: Vision and Technology Roadmap*. Atlanta, GA: TAPPI Press.

American Wood Preserver's Association. http://www.awpa.com/.

Arch Chemicals. http://www.wolmanizedwood.com/.

ASTM Standard A153. 2005. "Standard Specification for Zinc Coating (Hot-dip) on Iron and Steel Hardware." West Conshohocken, PA: ASTM International. www.astm.org.

ASTM Standard A653/A653M. 2007. "Standard Specification for Steel Sheet, Zinc-Coated (Galvanized) or Zinc-Iron Alloy-Coated (Galvannealed) by the Hot-Dip Process." West Conshohocken, PA: ASTM International. www.astm.org.

Athena Sustainable Materials Institute. *Athena Environmental Impact Estimator*, version 3.0.3. Kutztown, ON: Athena Sustainable Materials Institute.

Athena Sustainable Materials Institute. 2000, April. "Summary Report: A Life-cycle Analysis of Canadian Softwood Lumber Production." Prepared by Jamie K. Meil, Ottawa, Canada.

Austin Energy Green Building Program. 2007. *Sustainable Building Sourcebook*. Austin Energy. http://austinenergy.com/Energy%20Efficiency/Programs/Green%20Building/Sourcebook/e arthConstruction.htm.

Berge, Bjørn. 2000. *The Ecology of Building Materials*. Oxford: Architectural Press.

BuildingGreen. GreenSpec. Building Green, Inc. http://www.buildinggreen.com/menus/index.cfm Accessed October 30, 2007.

Chappel, S., ed. 1998. *The Alternative Building Sourcebook: For Traditional, Natural and Sustainable Building Products & Services*. Brownfield, ME: Fox Maple Press.

Composite Panel Association (CPA). "Certification Programs." http://www.pbmdf.com/Index.

Consortium for Research on Renewable Industrial Materials (CORRIM). 2005, August. *Life-cycle Environmental Perfor-*

mance of Renewable Building Materials in the Context of Residential Construction. Seattle: University of Washington, CORRIM.

Drengson, Alan, and Duncan Taylor, eds. 1997. *Ecoforestry: The Art and Science of Sustainable Forest Use*. Gabriola Island, BC: New Society Publishers.

Elvin, G. A. 2007. "Nanotechnology for Green Building." Green Technology Forum, June 2007. http://www.greentechforum.net/greenbuild.

Demkin, J., ed. 1998a. "Application Report 01: Light Framing." In *Environmental Resource Guide*. New York: John Wiley & Sons.

Environmental Building News (EBN). 2008. "Smaller Copper Particles, Smaller Environmental Impact for Treated Wood" Product Review. Brattleboro, Vermont: Building Green, Inc. Volume 17(2):8-9.

Environmental Building News (EBN). 2007. "Binders in Manufactured Wood Products." Brattleboro, VT: Building Green. Volume 16(10):10.

Environmental Building News (EBN). 2006. "Triton Logging Recovers Underwater Forests" Product Review. Brattleboro, Vermont: Building Green, Inc. 15(7):11–12.

Falk, Robert H. and David B. McKeever. (2004) "Recovering Wood for Reuse and Recycling: A United States Perspective". *Management of Recovered Wood Recycling, Bioenergy and Other Options*. Christos Gallis, editor. Thessaloniki, Greece, April 2004.

Falk, Bob. (2002). "Wood-Framed Building Deconstruction: A Source of Lumber for Construction?". *Forest Products Journal*, Madison, WI: Forest Products Society, Volume 52, No.3 pp 8–15.

Falk, B., and S. Williams. 1996. "Details for a Lasting Deck." In *Fine Homebuilding*. Newtown, CT: Taunton Press. No. 102, pp. 78–81, April/May.

Food and Agriculture Organization of the United Nations (FAO). 2005. *Global Forest Resources Assessment 2005*. FAO Forestry Paper 147. Rome: Food and Agriculture Organization of the United Nations.

Forest Certification Resource Center. "Search Tool." http://www.certifiedwoodsearch.org/searchproducts.aspx.

Forest Products Laboratory (FPL). 1999. *Wood Handbook: Wood as an Engineering Material*. Gen. Tech. Rep. FPL-GTR-113. U.S. Department of Agriculture, Forest Service, Forest Products Laboratory.

Forest Products Laboratory (FPL). 2005, April. "TechLine: New Uses for Old Lumber." Madison, WI: U.S. Department of Agriculture, Forest Service, Forest Products Laboratory.

Forest Products Laboratory (FPL). "Frequently Asked Questions about Wood Preservatives." USDA Forest Servuce. <.http://www.fpl.fs.fed.us>

Forest Products Laboratory (FPLa). "Research in Progress: Disposal of Chemically Treated Wood Products Used in Housing." RIP-4723-005. US Department of Agriculture, Forest Service, Forest Products Laboratory.

Forest Products Laboratory (FPLb). "Research in Progress: Remediating Treated Wood." RIP-4723-007. US Department of Agriculture, Forest Service, Forest Products Laboratory.

Forest Stewardship Council (FSC). http://www.fsc.org.

Forest Stewardship Council (FSC). "FSC Chain of Custordy Standard for Companies Supplying and Manufacturing FSC-Certified Products." FSC-STD-40-004 (Version 1-0) EN. FSC, 2004.

Forest Stewardship Council (FSC). 2005. *Designing and Building with FSC*. Developed by Forest Products Solutions. Washington, DC: Forest Stewardship Council.

Forest Stewardship Council (FSC). "FSC Controlled Wood Standard for Forest Management Enterprises." FSC-STD-30-010 (Version 2-0) EN. FSC, 2006.

Friends of the Earth http://www.foe.org/

Goverse, T., M. P. Heffert, P. Groenewegen, E. Worrell, and R. Smits. 2001. "Wood Innovation in the Residential Construction Sector: Opportunities and Constraints." *Journal of Resources, Conservation and Recycling* 34(1):53–74.

Greenpeace. 2004, November. "Good Wood Guide." Greenpeace.

Green Seal. 2005, February. *Green Seal's Choose Green Report*: Wood Finishes and Stains. Washington, DC: Green Seal.

Green Seal. 1993, May. *GS-11 Green Seal Environmental Standard for Paints*. 1st ed.. Washington, DC: Green Seal.

Gutowski, Timothy G. 2004, December. "Design and Manufacturing for the Environment." In *Handbook of Mechanical Engineering*. New York: Springer-Verlag.

Imhoff, Dan. 2005. *Building with Vision: Optimizing and Finding Alternatives to Wood*. Healdsburg, CA: Watershed Media.

International Agency for Research on Cancer (IARC). Monographs on the Evaluation of Carcinogenic Risks to Humans. Lyon, France: International Agency for Research on Cancer.

International Agency for Research on Cancer (IARC). http://www.iarc.fr/.

International Union for Conservation of Nature and Natural Resources (IUCN). "2006 Red List of Threatened Species Database." http://www.iucnredlist.org/ (accessed December 15, 2006).

IPCC. 2000. *Land use, Land-use change, and Forestry - Intergovernmental Panel on Climate Change Special Report* (eds. Watson R.T., Noble I.R., Bolin B., Ravindranath N.H., Verardo D.J., Dokken D.J.) Cambridge University Press, Cambridge.

Korthals Altes, Tristan. 2006, August. "Treated Wood in Transition: Less Toxic Options in Preserved and Protected Wood." *Environmental Building News* 15(8): 1, 11–19.

Korthals Altes, Tristan. 2007, March."New Treated Wood Uses Nonmetallic Biocides." *Environmental Building News* 16(3): 9–10.

Lippiatt, Barbara C. 2007. *BEES 4.0 Building for Environmental and Economic Sustainability Technical Manual and User Guide*. National Institute of Standards and Technology.

Metafore. "Environmental Assessment Tool." http://www.metafore.org/index (accessed November 11, 2007).

Miller, K. J., and T. Campbell. 2006. "Forest Certification and FSC." *Journal of Green Building* 1(1): 39–45.

National Council for Air and Stream Improvement. (NCASI) "Downloads Page." http://www.ncasi.org//Support/Downloads/.

National Institute of Standards and Technology. *BEES 4.0: Building for Environmental and Economic Sustainability*. http://www.bfrl.nist.gov.

New Life Millworks. http://www.newlifemillworks.com/.

Norris, G. A. 2006. "Life Cycle Perspectives on Wood and other Biobased Products." Sylvatica, Aug. 2006.

PureWood. http://www.purewoodproducts.com/ Accessed April 8, 2008

Rainforest Alliance. "SmartWood Program." http://www.rainforest-alliance.org/programs/forestry/index.html.

South Coast Air Quality Management District (SCAQMD). "Rule 1113, Architectural Coatings." Amended July 13, 2007. California South Coast Air Quality Management District.

Spiegel, Ross and Meadows, Dru. 2006. *Green Building Materials*. Hoboken, NJ: John Wiley & Sons.

Thompson, J.W., and K. Sorvig. 2000. *Sustainable Landscape Construction: A Guide to Green Building Outdoors*. Washington, DC: Island Press.

Timber Treatment Technologies. <http://www.timbersilwood.com/techcoverage.html> Accessed February 13, 2008.

U.S. Environmental Protection Agency (US EPA). "Ground Water & Drinking Water: Consumer Fact Sheet on Pentachlorophenol." http://www.epa.gov/safewater/contaminants (accessed September 12, 2006).

U.S. Environmental Protection Agency (U.S. EPA). "Pesticides: Topical & Chemical Fact Sheets: Chomated Copper Arsenate (CCA)." http://www.epa.gov/oppad001/reregistration/cca/.

U.S. Environmental Protection Agency (U.S. EPA), Office of Policy, Economics and Innovation. 2007, March. *Energy Trends in Selected Manufacturing Sectors: Opportunities and Challenges for Environmentally Preferable Energy Outcomes*. Prepared by ICF International.

U.S. Environmental Protection Agency (U.S. EPA). 1998. "National Volatile Organic Compound Emission Standards for Architectural Coatings, 40 CFR Part 59". Federal Register Vol.63, No. 176, September 11, 1998.

U.S. Green Building Council. 2005. *LEED-NC for New Construction Reference Guide, Version 2.2*. 1t ed.. Washington, DC: USGBC.

Western Wood Preservers Institute (WWPI), Wood Preservation Canada (WPC), The Southern Pressure Treaters Association (SPTA), and the Timber Piling Council (TPC).

2006, August. *Best Management Practices (BMPs) for the Use of Treated Wood in Aquatic and Sensitive Environments.* Vancouver, WA: WWPI.

Williams, R. S., and M. Knaebe. 1995, December. "The Finish Line: The Bark-Side/Pith-Side Debate." Madison, WI: U.S. Department of Agirculture, Forest Service, Forest Producs Laboratory.

Wilson, Alex. Personal Communication. December 16, 2007.

Wilson, Alex. 2006. "A White Paper to the USGBC Board: Dealing with Wood and Biobased Materials in the LEED Rating System." Washington, DC: U.S. Green Building Council.

Winterbottom, Daniel M. 2000. *Wood in the Landscape: A Practical Guide to Specification and Design.* New York: John Wiley & Sons.

chapter 11

Metals

Metals in site construction offer many advantages. Used appropriately, metal can be an enduring material with a longer life span than wood, concrete, or plastics. Many have a high strength-to-size ratio. A vast array of metal shapes, sheets, and prefabricated products are available, and metals can be cast or shaped into custom forms. The variety of metal finishes and alloys available offer a wide range of aesthetic possibilities.

These benefits must be weighed against serious environmental and human health impacts from mining, production, finishing, and use of metals. Impacts vary widely by metal type, product, and finish, yet are among the most significant of any construction material. Metal production uses large amounts of resources—often three to eight times the amount of metal actually produced, resulting in a huge amount of waste. This waste, some of which is considered toxic, is released to air, water, and soil where it can affect ecosystems and lead to negative human health effects. Mining of the vast quantity of resources required for metal production impacts habitats, air, and water around mining sites.

The potential for nearly endless recycling may be the most sustainable characteristic of metals. Use of both pre- and post-consumer scrap conserves substantial energy and reduces waste and pollution in the manufacture of new metals. And the metals recycling industry is generally well established and economically strong.

Longevity of metal products and installations is another key strategy in sustainable use of metals. A long use life can offset the substantial resource use and emissions and waste resulting from a metal's manufacture. If a metal product or structure remains for many years in the use phase, the negative impacts from its production can be "amortized" over a longer period, reducing their intensity. Appropriate use and specification of metals and metal finishes for a given application and site is critical to the sustainable use of metals as it can increase the use life. Specification of an inappropriate metal or metal finish can lead to rapid corrosion, yet in another site or application, the same specification may perform well for 50 years.

USE OF METALS

Steel and iron. Carbon steel, iron containing up to 1.7% carbon, is the most common metal used in the construction industry, used primarily in structural applications. With exposure to exterior conditions or moisture, carbon steel is extremely vulnerable to corrosion, so it is usually coated when used in site applications.

Worldwide, 1.2 billion tons of raw steel was produced in 2006. Of this, 96 million tons was produced in the United States and 187 million tons was produced in the

European Union. China was the largest producer of raw steel, with 420 million tons produced. This has been a cause for concern, as China's pollution regulations are not as stringent as those in the EU or the United States. In 2006, 46 million tons of raw steel were imported to the United States. Twenty-two percent of all primary steel produced in the United States was used in the construction sector (U.S. Geological Survey [USGS] 2007a).

Stainless steel may be the most commonly used material in site specialty applications due to its good corrosion resistance without finishes. In 2002 about 20 million tons of stainless steel was produced and 12 million tons of recycled stainless and other steel alloys was recycled back into new products.

Stainless steel is an iron alloy containing over 10.5% chromium and less than 1.5% carbon. There are numerous types of stainless steel, many of which also contain nickel, molybdenum, manganese, and selenium.

The most common types of stainless steel used in site construction are austenitic stainless steel types 304 and 316. Type 304 contains 18–20% chromium and 8–10.5% nickel. Type 316 contains 2–3% molybdenum and 10–14% nickel, both of which improve the stainless steel's corrosion resistance in chemically intensive en-

vironments (ASTM 2004). It is also more expensive than 304, which in some cases precludes its use.

One of the most important properties of stainless steel is its resistance to corrosion, which is provided by a passive surface layer formed by the chromium and sometimes nickel and molybdenum contents upon exposure to oxygen. This layer acts as a barrier between the metal and the environment, prohibiting corrosion. Seventeen percent of stainless steel that is produced in North America is used in the construction sector (Stainless Steel Information Center).

Aluminum use in construction has rapidly increased since the 1950s. It is a corrosion-resistant, lightweight, yet relatively structurally strong material that offers many opportunities for use in site construction, from site furnishings to guardrails to structures. Worldwide production of aluminum in 2005 was 31.9 million tons with 2.5 million tons produced in the United States. Fourteen percent of this aluminum was used for construction purposes (USGS 2007b).

Copper is used in landscape applications, primarily in sheet form, for flashing, caps, and panels, and in particulate form for lumber preservation treatments. Brass

Table 11–1 Alloying Elements for Various Architectural Metals

Base Metal	Alloying Element	Attribute
Aluminum	Copper	Improved strength
Aluminum	Manganese	Improved ductility
Aluminum	Silicon	Lower melting point
Aluminum	Magnesium	Improved finish
Copper	Tin	Color, lower melting point
Copper	Zinc	Color, strength
Iron	Carbon	Improved ductility and strength
Iron	Chromium	Improved corrosion resistance
Iron	Nickel	Improved corrosion resistance and hardness
Lead	Tin	Hardness, color
Nickel	Copper	Workability and color
Tin	Antimony	Workability
Zinc	Titanium	Workability

Source: Zahner 2005

and bronze—copper alloys with zinc, tin, aluminum, or nickel—are used in both cast and sheet forms.

Titanium, a relative newcomer to the construction industry, offers very high strength, light weight, and good corrosion resistance. Stainless Steel World estimates that close to 2,000 tons of titanium was used in architectural applications in 2005, with the majority used in roofing and cladding applications (Stainless Steel World). Other applications include paneling, sculptures, and plaques. The high cost of titanium prohibits its use in all but the most specialized applications.

Titanium, more commonly added to other metals as an alloy, is added to steel to produce ferro-titanium for increased corrosion resistance, and to stainless steel to reduce the carbon content. Titanium is added to aluminum to refine the grain size and to strengthen the metal. The majority of titanium used in construction is converted to titanium dioxide (TiO_2) for use as a pigment in paints (54%) and in plastics (27%; USGS 2007d).

Alloying elements in metals. While the following sections primarily discuss iron and steel, stainless steel, and aluminum, it is important to note that almost every metal used in construction contains alloying elements. Metals commonly used for alloys are shown in Table 11–1.

Environmental Impacts of Metal Production

Understanding human and environmental health impacts of the entire life cycle of metals can be quite complicated. There are hundreds of metal alloys used in construction materials in a staggering variety of products and finishes. Few life-cycle analyses (LCAs) have been completed for metal products, and where they exist, they are usually specific to a particular metal application or product. But impacts can vary widely between two different products made from the same metal, and between metal alloys and finishes. Impacts can also vary with "differences in environmental conditions, service life and other project-specific variables" (Houska and Young 2006).

MATERIALS ACQUISITION AND RESOURCE CONSUMPTION

The manufacture of metals requires significant inputs of raw materials, resulting in the depletion of resources, habitat destruction from mining, waste generation, and emissions releases to the environment. The large quantity of material that must be mined to yield metal resources is a significant impact in metal production. Ore wastes to metals ratios range from 3:1 for iron, 4:1 for aluminum, and up to 400:1 for copper (Demkin 1998b; Gutowski 2004). The greatest toxic releases in metals production result from the metals mining industry. Toxics Release Inventory (TRI) figures from 2005 show on-site land releases from metal mining totaled 1.17 billion pounds—about 27% of the TRI chemical releases from all industries combined.

Extraction. Most metal ore is surface mined through strip mining, open-pit mining, mountaintop removal, or dredging. These practices result in habitat destruction and soil loss. Downstream impacts from mine runoff are increased turbidity and pollution, lower aquatic productivity, increased biochemical oxygen demand, and increased deoxygenation of water bodies (Demkin 1998a).

Significant water pollution can result from runoff of mine tailings. Many metals exist with or occur as metallic sulfides. Once exposed at the surface they can oxidize into sulfates and sulfuric acid runoff. Mining for metals such as iron, copper, nickel, lead, and zinc can result in acid mine drainage (Gutowski 2004).

Beneficiation. The extraction and processing of beneficial materials from the mined materials includes milling, crushing, consolidation, washing, leaching, flotation, separation, and thermal processes. These activities are usually performed on or near the mine site to avoid transport of heavy waste materials. These processes result in large quantities of waste tailings and materials discarded at the mine.

Wastewater quality can be affected by leaching or disposal of the acids used to separate metals, some of which negatively affect water bodies around the mine. Water and acid runoff from mining and processing wastes can carry significant quantities of heavy metals and chemicals, potentially contaminating groundwater and surface water supplies. Disposal of spent solvents can also impact water quality. Windblown dust from large piles can pose adverse health effects in workers and communities surrounding the mines, and degrade land and water resources (Environmental Roadmapping Initiative [ERI] 2004b).

Iron and steel. The primary raw materials for iron and steel are iron ore, coal, and limestone. Iron, an abundant material, is estimated to compose about 5% of the earth's crust, and deposits of it are widespread. Other materials such as chromium, nickel, zinc, manganese, and cadmium are used to produce various alloys and coatings. Iron ore, coal, and limestone are primarily strip-mined, although some limestone is extracted from underground mines.

Aluminum. The primary raw material for aluminum is bauxite, a mineral found all around the world, but primary sources of bauxite for aluminum production are tropical and subtropical regions in South and Central America, Southeast Asia, Africa, and Australia. On average it requires four tons of bauxite to yield one ton of aluminum (U.S. EPA 2007b). The USGS estimates that domestic aluminum requirements can't be met by domestic supplies of bauxite, and while domestic non-bauxitic sources of aluminum are plentiful, processes

for using these resources to produce aluminum are not economically viable at this time, so they are not in use (USGS 2007b).

Bauxite is strip-mined, and it is estimated that bauxite mining destroys more surface area than any other ore mining. This destruction impacts the entire planet, as sensitive rain forests and tropical areas are the primary bauxite mining locations.

According to research by the International Aluminum Institute (IAI), the total annual area of land mined for bauxite has increased by 25% since 1998. However, the industry is starting to recognize and take steps to lessen the severe environmental impacts of this mining. The IAI has established a Bauxite Mining and Alumina Refining Task Force to foster better environmental practices in the industry. Some companies monitor the quality of surface water leaving the mine and, when the mine is closed, work to restore the land. Currently, full rain forest restoration attempts are rare; instead, land is turned to agricultural uses (IAI 2005).

After extraction, the bauxite is crushed and pulverized near the site, creating aluminum oxide along with other oxidized metals and contaminants, some of which leach into and pollute nearby waterways.

Copper. is mined primarily in open pits, with approximately two tons of overburden removed for every ton of copper ore mined; then just 0.7% of copper is in

Figure 11–1.

This view of the Berkeley Pit copper mine in Butte, Montana, taken by NASA records the impacts of metal mining activities on the environment and water quality. The large gray tailings pile of waste rock is adjacent to a heavy metal–laden tailings pond that at the time of this photo, 2006, was 275 ft deep. More than 400 tons of waste and by-products are mined for each ton of copper produced, and waste quantities are increasing as quality of the ores decreases. (Source: Image courtesy of Earth Sciences and Image Analysis Laboratory, NASA Johnson Space Center; http://eol.jsc.nasa.gov)

the ore. As a result, more than 400 tons of waste and by-products are mined for each ton of copper produced, and waste quantities are increasing as quality of the ores decreases (Demkin 1998b). A large quantity of copper mining takes place in developing countries where destruction of forests and streams is often less regulated, and restoration may be unlikely.

Water runoff from copper mining and processing wastes can carry significant quantities of heavy metals, potentially contaminating groundwater and surface water supplies. Copper is toxic to fish and aquatic organisms. Runoff from copper in use can impact sensitive ecosystems. Release of copper dust can be toxic to soil microorganisms and can disrupt microbial processes.

EMBODIED ENERGY OF METALS

Energy consumption for the production of metals varies by metal type, product, and manufacturing facility, but it is generally high compared with alternative building materials such as lumber or engineered wood. The primary processes of smelting and refining use the highest amounts of energy of any stage in the life cycle. Metals with the highest primary embodied energy are aluminum and titanium. Aluminum production's high energy consumption is somewhat offset by the use of cleaner hydroelectric energy sources.

The fact that embodied energy varies so widely by metal and even by metal products presents a challenge to quantifying the embodied energy of metals and use of the figures to make decisions about which metals to use. While embodied energy numbers are generally available for base metals, they do not often include all steps to get to a finished product. Instead most numbers reflect only materials acquisition and primary processing of the individual metal. And those that include product manufacturing usually do not include finishing.

Use of pre- and post-consumer scrap can substantially reduce energy use in metal production. For instance, use of aluminum scrap reduces energy use by 95% and use of steel scrap reduces energy use by 50%. Steel scrap recycling conserves a lower percentage of energy than aluminum because iron and steel have a very high melting point (see Figure 1–2 and Table 11–3).

Steel. Energy used in primary iron and steel manufacture accounts for 2.3% of total U.S. energy consumption and 9% of all U.S. manufacturing energy use (Energetics 2005). While the industry reduced the amount of energy used by 28% between 1990 and 2005, it still requires around 16.5 million Btu/ton to produce semifinished steel at integrated mills using the basic oxygen furnace and 5.7 million Btu/ton for flat-rolled EAF steel (U.S. EPA 2007b). Electric arc furnace (EAF) steelmaking is less than half as energy intensive as the basic oxygen furnace (BOF) process, partially due to the fact that EAFs use a higher percentage of steel scrap, eliminating the first and most energy-intensive step in the steel manufacture process, the conversion from iron ore to iron.

A 2005 *Steel Industry Marginal Opportunity Study* conducted on behalf of the U.S. Department of Energy (DOE) estimated that energy intensity reductions of 5.1 million Btu/ton for integrated steel-making and 2.7 million Btu/ton for EAF steel-making are technically feasible with implementation of industry best practices and commercially available technologies (Energetics 2005). While the new technologies are available, they may not

Table 11–2 Classes of Supply for Some Elements Related to Metal Manufacture.

Worldwide Supply	Elements Related to Metal Manufacture
Infinite supply	Silicon
Ample supply	Aluminum (Gallium), Carbon, Iron, Sulfur, Titanium
Adequate supply	Lithium, Phosphorus
Potentially limited supply	Cobalt, Chromium, Nickel, Lead (Arsenic, Bismuth), Platinum
Potentially highly limited supply	Copper, Mercury, Tin, Zinc (Cadmium), Silver, Gold

Source: Graedel and Allenby 1996

be economically feasible for some mills to implement (U.S. EPA 2007b).

Aluminum. One of the most severe environmental impacts resulting from the production of aluminum is the tremendous amount of electricity required for primary aluminum production. Twenty thousand kilowatt hours are required to refine one ton of aluminum. The Aluminum Association of North America estimates that the industry spends $2 billion per year to produce aluminum through the electrolytic process (Aluminum Association 2004).

Efforts to improve energy efficiency by the worldwide aluminum industry have resulted in a 5% decrease of average electrical energy required for electrolytic production per ton between 1990 and 2004. The IAI goals call for an additional 6% reduction by 2010 (IAI 2007a).

Stainless steel. Production of stainless steel uses approximately 60% more energy than that used to produce carbon steel. This is because of additional processing and higher temperatures required to melt and form the metal product.

Titanium has a very high melting point; therefore it requires substantial energy to produce. The high melting point can be an advantage in applications that must resist fire.

Energy use in secondary processes. Metal alloying and finishing can vary the energy use, emissions, and solid waste impacts of metals widely. Additional stages such as casting, shaping, rolling, and drawing can add, sometimes substantially, to the energy cost as some metals need to be melted in the secondary stages. Cold-rolled steel sheet has lower embodied energy than steel sheet that is hot rolled and formed. Thinner and smaller products may require more energy per unit of size than larger pieces (Houska and Young 2006).

The U.S. Department of Energy's Industrial Technologies Program on the metal casting industry estimates that a 22% reduction in energy use (and associated CO_2 emissions) is possible with use of energy-efficient equipment and processes. They estimate that these improvements would save 102 trillion Btus and 6.5 million tons of CO_2 per year (U.S. EPA 2006b).

ENERGY SOURCES

Embodied energy evaluation of metals is further complicated by the differing energy sources used to produce different metal types and even among manufacturers of the same metal. For instance, in the United States, 55% of energy used to produce aluminum is from relatively clean hydroelectric sources, yet aluminum production in the Middle East uses oil and gas energy sources. Iron and steel have substantially lower embodied energy than aluminum, yet energy sources for production are primarily natural gas and coal, which have relatively high CO_2, SO_2, and NO_x emissions. Differing energy sources may mean that embodied energy numbers are not a good indication of greenhouse gas emissions from the production of metals.

About half of the iron and steel industry's energy is derived from coal, a large part of which is used to produce coke for the blast furnace. The power used to produce aluminum comes from hydroelectric sources and environmental impacts from hydroelectric energy production are less than those of coal. Hydroelectric power plants don't release the high sulfur, nitrogen, and carbon gas emissions of fossil fuel–burning plants that con-

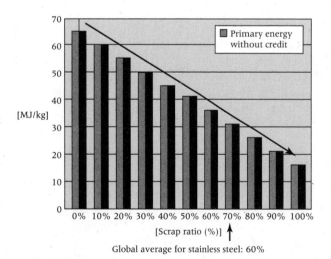

Figure 11–2.

This chart illustrates the primary energy of stainless steel in megajoules per kilogram. Primary energy is substantially reduced as the scrap content of stainless steel increases. (Source: Fujii et al. 2005)

Table 11–3 U.S. Metal Sector Energy Consumption and Energy Intensity, 2002

NAICS Code	Sector	Energy Consumption per Unit	Total Energy Consumption (trillion Btu)	Energy Consumption per Dollar Value of Shipments (thousand Btu [kBtu])
331111	Iron and steel	Integrated steelmaking 16.5 MBtu/ton EAF steelmaking 5.7 MBtu/ton	1,455	27.8
3313	Alumina and aluminum	13 kWh/kg for state-of-the-art facilities 20 kWh/kg for older Soderberg smelters	351	12.2
3315	Metal casting	Not available	157	5.6
332	Fabricated metal products	Not available	387	1.7

Source: U.S. EPA 2007b

tribute to acid rain and global warming. However, a few recent studies of large reservoirs behind hydroelectric dams have suggested that the submerged decaying vegetation may give off quantities of greenhouse gases similar to other sources of electricity. Other major impacts of hydroelectric power are flooding of vast areas of land for reservoirs, watershed impacts from amount and quality of downstream waters and soil, and fish migration barriers (Baird 2007) (see Table 11–4).

EMISSIONS, WASTE, AND TOXIC IMPACTS OF METAL PROCESSING AND MANUFACTURE

Environmental impact evaluation of metals tends to focus on embodied energy; however, toxic waste and emission releases to air, and to a lesser degree to water and soil can be a greater concern based on the sheer volume of waste material created during the metal production process. Billions of tons of waste, both solid and gaseous, result from the mining, production, manufacture, shaping, and finishing of metals. While increasing amounts of this waste are reused in beneficial ways either within or outside of the metal industry, and other waste is "neutralized," of greatest concern are the millions of pounds of toxic and criteria pollutant releases to air, and to a lesser degree to water.

After releases during the metal mining stages, the second greatest releases occur from primary metals processing such as ore refinement, coking, and smelting. Emissions and waste produced within these processes

Table 11–4 Energy Sources for Metals Processing and Manufacture, 2002

NAICS	Sector	Net Electricity	Coke and Breeze	Coal	Natural Gas	Other
331111	Iron and steel	13%	36%	3%	27%	21%[a]
3313	Alumina and aluminum	55%[b]	—	—	37%	7%
3315	Metal casting	34%	15%	1%	49%	1%
332	Fabricated metal products	42%	—	—	54%	4%

[a]This category largely consists of by-product fuels such as coke oven gas and blast furnace gas (which are coal based in origin).
[b]Primarily hydroelectric energy sources
Source: Adapted from U.S. EPA 2007b

for steel, iron, and aluminum are discussed in the individual metal sections below.

Huge reductions in emissions and waste can be achieved through use of metal scrap, avoiding the polluting refining and mining stages of metal manufacture. The Aluminum Institute estimates that 97% of aluminum production emissions can be reduced through use of scrap, and 60% of iron and steel production emissions are reduced through use of steel scrap.

Emission releases can be just as challenging to quantify for many reasons, some of which are similar to embodied energy evaluation. Emissions from manufacturing discrete metals and different metal products from the same metal vary widely. And impacts from metal finishes also vary between type of finish and finishing facility (see Table 11–5).

The EPA's Toxics Release Inventory (TRI) sector categories do not break down by all types of metal or all forms of a metal product, and Life-cycle Inventory (LCI) information is not available for most products. Therefore it is challenging to evaluate the relative emissions and waste of specific products (see Tables 11–6 and 11–7).

In addition, different facilities use varying manufacturing and finishing processes and have different types of pollution control equipment. Many sector reports attribute decreasing emissions to use of newer pollution control and processing technologies; however, not all facilities can or will upgrade their equipment. Lastly, industry data for the TRI inventories is self-reported by the industries themselves and not all facilities report.

Some significant impacts from metal mining and processing from 2005 TRI data are as follows:

- The primary metals sector, responsible for producing iron, steel, and aluminum among other metals, reported 479 million pounds of disposal or other toxic releases, 11% of total TRI releases. This quantity is up 3% from 2004.
- Overall air releases of persistent bioaccumulative toxins (PBTs) from the metals sector decreased from 2004–2005 by almost 27%.
- The metal mining sector releases of lead increased by 58 million pounds (17%) between 2000 and 2005.
- Primary metals lead releases decreased by 6.3 million pounds, or 18%, between 2000 and 2005.
- The metal mining industry was responsible for 3.7 million pounds, or 84%, of mercury or mercury compound releases in 2005. Releases of mercury and mercury compounds decreased by 420,000 pounds (9%).

Primary Iron and Steel Processing

While pollution controls, waste reuse, and new processes have reduced toxic pollutant and particulate releases and solid waste over the past years, the environmental and human health impacts of iron and steel processing are still quite significant just by the sheer volume of steel produced each year.

Solid waste. Waste generation from iron and steel production is a significant impact of the iron- and

Table 11–5 Criteria Air Pollutant Emissions by Metal Sector, 2002

NAICS	Sector	Energy-related CAP Emissions[a]	Non-energy-related CAP Emissions[a]	Total CAP Emissions[a]
3313	Aluminum	72,736 tons (13%)[b]	466,105 tons (87%)	538,841 tons
331111	Iron and steel mills	227,808 tons (27%)	622,836 tons (73%)	850,644 tons
3315	Metal casting	5,225 tons (7%)	67,420 tons (93%)	72,645 tons
332813	Metal finishing	111 tons (30%)	263 tons (70%)	374 tons

[a]Does not include carbon dioxide figures (see Table 11–8)

[b]According to the figure, energy-related CAP emissions are a relatively small fraction of total emissions; however, NEI data attribute emissions from the generation of purchased energy to the generating source, not the purchasing entity. Therefore, energy-related emissions from an electricity-dependent sector like aluminum will be underestimated.

Source: Adapted from U.S. EPA 2007b

Table 11–6 Total Greenhouse Gas Emissions in Teragrams of CO_2 Equivalents

Source	1990 (Tg CO_2 Eq.)	2005 (Tg CO_2 Eq.)	% change
Carbon dioxide (CO_2)			
Iron and steel production	84.9	45.2	−46.7
Aluminum production	6.8	4.2	−38.2
Ferroalloy production	2.2	1.4	−36.3
Zinc production	0.9	0.5	−44.4
Lead production	0.3	0.3	nc
Methane (CH_4)			
Iron and steel production	1.3	1.0	−23
Ferroalloy production	+	+	
Hydrofluorocarbons (HFCs), perfluorocarbons (PFCs), and sulfur hexafluoride (SF_6)			
Aluminum production	18.5	3.0	−83.7

Source: Adapted from U.S. EPA 2006a

steelmaking processes. In 1997 the steel industry generated around 39 million tons of solid wastes in the form of slags, sludge, and dust. About 42.5% of this total waste was recycled on-site, used for energy recovery in processing, or treated to remove pollutants. Another 47.5% was recycled off-site or treated, discharged, or disposed of off-site (Energetics 2005).

Increasing costs of solid waste disposal combined with the Resource Conservation and Recovery Act (RCRA) amendments have spurred the industry to recycle or reuse as much of its waste as possible. Slag, the largest single waste component of iron and steel production, is reused as aggregate base material in road and building construction, and aggregate in asphalt and concrete. Ground granulated blast furnace slag is also used as a partial substitute for portland cement in concrete.

Toxic releases. Of greatest concern is the large quantity of hazardous waste generated by iron and steel facilities. The National Biennial RCRA Hazardous Waste Report indicates that the iron and steel sector accounted for 1.3 million tons, or 4%, of all hazardous waste generated in 2003. Predominant hazardous wastes reported by the industry are emission-control dust or sludge (629,100 tons), spent pickle liquor (72,800 tons), and cadmium and chromium (Energetics 2005). The magnitude and type of these releases pose human and en-

vironmental health risks, as some of these releases are carcinogens, toxins, mutagens, and persistent bioaccumulative toxins (PBTs).

The 2003 TRI data show that iron and steel sector facilities report 636 million pounds of toxics released, disposed of, or managed through treatment, energy recovery, or recycling. Sixty-two percent of these were managed (usually recycled) and 38%, 242 million pounds, were disposed of or released to the environment. Of this, approximately 4.8 million pounds were released to air, 4.8 million pounds were released to water, and the remainder was released to land (see Table 11–9).

The annual normalized quantity of chemicals disposed of or released to the environment increased 171% from 1994 to 2003; however, releases to air and water remained relatively the same. These trends are likely caused by a combination of upgraded pollution control equipment and growth in the industry. The increased pollution control caused the quantity of chemicals that needed to be disposed of to increase (U.S. EPA 2006a).

When 90% of chemical releases from the iron and steel sector is weighted for toxicity using the EPA's Risk-Screening Environmental Indicators (RSEI) model, air releases of manganese, chromium, and lead account for 99% of the sector's toxicity-weighted results, and discharges to water—primarily lead, copper, and chromium—account for 1%. When weighted for toxicity, the sector's normalized air and water releases declined 69% from 1994 to 2003 (U.S. EPA 2006a).

Criteria air pollutants. In addition to the air releases of chemicals and compounds discussed above, the iron and steel industry is a significant source of emissions from combustion-related and manufacturing processes, such as volatile organic compounds (VOCs), particulates, sulfur dioxide (SO_2), nitrogen oxides (NO_x), carbon monoxide, and ammonia. Twenty-seven percent of emissions result from energy-related processes, and 73% result from processes such as coke making, sintering, iron making, steelmaking, and various shaping processes (see Tables 11–5 and 11–6).

Iron and steel operations are the greatest industrial source of fine particles, and the particles, resulting at many points in the process, are not easily captured. Emissions of fine particles less than 2.5 microns in diameter are one of the greatest concerns because they are small enough to get trapped in the lungs and are not easily cleared.

CO_2 release. Carbon intensities of iron- and steelmaking operations place the steel sector second only to the petroleum refining sector in industry contributions to greenhouse gas emissions (U.S. EPA 2007a). The two steelmaking processes, integrated steelmaking and EAF-based steelmaking, differ in the amount of CO_2 released. EAF-based steelmaking releases 2,150 lb./CO_2 per ton of steel, 57% less than the 4,988 lb./CO_2 per ton of steel from integrated steelmaking (Energetics 2005).

In addition to greenhouse gases released from energy combustion, nonfuel–related process-generated emissions of CO_2 and CH_4 are released in the production of iron and steel. Emissions of CO_2 and CH_4 from iron and steel production in 2005 were 45.2 Tg CO_2 Eq. and 1.0 Tg CO_2 Eq., respectively (U.S. EPA 2007a). These emissions are the highest of any industrial sector, just slightly greater than those of the cement industry.

Water. Seventy-five thousand gallons of water are required to produce one ton of steel. Water is used to cool equipment, furnaces, and steel; to produce steam; to remove scale from steel products; as a medium for lubricating oils and cleaning solutions; and in wet scrubbers for pollution control (Energetics 2005). Advances in manufacturing processes now recycle a large amount of this water; however, some water during the process, particularly that from coke making, is laden with pollutants, suspended solids, and heavy metals.

The Clean Water Act regulates discharges of toxic pollutants, suspended solids, oil, grease, and other pollutants; therefore process wastewater is filtered and/or clarified on-site prior to release to meet maximum effluent release guidelines set by the National Pollutant Discharge Elimination System (NPDES). Regulated pollutants from iron making and steelmaking are ammonia-nitrogen, phenols, cyanide, chromium, hexavalent chromium, lead, nickel, zinc, benzene, benzo(a)pyrene, naphthalene, and tetrachloroethylene.

Stainless Steel Production

Air, water, and waste impacts from production of stainless steel are greater than those of carbon steel. The impacts discussed above from the production of iron and steel are incurred for stainless steel, as iron ore production is the first step in its production. Then additional energy use and pollution impacts result from alloying the iron ore with metals such as chromium, nickel, manganese, and/or molybdenum.

The nickel and chromium added to impart strength and corrosion resistance to the steel have relatively high waste-to-ore ratios, resulting in removal of large amounts of material that quickly become waste after the ores are removed. Zones of nickel typically contain about 1% of the metal. Mining of nickel, chromium, manganese, and molybdenum is performed in either surface or underground mines. Most chromium, manganese, and nickel are imported to the United States. Recycling is the main domestic source of chromium (USGS 2007c).

Chromium, nickel, and manganese compounds are all regulated by the EPA as hazardous air pollutants (HAPs). Particulate emissions from these metals during crushing and smelting operations can pose health risks in workers, as all are toxic in high amounts. Manganese can affect the respiratory and central nervous systems and hexavalent chromium is considered a carcinogen (IARC).

Chromite ore smelting and ferrochromium production are energy-intensive processes requiring

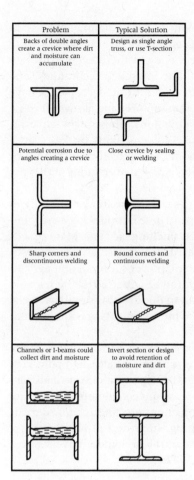

Problem	Typical Solution
Backs of double angles create a crevice where dirt and moisture can accumulate	Design as single angle truss, or use T-section
Potential corrosion due to angles creating a crevice	Close crevice by sealing or welding
Sharp corners and discontinuous welding	Round corners and continuous welding
Channels or I-beams could collect dirt and moisture	Invert section or design to avoid retention of moisture and dirt

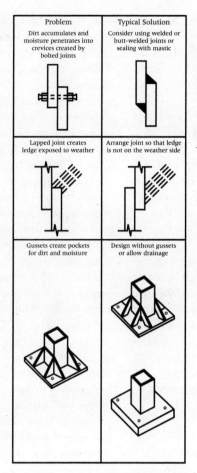

Problem	Typical Solution
Dirt accumulates and moisture penetrates into crevices created by bolted joints	Consider using welded or butt-welded joints or sealing with mastic
Lapped joint creates ledge exposed to weather	Arrange joint so that ledge is not on the weather side
Gussets create pockets for dirt and moisture	Design without gussets or allow drainage

Figure 11–3.

These figures from the Nickel Institute's *Stainless Steel in Architecture, Building, and Construction* publication illustrate problematic metal connection details that may encourage standing water and accumulation of chemicals that can lead to corrosion of metal and a reduced life of the structure. Typical solutions to the problems are offered. (Source: Nickel Institute, n.d.; Figures redrawn by John Wiley & Sons)

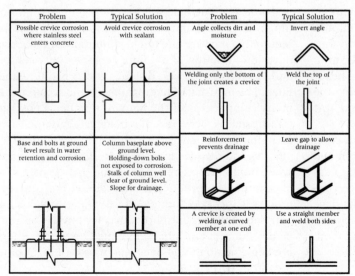

Problem	Typical Solution	Problem	Typical Solution
Possible crevice corrosion where stainless steel enters concrete	Avoid crevice corrosion with sealant	Angle collects dirt and moisture	Invert angle
		Welding only the bottom of the joint creates a crevice	Weld the top of the joint
Base and bolts at ground level result in water retention and corrosion	Column baseplate above ground level. Holding-down bolts not exposed to corrosion. Stalk of column well clear of ground level. Slope for drainage.	Reinforcement prevents drainage	Leave gap to allow drainage
		A crevice is created by welding a curved member at one end	Use a straight member and weld both sides

about 21.3 million Btus to produce one ton (Demkin 1998a).

Emissions of SO_2 from the processing of sulfide-containing ore are the primary concern of nickel smelting. Several tons of SO_2 is released for every ton of nickel produced.

In fabrication, fumes from welding and dust from grinding containing chromium, nickel, and molybdenum are assumed to pose worker health risks; however, there is much disagreement about the severity of the risks. The bioavailability of the fumes and dust is not well quantified (U.S. EPA "PBT and Toxic Chemical Program").

Primary Aluminum Processing

Aluminum production is a significant source of industrial pollutants. Aside from its high energy use, the major environmental and human health impacts from the primary smelting and manufacture of aluminum are greenhouse gas emissions from carbon dioxide and perfluorocarbons (PFCs) from aluminum smelting processes, and air emissions of polycyclic aromatic hydrocarbons (PAHs), inorganic fluorides, sulphur dioxide, and carbon dioxide (IAI 2007c).

Air emissions. The average smelting process for one ton of aluminum is responsible for the production of 1.7 metric tons of CO_2 from the consumption of carbon anodes and the equivalent of two tons of CO_2 from PFC emissions. In 1997, the worldwide primary aluminum industry was responsible for emitting 110 million tons of CO_2 equivalents, 50 million of which originated from the PFC compounds tetrofluormethane (CF_4) and hexofluormethane (C_2F_6). This produced 1% of the global human-induced greenhouse gas emissions (IAI 2007c).

While power generation for aluminum production may contribute fewer greenhouse gases than iron and steel, formation and release of perfluorocarbons (PFCs) from the aluminum smelting process are a large concern. PFCs are powerful global warming gases that have long atmospheric lifetimes. They are much more potent than carbon dioxide emissions from coal burning, with 1 kg of PFCs trapping equivalent heat to 6,500 kg of CO_2 (IAI 2007a).

PFCs are formed during the smelting process in events called anode effects. There is a possibility of controlling the frequency of these events through equipment modifications, improved techniques, and computer controls. In addition, modern plants have scrubbing equipment that captures and allows for reuse of 96%–99% of the emissions. These steps have reduced PFC greenhouse gas emissions by 74% since 1990, with an additional 6% reduction planned for 2010. This is a reduction equal to over 3 tons of CO_2 per ton of aluminum produced (IAI 2007c).

Aluminum smelting also releases inorganic fluorides as particulates and gases. These fluorides negatively impact vegetation around smelting facilities. Many smelting facilities are located in rural areas near forests, waterways (hydroelectric power sources), and agricultural land, all of which can be impacted by the releases. Large reductions (64%) in fluoride emissions have been made since 1990 due to improvements in pollution control equipment.

Other significant emissions of various stages of the aluminum production process are release of polycyclic aromatic hydrocarbons (PAHs); sulfur dioxide emissions from power generation, steam generation, anode plant ovens, and anode consumption; and carbon dioxide emissions from smelting. Improved production techniques and pollution control equipment have reduced these emissions (IAI 2007c).

Waste. Considerable solid waste is generated during the production of aluminum. Two tons of alumina are required to produce one ton of aluminum, and the production of one ton of alumina generates between 0.3 and 2.5 tons of bauxite residue, which is often landfilled. The industry is investigating methods to reuse as many components of the bauxite residue as possible. Caustic soda is recovered, as it holds value for the bauxite refining process. Leachate is also recovered from the landfills and recycled into the process. Bauxite residue, while nontoxic, has a high pH value (IAI 2005).

Another by-product of the aluminum smelting process is spent pot lining (SPL). While it contains carbon and other beneficial products for reuse, it also includes fluorine and small amounts of cyanide. Efforts are being made to find beneficial uses for SPL in other industries (IAI 2007c).

Water consumption and wastewater release. Manufacture of aluminum is water intensive, but less so than steel. Wastewater and sludge contaminants include aluminum, fluoride, nickel, cyanide, and antimony (Demkin 1998c).

Primary Copper Processing

Oxidation of copper in the smelter process produces sulfur dioxide; however, new technology has reduced emissions and the production of sulfuric acid from captured emissions results in a resalable by-product. Heating copper in smelting and in joining can release metal oxides fumes that can pose health risks for metal workers (Demkin 1998b).

Zinc Production

Zinc, used to galvanize steel, is mined primarily in the United States for use in the U.S. Impacts from zinc extraction are similar to those for iron and steel discussed above. Zinc and other metals in mine tailings can impact drinking water, and zinc is toxic to aquatic organisms.

The wastewater from zinc production facilities can contain metals and organics such as lead, cadmium, chromium, zinc, and toluene. Many zinc smelting facilities are listed as Superfund sites (Demkin 1998a).

SECONDARY PROCESSING OF METALS

Information on emissions and wastes for metal casting is not readily available by specific metals; instead it is combined into a metal casting sector report discussed in this section. In 2003, 8% of the 177 million pounds of waste generated by the metal casting industry alone was released to the air and 1% to water. Ferrous metal operations accounted for 94% by weight of these releases.

When 90% of chemical releases from metal casting are weighted for toxicity using the EPA's Risk-Screening Environmental Indicators (RSEI) model, air releases of manganese, chromium, nickel, lead, and diisocyanates account for 99% of the sector's toxicity-weighted results, and discharges to water, primarily lead and copper, account for 1%. Manganese and chromium releases decreased from 2000 to 2003 by 28% and 35%, respectively (U.S. EPA 2006c).

In addition to toxic emissions, the metal casting sector released thousands of tons of the following criteria air pollutants (U.S. EPA 2006b):

- 6,879 tons of nitrogen oxides (NO_x)
- 33,779 tons of particulate matter (PM_{10})
- 29,815 tons of fine particulate matter ($PM_{2.5}$)
- 5,064 tons of sulfur dioxide (SO_2)
- 22,868 tons of volatile organic compound (VOC) emissions

TRANSPORTATION OF METALS

Metal production is a global market, as metals are mined, produced, and distributed around the world. Even carbon steel, which historically has been regionally produced, is now a global commodity. Therefore transportation of metals at all stages of the life cycle can impose substantial environmental impacts.

The global metal production market has been influenced by economics of scale for increasingly specialized

Table 11–7 Primary Energy and Emissions to Produce One Metric Ton of Primary Metal from Ore[a]

Metal (1 kg)	Total Primary Energy (MJ)	CO_2 Emissions (kg)	Particulates (kg)	Chemical Oxygen Demand (COD) (kg)
Carbon steel	22,000	2,000	0.35	2.0
Stainless steel (304 2B)[b]	35,000	4,400	5.7	0.5
Aluminum	180,000	1,700	18	0.46
Zinc	29,000	1,900	—	—
Copper	70,000	4,200	33	1.3

[a]All figures unless otherwise noted are adapted from Houska 2006.

[b]These figures are for SS 304 2B with a 60% scrap ratio (the world average). Assuming a 20% scrap ratio, the total primary energy per metric ton of 304 2B is 54,000 MJ and 316 2B is 62,300 MJ.

Table 11–8 Embodied Energy and Carbon for Metal Products (One Metric Ton of Product)*

Metal Product (1 metric ton)	Embodied Energy (MJ)	Embodied Carbon (kg CO_2)	Comments
Aluminum, cast products	167,500	9,210	Recycled content assumed is 33%.
Aluminum, extruded	153,500	8,490	Recycled content assumed is 33%.
Aluminum, rolled	150,200	8,350	Recycled content assumed is 33%.
Brass	44,000	3,710	Recycled content assumed is 60%. Large data range, dependent on ore grade
Copper	47,500	3,780	Recycled content assumed is 46%. Large data range, dependent on ore grade
Lead	25,000	1,290	Recycled content assumed is 61.5%.
Steel, bar and rod	19,700	1,720	Assumed recycled material is 42.3%.
Steel, galvanized sheet	35,800	2,820	Figures for primary product
Steel, pipe	23,000	1,800	Assumed recycled material is 42.3%.
Steel, plate	45,400	3,190	Figures for primary product
Steel, section	22,700	1,790	Assumed recycled material is 42.3%.
Steel, sheet	20,900	1,640	Assumed recycled material is 42.3%.
Steel, wire	36,000	2,830	Assumed recycled material is 42.3%.
Stainless steel	51,500	6,150	Assumed recycled material is 42.3%. World average data is from Institute of Stainless Steel Forum (ISSF) for grade 304.
Titanium	498,090	unknown	Figures for primary product
Zinc	61,900	3,200	Assumed recycled material is 16%.

*These figures are based on embodied energy and embodied carbon data for metal products in the UK. Therefore they do not accurately represent embodied energy of metal products in North America. Instead they are used here to show a comparison of EE and EC among various metal products.

Source: Adapted from Hammond and Jones 2006

and modern production facilities that manufacture components for the least cost possible. It is not unusual for the raw materials for an aluminum light fixture to be mined in South America; refined into a slab in the United States; shipped to Germany for forming, specialized finishing, and incorporation into a light fixture product; and then shipped back to the United States for installation and use.

As transportation impacts vary so widely by each individual metal and metal product, embodied energy information for metals usually just includes primary processing energy use.

Transportation energy use is a significant impact of the raw materials acquisition phase of aluminum, as the majority of bauxite is mined outside of North America in the rain forests of South America and Southeast Asia. Ninety percent of U.S. bauxite used is shipped to Louisiana and Texas from rain forest mines for refining. Shipping energy use is substantial, as four tons of bauxite is shipped for every ton of aluminum produced.

There is some concern that specification of a recycled-content level for a metal can lead to additional transportation costs since the recycled content of metals is directly related to the amount of recycling in the region of the metal processing facility. Specification of higher recycled contents can result in additional shipping of secondary scrap materials.

Table 11-9 Toxics Release Inventory (TRI) Data for Total Disposal or Releases, 2005 (pounds)

SIC Code Industry	Industry	Total TRI Chemical Disposal and Releases in Pounds (Reduction from 2001 to 2005)	Total Hazardous Air Pollutants (HAPs) in Pounds	Persistent Bioaccumulative Toxic (PBT) Chemicals in Pounds[b]	Carcinogens[a] in Pounds
10	Mining—metals	1,169,176,121 (49% reduction) (3,480,956 lb. air 507,436 lb. water)	617,263,382 (496,917 lb. to air 158,361 lb. to water)	399,574,818 (88,370 lb. air 7,392 lb. water)	579,156,971 (104,172 lb. air 17,128 lb. water)
33	Primary metals (including iron, steel, aluminum, copper, titanium)	561,798,913 (6% reduction) (45,472,672 lb. to air 43,908,400 lb. to water)	146,784,664 (27,873,492 lb. to air 358,329 lb. to water)	35,219,177 (547,780 lb. to air 20,437 lb. to water)	65,970,872 (3,896,452 lb. to air 83,513 lb. to water)
34	Fabricated metals products	64,233,757 (15% increase) (32,602,667 lb. to air 1,937,490 lb. to water)	27,765,882 (22,564,623 lb. to air 17,508 lb. to water)	1,270,615 (23,672 lb. to air 4,220 lb. to water)	9,614,735 (4,133,289 lb. to air 11,945 lb. to water)

[a]For this analysis, the EPA included all TRI chemicals that appear as known or suspected carcinogens in one of three sources: National Toxicology Program (NTP), International Agency for Research on Cancer (IARC), and/or 29 CFR 1910, Subpart Z, Toxic and Hazardous Substances, Occupational Hazardous Safety and Health Administration (OSHA). There were 179 on the TRI list for 2005; 34 of the 179 carcinogens were not reported for 2005.

[b]Includes: Benzo (g,h,i)perylene, dioxin and dioxin-like compounds, lead, lead compounds, mercury, mercury compounds, polychlorinated biphenyls, polycyclic aromatic compounds, tetrabromobisphenol A. Releases are primarily lead and lead compounds.

Source: Adapted from U.S. EPA 2007c

Human Health Effects of Metals

While some metals, such as iron, copper, manganese, molybdenum, and zinc, in trace amounts are critical for human health, these same metals in larger doses can become toxic. Other metals, such as chromium, nickel, cadmium, lead, and mercury, have no known function in the mammalian body, and internalization and accumulation over time can be seriously harmful. Some metals such as copper are vital in trace amounts to humans but toxic to fish and aquatic organisms, even in relatively small amounts.

Persistence is a significant property of metals—they never degrade. Many organic pollutants break down with exposure to sunlight or heat; however, metals persist and will always remain a potential threat to their environment and to the health of living organisms. Metals such as lead, cadmium, and mercury are considered persistent bioac-

cumulative toxins (PBTs). PBTs are chemicals and compounds that do not easily break down, and accumulate in fatty tissues moving up the food chain, impacting health.

There are a number of pathways that metals travel into the environment and the human body. Uncaptured emissions of metal particulates, fumes, or gases from fossil fuel combustion or trash burning can be released to the air, where they are inhaled or deposited on soil, vegetation, or hard surfaces, where they are washed into stormwater runoff and then into water bodies. Industrial processes such as metal ore refining, metal finishing, cement production, and petroleum refining operations are major sources of metal pollutants as well. The EPA's sector report on metal finishing states that in 2003 99% of the Toxics Release Inventory (TRI) chemicals released by the sector were air releases of nickel and chromium. One percent was water releases of lead, copper, and chromium (U.S. EPA 2006c).

Wastewater from metal mines, manufacturing facilities, and finishing operations can carry metal particulates into water bodies, groundwater, and soils. Solid wastes such as sludge, slags, mud, and overburden can contain heavy metals that can leach into water and soils from mining sites, manufacturing facilities, and waste disposal sites. Discarded products containing metals or metal containing ash buried in landfills can leach into soils and groundwater.

An often overlooked pathway of metal migration into the natural environment is from metals in use, particularly older installations (N. Imm, personal communication, November 1, 2007). Metals such as copper, lead, or tin were used on older buildings in roofing applications, flashing, or piping. Trace amounts of these metals are slowly washed into rainwater and find their way into water bodies or soil, then into human bodies through water or food.

While not all metal pollution is in a bioavailable form, metal fumes, particulates, and liquids can find their way into the bodies of humans and living organisms through drinking water, food, and breathable air. Airborne metals, particularly fine particles less than 2.5 micrometers in diameter (PM 2.5), can lodge in the lungs without easy removal, working their way into the bloodstream. Metals borne on air can land many miles from the polluting source on agricultural lands or waterways and find their way into the food chain, then into the human body when consumed. Air-, water-, or soilborne metals can accumulate in reservoirs used for drinking water.

There are two types of metal poisoning in humans. Acute poisoning is primarily a risk for industrial workers exposed to metals on the job. Brief contact with high concentrations of metals may cause lung damage, skin reactions, and gastrointestinal problems. Chronic poisoning resulting from long-term exposure to low levels of metals is a greater concern for the public. Metals that accumulate in the body for a long time, such as cadmium, lead, methyl mercury, and tin, pose particular threats. Dust from arsenic, beryllium, cadmium, chromium, and nickel can cause lung cancer. See Table 11–11 for more information on sources of metal pollutants. Health and environmental risks of metals and metal compounds are summarized in Appendix B (see page 441).

Table 11–10 CERCLA Priority List of Hazardous Substances (Metals)[a]

Element	Rank on 2007 CERLA List
arsenic	1
lead	2
mercury	3
cadmium	8
chromium, hexavalent	18
chromium (VI) oxide	65
chromium	77
beryllium	42
cobalt	49
nickel	53
zinc	74
uranium	98
barium	109
manganese	117
copper	128
selenium	147
aluminum	187
silver	214

[a]These rankings by the Agency for Toxic Substances and Disease Registry are priority substances that are most commonly found at facilities on the National Priorities List (NPL) and which have been determined to pose the most significant potential threat to human health due to their known or suspected toxicity and potential for human exposure at NPL sites.

Source: ATSDR 2007

Sources of more information on metals pollution and health risks are listed below. Also refer to health impact resources listed in chapter 2:

- The National Institute for Occupational Safety and Health (NIOSH), Centers for Disease Control and Prevention, Department of Health and Human Services: http://www.cdc.gov/niosh/
- Air Toxics Website, Technology Transfer Network, U.S. Environmental Protection Agency: http://www.epa.gov/ttn/atw/
- Safewater, Ground and Drinking Water, U.S. Environmental Protection Agency: http://www.epa.gov/safewater/

Table 11–11 TRI Data: Metals Released from Metal Sectors, 2005 (Pounds)

Metal	SIC 10 Metal Mining	SIC Primary Metal Production	SIC Fabricated Metals	Total Releases from Metal Industry
	Total disposal or releases in lbs: / Air releases in lbs: / Water releases in lbs:	Total disposal or releases in lbs: / Air releases in lbs: / Water releases in lbs:	Total disposal or releases in lbs: / Air releases in lbs: / Water releases in lbs:	Total disposal or releases in lbs: / Air releases in lbs: / Water releases in lbs:
Aluminum (fume or dust)	—	3,061,189	268,818	3,330,007
		1,050,200	3,377	1,053,577
		2	—	2
Copper and copper compounds	108,384,957	27,424,979	1,610,154	137,420,090
	55,819	765,518	80,255	901,592
	17,301	37,392	7,507	62,200
Zinc (fume or dust) and zinc compounds	425,318,937	266,552,004	13,696,644	705,567,585
	117,889	3,189,565	396,821	3,704,275
	32,849	118,197	23,542	174,588
Chromium and chromium compounds[a]	7,665,070	19,409,400	2,424,427	29,498,896
	1,397	190,320	121,950	313,667
	685	41,907	2,169	44,761
Nickel and nickel compounds	5,385,423	4,454,103	1,690,986	11,530,512
	2,509	151,856	82,821	237,186
	4,250	18,128	5,815	28,193
Lead and lead compounds	394,533,618	34,015,371	1,237,509	429,786,498
	82,861	400,513	23,499	506,873
	7,386	19,999	4,193	31,578
Cadmium compounds	523,610	1,143,938	24,779	1,692,327
	1,937	4,327	2,631	8,895
	638	515	—	1,153
Mercury and mercury compounds	3,676,729	27,698	5,207	3,709,634
	4,908	10,469	21	15,398
	4	113	20	137
Manganese and manganese compounds	27,368,457	70,375,726	2,781,264	100,525,447
	14,439	984,597	95,627	1,094,663
	134,065	232,771	4,465	371,301

Continued

Table 11–11 TRI Data: Metals Released from Metal Sectors, 2005 (Pounds) *(Continued)*

Metal	SIC 10 Metal Mining — Total disposal or releases in lbs: / Air releases in lbs: / Water releases in lbs:	SIC Primary Metal Production — Total disposal or releases in lbs: / Air releases in lbs: / Water releases in lbs:	SIC Fabricated Metals — Total disposal or releases in lbs: / Air releases in lbs: / Water releases in lbs:	Total Releases from Metal Industry — Total disposal or releases in lbs: / Air releases in lbs: / Water releases in lbs:
Cobalt compounds	803,965 / 578 / 0	662,603 / 11,816 / 1,023	72,357 / 5,789 / 82	1,538,925 / 18,183 / 1,105
Arsenic and arsenic compounds	171,641,073 / 10,462 / 4,182	5,246,561 / 12,459 / 3,100	Arsenic only / 4,812 / 2,570 / 245	176,892,446 / 25,491 / 7,527
Barium and barium compounds	1,147,688 / 1,840 / 1,526	2,701,318 / 44,545 / 23,051	23,340 / 143 / 1,322	3,872,346 / 46,528 / 25,899
Beryllium compounds	5,990 / 130 / 0	53,367 / 420 / 33	2,881 / 2,599 / 0	62,238 / 3,149 / 33
Selenium compounds	457,967 / 849 / 250	458,161 / 20,638 / 1,547	—	916,128 / 21,487 / 1,797
Silver compounds	58,093 / 241 / 250	34,852 / 2,760 / 253	939 / 169 / 1	93,884 / 3,170 / 504
Thallium compounds	6,060,083 / 47 / 250	275,575 / 1,217 / 328	—	6,335,658 / 1,264 / 578
Antimony compounds	6,091,113 / 568 / 6,647	3,061,189 / 6,281 / 1,970	178,714 / 2,159 / 862	9,331,016 / 9,008 / 9,479
Vanadium and vanadium compounds[b]	4,307,830 / 14,190 / 110,250	1,084,696 / 11,694 / 36,581	0 / 0 / 0	5,392,526 / 25,884 / 146,831

[a]Except chromite ore mined in the Transvaal region
[b]Except when contained in an alloy
Source: U.S. EPA 2007c

Weathering and Durability of Metals

Relative longevity of metal structures may be their greatest advantage with respect to a site's sustainability. Previous sections have discussed some significant negative environmental and human health impacts of metal mining, manufacture, production, and finishing; however, if a metal structure can stay in the use phase for several decades, then these impacts may be offset by the resource savings of a durable structure. Therefore, selecting the appropriate metal type and finish for the structure and location will optimize performance, reduce corrosion and metal loss to the environment, and reduce the chance of premature replacement.

Sustainable choices of metals are directly related to their ability to resist corrosion. Metals used in exterior environments can be affected by corrosive conditions resulting from seawater contact, deicing salts, and industrial or urban pollution. Areas of particularly acidic rain, those with high airborne particulate levels and high sulfur/nitrous oxides and ozone amounts, require more corrosion-resistant metals. These potentially corrosive contaminants are made even stronger in hot, humid locations (see Tables 11–12—11–15).

The International Molybdenum Association has developed an evaluation system to determine a project location's corrosive environment, susceptibility of metals to corrosion, and aspects of metal structure design that may encourage corrosion. Use of this system is recommended as the first step in determining the grade of stainless steel to specify for a particular site; however, it may also be a useful system for evaluating a site to determine appropriateness of any metal type and finish. It is important to note that sites near each other can have widely varying conditions due to differing microclimates, localized conditions, or design details (see Table 11–16).

Categories of evaluation are as follows:

Environmental pollution levels from acid rain resulting from vehicular emissions and concentrated pollution in urban areas can result in oxidation and corrosion of metals. Industrial pollution such as sulfur and nitrogen oxides from coal combustion, released gases and chemicals, and airborne particles from industrial sites can also increase corrosion rates of some metals. Urban pollution level information can be obtained from the World Health Organization and the U.S. EPA (U.S. EPA Air Toxics).

Coastal and deicing salt exposure can corrode some metals. Humidity, high temperatures, fog, and mist will concentrate salt deposits on surfaces. Wind patterns will determine how far inland salts are carried in marine environments. Sites within five to ten miles from the shore are considered coastal; however, salt can be carried even farther. Stainless steel structures that are immersed in saltwater will require a super duplex, super ferritic, or 6% molybdenum super austenitic stainless steel (International Molybdenum Association [IMOA] 2002). Aluminum is most affected by coastal environments (Zahner 2005).

Deicing salts containing sodium chloride, calcium chloride, and magnesium chloride can corrode carbon steel and stainless steel adjacent to roads and sidewalks. Movement of deicing salts is affected by traffic speeds of nearby roads and wind patterns. Deicing salts can be carried half a mile from highways (IMOA 2002). Aluminum is less affected by deicing salts.

Local weather patterns such as fog, misty rain, or high humidity can combine with corrosive compounds to form an oxide film on a structure's surface that can lead to corrosion. High temperatures will hasten the rate of corrosion. Light rain will not remove surface contaminants from structures; however, areas that receive regular heavy rains or wind-driven rains—most of eastern North America can remove surface contaminants from exposed surfaces. This regular "cleaning" of surface deposits will reduce the risk of corrosion. In areas of light rain or arid environments, periodic manual cleaning may be required.

Design of the structure will affect the potential for corrosion of metal surfaces. Corrosive contaminants that are left on the surface of a metal can result in corrosion or staining. Roughness of the surface will determine adherence of contaminants. A rough surface can accumulate more contaminants and will make rain washing or manual cleaning less easy. Smooth finishes reduce the risk of corrosion staining. The finish grain orientation will also affect adherence of contaminants. Vertical finish grain orientations make it easier for rain to wash the surface and drain contaminants away. Horizontal grains tend to retain more contaminants.

Dirt and contaminants may accumulate more on sheltered components or horizontal surfaces, as rain may not wash the surfaces as easily. Where horizontal or sheltered elements are used, periodic manual cleaning may be necessary.

Crevices resulting from joined members or prefabricated meshes can trap water and corrosive contaminants as well. Eliminating crevices and using higher grades of stainless steel or corrosion-resistant finishes will avoid this risk (IMOA 2002). Galvanic relationships between adjacent metals should be considered to reduce the chance of corrosion. When two different metals are touching in the presence of corrosive conditions, the less noble metal can corrode. The greater the size of the differential electrical charge, the more chance exists for corrosion. Some oxides, such as the thick aluminum oxide developed during anodizing, will reduce electrical polarity (Zahner 1995). Coatings or plastic or rubber gaskets can inhibit galvanic corrosion.

Maintenance and cleaning of metal surfaces can reduce the risk of corrosive staining of metals. Contaminants must remain on the surface of a metal long enough and in high enough concentrations for corrosion to occur. If manual cleaning is regularly performed, it can prevent surface corrosive staining on some metals. Frequency of cleaning required will vary with type of metal and environmental conditions (IMOA 2002).

In addition to using the above evaluation criteria for selecting metal types and finishes, it is suggested that a sample of the finished metal be placed on-site to test for corrosion potential. The sample should be placed in such a way as to simulate the proposed design, and it should be exposed to environmental conditions for four to six months. In severe marine or industrial conditions, the sample exposure time may be reduced to six weeks. The IMOA and the Nickel Institute have published case studies of exterior use of stainless steel in a variety of environmental conditions (IMOA).

Iron and Steel Weathering

Most iron and carbon steel used in exterior applications must be finished, as oxide film that develops is porous and allows moisture and oxygen to penetrate. If unchecked, oxidation will corrode the entire metal thickness. Carbon steel has the highest rate of corrosion— average corrosion rate of 0.05–0.1 mm/year.

Iron oxide from corrosion runoff is generally nontoxic to organisms and humans; however, it can stain adjacent porous surfaces, potentially resulting in their

Table 11–12 Chemical Agents Found in the Environment and Their Effect on Metals

Chemical Agent	Major Source	Metal Affected	Result of Exposure
Sulfur	Combustion	Copper	Green patina
		Monel	Green/brown patina
		Lead	Dark patina
		Silver	Dark tarnish
Carbon	Carbon dioxide	Lead	Whitish oxide
		Zinc	Dark blue-gray patina
Chlorine	Sea	Aluminum	Pitting
	Deicing salts	Copper	Green-blue patina
		Stainless steel	Red spots
Silicon	Airborne blast particles and sealers	Stainless steel	Discoloration
		Titanium	Discoloration

Source: Zahner 2005

Table 11–13 Environments and Corrosion Potential

Most Severe
Marine
Coastal urban
Northern urban (road salts)
Urban industrial
Coastal
Urban
Urban: arid climate
Urban: protected
Arctic
Rural
Interior: entrances
Interior
Least severe
Interior: protected

Source: Zahner 1995

premature removal. Oxidation runoff from weathering steel, often left unfinished, contains small amounts of chromium and copper that can contaminate water and impact aquatic organisms.

Weathering steel, containing copper, develops a red iron oxide as it comes in contact with moist, humid air or water. Usually after a few months, the surface is en-

tirely covered with a light red-orange oxide. After a few years, the surface will appear red-brown. At this time, staining will be reduced, as the oxide is well adhered and dense on the metal surface; however, weathering steel is susceptible to deicing salts and other chlorides that will erode the oxide surface layer. Thinner sections of weathering steel should be painted on the unexposed side to reduce oxidation and thinning of the steel section. Weathering steel sheets should be avoided as they will not last long with a corrosion rate of .1 mm per year. Instead plate should be used (N. Imm, personal communication, November 1, 2007). Consideration should be given to protecting adjacent surfaces of concrete, stone, brick, and wood from oxide staining.

With the exception of stainless steel and weathering steel, all steels should be finished by galvanizing, powdercoating, painting, or another finishing method to ensure a long use life. Weathering steel can be finished with a clear sealer to prevent environmental contamination from oxide runoff; however, the clear finish will need to be reapplied every few years.

Stainless Steel Weathering

Stainless steel is specified in exterior structures for its corrosion resistance, durability, and aesthetic qualities. It is one of the most corrosion-resistant metals used in exterior applications, requiring no potentially toxic surface treatments such as galvanizing, anodizing, or electroplating. Its corrosion resistance means that when an appropriate type of stainless steel and finish are specified, the structure can last for 50 years or more. If the

Table 11–14 Characteristics of the Most and Least Corrosive Environments

Most Corrosive	Least Corrosive
High pollution levels, especially SO_2, chlorides, and solid particles	Low pollution levels
Low to moderate rainfall with moderate to high persistent humidity	Low rainfall with humidity or heavy, frequent rainfall
Moderate to high temperatures with moderate to high humidity and/or condensation	Low air temperatures, especially extended periods below 32°F
Frequent, salt-laden ocean fog and low rainfall	High air temperatures with low humidity
Sheltered locations exposed to salt or corrosive pollutants	

Source: Nickel Institute n.d.

Table 11–15 Metals for Different Environments

Environment		Metals
Rural environments		All metals
Urban, industrial environments	Best	Titanium
		316 stainless steel
		Copper
	Moderate	S304 stainless steel
		Painted aluminum
		Painted zinc-coated steel
		Zinc
	Poor	Aluminum
		Steel
		Brass and bronze
Coastal environments	Best	Titanium
		316 stainless steel
		Copper
	Moderate	S304 stainless steel
		Painted aluminum
		Painted zinc-coated steel
		Zinc
	Poor	Aluminum
		Steel
		Brass and bronze

Source: Adapted from Zahner 1995

structure is expected to be in use for a long time, this may offset the relatively high embodied energy of its manufacture, making it a good choice for sustainable sites.

It is important to specify the appropriate stainless steel and surface finish for the environmental condition of the site location, the project budget, and design of the structure to maximize the life of the structure. When stainless steel is exposed to oxygen, the chromium forms a thin, invisible protective passive film layer of chromium (III) oxide on its surface that prevents corrosion. However, stainless steel is not immune to corrosion, especially in environments of deicing salt exposure. There are many types of stainless steel with varying properties, some of which are less appropriate for some exterior situations. Stainless steel corrosion resistance improves with an increase of chromium, molybdenum, and nitrogen content.

Aluminum Weathering

When mill finish aluminum is exposed to oxygen, it forms a thin protective passive film layer of oxidation on its surface that prevents further corrosion; however, over time, the surface brightness will fade and dark gray mottling will occur. In addition, like any coating it can be eroded over time. Humid industrial and coastal environments will accelerate these effects. Aluminum is resistant to road salt spray in urban environments (Imm 2007). Cladding the aluminum with a more pure form of aluminum will help it remain brighter in appearance

Figure 11–4.

Figure 11–5.

This planter at April Philips Design Works' Bay Street Plaza is constructed from Cor-Ten steel with 95% recycled content. Use of one pound of recycled steel can save 5,000 Btus that would be required to produce primary steel. Use of recycled steel also saves resources, with a metric ton of recycled steel saving 1,134 kilograms of iron, 635 kg of coal, and 54 kg of limestone. (Photos from April Phillips Design Works)

Table 11–16 Stainless Steel Evaluation Selection System

Points	Section 1: Environment (Select the highest applicable score.)
0	Rural
0	Very low or no pollution
	Urban Pollution (Light industry, automotive exhaust)
0	Low
2	Moderate
3	High[a]
	Industrial Pollution (Aggressive gases, iron oxides, chemicals, etc.)
3	Low or moderate
4	High[a]
	Section 2: Coastal or Deicing Salt (Chloride) Exposure (Select the highest applicable score.) If there is exposure to both coastal and deicing salt, obtain assistance from a stainless steel corrosion expert.
	Coastal or Marine Salt Exposure
1	Low (> 1.6 to 16 km (1 to 10 miles) from saltwater)[b]
3	Moderate (30 m to 1.6 km (100 ft. to 1 mile) from saltwater)
4	High (< 30 m (100 ft.) from saltwater)
5	Marine (Some salt spray or occasional splashing)[a]
8	Severe Marine (Continuous splashing)[a]
10	Severe Marine (Continuous immersion)[a]
	Deicing Salt Exposure (Distance from road or ground)
0	No salt was detected on a sample from the site and no change in exposure conditions is expected.
0	Traffic and wind levels on nearby roads are too low to carry chlorides to the site and no deicing salt is used on sidewalks.
1	Very low salt exposure (≥ 10 m to 1 km [33 to 3,280 ft.] or 3 to 60 floors)[b]
2	Low salt exposure (< 10 to 500 m [33 to 1600 ft] or 2 to 34 floors)[b]
3	Moderate salt exposure (< 3 to 100 m [10 to 328 ft.] or 1 to 22 floors)[b]
4	High salt exposure (≤ 2 to 50 m [6.5 to 164 ft.] or 1 to 3 floors)[c]
	Section 3: Local Weather Pattern (Select only one.)
−1	Temperate or cold climates, regular heavy rain
−1	Hot or cold climates with typical humidity below 50%
0	Temperate or cold climate, occasional heavy rain
0	Tropical or subtropical, wet, regular or seasonal very heavy rain
1	Temperate climate, infrequent rain, humidity above 50%
1	Regular very light rain or frequent fog
2	Hot, humidity above 50%, very low or no rainfall[c]

Table 11-16 Stainless Steel Evaluation Selection System *(Continued)*

	Section 4: Design Considerations (Select all that apply.)
0	Boldly exposed for easy rain cleaning
0	Vertical surfaces with a vertical or no finish grain
−2	Surface finish is pickled, electropolished, or roughness ≤ R_2 0.3 μm (12μin)
−1	Surface finish roughness R_2 0.3 μm (12μin) < X = R_2 0.5 μm (20 μin)
1	Surface finish roughness R_2 0.5 μm (20μin) < X = R_2 1 μm (40 μin)
2	Surface finish roughness > R_2 1 μm (40μin)
1	Sheltered location or unsealed crevices[c]
1	Horizontal surfaces
1	Horizontal finish grain orientation
	Section 5: Maintenance Schedule (Select only one.)
0	Not washed
−1	Washed at least annually
−2	Washed four or more times per year
−3	Washed at least monthly
	Total Score (see Table 11-17)

[a]Potentially a highly corrosive location. Have a stainless steel corrosion expert evaluate the site.

[b]The range shows how far this chloride concentration has been found from small rural and large high-traffic roads. Test surface chloride concentrations.

[c]If there is also salt or pollution exposure, have a stainless steel corrosion expert evaluate the site.

Source: IMOA 2002

and resist corrosive effects for a longer period of time. Anodizing aluminum by immersion in a chemical bath results in a thicker, more controlled oxide layer that will resist corrosion longer as well. Specification of marine grade aluminum (5000 series or above) in coastal environments will better resist corrosion from airborne salts (Zahner 1995) and in urban environments will resist the effects of pollution.

Copper Weathering

Copper and copper alloys develop oxides that substantially change the appearance of the metal if allowed to fully mature. The oxide layer, called the patina, protects the metal from corrosive failure. Varying environmental conditions will produce different oxide effects. Dry environments will slow the oxidation process, and moist environments, industrial settings, and coastal ex-

posures will accelerate it. Copper will oxidize to a dark brown, then eventually a gray-green color. Copper alloys such as brass and bronze will oxidize to a deep brown color if left unfinished.

Appropriate acids and salts can be applied to the surface of copper to create a patina; however, these products should not be applied in the field as they can be toxic to soil and aquatic organisms (Imm 2007).

Titanium Weathering

Titanium is an inert material that is little affected by most environmental conditions. When titanium is exposed to oxygen, it rapidly forms a thin protective passive film layer on its surface that resists corrosive conditions. With prolonged oxidation in acid rain environments, titanium will form titanium carbide below the oxide layer.

Table 11–17 Stainless Steel Selection System Score Chart

Stainless Steel Selection	
Total Score	
0 to 2	Type 304/304L (UNS S30400, EN 1.4301, SUS 304) is generally the most cost-effective choice.
3	Type 316/316L (UNS S31600, EN 1.4401, SUS 316) or 444 (UNS S44400, EN 1.4521, SUS 444) is generally the most cost-effective choice.
4	Type 317L (UNS 31703, EN 1.4438, SUS 317L) or a more corrosion-resistant stainless steel is suggested.
≥ 5	A more corrosion-resistant stainless steel such as 2205 (UNS S32205, EN 1.4462, SUS 329J3L), 904L (UNS NO8904, EN 1.4539, SUS 890L), 317LMN (UNS S31726, EN 1.4439, SUS 317LN), super duplex, super ferritic, or a 6% molybdenum super austenitic stainless steel may be needed. If you obtain a score of 5 or above, a stainless steel corrosion expert with architectural experience should evaluate the site and design and suggest an appropriate stainless steel.

How can I reduce the score?

Some design changes that can improve performance and possibly change material requirements are as follows:

- Boldly expose components for better rain washing.
- Select smooth surface finishes.
- Use a vertical surface finish grain orientation.
- Eliminate horizontal surfaces.
- Eliminate or seal crevices.
- Design to facilitate and encourage a regular manual washing schedule.
- Add natural or artificial barriers to reduce deicing salt road mist exposure.

Source: IMOA 2002

Design the Metal Structure to Reduce Corrosion Potential

The design of a metal structure will affect the potential for corrosion of surfaces. Roughness of the surface will determine adherence of contaminants. A rough surface can accumulate more contaminants and will make rain washing or manual cleaning more challenging. Smooth finishes reduce the risk of corrosion staining. The finish grain orientation will also affect adherence of contaminants. Vertical finish grain orientations make it easier for rain to wash the surface and drain contaminants away. Horizontal grains tend to retain more contaminants.

Dirt and contaminants will accumulate more on sheltered components or horizontal surfaces, as rain may not wash the surfaces. Corrosive contaminants that are left on the surface of metals can result in corrosion staining. Where horizontal or sheltered elements are used, periodic manual cleaning may be necessary. Crevices resulting from joined members or prefabricated meshes can trap water and corrosive contaminants as well. Eliminating crevices will avoid this risk (IMOA 2002).

Exposed fasteners and rivets are more likely to provide places for water and pollutants to pond and corrode the metal. This could compromise the durability of the structure. Figure 11–3 illustrates metal design details that may increase the chance of corrosion and better alternatives to reduce the chance of corrosion.

Avoid Metals and Coatings That May Contaminate the Environment While in Use

Oxidation particles and mass loss of some metals can be washed off by water or worn off by wind or abrasion, dispersing metal oxides in water, air, or soil around metal structures. Negative impacts on these environments,

Table 11–18 Metal Weathering Characteristics and Potential Finishes

Metal and Expected Life Span	Color	Ten-year Aging Characteristics	Potential Finishes
Carbon steel	Gray-dark blue	Red rust if not finished, then major corrosion	Powder coating, thermal spray, vapor deposition, hot-dip galvanizing, painting
Galvanized steel 5 years in industrial applications, 11+ years in rural environments	Gray, light tint, bright	Gray-white (white rust will develop on the zinc coating), less reflective	Thermal spray, hot-dip galvanizing, cold-dip galvanizing
Aluminized steel 8–10 years in industrial exposures	Gray-white, bright	Light gray, less reflective	Usually left unfinished, but cut edges, deep scratches and fastener perforations will leave steel underneath vulnerable to corrosion. Painting is not recommended.
Weathering steel	Gray-dark blue	Dark red-brown Oxidation slows as oxide layer becomes more adherent and dense.	Staining is reduced as oxide layer becomes more adherent and dense; however, it can be clear finished in the field.
Stainless steel 316, 50 years	Chrome silver	No change	No finish required. Smoother mechanical finishes will resist staining better in harsh environments
Stainless steel 304 20–30 years	Chrome silver	Some staining in urban, industrial, or coastal environments	No finish required. Smoother mechanical finishes will resist staining better in harsh environments. Will need regular cleaning
Titanium	Soft gray with slight gold cast	Little change over time	No finish required, very inert material Can be mechanically finished with glass bead blasting or shot peening
Aluminum, mill finish	Silver-white	Gray, dull, some mottling	Anodizing, powder coating, painting
Aluminum, clear anodized	Gray-medium	Minimal color change over time	Anodizing, painting
Aluminum, alclad (coating of high purity aluminum) 30+ years in industrial environments	Shiny white, very reflective	Slightly mottled gray	No finish required
Zinc	Gray-blue tint	Dark bluish-gray color	No finish required
Copper	Reddish-pink	Gray-green patina	Clear finishes
Bronze	Reddish-gold	Gray-green patina	Clear finishes

Source: Adapted from Zahner 1995

creased concentrations of these metals can be hazardous for fish and crustaceans (Houska 2006). Care should be taken when selecting metals that will be used in sensitive or fragile environments.

A Swedish roof runoff study found concentrations of zinc (from galvanizing) and copper to be 10,000 times higher than typical drinking water concentrations, and both were in a bioavailable form. Stainless steel roofs were also tested, but runoff rates of chromium and nickel, both biological toxins, were found to be below typical drinking water concentrations (Houska 2006).

Another Swedish/Flemish study of chromium, nickel, and iron release from grades 304 and 316 stainless steel under atmospheric conditions found releases to be well below ecotoxic concentrations and recommended drinking water limits; however, it found that releases increased with grade of stainless steel. Releases of chromium (III) oxides from 316 stainless steel occurred at a rate of 0.2 to 0.7 mg/m^{-2}. Nickel was released at a rate of 0.3 to 0.8 mg/m^{-2} and iron was released at a rate of 10 to 200 mg/m^{-2} (Berggren et al. 2004).

Lead has a high rate of erosion during use and is a PBT that poses severe human health effects. Use of lead in building products has substantially decreased; however, lead-coated sheet metal is still used for flashing. Lead is also used for solder and is alloyed with tin, antimony, and bronze for various metal products.

Finishes and Applied Coatings for Metals

Without finishes or applied coatings, the life span of some metals in exterior applications would be just a fraction of their finished life span because of corrosion and wear. And, as discussed above, metals use such high amounts of energy for production and contribute so much to air and water pollution that if they will not have a long use life, this expenditure will not be worth it. Finishes protect the base metal from extreme oxidation leading to corrosion and premature failure of the metal structure, they protect the metal from the wear and tear of continuous use and environmental chemical exposure, they can harden the metal surface, and they impart aesthetic qualities such as color or reflectivity (see Table 11–18).

and resulting human exposures, vary by type of metal, local environments, and toxicity and bioavailability of the metal oxide particles. Some metals can cross toxicity thresholds at relatively low levels. For example, concentrations in water of copper as low as 0.002 mg per L or 0.007 mg of zinc per L are hazardous for algae. In-

While metal finishes will extend the useful life of a metal structure considerably, they can also pose substantial environmental and human health impacts. The metal finishing industry is one of the largest users of toxic chemicals and is responsible for managing large amounts of hazardous materials and wastes.

A 2006 EPA sector report on the metal finishing industry characterizes some impacts from the industry. Impacts are general as they are not broken down by type of finish or metals. In 2003, 632 metal finishing businesses reported 95 million pounds of chemicals released (this includes disposal) or managed through treatment, recycling, or energy recovery. Ten percent of this, 9.5 million pounds, was released (28%) or disposed of (72%) to the environment. The industry's release of toxics to air and water declined by 58% from 1994 to 2003.

Metals dominated these releases, with 59% zinc, chromium, and nickel. Nitrate compounds and nitric acid accounted for 16%. When chemical releases from metal finishing are weighted for toxicity using the EPA's Risk-Screening Environmental Indicators (RSEI) model, air releases of nickel and chromium account for 99% of the sector's toxicity-weighted results, and discharges to water, primarily lead, copper, and chromium, account for 1% (U.S. EPA 2006c).

The metal finishing sector accounted for 2% of all hazardous waste generated in 2003, with 582,000 tons reported. Of this, 331,000 tons was wastewater. Most of the hazardous waste reported by the industry was generated from plating and phosphating processes.

During some metal finishing processes, some metals in the finish are not captured on the base metal and can leave the process in wastewater sludge or solid waste. Some metal finishing industries are engaged in recovering metals from wastewater sludge. Water quality can also be affected by the large volumes of water used and metals released from plating baths, spent cleaning solutions, and spent bath solutions (U.S. EPA 2006c).

Opportunities for minimizing environmental and human health risks from metal finishes focus on managing and minimizing toxics and waste, reducing air emissions, and conserving water (U.S. EPA 2006c) (see Table 11–19).

Specify Factory Finishing Rather Than Field Finishing

Factory finishing of metals usually releases fewer toxic chemicals, wastes, and particulates than finishing metal in the field, as finishing facilities often employ pollution control equipment to minimize releases of pollutants and worker health risks. Factory finishing facilities are also better able to control the conditions in which the finish is applied, increasing the likelihood of durability and longevity. They can use materials more efficiently and are more likely to recycle overspray or excess finishing materials.

Specify Powder Coating Rather Than Solvent-based Coatings, Especially Spray Applied

Powder coating is a sprayed-on polymer or resin powder that adheres to metal through an electrostatic process. During the curing process, the powder liquefies, flows, and covers the metal. Many powders are similar to paint ingredients; however, most do not contain solvents, which can release VOCs and harmful fumes. Because powder coatings electrically adhere and bond to the metal, they have better adhesion than paints. They also result in a more uniform application than paint. Color variety is not as broad as paint. Some plastics used in powder coating are PVC and should be avoided.

As coating is in powder form, it does not require a solvent base. Powder coating is performed in a controlled factory environment, which allows for control of particulates and better worker safety precautions. Powder overspray is captured, contained, and reused with very little waste. Wastewater is often recycled in the process as well.

Recycling of powder-coated metal may be limited because of the mixed materials of plastic coating and metal. When powder-coated metal is recycled, fumes and emissions from heating the coating can pose a risk to air quality and worker health without pollution control measures.

Powder coating cannot be applied or touched up in the field. Scratches and nicks will need to be sanded down to the base metal and then primed and painted. It is difficult to match colors of paint to powder coating. This could result in premature removal of the structure.

Table 11–19 Metal Finish Types, Applications, and Environmental and Human Health Risks

Finish/Coating Type	Environmental and Health Risks, Recycling Potential	Additional Information
Chemical Processes Molecular interaction on metal surface to develop or break molecular bonds		
Anodizing involves dipping aluminum into an acid bath (sulfuric acid, nitric acid, phosphoric acid, nickel acetate, hexavalent chromium, and others) to create a controlled oxide layer that is thicker and more corrosion resistant and abrasion resistant than the oxide layer that naturally forms when aluminum is exposed to the atmosphere. The multistep process of anodizing requires cleaning and degreasing, followed by etching with sodium hydroxide, then anodic oxidation.	Anodic coatings are very durable, as they are grown from the aluminum itself and are not a surface-applied finish like paint that might crack or peel. Electricity, sometimes substantial amounts, is used to pass electrical currents through the acid solution. However, acid baths with varying levels of toxicity can lead to chemical burns and respiratory problems in workers. Surface etching preparations for anodizing involves use of sodium hydroxides. See "Etching" for risks of this process. The anodizing process does not involve VOCs or air pollutants, however. Wastewater can pose environmental risks if not controlled or neutralized. Some manufacturers recycle wastewater back into the system and reclaim and sell aluminum hydroxide from the process. Anodized finishes are chemically stable and nontoxic in use. Anodizing aluminum does not affect the recycling potential of aluminum. The integral color method of anodizing uses a lot of electricity to create the relatively thick oxide film. However, this process creates a very durable finish.	This is the most common finish for exterior applications, with a variety of colors available. "Protective" or "architecture class" anodic coatings are durable for exterior use and will help ensure that the aluminum structure will be in use for a long period. Anodic coatings can be clear or colored. Colored anodic coatings for exterior use have been limited to shades of brown, bronze, gray, or black; however, a process combining organic dyeing and electrolytic deposition is new to the market for exterior architectural applications. This process can produce vivid colors with a thick anodic coating that is saturated with organic dye before hardening and sealing.
Interference color uses a conversion treatment that converts the surface of a metal into a thick oxidation form and then creates an interplay of light with the two metal surfaces to create a color. By canceling portions of the light wave and reinforcing others, light interference causes a shift in wavelength perceived by the eye, resulting in a colored surface. This process is most common for stainless steel coloring; however, it is also used for titanium coloring.	Creation of the oxide layer has similar environmental impacts as aluminum anodizing, although other metals may require different chemical and electrochemical treatments to develop the film. Others will develop a clear oxide layer upon exposure to air.	Surfaces can oxidize further over time, especially in exterior conditions, reducing the color effects.

Table 11–19 Metal Finish Types, Applications, and Environmental and Human Health Risks *(Continued)*

Finish/Coating Type	Environmental and Health Risks, Recycling Potential	Additional Information
Chemical Processes (Cont'd.)		
Electroplating, also called *electrodeposition,* is a process of coating one metal onto the surface of another by immersing the metal in a solution and ions of the other metal. This develops an electrical potential but does not form a metallurgical bond. Chromium and nickel coatings are the most common. However, cadmium, copper, tin, zinc, lead, and platinum are also used in electroplating.	The electroplating process uses many toxic chemicals and results in substantial amounts of hazardous waste, some of which is released to air, water, and soil. Hexavalent chromium, cadmium, and nickel are all carcinogens posing risks to worker health. Electroplating may reduce the recycling potential of a metal because of the mixture of metals.	Chromium and nickel are very corrosion resistant; however, once they are damaged they do not function as galvanizing with its sacrificial action. Instead, the base metal that is exposed will corrode, possibly flaking the plating off. Vapor deposition processes are a cleaner alternative to electroplating.
Etching is a chemical treatment that etches the surface of a metal by dipping it in a caustic solution and dissolving the surface. Typical etching compounds are, for aluminum, hydrochloric acid; for copper and stainless steel, ferric chloride; and for titanium, hydrofluoric acid. Etching is often used as a pretreatment for anodizing or painting.	Solutions for etching are highly toxic and can pose risks of chemical burns, lung edema, scarring, and blindness for manufacturing workers if adequate protection is not used. Aquatic organisms in contact with wastewater from etching processes are at risk as well; however, many manufacturers adjust the pH of their wastewater and remove aluminum solids prior to release. Large amounts of hydrogen gas result from the combination of aluminum and sodium.[a]	Left uncoated, the surface will weather even more quickly than mill finishes because the surface is roughened by the etching.
Electropolishing involves placing a metal surface into an electrolytic solution and then passing a current through it to remove low conductive particles and foreign matter. This results in a finish with very high uniformity and a luster that is more corrosion resistant and homogeneous.	Electricity, sometimes substantial amounts, is used to pass electrical currents through the acid solution. However, acid baths with varying levels of toxicity can lead to chemical burns and respiratory problems in workers. Surface etching preparations for anodizing involves use of sodium hydroxides. See "Etching" for risks of this process. The anodizing process does not involve VOCs or air pollutants; however, wastewater can pose environmental risks if not controlled or neutralized.	

Continued

Table 11–19 Metal Finish Types, Applications, and Environmental and Human Health Risks *(Continued)*

Finish/Coating Type	Environmental and Health Risks, Recycling Potential	Additional Information
Deposition Processes A very thin layer of metal or metals is applied to the surface of another metal in such a way that a metallurgical bond is developed between the two metals. The deposited metal, acting as a barrier and sometimes a sacrificial metal, protects the base metal.		
Hot dipping is a finish that protects steel, iron, or copper from corrosion through a chemically bonded metal surface. The most common hot-dip coating is zinc; however, aluminum, tin, and lead are also used individually or in combination with zinc. The metal member is hot-dipped into the molten coating metal, forming a series of layers or alloy zones that transition from the base metal to the pure coating metal. A metallurgical bond between the coating and the base metal is formed. When it is exposed to exterior conditions, the zinc layer sacrifices itself, protecting the steel beneath both by coating it and, when breached, through cathodic protection.	Zinc is relatively nontoxic for humans; however, it can pose risks to aquatic organisms in wastewater from processing or runoff in use. Wastewater from zinc processing and galvanizing can contain heavy metals and toxic chemicals. Inhalation of vapors of zinc oxide during welding or brazing can cause "zinc fever," a debilitating but temporary illness. Zinc-coated steel may limit the member's ability to be recycled because of the mixed materials; however, if there are sufficient quantities, the zinc coating can be removed and recovered separately from galvanized products.	Zinc coatings are sensitive to sulfuric acid (a constituent of acid rain) and hydrochloric acid. Their life expectancy is eleven years for rural exposures, eight years for coastal exposures, and four years for industrial exposures. Galvanized steel can be painted, but there are risks of oxidation under the paint, compromising the paint surface. Longevity of hot-dipped metal finishes is directly related to the thickness of the coating.
Cold-dip zinc galvanizing is a 95% zinc-rich paint that is applied to metals. It is not a chemically bonded process; therefore it is not as durable as the hot-dip process.	Some cold-dip paints contain high levels of VOCs that can contribute to air pollution; however, some low-VOC versions are entering the market.	Cold-dip paints are less durable than hot-dip galvanizing.
Vapor deposition processes are metal finishes where simple evaporation and condensation of a metal in high vacuum occurs on the surface of a base metal, resulting in a very thin coating of metal. Several processes fall into this category: physical vapor deposition (most common in architectural applications), chemical vapor deposition, sputtering, and ion implantation. Vapor deposition deposits a variety of metals such as aluminum, chromium, cadmium, cobalt, copper, nickel, titanium, and zinc on steel or stainless steel (for coloring).	Vapor deposition is considered a less toxic alternative to electroplating, anodizing, hot-dip galvanizing, and cladding, as it does not require use of electrolytic solutions or plating baths. It does not require use of cadmium or hexavalent chromium. It uses less toxic chemicals and water, and substantially reduces the amount of hazardous waste generated. Vapor deposition uses substantial amounts of energy for application of the metal finish. Aluminum vapor deposition is considered one of the cleaner finishes.	Vapor deposition finishes are very thin, so they may not resist wear as well as thicker finishes. However, some, like titanium finishes, are very hard. The wide variety of vapor deposition finishes allows fasteners to be coated with a similar metal as the metal member to reduce the chance of galvanic corrosion (e.g., aluminum coating on steel bolts for an aluminum structure will reduce risk of galvanic corrosion).

Table 11–19 Metal Finish Types, Applications, and Environmental and Human Health Risks *(Continued)*

Finish/Coating Type	Environmental and Health Risks, Recycling Potential	Additional Information
Deposition Processes		
A very thin layer of metal or metals is applied to the surface of another metal in such a way that a metallurgical bond is developed between the two metals. The deposited metal, acting as a barrier and sometimes a sacrificial metal, protects the base metal.		
Thermal spray is a process of applying a thick coating of metal either in wire or powder form to a base metal using extremely high localized temperatures and high-velocity gases. Thermal spray techniques include plasma arc spray, wire flame spray, powder flame spray, electric arc spray, and high-velocity oxyfuel. Zinc and aluminum are the most common thermal spray materials. Like hot dipping, zinc coating will perform a sacrificial oxidation process.	Thermal spray processes are considered to be less toxic alternatives to electroplating, hot-dip galvanizing, and cladding techniques, as they do not require use of electrolytic solutions or plating baths. Thermal spray does not require use of cadmium or hexavalent chromium. It uses less toxic chemicals and water, and substantially reduces the amount of hazardous waste generated. There is limited information on health and environmental risks of thermal spray. Field spraying could release particulates and pollutants, as the conditions are less controlled than in a factory environment. Zinc is nontoxic for humans; however, it can pose risks to aquatic organisms in wastewater from processing or runoff in use. See "Hot Dipping" above for more information.	Reapplication in the field with specialized equipment is possible and is more durable than cold-dip painting. Thermal spray coatings may require some grinding, planing, or sanding, potentially producing airborne metal particles that may pose a risk to workers or environments around spraying facilities.
Powder coating is a sprayed-on polymer or resin powder that adheres to metal through an electrostatic process. During the curing process, the powder liquefies, flows, and covers the metal. Many powders are similar to paint ingredients; however, they do not contain solvents. Because powder coatings electrically adhere and bond to the metal, they have better adhesion than paints. They also result in a more uniform application than paint. Color variety is not as broad as paint.	As the coating is in powder form, it does not require a solvent base. Powder coating is performed in a controlled factory environment, which allows for control of particulates and better worker safety precautions. Powder overspray is captured, contained, and reused with very little waste. Wastewater is often recycled in the process as well. Some plastics used in powder coating are PVC and should be avoided. Recycling of powder-coated metal may be limited because of the mixed materials of plastic coating and metal. When powder-coated metal is recycled, fumes and emissions can pose a risk to air quality without pollution control measures.	Powder coating cannot be applied or touched up in the field. Scratches and nicks will need to be sanded to the base metal and then primed and painted. It is difficult to match colors of paint to powder coating. This could result in premature removal of the structure.

Continued

Table 11–19 Metal Finish Types, Applications, and Environmental and Human Health Risks *(Continued)*

Finish/Coating Type	Environmental and Health Risks, Recycling Potential	Additional Information
Deposition Processes		
A very thin layer of metal or metals is applied to the surface of another metal in such a way that a metallurgical bond is developed between the two metals. The deposited metal, acting as a barrier and sometimes a sacrificial metal, protects the base metal.		
Organic coatings, or paints, offer many color options and can be factory or field applied. Primer coats should be oil based, as water-based primers can corrode some metals and result in poor adhesion. Chips or scratches in the paint revealing steel will cause it to rust and deposit stains on the painted surface. Chips in painted aluminum revealing the aluminum will cause the aluminum to form a protective oxidation layer. Chemical etching or chromate conversion coatings are the two most common pretreatments for painted aluminum.	Paints for metal, often oil based, can contain VOCs, toxic chemicals, and heavy metals, resulting in air pollution and health risks. Corrosion can occur under paints, causing them to bubble and peel. Damage is mostly superficial, not structural; however, it can be an ongoing maintenance issue. Primers and paints can pose hazards to workers and the environment. Painted steel does not have as high a recycling value as unpainted steel. Pretreatments such as acid etching can pose hazards to workers and the environment. See "Etching" above.	Painted metal offers the advantage of easy color matching for touch-ups and long-term maintenance. This could improve the life span of the metal structure.
Enamel finishes for steel are fused glass coatings applied to steel surfaces at high temperatures (1,356°F to 1,598°F).	Enameling is an energy-intensive process.	
Clear coats are used to protect and reveal the natural metal; however, they should not be used as the sole source to prevent corrosion, but as added protection for metals and surface finishes that are corrosion resistant. *Siloxanes,* hybrid organic and inorganic organisilicon compounds relatively new to metal clear coating in exterior uses, create a chemical bond to the cleaned metal surface, preventing bubbling, peeling, and flaking. *Non–chemical bond clear coats* include paints, epoxies, powder coats, and nylonics that provide a clear finish for metal. Because they have no chemical bond with the metal, they are vulnerable to peeling, bubbling, flaking, and yellowing.	Siloxanes are factory-applied coatings where greater control of application can be achieved. Touch-ups can be performed in the field, but conditions must be well controlled for curing. Non–chemical bond clear coats can be applied in the field; however, they contain VOCs that can contribute to air pollution.	The life span of clear coats may be compromised on metals, such as handrails, that will receive wear and abrasion. The life span of siloxanes is expected to be around 25 years; however, the relative newness of the product indicates a short track record.

Table 11–19 Metal Finish Types, Applications, and Environmental and Human Health Risks *(Continued)*

Finish/Coating Type	Environmental and Health Risks, Recycling Potential	Additional Information
Mechanical Finishes		
The wide variety of mechanical finishes alter the surface texture and appearance of the metal surface through invasive mechanical means. Finishes include polishing, shot peening, rolling, dimpling, pressing, engraving, stamping, hydroforming, milling, expanding, and perforating.		
Mechanical finishes can be satin or polished, directional, or nondirectional. The surface of the metal will form a thin oxide film that if left unprotected will lead to corrosion. Uncoated mechanical finishes are uncommon on steel because they will quickly rust. They are primarily used to prepare steel to receive a coating such as paint or galvanizing. *Mill finish,* also called "as fabricated," is the surface finish that results from machining, rolling, extruding, or casting metal.	Environmental and health risks are minimal beyond the risks of production and fabrication of the metal. Some additional energy is used for applying the mechanical finish. Mechanical finishes do not impact the recycling potential of the metal product. Mechanical finishes on metal roughen the surface, increasing the surface area and exposing more metal to oxidation. Mechanical finishes on all metals, with the exception of stainless steel and titanium, should be given additional protection. Even rougher finishes can lower the stain resistance of stainless steel in areas of higher pollution or salt exposure.	Uncoated satin and mirror finishes are not common for exterior aluminum applications. Finishes are usually anodized or the metal is coated with thin layers of more corrosion-resistant aluminum alloys, paints, or ceramic coverings. Low-strength alloys (the purest aluminum) will maintain the best appearance when weathering. Higher strength alloys, containing copper or magnesium, will weather in more mottled tones. All require periodic cleaning to prevent discoloration.

ªInternational Occupational Safety and Health Information Centre

Sources: ATSDR; Imm 2007; U.S. EPA 1994; Zahner 1995, 2005; Spiegel and Meadows 2006

Where Possible, Specify Mechanical Finishes Rather Than Chemical

Specifying mechanical finishes such as buffing, grinding, polishing, or abrasive blasting on corrosion-resistant metals will reduce the use of resources and hazardous pollutant and waste release associated with applied chemical or electrical finishes.

Avoid Coatings That May Fail and Compromise the Longevity of the Structure

Coated metals may require more maintenance and repairs over the life of the structure. For example, powder-coated, galvanized, or painted metal may chip due to impact and wear. It is possible to apply paints or galvanizing in the field to repair the chips; however, some owners may decide to replace severely chipped or peeling structures before the expected useful life of the

metal has been met. If coating repairs are made, the suitable paint can release VOCs, harming air quality and posing human health risks.

In addition, coatings may fail and the metal may corrode prematurely, compromising the integrity of the metal structure. Stainless steel and aluminum offer some advantages, as they do not require coatings.

Avoid Finishes with Toxic Impacts to Environmental and Human Health

The U.S. EPA has identified cadmium plating materials, chromium plating materials, cyanide-based electroplating, and copper-/formaldehyde-based electroless copper solutions as toxic and/or polluting. Therefore, electroplating should be avoided or if necessary, a replacement technology listed by the U.S. EPA's National Risk Management Research Laboratory at the metal finishing website should be used (U.S. EPA National Risk Management Research Laboratory). Some recommended replacement technologies include metal stripping and zinc plating, noncyanide copper plating, ion vapor deposition (IVD), physical vapor deposition (PVD), chromium-free substances for some immersion processes, metal spray coatings, and trivalent chromium plating.

Recycling, Reuse, or Disposal of Metals

The trait of nearly endless recycling potential is the single most sustainable aspect of metals. Use of recycled metal reduces energy use, waste, and emissions associated with production of new metals. Most metals can be recycled multiple times into very high-value applications without compromising performance or downcycling. Because reuse of scrap saves producers the costs of primary metal manufacture, especially for energy-intensive aluminum, the market for secondary metals is strong, and scrap values, though they vary widely among metal types, are high. In 2000, 80.7 million metric tons of metal were recycled, valued at $17.7 billion. This was more than half of the metal supply by weight that year (USGS 2002) (see Table 11–20).

Use of recycled metal scrap in new metal products substantially reduces energy use and pollution emissions, and eliminates the mining impacts from acquisition of metal ores. Converting metal oxides into metals is the most energy- and pollutant-intensive step in metal manufacture, and use of scrap from both pre- and post-consumer uses can avoid this step. It is estimated that use of recycled aluminum content reduces energy use and air pollution by 95% and water pollution by 97% (Aluminum Association [AA] 2003). And while recovery of post-consumer metals can incur some environmental impacts, there are far less negative impacts on natural environments than mining imposes. For example, when one ton of steel is recycled, 2,500 pounds of iron ore, 1,400 pounds of coal, and 120 pounds of limestone are conserved (Steel Recycling Institute [SRI]).

It is important to note that use of recycled metal scrap does not completely eliminate the release of pollutants and toxins into the environment. Recycling aluminum results in tons of toxic sludge, steel recycling requires substantial energy since steel has a high melting point, and toxins are released from burning off paints and removal of surface alloys.

Separation of metal scrap from mixed waste varies by metal type. Iron and steel can be easily separated with magnets, and aluminum and copper can be separated with other types of electromagnetic processes. Mixed metals can be separated from each other using a fluidized bed that segregates metals according to their densities. Metals are recycled by adding them to the melt in furnaces where metal is being made, in which the properties of the metal are fully restored to a new metal.

There are some conditions that decrease the likelihood that a metal product will be recycled. Some finishes, such as electroplating, result in a mixed metal product that is not recyclable. Other finishes, such as powder coating or galvanizing, are technically removable for recycling but may pose toxic risks during their removal. Also, not all facilities are equipped to safely remove the finishes. Mixed-material assemblies such as light fixtures may not be easily recycled, as some labor to disassemble the product is required. Unless the metal is in high quantity or very high value, demolition contractors or recycling facilities may not find it worth the time.

Steel Recycling and Reuse

Steel, easily separated magnetically from other wastes, is one of the most recycled construction materials, with an average recycling rate of 75.7% in 2005 and 76 million tons recycled. The recycling rate in the construction industry was estimated to be 88% overall, with a 97% rate for structural beams and plates and a 65% rate for reinforcing bar and other products (SRI 2006).

Use of steel scrap is an integral part of steel manufacture because its use lowers the cost of producing new steel. It is less expensive to recycle steel than to mine virgin ore and process it to make steel. The Steel Recycling Institute estimates that in one year, the U.S. steel industry saves the equivalent energy to power 18 million homes by using recycled steel (SRI 2006). Over 5,000 Btus of energy are conserved with the use of one pound of recycled steel. Currently steel has a reasonably high scrap value that will undoubtedly increase

Table 11–20 U.S. Metal Recycling Statistics (in metric tons), 2005

Commodity	Recycled from New Scrap[a]	Recycled from Old Scrap[b]	Recycled[c]	Apparent Supply[d]	Percentage Recycled
Aluminum[e]	1,930,000	1,060,000	2,990,000	8,390,000	36
Chromium[f]	NA	NA	124,000	511,000	24
Copper[g]	769,000	182,000	951,000	3,170,000	30
Iron and steel[h]	NA	NA	65,400,000	122,000,000	54
Lead[i]	15,700	1,130,000	1,140,000	1,540,000	74.5
Magnesium[j]	53,400	19,400	72,800	167,000	44
Tin	2,280	11,800	14,000	46,500	30
Titanium[k]	NA	NA	25,700	—[l]	50
Zinc	302,000	43,100	345,000	1,170,000	29.5

[a]Scrap that results from the manufacturing process, including metal and alloy production. New scrap of aluminum, copper, lead, tin, and zinc excludes home scrap. Home scrap is scrap generated in the metal-producing plant.

[b]Scrap that results from consumer products.

[c]Metal recovered from new plus old scrap.

[d]Apparent supply is production plus net imports plus stock changes. Production is primary production plus recycled metal. Net imports are imports minus exports. Apparent supply is calculated on a contained weight basis.

[e]Scrap quantity is the calculated metallic recovery from purchased new and old aluminum scrap, estimated for full industry coverage.

[f]Chromium scrap includes estimated chromium-containing chemicals. Stocks include estimated chromium content of reported and estimated producer, consumer, and government stocks.

[g]Includes copper recovered from unalloyed and alloyed copper-based scrap, as refined copper or in alloy forms, as well as copper recovered from aluminum-, nickel-, and zinc-based scrap.

[h]Iron production measured as shipments of iron and steel products plus casting corrected for imported ingots and blooms. Secondary production measured as reported consumption. Apparent supply includes production of raw steel.

[i]Lead processors are segregated by primary and secondary producers. This segregation permits inclusion of stocks changes for secondary producers.

[j]Includes magnesium content of aluminum-based scrap.

[k]Percent recycled based on titanium scrap consumed divided by primary titanium sponge metal and scrap consumption.

[l]Withheld to avoid disclosing company proprietary data

Source: USGS 2007e

along with energy costs. Use of recycled steel also saves resources, with a metric ton of recycled steel saving 1,134 kg of iron, 635 kg of coal, and 54 kg of limestone (USGS 2004).

Reflecting the high recycling rates, more than 62% of the average steel product produced in the United States is recycled content. Some steel products used in construction contain close to 100% recycled content while others are just 25%–35%. Potential recycled contents are determined by the two modern types of steelmaking facilities, the basic oxygen furnace (BOF) and the electric arc furnace (EAF). The BOF steelmaking process, used in 45% of steel pro-duction in 2005, optimally uses between 25% and 35% steel scrap to produce new steel (U.S. DOE 2007). An estimated 16% of this is post-consumer steel (National Institute of Building Sciences 2007). Typical construction products produced by the BOF process are those whose major characteristic is draw-ability, such as hollow structural sections, studs, decking, and plate. The EAF process, used in 55% of new steel production, uses 95%–100% steel scrap in new steel production for products whose major required characteristic is strength (U.S. DOE 2007). An estimated 67% of steel recycled into EAF processes is post-consumer content. These products include reinforcing bars, structural beams and columns, shapes and angles, and plates (Steel Recycling Institute).

The global demand for steel products far outpaces the amount of recycled scrap available by a factor of two; therefore new steel from primary sources must be produced. There is some concern that specifying steel products with high recycled content will drive up the price of steel made by the EAF process. There is also concern that transportation impacts will increase, as 100% recycled steel may not be available in some locations (Addis 2006).

Steel coatings can inhibit recycling of steel members, and removal of finishes such as galvanizing and powder coating can release toxins or add minor contaminants to the new production process; however, these impacts are viewed as minor compared with the positive energy and resource savings of using recycled steel.

Stainless Steel

Stainless steel is highly recyclable with a very high scrap value. Worldwide the average recycled content of stainless steel is 60%, with the typical remelt rate between 65% and 85% of the furnace charge in North America (Specialty Steel Industry of North America). Like carbon steel, the demand for new stainless steel products outweighs the nearly 100% recycling rate of stainless steel.

Aluminum

As a result of the high monetary and environmental costs of refining and producing aluminum, aluminum recycling has become a very strong secondary market. Forty-four percent of all aluminum production in the United States in 2005 was secondary production from pre-consumer scrap (60%) and post-consumer recycling (40%; USGS 2007e). The end-of-life (EOL) collection ratio for aluminum used in construction was 70% in 2005 (Houska 2006), with a range of recycled content from 100% in aluminum castings to 0% in sheet stock. Like steel and stainless steel, demand for new aluminum exceeds the supply of used metal.

Aluminum has a low melting temperature and therefore can be recycled with relatively low energy inputs. The practice of recycling aluminum scrap and

Figure 11–6.
Reclaimed truck tailgates are used as guardrails for a third-floor deck at Leger Wanaselja's Adeline Street remodel. (Photo from Leger Wanaselja Architects)

post-consumer products uses less than 5% of the energy (and produces less than 5% of the greenhouse gases) required to produce aluminum from virgin materials in primary processes because the energy-intensive refining stage is bypassed. Use of both pre- and post-consumer aluminum scrap has reduced the average energy used to produce aluminum in the United States by 57% (AA 2003). The International Aluminum Institute estimates that worldwide post-consumer recycling of aluminum saves 84 million tons of greenhouse gas emissions per year.

Release of toxic by-products, emissions, and pollutants is substantially reduced as well, with savings of four pounds of chemical by-products for every pound of aluminum recycled (IAI 2007b).

Using recycled aluminum avoids the habitat destruction required for strip mining of bauxite, aluminum's feedstock, as for every ton of recycled aluminum eight tons of bauxite is saved. Use of recycled aluminum scrap also reduces water pollution by 97%, as the pollutant-laden smelting stage for primary aluminum is eliminated (IAI 2007b).

A high priority of the North American aluminum industry is to increase the recycling rate of aluminum and establish the industry as a "leader in sustainability." The Aluminum Association's 2003 "Aluminum Industry Technology Roadmap" states a performance target goal of a 100% recycling rate for aluminum products by 2020 (AA 2003).

Copper

The extensive costs of mining, processing, and disposing of waste from copper material acquisition is the primary reason for the high recycling value and rate of copper, which has an EOL collection rate of greater than 90%. The average copper product used in construction (with the exception of copper wire) has a recycled content of between 75% and 95% (Houska 2006).

SPECIFY METALS WITH RECYCLED CONTENT

There are two ways to evaluate recycled metals. The first is to evaluate metal products by the percentage of their recycled content, which is defined by the amount of scrap material input in the production of the metal product. However, these numbers could be inflated if inefficient production generated a lot of scrap or waste, if there are

many premature failures of the metal products, or if low quality material is used as feed (Houska 2006).

Recycled content of metal products varies widely by the type of product. For example, some metal products, such as aluminum sheet metal, have very little recycled content due to specific material requirements (Houska 2006). Stainless steel is 100% recyclable for a theoretically unlimited number of times with no downcycling. And stainless steel has a very high recapture rate as do copper and steel because of their high scrap value; however, its long service life and rapid growth in production means that there is a shortage of scrap, so actual recycled

Figure 11–7.
Oxbow Park designers Nate Cormier and Laura Haddad hunted for "obtainium" in local scrap yards. Tools, gears, and other artifacts from the industrial Georgetown neighborhood were embedded in artful concrete walls. (Photo by Allen Cox)

content of stainless steel products may not be very high (Houska 2004).

Specify Metals with High Recycling Potential

Examination of the recycling potential of a product is equally important to the recycled content of a product. End-of-life (EOL) collection ratios, also called reclamation rates, indicate the percentage of a material that is recycled at the end of a product's useful life. Most EOL ratios are higher than recycled contents. Some argue that this may be a more relevant indicator of environmental impact than recycled content (Houska 2006). Some products, such as sheet aluminum, with little or no recycled content can be recycled into other high-quality aluminum products. An examination of EOL collection ratios for aluminum products shows a recycling rate of 70% for products used in construction.

EOL separation and recycling can be ensured by specification of appropriate finishes, products, and connections that will facilitate disassembly and recycling rather than demolition and landfilling at the end of the structure's life. This is discussed in later sections. EOL collection is also influenced by scrap values. For instance, copper and aluminum are at current high price levels and stainless steel is also high, increasing the likelihood that products made from these materials will be recycled (Houska 2006).

While reclamation rates are equally important to minimize environmental impact of metal specification, they are not currently considered by the LEED system. Instead LEED credits related to material recycling address recycled content of materials.

Figure 11–8.

SALVAGE AND REUSE METAL MEMBERS

Salvaging and reusing metal members whole will save energy use and emissions that occur from secondary smelting, forming, and finishing of recycled metals. Structural steel, stainless steel, and, to a lesser extent, aluminum are made in standard sections and grades (strengths). This means that structural metal members can be easily reused in whole form without the regrading that must occur with use of salvaged wood. Use of some salvaged metals may require field finishing techniques to prevent corrosion.

DETAIL METAL STRUCTURE TO MAKE END-OF-LIFE SCRAP COLLECTION, SEGREGATION, AND REUSE OR RECYCLING EASIER

Careful design of the metal structure can make EOL material separation easier, increasing the likelihood of recycling after the structure's useful life. Use of mechanical fasteners rather than welded connections can make it easier to disassemble the structure for recycling of metals and other components. Highly corroded pieces with significant metal loss can limit the scrap value of a metal, reducing the chances that it will be recycled.

Some coated metals or mixed metal assemblies can present challenges to EOL recycling, and if the components being removed are not numerous or large enough, recycling may not occur. Electroplated metals are not usually recyclable because of the mixed metals. Galvanized or powder-coated metals are recyclable; however, removal of the finish requires special facilities and can release air and water toxics. Removal and recycling of zinc coatings is increasingly done.

REDUCE METAL WASTE

Metal and metal finishing waste can be reduced by ordering prefabricated materials, products, and structures. If structures are at least partially fabricated in a factory setting, scrap and excess finish materials can be more easily recycled into other processes. Fabrication and finishing of metal on-site may result in more waste.

REDUCE METAL MEMBER SIZES AND THICKNESSES

High-strength stainless steel alloys and titanium, both relatively high in embodied energy, are very strong

Figure 11–9.
The shoulder hedge frame at Gustafson Guthrie and Nichol's Lurie Garden in Chicago's Millennium Park encloses a fifteen-foot-high topiary hedge on the perimeter of the garden. While it is intended to be a permanent structure, the powder-coated steel frame has bolted connections which could allow for disassembly and reuse of the frame members. (Design by Gustafson Guthrie and Nichol, Ltd; Photos by Meg Calkins)

metals offering potential for reduced section sizes and sheet thicknesses. For a given span, steel may require more material than stainless steel and titanium, and aluminum may require even more material than steel (Houska 2004).

CONSIDER MAINTENANCE AND CLEANING REQUIREMENTS OF METALS

Maintenance requirements are an important consideration in metal selection, as the structure will be in use for a long period of time. Maintenance and cleaning of metal surfaces can extend the life span of a metal structure and reduce the risk of corrosive staining of metals and metal runoff pollution. Contaminants must remain on the surface of a metal for long enough and in high enough concentrations for corrosion to occur, so if manual cleaning is regularly performed it can prevent surface corrosive staining. Frequency of cleaning required will vary with type of metal and environmental conditions (IMOA 2002).

Stainless steel may have the simplest maintenance requirements, as it can be cleaned with a nontoxic mild detergent and water solution with a degreaser as needed. Frequency of cleaning will directly relate to the environmental conditions of the site and to the grade of stainless steel. This simple maintenance regimen may help to offset the higher first costs of stainless steel.

Questions to Ask When Specifying Metals for Use in Sustainable Sites

- What are the potential air, water, and soil pollution impacts of the metal in extraction, production, manufacture, and fabrication?
- Will the metal structure last the expected duration of the landscape?
- Is the metal structure reusable or recyclable?
- Are corrosion-protective coatings required?
- Do they off-gas VOCs, pose health risks to workers or users, or contribute to air, water, or soil pollution?
- Is there a risk of coating loss to the environment due to wear or spalling?
- Does the coating limit recyclability of the metal member?
- How much metal may enter the environment from corrosion carried by runoff? Is the corrosion hazardous?
- What are the maintenance requirements of the metal structure? Will hazardous cleaners or new protective coating applications be required to maintain the structure?

Source: Adapted from Houska 2004

Coated metals can require frequent touch-ups and repairs throughout their life cycle, and chips can expose the base metal, which may lead to corrosion.

Copper and Cor-Ten steel require periodic sealing to maintain the desired corrosion layer. Metal sealants can also contain VOCs and hazardous compounds.

The Future of Metals

INDUSTRY EFFORTS TO REDUCE HEALTH AND ENVIRONMENTAL IMPACTS OF METAL MANUFACTURE

Increased attention is being paid to the environmental impacts of metal production by environmental and human health organizations, policy makers, and metal industry groups and producers. The U.S. EPA, the U.S. DOE, researchers, and metal trade associations have teamed in several efforts to better quantify these impacts, and set both voluntary and mandated goals for reducing them. The result has been sometimes substantial reductions in energy use and release of toxic chemicals, greenhouse gases, and hazardous wastes over the past ten years. The metal finishing industry is somewhat lagging behind this effort, as many finishing shops are small operations without resources for improved pollution control equipment and energy efficiency measures.

Both steel and aluminum sectors are participants in the Department of Energy's (DOE) Industrial Technologies Program (ITP), as they are classified as "Energy Intensive Industries." The program's goals for all sectors include the following (2007):

- Between 2002 and 2020 contribute to a 30% decrease in energy intensity.
- Between 2002 and 2010 commercialize more than ten industrial energy efficiency technologies through research, development, and demonstration (RD&D) partnerships.

Steel

Though still contributing significant amounts of pollutants to air, water, and soil and using copious amounts of energy, the steel industry has made substantial progress toward reducing pollutant emissions and energy and water use. In a 2000 report for the Department of Energy, the steel industry claims to have spent $10 billion over the past 30 years to improve its environmental record, with 65% of that going to controlling air emissions to comply with the 1990 Clean Air Act (Energetics 2005).

The industry's investments in pollution control have improved its environmental track record. Its self-stated accomplishments in the 2000 report are as follows:

- Over 95% of the water used in producing and processing steel is recycled.
- Discharges of air and water pollutants have been reduced by over 90% since 1980.
- Solid waste production, with the exception of slag, has been reduced by over 80%. Much of the waste is recycled back into the process or into other industries.
- Many hazardous wastes are recycled or recovered for reuse.
- The recycling rate of steel was 68% at the time of the report publication in 2000 and is now even higher (Energetics 2005).

The American Iron and Steel Institute (AISI) collects data from its member companies on energy intensity, GHG emissions, material efficiency, steel recycling, and implementation of environmental management systems. By joining Climate VISION, it has committed to improving member energy efficiency by 10% by 2012 from 2002 levels (AISI 2007).

Aluminum

Like the steel industry, the aluminum industry has made substantial improvements to its manufacturing processes that have decreased emissions and energy use in recent decades. In 2003, the International Aluminum Institute conducted a life-cycle analysis and survey of companies around the world that represent more than 75% of the world's aluminum production, focusing on examination of manufacturing techniques and the resulting environmental and economic impacts. The result of the ongoing study is a set of twelve voluntary objectives and 22 performance indicators for reducing the environmental impacts (and economic costs) of aluminum by 2010 (IAI 2005).

Similar efforts are ongoing in North America as the Aluminum Association and the U.S. Department of Energy's Industrial Technologies Program teamed to produce a vision and technology roadmap for the industry,

also released in 2003. It sets strategic goals and industry-wide voluntary performance targets for achievement by 2020. Fewer of the North American goals set quantifiable performance targets than the International Aluminum Institute effort set. However, some North American companies participated in the IAI effort.

A growing concern of the rising cost of energy and increasing pollution-control standards in North America may mean that more iron, steel, and aluminum will be produced in countries such as China and Russia where there are less stringent pollution controls or where energy costs are lower. And because aluminum is so lightweight, it is relatively inexpensive to ship long distances.

NANOTECHNOLOGY AND METALS

Nanotechnology and Steel

Recent developments in nanotechnology offer the potential to improve the performance of metals, particularly steel, while reducing some environmental impacts. However, it is important to note that the human and environmental health impacts of many nanomaterials are relatively unknown. Nanocomposite steel, a mix of steel and carbon nanotubes, is not yet available in structural dimensions but may offer a stronger, lighter weight structural material in the future. Carbon nanotubes are formed from very strong nanoscale sheets of carbon molecules rolled in cylinders. Thermally and electrically conductive, they are up to 250 times stronger than steel and 10 times lighter (Elvin 2007).

Techniques of fabricating metals by weaving them into ultrafine lattice structures have been developed resulting in strong, lightweight metals. Steel produced with a nanoscale lath structure similar to plywood is currently used in reinforcing bar. While more expensive than conventional rebar, it is more durable and corrosion resistant, so life-cycle costs may be less. Also, less rebar is required since it is stronger, saving on material and labor costs (Elvin 2007).

Nanotechnology is improving steel welds and the heat-affected zone (HAZ) of welded areas by adding magnesium and calcium nanoparticles. This reduces the size of HAZ grains to around one-fifth of their standard size, resulting in increased weld strength and toughness and a longer-lasting metal structure (Elvin 2007).

Nanotechnology and Metal Finishes

Recently developed nanotech finishes may offer safer, more efficient options than traditional methods. New nanopolymer coatings can protect metals from corrosion through a very thin polymer film. This film is a high-density, cohesive, extremely thin layer that is said to deliver better corrosion protection and paint adhesion without use of heavy metals, solvents, or heating. For instance, some coatings exceed the properties of chrome coatings (wear resistance, corrosion resistance) without use of chromium. Other nano coatings are made from ceramic nanoparticles.

In addition to corrosion protection and paint adherence, nano coatings offer ease of cleaning and protection of the structure from graffiti paint, which will not adhere to the surface (Elvin 2007).

REFERENCES

Addis, B. 2006. *Building with Reclaimed Components and Materials: A Design Handbook for Reuse and Recycling.* London: Earthscan.

Agency for Toxic Substances and Disease Registry (ATSDR). "ToxFAQs." U.S. Department of Health and Human Services. http://www.atsdr.cdc.gov/toxfaq.html (accessed between May 2006 and November 2007).

The Aluminum Association, Inc. 2003, February. "Aluminum: Industry Technology Roadmap." D.C.: The Aluminum Association.

The Aluminum Association, Inc. 2004. "Issues Facing the Industry." http://www.aluminum.org/Content/NavigationMenu/The_Industry/-Impacts/Impacts.htm.

American Iron and Steel Institute (AISI). 2007. "Climate Vision." http://www.climatevision.gov/sectors/steel/index.html.

American Society for Testing and Materials (ASTM), Society of Automotive Engineers (SAE). 2004. *Metals & Alloys in the Unified Numbering System.* 10th ed.

Agency for Toxic Substances and Disease Registry. 2007 CERCLA Priority List of Hazardous Substances, Agency for Toxic Substances and Disease Registry, Department of Health and Human Services, http://www.atsdr.cdc.gov/cercla/

Baird, S "Hydro-Electric Power." Ecology Comunications http://www.ecology.com/archived-links/hydroelectric-energy/index.html. Accessed July 14, 2007.

Demkin, J., ed. 1998a. "Application Report 09: Structural Framing." In *Environmental Resource Guide.* New York: John Wiley & Sons.

Demkin, J., ed. 1998b. "Application Report 10: Metal and Plastic Plumbing Pipe." In *Environmental Resource Guide.* New York: John Wiley & Sons.

Demkin, J., ed. 1998c. "Materials Report 09510: Acoustical Ceiling Systems." In *Environmental Resource Guide.* New York: John Wiley & Sons.

Elvin, G. A. 2007, June. "Nanotechnology for Green Building." Green Technology Forum. http://www.greentechforum.net/greenbuild.

Energetics. 2005, September. *Steel Industry Marginal Opportunity Study.* Prepared for U.S. Department of Energy Office of Energy Efficiency and Renewable Energy Industrial Technologies Program.

Environmental Roadmapping Initiative (ERI). 2004a. "Iron and Steel: Impacts, Risks and Regulations, Summary." Ann Arbor, MI: National Center for Manufacturing Sciences, August 10, 2004.

Environmental Roadmapping Initiative (ERI). 2004b. "Mining: Impacts, Risks and Regulations, Summary." Ann Arbor, MI: National Center for Manufacturing Sciences, August 10, 2004.

Fujii, Hiroyuki et al.(2005) "How to Quantify the Environmental Profile of Stainless Steel."

Graedel, T.E. and Allenby, B.R., 1996. *Design for Environment.* Upper Saddle River, New Jersey Prentice Hall.

Gutowski, Timothy G. 2004. *Design and Manufacturing for the Environment. For the Handbook of Mechanical Engineering.* Ed. K.H. Grote and E.K. Antonsson. Springer-Verlag, in press.

Hammond, G., and C. Jones. 2006. *Inventory of Carbon and Energy.* Version 1.5 Beta. Bath, UK: University of Bath, Department of Mechanical Engineering. http://www.bath.ac.uk/mech-eng/sert/embodied/

Houska, C. 2004. "Stainless Steel's Sustainable Advantage." *The Construction Specifier* 57(8): 52–60.

Houska, C. and S.B. Young 2006. "Comparing the Sustainability of Architectural Metals." *The Construction Specifier* 59(7): 80–91.

Imm, N. 2007. "Metals." In *Landscape Architectural Graphic Standards,* ed. L. Hopper. Hoboken, NJ: John Wiley & Sons,. pp. 495–500.

International Agency for Research on Cancer (IARC). *Monographs on the Evaluation of Carcinogenic Risks to Humans.* Lyon, France: International Agency for Research on Cancer.

International Aluminum Institute (IAI). 2005. *Aluminum for Future Generations.* Sustainability Update 2005.

International Aluminum Institute (IAI). 2007a. "Greenhouse Gases." http://www.world-aluminium.org/Sustainability/Environmental+Issues/Greenhouse+gases.

International Aluminum Institute. 2007b. "Recycling." http://www.world-aluminium.org/Sustainability/Recycling.

International Aluminum Institute (IAI). 2007c. "Smelter Emissions." http://www.world-aluminium.org/Sustainability/Environmental+Issues/Smelter+emissions.

International Molybdenum Association (IMOA). 2002, September. "*Which Stainless Steel Should I Specify for Exterior Applications?*" Prepared by Catherine Houska. Architecture, Building and Construction series. Publication IMOA/ABC 00, 4 pages.

International Occupational Safety and Health Information Centre (IOSHIC). http://www.ilo.org/public/english/protection/safework/ (accessed May 14, 2007). International Labor Organization (ILO).

International Stainless Steel Forum (ISSF). "The Recycling of Stainless Steel." http://www.worldstainless.org/ISSF/Files/Recycling/Flash.html.

National Institute of Building Sciences. 2007. *Whole Building Design Guide.* http://www.wbdg.org/.

Nickel Institute. "Stainless Steels in Architecture, Building and Construction" Prepared by C. Houska, Technical Marketing Resources, n.d.

Specialty Steel Industry of North America (SSINA). "The Stainless Steel Information Center: Green Material." http://www.ssina.com/index2.html.

Spiegel, Ross and Meadows, Dru. 2006. *Green Building Materials.* Hoboken, NJ: John Wiley & Sons.

Stainless Steel World. *Architecture.* The Netherlands: KCI Publishing B.V. Zutphen. http://www.stainless-steel-world.net/titanium/ShowPage.aspx?pageID=206.

Stanford Research Institute (SRI). April 2, 2006 press release

Steel Recycling Institute (SRI). 2006–2007. "Buy Recycled with Recyclable Steel." www.recycle-steel.org.

Steel Recycling Institute (SRI). 2006–2007. "Representing America's Number One Recycled Material." www.recycle-steel.org.

Steel Recycling Institute (SRI). "Steel Takes the LEED with Recycled Content." www.recycle-steel.org.

Thompson, J. W., and K. Sorvig. 2000. *Sustainable Landscape Construction: A Guide to Green Building Outdoors.* Washington, DC: Island Press.

Toxics Release Inventory Explorer (TRI) Data. 2005. http://www.epa.gov/tri-efdr/.

U.S. Department of Energy (US DOE) Office of Industrial Technologies. 2000. Energy and Environmental Profile of the U.S. Iron and Steel Industry. Prepared by Energetics, Incorporated, August 2000.

U.S. Department of Energy (U.S. DOE). Industrial Technologies Program. May 1, 2007. "Steel Industry of the Future." http://www.eere.energy.gov/industry/steel.

U.S. Environmental Protection Agency (U.S. EPA) 1994. "Guide to Cleaner Technologies, Alternative Metal Finishes." EPA/625/R-94/007. Washington D.C.: US EPA.

U.S. Environmental Protection Agency (U.S. EPA). 2006a. "Iron and Steel Sector." 2006 Sector Strategies Performance Report. Sector Programs, U.S. EPA.

U.S. Environmental Protection Agency (U.S. EPA). 2006b. "Metal Casting Sector." 2006 Sector Strategies Performance Report. Sector Programs, U.S. EPA.

U.S. Environmental Protection Agency (U.S. EPA). 2006c. "Metal Finishing Sector." 2006 Sector Strategies Performance Report. Sector Programs, U.S. EPA.

U.S. Environmental Protection Agency (U.S. EPA). 2007a. "Inventory of U.S. Greenhouse Gas Emissions and Sinks, 1990–2005." April 2007. Report EPA 430-R-07–002.

U.S. Environmental Protection Agency (U.S. EPA). Office of Policy, Economics and Innovation. 2007b. "Energy Trends in Selected Manufacturing Sectors: Opportunities and Challenges for Environmentally Preferable Energy Outcomes." Prepared by ICF International, March 2007.

U.S. Environmental Protection Agency (US EPA). 2007c. "2005 Toxics Release Inventory (TRI) Public Data Release Report". EPA 260-R-07–001. Public data release March 2007.

U.S. Environmental Protection Agency (U.S. EPA). National Risk Management Research Laboratory. "Metal Finishing." http://www.epa.gov/nrmrl/std/mtb/metal_finishing.htm.

U.S. Environmental Protection Agency (U.S. EPA). Technology Transfer Network. Air Toxics Web Site. http://www.epa.gov/ttn/atw/orig189.html (see also report released in 2006 at)

U.S. Geological Survey (USGS). 2002. "Materials in the Economy" Material Flows, Scarcity, and the Environment, U.S. Geologic Survey Circular 1221.

U.S. Geological Survey (USGS). 2004. "Iron and Steel Scrap." In *2002 Minerals Yearbook.* Washington, DC: U.S. Geological Survey.

U.S. Geological Survey (USGS). 2007a. "Iron and Steel." In *2005 Minerals Yearbook.* Washington, DC: U.S. Geological Survey.

U.S. Geological Survey (USGS). 2007b. "Aluminum and Alumina." In *2005 Minerals Yearbook.* Washington, DC: U.S. Geological Survey.

U.S. Geological Survey (USGS). 2007c. "Chromium." In *2005 Minerals Yearbook.* Washington, DC: U.S. Geological Survey.

U.S. Geological Survey (USGS). 2007d. "Titanium and Titanium Dioxide." In *2005 Minerals Yearbook.* Washington, DC: U.S. Geological Survey.

U.S. Geological Survey (USGS). 2007e. "Metals—Recycling." In *2005 Minerals Yearbook.* Washington, DC: U.S. Geological Survey.

Zahner, William L. 1995. *Architectural Metals: A Guide to Selection, Specification, and Performance.* New York: John Wiley & Sons.

Zahner, William L. 2005. *Architectural Metal Surfaces.* New York: John Wiley & Sons.

chapter **12** | # Plastics and Rubber

Over the past five decades, plastics have become one of the more common materials in site construction. Numerous products are made from plastics or have plastic components or coatings. This rapid growth is part of the trend in building products toward use of more sophisticated materials involving more complex manufacturing processes. The most common plastic-based products in site construction are pipes, drainage and irrigation systems, plastic and composite lumber, and modular fence and rail panels. Some metal products such as chain link, bike racks, and playground equipment are coated with plastics for protection, and many paints, coatings, adhesives, and joint compounds contain polymers as well.

Plastics offer several benefits for site construction. Some can be durable, waterproof, decay resistant, flexible, integrally colored, inexpensive, and low maintenance. They can incorporate substantial recycled content, can be recycled themselves, and are relatively lightweight, conserving transportation energy use. Plastic lumber can reduce pressure on forests by replacing use of old-growth and pressure-treated lumber. And plastic pipes can replace energy- and pollution-intensive metal pipe.

But there are some drawbacks to plastic use as well. Plastics are made from nonrenewable fossil fuel feedstocks and additional fuels are consumed in their production. Waste and emissions from some plastics, by-products, and chemical additives can release toxins, such as dioxins, furans, and heavy metals, during both production and disposal. Among the most serious of impacts is the 28.9 million tons of plastics that are disposed of in the U.S. municipal solid waste stream each year—11.8% of all municipal solid waste (U.S. EPA 2006b). With the exception of some HDPE products, most plastics are disposed of in landfills or incinerators, as the recycling infrastructure for plastics faces challenges that limit the activity.

Despite these drawbacks, plastics are a viable alternative for some site construction products, and it is important to emphasize that not all plastics pose equal environmental and human health risks. This chapter will discuss characteristics, risks, and benefits of the six primary plastics used in site construction products. They are high-density polyethylene (HDPE), cross-linked polyethylene (XLPE or PEX), polypropylene (PP), polyvinyl chloride (PVC), polystyrene (PS), and acrylonitrile butadiene styrene (ABS). Polyisoprene and synthetic rubbers will be discussed later in the chapter.

PLASTICS USE

One hundred and thirteen billion pounds of plastic resin were produced in North America in 2006. Of this, 38.6 billion pounds were polyethylenes (most commonly HDPE and LLDPE) and 14.9 billion pounds were PVC, approximately 75% of which is used in construction.

Packaging is the largest consumer category of plastics (29%), resulting in a relatively short use phase for a large proportion of plastics. Plastics in construction comprise about 19% of the total and usually have a longer useful life (Plastics Industry Producers' Statistics Group 2007).

While PVC is not the most commonly used plastic overall, it is by far the most commonly used plastic in the construction industry, with an estimated 11.5 billion pounds used annually in piping, siding, flooring, windows, electrical wire, cable, and other products. The American Plastics Council estimates that PVC use in fencing, decking, and signage is growing at a rate of 8.1% each year (American Plastics Council [APC] 2000).

PLASTIC BASICS

The majority of plastics are derived from natural gas or crude oil, which, after refining and processing, generates monomers, the building blocks of plastics. Monomers are then processed in a variety of combinations and routes to form chainlike polymers. This process is called polymerization and it results in an array of plastics with widely varying properties. Chemical additives are mixed into many plastics to impart properties of flexibility, workability, color, UV resistance, heat stabilization, and impact resistance. Some additives compose a significant percentage of the final product.

Plastics can be hard or soft, rigid or flexible, clear or brightly colored. While the majority of polymers are synthesized from oil derivatives, exceptions are natural rubber, cellulose, and a very limited but growing number of other biobased feedstocks (see Table 12–1).

There are two broad groups of plastics.

Thermoplastics, comprising the majority of plastics in use today, will soften repeatedly in heat and obtain their shape by cooling. This reshaping process can be repeated multiple times, making thermoplastics ideal for recycling. Thermoplastic products are usually manufactured from solid pellets. Polyethylenes (HDPE, PET, LDPE, LLDPE, and XLPE), polypropylene (PP), polystyrene (PS), and polyvinyl chloride (PVC) are the main thermoplastic polymers that are used in site construction products.

Thermoset plastics undergo an irreversible chemical reaction with heating, pressurization, or reacting with a hardening agent, which forms cross-link bonds of polymers. The bonds are durable and heat resistant, but can fail in extreme heat. Most thermoset polymers are not recyclable as they are not easily remelted or refabricated. Thermoset polymers used for site construction materials are primarily found in paints, coatings, adhesives, and glues. They include epoxies, phenolic polyurethanes, unsaturated polyester, and urea-formaldehyde (U.S. EPA 2006a). PEX piping is a thermoset plastic that is used in some hot water building applications. It is sometimes used in pavement deicing applications and occasionally for other site piping uses.

Environmental and Human Health Impacts of Plastics

While plastics offer many benefits, some pose risks to human and environmental health in many phases of their life cycles. Severity of impacts varies widely among plastic types, with the strongest from hazardous constituents and intermediaries of PVC, ABS, and polystyrenes. Polyethylenes and polypropylene, while still posing some risks, are comparatively benign. Also, risk characterizations are hotly debated. Comprehensive life-cycle assessment information is not available for most plastics used in construction; however, concerns about health risks of PVC and some adhesives have resulted in a large body of research on these polymers and their additives. There is enough information on other plastics to generally characterize their health and environmental risks, and with growth of the green building movement worldwide, new research is becoming available all the time. General impacts of plastics are discussed in this section and impacts and risks associated with PVC are summarized in Table 12–2.

While the hazards and risks of some plastic production, use; and disposal are generally accepted as existing, experts and stakeholders disagree on their severity and extent. For instance, the presence of dioxins in ash from incinerated PVC products has been documented, but the amount leaching into groundwater from landfills is unknown.

Table 12–1 Plastic Types Common to Site Construction

Type of Plastic, Resin Code, and Annual Production[a]	Characteristics of the Plastic and Its Use in Site Applications
High-density polyethylene (HDPE) Resin code #2 17.6 billion pounds	HDPE is created by the polymerization of ethylene. It is characterized by its ease of forming, low cost, and resistance to breakage. It has higher tensile strength and density than LDPE. It is opaque and can stand higher temperatures than LDPE (230°F continuously, 248°F for short periods). HDPE is easily recyclable and many site products are made from post-consumer recycled HDPE. Common site products made from HDPE include plastic lumber, sewer pipes, flexible irrigation line, and storm water structures. While the production of polyethylenes doesn't pose the extent of health risks of PVC and ABS, their production can be a source of pollution from the extraction of fossil fuels to air emissions of combustion fuels used in processing. Polyethylene processing is more limited than PVC or ABS, producing fewer pollutants, and waste can be recycled during the processes of manufacture. Polyethylenes (polymer codes #1, 2, and 4), with the exception of cross-linked polyethylene (XLPE or PEX), are the most recycled and recyclable plastics. In 2005, 8.8% of HDPE products were recycled. Recycling infrastructure for polyethylenes is widely in place and they can be either mechanically or chemically recycled into new products. Theoretically, polyethylenes can be recycled numerous times without significant change to their properties because of the lack of cross linking between their polymer chains.
Low-density polyethylene (LDPE) Resin code #4 7.8 billion pounds	Like HDPE, LDPE is created by the polymerization of ethylene. LDPE is opaque white or translucent and used for flexible products. It has lower tensile strength and density than HDPE, and will soften at lower temperatures than HDPE. While it is a very common material, particularly in packaging, it is not used in site applications as often. It is recyclable and is commonly recycled into plastic lumber along with HDPE. Common site uses are geomembranes and geotextiles.
Linear low-density polyethylene (LLDPE) Resin code #4 13.1 billion pounds	LLDPE is a linear polymer made by copolymerization of ethylene with longer chain polyolefins. It has a higher tensile strength and impact puncture resistance than LDPE. It is very flexible, elongates under stress, and has good UV resistance. Site applications include geomembranes, flexible tubing, and cable covering.
Cross-linked polyethylene (PEX or XLPE)	XLPE is produced by compounding LDPE with a cross-linking agent such as dicumyl peroxide. This forms a material that has good mechanical properties at relatively high temperatures (rated maximum is 90°C and emergency rating of 140°C). XLPE is primarily used for insulation of electrical cables or hot water pipes.
Polypropylene (PP) Resin code #5 18.3 billion pounds	PP is made from the monomer propylene. It is resistant to many chemical solvents and acids. It is less tough and more brittle than HDPE and less flexible than LDPE. It is rugged and has a good resistance to fatigue. Site applications include geotextiles, geomembranes, pipe, and synthetic fiber reinforcing in concrete.
Polyvinyl chloride (PVC) Resin code #3 14.9 billion pounds	PVC, also called vinyl, is produced by polymerization of the monomer vinyl chloride. At least 50% of its mass by weight is chlorine, using about a third of all chlorine production. It is lightweight, durable, and highly adaptable to many uses, and it is the most common plastic used in the construction industry. It can be modified in many ways with additives to impart specific properties. For example, phthalate plasticizers can be added to make PVC flexible, or UV inhibitors can be added to slow UV degradation. In use, PVC is relatively inert except when exposed to heat or UV rays, which can break down the plastic and/or release harmful toxins and heavy metals from additives. PVC poses heath risks in manufacture and disposal, discussed in greater detail in Table 12–2. Site applications of PVC include pipe, decking, fencing, and many others.

Continued

Table 12–1 Plastic Types Common to Site Construction *(Continued)*

Type of Plastic, Resin Code, and Annual Production[a]	Characteristics of the Plastic and Its Use in Site Applications
Acrylonitrile butadiene styrene (ABS) Resin code #ABS 1.2 billion pounds	ABS is produced by copolymerizing the acrylonitrile and styrene monomers in polybutadiene rubber. ABS is a strong, rigid, and tough polymer used in site applications in piping. ABS poses some health risks in manufacture and disposal. All three petrochemical components of ABS are potentially harmful to human health. Fugitive emissions from the components during polymerization can pose health risks to workers and the surrounding community. Acrylonitrile can cause respiratory irritation and central nervous system effects, and is a known carcinogen (International Agency for Research on Cancer [IARC]). Styrene and butadiene can irritate eyes and the central nervous system as well (Agency for Toxic Substances and Disease Registry [ATSDR]). Butadiene-1,3 is an IARC probable carcinogen, as well as a European Union Category 2 mutagen, and reproductive/developmental toxicant according to the State of California (Proposition 65). Styrene, which is also the building block of polystyrene, is an IARC possible human carcinogen (Group 2B). Catalytic cracking of petroleum for ABS can release wastewater containing the known carcinogen phenol in addition to oil, sulfides, cyanides, and ammonia. Manufacturing waste can be recycled within the process. Like PVC, ABS is technically recyclable; however, limited use of the material means that the market for recycling it is still more limited. The infrastructure is not in place for return of ABS to manufacturers or to recycling facilities, so little is recycled. However, as European manufacturers are increasingly required to take back their products for reuse or recycling, the industry may grow. Like PVC, ABS can't be commingled with other plastics in recycling because of its ingredient incompatibility with polyethylenes. Research on fugitive emissions risk of ABS incineration is not currently available.
Polystyrene (PS) Resin code #6 6.3 billion pounds 6% of total production	Polystyrene is produced by the polymerization of styrene and benzene. It is a colorless hard plastic with limited flexibility. It can be cast into molds with fine detail. It can also be foamed with a foaming agent into expanded products. It is used as a coating in landscape products and as insulation in buildings. Polystyrene (PS) manufacture includes benzene, a known carcinogen; ethyl benzene, a suspected carcinogen; and styrene, a known neurotoxin, suspected carcinogen, and hormone-disrupting chemical. When ignited, polystyrene releases a wide variety of polycyclic aromatic hydrocarbons (PAHs). It is easily ignited and because of its toxic potential, some codes prohibit its use in exposed building applications.
Rubber, natural and synthetic	Rubber is an elastic hydrocarbon polymer that occurs naturally as latex in the sap of several plants. The most common plant from which rubber is harvested is the para rubber tree. Rubber can also be synthetically produced from a variety of petroleum-based monomers, such as isoprene, butadiene-1,3, chloroprene, and isobutylene, combined to produce various chemical and physical properties. Rubbers, both natural and synthetic, are used in site construction applications in gaskets, sealants, surfacings, liners, hoses, and other capacities. Constituents of rubbers are polymers (either raw or synthetic rubber or some combination), carbon black (the primary filler for strength and color), oils, and miscellaneous chemicals. Chemicals used act as processing aids, vulcanizing agents or activators, accelerators, age resisters, fillers, or softeners. Like plastics, rubber mixes vary widely depending on the required characteristics of the end use.

Table 12–1 Plastic Types Common to Site Construction *(Continued)*

Type of Plastic, Resin Code, and Annual Production[a]	Characteristics of the Plastic and Its Use in Site Applications
	Primary environmental concerns during rubber manufacturing are fugitive emissions and VOC emissions that can result from heating rubber products, as well as chemical additives or solvent evaporation emissions that are not contained or may be spilled or leaked. Some major chemicals that may be released are phenol, ammonia, dibutyl phthalate, dioctyl phthalate, bis(2-ethylhexyl) adipate, and zinc, nickel, cadmium, and lead compounds. Wastewater from production processes can contain zinc and other hazardous chemicals. Solid wastes with particulates from grinding operations and disposal of used lubricating and process oils are also a concern. Scorched rubber is a major solid waste source that is generally not able to be reprocessed.
	The largest environmental concern related to the rubber product life cycle is the disposal of scrap tires—the primary source of rubber in municipal solid waste. Millions of tires, primarily made from synthetic rubber, sometimes with steel or fiber reinforcing, are removed from use and placed into the waste stream at the equivalent rate of one passenger tire per person per year. Of the 299 million scrap tires generated in 2005, an estimated 259 million, or 87%, were recovered for beneficial uses such as rubberized asphalt, fill, surfacing, or energy recovery. This is a good recycling rate; however, accumulation of the unused tires, and tires from previous years in tire piles and landfills, can pose environmental and human health hazards.

[a]Plastics Industry Producers' Statistics Group 2007

Sources: Azapagic et al. 2003; EBN 2001; Platt, Lent, and Walsh 2005; Rubber Manufacturers Association 2006; Tom Lent, personal communication, November 10, 2007; Demkin 1998; U.S. EPA 1981; U.S. EPA 2006b

Feedstocks

Feedstocks for almost all plastics are derived from petroleum and/or natural gas. The petrochemical industry uses approximately 10% of all fossil fuels consumed (EBN 2001). Extraction and processing of these nonrenewable fossil fuels generate both toxic and nontoxic by-products that pollute waters, sediment, and air. Processing and distillation can release VOCs and mercaptans, affecting human health, and wastewater containing emulsified and free oils, sulfides, ammonia, phenols, heavy metals, and suspended and dissolved solids. Releases can lead to increased biochemical oxygen demands (BODs), eutrophication, environmental poisoning, and consumption of toxics by wildlife (Demkin 1998). Substantial reductions in use of fossil fuels for feedstocks can be achieved by specifying recycled-content plastics.

Toxic Releases

Through regulation in the United States and Europe, releases of toxins during materials preparation and manufacture are becoming better controlled; however, some fugitive emissions are still released, impacting workers and surrounding communities. Greater risks are posed by plastics manufacturers in countries without stringent health and environmental regulations; therefore the source as well as the type of resin should be considered during specification of plastic products (EBN 2001).

The 2005 EPA "Profile of the Rubber and Plastics Industry" by the Office of Compliance's Sector Notebook Project states the following general concerns in plastic product manufacture:

- Chemicals used as additives in plastics, such as phthalates, lead, cadmium, stearic acid, alkylated phenols, quaternary ammonium compounds, benzophenones, butane, and pentane, can be released through spills, leaks, or fugitive dust emissions.
- Toxic pollutants, including BEHP, di-n-butyl phthalate, dimethyl phthalate, phenol, zinc, BOD5, oil, and grease, can be released in wastewater.
- Accidental plastic pellet release is a wildlife ingestion concern.

Toxics Release Inventory (TRI) data show that the Rubber and Miscellaneous Plastic Products (RMPP) industry managed 205 million pounds of TRI chemical waste in 2001 (U.S. EPA 2006a). TRI chemicals released include styrene, toluene (toluene diisocyanates), dichloromethane, carbon disulfide, trichloroethylene, lead compounds, polycyclic aromatic compounds, nitrate compounds, zinc compounds, and ammonia.

Embodied Energy

Embodied energy varies among resins and among the wide variety of plastic products. Most thermoplastics have a lower embodied energy than thermoset polymers. In some analyses, PVC has the lowest embodied energy of thermoplastics because so much of the feedstock is chlorine, which uses little energy to extract from brine. Plastics have a relatively low embodied energy when compared to metals; however, in a true life-cycle comparison, longevity of the product in use and toxic impacts would figure into the equation, and plastic products on average are not designed to last as long as metal products. The figures for embodied energy of plastics given in Table 12–3 are based on the plastic's mass, and as plastics are more lightweight than alternative materials, the embodied energy is relatively low.

Less energy is used to transport plastics than some alternative materials, as plastics are of lighter weight than steel, aluminum, concrete, and stone. An exception is plastic lumber, which is heavier than wood. While plastics are lightweight, they are often produced in highly centralized facilities, so transportation distances can be long.

Embodied Carbon

The production of plastics results in the release of small amounts of CO_2 and CH_4 emissions relative to other construction materials, with primary CO_2 released from fossil fuel combustion to power production machinery. Much of the carbon in petrochemical feedstocks for plastics and rubber is stored in products until they are combusted after disposal. The Inventory of Greenhouse Gas Emissions and Sinks estimates that an average of 61% of carbon consumed in the feedstocks of plastics was stored in the product, while 39% was emitted in production in the form of CO_2. Emissions of CH_4 from petrochemical production (equal to 1.1 Tg CO_2 Eq.

[52 Gg] in 2005) result from the production of carbon black, ethylene, ethylene dichloride, and methanol (U.S. EPA 2007).

Construction Impacts

Construction impacts of plastic products vary widely. Methods of joining plastics range from mechanical fasteners to solvent cements to heat fusion. Some plastic products, such as porous paving grids, are joined by interlocking elements requiring no cements or fusion. The most serious risks of plastics in construction are posed by solvent cements and heat fusion techniques. PVC and ABS pipe are joined by solvent cements that are usually a mixture of solvents and plastic resins. Common solvents contain high levels of VOCs, yet in some cases lower-VOC formulations are available.

Use Phase

The use phase of many plastics in construction applications tends to be relatively long compared with other consumer plastic products. Plastic construction products can be durable, impervious to moisture, and resistant to insects and fungi, so they perform well in ground contact applications. However, plastics are vulnerable to UV degradation and extreme temperatures, and some plastics such as PVC will lose strength as they age. Additives such as titanium dioxide are used to inhibit UV degradation. Many plastics are integrally colored and will not need regular maintenance coatings such as paint, stains, or sealers. PVC, and also possibly ABS and polyurethane, may pose a hazard during building fires. PVC releases hydrochloric acid before the material ignites. After ignition, dioxins are released. ABS and polyurethane emit hydrogen cyanide and carbon monoxide when burned. Halogenated flame retardants (HFRs) are often added to polyurethane to counteract this problem; however, HFRs pose health risks as well (Healthy Building Network [HBN] Pharos Project).

Disposal

The greatest environmental and human health risks may occur during the disposal phase of plastics. Twenty-eight million tons of plastics entered the municipal solid waste (MSW) stream in the United States in 2005. This is about 11.8 % of all municipal solid waste by weight. As use of plastics increases, so does the amount of

Table 12–2 Life-cycle Impacts of Polyvinyl Chloride (PVC) Plastics

Feedstocks	The major raw materials are ethylene and elemental chlorine. Chlorine is derived from either rock salt or saltwater brine, and its use in PVC accounts for about 25% of all chlorine produced. While the resource is abundant, there are many concerns resulting from the quantities of organochlorine by-products, such as dioxins, that are formed during the PVC preparation process and released as fugitive emissions to the environment, where they can affect the health of organisms, including humans.[a]
	Chlorine gas, acutely hazardous if inhaled, is on the EPA's list of extremely hazardous substances. Chlorine is reacted with ethylene to form ethylene dichloride (EDC); then EDC is cracked to become the vinyl chloride monomer. EDC is classified as a probable carcinogen by the U.S. EPA. Chronic exposure to EDC has also been linked to liver, kidney, and nervous system problems.[b]
	Vinyl chloride is ranked number four, behind only lead, mercury, and arsenic, on the Department of Health and Human Services CERCLA Priority List of Hazardous Substances. The vinyl chloride monomer is a known human carcinogen, and while strictly controlled, has been linked to liver, blood, and brain cancers in PVC manufacturing workers.[c]
	The transport of vinyl chloride has been declared "ultrahazardous" by the National Toxicology Program, resulting in emergency legislation early in 2005 banning truck or train transport of vinyl chloride through the District of Columbia.[d]
	Some communities adjacent to PVC plants have been displaced by releases of hazardous levels of vinyl chloride into their air and water.[e]
Embodied energy	PVC uses the least amount of fossil fuels of the plastics discussed in this chapter because its composition is at least 50% chlorine by weight.[f]
By-products	The most harmful by-products of PVC production and disposal are dioxins, a family of persistent bioaccumulative toxins (PBTs) that do not easily break down and accumulate in fatty tissues, moving up the food chain. Dioxins are released in emissions from PVC production and from incineration or accidental burning of PVC products. While the health risks that dioxins pose are widely acknowledged, their severity and the actual degree of human exposure is still debated. In a 2003 EPA reassessment, 2,3,7,8-Tetrachloro-dibenzo-p-dioxin (TCDD), a common dioxin, was classified as a carcinogen and other dioxins as probable carcinogens. Dioxins can alter the fundamental growth and development of cells in ways that have the potential to lead to suppression of the immune system, endocrine disruption, and birth defects.[g]
Additives	Some PVC products require additives to impart special properties to the finished plastic product, yet some of these additives pose health and environmental risks. As PVC is inherently rigid and brittle, phthalate plasticizers are added (in amounts of up to 60% of the product's weight) to make flexible vinyl products such as drip irrigation tubing, garden hoses, and lawn edging. Some studies have shown that phthalates are released into the environment during PVC manufacture and disposal in landfills or incinerators.[a] Diethylhexyl phthalate (DEHP), the most common PVC plasticizer, is a Semi-volatile Organic Compound (SVOC) that off-gasses much more slowly than VOCs, so DEHP can be emitted to air or by attaching to dust for years while the product is in use.[h] In disposal, it can leach into groundwater and drinking water from PVC products disposed of in landfills. DEHP can negatively affect reproduction, liver, and kidney function of some organisms at low levels.[b] Research has recently linked DEHP to abnormal reproductive tract development in male babies and an increasing body of science is now associating DEHP and other phthalates with asthma and other bronchial problems.[e]

Continued

Table 12–2 Life-cycle Impacts of Polyvinyl Chloride (PVC) Plastics

Additives	Metal stabilizers such as lead, cadmium, and tin are also added to PVC to extend the life of some products, yet these metals are PBTs and neurotoxins for humans. While lead is no longer used in PVC water supply pipes, significant quantities of lead have been found in water flowing from PVC pipes already in use.[a]
Disposal—incineration	Disposal of PVC is a major environmental and human health issue, as an estimated 1.6 million tons are discarded each year with only a negligible amount recycled.[i] Incineration of PVC can release hydrogen chloride gas, dioxins, and heavy metals. The metals may react with the HCl to form metal chlorides, which are relatively difficult to remove from flue gases.[j] While incineration of waste is strictly regulated in the United States, the ash containing these chemicals is disposed of in landfills and can seep into groundwater.
Disposal—unregulated and accidental burning	Additionally, uncontrolled burning of PVC products in landfill fires, backyard trash piles, or building or car fires can release large amounts of dioxins into the air and soil.[e] The U.S. Green Building Council's TSAC report comparing several building materials with PVC states that the "risk of dioxin emission puts PVC consistently among the worst materials for human health impacts."[k] Prior to ignition at relatively low temperatures, PVC releases hydrogen chloride gas, which becomes hydrochloric acid, an extremely toxic and potentially deadly substance, on contact with moisture.[b]
Disposal—Landfills	In landfills, PVC will not break down easily. and leaching of toxins such as phthalate plasticizers or dioxins into soil and groundwater can pose a hazard, especially in landfills without liner protection.
Recycling	While PVC is technically recyclable, not much is as its chlorine content prevents commingling with other plastics and the wide variety of additives (e.g., plasticizers, UV inhibitors) in PVC that impart specific properties to the first product complicate the recycling of PVC products. The equipment required to recycle PVC and contain any harmful emissions released during the recycling process is expensive, so the infrastructure to collect and recycle PVC is not widely available. If a PVC product finds its way into a group of other plastics, it can contaminate the entire batch, rendering it unrecyclable. The Association of Postconsumer Plastic Recyclers discourages the use of PVC for plastic components because of its limited recyclability.[l]

[a]Thornton 2002

[b]ATSDR

[c]Steingraber 2004

[d]National Toxicology Program

[e]HBN Pharos Project

[f]Platt et al. 2005

[g]EPA 2003

[h]Tom Lent, personal communication, November 10, 2007

[i]U.S. EPA 2006b

[j]Demkin 1998

[k]U.S. Green Building Council 2007

[l]Association of Postconsumer Plastic Recyclers

Table 12–3 Embodied Energy and Carbon Emissions to Produce One Kilogram of Material*

Material (1 kg)	Embodied Energy (EE) (MJ)	Feedstock Energy (Included in EE Figures) (Mj)	Embodied Carbon (EC) (kg CO$_2$)	Comments
PVC, general	77.2	28.1	2.41	Based on the market average use of types of PVC in the European construction industry
PVC pipe	67.5	24.4	2.5	
PVC, injection molding	95.1	35.1	2.2	
High-density polyethylene (HDPE)	76.7	54.3	1.6	
HDPE pipe	84.4	55.1	2	
Low-density polyethylene (LDPE)	78.1	51.6	1.7	
General polyethylene	83.1	54.4	1.94	Based on average use of types of PE in European construction
ABS	95.3	48.6	3.1	
Nylon 6	120.5	38.6	5.5	
Polycarbonate	112.9	36.7	6	
Polypropylene, injection molding	115.1	54	3.9	
Expanded polystyrene	88.6	46.2	2.5	
Polyurethane	72.1	34.67	3	

*Assumptions and notes:

Figures are based on several records of EE and EC published for EU plastic products. It is assumed that figures for the United States would differ slightly; however, these figures can offer a useful snapshot comparison among plastic types.

Parameters are cradle to gate.

EE range is ± 30%.

The majority of records examined for these figures included feedstock energy.

Source: Adapted from Hammond and Jones 2006

plastic waste, especially since plastic packaging, used for a short time, is the greatest market segment. While the use phase of plastics in construction may be the longest of any plastic product category, the sheer volume of plastics in construction poses a huge disposal problem. With only a 5.7% recycling rate in 2005, the majority of plastics have a linear consumption pattern where products are used once, discarded, and disposed of in landfills or incinerators (U.S. EPA 2006b).

The characteristics of durability and resistance to decay that are desirable during the use phase make plastics problematic in disposal. They can take hundreds of years to break down in a landfill. The risk of toxic fugitive emissions during incineration renders this disposal method problematic for some plastics as well. Recycling may be the best method to deal with plastics at the end of their use phase; however, not all plastics are easily recycled and recycling plastics, with few exceptions, results in a "downcycled" product. Additives in plastics can be a concern in MSW landfills, as they can leach into the environment as plastics degrade. Plastics contribute 28% of all cadmium and 2%

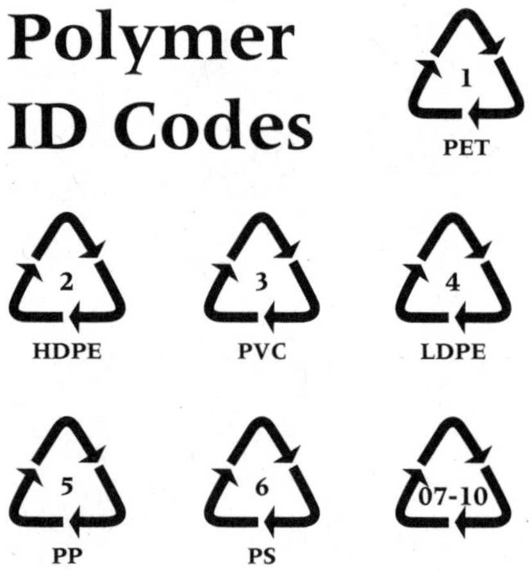

Polymer ID Codes

Figure 12-1.

The Society of the Plastics Industry, Inc. (SPI) developed a resin identification system to meet recyclers' needs for providing manufacturers with a consistent, uniform system that applies to plastic products nationwide. Products will either have the code printed on them or on the product packaging and literature. Products with code 3 should be avoided, as they are polyvinyl chloride. Items with a 7 are generally not recyclable. (Society of the Plastics Industry; Illustration by John Wiley & Sons)

of all lead found in MSW (U.S. EPA 2006a). A detailed discussion of plastics disposal methods follows descriptions of disposal options for the individual plastics later in the chapter.

Reducing Use of Plastics

The most sustainable waste management method for plastics is reduction at the source. Using less plastic and maximizing the useful life of plastic products will reduce the volume of plastic waste. Plastic packaging is commonly used for all types of site construction materials. As packaging has a very short life, plastic waste is created quickly. Specifying products with minimal packaging or whose manufacturers will take back and reuse/recycle the packaging can minimize plastic waste. Efforts to dematerialize packaging are increasing in Europe, as the EU has begun to require manufacturers to take back packaging and take steps to reduce the volume of packaging used (Azapagic et al. 2003).

Specifying plastic products that minimize use of resources in production and are easy to disassemble and recycle will minimize waste and resource use. Durability and appropriateness for the application will keep plastics in use longer, further minimizing waste. For example, PVC fencing panels appear to be an inexpensive, low-maintenance choice; however, in climates with extreme low and high temperatures, the PVC will weaken relatively quickly and may require replacement within a decade. A fence made from HDPE plastic lumber (often with 100% recycled content) may cost more, but

Table 12-4 Plastics in U.S. Municipal Solid Waste, 2005

Product Category Total Plastics in MSW, by Resin	Generation (Thousand Tons)	Recovery		Discards (Thousand Tons)
		(Thousand Tons)	(Percent of Generation)	
PET	2,860	540		2,320
HDPE	5,890	520		5,370
PVC	1,640			1,640
LDPE/LLDPE	6,450	190		6,260
PP	4,000	10		3,990
PS	2,590			2,590
Other resins	5,480	390		5,090
Total Plastics in MSW	**28,910**	**1,650**	**5.7%**	**27,260**

Some detail of recovery by resin omitted due to lack of data.

This table understates the recovery of plastics due to the dispersed nature of plastic recycling activities.

Source: U.S. EPA 2006b

some are guaranteed to last 50 years (Minnesota Pollution Control Agency 2006).

In some ways, the use of plastics can save energy resources as compared to other products. One study of packaging in the use phase concluded that the use of nonplastic packaging would increase overall packaging consumption by 291% by weight, with a corresponding increase in manufacturing energy of 108% and a 158% increase in volume of waste (Azapagic et al. 2003). These estimates do not include other phases such as raw material extraction and processing or post-consumer waste management. Transportation of comparatively lightweight plastics can also reduce fuel use.

REUSE AND RECYCLE PLASTICS

Reuse and/or recycling of plastics turns waste into resources for new products, conserving use of virgin fossil fuels and reducing the associated impacts of their extraction and processing. The strength and durability of plastics makes some products good candidates for reuse in new applications without recycling. Some manufacturers of plastic products will take back the product and reuse the component parts in new products. This remanufacturing process is gaining acceptance in the auto, electronic, and electrical industries (Azapagic et al. 2003). In the construction industry, manufacturer take-backs and remanufacture are just beginning in the furniture and carpet industries. Theoretically there are some products used in site construction that could be reused whole (e.g., plastic porous paving webs or plastic lumber); however, at the time of this printing no known manufacturing take-back programs exist for site construction products. Some products are undoubtedly reused within informal reuse structures.

Some obstacles to reuse of plastic products are as follows:

- **Weak material recovery structures.** As products are dispersed in the marketplace, it is difficult for a manufacturer to recover products for reuse. A solution to this dilemma is for manufacturers to lease their product to customers and take the product back at the end of its useful life. A successful example of this product-leasing structure is Xerox leasing machines to customers and taking the machines back

after their useful life is over and reusing some of the parts in new copiers. In the construction industry, some products are not taken back by the manufacturer, but by salvage yards that resell reclaimed products to new owners. However, these structures can be weak as well, since finding appropriate quantities and types of products can present a challenge.

- **Product design for reuse.** Reuse of plastic products, either in whole or part, is dependent on the design of the product and how easy it is to disassemble from its current installation. Some plastic products, such as fuse- or solvent-welded pipe, can't be disassembled without damage to the product. Nonpressurized HDPE pipe can potentially be reused if a compression band connection is used.

- **Customer perceptions.** The last major obstacle to plastics reuse is the perception of customers that they will be purchasing a product that is not brand-new. If the price of the product is substantially lower than a comparable new product, then the customer may be more likely to accept one that is used (Azapagic et al. 2003).

Plastics Recycling Processes

Plastics can be recycled multiple times to yield new polymeric materials and products. There are three ways to recycle plastics: mechanical recycling, chemical recycling, and energy recovery, also called waste to energy. Mechanical recycling and chemical recycling are called material recycling because they recycle plastics back into usable plastic or composite products. Energy recovery uses the energy produced from burning the plastics.

Mechanical recycling uses mechanical and physical means such as melting and reforming or grinding and extruding to transform waste plastics into new products. The plastics waste must be clean and homogeneous, which requires accurate sorting by type. This often presents a challenge, as obtaining clean homogeneous waste streams can increase recycling costs that are then passed on in increased product costs. For example, plastic lumber that is 100% HDPE is more expensive than plastic lumber that is made from mixed plastics. However, 100% HDPE is likely stronger, more durable, and can be recycled multiple times into new

HDPE products. Generally, most thermoplastics can be recycled; however, the recycling often results in a "downcycled" conversion to a lower-grade product. Most thermoset plastics can't be recycled; therefore reuse of their component parts is the best strategy.

Chemical recycling uses chemicals to break the polymers down into their chemical constituents and converts them into useful products such as monomers and/or basic chemicals. Chemical recycling processes are used for mixed plastics, which require less separation actions. Chemical recycling processes pose more risks to human and environmental health due to the heating of polymers and use of chemicals, as there is potential for release of fugitive emissions during recycling.

Energy recovery, where the caloric value of plastic products is recovered as energy, is another option for plastics in the waste stream that are not recyclable. Energy recovery can be achieved by direct incineration to generate steam, hot water, and/or electricity in waste-to-energy (WTE) plants. These WTE plants have controlled combustion with extensive air pollution controls and ash management systems in compliance with government regulations for air, water, and solid waste emissions. Concerns remain about both fugitive emissions and the rigorousness of federal emissions standards.

Polymers can also be incinerated directly in production processes, such as cement kilns, to replace other fuels. Emission controls are required for these plants as well; however, some fugitive emissions are most likely released. While energy recovery is the most downcycled recycling process, destroying the polymer, the majority of post-consumer plastics are disposed of in this way due to the challenges in collection for plastics recycling.

The two other methods of disposal of plastics are incineration without energy recovery and disposal in landfills. Today, the majority of plastics are disposed of in one of these ways. Incineration without energy recovery only reduces the volume of solid waste (as much as 90%); however, the energy-producing potential of fossil fuel–based polymers is lost. Concerns about fugitive emissions of dioxins, furans, heavy metals, and

other HAPs exist despite pollution control measures in incinerators. Some of these emissions are persistent bioaccumulative toxins. Disposal of ash from incineration in landfills can pose an environmental hazard, as these hazardous constituents can remain in the ash.

Disposal of plastics in landfills wastes valuable resources and consumes high volumes of space for products that will not easily decompose. Concerns also exist about leaching of toxins from plastics in unlined landfills or landfill fires.

The Plastics Recycling Industry

Given concerns about incineration and landfill disposal techniques, coupled with a limited supply of fossil fuels, worldwide efforts to recycle plastics are rapidly growing. These efforts are spurred in part by increasing legislation and voluntary incentives aimed at product manufacturers and the construction industry in the European Union and to a lesser degree in North America. EU directives require manufacturers to reduce packaging waste and recover, reuse, and recycle a percentage of their product after use. They also offer economic incentives for manufacturers, such as carbon taxes and tradable pollution permits, to take steps to recycle and reuse plastics waste (Azapagic et al. 2003).

In North America, more than 1,800 businesses are involved in recycling plastics, and construction and demolition (C&D) and curbside waste collection programs are growing but are still very limited (Association of Postconsumer Plastic Recyclers). Logistical problems in collection and separation still plague the plastics recycling industry and as a result, the plastics industry recycled only 5.7% of its product in 2005 (U.S. EPA 2006b). Projections for growth of plastics recycling in the United States estimate an annual increase of 3%. Recycling rates for plastics used in construction are far lower, primarily because of the low cost of C&D landfills and the relative light weight of plastics keeping landfill tipping fees based on weight low. Plastics recycling facilities for C&D waste are not consistently available in all regions.

SPECIFY RECYCLED-CONTENT CONSTRUCTION PRODUCTS

Despite relatively low plastic recycling rates, the large volume of plastics in the waste stream has resulted in

Table 12–5 Landscape Products Made from Recycled Plastic and Rubber

Product	Post-consumer Content EPA CPG Recommendations[a]	Total Recovered materials content EPA CPG Recommendation[a]	Materials and Comments
Decking	75%–100%	100%	HDPE and/or commingled plastics Most are a combination of post-consumer and recovered plastic materials. 50-year guarantee Nonstructural Recycled-content thresholds will exclude PVC products.
Composite decking	60%–100%	100%	HDPE and LDPE combined with waste wood fiber Can be painted and sanded Some can be used in structural applications.
Fencing	40%–60%	100%	Usually HDPE Recycled-content thresholds will exclude PVC products.
Timbers and posts, raised beds, retaining walls, and terracing	25%–100%	75%–100%	HDPE
Timbers and posts, raised beds, retaining walls, and terracing	50%	100%	Mixed plastics
Timbers and posts, raised beds, retaining walls, and terracing	75%	95%	HDPE/fiberglass
Timbers and posts, raised beds, retaining walls, and terracing	50%–100%	95%–100%	Other mixed resins and biocomposites
Edging	30%–100%	30%–100%	
Railings	75%–100%[b]	100%[b]	HDPE, commingled plastics, or composite lumber Recycled-content thresholds will exclude PVC products.
Park benches and picnic tables, plastic	90%–100%	100%	Plastic (single, HDPE, or mixed resins)
Park benches and picnic tables, plastic composites	50%–100%	100%	Plastic composites (HDPE and/or LDPE and/or composites mixed resins combined with waste wood fiber or fiberglass)
Construction/snow fencing	60%–100%	90%–100%	HDPE

Continued

Table 12–5 Landscape Products Made from Recycled Plastic and Rubber *(Continued)*

Product	Post-consumer Content EPA CPG Recommendations[a]	Total Recovered materials content EPA CPG Recommendation[a]	Materials and Comments
Playground equipment, plastic	90%–100%	100%	Plastic (mixed resins or HDPE)
			U.S. Consumer Product Safety Commission (CPSC) Publication No. 325 and ASTM standard F-1487–95
Playground equipment, plastic composites	50%–75%	95%–100%	Plastic composites (HDPE and/or LDPE and/or mixed resins combined with waste wood fiber or fiberglass)
			U.S. Consumer Product Safety Commission (CPSC) Publication No. 325 and ASTM standard F-1487–95
Playground surfaces	90%–100%	—	Plastic or rubber
			See also ASTM specification F1292.
Running tracks	90%–100%	—	Plastic or rubber
Bike racks	100%	100%	HDPE
Garden hoses	60%–65%		Rubber and/or plastic
			See also ASTM D3901 Consumer Specification for Garden Hose and Green Seal GC-2: Watering Hoses
Soaker hoses	60%–70%		Rubber and/or plastic
			See also Green Seal GC-2: Watering Hoses
Patio blocks, rubber	90%–100%	—	Rubber or rubber blends
			Made from airplane and truck tires
Patio blocks, plastic	—	90%–100%	Plastic or plastic blends
Tree grates	100%		Post-consumer high-density polyethylene (HDPE)
			Lighter than steel tree grates
			Often require support by aggregate under grate
Tree guards	100%		Post-consumer high-density polyethylene (HDPE)
			Some combine HDPE and LDPE.
			Some products have much lower recycled-content ranges.
Tree root barriers	26%–50%		Recycled polypropylene
Bollards	95%–100%		Post-consumer polyethylene materials
			HDPE, LLDPE, and LDPE
			The weatherproof, rot-proof bollards are lighter than metal and can be longer lasting than wood.

Table 12–5 Landscape Products Made from Recycled Plastic and Rubber *(Continued)*

Product	Post-consumer Content EPA CPG Recommendations[a]	Total Recovered materials content EPA CPG Recommendation[a]	Materials and Comments
Parking stops		100%	Plastic and/or rubber
Nonpressure pipe	100%	100%	HDPE
Nonpressure pipe	5%–15%	25%–100%	PVC
			See also ASTM F1960, F1732, and others
Sound barriers	75%	75%	

[a]U.S. EPA Comprehensive Procurement Guidelines
[b]CIWMB

the development of many construction products with recycled plastic content. Growth of the LEED system, which offers points for use of recycled-content products, state waste reduction mandates, and federal encouragement to "buy recycled," have contributed to the huge growth in recycled plastic products industries.

"Greening" Plastics Specifications and Product Selection

- Only specify plastic products that number each component of the product. Avoid use of number 3, PVC. HDPE is number 2, LDPE is number 4, and ABS is ABS.

- Look for products with recycled-content minimums of 25% post-consumer or 40% total recycled content. Ideal recycled content is much higher. Refer to the EPA's Comprehensive Procurement Guidelines for percentages by product.

- Carefully examine product literature for composite materials, especially in fencing, decking, and artificial turf, as many products contain some PVC or vinyl.

- Tell suppliers and manufacturers of products containing PVC why you are not specifying their product. Manufacturers like to be aware of designers' needs and values, hence all the ads for "green" products that have even the smallest recycled content.

The U.S. EPA has developed Comprehensive Procurement Guidelines (CPG) for public agency purchasing that define recommended recycled-content percentages for a wide variety of products. These guidelines, based on actual recycled-content products available in the industry, break recycled content down into the categories of "post-consumer recovered content" and "total recovered content."

Post-consumer recovered content reflects "a material or finished product that has served its intended use and has been diverted or recovered from waste destined for disposal, having completed its life as a consumer item."

Recovered materials, which include post-consumer materials, are defined as "waste materials and byproducts that have been recovered or diverted from solid waste, but does not include materials and byproducts generated from, and commonly reused within, an original manufacturing process."

Table 12–5 lists common site construction materials with recycled plastic content. For each material, CPG-recommended recycled-content percentages are given. Where the CPG guidelines do not address a particular product, industry ranges are given based on information on recycled-content products recommended by the California Integrated Waste Management Board's (CIWMB) *Recycled-Content Products Directory.*

Table 12–6 Common Plastic Site Products and Their "Greener" Alternatives

Product/Application and Common Plastics Used	Alternatives with Fewer Environmental and Human Health Impacts*
Irrigation pipe, pressurized (PVC, PE, ABS)	HDPE fuse weld produces stronger pipe, but requires special joining equipment for pressurized lines. Metallocene polyolefins are in development.
Irrigation pipe, non-pressurized (PVC)	HDPE, PEX
Irrigation pipe connectors (PVC)	HDPE, PE widely available
Irrigation drip lines and soaker hoses (PVC, HDPE)	HDPE widely available
Garden hoses (PVC)	PVC substitutes are difficult to locate. Some vinyl hoses have recycled rubber content (around 50%). PP
Storm water pipe (PVC, concrete)	HDPE fuse weld produces stronger pipe, but requires special equipment for joining. Growing market
Wastewater pipe (PVC, concrete)	HDPE, concrete, vitrified clay Many codes require PVC.
Drain structures (PVC, concrete)	Concrete
Drainage mats (HDPE)	HDPE
Conduit (PVC)	HDPE, steel
Wiring (PVC)	Polyethylene (only a few products available)
Junction boxes (PVC, steel)	HDPE, steel
Downspout extensions (PVC)	HDPE
Root barriers (PVC)	HDPE
Tree guards (PVC, steel)	HDPE, steel
Lawn edging (HDPE, steel, aluminum, PVC)	HDPE, steel, aluminum
Geotextiles (PVC, LDPE, PP)	LDPE, PP
Geomembranes/pond liners (PVC, LDPE, PP)	LDPE, PP
Artificial turf (PP, PVC is small component)	Ask manufacturers if their product contains PVC; if so, avoid it.
Coated wire mesh fencing (PVC, polyester coating)	Polyester coating is more durable.
Fencing, gates, trellises, and lattice (PVC)	HDPE, PE, composite lumber, wood, bamboo, willow Completely comparable alternatives are hard to find. Most alternatives don't come preassembled like PVC products, but some can be worked like wood. PVC is still the least expensive.

Table 12–6 Common Plastic Site Products and Their "Greener" Alternatives *(Continued)*

Product/Application and Common Plastics Used	Alternatives with Fewer Environmental and Human Health Impacts*econom
Decking (PVC, HDPE, composite lumber)	HDPE, composite lumber PVC decking market is rapidly growing and economic costs may be lower.
Railings (PVC—preassembled panels, HDPE)	HDPE, PE, composite lumber Completely comparable alternatives are hard to find. Most alternatives don't come preassembled like PVC products, but some can be worked like wood. PVC is still the least expensive.
Docks (HDPE, PVC, composite lumber—some contain fiberglass)	HDPE, PE, composite lumber with wood fiber (Fiberglass can be a mechanical irritant to skin.)
Outdoor furniture (PVC, metal, some HDPE)	Metal, HDPE
Umbrella fabric (PVC, LDPE, PP, nylon)	LDPE, PP, nylon
Pool and grill covers (PVC)	PP, LDPE PVC substitutes are difficult to locate.
Signs (variety of materials, including PVC)	Read manufacturer's literature carefully for composite material content; avoid PVC content.

*Note: These alternatives are comparable in performance. In some cases the cost may be higher.

Sources: EBN 2001; Harvie and Lent 2002; HBN 2005; U.S. EPA Comprehensive Procurement Guidelines; CIWMB

Plastic Pipe and Tubing

Plastics are one of the most common materials used in piping applications. They are inexpensive, lightweight, relatively durable, easy to install, and can be rigid or flexible as required. While HDPE, PEX, and ABS are used, PVC is the most common pipe material, and in many cases the industry standard for multiple site applications. PVC pipe is used for water lines that are pressurized, as it has good tensile strength. It is rigid, but when flexibility is needed, plasticizers can be added to create flexible pipe. It is lightweight in comparison with cast iron or other metals. The glue fitting joinery is simple (although it poses health risks in construction), and PVC elbows and other fittings are readily available. It is inexpensive, and most importantly, it is the industry standard for many pipe applications, holding firm in countless standard specs for both public agencies and private firms.

While PVC pipe offers many performance benefits, as discussed above it poses many human and environmental health risks, so specifying alternatives to PVC should be a high priority when designing sustainable sites. In some piping applications alternatives to PVC can offer many of the same benefits and are easily used. In other applications, PVC pipe may be required by code, or contractors may not be equipped to install alternative material pipes.

High-density polyethylene (HDPE) is a good substitute for PVC pipe applications such as irrigation pipe, both pressurized and nonpressurized; sewer pipe; storm water drainage pipe; and wastewater pipe (Harvie and Lent 2002). It is a more benign plastic as it is chlorine-free, requires fewer additives, and is easily recycled. PVC is more resistant to combustion, but will smolder, releasing toxic hydrochloric gases before combustion. HDPE has a higher abrasion and chemical resistance than PVC and is less susceptible to surge shocks since it is more flexible.

Cross-linked polyethylene (PEX) is a good substitute for PVC in pipe situations that might be exposed to higher-temperature liquids, such as water supply pipe, sewer pipe, drainage pipe, or drain, waste, vent pipe (DWV). PEX tubing is lightweight, flexible, durable, and able to withstand temperatures up to 200°F (Partnership for Advancing Technology in Housing [PATH]).

Acrylonitrile butadiene styrene (ABS) pipe is not chlorinated, but it contains hazardous constituents resulting in hazardous by-products. It is difficult to recycle and is only marginally better than PVC (Harvie and Lent 2002).

Both HDPE and PEX pipe are flexible, so they are delivered to the site in long rolls as opposed to the rigid, shorter lengths of PVC. The longer lengths mean that there are fewer fittings, connections, and elbows than PVC, and fewer places that may leak. Labor may also be reduced with fewer connections. HDPE and PEX can be used in some trenchless pipe applications, while PVC cannot. Also, the flexibility of HDPE results in less ruptures from digging and construction around the pipes than PVC (Harvie and Lent 2002).

High-density polyethylene (HDPE) and cross-linked polyethylene (PEX) are good PVC piping alternatives for some pipe and conduit applications; however, using them can be challenging because they are not the industry standard in the United States. Contractors may resist use of these alternatives because they are not familiar with them. While material costs are lower, installed costs of HDPE piping can be higher because contractors need to use special welding equipment to join pressurized pipes. The nonpressurized HDPE drain lines use simple bell and spigot/slip fittings that don't require the fusing equipment. PEX fittings are available in both mechanical compression and crimping styles, depending on the application and manufacturer.

HDPE pipe is more commonly used in storm water applications. HDPE is also used for underground storm water retention structures. In wastewater applications, PVC is often required by codes because of its corrosion resistance to hydrogen sulfide, its durability, and economics.

In irrigation applications, HDPE and PEX are comparable alternatives to PVC for all irrigation components. In pressurized applications, a good substitute to PVC is HDPE for reasons discussed above. Drip irrigation components and soaker hoses can also be found in HDPE.

Plastic and Composite Lumber

The environmental concerns of forest overharvesting, the toxicity risks of lumber pressure-treatment methods, and plastic waste disposal problems combined with the performance and maintenance concerns of exterior use of wood lumber have resulted in rapid growth of the plastic lumber market. And, as interest in plastic lumber and composites as a viable wood substitute in some applications has grown, improvements over early products have been made in mechanical properties and performance. Price has decreased and availability has increased. In addition, ASTM test procedures have been developed for testing and standardizing performance properties of plastic lumber, making product comparison, selection, and specification clearer (Robbins 2005).

Plastic lumber is nominally sized, resin-based lumber available in both solid and hollow profiles that can be substituted for wood in some applications. Plastic lumber usually has a minimum of 50% plastic content by weight, and some lumber incorporates additional materials such as fiberglass. Plastic lumber is capable of incorporating 100% recycled materials; however, recycled content varies widely among plastic lumber brands.

Plastic Lumber

There are two types of plastic lumber available:

Single-resin plastic lumber is made from one type of plastic, usually HDPE or PVC. Use of only one type of plastic generally leads to a more consistently performing product. HDPE plastic lumber usually has a relatively high recycled content. PVC plastic lumber is almost entirely comprised of virgin material as the recycling market for PVC is extremely limited. As HDPE plastic lumber is not mixed with other resins, it can be recycled into new products after its useful life; however, recycling prospects for PVC are lower due to the scarcity of markets. Costs of separation and sorting during recycling processes make some single-plastic recycled products more expensive than plastic lumber made from commingled plastics or biocomposite products.

Commingled plastic lumber is made with two or more plastics that are commingled into one product. It is generally less expensive than purified plastic lumber. However, differing plastic properties may make the finished product more variable in performance, as different resins can have different tolerances for heat, chemicals, and stresses. Both types of plastic lumber lack the stiffness and strength of wood.

Composite Lumber
Composite lumber is produced by blending other materials, such as fiberglass or wood waste (e.g., sawdust and other cellulose-based fiber fillers such as peanut hulls, bamboo, straw, or digestate), with recycled plastics to form a composite product. Materials and mix proportions vary widely. If the biological content is greater than 50%, ASTM classifies it as biocomposite lumber. The addition of materials other than plastic can provide some reinforcing to the plastic and allows use in structural applications. Mixing resins (a synthetic material) with wood or glass fibers renders the composite lumber nonrecyclable.

Figure 12–2.
Solid 100% recycled HDPE plastic lumber is available in a variety of colors, some of which have a faux wood grain. This plastic lumber, made from recycled milk and water bottles, is ideal for deck boards because it is decay resistant; however, it is generally not recommended for structural applications. (Photo from Casual Living Products Unlimited, LLC)

The State of the Plastic and Plastic Composite Lumber Industry

In 2004, the North American market for wood- and natural-fiber plastic composites and plastic lumber was estimated at 2.2 billion pounds. With an average annual growth rate of 9.5%, the industry is expected to reach 3.6 billion pounds in 2009. This recent rapid growth may be partially due to the 2003 phaseout of CCA lumber preservative treatments for most uses.

Some recent trends (Robbins 2005):

- Biocomposites are the fastest-growing segment of the plastic lumber industry, comprising a large portion of the total market. Biocomposites combine wood or other biological materials (e.g., flax, rice hulls) within a thermoplastic matrix. These materials are less expensive than pure HDPE products, as the cost of the plastic is higher.
- The PVC decking industry has grown rapidly in the past few years, replacing more expensive HDPE decking materials.
- Fiberglass-reinforced plastic lumber has grown slowly, but shows promise as a product with structural capabilities that some other products in the industry do not have.

Biocomposites combine wood waste or other biological materials, such as flax or rice hulls, within a thermoplastic matrix, often LDPE.

Fiberglass-reinforced lumber is a combination of HDPE reinforced with fiberglass. It offers better strength and stiffness and is often better suited for structural applications. EPA comprehensive procurement guidelines for fiberglass-reinforced lumber recommend 75% post-consumer content and a total of 95% total recovered material content (U.S. EPA CPG).

ENVIRONMENTAL IMPACT CONSIDERATIONS OF PLASTIC AND COMPOSITE LUMBER

It is important to note that not all plastic lumber can be considered a "green" material. Environmental impacts

Table 12–7 Plastics Recycling Rates and Use in Plastic Lumber Applications

Plastic	Common Uses of Material	Generation (Thousand Tons)	Recovery (Thousand Tons)	Recovery (Percent of Generation)	End Use in Plastic Lumber (Thousand Tons)
HDPE	Containers for milk, juice, water, laundry detergent; margarine tubs; cereal box liners; trash and retail bags	4,830	420	8.7	33.6
LDPE	Grocery bags, bread bags, frozen food bags, sandwich bags, produce bags, trash can liners	5,740	150	2.6	108.8
PET	Soft drink, juice, and cooking oil bottles; peanut butter and salad dressing bottles; oven-safe food trays	2,900	430	17.3	17.2

Sources: APC 2007; U.S. EPA 2006b

vary widely depending on materials used, recycled content, and potential for recycling after use.

Materials for plastic lumber. Most plastic lumber products are made from high- and low-density polyethylenes (HDPE and LDPE), but PVC plastic lumber use is growing, as snap-together connections and prefabricated structures such as fence panels offer ease of construction. Other plastic lumber is made from a mix of resins collected from post-consumer recycling programs.

Generally, plastic lumber products made from polyethylenes (HDPE and LDPE) are preferred, given the fewer chemical hazards associated with their manufacture and disposal. PVC and polystyrene pose more risks to human and environmental health (refer to the plastic resin discussions earlier in this chapter).

Fiberglass is added to some plastic lumber products for reinforcing and increased load-bearing abilities. Fiberglass can be a skin irritant, and surface fiberglass should be removed from structures where human or animal skin will contact the material (Platt et al. 2005). Fiberglass, affecting the lungs in a similar but lesser way than asbestos, has been linked to pulmonary disease.

Plastic lumber also can contain additives—such as colorants, coupling agents, stabilizers, blowing agents, reinforcing agents, foaming agents, and lubricants—to help tailor the end product to the target area of application (Platt et al. 2005). Some of these additives can pose health and environmental risks.

Recycled content quantities of plastic and composite lumbers vary widely from zero recycled content to 100% recycled content. Products with high recycled content, particularly post-consumer recycled content, should be favored to minimize virgin resource use and reduce plastic waste. Plastic lumber made from HDPE and LDPE generally has a higher recycled content than plastic lumber made from PVC or composite plastic lumber. Most PVC products contain no post-consumer recycled content and low total recycled content. Composite products that contain post-industrial wood waste from wood processing generally incorporate 50%–100% recycled content. Plastics that incorporate auto-shredder fluff should be avoided because they may contain heavy metals and other toxic chemicals (Platt et al. 2005).

End-of-life recyclability is an important consideration when specifying a plastic lumber product. Plastic lumber is a durable product and is expected to have a long use life; however, if a product is not recyclable, it will eventually contribute to the plastic waste stream and wind up in a landfill or incinerator. Using recycled con-

Table 12–8 Preferability, Health Issues, and Recyclability of Plastic and Composite Lumber Materials

	Type of Plastic	Other Common Applications	Health Issues	Recyclability
Prefer	High-density polyethylene (HDPE)	Milk and water jugs, detergent containers, trash bags	HDPE does not require toxic plasticizers such as phthalates. Some applications use flame-retardant additives, which if brominated are toxic.	High potential for mechanical recycling. HDPE bottles are collected in most curbside recycling programs. In 2001, 28% of HDPE milk and water bottles were recycled.
	Low-density polyethylene (LDPE)	Dry-cleaning, trash, produce, and bread bags; shrink-wrap; containers for dairy products	LDPE does not require toxic plasticizers such as phthalates. Some applications use flame-retardant additives, which if brominated are toxic.	Technically it can be recycled, but actual recycling levels are under 3%. Infrastructure of collection of LDPE wrap and bags is not well developed.
	Polystyrene (PS)	Foam insulation, packaging peanuts, plastic utensils, meat trays, egg cartons, take-out containers, single-use disposable cups	PS production uses benzene (a known human carcinogen), styrene, and butadiene-1,3 (suspected human carcinogenic substances). Styrene is a neurotoxin and is known to be toxic to the reproductive system. PS releases toxic chemicals when burned.	Recycling level is negligible, less than 1%.
Avoid	Polyvinyl chloride (PVC or vinyl)	Most PVC is used in building materials such as pipes, siding, membrane roofing, flooring, and wind frames, as well as in other consumer products such as shower curtains, beach balls, and credit cards.	PVC is made from the vinyl chloride monomer, a known human carcinogen. PVC has a high chlorine and additive content. Toxic additives such as phthalate softeners are not bound to the plastic and leach out. PVC releases dioxin and other persistent organic pollutants during its manufacture and disposal.	Recycling level is negligible. At trace quantities, PVC can interfere with the recycling of other resins, such as HDPE and polyethylene terephthalate (PET) used in soda and water bottles.

Source: Platt et al. 2005

tent and recyclable plastic lumber that can be part of a closed-loop system will minimize resource use and waste for multiple generations of use.

Specifying plastic lumber made from a single plastic resin (usually HDPE) will maximize the recyclability of the product. Plastic lumber made from 100% mixed resins is more difficult to recycle, as there are limited markets for it, and if it is recycled it will be downcycled into a lesser product. Composite lumber made with fiberglass, PVC, or wood fibers is most likely not recyclable since different materials are permanently mixed in one product. Manufacturers of the product may take

it back for reuse in new products, but the prospects for this are very limited and there is some question about the strength properties of the material after being in use for several years (PATH).

PERFORMANCE PROPERTIES OF PLASTIC LUMBER

Like environmental impacts, performance characteristics of plastic and composite lumber can vary widely, and performance is determined by material composition and product shape. ASTM developed test methods that have made it clearer to identify and measure performance properties among plastic lumber types. Table 12–9 discusses some basic performance properties as they compare among types of plastic and composite lumber, and with wood.

Plastic lumber is available in hollow, solid, and structural solid grades. Hollow-grade plastic lumber can be used for light-load applications such as low-load deck surfaces, fences, and deck rails. Solid-grade plastic lumber, heavier than hollow grade, is used for medium-load deck surfaces, benches, picnic tables, planters, and fences. Structural-grade plastic lumber is usually composite lumber with fiberglass or wood fiber that provides reinforcing and reduces expansion and contraction of the product.

COSTS OF PLASTIC LUMBER

Costs of plastic and composite lumber are generally higher than competing wood lumber materials; however, when maintenance and life-cycle costs are factored in, plastic and composites are less expensive. An examination of maintenance costs for an 800-square-foot deck found that after five years a cedar deck will cost $2,000 more and a pressure-treated deck will cost $900 more than a comparable plastic lumber deck. Treated and untreated wood requires the yearly or biyearly application of sealants to prevent degradation.

The EPA Greenscapes program offers a decking cost calculator that compares the cost of building a new deck

Table 12–9 Properties of Plastic and Composite Lumber

Property	Plastic Lumber Characteristics	Composite Lumber Characteristics
Thermal performance, creep, and deflection	The most significant difference between wood and plastic lumber is sensitivity to higher temperatures. Plastic lumber's structural behavior is different when it is warm than when it is cold. When warm, it has a higher flex modulus than wood and it can be susceptible to creep (bending or sagging) under heavy loads and high temperatures. Spacing of joists with 1 × 6 plastic lumber deck boards may need to be closer together (e.g., 12 inches oc) than with wood lumber (e.g., 16 inches or 24 inches oc). PVC lumber can become brittle at lower temperatures.	Composite lumber also performs differently than wood at higher temperatures and exhibits similar, but less extreme, thermal behavior as plastic lumber.
Expansion and contraction	Plastic lumber has a relatively high rate of expansion and contraction, necessitating connections that accommodate this behavior. The average rate of expansion and contraction is one-fourth inch per eight-foot length with a 50° temperature change. One supplier offers the following formula for calculating expansion across the length of a member: .00007 × (length of board in inches) × (°F of temperature change) = dimension of expansion or contraction in length.	Composite lumber generally has a lower rate of expansion and contraction, but is still higher than wood lumber.
Structural capabilities	Not as structurally strong as wood—joist spacing may need to be closer together for plastic lumber decking.	Composites are usually stronger than plastic lumber and are often available in structural grades. Joist spacing with some composite decking can be as much as 24-inch oc.
Density and weight	Plastic lumber is heavier than wood of the same dimensions, resulting in an increased dead load for some structures. Hollow profiles and foaming agents decrease the weight of plastic lumber.	Composite lumber is heavier than wood of the same dimensions, resulting in an increased dead load for some structures. Hollow profiles and foaming agents decrease the weight of composite lumber.
Weathering and UV exposure	While surface color of plastic lumber can fade slightly, UV rays do not degrade the mechanical properties of plastic lumber. Plastic lumber has very low moisture absorption. Because of its resistance to decay, plastic lumber is good in ground contact applications and marine environments.	While surface color of composite lumber can fade slightly, UV rays do not degrade the mechanical properties of composite lumber. Composite lumber has very low moisture absorption, although some with wood fiber may need to be sealed. Because of its resistance to decay, composite lumber is good in ground contact applications and marine environments.

Continued

Table 12–9 Properties of Plastic and Composite Lumber *(Continued)*

Property	Plastic Lumber Characteristics	Composite Lumber Characteristics
Durability	Plastic lumber is quite durable, with a range of guarantees from ten years to a lifetime. Most will not splinter or peel. Some warping can occur with some 100% plastic lumber; however, improved properties may lessen the chance that this will happen. Plastic lumber has good stain resistance, as it is relatively nonporous. Graffiti is relatively easily removed from plastic lumber. Solvents will remove paint and pens, and plastic lumber can be sanded to remove additional marks. A heat iron can be used to remove deep etching.	Composite lumber is quite durable, with a range of guarantees from ten years to a lifetime. Most will not splinter or peel. Composite lumber has good stain resistance, as it is relatively nonporous. Graffiti is relatively easily removed from composite lumber. Solvents will remove paint and pens, and plastic lumber can be sanded to remove additional marks.
Color	Plastic lumber is integrally colored and available in a very wide variety of colors. It does not require paint or stain. Some colors of plastic lumber may fade with continuous UV exposure. This will be most obvious with brighter or more intense colors, and earth tones will fade less. Some plastic lumber contains stabilized UV-graded pigments; however, some fading can still occur.	Most composite lumber is integrally colored and available in a very wide variety of colors. It does not require paint or stain. Some composite lumber can be painted if so desired. Some colors of composite lumber may fade with continuous UV exposure. This will be most obvious with brighter or more intense colors, and earth tones will fade less.
Insect resistance	Plastic lumber is resistant to insects (e.g., termites and marine borers) and decay.	Composite lumber is resistant to insects (e.g., termites and marine borers) and decay.
Constructability	Most plastic lumber can be cut and shaped, and structures fabricated, with standard woodworking tools. Nails can be used, but expansion may loosen joints, so screws and bolts are recommended. Some plastic lumber brands require a fastener system that is proprietary. Plastic lumber profiles can be different from standard lumber, although standard dimensions are usually consistent. Hollow profiles will need end pieces to cover the profiles from the end. Some PVC decking and rails can't be field cut. The deck and rails need to be designed to existing modular sizes. Cellular PVC lumber profiles can be welded like PVC pipe or cut, milled, and fastened like wood.	Some composite lumber can be cut and shaped, and structures fabricated, with standard woodworking tools. Nails can be used, but expansion may loosen joints, so screws and bolts are recommended. Some composite lumber brands require a fastener system that is proprietary. Composite lumber profiles can be different from standard lumber, although standard dimensions are usually consistent. Hollow profiles will need end pieces to cover the profiles from the end. Some composite decking and rails can't be field cut. The deck and rails need to be designed to existing modular sizes.

Table 12–9 Properties of Plastic and Composite Lumber *(Continued)*

Property	Plastic Lumber Characteristics	Composite Lumber Characteristics
Toxicity	As plastic lumber is decay and insect resistant, it does not require treatment with toxic heavy metals such as copper, chromium, or arsenate as does wood for exterior applications. HDPE plastic lumber is relatively nontoxic to humans and aquatic organisms, so it is good in ground contact applications and marine environments. Plastic lumber made from PVC has negative associated health and environmental impacts as discussed above.	As composite lumber is decay and insect resistant, it does not require treatment with toxic heavy metals such as copper, chromium, or arsenate as does wood for exterior applications. Composite lumber is relatively nontoxic to humans and aquatic organisms, so it is good in ground contact applications and marine environments. Composite lumber with PVC content has negative associated health and environmental impacts as discussed above.
Maintenance	Plastic lumber structures require relatively little maintenance as compared with wood lumber, which must be sealed, stained, or painted every few years.	Composite lumber structures require relatively little maintenance as compared with wood lumber, which must be sealed, stained, or painted every few years.
Slip resistance	There is limited data on the slip resistance and coefficient of friction of plastic lumber as compared to wood lumber. Varying conditions such as shoe sole type and wet or dry surfaces will produce different effects. Anecdotal evidence suggests that plastic lumber can be more slippery than wood. Some plastic decking is textured with imitation wood grain or other deformations to aid slip resistance.	There is limited data on the slip resistance and coefficient of friction of composite lumber as compared to wood lumber. Varying conditions such as shoe sole type and wet or dry surfaces will produce different effects. Anecdotal evidence suggests that composite lumber can be more slippery than wood. Some composite decking is textured with imitation wood grain or other deformations to aid slip resistance.
Flammability	Plastic lumber is relatively flame resistant. PVC is more resistant to combustion, but will smolder, releasing toxic hydrochloric gases before combustion.	Composite lumber is relatively flame resistant. PVC is more resistant to combustion, but will smolder, releasing toxic hydrochloric gases before combustion.

Sources: ASTM D6662; ASTM D7032; PATH; Plastic Lumber Yard; Platt et al. 2005; U.S. EPA Greenscapes; Winterbottom 1995

with plastic or composite lumber with the cost of building a wood lumber deck. The calculator offers life-cycle comparisons of many types of plastic, composite, and wood lumber. Average prices can be used, or users can plug in their own specific prices. Table 12–10 demonstrates a cost comparison using the EPA Greenscapes Decking Cost Calculator (U.S. EPA Greenscapes).

PLASTIC FENCES, GATES, AND TRELLISES

Use of PVC fencing and railings is a rapidly expanding market, as they are inexpensive, don't require painting or much maintenance, and come preassembled in panels that are quick and simple to install. There is also a wide variety of arbors, gazebos, lattice, and gates that are quick and easy to snap together.

There is no one product that can be a perfect substitute for PVC fencing and landscape structures, offering the range of shapes and ornamentation and ease of construction that vinyl fencing provides. Plastic lumber made from HDPE or composite materials are widely available alternatives. Polyethylene-coated composite lumber and hollow HDPE fencing and decking products, very similar to vinyl, are manufactured by only a few companies but are gaining a share of the market. Manufacturers claim that these products will last longer than

Figure 12–3.
Composite lumber is made with a combination of wood fiber, often wood waste, or fiberglass and plastic. Some composite lumber is made from all virgin materials; others contain some recycled content. Look for products with high recycled content and avoid composites with PVC content. Some composite lumber is appropriate for use in structural applications. It is often sold in hollow sections because of its weight. (Photo from RENEW Plastics)

PVC, which is susceptible to failure in extreme cold temperatures and is said to lose strength as it ages. These products can also be cut and joined in a manner similar to wood, whereas PVC has special connections that accommodate its high thermal expansion and contraction. The hollow HDPE products have a thicker wall, making the product stronger and more durable. Some companies offer both vinyl and HDPE fence, gate, and decking products, so careful examination of the product literature is critical.

Vinyl-coated chain-link fencing offers a range of colors and weather protection for metal fences. An alternative material is a polyester powder coating that is electrostatically applied to the chain link. While the polyester powder coating is not without environmental impacts, it still appears to be less harmful than vinyl. Some manufacturers offer both options and will guarantee the vinyl coating for twelve years and the polyester coating for fifteen years.

Table 12–10 Decking Alternatives Cost Analysis for a 600-square-foot Deck

Deck Material	Initial Cost	Cost of Maintenance (annual)	Three-year Cost	Ten-year Cost	Average Annual Cost over Lifetime
Recycled HDPE plastic lumber	$6,551	$0.00	$6,551	$6,551	$282
Recycled plastic/wood composite	$5,121	$0.00	$5,121	$5,121	$219
Cedar/redwood	$5,745	$499	$7,242	$11,637	$1,093
Pressure-treated southern yellow pine	$4,029	$499	$5,526	$9,921	$961

Source: Adapted from U.S. EPA Greenscapes

Table 12–11 ASTM Standards Related to Plastic and Composite Lumber

D6108	Standard Test Method for Compressive Properties of Plastic Lumber and Shapes
D6109	Standard Test Method for Flexural Properties of Unreinforced and Reinforced Plastic Lumber and Related Products
D6111	Standard Test Method for Bulk Density and Specific Gravity of Plastic Lumber and Shapes by Displacement
D6112	Standard Test Methods for Compressive and Flexural Creep and Creep-Rupture of Plastic Lumber and Shapes
D6117	Standard Test Methods for Mechanical Fasteners in Plastic Lumber and Shapes
D6341	Standard Test Method for Determination of the Linear Coefficient of Thermal Expansion of Plastic Lumber and Plastic Lumber Shapes between 30°F and 140°F (34.4°C and 60°C)
D6435	Standard Test Method for Shear Properties of Plastic Lumber and Plastic Lumber Shapes
D6662	Standard Specification for Polyolefin-Based Outdoor Structural-Grade Plastic Lumber
D7031	Standard Guide for Evaluating Mechanical and Physical Properties of Wood-Plastic Composite Products
D7032	Standard Specification for Establishing Performance Ratings for Wood-Plastic Composite Deck Boards and Guardrail Systems (Guards or Handrails)

Figure 12–4.

This composite lumber deck with high recycled content at the Shure, Inc., Prairie Garden in Niles, Illinois, emulates the movement of water as it traverses a series of rain garden cells at the facility. (Photo © Conservation Design Forum, 2008. All rights reserved. www.cdfinc.com)

Table 12–12 BEES Comparison of Cedar and Vinyl Siding

Impact[a]	Units	Cedar Siding[b]	Vinyl Siding[b]
Embodied energy by fuel renewability	Nonrenewable energy (MJ/unit)	12.20	27.57
	Renewable energy (MJ/unit)	24.50	0.66
Acidification	Mg H+ equivalents	241.56	869.90
Criteria air pollutants	micro DALY (disability-adjusted life years)	0.09	0.24
Ecological toxicity	g 2,4-D (2,4-dichlorophenoxy-acetic acid) equivalents	2.45	5.83
Eutrophication	g N (nitrogen) equivalents	0.53	0.19
Fossil fuel depletion	MJ (megajoules)	1.59	3.67
Global warming	g CO_2 equivalents	726.88	1,107.93
Habitat alteration	Threatened & endangered species/unit	0.00	0.00
Indoor air quality	g VOC	0.00	0.00
Ozone depletion	g CFC-11 equivalents	0.00	0.00
Smog	g NO_x equivalents	3.58	3.49
Water intake	Liters	7.27	0.22
Human health	g C_7H_8 (toluene) equivalents	51,369.51	390,692.18
Economic performance[a]	**Present value $**	**34.40**	**15.60**
Environmental performance[a]	**Weighted score (EPA weights)**	**7.70**	**42.30**

[a]Note: In all values, including overall performance, lower values are better.

[b]Assumptions (see BEES Reference Guide for more detailed information on assumptions):

The functional unit for both products is 0.09 m² (1 ft.²) of material.

Transport from manufacturing to use for both products is 500 miles.

Cedar siding beveled 1.3 cm (½ in.) thick and 15 cm (6 in.) wide is studied. Cedar siding is assumed to be installed with galvanized nails 41 cm (16 in.) on center and finished with one coat of primer and two coats of stain. Stain is reapplied every ten years.

Horizontal vinyl siding 0.107 cm (0.042 in.) thick and 23 cm (9 in.) wide installed with galvanized nail fasteners is studied. The nails are assumed to be placed 41 cm (16 in.) on center.

Source: National Institute of Standards and Technology 2006

BEES 4.0 Comparison of Cedar and Vinyl Siding

While cedar and vinyl siding are not generally used in site structures, the comparison of the above materials offers a useful, if limited, snapshot comparison of potential decking materials. Ideally, BEES would offer a comparison between wood decking, plastic lumber decking, and composite decking or a comparison between wood structural lumber and composite structural lumber. However, they currently do not.

The table above compares environmental and human health impacts of cedar and vinyl siding using data from BEES version 4.0. Basic information about BEES is discussed in detail in chapter 3.

Recycled Tires in Site Construction Products

Many states are working to clean up tire piles by exploring beneficial uses for scrap tires. State highway departments are incorporating crumb rubber from scrap tires in asphalt and asphalt surfacing applications (discussed in chapter 8). Crumb rubber used as fill or subbase is also gaining use.

A huge market for scrap tires is incineration for energy recovery, particularly in manufacturing settings such as cement plants. While energy is recovered, concerns about release of toxins and heavy metals from the tires have caused some states to ban the practice.

In addition to road paving and fill uses, ground rubber from tires is used in landscape applications such as playground surfaces, both bound and unbound; run-

Table 12–13 Scrap Tire Markets in the United States (2005)

Market	Millions of Tires	Percent
Tire-derived fuel	155.09	52
Civil engineering uses	49.22	16
Ground rubber	37.47	12
Export	6.87	2
Cut/punched/stamped	6.13	2
Miscellaneous/agriculture	3.05	1
Electric arc furnace	1.34	15
Total use	259.17	87
Land disposal	38.9	13

Source: Adapted from RMA 2006

- **Paving and surfacing** applications are made by adding crumb rubber to a binder and then placing it. The most common example of this is asphalt rubber used on highways, streets, parking lots, and paths. Asphalt rubber offers performance advantages such as increased pavement life because of its greater flexibility over traditional aggregate asphalt, less road noise, and increased traction.
- **Ground rubber** is used in turf topdressing applications and in turf soil.
- **Whole form** use of tires in site applications includes retaining walls, erosion control, and dock bumpers. Whole tires packed with soil and rammed are being used as structures for houses and skate parks. The tires serve as the structure and then are covered with concrete or other surfaces.

ning surfaces; athletic field turf amendments; and rubber sidewalks. A report prepared by the Tellus Institute calculates that the market for these nonroad ground rubber applications can be large enough to recover and use all scrap tires currently in landfills or tire piles (Stutz et al. 2003).

Some benefits from using ground rubber from scrap tires in site uses are potential cost savings, use of a local material, improved product performance, and safety ratings. Environmental benefits are reuse of a waste material, saving virgin resources and landfill space, and lower greenhouse gas emissions than would have been released from drilling and refining virgin petroleum resources.

Thirty-three million scrap tires are ground into products each year. Ground or crumb rubber (rubber particles sized three-eighths inch or less) can be used in relatively high percentages, many 100%, in the following applications:

- **Loose cover** ground rubber provides a cushioned surface when placed under or around playground equipment. It can also be used as mulch in planting beds.
- **Rubber surfacing products** are precast tiles and mats or poured-in-place surfacing. Examples of this are mat playground surfacing, running tracks, or rubber sidewalks (see Figures 12–5 and 12–6).

Figure 12–5.
Rubberized paving units made from crumb rubber from recycled tires are installed on a city sidewalk in Seattle. If tree roots cause the pavers to heave, they can be individually lifted out and re-leveled. (Photo from Rubbersidewalks, Inc.)

New Developments and the Future of Plastics

Plastics are rapidly gaining larger and larger shares of the construction products market. While plastics used in construction have a relatively long use phase, there is a growing plastic waste disposal crisis that will only intensify as plastics use increases. This waste crisis coupled with concerns about toxic by-products and consumptive petroleum product use is spurring increasing regulation and incentives for reduction of use and recycling. It is also encouraging research into new polymers with more sustainable properties and new uses for recycled plastics.

PLASTICS AND GOVERNMENT REGULATION

As long as plastic is inexpensive to produce and dispose of, plastic consumption will continue to increase. There is no incentive to either consumers or manufacturers to reduce consumption, to reduce packaging, or to recycle plastics. Therefore, government entities are critical to slowing and even reversing the trend toward rapid plastic consumption and waste.

The U.S. EPA has endorsed use of recycled plastic products through the Comprehensive Procurement Guidelines and Environmentally Preferable Purchasing programs, but federal legislation and incentives to reduce use or recycle plastics are virtually nonexistent in the United States. Some states and municipalities, particularly those with limited landfill space, have made substantial recycling efforts, followed with policies, and recycling industries thrive in those locales. Other municipal recycling programs don't collect plastics at all, so consumers must make an extra effort to recycle them.

Several products have been developed that incorporate recycled plastic content; however, difficulties in plastics separation and scarcity of recycling facilities mean that plastics are recycled at lower levels and a consistent supply of recycled plastics for new products is not always available.

The EU and other European governmental organizations have better recognized the plastics waste crisis and are taking steps through many measures to slow it down. The EU's policy emphasis has shifted recently to the principle of "producer responsibility"—giving the producers the responsibility for recycling, recovery, and reuse of their products. This has been accomplished in the following ways (Azapagic et al. 2003):

Voluntary incentives such as tax credits or other support for take-back programs, carbon credits, or product stewardship activities are aimed at manufacturers/producers.

Market-based instruments such as carbon taxes, packaging taxes, and fees based on production volumes are in place. Waste removal fees based on volume of waste are levied at consumers, encouraging reduction of use and recycling efforts.

Regulatory measures are imposed on manufacturers, such as mandatory recycling, take-back programs, and packaging reduction percentages based on volume of product produced.

Reduction of PVC use. Policy makers in European countries and some U.S. states and municipalities are addressing reductions in PVC use. The United Nations Stockholm Convention aims to reduce releases of persistent organic pollutants (POPs), including PVC dioxins, and the European Union is debating the REACH proposal, a policy requiring the registration of all toxic chemicals, including vinyl chloride, the monomer of PVC (Ackerman 2005).

In 2002, the Seattle City Council passed Resolution 30487, which directs city departments to reduce the use of materials that contain or emit persistent bioaccumulative toxins (PBTs), including PVC. Seattle's Office of Sustainability and Environment developed an implementation plan focusing on reducing PVC in building materials in city projects. And the state of New York and cities of San Francisco and Boston are also encouraging less use of products that contain PBTs (Seattle City Council 2002). Even some major corporations such as Microsoft, Sony, Wal-Mart, General Motors, and Honda are exploring PVC-free alternatives.

One positive by-product of the PVC debate is the increasing research on the harmful aspects of PVC, so hazards that were relatively unproven ten years ago are better understood today. And as the dialogue moves into the construction industry through efforts of organizations like Healthy Building Network and the U.S.

Figure 12–6.
Rubberized sidewalk paving units, incorporating around five scrap tires per unit, lock in place with pins and slots and are laid on a gravel aggregate base. (Photo from Rubbersidewalks, Inc.)

Table 12–14 Landscape Products Made from Recycled Rubber

Product/Material	Post-consumer Content (EPA CPG Recommendations)[a]	Other Standards	Comments
Playground surfaces	Rubber 90%–100%	See also ASTM specification F1292 and F2223–04	
Running tracks	Rubber 90%–100%		
Garden hoses	60%–65% rubber and/or plastic	See also ASTM D3901 Consumer Specification for Garden Hose and Green Seal GC-2: Watering Hoses	
Soaker hoses	60%–70% rubber and/or plastic	See also Green Seal GC-2: Watering Hoses	
Patio blocks, rubber	Rubber or rubber blends 90%–100%		Made from airplane and truck tires
Rubberized asphalt	15%–20%[b]	ASTM D6114–97(2002) Standard Specification for Asphalt-Rubber Binder	Can be mixed in asphalt binder or as aggregate in asphalt
Asphalt fill	100%		

[a]U.S. EPA CPG
[b]Turner Fairbank Highway Research Center

Green Building Council, designers and policy makers will start to investigate alternative products and materials.

NEW AND IMPROVED POLYMERS

Maybe more than any other building material, innovations in plastics chemistry continue to be developed. And by all accounts, plastics will continue to gain use in the construction market as their properties improve. The formation of new polymer chains, development of biopolymers, breakthroughs in precision polymerization techniques, and development of nanomaterials for plastics all provide limitless possibilities for the future of plastics. Many new developments are spurred by performance improvement or cost-saving concerns; however, there is some attention being paid to environmental health concerns by finding replacements for petroleum feedstocks, developing viable alternatives to PVC, and increasing the durability of plastics.

Composite plastics. Many plastic improvements result from the addition of materials, other than resins, to form composite plastic materials that possess positive qualities of both the plastic and the other material. Aluminum or stainless steel are added to plastics to impart strength, durability, or finish characteristics while still maintaining flexibility. For example, aluminum has been combined with HDPE to produce shadecloth that is reflective, weather resistant, UV radiation stabilized, and flame retardant (Beylerian, Dent, and Moryadas 2005). Glass and ceramics are also combined with plastics to form composite materials with increased abrasion resistance and strength. Road striping tape composed of microcrystalline ceramic beads bonded in a polyurethane topcoat provides bright permanent color and three-dimensional patterns that are highly abrasion resistant (Beylerian et al. 2005).

Nanocomposite polymers are pushing some plastics beyond their traditional limitations, particularly in areas of strength and durability. For instance, ultrafine platelets of alumino-silicate clay plates that are 50 Å/5 nm thick offer strengthening and surface gloss improvements beyond what would be expected for their volume. The resulting composite plastic has much improved properties such as increased strength, improved impact resistance, and dimensional stability. Potential for use of this in

plastic lumber could make it structurally competitive with some metals. Other nanoplastics under development are reinforced with bamboo fibers, glass microspheres or fibers, or carbon nanotubes (Elvin 2007).

Nanocoatings are a large area of recent and future developments in plastics. They can offer improved impact resistance and durability while some use less toxic/low-VOC chemicals that perform as well or better than traditional formulations. Nanorods dispersed in coatings that collect solar energy are also being developed.

Metallocene polyolefins are a new type of polyolefin that offers better control over where the side chains of polymers form, offering the advantage of cleaner, more controlled polymerization. This results in the opportunity for more precisely engineered and specific properties, including density, strength, flexibility, elasticity, tensile strength, and temperature resistance. Metallocene polyolefins may offer a replacement plastic for PVC and other plastics with high environmental and human health impacts (EBN 2001), yet despite this promising potential, few products are available in construction applications.

Bioplastics are plastics derived from plant sources such as cornstarch, soy, polylactides (PLA), or cellulosic materials. Bioplastics are considered a preferable alternative in some applications to petroleum-based plastics because they are made from renewable resources and many are biodegradable. Yet they are not without environmental impacts, and their property of biodegradability gives them limited use in site applications that are exposed to weather and microbes that can break them down prematurely. Even though the feedstock of bioplastics is renewable, their production requires inputs of fossil fuel for fertilizers and pesticides to grow the crops, and fuel to power the farm machinery and processing and production equipment. An LCI, prepared for the Athena Sustainable Materials Institute, of cold drink cups, window film, foam meat trays and water bottles made from polylactic acid (PLA)—one of the more common bioplastics—and petroleum-based high-impact polystyrene (HIPS), PP, and PET found that the total energy required to produce the PLA products was not lowest in most applications (Athena Sustainable Materials Institute 2006).

As with any biobased materials, there are concerns about the environmental impacts of the volume of crops that must be grown for biobased materials and the water, fertilizer, and pesticide inputs. There is also some concern about the diversion of land away from food crops (Athena Sustainable Materials Institute 2006).

Some bioplastics are considered biodegradable or compostable, yet in actual practice this may be less easily executed. Studies have shown that other biobased products, such as newspapers, do not easily break down, so there is an assumption that bioplastics may not either. Incineration of bioplastics may be more beneficial than incineration of petroleum-based plastics that release CO_2, and possibly CO and toxic emissions. PLA incineration will also release CO_2, but it is of biomass origin, so its return to the atmosphere is part of the natural cycle (Athena Sustainable Materials Institute 2006).

Some bioplastics can be composted, yet most are not suitable for home composting; instead they will need to be commercially composted at higher temperatures. Most consumers have limited access to commercial composters, so the likelihood of composting bioplastics may be limited.

In site applications bioplastics are currently in limited use for packaging. There is potential for their use in biodegradable applications such as erosion control fabrics. Biobased plastics are discussed in greater detail in chapter 13.

Should Plastics Be Specified or Avoided?

The answer is both yes and no, as it depends on what plastic is specified. Some plastics, especially those with high recycled content, may be the best material for a given application. After all, plastics are affordable, waterproof, lightweight, and durable. The Healthy Building Network summarizes many green building organizations, opinions in the following way: "While no plastic is environmentally benign, our analysis concludes that the polyethylenes possess lesser chemical hazards and associated environmental health impacts, making them environmentally preferable to those that have greater hazards and impacts such as PS and PVC" (Platt et al. 2005).

While the environmental and health impacts of PVC have been proven by many research studies, vinyl industry groups point to other studies (some of which they sponsored) that show far fewer harmful effects of PVC. Many hazards are proven; yet in some cases the degree of exposure that causes harm is not well understood.

As the debate continues over just how harmful PVC really is, there are many green building industry leaders who argue for approaching the PVC issue within the framework of the Precautionary Principle adopted by the UN Conference on the Environment and Development in 1992. This principle reads: "Where an activity raises threat of harm to the environment or human health, precautionary measures should be taken even if some cause and effect relationships are not fully established." Some believe that the consequences of waiting for higher levels of proof may be costly and/or irreversible.

As metallocene polyolefin production technologies bring some properties of PVC to polyolefins, this new generation of polyolefins may eventually replace PVC with a healthier, yet comparable plastic.

References

Ackerman, Frank. 2005. "REACH: Europe's Precautionary Chemicals Regulation." Center for Progressive Reform. Medford, MA.

Agency for Toxic Substances and Disease Registry (ATSDR). "ToxFAQs." U.S. Department of Health and Human Services. http://www.atsdr.cdc.gov/toxfaq.html (accessed between May 2006 and November 2007).

American Plastics Council (APC). "Plastics Industry Producers' Statistics Group." American Chemistry Council, Plastics Division. http://www.americanchemistry.com/s_acc/sec_news_article.asp?CID=206&DID=2377 (accessed February 17, 2007).

American Plastics Council. "2000 National Post-consumer Plastics Recycling Report." American Chemistry Council, Plastics Division.

American Plastics Council. 2007, March. "Plastic Packaging Resins." Arlington:American Chemistry Council, Plastics Division.

ASTM Standard D6662. 2007. "Standard Specification for Polyolefin-Based Outdoor Structural-Grade Plastic Lumber." West Conshohocken, PA: ASTM International, www.astm.org.

ASTM Standard D7032. 2008. "Standard Specification for Establishing Performance Ratings for Wood-Plastic Composite Deck Boards and Guardrail Systems (Guards or Handrails)." West Conshohocken, PA: ASTM International, www.astm.org.

Association of Postconsumer Plastic Recyclers. "Technical Resources: PVC Bottles." http://www.plasticsrecycling.org/ (accessed October 20, 2007).

Athena Sustainable Materials Institute. 2006, November. "Life Cycle Inventory of Five Products Produced from Polylactide (PLA) and Petroleum-based Resins." Prairie Village, KS: Franklin Associates.

Azapagic, A., A. Emsley, and I. Hamerton. 2003. *Polymers: The Environment and Sustainable Development.* New York: John Wiley & Sons.

Beylerian, G. M., A. Dent and A. Moryadas. 2005. *Material ConneXion: The Global Resource of New and Innovative Materials for Architects, Artists and Designers.* New York: John Wiley & Sons.

California Integrated Waste Management Board (CIWMB). *Recycled-content Products Directory.* http://www.ciwmb.ca.gov/RCP/.

Demkin, J., ed. 1998. "Application Report 10: Metal and Plastic Plumbing Pipe." In *Environmental Resource Guide.* New York: John Wiley & Sons.

Elvin, G. A. 2007, June. "Nanotechnology for Green Building." Green Technology Forum. http://www.greentechforum.net/greenbuild.

Environmental Building News. 2001. "Plastics in Construction: Performance and Affordability at What Cost?" *Environmental Building News* . Brattleboro, VT: Building Green, 10:7.

Hammond, G., and C. Jones. 2006. "Inventory of Carbon and Energy." Version 1.5 Beta. Bath, UK: University of Bath, Department of Mechanical Engineering.

Harvie, J., and T. Lent. 2002. "PVC-Free Pipe Purchasers' Report." Washington, DC: Healthy Building Network.

Healthy Building Network, Pharos Project. "Asmthman-PVC-Phthalates Science." http://www.pharosproject.net/ wiki/. Healthy Building Network.

International Agency for Research on Cancer. 2006. "Complete List of Agents Evaluated and Their Classification." http://monographs.iarc.fr/ENG/Classification/.

Minnesota Pollution Control Agency. 2006, June. "Plastic Lumber and Outdoor Furniture." http://www.pca.state.mn.us/oea/epp/plasticlumber.cfm.

National Institute of Standards and Technology. 2006. *BEES 4.0: Building for Environmental and Economic Sustainability.* http://www.bfrl.nist.gov.

National Toxicology Program, Department of Health and Human Services. http://ntp.niehs.nih.gov/.

Partnership for Advancing Technology in Housing (PATH). "Technology Inventory Factsheets." http://www.toolbase.org/TechInventory/ViewAll.aspx.

Plastic Lumber Yard. http://www.plasticlumberyard.com.

Platt, B., T. Lent, and B. Walsh. 2005, October. "Guide to Plastic Lumber." Healthy Building Network. Washington, DC: Institute for Local Self-Reliance.

Robbins, Alan E. 2005. "State of the Recycled Plastic Lumber Industry: The Plastic Lumber Industry in Competition Markets." Presented at he annual meeting of the Plastic Lumber Trade Association, Pittsburgh, PA.

Rubber Manufacturers Association (RMA). 2006. "U.S. Scrap Tire Markets 2005." Washington, DC: RMA.

Seattle City Council. 2002, July. Resolution 30487: A Resolution Relating to Persistent, Bioaccumulative, Toxic Chemicals (PBTs).

State of California Environmental Protection Agency. Office of Environmental Health Hazard Asssessment. 2007, June. Proposition 65. "Chemicals Known to the State to Cause Cancer or Reproductive Toxicity."

Steingraber, Sandra. 2004, April. "Update on the Environmental Health Impacts of Polyvinyl Chloride (PVC) as a Building Material: Evidence from 2000–2004. A commentary for the U.S. Green Building Council." New York: Healthy Building Network.

Stutz, J., S. Donahue, E. Mintzer, and A. Cotter. 2003. *Recycled Rubber Products in Landscaping Applications.* Boston, MA: Tellus Institute.

Joe Thornton, P. D. (2002) "Environmental Impacts of Polyvinyl Chloride (PVC) Building Materials." Washington D.C.: Healthy Building Network.

Turner Fairbank Highway Research Center (TFHRC). 2004. *User Guidelines for Waste and By-product Materials in Pavement Construction.* McLean, VA: Turner Fairbank Highway Research Center, Federal Highway Administration. http://www.tfhrc.gov/hnr20/recycle/waste/begin.htm.

U.S. Environmental Protection Agency (U.S. EPA). 1981. "Chapter 6: Petroleum Industry, Section 6.1 Synthetic Rubber." *AP 42.* 5th ed. Clearinghouse for Inventories and Emissions Factors, Technology Transfer Network, U.S. EPA.

U.S. Environmental Protection Agency (U.S. EPA). 2003. "Exposure and Human Health Reassessment of 2,3,7,8-Tetrachlorodibenzo-p-Dioxin (TCDD) and Related Compounds, National Academy Sciences (NAS) Review Draft." National Center for Environmental Assessment, December 2003.

U.S. Environmental Protection Agency (U.S. EPA). "Comprehensive Procurement Guidelines." http://www.epa.gov/cpg

U.S. Environmental Protection Agency (US EPA). 2005. "Profile of the Rubber and Plastics Industry, 2nd Edition." EPA Office of Compliance Sector Notebook Project, U.S. EPA. February 2005.

U.S. Environmental Protection Agency (U.S. EPA). 2006a. "Plastics and Rubber." *2006 Sector Strategies Performance Report.* Sector Programs, U.S. EPA.

U.S. Environmental Protection Agency (U.S. EPA). Office of Solid Waste. 2006b. "2005 Municipal Solid Waste in the United States: Facts and Figures." EPA530-R-06–011. October 2006.

U.S. Environmental Protection Agency (U.S. EPA). 2007, April. "Inventory of U.S. Greenhouse Gas Emissions and Sinks, 1990–2005." Report EPA 430-R-07–002.

U.S. Environmental Protection Agency (U.S. EPA). "Comprehensive Procurement Guidelines Glossary of Terms." http://www.epa.gov/epaoswer/non-hw/procure/glossary.htm#recovered (accessed February 5, 2007).

U.S. Environmental Protection Agency (U.S. EPA), Greenscapes. "Cost Calculator." http://www.epa.gov/epaoswer/non-hw/green/tools/decking.pdf.

U.S. Green Building Council, LEED Technical and Scientific Advisory Committee (TSAC) PVC Task Group. 2007, February. "Assessment of the Technical Basis for a PVC-Related Materials Credit for LEED." Washington D.C.: USGBC.

Winterbottom, Daniel. 1995. "Recycled Plastic Lumber." *Landscape Architecture Magazine* 85(1): 34–36.

chapter 13

Biobased Materials

BY RUTH STAFFORD

Introduction

Biobased materials and products are derived from renewable organic constituents of plants and animals. Biomass sources for these products can include agricultural crops and residues, forest products and residues, animal wastes, and biobased post-industrial and post-consumer solid waste (U.S. Department of Energy 2002). This chapter primarily covers short-cycle biobased materials and products that have applications in site construction. Plant-based feedstocks for these products typically are harvested within a ten-year cycle, as indicated in LEED rating systems (U.S. Green Building Council 2005). Examples of these feedstocks include fiber crops, bamboo, agricultural residues, and plant seed oils. Some products made from lumber processing waste are mentioned in this chapter as well, although the bulk of lumber and wood products is addressed in chapter 10.

Biobased construction products can offer several benefits. Many are biodegradable, are nontoxic, and do not create hazardous waste by-products. By displacing petroleum-based products, use of biobased products can help reduce emissions of greenhouse gases and other pollutants, in addition to lessening dependence on nonrenewable resources. Biobased products made from agricultural wastes prevent these materials, which would otherwise be burned in many instances, from adding to particulate air pollution. From an agricultural industry perspective, biobased materials are beneficial because they expand the market of agricultural products, contributing to stable commodity prices and enhancing rural economies (McNeil Technologies 2005). Costs of biobased products relative to comparable conventional products vary greatly; some are much less expensive, while others can be more expensive.

Although they are made from renewable resources, biobased products are not without impacts. For products derived from agricultural feedstocks, there are potential effects associated with cultivation, as agricultural practices can be petroleum-intensive (Morris 2006). Production of these biobased feedstocks uses petroleum to operate machinery, transport products, and serve as the basis of synthetic chemical inputs; as a result, cultivated biobased products are not carbon neutral (Miller, Landis, and Theis 2007). Air and water pollution can result from fertilizer use (especially nitrogen and phosphorus), and pesticide application can harm plants and animals that are not intended targets of pesticides. Although increased fertilizer use has improved crop yields (resulting in more land-efficient production), plants do not take up all the applied nutrients—leading to excessive nutrient pools that can be leached into water or volatilized into air (Tilman et al. 2002). Nitrogen inputs in particular have a variety of potentially significant environmental effects, with consequences for air and water quality that result from release of reactive nitrogenous compounds. It is estimated that agricultural uses have doubled yearly terrestrial nitrogen inputs, with negative consequences (Tilman et al. 2002). These effects include eutrophication and oxygen depletion of water bodies, ozone depletion in the stratosphere and ozone production at ground level, and increased N_2O concentrations (which increase global warming potential; Miller et al. 2007; Tilman et al. 2002). Soil erosion also is a serious consequence of some cropping practices—not only does eroded soil decrease land fertility, but also airborne soil particles contribute to air pollution, and sedimentation of eroded soil can impair receiving waters by increasing turbidity and chemical pollution (Schueler and Holland 2000). Moreover, the resulting reduced soil fertility increases the need for chemical and water inputs to grow future crops (Tilman et al. 2002). Supplemental irrigation reduces water availability for competing uses, exacerbating water supply problems in some regions (Tilman et al. 2002). Agriculture is land-intensive, with approximately half of the world's usable land already devoted to crop production and pastureland (Tilman et al. 2002). This removes land from use for other functions, such as wildlife habitat or buffering waterways (Millennium Ecosystem Assessment 2003). The direct loss of natural plant and animal communities resulting from intensive agriculture, coupled with pollution from fertilizers and pesticides, has compromised the effectiveness of services such as water treatment provided by ecosystems (Tilman et al. 2002). In addition to these impacts, there are crops that have been genetically engineered using recent innovations in biotechnology, and the potential environmental impacts of these genetically modified organisms are still being assessed (Wolfenbarger and Phifer 2000). Finally, by diverting more crop products to biobased materials, less is available for food. This consequence already has been anticipated because of the increased demand for biofuels, with food prices predicted to increase up to 50% by 2016 as a result (Doornbosch and Steenblik 2007). If biobased products also reduce food supply, continued pressure will be exerted on food prices, making daily subsistence more costly.

There are conflicting opinions on the energy use and other impacts of biobased products. For example, some reports indicate that more energy is required to produce a unit of fuel ethanol than is actually available in the fuel; however, others dispute these results because of the methods used in the analysis—their studies suggest that fuel ethanol is more energy-efficient than petroleum fuel (Kim and Dale 2004). Studies comparing biobased with petroleum-based materials support the notion that biobased materials have less of a negative impact in terms of climate change (Miller et al. 2007). However, with the majority of analyses focused on climate-related effects (e.g., greenhouse gas emissions), other potentially problematic impacts have not been evaluated as carefully. Because the ability to fully analyze impacts and benefits of biobased products is still being developed, the advantages of their use must be reassessed as more information becomes available in the future.

USE OF BIOBASED MATERIALS

Biobased materials were used extensively in pre-industrial societies, but have been replaced largely by materials manufactured from petroleum and other non-renewable resources since the early 1800s. This trend accelerated during the 1900s, with increased diversity of products made from petroleum resources. In 1900, about 41% by weight of the 161 million metric tons of materials used in the United States was derived from renewable feedstocks, including agricultural and forest products (Matos and Wagner 1998). By 1995, material consumption increased to 2.8 billion metric tons, although renewable materials comprised only about 8% by weight of the material stream by this time; the rate of decline was especially pronounced during the first half of the twentieth century (Matos and Wagner 1998). The downward trend in renewable material use reflects changes in the U.S. economy, as it transitioned from agricultural to industrial and service-based during this period.

Since the 1970s, biobased materials have experienced greater attention and use in construction and other industries. This has resulted from several factors (Kim and Dale 2004; Morris 2006). Awareness of the environmental costs of fossil fuel use has spurred the search for alternatives. These costs include increased rates of greenhouse gas emissions, rapid depletion of nonrenewable petroleum resources, waste disposal concerns for petroleum-based materials (such as plastics), and risk of environmental contamination associated with fossil fuel use, petroleum-based material processing, and accidental spills (Millennium Ecosystem Assessment 2003). In addition, monetary costs of petroleum-based products are increasing because of fossil fuel depletion, geopolitical issues, and a regulatory environment that has raised production costs of petroleum- and mineral-based products. Finally, technological advances in biobased research and development have lowered the cost of producing many biobased products, making them more competitive with conventional products.

Biobased products are poised for more significant growth in market share. For instance, the current production level of products made from refined biobased chemicals (e.g., starch, polymers, oils, etc.) is about 12.4 billion pounds. The total biobased plus non-biobased production of these materials, however, is measured in hundreds of billions of pounds, which indicates substantial growth potential for the biobased industry (U.S. Department of Energy 2002). Several federal agencies routinely purchase biobased products, such that these comprised 20% of total buying in 2006, up from less than 2% in 2000 (Kim C. Kristoff [President, GEMTEK Products], personal communication). The U.S. government has acknowledged this growth potential and set vision goals for biobased products to comprise 12% of the market by 2010, 18% by 2020, and 25% by 2030 (U.S. Department of Energy 2002).

Despite the recent increase in their use, there are several obstacles to widespread production and use of biobased products (McNeil Technologies 2005). For products derived from agricultural residues, the seasonal nature and geographic variation in residue availability can be difficult for manufacturers of biobased products to manage. Residues need to be stored to ensure a constant supply for manufacturers. The bulky nature of agricultural wastes also limits the distance they can be transported to a processing facility in a cost-effective manner.

The use of biobased feedstocks often necessitates changes in production technologies and equipment needs for manufacturers of biobased products, which can increase the cost of these products as they are being

Table 13–1 Major Categories of Biobased Product Inputs

Input Category	Example of Biobased Material or Product Used for Site Construction
Recycled and reprocessed biobased waste	Cellulose fiber mulch (e.g., newsprint)
Agriculture and timber industry waste by-products	Coir erosion control products
	Straw mulch and erosion control products
	Straw bale
	Cellulose fiber mulch
Cultivated or harvested materials	Jute erosion control products
	Rope or twine
	Tackifiers
	Soil stabilizers and aggregate binders
	Concrete and asphalt release agents
	Concrete curing agents
	Bamboo products

introduced into the market. This contrasts with a well-developed production and distribution infrastructure for petroleum, contributing to the relatively low cost of petroleum-based products and making it difficult for biobased materials to be economically competitive (Singh et al. 2003).

Some biobased products are more costly because of their smaller scale of production, and this may be limiting the use of these products by consumers—although surveys indicate that the typical buyer of a biobased product may be willing to spend between 10% and 20% more for the biobased product (McNeil Technologies 2005). Local availability of biobased site construction products may be more of a limiting factor than cost differential for adoption of biobased products. In construction, modifications of equipment or installation and application procedures may be necessary, which may present challenges. Also, current building codes may not allow the use of biobased products.

There are three broad categories of biobased materials and products with varying life-cycle impacts (Table 13–1). Some products are made from recycled and re-processed biobased waste, such as paper. Biobased products also can be derived from waste by-products of the agriculture and timber industries. Finally, products can be made from materials that are specifically cultivated or harvested for that use.

According to the Biobased Manufacturers Association (BMA), a product is considered biobased if it contains 90% or more biomaterial content (by mass or volume, depending on whether the product is a solid or liquid; the percentage excludes inorganic materials in the product, including water). Products with less than 90% biomaterial composition still can be considered as having biobased content.

The United States Department of Agriculture (USDA) has specified minimum biobased content levels of products in several categories, as part of the Federal Biobased Products Procurement ("BioPreferred") Program. Through this program, an extensive list of products eventually will be designated by the USDA for minimum biobased content, and will be included in the BioPreferred listing of recommended procurement items. Products are being evaluated for their life-cycle impacts using the BEES (Building for Environmental and Economic Sustainability) program. Table 13–2 lists the minimum biobased content for construction-related materials indicated in the USDA final and proposed regulations and for product types in the early stages of evaluation.

Biobased Materials and Their Applications for Sustainable Sites

The applicability of biobased materials to outdoor uses varies depending on the properties of a given product and how it is installed on the site. A major consideration is compatibility between a product's susceptibility to degradation and the desired level of durability in a given application. Some very common biobased products, such as building panels made from agricultural residues, are readily used in building interiors but cannot be used in the landscape because they will be compromised by exposure to rain, wind, and sunlight.

Current uses of biobased materials in the landscape primarily involve soil- and pavement-related work, such as controlling erosion, amending soil, stabilizing aggregate pavement, and working with concrete. Biobased materials also can be used for site furnishings and structures. Ongoing research and technological advances may expand the applications of biobased materials and composite materials that have biobased content. The following sections discuss broad categories of currently available biobased materials and their use in landscape and site work.

JUTE, COIR, STRAW, AND RECYCLED FIBER FOR EROSION CONTROL, REVEGETATION, AND MULCHING

Geotextiles and mulches made from natural fibers are used primarily to control soil erosion and stabilize slopes, usually in conjunction with revegetation efforts (Environmental Building News 1997b). Mulches also are used to improve soil moisture retention, reduce weeds, and moderate soil temperatures, all of which benefit the survival and growth of desired plants. In considering the need for erosion control products, it should be noted that soil with higher organic matter content is less likely to erode—in some situations, simply amending soil with organic material may lower (or

Table 13–2 USDA-Specified Biobased Content of Selected Product Types

Phase of Designation	Product Type	Minimum Biobased Content (Percent)
USDA Rounds 1–4 Designations		
USDA Round 1 Designation (final rule)	Mobile equipment hydraulic fluids	44
	Roof coatings	20
	Water tank coatings	59
	Penetrating lubricants	68
USDA Round 2 Designation (proposed rule)	Adhesive and mastic removers	58
	Insulating foam for wall construction	8
	Composite panels	26
	Fertilizers	71
	Metalworking fluids	40
	Sorbents	52
	Graffiti and grease removers	21
USDA Round 3 Designation (proposed rule)	Stationary equipment hydraulic fluids	46
	Glass cleaners	23
	Dust suppressants	66
	Carpet	7
USDA Round 4 Designation (proposed rule)	Concrete and asphalt release fluids	87
	Cutting, drilling, and tapping oils	64
	Durable plastic films	61
	Wood and concrete sealers	79
USDA Biobased Content Suggestions for Several Other Categories under Evaluation		
Building Materials and Composites	Construction materials	85
	Molded reinforced composites	10
	Insulating foams and films	15
	Components of mixed system products	25
Fibers, Papers, and Packaging	Fibers	90
	Fiber composites	30
	Woven fiber products	75
Landscaping Materials, Compost, and Fertilizer	Landscaping materials	100
	Compost	100
Plastics	Biodegradable foams	50
	Durable foams	15
	Water-soluble polymers	50
	Compostable molded products	75
	Molded plastics and composites/biobased resins	10
	Molded composites/biobased fibers	20
	Synthetic fibers	50
Paints and Coatings	Formulated product	20

Sources: Environmental and Energy Study Institute 2004; USDA 2006a, 2006b, 2006c

eliminate) the need for supplemental erosion control measures.

Natural-fiber geotextiles and mulches can replace synthetic plastic products that usually are made from polypropylene (PP) or polyethylene (PE). These natural-fiber products are derived from materials representing different life-cycle phases. They can be a) cultivated and harvested specifically for these uses, such as jute and other annual or short-cycle fiber crops; b) agricultural by-products of crop processing, such as coir (coconut fiber) and straw from grain crops (e.g., wheat straw and rice straw); or c) made using post-industrial or post-consumer fibers, such as cellulose (from recycled paper and cardboard) and natural textile fibers.

The type of erosion control or mulch product used and its installation will vary depending on slope, anticipated runoff velocities, and desired degree of persistence in the landscape. Manufacturers of geotextiles and tackifiers often have installation guidelines that are specific to each product. In addition, standard specifications for rolled erosion control products, which include natural-fiber geotextiles discussed here, have been developed by the Erosion Control Technology Council and are updated periodically (Erosion Control Technology Council 2006). The U.S. Environmental Protection Agency (EPA) also has recommended best management practices (BMPs) for erosion and sediment control, including use of geotextiles, mulching, fiber rolls, compost blankets, compost filter berms, and compost filter socks (U.S. Environmental Protection Agency 2006). Finally, individual state agencies and municipalities may have their own construction and product specifications for erosion control and mulch products.

Environmental Impacts and Benefits

Because they are made from minimally processed plant material, natural-fiber geotextiles and mulches are biodegradable. As a result, these products can be left to decompose in place and amend the soil; they do not have the waste-disposal concerns of their synthetic counterparts. Moreover, because synthetic geotextiles and mulches use petroleum-based feedstocks, their use has impacts associated with nonrenewable resource use and chemical processing. Use of coir and biobased mulches (straw and post-consumer or post-industrial cellulose waste) is beneficial by keeping these waste materials out of landfills or from being burned. However, straw mulches can be a source of unwanted seeds; using straw mulch during revegetation may have the unintended consequence of spreading potentially invasive plants (Beyers 2004; Kruse, Bend, and Bierzychudek 2004), so it is important that weed-free straw is specified and that the straw does not inadvertently pick up unwanted seeds before being applied in the landscape. Another concern with mulching is that it may interfere with reestablishment of native vegetation following natural disturbances, by reducing sunlight to seeds and seedlings, physically interfering with plant emergence, lowering nitrogen availability as it decomposes, and preventing contact of seeds with soil if seeds arrive after mulch is installed (Kruse et al. 2004). As a result, it is important that the choice of mulch or erosion control product is compatible with site conditions, erosion potential, and revegetation procedures.

The primary input for jute cultivation is human labor, which minimizes energy-use impacts typically associated with mechanized agriculture (Environmental Building News 1997b). It also appears that chemical pesticides or fertilizers are seldom used to produce jute, which minimizes pollution and fossil fuel inputs (Environmental Building News 1997b). Recent LCA (life-cycle analysis) research comparing impacts of natural fibers with synthetic fibers supports these assertions. For example, the production of petroleum-derived polypropylene uses about ten times the energy than for jute, and polypropylene production also leads to higher carbon dioxide (CO_2) emissions. However, there are impacts associated with the processing of both jute and coir fibers. The traditional process for jute is a water retting procedure, in which the stems are submerged in water for fifteen to eighteen days and subjected to microbial action, facilitating fiber harvest. This process can increase organic loads in rivers, lakes, and estuaries (Karus, Kaup, and Lohmeyer 2000), and can cause eutrophication and unpleasant odors (van Dam and Bos 2004). There are indications that water retting may be on the decline, as more environmentally friendly techniques, such as ribbon retting, become adopted (van Dam and Bos 2004). Coir fibers are processed in a similar fashion, in which the fibers are removed from coconut husks that have been soaked in water. In this case, the soaking time is much longer (three to six months), and the resultant fermentation process pollutes the water and releases methane, a powerful greenhouse gas (van Dam and Bos 2004). These effects can be reduced by a semimechanized procedure that reduces soaking time (although with energy-use impacts from machine operation), and by implementing biological wastewater treatment. An additional impact of using jute and coir in North America comes from transporting these materials overseas from where they are cultivated, plus additional overland transport to destinations across North America. An alternative to reduce some of these transportation impacts would be the use of geotextiles made with hemp fibers grown in North America (primarily Canada), although hemp geotextile availability would need to increase to make this a viable alternative (Small and Marcus 2002).

A significant environmental benefit of natural geotextiles and mulches involves water retention and conservation (Huang et al. 2005; Ji and Unger 2001; Zink and Allen 1998). By covering the soil, these products directly reduce water evaporation from the soil. The ability of some of the natural fibers to absorb water also helps trap surface runoff, with these fibers acting as a water reservoir for plants. An important property of mulching is to moderate soil temperature; in hot weather, this cooling effect also reduces evaporation of water from soil. These water-related benefits can facilitate new plant establishment and growth, and also reduce the need for irrigation.

Another major benefit of natural-fiber rolled erosion control products (RECPs) and mulches is their biodegradability. Synthetic geotextiles resist degradation, remaining in the soil unless removed later (which is costly and potentially disruptive to soil; van Dam and Bos 2004). Natural-fiber RECPs persist about two to five years on-site (coir generally lasts longer than jute), while some synthetics can remain 25 years or more (Rickson 2006). As natural geotextiles degrade, they provide the added benefit of soil enrichment with nutrients and organic matter (Rickson 2006). Loose straw and recycled-fiber mulches tend to decompose more quickly than natural geotextiles, and likewise add organic matter to soil. Initial decomposition of natural geotextiles and mulches, especially those with higher carbon-nitrogen ratios, may tie up nitrogen that might otherwise be available for plants (Kruse et al. 2004). Depending on the circumstances, this may have negative or positive impacts. This effect was found to actually benefit the survival and growth of native perennials in a restoration project because these plants outcompeted invasive plants that tend to require higher levels of readily available soil nutrients (Zink and Allen 1998). In addition, one study showed that when partially degraded straw mulch was incorporated into soil, the resultant immobilization of nitrogen reduced leaching of nitrate from the soil (Döring et al. 2005). This keeps nitrogen in the local soil system and eventually available for plant growth. In general, the increased organic matter from decomposition of natural-fiber mulches and geotextiles provides a favorable environment for beneficial soil microbes that decompose matter and recycle nutrients. The result is increased microbial biomass and activity that ultimately enhances soil conditions and nutrient availability for plants (Tu, Ristaino, and Hu 2006; Zink and Allen 1998).

Mulches

Biobased materials commonly used in mulching include straw (for loose applications) and cellulose fibers, such as recycled paper, cardboard, and wood pulp (for hydraulic applications; Figures 13–1 and 13–2). Hydraulic mulches frequently combine mulch with seed and sometimes fertilizer in a single application step. Although this may be convenient and cost-effective, the small fiber sizes required for these mulches to pass through pumps of the application equipment can render them less effective as erosion control agents (Lancaster and Austin 2003). Tackifiers also may be included with hydraulically applied mulch. A tackifier is a viscous liquid that helps bind the fibers to each other and to underlying soil, improving mulch stability in sloped areas. Tackifiers can be produced from several sources, including biobased materials (e.g., starch, and powdered guar and psyllium gums), as well as petroleum products (e.g., asphalt emulsions and petroleum distillates) and synthetic polymers (Carlson 2003; Lancaster and Austin 2003). Loose straw mulches may be spread by hand or machine-blown onto soil that often is seeded or planted with seedlings. To help anchor straw mulch to soil, it is "crimped" into the soil with dull coulter disks or by hand (using a shovel), and may be covered with a mulch control netting for extra protection in windy

Figure 13–1.
A large coverage area is afforded by hydraulically applied mulch. Biobased mulch will gradually decompose and can use recycled fiber material. (Photo from Ruth Stafford)

Figure 13–2.
The finer texture of hydraulic mulch contrasts with shredded bark mulch. (Photo from Ruth Stafford)

conditions or sloped areas. Loose mulch also may be anchored with a sprayed-on tackifier.

Natural mulches perform as well as synthetics by reducing erosion and providing enhanced conditions for plant growth. Research has demonstrated the ability of natural-fiber mulches, especially straw, to reduce erosion for the benefit of new vegetation (Beyers 2004; Döring et al. 2005). By suppressing weeds, natural-fiber mulches can increase growth of desired plants, even after the mulches have partially deteriorated, especially when the result is a fibrous cover that functions like organic litter (Haywood 1999). Organic mulches also improve water availability through reducing evaporation of water from soil, leading to increased plant growth (Huang et al. 2005; Zink and Allen 1998). Other potential effects of straw mulch include reducing infestation of plants with disease-carrying insects (by disorienting them through reflection of ultraviolet light; Summers, Mitchell, and Stapleton 2004) and lowering the likelihood of direct plant infection by soilborne pathogens (Ellis, Wilcox, and Madden 1998).

Natural mulches are best used as a temporary measure on sites that do not require the extra strength and cost of RECPs. RECPs should be considered instead of mulches in the following situations (Kansas City Metropolitan Chapter APWA 2003):

- In an area needing protection longer than eight months (up to two to five years)
- In windy areas that prevent satisfactory application of loose or hydraulic mulches
- In areas that will experience concentrated flow of runoff
- For slopes steeper than 3:1 (H:V)

Before applying mulch, the site must be prepared. After any grading, remove larger rocks, stumps, and other debris. Divert runoff from areas above the site to be mulched. Apply mulch immediately after seeding an area, and mulch areas that cannot be seeded. See Table 13–3 for a summary of specifications for natural-fiber mulches.

Geotextiles

Natural-fiber geotextiles typically are made from jute or coir (Figures 13–3 and 13–4); wood excelsior (thin wood shavings, usually from aspen trees) can be used in blanket-type geotextiles as well. Jute is an annual crop, with most production occurring in India and Bangladesh. Most natural-fiber geotextiles are produced as rolled erosion-control products (RECPs; these also can be produced from synthetic fibers), in which the materials are assembled into one of the following product types (descriptions from Lancaster and Austin 2003):

Mulch control netting. This product consists of a fairly open-weave fiber net that normally is used to keep applications of loose mulch in place. The netting is anchored with stakes or large staples. This application is considered more stable than applied hydraulic mulches, and less stable than open-weave textiles or erosion control blankets.

Open-weave textile. For this product, fibers are woven much more tightly than mulch control netting, allowing the geotextile to be used for erosion control without any loose mulch underneath. Because open-weave textiles have greater tensile strength than mulch control netting, they can be used on steeper slopes and in some turf-reinforcement applications.

Erosion control blanket. This geotextile is more of a "sandwich," where a layer of degradable fibers (e.g., straw, coir, wood excelsior) is attached to a binding layer of woven textile or netting, which can comprise either a natural fiber (often jute) or a plastic mesh (which is typically UV-degradable). The binding layer can be on one or both sides of the fiber layer. The strength and durability of an erosion control blanket depends on its material composition and method of attaching the layers (e.g., woven or glued). These products typically are used for areas that need longer-term erosion control or have higher erosion potential, such as steep slopes and low-flow channels or swales that will be revegetated.

Natural geotextiles perform as well as or better than synthetics for controlling soil loss through erosion (Sutherland 1998). One study compared the effectiveness of woven jute and coir netting with nylon and polypropylene geomats (Rickson 2006). The results indicate that soil loss due to rain splash decreases with the following geotextile features: high percentage area of

Table 13–3 Design and Specification Recommendations for Natural-Fiber Mulches

Mulch	Properties	Application
Straw (loose)	From wheat, rice, oat, barley, or rye Should be dry, unchopped, unweathered, and free of weed seeds and rot Should not have been used as animal bedding	Apply a minimum two to three tons/acre (more for steep slopes and channels) to a uniform depth of two to three inches. Straw may be blown by machine or distributed by hand. At least 80% of the soil surface should be covered by the mulch. If mulch is to be anchored using a tackifier, first roughen surface and fill areas with a crimping- or punching-type roller, or by track-walking. Extend mulch cover into existing vegetation and adjacent stabilized areas. Anchor either by covering with mulch control netting, crimping/punching into the soil (by hand or machine), or spraying with an organic-based tackifier. Netting may be used on large, steep areas that can't be machine-crimped. If anchoring by crimping or roller-punching, use a machine crimper (serrated disks four to eight inches apart, done in two directions with final pass parallel to contours) or roller (with straight studs at least eight inches apart, six inches long, four to six inches wide, and ca 0.75 inch thick). Punching is not as effective in sandy soils. For areas that are small, rocky, steep (> 3:1 H:V), or have wattles in place, anchor by hand, using a shovel to punch straw into soil about four inches so it stands upright. For small, steep slopes or rocky areas, mulch also may be anchored using a tackifier. The tackifier should be organic, biodegradable, and made from psyllium, guar gum, starch, or other suitable organic substance. Mix tackifier with water and apply over the mulch according to manufacturer's specifications, or apply at a rate of 125 lb./acre or 178 lb./acre in windy conditions. Do not apply tackifier during or just before rain.
Hydraulic mulch: paper	Should contain 100% post-consumer recovered materials (e.g., newsprint, magazines, and other waste paper)	Apply a minimum 1.5 to 2 tons/acre (or twice this amount for areas especially susceptible to erosion). Avoid application during hot, dry conditions. May be applied in combination with tackifier and/or seed and fertilizer. Use a power mulcher or hydroseeder to apply hydraulic mulch. The tackifier should be organic, biodegradable, and made from psyllium, guar gum, starch, or other suitable organic substance. Mix with water and apply at the manufacturer's specified rate.
Hydraulic mulch: wood	Should contain 100% recovered wood and wood waste Should not have sawdust or substances that could inhibit seed germination or plant growth	Apply a minimum one to two tons/acre, as slurry with a stabilizing emulsion or tackifier. If used with a tackifier, first roughen surface with a crimping- or punching-type roller, or by track-walking. Mulch needs about 24 hours to dry before rainfall to be effective for the duration of the rainy season. May be applied in combination with seed and fertilizer. Use a power mulcher or hydroseeder to apply hydraulic mulch. The tackifier should be organic, biodegradable, and made from psyllium, guar gum, starch, or other suitable organic substance. Mix with water and apply at the manufacturer's specified rate or 2% to 5% by weight.

Sources: Barr Engineering Company 2001; California DOT 2003; California Stormwater Quality Association 2003; Geosyntec Consultants 2005; Idaho Department of Environmental Quality 2005; Kansas City Metropolitan Chapter APWA 2003; U.S. Environmental Protection Agency 1995

Figure 13–3.

Figure 13–4.
Jute textile, with a relatively open weave, is used on a recently graded and planted slope. Woven geotextile can be used for sloped areas (as shown) as well as flatter sites. The biobased fabric gradually decomposes, and its texture helps reduce the velocity (and erosive potential) of runoff. (Photos from Ruth Stafford)

soil covered by the product, high water retention and ability to pond water (both of which weigh down the geotextile and increase its contact with soil), and rough texture. Natural geotextiles, especially blankets or mats and the more densely woven fabrics, have these characteristics. In addition, these same features enable natural geotextiles (especially jute, and coir to a lesser extent) to outperform synthetic products in controlling soil loss from overland flow of water runoff. In particular, the rough texture of natural geotextiles reduces the velocity and increases the depth of runoff, which decreases the erosive potential of overland flow (Rickson 2006). Another study of RECPs revealed that the effectiveness of erosion control is associated with geotextile structure (Sutherland and Ziegler 2006). In this case, both natural and synthetic RECPs were tested for their ability to control erosion and were classified as either open-weave (OW) products (i.e., a grid fiber network with regular square or rectangular openings) or randomly oriented fiber (ROF) systems. This study did not compare the performance of natural versus synthetic fiber types, each of which was represented in the OW and ROF products. Both OW and ROF geotextiles led to significantly reduced sediment output compared with bare-earth controls. However, ROF geotextiles were generally more effective than OW systems, probably because the openings in OW products can still allow rain splash detachment of soil particles, and because the fibers in some ROF systems are more likely to integrate with the soil surface. This suggests that geotextile structure is an important consideration when selecting a product for especially high-stress conditions, such as steeper slopes that will experience overland water flow.

Although biodegradability is a benefit of natural geotextiles, it can limit their range of uses in the landscape. Natural-fiber geotextiles generally are not as durable as synthetic products (Haywood 1999). Geotextiles are used not only to control erosion and stabilize slopes (see Table 13–4), but also to separate materials (e.g., aggregate and subsoil), act as a filter in drainage applications, and reinforce soils, paving, and steep vegetated drainage channels (Harris and Dines 1998; Lancaster and Austin 2003; Rickson 2006). In most of these other situations, the long-term durability of synthetic geotextiles is needed for proper functioning of the installation.

Wattles

In addition to RECPs, wattles are another erosion control product consisting of a tube of fibrous material (often coir or rice straw, as well as wood excelsior) held within a natural-fiber or other degradable netting (Figures 13–5 and 13–6). In addition, they can be formed from tightly rolled natural-fiber textiles. Wattles also are known as fiber logs or fiber rolls, and can be used as a more effective biobased alternative to straw bales and silt fences (Keating 2003). Wattles are shaped like long tubes, up to 25 feet long, and normally are used to control erosion on slopes and trap sediment along curbs and before reaching storm drains. On slopes, they are placed at the top and base, as well as along the face (parallel to contours at regular intervals), and work like check dams to slow runoff velocity and trap sediment (ISU Center for Transportation Research and Education 2006). Wattles may be seeded or combined with RECPs or loose mulch (Keating 2003). In addition to wattles, compost filter socks have similar structure and function. They comprise a compost-filled mesh tube, and can be used for erosion control and filtering runoff. A specialty type of wattle is made from willow cuttings that are bundled together. Unlike fiber wattles, willow wattles are living materials. They can be produced in a range of lengths and diameters, depending on specific needs. Willow wattles usually are employed to stabilize banks adjacent to streams and other water bodies, by taking advantage of the willow cuttings' propensity to develop new roots.

Fiber wattles usually are placed along slopes. Site characteristics, desired longevity, and product availability will influence the material and dimensions of wattles. Those made with coir typically last two to five years, while straw wattles last one to two years; wattles made with photodegradable plastic netting also tend to last longer than those made with natural-fiber netting. If using straw wattles, specify that they are made using weed-free straw. Wattle length can range from 10 to 25 feet, and diameter usually is between 6 and 20 inches (common diameters are nine and twelve inches; ISU Center for Transportation Research and Education 2006). They are used more for controlling sheet flow and trapping sediments, and should be limited to areas where the rate of concentrated runoff flow is less than 0.5 cfs (ISU Center for Transportation Research and Education 2006; see Table 13–5).

Table 13–4 Suggested Specifications for Natural-Fiber RECPs

| RECP | Slope Applications[a] | | Channel Applications Max. Shear Stress[b] | Min. Tensile Strength[c] |
	Max. Gradient (H:V)	C Factor		
Ultra-short-term (ca. 3 months):				
MCN[d]	5:1	≤ 0.10 @ 5:1	0.25 lb./ft.^{2} (12 Pa)	5 lb./ft. (0.073 kN/m)
Netless RECBs[e]	4:1	≤ 0.10 @ 4:1	0.5 lb./ft.^{2} (24 Pa)	5 lb./ft. (0.073 kN/m)
Single-net ECBs and OWTs[f]	3:1	≤ 0.15 @ 3:1	1.5 lb./ft.^{2} (72 Pa)	50 lb./ft. (0.73 kN/m)
Double-net ECBs[g]	2:1	≤ 0.20 @ 2:1	1.75 lb./ft.^{2} (84 Pa)	75 lb./ft. (1.09 kN/m)
Short-term (ca. 12 months):				
MCN[d]	5:1	≤ 0.10 @ 5:1	0.25 lb./ft.^{2} (12 Pa)	5 lb./ft. (0.073 kN/m)
Netless RECBs[e]	4:1	≤ 0.10 @ 4:1	0.5 lb./ft.^{2} (24 Pa)	5 lb./ft. (0.073 kN/m)
Single-net ECBs and OWTs[h]	3:1	≤ 0.15 @ 3:1	1.5 lb./ft.^{2} (72 Pa)	50 lb./ft. (0.73 kN/m)
Double-net ECBs[g]	2:1	≤ 0.20 @ 2:1	1.75 lb./ft.^{2} (84 Pa)	75 lb./ft. (1.09 kN/m)
Extended-term (ca. 24 months):				
MCN[i]	5:1	≤ 0.10 @ 5:1	0.25 lb./ft.^{2} (12 Pa)	25 lb./ft. (0.36 kN/m)
ECBs and OWTs[j]	1.5:1	≤ 0.25 @ 1.5:1	2.00 lb./ft.^{2} (96 Pa)	100 lb./ft. (1.45 kN/m)
Long-term (ca. 36 months):				
ECBs and OWTs[g]	1:1	≤ 0.25 @ 1:1	2.25 lb./ft.^{2} (108 Pa)	125 lb./ft. (1.82 kN/m)

[a]C factor and shear stress for MCN to be obtained with netting used along with preapplied mulch. C factor calculated as ratio of soil loss from RECP-protected slope (tested at specified or greater gradient, H:V) to ratio of soil loss from unprotected (control) plot in large-scale testing. Acceptable large-scale test methods may include ASTM D6460, or other independent testing deemed acceptable by the engineer.

[b]Required minimum shear stress RECP (unvegetated) can sustain without physical damage or excess erosion (> 12.7 mm or 0.5 inch soil loss) during a 30-minute flow event in large-scale testing. The permissible shear stress levels established for each performance category are based on historical experience with products characterized by Manning's roughness coefficients in the range of 0.01–0.05. Recommended acceptable large-scale testing protocol may include ASTM D6460, or other independent testing deemed acceptable by the engineer.

[c]Minimum average roll values, machine direction using ECTC Mod. ASTM D5035.

[d]Mulch control netting (ultra short- and short-term): a woven biodegradable natural fiber or photodegradable synthetic mesh netting

[e]Netless rolled erosion control blankets: natural fibers mechanically interlocked and/or chemically bonded to form a blanket

[f]Single-net erosion control blankets and open-weave textiles (ultra short-term): degradable natural fibers mechanically bound together by a single, fast-degrading synthetic or natural fiber netting, or an open-weave textile of fast-degrading natural yarns or twines woven into a continuous matrix

[g]Double-net erosion control blankets: degradable natural fibers mechanically bound together between two fast-degrading synthetic or natural fiber nettings

[h]Single-net erosion control blankets and open-weave textiles (short-term): degradable natural fibers mechanically bound together by a single degradable synthetic or natural fiber netting to form a continuous matrix, or an open-weave textile of degradable natural yarns or twines woven into a continuous matrix

[i]Mulch control netting (extended-term): a slow-degrading natural fiber netting

[j]Erosion control blankets and open-weave textiles (extended- and long-term): slow-degrading natural fibers mechanically bound together between two slow-degrading synthetic or natural fiber nettings to form a continuous matrix, or an open-weave textile of slow-degrading natural yarns or twines woven into a continuous matrix

Source: Adapted from Erosion Control Technology Council 2006

BIOBASED PRODUCTS IN CONCRETE AND PAVEMENT APPLICATIONS

Biobased materials are available for use in several concrete and pavement applications: as form release and curing agents for cast concrete, and as binding agents for aggregate. Conventional form release agents are petroleum-based, such as oil or kerosene. These materials are used to facilitate removal of concrete formwork after the concrete has set. More recently, biobased alternatives (typically made from plant seed oils) have been developed that have lower environmental impacts

Figure 13–5.

Figure 13–6.
Fiber wattles are placed along a slope to catch sediment and debris. Fiber wattles will decompose in place and provide a use for agricultural waste such as straw fiber. They may be used alone or in combination with other erosion control methods such as geotextiles. (Photos from Ruth Stafford)

Table 13–5 Wattle Spacing

Slope (H:V)	Wattle Spacing	
	9" Diameter	12" Diameter
< 4:1	20 ft.	40 ft.
2:1 to 4:1	15 ft.	30 ft.
≥ 2:1	10 ft.	20 ft.

Source: ISU Center for Transportation Research and Education 2006

than petroleum-based release agents. Concrete curing agents, which help newly poured concrete cure at a proper rate, also traditionally have been petroleum-based. As with form release agents, other products have become available as an alternative, with reduced negative effects compared with petroleum-based curing agents. Among these newer products are biobased agents, often made from soy.

Low-impact and reduced-traffic aggregate surfaces may be installed incorporating a plant-based binder, which can increase the durability and erosion resistance of an aggregate surface. The binder frequently is derived from psyllium (*Plantago* sp.) seed coats, which contain a mucilage that helps bind aggregate. Plant-derived binders are a biobased alternative to organic petroleum emulsions and synthetic polymer products, which are petroleum-based materials. It should be noted that tree-resin emulsion binders also are available for paving applications (to bind aggregate and soil). Although not made from short-cycle biobased materials (they are a by-product of lumber processing), they nonetheless present another alternative to petroleum and synthetic polymer binders used for aggregate pavements (Maher et al. 2005).

Performance

Biobased form release and concrete curing agents appear to perform comparably to their petroleum-based counterparts (Environmental Building News 1997a). Biobased form release agents generally are tested against industry performance standards (U.S. Dept. of Agriculture 2006c). Indeed, some biobased form release agents can provide a smoother finish that is less likely to have "bug holes" (Bleck et al. 2005). Plant-based aggregate binders can make paved surfaces appear more naturalistic than asphalt-stabilized pavement. However, biobased aggregate binder made from psyllium is not as durable as asphalt-based binder for higher-traffic applications, although surfaces expected to have lighter traffic loads (e.g., trails and driveways) may be suitable for psyllium-bound aggregate. These surfaces also may be less firm than aggregate bound with other materials. In a study that evaluated the firmness and stability of limestone aggregate stabilized with either psyllium-based binder, tree-resin binder, or a polyurethane binder, the psyllium-stabilized surface showed more wear and was less firm than surfaces stabilized with the other two materials (National Center on Accessibility). Trail firmness was evaluated using a rotational penetrometer, which measures the depth of penetration into a ground or floor surface; greater penetration indicates a less firm surface. Trail firmness and surface wear results for the three different stabilized surfaces, plus a control (unstabilized) limestone aggregate surface, are shown in Table 13–6. Recommended performance specifications for a dry surface to be considered "firm" is 0.3 inch or less penetration, and "moderately firm" is greater than 0.3 inch up to 0.5 inch (Axelson and Chesney 1999).

Environmental Impacts and Benefits

Using plant-based form release agents, curing agents, and aggregate binder displaces petroleum-based and synthetic polymer products, which have nonrenewable resources as their feedstock. However, biobased products made from crop plants have negative impacts associated with agricultural production, which includes fossil fuel use. On the positive side, these plant-based materials have little or no VOC (volatile organic compound) content, as compared with conventional products (Bleck et al. 2005). By not using petroleum-based products, workers are not exposed to these noxious (and potentially carcinogenic) fumes, which can cause respiratory and eye irritation (Butler et al. 2000). This concern is more pronounced for paving applications and for precast concrete products that are produced indoors.

There are other benefits to using biobased materials in concrete and paving applications. For example, because biobased form release agents are nontoxic and biodegradable, they do not have the potential to contaminate soil or water with standard use, unlike petroleum-based

Table 13–6 Firmness and Wear of Aggregate Surfaces Stabilized with Different Materials

Surface Application	Surface Penetration	Surface Wear
Unstabilized limestone aggregate (quarter minus)	0.10–0.90 inch	Shows more wear and degradation than stabilized surfaces. More unstable when wet.
Limestone aggregate stabilized with psyllium binder	0.36–0.59 inch	Shows more wear than the other two stabilized surfaces, although it is an improvement over unstabilized aggregate. Test surface shows breakdown along edges of trail.
Limestone aggregate stabilized with tree-resin binder	0.05–0.08 inch	Shows relatively little wear. Surface is sufficiently stable for use by those with impaired mobility.
Limestone aggregate stabilized with polyurethane binder	0.009–0.03 inch	Shows less wear than the other three surfaces.

Source: National Center on Accessibility

agents. For projects that require environmental review, use of these biobased form release agents instead of petroleum products may expedite permitting (Environmental Building News 1997a). As another example of an environmental benefit, use of psyllium-based aggregate binders results in a permeable surface, which can reduce storm water runoff and its associated impacts.

Specification

Because biobased products used in concrete and paving applications tend to be proprietary products, it is necessary to follow manufacturers' recommended guidelines for installation and use. Table 13–7 outlines recommendations for biobased product specifications.

Table 13–7 Design and Specification Recommendations for Biobased Materials in Concrete and Pavement Applications

Product	Product Specifications
Form release agent	Colorless, 100% biodegradable, plant oil–based agent (soy, rapeseed, or other plant) Minimum biobased content of 87%, with low or no VOC content (maximum 55 grams/liter) Shall not bond with or stain concrete or interfere with subsequent application of coatings and finishes Shall not contain diesel fuel, petroleum-based lubricating oils, waxes, or kerosene
Concrete curing agent	Organic, biobased concrete curing compound Should have low or no VOC content (maximum 55 grams/liter)
Psyllium aggregate binder	Colorless, odorless, nontoxic organic binder Should bind decomposed granite or crushed $3/8$" or $1/4$" minus aggregate to produce a firm surface

Sources: Form release agent: Bleck et al. 2005; Unified Facilities Guide Specification 2006; U.S. Department of Agriculture 2006c.
    Concrete curing agent: Bleck et al. 2005
    Psyllium aggregate binder: Riverside County, CA, Transportation and Land Management Agency

BAMBOO PRODUCTS

Bamboo is a plant with a great range of applications in the landscape, either as living plants or building materials and finished products from harvested bamboo. It has been used extensively (and for millennia) as a building material in regions where it naturally occurs (Farrelly 1984; Oprins and van Trier 2006). There are up to 1,500 bamboo species distributed worldwide among about 76 genera (Farrelly 1984), with the greatest species diversity in Asia (especially China) and Central and South America (Oprins and van Trier 2006). In addition, Asian species have been brought to the Western hemisphere for horticultural purposes and cultivation for other uses (Stangler 2001). The use of bamboo is expected to remain strong and perhaps increase, especially in areas where timber is in short supply. For many uses in the landscape, bamboo can provide an alternative to wood, concrete, steel, and plastic.

The short-cycle, biobased aspect of bamboo materials and products results from the nature of the plant. It is a member of the grass family (*Gramineae* or *Poaceae*; subfamily *Bambusoidae*; Mabberley 1989), and individual stems, known as culms, typically are harvested within three to five years (Stangler 2001). The culm is the primary material used in bamboo products. Culm growth rates and heights vary among species and with environmental conditions, and can be impressive. For example, one investigation in Japan measured a culm that grew over 47 inches in 24 hours; more typical daily growth rates range between three and sixteen inches for the larger bamboo species (Farrelly 1984). Final culm height generally depends on the species, and ranges from less than one foot up to 120 feet (Farrelly 1984). After a rapid start, culm growth both vertically and in diameter levels off after several months, and is followed by hardening as it matures over the next several years (Oprins and van Trier 2006); its typical life span is five to ten years (Farrelly 1984). Although bamboo technically is not woody (it lacks the secondary cell wall thickening of wood; Mabberley 1989), mature culms have great strength and hardness because their fibrous cell walls are highly lignified; they contain silicon dioxide and have a silica content approaching 5% (Oprins and van Trier 2006; Stangler 2001).

Bamboo traditionally is processed as either cut poles (culms), large culms split lengthwise and flattened into boards, or split culms woven into panels (Farrelly 1984). Bamboo poles and boards are used in structures such as pavilions, bridges, and scaffolding, and in fences, gates, screens, trellises, furnishings, and accessories or decorative items. Woven bamboo panels have uses as screens and decorative fence or façade treatments. Because bamboo is a rapidly renewable and versatile material with characteristics similar to wood, its use as an alternative to wood has expanded rapidly in recent years, particularly in building interiors (e.g., laminate flooring and panels, chipboard, and fiberboard). Moreover, laminated and sealed bamboo is expanding the versatility of product offerings for outdoor use (Farrelly 1984). This includes use as a deck surfacing and in contemporary-styled outdoor furniture. In addition, corrugated bamboo panels (made from resin-coated, laminated panels) are used as an alternative to asbestos for roofing in many developing countries (Oprins and van Trier 2006).

Performance

Bamboo's structural characteristics allow it to perform comparably to wood and other materials in several respects. First, it is a lightweight material with a high strength-weight ratio (Oprins and van Trier 2006), has a very hard surface, and requires few tools or specialized equipment for installation (Van der Lugt, van den Dobbelsteen, and Abrahams 2003). However, at this point bamboo is perhaps a less workable and flexible material overall compared with both plastic and wood, although this may change if bamboo becomes increasingly used in composite products containing wood and/or plastic. Bamboo has high tensile strength and outperforms steel in terms of elasticity (Oprins and van Trier 2006). Bamboo plywood (also known as plybamboo, plyboo, or lamboo) is similar to conventional plywood but is more elastic (Dethier et al. 2000). Small bamboo poles or split culms also have been used to replace metal rods to reinforce concrete in Asian countries (Farrelly 1984). Bamboo as a potential concrete-reinforcement material has been studied in the United States and several European countries. For example, experiments in South Carolina in the mid-1900s evaluated structural properties of bamboo-reinforced concrete. Results then indicated that these reinforced beams can carry two to three times the load of unreinforced concrete. In addition, unseasoned culms (up to 0.75 inch in diameter) can reinforce concrete slabs and other components not needed for critical load-bearing applications (Farrelly 1984).

Some of bamboo's physical features contribute to potentially problematic issues in terms of performance. Minimally processed culms can develop cracks, and the hard outer surface can be slippery when wet (Van der Lugt et al. 2003). Also, when working with bamboo poles, joining them is a critical issue—it is labor intensive, and the joints can be a major limitation on the load-bearing capacity of bamboo structures (Hopper 2006). For less critical applications, bamboo may be joined simply by tying it with rope or using mortise and tenon joints. Stronger joints are made using a bolt through the culms to be joined; the hollow spaces may be filled with concrete or mortar to minimize the likelihood that the connection will compress the culms.

Because they are plant-based materials, bamboo products are susceptible to attack by insects and microbes; this vulnerability to deterioration is an issue that limits more widespread use of bamboo in the landscape (Oprins and van Trier 2006). The external surface of the culm is quite resistant, but the internal portion is not. Insect pests include beetles, which are attracted to bamboo's fairly high starch content. Carbohydrate levels are greatest in younger culms and diminish over time, which is one reason for harvesting older culms (Farrelly 1984). Additional curing after harvest further lowers carbohydrate content in culms, making them less susceptible to insect and microbial attack. Several traditional curing methods are used to reduce carbohydrates in culms: these include water leaching, gentle heating, exposure to sun or smoke, soaking first in water and then in oil, or using chemical preservatives (which have their own environmental impacts; Dethier et al. 2000; Farrelly 1984). Additional processing is continued by air-seasoning, where culms are stored and allowed to dry and strengthen in a sheltered area with good air flow.

Like some kinds of wood used in the landscape, untreated bamboo weathers quickly when exposed to moisture and UV (ultraviolet) light, which also can make it more vulnerable to fungal attack. Its durability can be extended with the application of stains and sealers; more effective products include polyurethane and UV-protective sealers that are water-based (Stangler 2001). Outdoor bamboo structures will last longer if they are inspected each year for signs of degradation and maintained as needed. This can include washing off soil and other debris (paying special attention to joints), and reapplying sealer if necessary. It also is important to keep bamboo structures from direct contact with damp soil, by placing them on concrete footings, for example.

There is much variation in bamboo materials for construction and other uses because of the variety of species harvested and methods of processing and curing bamboo. As a result, there are concerns with quality control and uniformity of material, some of which can be addressed with improved management of cultivated bamboo, heating culms to straighten them, and adopting bamboo testing standards (Van der Lugt et al. 2003). Although bamboo has been used for a long time, adopting it for use in structural applications in the United States likely will require extra time to work with permitting agencies and to conduct additional tests on bamboo structural capacity (Van der Lugt et al. 2003).

Environmental Impacts and Benefits

Because bamboo plants generally are grown with few chemical inputs, impacts associated with their cultivation are relatively low. Compared with plastic products (e.g., fencing), bamboo is a renewable, biobased material that does not pollute; its ability to substitute for plastic products is expected to increase in the future (Farrelly 1984). Moreover, bamboo's high growth rate allows it to have up to 25 times greater yield than timber (Dethier et al. 2000). Compared with bamboo, which resprouts from underground roots and rhizomes after harvest, a tree takes many more years to be replaced by intensive reforestation procedures (Dethier et al. 2000; Oprins and van Trier 2006). In addition, conventional logging and reforestation practices can have severe environmental consequences resulting from soil erosion and effects on habitat and water quality. However, bamboo's rapid growth rate and ability to recover from harvesting contribute to its being potentially invasive, depending on the species, extending into areas not originally intended for bamboo cultivation (Farrelly

1984). With careful management and species selection, this can be less of a problem.

Very little quantitative and broad-based information is available concerning comparative impacts and benefits of bamboo as an alternative to wood, plastic, metal, and concrete. However, a recent study examined environmental impacts of bamboo used in western Europe by conducting a life-cycle analysis (LCA) of bamboo culms from Costa Rica and bamboo panels produced in China (Van der Lugt et al. 2003). The culms were compared with steel, concrete, and sustainably harvested lumber for use in bridges (as columns, beams, and rails). The LCA revealed that most of bamboo culms' environmental cost is associated with transporting the materials overseas from Costa Rica to Europe. Comparison with the other materials indicates that the annualized environmental costs of bamboo culms are lower than steel, concrete, and lumber. This particular analysis estimated that the environmental costs of steel and some types of lumber are about twenty times higher than bamboo, and the annualized environmental cost of concrete is about twelve times higher. Two main reasons account for the lower environmental cost of bamboo culms: 1) bamboo's physical properties (a hollow tube) allow it to perform more efficiently per unit of material mass than the other materials; and 2) bamboo culms have relatively simple processing methods with much lower energy and other inputs. In terms of annualized monetary costs, bamboo culms are competitive with wood, but steel outperforms the other materials in this measure because of its longer life span. In the same report, a similar LCA compared bamboo panels made in China with panels made from various wood products and cementitious wood fiberboard (Van der Lugt et al. 2003). The panels are used in parquet, veneer, and other covering applications. Compared with bamboo culms, bamboo panels have more complex and energy-intensive processing methods, including bleaching and laminating. Based on the LCA, the main environmental costs of bamboo panel production are associated with bleaching (using hydrogen peroxide) and overseas transportation; the bleaching costs are more than double the transport costs. Bamboo panels varied in their environmental costs compared with panels made from other materials. Panels made from bamboo had lower environmental costs than those made from standard-harvest wood (pine and

tropical) and cementitious fiberboard. However, the environmental performance of bamboo panels was lower than those produced from sustainably harvested wood and 100% waste wood. The study's authors suggest that the environmental performance of bamboo panels would be greatly improved if production methods can reduce or eliminate the impacts of bleaching the bamboo (Van der Lugt et al. 2003). It also is evident that the environmental costs of bamboo can be lowered by having production and processing areas located such that overseas transport of bamboo products is not necessary; the study revealed that overland transport impacts are very low in comparison.

As mentioned in the LCA study, the use of chemicals in bamboo processing presents a major environmental impact of this biobased material. Almost all methods to treat bamboo for protection from insect and microbial attack involve toxic chemicals, although less negative alternatives are available and include traditional curing methods, such as smoking (Oprins and van Trier 2006). In addition, the more intensively processed laminated bamboo panels have greater environmental impacts. For example, processing plants that produce bamboo flooring tend to use great amounts of energy for kiln drying, compressing, and milling sheets. To mitigate this impact, some factories use waste bamboo biomass and sawdust to provide some of this energy (Oprins and van Trier 2006).

Anticipated future demand for bamboo has raised concern about overexploitation of natural (uncultivated) bamboo groves, which supply much of the world's bamboo (Oprins and van Trier 2006). Future bamboo needs should be increasingly met by commercial bamboo plantations that are well managed and minimize impact on naturally occurring plant communities. In terms of source material location, India currently has much of the world's bamboo plantations (Farrelly 1984). More globally widespread bamboo cultivation would ensure that supplies are closer to where they are used, to reduce the effects associated with overseas transport of the material.

Specification

Many bamboo products, such as furniture, gates, and fencing, are available fully or partially preassembled, and selection is based on product availability, cost, and aesthetics. There may be other situations, however, where an application that uses bamboo is tailored specifically for a site, and bamboo materials will need to be selected accordingly for the project. This can present a challenge for material specification. Bamboo culms vary greatly in length, diameter, thickness, and straightness; these different parameters all affect bamboo's structural and mechanical properties and its workability. If available bamboo poles exhibit this variation, it may be better to use them for situations where measurement precision is less critical (e.g., temporary outdoor structures), as a veneer or finish material, or for small-scale projects (e.g., footbridges; Van der Lugt et al. 2003). It also is helpful to simplify design and joining methods to the greatest extent, and to pre-assemble portions of bamboo structures. In addition, when developing a procurement schedule for bamboo (especially whole culms for structures and other outdoor uses), it is important to factor additional time that may be needed for bamboo processing (curing and slow-drying) and transportation, if the material is not already in stock at a bamboo supplier (Van der Lugt et al. 2003).

The variation in bamboo building materials has been long recognized, and bamboo grading and certification processes are being developed. The Evaluation Service of the International Conference of Building Officials (ICBO) released its *Acceptance Criteria for Structural Bamboo* (AC162) in March 2000 (http://www.icc-es.org/criteria/pdf_files/ac162.pdf). This document includes bamboo test methods and data analysis, allowable design stress criteria and other design considerations, and recommendation of ASTM D5456–98 as a quality control standard. It also references the January 2000 version of the *Standard for Determination of Physical and Mechanical Properties of Bamboo,* which was proposed by the International Network for Bamboo and Rattan (INBAR) (http://www.inbar.int/). This standard has guidelines for testing the following properties of bamboo: moisture content, mass per unit of volume, shrinkage, compression, bending, shear, and tension. As these standards become refined and

Figure 13–7.
A straw bale garden wall is finished with stucco to protect the straw from moisture. Straw bale uses nontoxic agricultural waste as a construction material, and the thickness of straw bale walls provides an excellent sound barrier. (Photo from Gayle Borst)

adopted in different countries, they should facilitate evaluation of bamboo materials for project use and permitting.

STRAW BALE IN THE LANDSCAPE

The use of straw bale as a construction material has increased since the 1990s. Straw bale is densely packaged waste straw from areas where grain crops are produced. After the grain is harvested, the straw residues are mechanically harvested in the form of compressed bales (generally three to four feet long, weighing between 50 and 85 pounds); straw sources include rice, wheat, barley, oat, flax, and rye (U.S. Department of Energy 1995). Straw bale is most commonly used in the construction of single-family dwellings and accessory structures. It is an increasingly popular building material not only because it is considered a more sustainable alternative to lumber, but also because it has excellent insulation and noise reduction properties (Magwood, Mack, and Thierren 2005). After a building's straw bale walls are in place, plaster is applied to the exterior and interior surfaces, forming a type of "sandwich" that contributes to the wall's insulative value and thermal mass. The plaster also protects the straw bales from moisture and damaging pests, and the strong bond of the plaster with the straw bales helps the wall withstand compressive and shear forces (Magwood et al. 2005).

Straw bale has been used less frequently to construct landscape features in addition to buildings—primarily garden walls and seating (Figures 13–7 and 13–8). As such, straw bale may be used to displace lumber and masonry, including concrete block. Straw bale walls may be a range of shapes and heights, and can incorporate gates, clear openings, and niches or decorative relief designs carved into the straw. Similarly, outdoor seating made from straw bale can have numerous configurations and sizes, depending on the number and arrangement of bales used. Like straw bale buildings, straw bale landscape structures must be finished with plaster for strength and protection from the elements. Tiles and other durable objects may be embedded in the plaster for decorative effects.

Four different plaster types typically are used with straw bale: stucco, lime, earth, and gypsum (Magwood et al. 2005). All except gypsum are suitable for exterior

Figure 13–8.

Its modular nature gives straw bale great versatility as a material, and structures can be customized easily to include openings and decorative treatments. (Photo from Gayle Borst)

applications, including building exteriors and site structures. Stucco, or masonry cement, combines portland cement with a lime binder and is commonly used and widely available. Lime used for plaster can be either hydraulic lime or "Type S" hydrated lime (the latter is more common). Earthen plasters are made with native soil containing some clay and sand (soil may need to be supplemented with additional clay or sand for suitable texture); this kind of plaster is relatively inexpensive, but is generally not as durable with frequent rain. These plasters vary in their physical properties and environmental impact and are discussed further in chapter 6. Portland cement–only plaster is not recommended for use with straw bale because 1) it does not allow the straw to breathe (thereby trapping moisture and potentially damaging the structure), 2) it is not as easy to work with compared to the other plasters, and 3) its production is highly energy-intensive, with high environmental impacts (Magwood et al. 2005).

Environmental Impacts and Benefits

Long touted as an alternative to lumber and other common building materials, straw bale structures incorporate materials that can have lower embodied energy and fewer environmental impacts (Minke and Mahlke 2005). It is estimated that using straw bales in buildings can reduce the need for lumber by one-third to one-half in these buildings (Elizabeth and Adams 2005). Not only does straw bale displace other building materials, but it also provides a market for an abundant agricultural waste product. Agricultural straw poses disposal issues because it does not decompose rapidly. Excess straw frequently is burned as a result, contributing to particulate air pollution (Elizabeth and Adams 2005). As more restrictions are placed on this burning, the straw bale building market provides an outlet for this material. Another benefit of straw bale comes from its ability to act as a sound barrier. Straw bale garden walls may help reduce noise from adjacent areas, providing a quiet and restful place for people (Minke and Mahlke 2005; Steen et al. 2005).

A potentially great environmental impact of straw bale structures results from their need for a plaster finish. The more durable stucco and lime plasters require a great deal of energy for their production (more so for stucco because it contains cement). If a straw bale wall uses plaster with high cement content, the amount of cement used to finish the wall may be comparable to the amount used in a similar concrete masonry unit wall (Steen et al. 2005). Another possible impact may result if waste straw is continually harvested for use in straw bales and other waste straw products. Normally, some agricultural residues are often left on fields to help reduce erosion when fields are left fallow and to gradually enrich the soil as they slowly break down. If too much waste straw is removed to make building and other products, the result could be loss of soil and/or soil organic matter for field crops. Finally, although straw bale usually has low embodied energy, this advantage could be negated if straw bale comes from a distant source, as transportation energy inputs increase. Because grain crops are fairly ubiquitous, this impact may be alleviated by specifying local straw sources.

Performance and Specification

The performance of a straw bale structure depends on the condition of the bales, as well as proper installation and plaster finishing. In terms of straw bale quality, avoid bales that are more prone to decomposition; the bales should be well-compressed. The following guidelines (U.S. Department of Energy 1995) are useful for selecting straw bales to be used in structures:

- Straw bales should be stored to facilitate drying and minimize water intrusion; they should have a maximum moisture content of 14%.
- Choose straw bales that are virtually free of residual seed heads, as these will attract pests and microbes, and facilitate decomposition of straw within the structure.
- Avoid straw bales that are tied with natural fibers— opt instead for those tied with baling wire or polypropylene fibers, to ensure that the bales remain well-compressed.
- Straw bale length should be about twice its width, which makes it easier to build with the bales in a running bond pattern.
- Straw bales may be purchased from farmers, wholesalers, and retail outlets (e.g., farm and feed supply stores); they are generally less expensive right after harvest.

The design and construction of straw bale features must minimize the likelihood of water getting trapped within the straw bale, because this can lead to early degradation of the straw and compromise the structural integrity of the plastered straw bale. There are several ways to protect straw bale structures from water damage (Minke and Mahlke 2005; Steen et al. 2005):

- Site the structure above grade on a well-drained foundation, being sure that water cannot be wicked up into the straw from the ground.

- Apply several coats of plaster, allowing adequate curing time between coats.
- The plaster on horizontal surfaces may need to be capped with an impervious material (e.g., tile) or treated with a water-repellent coating to minimize the chance that standing water is absorbed into the plaster and infiltrates the straw.
- For additional protection from rain and melting snow, use an overhead structure or incorporate roofing material in the design, to shed water away from the structure.

Government Support for Biobased Materials

There are many U.S. government programs that encourage use of alternatives to petroleum. The programs that support the biobased product industry have been designed for consistency with federal energy and agricultural policies, and to help overcome obstacles to biobased market growth. The policies support research and development, and they also target procurement practices to help increase market demand for biobased products.

Presidential Executive Orders
Two executive orders have been especially important in broadening the use of biobased products. Executive Order 13101, "Greening the Government through Waste Prevention, Recycling, and Federal Acquisition," was issued in 1998. Among other things, it directs U.S. agencies to purchase products that contain recycled-content materials and to procure products that are environmentally preferable (" . . . products or services that have a lesser or reduced effect on human health and the environment when compared with competing products or services that serve the same purpose"; *Federal Register* 63, no. 179, 1998). The following year, Executive Order 13134 was issued: "Developing and Promoting Biobased Products and Energy." Its intent is to "stimulate the creation and early adoption of technologies needed to make biobased products and bioenergy cost-competitive in large national and international markets" (*Federal Register* 64, no. 157, August 16, 1999).

To do this, it requires establishing an Interagency Council on Biobased Products and Bioenergy to prepare an annual strategic plan for national goals concerning biobased products and bioenergy, with consideration of rural economic interests, energy security, and environmental protection. Executive Order 13134 also requires the establishment of the Advisory Committee on Biobased Products and Bioenergy and the National Biobased Products and Bioenergy Coordination Office.

Legislation
The Biomass Research and Development Act of 2000 was created by the U.S. Congress to support research programs for producing power, fuels, materials, and chemicals from biobased feedstocks (U.S. Department of Energy 2002). In 2002, additional support for the biobased industry was outlined in the Farm Security and Rural Investment Act (FSRIA). This legislation established a federal purchasing program to help expand the market for biobased products. FSRIA also defined a biobased product as "a product determined by the Secretary to be a commercial or industrial product (other than food or feed) that is composed, in whole or in significant part, of biological products or renewable domestic agricultural materials (including plant, animal, and marine materials) or forestry materials" (2002). The framework of the purchasing program, known as the Federal Biobased Products Preferred Purchasing Program (also called FB4P or "BioPreferred"), was established by the U.S. Department of Agriculture (USDA) in 2005. In it, the USDA began suggesting standards for minimum biobased content of different kinds of biobased products, and soon after the agency designated the first product types that meet procurement requirements of the program. The list of designated products has been growing since the program began; it is possible that more than 100 product types may be designated for biobased procurement, as they become more thoroughly researched and receive biobased content recommendations (Office of the Federal Environmental Executive 2006).

Anticipated Biobased Product Development and Improvements

Because of the increasing recognition of, and demand for, more sustainable approaches to creating built environments, it is expected that the use of biobased materials covered in this chapter will expand. This mirrors trends in biobased product use for other applications, such as biofuels and their processing coproducts, biomass energy, nonwood pulp and paper, novel industrial lubricants and solvents, composite materials, and biobased packaging. In addition, technological advances are making possible new biobased materials and products. Through this evolving industrial biotechnology, naturally occurring biochemical pathways and microbial processes are applied to industrial practices, such as synthesizing chemicals and facilitating large-scale production of biobased products. These processes generally involve breaking down biobased feedstocks into basic chemical building blocks (e.g., starch, cellulose, oils, proteins) that then can be synthesized into a broad array of polymers, fuels, more environmentally friendly solvents, and other specialty chemicals (Singh et al. 2003).

Biobased plastics (bioplastics) and composite materials with partial or complete biobased content are especially promising materials for increased use in buildings and the landscape. Biocomposites present an alternative to composite materials that usually contain glass fibers embedded in a petroleum-based plastic matrix (Fowler, Hughes, and Elias 2006). Biocomposites are composed of natural fibers (e.g., flax, hemp, kenaf) in a matrix consisting of either petroleum-derived plastic (e.g., polypropylene, polyethylene) or, increasingly, a biobased material made from starch plastics, polylactides (PLA), soy plastics, cellulosic plastics, or microbial-produced polymers (Mohanty, Misa, and Drzal 2002). Currently, biocomposites are most frequently used in the automotive industry for interior panels: because the natural fibers produce a lighter-weight panel compared with glass-fiber composites, these panels help reduce vehicle weight and improve fuel economy (Fowler et al. 2006). However, biocomposites have found uses in building applications, such as a solid surface material that can be used indoors or to clad exterior walls, and more commonly plastic lumber, which can be used outdoors as a decking and fencing material and has been commercially available for several years.

Biocomposites are more environmentally friendly than petroleum-derived products; this is more pronounced for completely biobased composites than for composites containing natural fibers in a petroleum-based matrix. Biocomposites use rapidly renewable feedstocks and have lower production energy requirements. Completely biobased composites are more readily degradable, which improves upon the waste disposal issues associated with the conventional composites; however, other composites with biobased content are less degradable and can be difficult to recycle, especially if the products contain a mix of bioplastics and petroleum-based plastics. The general environmental advantages of biocomposites have been supported by a review of twenty different LCA studies involving biobased polymers and natural fibers in composite products (Patel et al. 2003). Although there is much variation, biocomposites generally exhibit reduced energy consumption and greenhouse gas emissions than their petroleum-based counterparts.

Bioplastics and biocomposites do face challenges to gaining market share. Natural fibers perform well and are fairly low cost, so their use in composites has faced few barriers. On the other hand, bioplastics (on their own and in biocomposites) currently are not economically competitive with petroleum-derived plastics, in part because of the high costs associated with developing this market in the face of well-established petroleum-based product development and distribution (Singh et al. 2003). This is expected to change as production of bioplastics increases and unit costs correspondingly decrease, and as technological barriers are overcome to help lower production costs (Mohanty et al. 2002; Morris 2006). Technical concerns also are hampering efforts to develop biobased matrices that are compatible with natural fibers in composite materials, in terms of both performance and manufacturing processes; these challenges will require ongoing investment (Fowler et al. 2006). Another issue with biobased plastics is producing them so that they remain stable and functional during their intended use, but then biodegrade when disposed of. This challenge is being addressed by producing bioplastics with "triggered" degradability, in which degradation commences when the material is exposed to factors associated with composting environments (Mohanty et al. 2002).

In spite of these challenges, the strong recent growth in bioplastics and biocomposites is predicted to continue (Fowler et al. 2006), and biobased products in general have a share in a potentially large market (U.S. Department of Energy 2002). There clearly is great opportunity for expanded use of biobased products and corresponding displacement of products made from nonrenewable resources.

RESOURCES

Biobased Information System http://biobased.org/index.php
Biobased Manufacturers Association
    http://www.biobased.org/association/overview.php
California Straw Building Association
    http://strawbuilding.org/
Development Center for Appropriate Technology
    http://www.dcat.net/
Ecological Building Network
    http://www.ecobuildnetwork.org/index.htm
Erosion Control Technology Council http://www.ectc.org/
International Network for Bamboo and Rattan
    http://www.inbar.int/
New Uses Council http://www.newuses.org/
U.S. Department of Agriculture BioPreferred Program
    http://www.biobased.oce.usda.gov/fb4p/
U.S. Environmental Protection Agency GreenScapes Program http://www.epa.gov/greenscapes/

REFERENCES

Axelson, Peter W., and Denise Chesney. 1999. "Accessible Exterior Surfaces: Technical Article." Prepared for U.S. Architectural and Transportation Barriers Compliance Board. http://www.access-board.gov/research/Exterior%20 Surfaces/exteriorsarticle.pdf (accessed May 19, 2007).

Barr Engineering Company. 2001. "Minnesota Urban Small Sites BMP Manual: Stormwater Best Management Practices for Cold Climates." Prepared for the Metropolitan Council. http://www.metrocouncil.org/environment/ Watershed/BMP/manual.htm (accessed March 10, 2007).

Beyers, Jan L. 2004. Postfire seeding for erosion control: Effectiveness and impacts on native plant communities. *Conservation Biology* 18(4): 947–56.

Bleck, Regina, Eduardo del Valle, Walter Kanzler, Michael Kornitas, and William Bobenhausen. 2005. *Sustainable Design Guidelines: High Performance Campus Design Handbook, Volume II.* Newark, NJ: New Jersey Higher Education Partnership for Sustainability.

Butler, Mary Ann, Gregory Burr, David Dankovic, R. Alan Lunsford, Aubrey Miller, Mimi Nguyen, Larry Olsen, Douglas Sharpnack, John Snawder, Leslie Stayner, Marie Haring Sweeney, Alexander Teass, Joann Wess, and Ralph Zumwalde. 2000. *Hazard Review: Health Effects of Occupational Exposure to Asphalt.* DHHS/NIOSH Publication No.

2001–10. Cincinnati, OH: U.S. Department of Health and Human Services and National Institute for Occupational Safety and Health.

California Department of Transportation. 2003. *Construction Site Best Management Practices (BMPs) Manual.* http://www. dot.ca.gov/hq/construc/stormwater/CSBMPM_303_Final. pdf (accessed April 15, 2007).

California Stormwater Quality Association. 2003. *Stormwater Best Management Practice Handbook: Construction.* http://www. cabmphandbooks.com/Documents/Construction/Construction.pdf (accessed April 15, 2007).

Carlson, Brett. 2003. Tackifiers put to the test: Erosion and sediment control comes to a natural conclusion. *Land and Water* 47(4): http://www.landandwater.com/features/ vol47no4/vol47no4_1.php (accessed March 11, 2007).

Dethier, Jean, Walter Liese, Frei Otto, Eda Schaur, and Klaus Stephens. 2000. *Grow Your Own House: Simón Vélez and Bamboo Architecture.* Weil am Rhein, Germany: Vitra Design Museum.

Doornbosch, Richard, and Ronald Steenblik. 2007. "Biofuels: Is the Cure Worse Than the Disease?" Prepared for the Organisation for Economic Cooperation and Development. http://www.oecd.org/dataoecd/9/3/39411732.pdf (accessed November 9, 2007).

Döring, Thomas F., Michael Brandt, Jürgen Heß, Maria R. Finckh, and Helmut Saucke. 2005. Effects of straw mulch on soil nitrate dynamics, weeds, yield and soil erosion in organically grown potatoes. *Field Crops Research* 94: 238–49.

Elizabeth, Lynne, and Cassandra Adams, eds. 2005. *Alternative Construction: Contemporary Natural Building Methods.* New York: John Wiley & Sons.

Ellis, M. A., W. F. Wilcox, and L. V. Madden. 1998. Efficacy of metalaxyl, fosetyl-aluminum, and straw mulch for control of strawberry leather rot caused by *Phytophthora cactorum*. *Plant Disease* 82(3): 329–32.

Environmental and Energy Study Institute. 2004, January. *Summary of USDA Guidelines for Designating Biobased Products for Federal Procurement.* http://www.eesi.org/programs/ agriculture/Summary%209002%20Proposed%20Regs. PDF (accessed January 27, 2007).

Environmental Building News. 1997a, January. "A Green Release Agent for Concrete Forms." *Environmental Building News.* 6(1).

Environmental Building News. 1997b, November. "Natural-Fiber Erosion-Control Fabrics (Product Review)." *Environmental Building News.* 6(10).

Erosion Control Technology Council. 2006. *Standard Specification for Rolled Erosion Control Products.* St. Paul, MN: Erosion Control Technology Council.

Farrelly, David. 1984. *The Book of Bamboo.* San Francisco, CA: Sierra Club Books.

Fowler, Paul A., J. Mark Hughes, and Robert M. Elias. 2006. Biocomposites: Technology, environmental credentials and market forces. *Journal of the Science of Food and Agriculture* 86: 1781–89.

GeoSyntec Consultants. 2005. *Erosion and Sediment Control Manual*. Portland, OR: State of Oregon, Department of Environmental Quality.

Harris, Charles W., and Nicholas T. Dines, eds. 1998. *Time-Saver Standards for Landscape Architecture: Design and Construction Data*. 2nd ed. New York: McGraw-Hill.

Haywood, James D. 1999. Durability of selected mulches, their ability to control weeds, and influence growth of loblolly pine seedlings. *New Forests* 18:263–76.

Hopper, Leonard J., ed. 2006. *Landscape Architectural Graphic Standards*. Hoboken, NJ: Wiley.

Huang, Yilong, Liding Chen, Bojie Fu, Zhilin Huang, and Jie Gong. 2005. The wheat yields and water-use efficiency in the Loess Plateau: Straw mulch and irrigation effects. *Agricultural Water Management* 72:209–22.

Idaho Department of Environmental Quality. 2005. "IDEQ Storm Water Best Management Practices Catalog." http://www.deq.idaho.gov/water/data_reports/storm_water/catalog/ (accessed March 10, 2007).

Iowa State University Center for Transportation Research and Education. 2006. *Iowa Statewide Urban Design and Specifications: Design Manual (Supplemental Design Standards)*. http://www.iowasudas.org/supplemental_design/ (accessed April 21, 2007).

Ji, Shangning, and Paul W. Unger. 2001. Soil water accumulation under different precipitation, potential evaporation, and straw mulch conditions. *Soil Science Society of America Journal* 65:442–48.

Kansas City Metropolitan Chapter, American Public Works Association. 2003. "Division II Construction and Material Specifications: Section 2150 Erosion and Sediment Control." http://www.kcmo.org/pubworks/stds/spec/Temp/APWA2100.pdf (accessed March 11, 2007).

Karus, Michael, Markus Kaup, and Dalke Lohmeyer. 2000. *Study on Markets and Prices for Natural Fibres (Germany and EU)*. Hürth, Germany: Nova Institute for Ecology and Innovation.

Keating, Janis. 2003, July/August. A tale of two wattles. *Erosion Control*. http://www.forester.net/ecm_0307_tale.html (accessed February 3, 2007).

Kim, Seungdo, and Bruce E. Dale. 2004. Cumulative energy and global warming impact from the production of biomass for biobased products. *Journal of Industrial Ecology* 7(3–4): 147–62.

Kruse, Renee, Eric Bend, and Paulette Bierzychudek. 2004. Native plant regeneration and introduction of non-natives following post-fire rehabilitation with straw mulch and barley seeding. *Forest Ecology and Management* 196:299–310.

Lancaster, Tim, and Deron N. Austin. 2003. *Classifying Rolled Erosion-Control Products: A Current Perspective*. St. Paul, MN: Erosion Control Technology Council.

Mabberley, D. J. 1989. *The Plant-Book: A Portable Dictionary of the Higher Plants*. Cambridge: Cambridge University Press.

Magwood, Chris, Peter Mack, and Tina Thierren. 2005. *More Straw Bale Building: A Complete Guide to Designing and Building with Straw*. Gabriola Island, BC: New Society Publishers.

Maher, Michael, Chris Marshall, Frank Harrison, and Kathy Baumgaertner. 2005. *Context Sensitive Roadway Surfacing Selection Guide* (Federal Highway Administration Report No. FHWA-CFL/TD-05–004). Lakewood, CO: Federal Highway Administration, Central Federal Lands Highway Division.

Matos, Grecia R., and Lorie A. Wagner. 1998. Consumption of materials in the United States, 1900–1995. *Annual Review of Energy and the Environment* 23:107–22.

McNeil Technologies. 2005. *Colorado Agriculture IOF Technology Assessments: Biobased Products*. Denver: State of Colorado, Governor's Office of Energy Conservation and Management.

Millennium Ecosystem Assessment. 2003. *Ecosystems and Human Well-being: A Framework for Assessment*. Washington, DC: Island Press.

Miller, Shelie A., Amy E. Landis, and Thomas L. Theis. 2007. Environmental trade-offs of biobased production. *Environmental Science & Technology A-Page Magazine* 41(15): 5176–82.

Minke, Gernot, and Friedemann Mahlke. 2005. *Building with Straw: Design and Technology of a Sustainable Architecture*. Basel, Switzerland: Birkhäuser.

Mohanty, A. K., M. Misa, and L. T. Drzal. 2002. Sustainable bio-composites from renewable resources: Opportunities and challenges in the green materials world. *Journal of Polymers and the Environment* 10(1–2): 19–26.

Morris, David. 2006. The next economy: From dead carbon to living carbon. *Journal of the Science of Food and Agriculture* 86:1743–46.

National Center on Accessibility. *A Longitudinal Trail Research Program on Soil Stabilizers*. http://www.ncaonline.org/trails/soil-study.shtml (accessed May 3, 2007).

Office of the Federal Environmental Executive. 2006. Closing the Circle News. Issue 41 (Fall).

Oprins, Jan, and Harry van Trier. 2006. *Bamboo: A Material for Landscape and Garden Design*. Basil, Switzerland: Birkhäuser.

Patel, Martin, Catia Bastioli, Luigi Marini, and Eduard Würdlinger. 2003. "Environmental Assessment of Biobased Polymers and Natural Fibres." In *Biopolymers (Volume 10): General Aspects and Special Applications*, ed. A. Steinbüchel. Weinheim, Germany: Wiley.

Rickson, R. J. 2006. Controlling sediment at source: An evaluation of erosion control geotextiles. *Earth Surface Processes and Landforms* 31:550–60.

Riverside County, California, Transportation and Land Management Agency. "Ordinance 461 Specifications." http://www.tlma.co.riverside.ca.us/ordinances/ord461_specs.pdf (accessed May 19, 2007).

Schueler, Thomas R., and Heather K. Holland, eds. 2000. *The Practice of Watershed Protection*. Ellicott City, MD: Center for Watershed Protection.

Singh, Surendra P., Enefiok Ekanem, Troy Wakefield, Jr., and Sammy Comer. 2003. Emerging importance of bio-based products and bio-energy in the U.S. economy: Information dissemination and training of students. *International Food and Agribusiness Management Review* 5(3): http://www.ifama.org/tamu/iama/nonmember/OpenIFAMR/Articles/v5i3/singh.PDF (accessed January 1, 2007). Small, Ernest, and David Marcus. 2002. "Hemp: A New Crop with New Uses for North America." In *Trends in New Crops and New Uses,* ed. J. Janick and A. Whipkey. Alexandria, VA: ASHS Press.

Stangler, Carol A. 2001. *The Art and Craft of Bamboo*. New York: Lark Books.

Steen, Bill, Athena Swentzell Steen, and Wayne J. Bingham. 2005. *Small Strawbale: Natural Homes, Projects & Designs*. Salt Lake City, UT: Gibbs Smith.

Summers, Charles G., Jeffrey P. Mitchell, and James J. Stapleton. 2004. Management of aphid-borne viruses and *Bemisia argentifolii (Homoptera: Aleyrodidae)* in zucchini squash by using UV reflective plastic and wheat straw mulches. *Environmental Entomology* 33(5): 1447–57.

Sutherland, Ross A. 1998. Rolled erosion control systems for hillslope surface protection: A critical review, synthesis and analysis of available data. II. The post-1990 period. *Land Degradation & Development* 9:487–511.

Sutherland, Ross A., and Alan D. Ziegler. 2006. Hillslope runoff and erosion as affected by rolled erosion control systems: A field study. *Hydrological Processes* 20:2839–55.

Tilman, David, Kenneth G. Cassman, Pamela A. Matson, Rosamond Naylor, and Stephen Polasky. 2002. Agricultural sustainability and intensive production practices. *Nature* 418:671–77.

Tu, Cong, Jean B. Ristaino, and Shuijin Hu. 2006. Soil microbial biomass and activity in organic tomato farming systems: Effects of organic inputs and straw mulching. *Soil Biology and Biochemistry* 38:247–255.

Unified Facilities Guide Specification UFGS-03 30 30 00.00 20, July 2006. http://www.wbdg.org/ccb/DOD/UFGS/UFGS%2003%2030%2000.00%2020.pdf (accessed April 21, 2007).

U.S. Department of Agriculture. 2006a. 7 CFR Part 2902. "Designation of Biobased Items for Federal Procurement." *Federal Register* 71, no. 51, March 16, 2006.

U.S. Department of Agriculture. 2006b. 7 CFR Part 2902. "Designation of Biobased Items for Federal Procurement (Proposed Rule)." *Federal Register* 71, no. 159, August 17, 2006.

U.S. Department of Agriculture. 2006c. 7 CFR Part 2902. "Designation of Biobased Items for Federal Procurement (Proposed Rule)." *Federal Register* 71, no. 196, October 11, 2006.

U.S. Department of Energy. 1995. *House of Straw: Straw Bale Construction Comes of Age*. Washington, DC: USDOE Office of Energy Efficiency and Renewable Energy. http://www.kcmo.org/pubworks/stds/spec/Temp/APWA2100.pdf (accessed September 29, 2007).

U.S. Department of Energy. 2002. *Vision for Bioenergy and Biobased Products in the United States*. Washington, DC: USDOE.

U.S. Environmental Protection Agency. 1995. *RMAN for Items Designated in the Comprehensive Procurement Guideline: Supporting Analyses*. Washington, DC: U.S. EPA. Office of Solid Waste.

U.S. Environmental Protection Agency. 2006. NPDES Construction Site Stormwater Runoff Control. http://cfpub.epa.gov/npdes/stormwater/menuofbmps/index.cfm?action=min_measure&min_measure_id=4 (accessed February 17, 2007).

U.S. Green Building Council. 2005. *LEED-NC Green Building Rating System for New Construction and Major Renovations (Version 2.2)*. Washington, DC: U.S. Green Building Council.

van Dam, Jan E. G., and Harriëtte L. Bos. 2004. "The Environmental Impact of Fibre Crops in Industrial Applications. Background report for December 2004 Consultation on Natural Fibres." Rome: Food and Agriculture Organization of the United Nations. Van der Lugt, P., A. van den Dobblesteen, and R. Abrahams. 2003. Bamboo as a building material alternative for western Europe? A study of the environmental performance, costs and bottlenecks of the use of bamboo (products) in western Europe. *Journal of Bamboo and Rattan* 2(3): 205–23.

Wolfenbarger, L. L. and P. R. Phifer. 2000. The ecological risks and benefits of genetically engineered plants. *Science* 290(5499): 2088–93.

Zink, Thomas A., and Michael F. Allen. 1998. The effects of organic amendments on the restoration of a disturbed coastal sage scrub habitat. *Restoration Ecology* 6(1): 52–58.

Material (1 Metric Ton)	Embodied Energy (MJ/Metric Ton)	Embodied Carbon (kg CO_2/Metric Ton)	Notes*
Hot-mix asphalt pavement, 0% RAP	10,583[b]	185[b]	Includes feedstock energy value Figures based on Canadian average application System boundary is cradle to asphalt plant gate
Hot-mix asphalt pavement, 20% RAP	8,890[b]	177[b]	Includes feedstock energy value Figures based on Canadian average application System boundary is cradle to asphalt plant gate
Portland cement	5,232[b]	908[b]	Canada Average figures
Portland cement, 25%–30% fly ash	3,450[a]	585[a]	
Portland cement, 64%–73% slag	2,350[a]	279[a]	
Concrete	990[a]	134[a]	Unreinforced 20 Mpa (3,000 psi) compressive strength
Concrete pavement	790[b]	116[b]	Canada average figures for 30 MPa with 13% Fly Ash and 18% Blast Furnace Slag System boundary is cradle to concrete plant gate Excludes reinforcing steel
Concrete, steel reinforced 1%	1,810[a]	222[a]	
Precast concrete	2,000[a]	215[a]	
Concrete masonry units (CMU)	1,855[c]	180[c]	Figures based on Toronto average CMU System boundary is CMU plant gate
Clay brick, general	4,584[c]	232[c]	Figures based on Canadian average clay brick System boundary is brick plant gate
Engineering bricks	8,200[a]	850[a]	

Continued

Material (1 Metric Ton)	Embodied Energy (MJ/Metric Ton)	Embodied Carbon (kg CO_2/Metric Ton)	Notes*
Mortar (1:3 cement-sand mix)	1,520[a]	228[a]	
Mortar ($1^1/_2$:$4^1/_2$ cement-lime-sand mix)	1,640[a]	251[a]	
Mortar (1:2:9 cement-lime sand mix)	1,330[a]	198[a]	
Tile	9,000[a]	430[a]	
Soil cement	850[a]	140[a]	Quantity of cement not specified
Rammed earth	450[a]	24[a]	Quantity of cement not specified
Aggregate	150[a]	8[a]	
Granular base	90[b]	7[b]	System boundary is Canadian average from cradle to road building site 50/50 fine and coarse aggregate
Granular sub-base	75[b]	6[b]	System boundary is Canadian average from cradle to road building site
Stone/gravel chippings	300[a]	16[a]	
Local granite	5,900[a]	317[a]	
Imported granite	13,900[a]	747[a]	To UK from Australia
Limestone	240[a]	12[a]	
Sand	100[a]	5.3[a]	
Lime (hydrated)	5300[a]	1290[a]	
Aluminum, cast products	167,500[a]	9,210[a]	Assumed recycled content is 33%.
Aluminum, extruded	153,500[a]	8,490[a]	Assumed recycled content is 33%.
Aluminum, rolled	150,200[a]	8,350[a]	Assumed recycled content is 33%.
Brass	44,000[a]	3,710[a]	Assumed recycled content is 60%. Large data range, dependent on ore grade
Copper	47,500[a]	3,780[a]	Assumed recycled content is 46%. Large data range, dependent on ore grade
Lead	25,000[a]	1,290[a]	Assumed recycled content is 61.5%.
Steel, bar and rod	19,700[a]	1,720[a]	Assumed recycled content is 42.3%.
Steel, galvanized sheet	35,800[a]	2,820[a]	Figures for primary product
Steel, pipe	23,000[a]	1,800[a]	Assumed recycled content is 42.3%.

Material (1 Metric Ton)	Embodied Energy (MJ/Metric Ton)	Embodied Carbon (kg CO_2/Metric Ton)	Notes*
Steel, plate	45,400[a]	3,190[a]	Figures for primary product
Steel, section	22,700[a]	1,790[a]	Assumed recycled content is 42.3%.
Steel, sheet	20,900[a]	1,640[a]	Assumed recycled content is 42.3%.
Steel, wire	36,000[a]	2,830[a]	Assumed recycled content is 42.3%.
Stainless steel	51,500[a]	6,150[a]	Assumed recycled content is 42.3%. World average data from Institute of Stainless Steel Forum (ISSF) for grade 304
Titanium	498,090[a]	unknown[a]	Figures for primary product
Zinc	61,900[a]	3,200[a]	Assumed recycled content is 16%.
PVC, general	77,200[a]	2,410[a]	Based on the market average use of types of PVC in the European construction industry
PVC pipe	67,500[a]	2,500[a]	
PVC injection molding	95,100[a]	2,200[a]	
General polyethylene	83,100[a]	1,940[a]	Based on average use of types of PE in European construction
High-density polyethylene (HDPE)	76,700[a]	1,600[a]	
HDPE pipe	84,400[a]	2,000[a]	
Low-density polyethylene (LDPE)	78,100[a]	1,700[a]	
ABS	95,300[a]	3,100[a]	
Nylon 6	120,500[a]	5,500[a]	
Polycarbonate	112,900[a]	6,000[a]	
Polypropylene, injection molding	115,100[a]	3,900[a]	
Expanded polystyrene	88,600[a]	2,500[a]	
Polyurethane	72,100[a]	3,000[a]	
Softwood lumber (small dimension, green)	2,226[d]	132[d]	2 × 6 and smaller products System boundary is cradle to average U.S. site
Softwood lumber (small dimension, kiln dried)	9,193[d]	174[d]	2 × 6 and smaller products System boundary is cradle to average U.S. site
Softwood lumber (large dimension, green)	1,971[d]	101[d]	2 × 8 and larger products System boundary is cradle to average U.S. site

Continued

Material (1 Metric Ton)	Embodied Energy (MJ/Metric Ton)	Embodied Carbon (kg CO_2/Metric Ton)	Notes*
Softwood lumber (large dimension, kiln dried)	9,436[d]	179[d]	2 × 8 and larger products System boundary is cradle to average U.S. site
Glulam beams	20,440[d]	505[d]	System boundary is cradle to average U.S. site
Parallel strand lumber	17,956[d]	529[d]	System boundary is cradle to average U.S. site
Laminated veneer lumber	10,431[d]	262[d]	System boundary is cradle to average U.S. site
Plywood	15,000[a]	750[a]	

*Note: System boundaries are cradle to plant gate unless otherwise noted.

[a]Hammond, G. and C. Jones. 2006. "Inventory of Carbon and Energy." Version 1.5 Beta.Bath, UK: University of Bath, Department of Mechanical Engineering. All data is for materials used in the UK. Data was collected from UK and EU sources and worldwide averages. Values may vary from U.S. figures but are useful for comparisons among materials.

[b]Athena Sustainable Materials Institute. 2006. "A Life Cycle Perspective on Concrete and Asphalt Roadways: Embodied Primary Energy and Global Warming Potential." Submitted to Cement Association of Canada. Merrickville, ON: Athena Sustainable Materials Institute.

  -Figures converted from cubic meters, assumed density of asphalt pavement is 721 kg/m^3, assumed density of concrete is 2,354 kg/m^3).

  -Figures for CO_2 are total CO_2 equivalents.

[c]Athena Sustainable Materials Institute. 1998. "Life Cycle Analysis of Brick and Mortar Products". Prepared by Venta, Glaser & Associates, Ottawa, Canada.

[d]ATHENA® Impact Estimator for Buildings, version 2.0. Athena Sustainable Materals Institute, Merrickville, Ontario, Canada.

  -Figures converted from cubic meters, assumed density of softwood lumber is 550 kg/m^3, assumed density of parallel strand lumber is 630 kg/m^3, assumed density of laminated veneer lumber is 600 kg/m^3).

  -Figures for CO_2 are "Global Warming Potential" total CO_2 equivalents.

IMPACT CLASSIFICATIONS:

HAP =	Hazardous air pollutant
PBT =	Persistent bioaccumulative toxin
P-PBT =	Priority persistent bioaccumulative toxin by EPA, http://www.epa.gov/pbt/pubs/cheminfo.htm
W-PBT =	Washington State PBT list, http://www.ecy.wa.gov/programs/eap/pbt/pbtfaq.html
CERCLA =	CERCLA Priority List of Hazardous Substances, Agency for Toxic Substances
IARC group =	Group 1: The agent is *carcinogenic to humans.*
	Group 2A: The agent is *probably carcinogenic to humans.*
	Group 2B: The agent is *possibly carcinogenic to humans.*
	Group 3: The agent is *not classifiable as to its carcinogenicity to humans.*
	Group 4: The agent is *probably not carcinogenic to humans.*
DWC =	Drinking water contaminant, http://www.epa.gov/safewater/contaminants/index.html#inorganic
GHG =	Principal greenhouse gas
High GWP =	High global warming potential gas
I-GHG =	Indirect greenhouse gas
CAP =	Criteria air pollutant

Table B–1 Sources, Environmental Impacts, and Health Effects of Select Hazardous Air Pollutants (HAPs) Related to Construction Materials

Groups of Pollutants and Individual Pollutant and EPA or Other Classification	Major Sources (Related to Power Generation and Construction Materials)	Health and Environmental Impacts
Volatile organic compounds (VOCs) CAP	VOCs volatilize and off-gas from materials and products, impacting air quality. They are released from materials as a gas into the air as the material dries or cures. A wide range of carbon-based molecules are VOCs, including aldehydes, ketones, and hydrocarbons. Not all VOCs are hazardous air pollutants. Some are toxic, but others are not.[b] The largest energy-related sources of VOCs are fugitive emissions from fuel storage tanks and pipelines; and also from solvent use and incomplete combustion. Methane is a major VOC. In construction materials, VOCs originate from solvents, adhesives, cleaners, finishes, paint, stains, engineered wood products, metal coatings, and many other products. Common VOCs are formaldehyde, acetaldehyde, toluene, and benzene.[d]	VOCs can be directly inhaled or attached to dust that is inhaled, producing negative health effects. They can also leach directly from the material into water. VOCs can cause respiratory illness, including asthma; they can irritate eyes and the respiratory system. Some VOCs are known or suspected carcinogens.[a] Others are acute or chronic toxicants. VOCs that off-gas from materials in interior spaces can contribute to sick building syndrome. Some VOCs react with nitrogen oxides and sunlight to form ground-level ozone and smog; some damage vegetation or water quality.[a] Methane is a potent greenhouse gas.

Groups of Pollutants and Individual Pollutant and EPA or Other Classification	Major Sources (Related to Power Generation and Construction Materials)	Health and Environmental Impacts
Semivolatile organic compounds (SVOCs)	SVOCs release more slowly from materials and products over a longer period of time—sometimes years. They can attach to soil or dust particles.[d] SVOCs originate from phthalates in PVC and other products, halogenated flame retardants, products using perfluorochemicals (PFCs), and other materials.	SVOCs can cause a range of health and environmental impacts as discussed for individual compounds below.
Polycyclic aromatic hydrocarbon compounds (PAHs) W-PBT HAP P-PBT CERCLA #7	PAHs are usually complex mixtures of compounds that form from incomplete combustion. Formed primarily from fossil fuel combustion, coal, coal tar, and coke ovens, But also from bitumen and asphalt production plants, asphalt roads, aluminum production, some wood preservatives, and wood product manufacturers.[c,f]	Humans are exposed to PAHs primarily through breathing them in air. However, they can be ingested from water. Some PAHs are known or suspected human carcinogens.[c] Some are PBTs. Some are reproductive toxins. PAHs enter water through discharges from industrial and wastewater treatment plants. Most PAHs do not dissolve easily in water. They stick to solid particles and settle to the bottoms of lakes or rivers. Microorganisms can break down PAHs in soil or water after a period of weeks to months. In soils, PAHs are most likely to stick tightly to particles; certain PAHs move through soil to contaminate underground water. PAH contents of plants and animals may be much higher than PAH contents of soil or water in which they live.[i]
Mercury P-PBT W-PBT HAP CERCLA #3 IARC Group 3	Predominantly emitted to the air by the combustion of fossil fuels (mostly coal) and waste[c] In construction materials, mercury is used for stabilizers or other additives. It can also be released when chlorine is manufactured in the mercury cell process for PVC production, among other things.[d]	Mercury exposure at high levels can harm the brain, heart, kidneys, lungs, and immune system of people of all ages. Research shows that most people's fish consumption does not cause a health concern. However, it has been demonstrated that high levels of methylmercury in the bloodstream of unborn babies and young children may harm the developing nervous system, making the child less able to think and learn.[ef] Mercury in the air eventually settles into water or onto land where it can be washed into water. Once deposited, certain microorganisms can change it into methylmercury, a highly toxic form that builds up in fish, shellfish, and animals that eat fish. Fish and shellfish are the main sources of methylmercury exposure to humans. Birds and mammals that eat fish are more exposed to mercury than other animals in water ecosystems. Similarly, predators that eat fish-eating animals may be highly exposed. At high levels of exposure, methylmercury's harmful effects on these animals include death, reduced reproduction, slower growth and development, and abnormal behavior.[ef]

Continued

Groups of Pollutants and Individual Pollutant and EPA or Other Classification	Major Sources (Related to Power Generation and Construction Materials)	Health and Environmental Impacts
Dioxins and furans P-PBT W-PBT HAPs IARC Group 1 (2, 3, 7, 8 TCDD and others)	The term *dioxin* is commonly used to refer to a family of toxic chemicals that all share a similar chemical structure and a common mechanism of toxic action. This family includes seven of the polychlorinated dibenzo dioxins (PCDDs), ten of the polychlorinated dibenzo furans (PCDFs), and twelve of the polychlorinated biphenyls (PCBs).[h] Dioxins are released from cement kilns,[c] PVC production, incineration of municipal solid waste, secondary copper smelting, coal-fired power plants, backyard burning of household waste, and landfill fires.[c,h]	Because dioxins are widely distributed throughout the environment in low concentrations and are persistent and bioaccumulated, most people have detectable levels of dioxins in their tissues. These levels, in the low parts per trillion, have accumulated over a lifetime and will persist for years, even if no additional exposure were to occur. This background exposure is likely to result in an increased risk of cancer and is uncomfortably close to levels that can cause subtle, adverse, noncancer effects in animals and humans. Dioxins have been characterized by the U.S. EPA as likely to be human carcinogens and are anticipated to increase the risk of cancer at background levels of exposure. In 1997 the International Agency for Research on Cancer classified 2,3,7,8, TCDD, the best studied member of the dioxin family, as a known human carcinogen. 2,3,7,8 TCDD accounts for about 10% of our background dioxin risk. Effects specifically observed in humans include changes in markers of early development and hormone levels. At much higher doses, dioxins can cause a serious skin disease in humans called chloracne.[h] Dioxins can be commonly detected in air, soil, sediments, and food. Dioxins are transported primarily through the air and are deposited on the surfaces of soil, buildings and pavement, water bodies, and the leaves of plants. Most dioxins are introduced to the environment through the air as trace products of combustion. The principal route by which dioxins are introduced to most rivers, streams, and lakes is soil erosion and storm water runoff from urban areas. Industrial discharges can significantly elevate water concentrations near the point of discharge to rivers and streams.[gh]

Groups of Pollutants and Individual Pollutant and EPA or Other Classification	Major Sources (Related to Power Generation and Construction Materials)	Health and Environmental Impacts
Vinyl chloride HAP CERCLA #4 IARC Group 1	Vinyl chloride is a colorless organic gas with a sweet odor. It is used in the manufacture of numerous products in building and construction, the automotive industry, electrical wire insulation and cables, piping, industrial and household equipment, and medical supplies, and is depended upon heavily by the rubber, paper, and glass industries.[e] Most vinyl chloride is used to make polyvinyl chloride (PVC) plastic and vinyl products.	Acute (short-term) exposure to high levels of vinyl chloride in the air has resulted in central nervous system (CNS) effects, such as dizziness, drowsiness, and headaches in humans. Chronic (long-term) exposure to vinyl chloride through inhalation and oral exposure in humans has resulted in liver damage. Cancer is a major concern from exposure to vinyl chloride via inhalation, as vinyl chloride exposure has been shown to increase the risk of a rare form of liver cancer in humans. The U.S. EPA has classified vinyl chloride as a Group A, human carcinogen.[c] Its major release to the environment is emissions and wastewater at polyvinyl chloride (PVC) plastics production and manufacturing facilities. Small quantities of vinyl chloride can be released to food since it is used to make food wrappings and containers. Vinyl chloride released to soil will either quickly evaporate, be broken down by microbes, or may leach to the groundwater. It rapidly evaporates from water, but does not degrade there. It will not accumulate in aquatic life.
Hexachlorabenzene P-PBT W-PBT HAP IARC Group 2B	HCB is no longer directly used, although it is a by-product from some manufacturing processes. By-product from making chlorine-containing compounds, chlorination treatment of process water and wastewater, incineration of municipal and hazardous wastes, and making chemical solvents (chemicals used to dissolve other chemicals).[c]	Chronic (long-term) oral exposure to hexachlorabenzene in humans results in a liver disease with associated skin lesions. The U.S. EPA has classified hexachlorabenzene as a probable human carcinogen (Group B2) and a PBT. Hexachlorabenzene has been listed as a pollutant of concern to to the EPA's Great Waters Program due to its persistence in the environment, potential to bioaccumulate, and toxicity to humans and the environment.[c]
Benzene HAP CERCLA #6 IARC Group 1	Emissions from oil and natural gas production, petroleum refining, burning coal and oil, coke ovens, and motor vehicle exhaust Used as a solvent for waxes, resins, oils, paints, plastics, and rubber[c]	Acute (short-term) inhalation exposure of humans to benzene may cause drowsiness, dizziness, and headaches, as well as eye, skin, and respiratory tract irritation, and, at high levels, unconsciousness. Chronic (long-term) inhalation exposure in occupational settings has caused various disorders in the blood, including reduced numbers of red blood cells and aplastic anemia. Reproductive effects have been reported for women exposed by inhalation to high levels, and adverse effects on the developing fetus have been observed in animal tests. Increased incidences of leukemia (cancer of the tissues that form white blood cells) have been observed in humans occupationally exposed to benzene. The U.S. EPA has classified benzene as a Group A, human carcinogen.[c]

Continued

Groups of Pollutants and Individual Pollutant and EPA or Other Classification	Major Sources (Related to Power Generation and Construction Materials)	Health and Environmental Impacts
Acrylonitrile HAP IARC Group 2B	Acrylonitrile is primarily used in the manufacture of acrylic and modacrylic fibers. It is also used as a raw material in the manufacture of plastics.[c] Acrylonitrile may be released to the ambient air during its manufacture and use, from landfills, and through incineration of sewage sludge.	Exposure to acrylonitrile is primarily occupational: Acute (short-term) exposure of workers to acrylonitrile has been observed to cause mucous membrane irritation, headaches, dizziness, and nausea. No information is available on the reproductive or developmental effects of acrylonitrile in humans. Based on limited evidence in humans and evidence in rats, the U.S. EPA has classified acrylonitrile as a probable human carcinogen (Group B1).[c]
1,3-Butadiene HAP IARC Group 1	From motor vehicle exhaust, manufacturing and processing facilities, and production of synthetic plastics and rubber[c]	Although 1,3-butadiene breaks down quickly in the atmosphere, it is usually found in ambient air at low levels in urban and suburban areas.[c] Acute (short-term) exposure to 1,3-butadiene by inhalation in humans results in irritation of the eyes, nasal passages, throat, and lungs. Epidemiological studies have reported a possible association between 1,3-butadiene exposure and cardiovascular diseases. Epidemiological studies of workers in rubber plants have shown an association between 1,3-butadiene exposure and increased incidence of leukemia. Animal studies have reported tumors at various sites from 1,3-butadiene exposure. The U.S. EPA has classified 1,3-butadiene as a Group B2, probable human carcinogen.[c]
Coke oven emissions HAP IARC Group 1	A mixture of coal tar, coal tar pitch, and creosote, containing chemicals such as benzo(a)pyrene, benzanthracene, chrysene, and phenanthrene. Coke oven emissions may occur from coke ovens and facilities associated with the manufacture of aluminum, steel, and graphite as well as electrical and construction industries.[c] Chemicals recovered from coke oven emissions are used as raw materials for plastics, solvents, dyes, drugs, waterproofing, paints, pipecoating, roads, roofing, insulation, and pesticides and sealants.[c]	Exposure to coke oven emissions may occur for workers in the aluminum, steel, graphite, electrical, and construction industries. Chronic (long-term) exposure to coke oven emissions in humans results in conjunctivitis, severe dermatitis, and lesions of the respiratory system and digestive system. Cancer is the major concern from exposure to coke oven emissions. Epidemiologic studies of coke oven workers have reported an increase in cancer of the lung, trachea, bronchus, kidney, prostate, and other sites. Animal studies have reported tumors of the lung and skin from inhalation exposure to coal tar. The U.S. EPA has classified coke oven emissions as a Group A, known human carcinogen.[c]

Groups of Pollutants and Individual Pollutant and EPA or Other Classification	Major Sources (Related to Power Generation and Construction Materials)	Health and Environmental Impacts
Ethylene dichloride HAP	Ethylene dichloride is primarily used in the production of vinyl chloride as well as other chemicals. It is used in solvents in closed systems for various extraction and cleaning purposes in organic synthesis. It is also added to leaded gasoline as a lead scavenger. It is used as a dispersant in rubber and plastics, as a wetting and penetrating agent.[e]	Inhalation of ethylene dichloride in the ambient or workplace air is generally the main route of human exposure. The compound may be released during its production, storage, use, transport, and disposal. Exposure may also occur through the consumption of contaminated water. But usually ethylene dichloride will evaporate quickly into the air from the water or soil. Exposure to low levels of ethylene dichloride can occur from breathing ambient or workplace air. Inhalation of concentrated ethylene dichloride vapor can induce effects on the human nervous system, liver, and kidneys, as well as respiratory distress, cardiac arrhythmia, nausea, and vomiting. Chronic (long-term) inhalation exposure to ethylene dichloride produced effects on the liver and kidneys in animals. Information is limited on the reproductive or developmental effects of ethylene dichloride in humans. Decreased fertility and increased embryo mortality have been observed in inhalation studies of rats. Epidemiological studies are not conclusive regarding the carcinogenic effects of ethylene dichloride, due to concomitant exposure to other chemicals. Following treatment by gavage (experimentally placing the chemical in the stomach), several tumor types were induced in rats and mice. The U.S. EPA has classified ethylene dichloride as a Group B2, probable human carcinogen.[ce]
Formaldehyde (VOC) HAP CERCLA #247 VOC IARC Group 1	Used mainly to produce resins used in manufactured wood products and as an intermediate in the synthesis of other chemicals[c]	The highest levels of airborne formaldehyde have been detected in indoor air, where it is released from various consumer products such as building materials and home furnishings. Formaldehyde has also been detected in ambient air; the average concentrations reported in U.S. urban areas were in the range of 11 to 20 parts per billion (ppb). The major sources appear to be power plants, manufacturing facilities, incinerators, and automobile exhaust emissions.[c] Exposure to formaldehyde may occur by breathing contaminated indoor air, tobacco smoke, or ambient urban air. Acute (short-term) and chronic (long-term) inhalation exposure to formaldehyde in humans can result in respiratory symptoms and eye, nose, and throat irritation. Limited human studies have reported an association between formaldehyde exposure and lung and nasopharyngeal cancer. Animal inhalation studies have reported an increased incidence of nasal squamous cell cancer. The U.S. EPA considers formaldehyde a probable human carcinogen (Group B1).[c]

Continued

Groups of Pollutants and Individual Pollutant and EPA or Other Classification	Major Sources (Related to Power Generation and Construction Materials)	Health and Environmental Impacts
Methylene chloride CERCLA #81	Methylene chloride is predominantly used as a solvent in paint strippers and removers; as a process solvent in the manufacture of drugs, pharmaceuticals, and film coatings; as a metal cleaning and finishing solvent in electronics manufacturing; and as an agent in urethane foam blowing. Other sources of emissions are landfills and wastewater processing.[c]	The acute (short-term) effects of methylene chloride inhalation in humans consist mainly of nervous system effects, including decreased visual, auditory, and motor functions, but these effects are reversible once exposure ceases. The effects of chronic (long-term) exposure to methylene chloride suggest that the central nervous system (CNS) is a potential target in humans and animals. Human data are inconclusive regarding methylene chloride and cancer. Animal studies have shown increases in liver and lung cancer and benign mammary gland tumors following the inhalation of methylene chloride. The U.S.EPA has classified methylene chloride as a Group B2, probable human carcinogen.[c]

[a]U.S. Environmental Protection Agency (U.S. EPA). Office of Policy, Economics, and Innovation. 2007. *Energy Trends in Selected Manufacturing Sectors: Opportunities and Challenges for Environmentally Preferable Energy Outcomes.* Prepared by ICF International, March 2007.

[b]http:www.epa.gov/climatechange/emissions/

[c]http://www.epa.gov/ttn/atw/

[d]http://www.pharosproject.net/wiki/index

[e]http://www.epa.gov/safewater/contaminants/index

[f]http://www.epa.gov/mercury/about.htm

[g]http://www.npi.gov.au/database/substance-info/profiles/

[h]http://www.epa.gov/pbt/pubs/dioxins.htm

[i]http://www.atsdr.cdc.gov/tfacts69.html

Table B–2 Sources, Environmental Impacts, and Health Effects of Select Heavy Metals Related to Construction Materials

Metal and EPA or Other Classification	Major Sources (Related to Construction Materials)	Health and Environmental Impacts
Lead CAP P-PBT W-PBT HAP CERCLA #2 IARC Group 2B	Sources of air emissions of lead include combustion of solid waste, coal, and oils, and emissions from iron and steel production and lead smelters.	Exposure to lead can occur from breathing contaminated workplace air or house dust or eating lead-based paint chips or contaminated dirt. Lead is a very toxic element, causing a variety of effects at low dose levels. Brain damage, kidney damage, and gastrointestinal distress are seen from acute (short-term) exposure to high levels of lead in humans. Chronic (long-term) exposure to lead in humans results in effects on the blood, central nervous system (CNS), blood pressure, kidneys, and Vitamin D metabolism. Children are particularly sensitive to the chronic effects of lead, with slowed cognitive development, reduced growth, and other effects reported.[c]
Chromium, compounds HAP CERCLA #18 IARC Group 1 (IV) IARC Group 3 (III)	Sources include combustion of coal and oil, electroplating, vehicles, iron and steel plants, and metal smelters. Ore refining, chemical and refractory processing, cement-producing plants, automobile brake lining and catalytic converters for automobiles, leather tanneries, and chrome pigments also contribute to the atmospheric burden of chromium.[c] Chromium occurs in the environment primarily in two valence states: trivalent chromium (Cr III) and hexavalent chromium (Cr VI). Exposure may occur from natural or industrial sources of chromium.	Hexavalent chromium is the most toxic form. The general population is exposed to chromium (generally chromium (III) by eating food, drinking water, and inhaling air that contains the chemical. The respiratory tract is also the major target organ for chromium (III) toxicity, similar to chromium (VI). Chromium (III) is an essential element in humans. The body can detoxify some amount of chromium (VI) to chromium (III). The respiratory tract is the major target organ for chromium (VI) toxicity, for acute (short-term) and chronic (long-term) inhalation exposures. Shortness of breath, coughing, and wheezing were reported from a case of acute exposure to chromium (VI), while perforations and ulcerations of the septum, bronchitis, decreased pulmonary function, pneumonia, and other respiratory effects have been noted from chronic exposure. Human studies have clearly established that inhaled chromium (VI) is a human carcinogen, resulting in an increased risk of lung cancer. Animal studies have shown chromium (VI) to cause lung tumors via inhalation exposure.[c] Emissions of chromium are predominantly of trivalent chromium, and in the form of small particles or aerosols. Chromium is a naturally occurring element in rocks, animals, plants, soil, and volcanic dust and gases. The chromium (III) compounds are sparingly soluble in water and may be found in water bodies as soluble chromium (III) complexes, while the chromium (VI) compounds are readily soluble in water.[c] High chronic toxicity to aquatic life. Chromium particles adhere to soil and sediment particles.

Continued

Metal and EPA or Other Classification	Major Sources (Related to Construction Materials)	Health and Environmental Impacts
Nickel, compounds HAP CERCLA #55 IARC Group 2b IARC Group 1 (compounds)	Sources include utility oil and coal combustion, nickel metal refining, lead smelting, and manufacturing facilities. Nickel is used for nickel alloys, electroplating, batteries, coins, industrial plumbing, spark plugs, machinery parts, stainless steel, nickel-chrome resistance wires, and catalysts.[a] Combined with other alloys such as chromium and molybdenum to form stainless steel. Increases corrosion resistance and tensile strength without reducing ductility. Also added to copper to produce monel with high corrosion resistance or as a plating metal.[e]	Nickel is found in ambient air at very low levels as a result of releases from oil and coal combustion, nickel metal refining, sewage sludge incineration, manufacturing facilities, and other sources.[c] Nickel compounds are classified as carcinogens, and nickel metals and alloys are considered possible carcinogens. Individuals also may be exposed to nickel in occupations involved in its production, processing, and use, or through contact with everyday items such as nickel-containing jewelry and stainless steel cooking and eating utensils, and by smoking tobacco.[a] Nickel is an essential element in some animal species, and it has been suggested it may be essential for human nutrition. Nickel dermatitis, consisting of itching of the fingers, hands, and forearms, is the most common effect in humans from chronic (long-term) skin contact with nickel. Respiratory effects have also been reported in humans from inhalation exposure to nickel. Human and animal studies have reported an increased risk of lung and nasal cancers from exposure to nickel refinery dusts and nickel subsulfide. Animal studies of soluble nickel compounds (i.e., nickel carbonyl) have reported lung tumors. The U.S. EPA has classified nickel refinery dust and nickel subsulfide as Group A, human carcinogens, and nickel carbonyl as a Group B2, probable human carcinogen.[c]
Arsenic HAP CERCLA #1 IARC Group 1	Arsenic air emissions are predominantly a result of the burning of coal or fuel oil, from metal smelters, iron foundries, and burning of wastes. The major use for inorganic arsenic is in wood preservation.[c]	For most people, food is the major source of exposure to arsenic. Inorganic arsenic exposure in humans, by the inhalation route, has been shown to be strongly associated with lung cancer, while ingestion of inorganic arsenic in humans has been linked to a form of skin cancer and also to bladder, liver, and lung cancer. The U.S. EPA has classified inorganic arsenic as a Group A, human carcinogen. Acute (short-term) high-level inhalation exposure to arsenic dust or fumes has resulted in gastrointestinal effects (nausea, diarrhea, abdominal pain); central and peripheral nervous system disorders have occurred in workers acutely exposed to inorganic arsenic.[c]

Metal and EPA or Other Classification	Major Sources (Related to Construction Materials)	Health and Environmental Impacts
Manganese CERCLA #115	Metallic manganese is used primarily in steel production to improve hardness, stiffness, and strength. It is also used in carbon steel, stainless steel, and high-temperature steel, along with cast iron and superalloys. Manganese can also be released into the air by combustion of coal and oil, residential combustion of wood, iron and steel production plants, and power plants.[d]	Manganese is essential for normal physiologic functioning in humans and animals, and exposure to low levels of manganese in the diet is considered to be nutritionally essential in humans. Chronic (long-term) exposure to high levels of manganese by inhalation in humans may result in central nervous system (CNS) effects. Visual reaction time, hand steadiness, and eye-hand coordination were affected in chronically exposed workers. A syndrome named manganism may result from chronic exposure to higher levels; manganism is characterized by feelings of weakness and lethargy, tremors, a masklike face, and psychological disturbances. Respiratory effects have also been noted in workers chronically exposed by inhalation. Impotence and loss of libido have been noted in male workers afflicted with manganism.[c]
Cadmium W-PBT HAP CERCLA #8 IARC Group 1	Sources are mainly from the burning of fossil fuels such as coal or oil. Also emitted into the air from zinc, lead, or copper smelters.[f] Mined in association with zinc, it is used to galvanize metal, in electroplating to create special metal alloys and solders, and as a pigment in paints and plastics.[e] Zinc mining, anodizing, metal processing, electroplating, plastics, and dye manufacture are sources contributing to water and soil releases.[e]	Cadmium attaches to fly ash carried widely in the air for a week, then settles and attaches to clay soils. Cadmium from soil, water, and sediments is taken up by plants and animals and enters the human food supply. It is not metabolized. Limited bioconcentration has been documented. For nonsmokers, food is generally the largest source of cadmium exposure. Cadmium levels in some foods can be increased by the application of phosphate fertilizers or sewage sludge to farm fields.[f] The acute (short-term) effects of cadmium in humans through inhalation exposure consist mainly of effects on the lung, such as pulmonary irritation. Chronic (long-term) inhalation or oral exposure to cadmium leads to a buildup of cadmium in the kidneys that can cause kidney disease. Cadmium has been shown to be a developmental toxicant in animals, resulting in fetal malformations and other effects, but no conclusive evidence exists in humans. An association between cadmium exposure and an increased risk of lung cancer has been reported from human studies, but these studies are inconclusive due to confounding factors. Animal studies have demonstrated an increase in lung cancer from long-term inhalation exposure to cadmium. The U.S. EPA has classified cadmium as a Group B1, probable human carcinogen.[c]

Continued

Metal and EPA or Other Classification	Major Sources (Related to Construction Materials)	Health and Environmental Impacts
Copper CERCLA #133 DWC	Used as a base metal or added to carbon steel for resistance to atmospheric corrosion.[e]	Heating copper in smelting and in joining can release metal oxide fumes that can pose health risks for metal workers. Water runoff from copper mining and processing wastes can carry significant quantities of heavy metals, potentially contaminating ground- and surface water supplies. Copper is toxic to fish and aquatic organisms. Runoff from copper in use can impact sensitive ecosystems. Release of copper dust can be toxic to soil microorganisms and can disrupt microbial processes.[e]
Brass and bronze	Copper alloys	Some brasses contain lead as an alloying constituent. If the brass alloy contains less than 8% lead, it is considered "lead free." This could be a concern with brass fittings for water sources.[e] Water runoff from copper mining and processing wastes can carry significant quantities of heavy metals, potentially contaminating ground- and surface water supplies. Copper is toxic to fish and aquatic organisms. Runoff from copper in use can impact sensitive ecosystems. Release of copper dust can be toxic to soil microorganisms and can disrupt microbial processes.[e]
Aluminum CERCLA #186 IARC Group 1 (aluminum production)	Used as a base metal or alloy added to steel for surface hardening or copper for bronze	Aluminum can be a neurotoxin if large amounts are ingested. It can alter the blood-brain barrier.[a]
Thallium DWC	By-product of ore processing	Thallium leaching from ore processing applications is the largest source of the metal contamination in drinking water.[c]

[a]Agency for Toxic Substances and Disease Registry (ATSDR). "ToxFAQs." U.S. Department of Health and Human Services, http://www.atsdr.cdc.gov/toxfaq.html (accessed between May 2006 and November 2007).

[b]Stockholm Convention on Persistent Organic Pollutants http://www.pops.int/

[c]U.S. Environmental Protection Agency (U.S. EPA). Technology Transfer Network, Air Toxics http://www.epa.gov/ttn/atw/allabout.html (accessed between May 2007 and November 2007)

[d]U.S. Environmental Protection Agency (U.S. EPA). Persistent Bioaccumulative and Toxic Chemical Program http://www.epa.gov/pbt/ (accessed between May 2007 and November 2007)

[e]Zahner, William L. 1995. *Architectural Metals: A Guide to Selection, Specification, and Performance.* New York: John Wiley & Sons.

[f]http://www.pharosproject.net/wiki/index

Index

Numbers in italic indicate illustrations.

A

Acidification, 15, 18
Acid rain, 18
Acrylonitrile butadiene styrene (ABS), 373–374, 376, 378, 381, 387–390
Adobe bricks, 149–150, 152–155, *156*
Agency for Toxic Substances and Disease Registry (ATSDR), 23
Aggregate pavements, 255–263
    design and specification considerations, 257
    environmental impacts, 256
    gradations, 255–256
    porous, 256–257
    stabilized, 257–261, 423–424
Aggregates, natural, 109–110
    construction and use impacts, 241–242
    embodied carbon, 239
    embodied energy, 239
    emissions, 240–241
    energy use, 109
    environmental and human health impacts, 109–110, 237–242
    mine reclamation, 240
    mining and processing, 109–110, 237–241, *238*
    transportation impacts, 240–241
    use, 235–237
    waste, 238–239
Aggregates, recycled, 122–128, 242–253, *245*. *See also* specific materials
    applications of, 244
    benefits and limitations of use, 242–243
    sources, 242–244
Air pollution, 15, 17
Aluminum, 328–341, 343, 345–346, 348, 351, 353, 356–357, 360–364, 367, 369
Andropogon Associates, *254*
Arbors, wood, *282*
Arkin Tilt Architects, *292, 298*
Arnold Associates, *262*
Asphalt cement:
    polymer modifier, 212
    production, 201
Asphalt pavement, 199–233. *See also* Asphalt cement; Asphalt pavement surfaces; Blast furnace slag; Cullet, glass; Foundry sand; Mineral processing waste; Plastics, recycled; Resin-modified pavement; Stabilized surfacings; Steel slag; Synthetic binder

concrete pavement; Tires, recycled; Urban heat island effect
    alternatives to, 229–230
    asphalt basics, 199–200
    cold-mix, 207
    cold in-place recycling, 208–209
    comparison with concrete, 204–205
    environmental impacts of, 200–202, 204–205
    foamed, 206–207, *210*
    full depth reclamation, 209
    hot in-place recycling, 209
    human health impacts of, 202–204
    placement, 204–205
    porous, 223–227 *223, 225, 227*
    production emissions, 201–204
    production energy use, 201
    raw materials acquisition, 200–201
    recycled aggregates for, 207–212
    recycled asphalt pavement, 208–209
    research organizations, 231
    rubberized asphalt concrete, 209–211, *211*
    use and maintenance, 204
    using less binder, 207
    warm mix, 205–206, *206*
Asphalt pavement surfaces, 216, 219–223
    cape seal, 220
    chip seal, 220
    fog seal, 222
    microsurfacing, 220
    open graded friction course, 221
    otta seal, 221
    sand seal, 221
    scrub seal, 222
    sealants, 223
    shot abraded, *219*
    slurry seal, 222
    ultra-thin friction course, 222
    ultra-thin white topping, 221
Asphalt stabilized soil, 172
Athena EcoCalculator, 64–65
Athena Environmental Impact Estimator, 64–65, 111, 184, 186, 277
Athena Sustainable Materials Institute, 64–65, 201, 205
Atmospheric lifetimes (years) of GHG, 16

B

Backflows of materials, 26
Bamboo, 425–428, 433
    environmental impacts and benefits of, 426–427

specification of, 427–428
BEES, Building for Environmental and Economic Sustainability, 27, 63–64, 279, 400
    BEES Stakeholder Panel, 64
    BEES Criteria, 64, *64*
Biobased Manufacturer's Association, 412
Biobased materials, 409–435. *See also* specific materials; Strawbale construction; USDA-Specified Biobased Content
    benefits of use, 409–412
    categories of inputs, 411
    challenges to use, 409–412
    for concrete and pavements, 421, 423–424
    for erosion control, reveg and mulching, 411–423
    government support for, 431–432
    impacts of use, 409–412
    product development, 432–433
    resources for, 433
Biofuels, 32–33
Biomimicry, 44
Blast furnace slag, 246–248
    air cooled, 125–126
    expanded, 125–126
    ground granulated, 117–119, 121–122
    palletized, 125–126
Blended cements, 106, 113–114, 120–122
Brass, 329, 340, 348, 351
Brick, 179–197. *See also* Brick paving; Brick walls; Cement mortar
    construction impacts, 186
    crushed, 127, 251
    dry press, 179
    production embodied energy, 182–183
    production emissions, 183–184
    end of life, 194, 196
    environmental impacts of, 180–187
    extruded, 179
    human health impacts of, 180–187
    life-cycle analysis, 184, 186
    manufacturing, 182–184
    minimizing manufacturing impacts, 185
    molded, 179
    production, 179–180, *180*
    raw materials, 180–182
    reducing impacts, 186–196
    salvaged brick, 196
    transportation, 184–185
    water use in production, 184

WILEY BOOKS ON Sustainable Design

Environmental Benefits Statement